KRLA ARCHIVES

KRLA
*Chronological Archives
Volume 6*
November 19, 1966, to April 8, 1967

KRLA ARCHIVES

Rumors of the Beatles splitting had been reported in the past but the suspicions were refuted and coverage continued. The Monkees, the manufactured for marketing band caught on fire in all media. American bands like The Association, Simon & Garfunkle, The Dave Clark Five, Neil Diamond, joined the old faithfuls in demanding attention from the teen age public. Brian Wilson and the Beach Boys continued to command attention and print space. And Sonny and Cher continued to reign in pop music coverage.

The articles didn't limit themselves to the rock stars themselves. Entire articles were dedicated to who the stars were dating...or breaking up with, at any given moment. And articles on religion, the generation gap and riots began making their way into the spotlight even in The KRLA Beat, as did pieces on the military draft and riots. Comedians like Bill Cosby and Phyllis Diller were given print space, as well.

In presenting these original issues, we've moved a few of the pages around to ensure that the spreads still lined up. Not a big deal to most people unless you are severly OCD and have access to the original issues.

Copyright © 2016 White Lightning Publishing

KRLA ARCHIVES

KRLA BEAT

Volume 2, Number 28   November 19, 1966

Keith Relf Denies Yardbird Split-Up

Despite rumors to the contrary, Keith Relf revealed to *The BEAT* in an exclusive interview that he has no intentions of leaving the Yardbirds.

Keith was visibly upset that someone had actually printed, without any basis whatsoever, that he was ready to quit the group. He said he had no idea what had prompted a British paper to print what he termed absolute "lies" regarding his relationship with the Yardbirds.

Keith further added that although he had cut a single record some months ago, "Mr. Zero," he did not think he would do so again but would, instead, sing only with the Yardbirds.

The rumors of Jeff Beck's departure have, of course, been running full-speed ahead for quite some time but the Yardbirds were adamant in their denial of any break-up in the group.

During the Yardbirds' last American tour, Jeff's tonsils gave him so much trouble that they were finally removed in a San Francisco hospital. Consequently, Jeff was forced to miss a large centage of the group's dates. He has now fully recovered, and barring any accidents, will perform with the Yardbirds on their entire current U.S tour.

While in Hollywood the group taped a "Milton Berle Show" and, thus, became the first self-contained British group to appear on the show. Also, during their Southern California stop-off, the Yardbirds paid a visit to the set of "The Monkees." It was their first visit to an American movie studio and the boys seemed to enjoy it thoroughly.

Beatles' Film Another Solo?

The Beatles have been making a lot of solo appearances lately, and if things go as scheduled the four Britons may not even be viewed as a group in their forthcoming film.

Tentative plans reveal John, Paul, George and Ringo will all make appearances in the film, but probably never at the same time. Filming is scheduled to begin in January.

One of the Beatles will have the leading role and will portray a character with a split personality. He will imagine he is four different people—himself plus the other three Beatles.

The lead Beatle has not yet been selected. The film will also have a leading lady, who will be in separate scenes with all four Beatles.

The idea of solo shots was submitted by scriptwriter Owen Holder and approved by Brian Epstein. Four different story lines have been written around the basic plot and one is expected to be approved very soon.

London sources are speculating that due to the film's unusual story line fewer songs will be used than in either "Help" or "A Hard Day's Night." But John and Paul are expected to write a full score of incidental music.

Beatle John Lennon has redeemed himself, in the eyes of his business partners anyway.

Northern Songs Co., a Beatle-owned music publishing firm which took a sharp drop on the stock market when Lennon made his infamous remarks about Christianity, will pay shareholders a big 40 per cent this year.

The company announced that current profits this year total $1.7 million.

... BEAU BRUMMELS (l. to r.) Sal, Don, John, Ron and Ron split due to health and the draft board.

Brummels 'Killed' By Health, Draft Board

The unavailability of three members of the Beau Brummels to conduct tours and personal appearances has forced the disbandment of the group, a spokesman for the Brummels told *BEAT* reporters in an exclusive interview.

Carl Scott, Brummels' manager, said his group would withdraw from public appearances entirely rather than replace Ron Elliot, Don Irving and Ron Meagher.

Scott said, however, the group may still record together and use the same name.

Elliot's poor health has not allowed him to tour with the Brummels for quite some time now, but it was the loss of Irving and Meagher that finally forced the split. Both musicians were drafted into the Military last month.

Scott said the Brummels accepted with optimism the decision for the split. "They look at it more as a beginning than as an end," he said.

Career Plans

He said Valentino, Elliot and John Peterson all have immediate plans for their careers. Elliot will devote almost full time to record production and Valentino is expected to do solo singing on the Reprise label.

Peterson, a drummer, will continue to work with Valentino.

The Beau Brummels had been an established group only slightly more than two years, but achieved widespread popularity during that time. They were voted best new group of 1965 in a poll taken by The BEAT.

The group was responsible for a string of top selling records. Their first and biggest, "Laugh Laugh," sold more than 500,000 copies here and was one of America's biggest exports to England.

Once the group was established, however, it encountered legal problems. Declan Mulligan, an original member of the Brummels who left the group and returned to his native Ireland, filed a $1,250,000 suit against his former mates early this year.

Allegations

Mulligan alleged he was the founder of the Brummels and he charged he had been frozen out of the group by the other four members.

But Mulligan's charges were never publicly substantiated as he settled out of court for a comparatively nominal $1,500.

The group had a steady tour of road duty during 1966. Their final club date was at the Whiskey-A-Go-Go in Hollywood, where they closed in mid-October.

SUPREME, DIANA ROSS, VICTIM OF MAGNIFICENT 'MARRIAGE' HOAX

The pop farce of the year was pulled off at the expense of Supreme lead singer, Diana Ross, and her Motown chief, Berry Gordy.

Last Friday night, a girl called up a New York radio station claiming to be Diana's secretary and informed the station that the Supremes' lead singer had married Berry Gordy.

Since it was Friday night, everyone at Motown had left the office and consequently the "marriage" could be neither confirmed nor denied. According to a Motown official: "The news was put out in a bulletin and things went from there."

Wedding gifts and congratulatory notes have been pouring into the Motown offices ever since. All gifts are, naturally, being returned but some of them are so expensive that the temptation *not* to keep them is demanding great will power.

Following the "marriage" announcement the rumor that the Supremes are breaking up is running rampant but according to Motown the whole thing is a gigantic hoax and the Supremes are definitely not going to change members.

DIANA ROSS AND BERRY GORDY — "Happily married" — not really.

Inside the BEAT
Letters To The Editor 2
Eric Burdon Names Animals 3
Teens Discuss Religion 4
Standells Thrown Out 5
Bill Cosby Wins Four Goldies 6
Man-Made Monkees 7
Discussion 10
Association Schedule 11
Herman A Smash 12
Visit With Tommy Roe 13
For Girls Only 14
Left Banke Communicate 15

KRLA ARCHIVES

Letters TO THE EDITOR

POEM FOR 'LOVERS'

Dear BEAT:
I read the book "Only Lovers Left Alive" (which as you know is to be the Stones' film as well) a few months ago, before I knew about the film. Afterwards, I wrote a poem concerning the beginning—after the adults were gone. I'd like to share it with you.

The younger generation started speaking up again.
   We told them what we wanted—and then we did not waive.
Our parents stood 'round saying we would drive them to their graves.
   Ah, yes it's true that's what we did—thru no fault of our own,
We stand for what we believe in, and that they should have known.
   The world is in a better state—though not much I should say,
Gangs and groups have formed all around and more form every day.
Months have passed since the crisis, and winter's coming on,
   The birds have gone, the wind grows cold, and frost lies on the lawn.
One thing good about the world—racial prejudice has passed,
   We all fight for each other, and no one's an outcast.
—Sharlene Swinson

UPSET

Dear BEAT:
This is in response to the letter, "Sir Douglas Poor Rep." It really upset me because I like John York who is in the Quintet. He is a groovy guy. When I met John he was shy but friendly. He did not leave me with the impression that he was "an under-fed, homeless misfit." He was very polite and I liked him right away.

I've been writing to John since I met him in September, I received a letter from him. I'll always treasure that letter because it was written from the heart. John proved what I knew a long time ago, that he's a beautiful person!

I only hope that more teenagers will "practice what they preach" by not judging the Quintet by how they look but by evaluating them as individuals who have faults like you and I.
Marcy

FINKING ON RUSS

Dear BEAT:
So, the Association is finally getting the recognition they deserve! Wonder of wonders! I never thought it would happen. A good, extremely talented, no-gimmick group getting ahead, I mean.

For so long, the only pictures and articles on the Association to be found anywhere were found right in the pages of The BEAT. For that foresight, I congratulate you.

Anyway, the reason I am writing is simple. I dig Russ Giguere and would like to know all about him. Since you know him as well as anybody, I am, naturally, writing to you for help. Please, tell me all you know about Russ.
Cyn Ellington

That's a rough assignment, Cyn. We hardly know where to begin. Russ is an intelligent, extremely friendly, fun-loving person. He has a wild passion for buttons and is forever popping into our offices to see if we've received any new ones. He always has a favorite word with which to punctuate his speech. He used to go around saying "repent" all the time but now has forsaken that for "pleasant."

Success has gone to Russ' head—sort of. He never owned a car and declared that they were rather useless as he never went anywhere he couldn't walk. However, following the chart-topping "Cherish" Russ has purchased a car! "A racy, black convertible," he says. The year and make? A 1959 Volkswagen. Why? "Because that's all the money I had in my pocket at the time."

What else can we say, Cyn? The guy's out of sight!
The Editor

MONKEES OFF?

Dear BEAT:
I've just read an article in a newspaper with the ratings of the new television shows and it says that The Monkees might go off the air! That made me mad because everyone I know watches The Monkees. So, if you're as nutty about The Monkees as I am help save The Monkees by writing to Program Director, NBC TV, 3000 West Alameda Ave., Burbank, California 91503.

Even if a show's ratings are low, your letters can help keep it on. So, tell all your friends to write and say how good the show is. The more letters, the better. Thank you very much.
Shannon McMahon

While it's true that the initial ratings on new television shows, indicates that The Monkees ratings are not all they could be, the axe has not, as yet, been lifted. However, we're sure the Monkees themselves would appreciate your letters regarding their continuance on the air.
The Editor

MOTHERS 'IN' BUT LEFT OUT

Dear BEAT:
In reference to the October 22 article on "Electronic Music," I would like to say that the Mothers of Invention's new album, "Freak Out," is full to the brim with electronic gadgets. This album is strictly out of sight and the best in my collection.

Thanks also to the great new Beach Boys' album, "Pet Sounds." A groovy set of grooves. Thanks again.
Scott Lyon

CHERISHED

Dear BEAT:
I feel that congratulations are in store for Debbie Davis, as well as a great big "THANK YOU!"

For many months, you have been printing letters either condemning or standing behind various entertainers. But never have you printed a letter as "cherished" as Debbie's.

Needless to say, I'm an Association fan all the way but I'm not quick to put down any other group. It's just that they're beautifuller than anyone else!
A Terry Kirkman fan forever

P.F. ON HERMAN

Dear BEAT:
A few months ago a friend and I went to a local night club to see some friends of ours who were playing there at the time. P.F. Sloan was also there and during one of their breaks he came over to talk to them. I overheard him say that Peter Noone puts on his English accent. This remark made me mad because I know Peter personally and his accent, to my knowledge, is genuine.

I can't understand P.F. Sloan's basis for such a remark. He has worked with Peter and written songs for him.
"Anonym"

MICKEY ROONEY BAND

Dear BEAT:
First of all, I'd like to tell you how much I love your newspaper. The articles and pictures are all really great and I especially luv Shirley Poston's column.

Could you please tell me where I can write to the Monkees? They are absolutely the greatest thing since the Beatles (yeah!!). I luv all four of them.

I noticed a few weeks ago that someone wrote you a letter telling you about a certain group she wanted to be discovered. Well, I have a group that wants discovering too. It's the Mickey Rooney Jr. Band. They have been on television a few times but I've never heard them played on the radio or mentioned in The BEAT.

Their latest record, "The Choice Is Yours," is really good. It was written by their bass guitar player, Johnny Blanchard. The other members are Mickey Rooney Jr., Carmine Sardo and Russ Haney. This group really deserves some recognition.
Louise Bensema

You may write to the Monkees at 1334 North Beechwood Drive, Hollywood 28, California 90028.
The Editor

KEITH LOOSE

Dear BEAT:
Help! I just read in a teen magazine that Keith Richard is engaged. Is he? If he is, I'm going to commit suicide or something! The magazine said something like "and there was Keith Richard, dragging his fiancee, Linda Keith, with him."

Please tell me whether this is true or not. Thank you very much.
Toni DeVito

Relax, Toni, you needn't do anything as drastic as commit suicide. Keith is not engaged to Linda Keith or anyone else. At one time, Keith and Linda were going together but it is now a "thing of the past." As a matter of fact, Keith doesn't even have a steady girlfriend anymore.
The Editor

MISSED 'EM

Dear BEAT:
We were shocked to find that in your article, "Funny Men Coming Into The Teen Age," you completely overlooked the Bay Area's own comedy team, The Congress of Wonders.

In case you haven't heard, and you should have by now, they are three very groovy guys who perform the written works of John Lennon (yes, the Beatle) as well as their own material.

We really don't see how you could have missed them but we might suggest that you make amends to an awful lot of loyal fans by printing this letter and writing an article on a group that deserves a lot more attention than the silence you gave them.
Karen Meile
Deborah Henriques

DAVID'S COOL

Dear BEAT:
It may surprise you to get a letter from so far away and I do hope you will publish it in The BEAT. You see, I'm a very great fan of David McCallum's and I would like to say a few words about an interview in a U.S. magazine (not The BEAT). The reporter concerned made some sarcastic remarks about David being Scottish and I wish to point out that us Scots don't run around in kilts shouting "Hoot mon" at the top of our voices!

I live very near Glasgow, where David was born and spent most of his childhood and, in my opinion, the people are the friendliest you could find anywhere.

So, I do hope that the reporter who wrote the article reads this and understands that there's nothing wrong with David being a "braw Scots laddie." Also, I'm truly sorry that he's lost his accent.
Janice Pitkethly

TEMPTATIONS

Dear BEAT:
I would like some information on how I could write to The Temptations, mainly Eddie Kendricks. I think he is so fine!

Please! Don't let me down.
Alexis Smith

You can write to the Temptations at 2648 West Grand Blvd., Detroit, Michigan.
The Editor

STONES' GIGGLE

Dear BEAT:
May I be among the first of the girls to comment on the Rolling Stones' "mothers" picture? It is not merely a "giggle." It's a scream. Very good, boys. If it begins a good old-fashioned controversy, as I'm sure it will, what little faith I have left in mankind will be destroyed.

So, rave on, fellow Americans, since you seem to have nothing better to do. I'm waiting for you all to tear into Peter Noone for being so inexcusably clumsy as to smash his fingers in an elevator door. I really think this calls for a Hermits' bonfire.

Sorry, I didn't mean to get carried away but I can take only so much. Let me terminate this tirade by saying—it's none of our business what any of the pop stars do. They don't ask us to love them; we love them because they are lovable, not to mention talented.

If they want to chip their teeth, chop up dolls, pose as mothers, punch disc jockeys, smash their fingers, say they are more popular than Jesus in England, play the sitar, play the field, or stand on their heads in a purple snowdrift, why, let's let them. Okay?

To the Stones again—great photo fellows.
Corey Clarke

KRLA ARCHIVES

On the BEAT
By Louise Criscione

In order to keep things from becoming too terribly dull, a new Yardbird rumor is making the pop rounds. Of course, we've heard the "Jeff Beck to leave Yardbirds" rumor so many times now that the whole thing is a gigantic drag. So, the latest rumor has Keith Relf departing! The rumor has reached such proportions in England that a spokesman for the group was forced to issue a denial.

However, the rumor-people are sticking to their guns and continue to prophesize that Keith will soon leave the Yardbirds due to poor health. It is true that Keith has been in poor physical condition for several years and, in fact, in 1964 was hospitalized with a punctured lung. At that time, Keith *did* consider leaving the group because he felt he would only pull them down. Luckily, Keith reconsidered and remained with the Yardbirds. I, for one, believe this latest rumor is just that—a rumor. The day it becomes fact, you can kiss the Yardbirds goodbye. Without Keith they don't exist.

Tops Do It

Congratulations are in order for the swinging Four Tops. Why? Because in two weeks they've managed to knock all competition out of their path and have snatched the number one position in England with their fantastic "Reach Out I'll Be There." The disc has already made it to the top spot in the U.S. and I suppose the English didn't want to be different so they hurriedly sent the Tops to the heights of their charts too. A wise decision anyway you look at it.

You must admit that there is nothing like a nice little squabble between two pop groups. So, just to oblige everyone, the Hollies and the Small Faces had a rousing argument over which group would top the bill on their current British tour. The Hollies say they have top billing and the Small Faces declare that they were supposed to receive equal billing with the Hollies. As a result, the Small Faces missed two of the tour dates when neither group would compromise.

Hollies Sound Off

On the American scene, the Hollies may be sorry they're sounding off so much lately. They've cancelled the Dick Clark tour because they didn't want to play ballrooms, have nixed their projected film because they refuse to sing on screen, decided to make themselves relatively scarce so that fans will want to see them and they will only come to America for the Herman tour in December "if the money's right." Somebody ought to clue them in that absence doesn't necessarily make the U.S. heart grow fonder.

Not to be outdone by *anyone*, the Association is putting out a book of their own. Besides the usual pictures, etc., each member of the group has written his own autobiography for the book and Russ has contributed the forward. Other Associated literary works will also be included and you can expect the book in time for Christmas presents. That, of course, does not mean you'll *get* it by Christmas.

Meanwhile, everyone is having a field day suing the group. Funny what success will do for you. Make a little money and everyone wants to stick his fingers in the pie. I imagine it's enough to make a person wish he was still unknown and broke 'cause at least then you know who your friends are.

Scott Collapses

Scott Walker continues along his collapsing route. This time he collapsed in a dressing room in London. Says the group's co-manager, Maurice King: "Scott was taken ill suddenly. His eyes puffed up and he could hardly see. He had taken some tablets to calm his nerves and I think they must have upset him."

On the heels of the news that the Stones had failed to send "Have You Seen Your Mother, Baby, Standing In The Shadow?" to the top of the British charts, three of their devoted fans decided to take matters into their own hands. Accordingly, each fan stomped into their nearest London record store with the purpose of purchasing ten copies of the single each. Unfortunately, it didn't help much as the Stones toppled down another notch on the record charts.

... KEITH RELF

... MICK JAGGER

Eric Burdon's Announced His New Group Members

Eric Burdon finally unveiled his new group last week after his split with the original Animals almost two months ago. Burdon's new Animals made their debut at Finsbury Park Astoria on the opening date of the Burdon-Georgie Fame-Chris Farlowe tour.

Speculations that as many as two members of the former group would remain with Burdon were nixed as Hilton Valentine, Chas Chandler and Dave Rowberry have all departed.

Drummer Barry Jenkins is the lone original Animal retained by Burdon. The new group, which is alleged to be nothing more than back-up accompanyment for Burdon's solos, will keep the name, Animals.

Burdon dipped into other English groups to replace the original trio.

The new Animals are:

Tom Parker—organist. He is Crispian St. Peter's musical director and formerly played with the Mark Leeman Five. Parker's presence, however, may be only temporary. He is expected to continue working with Crispian when the latter returns from a lengthy tour of Australia.

Johnny Weilder—lead guitarist. He is a 19-year-old Londoner who was a one-time member of Johnny Kidd's Pirates and John Mayall's Bluesbreakers.

Danny McCulloch—bass guitarist. He played with Screamin' Lord Sutch and Red Price, and has backed Jerry Lee Lewis and John Lee Hooker.

... ERIC KEEPS JENKINS AND FIRES THE OTHERS.

KINKS GET THEIR L.P. RELEASED

After weeks of waiting and legal hassles, the Kinks have successfully negotiated for the release of their new L.P. The record was released in England Oct. 28.

The lengthy hold-up was terminated recently when Kink Ray Davies and manager Robert Wace flew to America and teamed with business manager Allen Klein to settle the dispute.

Release difficulties and hang-ups in their personal appearance schedule recently had the Kinks almost at a standstill. They broke several engagements which prompted their ban in several Scandanavian countries.

But at least now they can release their records and it looks like they're on the move again, although no plans have been set for the release of a new single. "Right now there is nothing in the can," a Kink spokesman said.

Now that contractural difficulties have been settled, however, the group is expected to head for the recording studios shortly.

BILL FOR ROYAL SHOW INCLUDES U.S. STARS

England's Royal Variety Performance, following in the wake of criticism of its tentative booking bill, has announced it will feature some of America's biggest name entertainers this year.

Americans Gene Pitney, Sammy Davis, Jerry Lewis, Wayne Newton and Henry Mancini will all appear on the show that features foremost entertainers from all over the world. The Queen-Mother will attend the show.

The show, however, has been criticized by British press for allegedly breaking certain practices and completely ignoring beat groups for the first time in many years.

There are two noticeable absentees on the bill—there will be no English female vocalist or beat groups. In addition, only two groups of any sort will be included in the long line of celebrities.

The Seekers and the Bachelors, both clean-cut, conservative groups, were the lone groups to receive invitations to the exclusive event.

The refusal to book more groups on this year's show probably stems from the Beatles' refusal to appear on the program when they were asked last year. There is no evident explanation for leaving off a British songstress, however.

Last year, Dusty Springfield and Shirley Bassey appeared and it was believed either Cilla Black or Petula Clark would perform this year. But neither was asked.

The Royal Variety Show is Britain's gala tribute to the music industry and is annually aired at the London Palladium. It takes place Nov. 14 and will be on nationwide TV in England.

The invitation of the five American performers, especially Pitney, came as no surprise to English observers. Pitney is one of America's most consistently popular singers with British fans.

Pitney, now on a promotional visit to England, delayed his trip to the country for more than a month in an effort to enable him to take part in the show.

KRLA ARCHIVES

TEEN PANEL

Is Religion Dead, Dying Or Alive?

In this issue, the members of The BEAT teen panel exchange views on the subject of religion. Participating are Andrea – 16, Jean – 17, Karl – 18, and Brian – 19.

If you would like to be a member of a future panel, or would like to suggest a topic, please send a postcard to The BEAT.

Karl – "As far as I'm concerned, John Lennon has already summed it all up."

Andrea – "Don't tell me we're going to get off on *that*. His comment has been hashed and rehashed and I'm sick of hearing about it."

Karl – "Then my opinion would make you just as sick. I agree with him."

Sick

Andrea – "I didn't say his opinion made me sick. I said I'm sick of hearing about it. All he said was that there's less interest in religion today. Hundreds of ministers say that every Sunday. They don't make headlines. People just made a big deal out of it."

Karl – "Sure, but that proves what he said was right. The only people who were genuinely upset over it were kids who got the wrong idea and felt like they were being forced to choose between the Beatles and religion. All the rest just used his opinion to get publicity for themselves, or to have something to sound off about. Those guys in Alabama who started the whole thing – they probably haven't been to church for ten years. It wasn't a protest, it was a promotion. 'Good Christians' don't start bonfires. Nothing like this has happened since Hitler's book-burnings. Lennon was so right."

Jean – "I think he was right, too, but I think his comment helped religion more than harmed it. It really made some people wake up and take a look at their own lives. I'll bet church attendance has gone up a lot since August."

Andrea – "I said I was sick of hearing about this and here I am talking about it, but oh, well. I agree it helped like you said, but you also mentioned the word harm. You didn't elaborate on that. How much harm did it do, in your opinion, I mean, and what kind of harm?"

Harm

Jean – "That's a good question, but I can't answer it. I hadn't thought about it that way. I have thought about the possible harm it could do to the Beatles, but not to religion. I don't know if anything could actually *harm* religion."

Brian – "Not on an over-all basis, you mean. No one event or person is powerful enough to have that much effect on millions of people. But Lennon's remark didn't do the Christian religion a whole lot of good in one way, although it may have helped in another. I don't see how any devout Christian who is also an intelligent person could help but be appalled by the way some of his fellow-Christians acted. Some of them probably stopped going to church when they found out how narrow some of the other members really are."

Jean – "I doubt that. Maybe a few did, but most people don't change their minds that suddenly, or their church. Besides, what other people in a church do isn't really that important. What's important is whatever there is between yourself and what you believe in. Still, it does get you to thinking when people don't practice what they preach. It's like parents telling you not to do a certain thing and then doing it themselves. It makes you wonder. I don't know if this is good or bad."

Karl – "If what's good or bad? Wondering about your parents or wondering about religion?"

Jean – "About religion. People always 'wonder' about each other – that's natural. But it seems almost *un-*natural to start probing into beliefs you've had all your life. There's a lot wrong with a lot of 'good Christians,' but they'd be worse if they didn't have their faith to keep them in line. Whether you disagree or agree with the Christian religion, you've got to admit its basic principles are valid."

Teaches Love

Karl – "Sure they are. It teaches kindness and fairness and honesty and brotherhood; it all boils down to one word – *love*, and that's good. There should be more of it. But it's the rest of it that throws me. You aren't allowed to think of Christ as a great man and a profound philosopher. If your feelings stop there and don't go any further, you're doomed according to most churches. Even if you're the best person in the world, and follow the principles to the letter, they say you're still going to wind up in Hell if you don't go along with the intangible parts of the faith."

Brian – "Are you talking about believing there is a God and accepting the divinity of Christ?"

Karl – "Yeah, partly. I mean there's proof that those basic principles are real. All you have to do is look around you. But there isn't any proof about the other, starting right from the Creation. It isn't easy to believe all of it when you live in a scientific society, and most churches say you've *got* to believe all of it. Some of them even say you can be a bastard all your life and never do one right thing and then turn around on your deathbed and say you believe and everything's okay. I can't buy that."

Andrea – "You keep saying churches-say-this and churches-say-that. I think that situation is what makes it so difficult for some people to accept religion. There are so many churches and doctrines, and that's okay I guess, but the trouble is, some of them think they're the *only* ones who are right. I mean, they're very *adamant* about it. If you don't go to that church and do what that church says, you're out of luck. That doesn't make sense. The Christian religion is based on the Bible, and that's been translated and re-translated and interpreted and re-interpreted, and sometimes *mis*-interpreted. I don't have any problems believing there's a God, but a lot of people have problems figuring out what *version* to believe. Who's wrong and who's right? And really, who has the right to say anyway? What *person*, I mean, is qualified to tell you what the Bible

Brian – "How do you know there's a God?"

Andrea – "I don't. I *believe* there is. There's a difference, you know."

Brian – "Why do you believe this?"

Andrea – "How do *I* know? Because I was taught to believe it, and because I want there to be one. I just think there is one. All of this couldn't have just *happened*."

Brian – "Ever heard of the theory of evolution?"

Andrea – "No, I just got off the boat this morning. Of course I've heard of it. It could be right, but I could be right too. I think it's pointless for you to ask questions like 'how do you know there's a God?' I can't prove there is and you can't prove there isn't, so why even talk about it?"

Brian – "Sorry about that. Next question. Do you believe exactly as you were taught, or do you have some of your own *versions*, as you put it."

Andrea – "I pretty much agree with the church I go to. The things I don't agree with, I have my own opinions about. My church isn't down on every other faith, and doesn't have a lot of additional man-made rules and regulations. They do have certain ways of their own, but they aren't offensive or illogical, like thinking only Protestants are going to Heaven and it's just too bad about the Catholic and Jewish religions. I couldn't accept that for five minutes. Fortunately, I haven't had to try."

Karl – "How does your church feel about other religions, like Buddhism?"

Andrea – "I've never even heard the subject mentioned in church."

Other Faiths?

Karl – "How do you feel about the other faiths?"

Andrea – "I don't know very much about them. I do know that Buddhism started in the sixth century – the sixth century B.C. – and I only remember that because I looked the word up in the dictionary once to see how it was spelled. But from what I've heard, it seems like all major religions in the world worship a central figure, and have the same basic principles. I'd say we're all just worshipping the same God in different ways. Which is great unless you get to thinking your way is the *only* way."

Jean – "Do you think people who don't believe in God will go to Hell, even if they live good, responsible lives?"

Andrea – "Why is everyone picking on *me*? I'm not a theologian."

Jean – "We aren't picking on you – we're just interested. You don't have to answer the question if you don't want to."

Andrea – "Well, I'd like to be able to, but I can't. I haven't decided yet."

Brian – "What's holding you up?"

...LENNON MAKING THEM THINK?

Andrea – "What are you trying to make me say? That I don't know whether I believe there even is a Hell? Okay, I *admit it*. I *do not know* what I believe about this."

Brian – "Why do you doubt its existence, which you obviously do or you wouldn't be worrying about it."

Andrea – "Oh, for God's sake. I'm not *worrying* about it. I'm thinking it *over*. I don't doubt the existence of life after death; I'm just not sure this part of it has been interpreted correctly. It doesn't seem to me that all the people in the world, and all the people who have lived and will live can possibly be separated into two rigid categories like Good and Bad. We're human beings and a lot of things contribute to what we do with our lives. Hardly anybody is that *Good* and hardly anybody is that *Bad* unless they have a screw loose or were raised like some kind of animal. I get the creeps just saying this, because it sounds like I'm trying to re-write the Bible: I'm not. I'm not questioning it either. I'm only questioning the man-made interpretation of this particular subject."

Creeps?

Jean – "I know exactly what you mean by the creeps."

Brian – "I don't."

Jean – "Were you brought up in a religious home, or have you gone to church a lot?"

Brian – "Well, I wasn't brought up by a bunch of savages, and I went to church regularly – sort of – until I started high school, but I don't think you could call mine a *religious* home."

Jean – "That explains why you don't know about the creeps. When you're brought up in a religious atmosphere, or where religion is an integral – I never *could* say that word right – part of the atmosphere around you, you get a funny feeling when you start sorting things out for yourself. Not just because you're questioning what you've been taught. Also because the questions either have no answers, or have so *many* answers, you don't know which one is the right one."

Brian – "You know what that feeling is, don't you? It's fear. Religion has a lot of good things about it, but fear isn't one of them. That may account for why girls are more religious than boys. Girls scare easier. There are other reasons too, I suppose. Boys are more interested in...in other activities."

Andrea – "I had a feeling you'd get around to that subject sooner or later."

Not Mine

Brian – "Relax. You aren't my type."

Jean – "If we can get back to the previous subject, what I felt may have been fear. I don't know. Whatever it was, it doesn't happen to me any more. I've already gone through that period of trying to figure everything out, and I finally gave up. Now I can accept the existence of God without picking at details and sitting around driving myself nuts wondering who Adam and Even's sons married and how this or that could possibly have happened. I've stopped worrying about the details. Like I said before, the basic principles are valid, and that's what really matters, I still don't know if it's good or bad to feel this way, but that's the way I feel."

Andrea – "I think it's my turn to pick on someone. Brian, I'd like to know if you believe in God?"

Brian – "So would I."

Andrea – "Why don't you *know* whether you believe?"

Turn to Page 6

KRLA ARCHIVES

Vaudeville's Best Is Bouncing Back!

Oh! For those good old days... times that were the heyday of the hip flask, raccoon coat and bulky sweater with a large college letter plastered across the front. Oh! What has become of the Model T's, the Al Jolsons and the unquestioned master, Rudy Vallee and his crooning, swooning sounds?

Well, hip flasks still serve some useful purpose, but raccoon coats and bulky letter sweaters were buried with the 30's. Model T's are now the property of middle-aged antique auto enthusiasts. Al Jolson is dead and Rudy Vallee is grey where he is not bald.

Ghosts

But wait... there is some salvage from that golden era. Like ghosts, those unmistakeable sounds of Rudy Vallee and his former contemporaries have come back from the dead to haunt the music industry. And a real, honest-to-goodness vaudeville band is making all the noise with those sounds of the past.

Appropriately, the group is labeled The New Vaudeville Band and all the nasal crooning is about a thing called "Winchester Cathedral." Ironically, The New Vaudeville Band is from Olde England.

What inspired the group's reversion to antique music? "Junk," answers Geoff Stephens with a wink.

Geoff is the leader of this merry band, and he has a keen interest in relics from the past. Geoff has an immense admiration for the sounds of the 30's and he has been scouring antique shops in London for some time in search of material.

For the group's next record, Geoff says, a song popular 35 years ago might be recorded. But a follow-up for "Winchester Cathedral" will be difficult. The disc is currently number three in England and is gaining more and more momentum in the States every day.

Is the song just a novelty item or do fans really dig this wild new, old-fashioned flavoring? The group has been touring with Dusty Springfield and Geoff says "the reaction was very good.

"We only had a small spot on the tour – about 12 minutes – and basically it went down very well," continued Geoff. "It was a bit weird. We did 'Day Dream' and even 'Batman' and a James Brown number! It was a bit tricky at first to see what the audiences would like. They seem to like the vaudeville stuff so they'll get more numbers like 'Lady Godiva' and 'Mrs. Applebee.'"

Geoff was the soloist when the record was originally cut but he now has a full group with him. The line-up is Hugh Watts (trombone), Nick Wilser (guitar), Ian Green (piano and organ), Bobby Kerr (trumpet and vocals), Neil Korner (bass guitar) and Henry Harrison (drums.)

Permanent?

"I hope this will be permanent," said Geoff. "We are aiming basically to do what I call modern good time numbers and some really old numbers.

"A follow-up single to 'Winchester' will be difficult. I've written a thing called 'Shirl' but I have also got to do another song to take along to the company.

"But you've got to be careful with follow-ups now. You can't get away with similar follow-ups in this country any more. We can't do another 'Winchester Cathedral' but we've got to do something with the same recognizable sound that people can identify."

...BRIAN JONES AND MICK JAGGER are greeted at the airport by three of the Standells

Hotels Nix Standells

The prejudice of some people in America is really amazing. The Standells were the latest victims of narrow-mindedness when they were turned out of three different Chicago hotels because their hair is longer than the hotels' management deemed necessary.

The Standells had previously made hotel reservations but when the group turned up in person the hotels took one look at their hair and informed them that their reservations were cancelled.

This is only the latest in a long string of insults aimed at pop groups whose hair is not trimmed to Yul Brynner length. Hotels have become notorious for tearing up reservations and practically every group who tours the country returns home with the news that hotels, restaurants, Disneyland and other such "public" places have refused them admittance because of their hair.

A segment of the American population apparently feels that the right to choose one's own hair style is not a freedom guaranteed in the U.S. Constitution. But the situation really gets ridiculous when the Yardbirds are thrown out by a hotel which was, at that time, housing a mule; when hair, or lack of hair, is a requirement to get into Disneyland; and when the Standells are not allowed to stay in three hotels because they're not bald.

The whole thing makes people wonder if George Washington, Benjamin Franklin and Davy Crocket faced the same problems during their lifetimes. Were our Founding Fathers kicked out of hotels because they wore wigs? Or maybe they were thrown out if they *failed* to wear wigs!

'in' people are talking about...

What's happened to the Beatles and wondering if they're going to forsake togetherness for solo jobs on a permanent basis... What the Supremes are saying in Morse Code or if they're really not saying anything and just hanging us on... How far that Clarksville Train went when the entire background music was provided by studio musicians... How with legs like theirs it's no small wonder the Stones are hiding in the shadow... Beauty being only skin deep and the beauties protesting that the whole concept is a gigantic lie... Where P&G found their Lady Godiva and deciding it was probably under some rock in the middle of the Sahara.

PEOPLE ARE TALKING ABOUT the Beach Boys finally getting some good vibrations on wax... Whether Billy Stewart has a speech problem or does it on purpose... Why Mitch seems to feel that he has to put two different songs on one record and wondering if perhaps he has a difficulty counting or if he believes that two always wins out over one... What tears Percy up... Why Terry kisses hands and Russ only offers a lick of chocolate candy... How groovy Tommy's new house is and wishing he'd have a party up there. Doing the Philly Dog but giving up on the idea because they'd only look like idiots grooving out of their bag... How sweet it is that Lou digs low-down sneaks.

PEOPLE ARE TALKING ABOUT the going rate on anything that ultra-cool Bill Cosby has touched and how big your points soar if you can honestly (or dishonestly) say you know him... Run, run, look and see and wondering if Brian's reverting to his first grade days... How many records the Hollies are going to release before they get off their "stop" kick... Whether or not Dean really drinks and what a giggle it would be if the guy doesn't guzzle a drop... If Ronnie Dove really doesn't want to know how come he keeps asking... Whether or not it's true that Davy's father wouldn't let him into the house until he had his hair cut — twice.

PEOPLE ARE TALKING ABOUT how popular the Association is now and kicking themselves for not being nicer to the guys when they were struggling to move because now they have to stand in line to tell the world that *they* discovered the Association and how some people are even willing to go to court over "discovery right"... How the Monkees could possibly be receiving such low ratings when so many people watch the show and deciding that perhaps the ratings are fixed against long-haired groups... How heaven must have *really* sent the Elgins since no one has any pictures or information on the group... When it's going to be Herman's turn to get burned... The Mama's and Papa's leaving the pop world – either voluntarily or unvoluntarily.

PEOPLE ARE TALKING ABOUT what would happen if Elvis got a butch haircut and deciding it probably wouldn't make much difference since no one ever sees him anyway... Sonny and Cher falling from front page news to a middle-of-the-paper picture – occasionally... How long it will take groups to change members so many times that they kill themselves and the scene reverts back to solo artists... The state of the pop charts when Pat Boone and Dean Martin get their records on it and that's not even counting Frank Sinatra and Roger Williams... Whether or not the influx of hype artists will ever end... Gerry swinging a girl and getting a medium-sized hit out of it and deciding that he definitely received better results from the ferry – Why the national "news" magazines are finally recognizing the existence of pop artists but limited it to interviews with the Spoonful.

PEOPLE ARE TALKING ABOUT the fact that only nine British artists are included in this week's national top one hundred songs and how groovy it is to have Americans back ruling the pop roost... Who "inspired" John to go ahead and work with Paul on "All In Good Time"... What happened to the Young Rascals... How fast so-called psychedelic music is becoming a thing of the past and how even the hippies would rather switch than fight... Gary Alexander's praise for "I Spy" and how sweet it is to see him actually conforming to something for a change... The problems mini-skirts present.

PEOPLE ARE TALKING ABOUT Winchester Cathedral and wondering if the lead singer has a nasal problem and deciding that it doesn't matter because the record is a hit – nasal or no nasal... How tall Johnny Rivers is in his stocking feet... Them who has getting and them who ain't remaining the same but swinging anyway... Staging a giant, nation-wide protest to lower the drinking age but changing their minds because bartenders dig such big tips... How absolutely broad-minded the younger generation is and how groovy it would be if adults followed our example and stopped being anti-everything.

KRLA ARCHIVES

PICTURES in the NEWS

...JOHNNY MATHIS AND PAUL McCARTNEY grin understandingly as Ringo Starr does his very best to explain a point.

THE COUNT FIVE made the news by turning down a million dollars in favor of continuing their education. The group was offered a million dollars to tour the United States but the boys feel that their education definitely comes first and nixed the deal in spite of the big money.

GENE CLARK has turned from the Byrds to the Gene Clark Group and is now going strictly solo. His first single for Columbia is "Echoes" and his debut album is due out sometime during January.

PETULA CLARK has just opened her second stint at the world famous Copacabana in New York to a standing-room-only audience. Pet wowed the packed audience with her hits, old standards and original material. Her latest pop smash, "Who Am I," is flying up the world's charts and the international singing star is slowly but surely making the rounds of the top musical shows in the States.

COSBY, ASSOCIATION WIN GOLD RECORDS

Bill Cosby, the ultra-cool star of "I Spy," has set a new record. All four of Cosby's albums—"Wonderfulness," "Why Is There Air?", "I Started Out As A Child" and "Bill Cosby Is A Very Funny Fellow, Right?"—have been certified by the Record Industry Association of America as having sold one million dollars worth of records. This means that Cosby has sold more records than an other comedian on wax!

What is even more unique is the fact that all four of Cosby's LP's were certified at the same time, enabling him to snatch the laugh crown with no trouble at all. No comedian has ever sold that many records but, then, perhaps no other comedian has ever appealed to such a large age group. Teens as well as their parents and grandparents all dig Cosby's brand of humor and show it by purchasing his albums en masse.

Besides Bill Cosby's four Gold Records, the RIAA certified one single as a million seller. The single to receive a Gold Record was "Cherish" by the Association. It is the group's first million seller as well as the first million seller ever to be released on the Valiant label.

Milton Berle presented the Gold Record to the Association on his national television show and announced that due to audience-response he was forced to have the Association back on his show a short three weeks after their debut appearance.

The Association is also scheduled for an appearance on "Ed Sullivan" but no date has yet been set. They're currently recording a follow-up to their first album, "And Then Along Comes The Association."

The only other album certified for a Gold Record this time around was "The Best Of Al Hirt." It marked the fourth million seller for Hirt. His previous million sellers were "Honey In The Horn," "Cotton Candy" and "Sugar Lips."

Although most people outside of the record industry are notoriously unaware of the fact, a gold record is extremely difficult to come by and is rarely won. For instance, of all the singles currently in the top one hundred in the nation only one has sold a million. And that one is "Cherish."

Teens Discuss Religion

(Continued from Page 6)

Brian—"Because I haven't much cared one way or another. I never really thought much about it until recently. I'm working it out, though, with your help of course."

Karl—"If you two can stop long enough, I want to say something. Jean brought up a good point. My big hassle about religion has been the details, and their credibility. That really doesn't make much sense. It's like worrying about a few notes in a symphony—let's hear it on those violins, folks. I also have a question. Why is it that people in small towns tend to be far more religious than people who live in a large city?"

Small Town

Brian—"I should know. I used to live in one. In a small town, there's nothing to do and most of your social life centers around the church you go to. Small town people aren't really more religious, they just spend more time at church because there's no place else to go, and they're more narrow. They just hear someone else's ideas of what's going on in the world, instead of seeing it for themselves."

Jean—"There are people like that in cities, too. That's about the only bad thing about religion. That and the people who use it for an escape, and pray for miracles instead of going out and working for what they want, or go through a lifetime of self-imposed misery just because they're hoping it's going to be different in the hereafter. The *here* is just as important."

Andrea—"There are a couple of other bad things about religion—people who *use* religion, I mean. I can't stand people who won't do anything to make the world better and then try to pass off their lack of participation by saying the world is *supposed* to get worse because the Bible says that's what it'll do. I know there are some pretty terrifying prophecies in the Bible, but again, they're a matter of interpretation, and translation. This kind of person is the sort who loves to be pessimistic and refuses to admit there are many wonderful things in the world, and that it could get so much better if everyone would try harder."

Amen

Jean—"Amen."

Karl—"What I can't stand are people who bring their kids up in a strict-strict church and even keep them away from the social life at school—such as it is. You'd think they'd be wanting to prepare their kids to cope with the world instead of hiding them away from it. Maybe it's okay for the kids who grow up that way and decide to stay in hiding, and live in a church instead of a society. Anyway, it's their decision and their problem. But it's not okay for the kids who change their minds and then get smacked in the face by a life they know nothing about. Kids like this really go off the deep end sometimes when they have to face a world they're not ready for, and I don't think they're to blame. Their parents are."

Sheltered

Andrea—"I knew a girl who did just that. She'd been so sheltered and so repressed, she went *ape* when she got out in the world, and she ended up ... well, never mind what she ended up, but what happened to her wasn't her fault."

Brian—"Are you, by any chance, talking about yourself?"

Andrea—"No, I am *not*. And I'd appreciate it if you'd never speak to me again as long as I live."

Brian—"That's a *terrible* way to talk to someone you may have just converted. I thought you would want to be the very *first* to know when I make up my mind."

Andrea—"I just won't sleep a *wink* until I hear from you."

Brian—"On second thought, don't relax, either."

KRLA ARCHIVES

Purify 'Bros.' Really Cousins

By George Lincoln Culver

"Purifyin' soul sounds"...that's what you're going to hear from James and Bobby, the Brothers Purify, (who aren't brothers at all, but cousins). Just 22-years-old, James confines his soulful talents to singing, and plays no instruments on the stage. Bobby, however, spent four of his 24 years as a member of a band, playing and singing, as well as backing up other top-name artists.

Both James and Bobby enjoy singing hard-core rhythm and blues, preferably with a solid beat. Interestingly enough, however, the record which soared to the top of the nation's charts—both pop and R&B, "I'm Your Puppet"—was a source of great aggravation before its release.

James insisted that the song was too slow and not really "bluesy" enough, but Bobby prevailed upon the younger Purify to record the tune anyway. Once recorded, James still had his doubts about releasing the disc, but Bobby teamed up with the boys' manager, Don Schroeder, and together they convinced James that this was, indeed, the right one.

Just a few turntables and a smash hit later, James confided to us on the set of "Action" that perhaps he *had* been wrong, after all!

Both boys enjoy listening to the pop and R&B stations when they get an opportunity, and agree that James Brown has to take top honors in their performers' popularity poll. After James? Well, you can't forget Lou Rawls and Otis Redding!

We spoke about the recent developments in popular music, and both James and Bobby were quite happy to see that R&B had finally become a strong and lasting influence on the pop charts of the country.

We discussed the recent charges of obscenity which have been hurled at popular music, but James just laughed them off, explaining that there were, of course, *some* questionable lyrics now, but "if they were *really* that dirty they wouldn't be played on the radio!"

The future holds another single—not yet recorded—and a new album which the boys will begin cutting as soon as they have finished their current cross-country tours.

Motion pictures are also beckoning to the Purify Brothers, and both James and Bobby eagerly await an opportunity to try their hands at the art of "flick-making."

Man-Made Monkees

By Louise Criscione

Most groups happen. The Monkees were made. If they weren't intentionally created, it is conceivable that they would not exist for it is highly unlikely that the four of them would ever have met. They're about as different as any four human beings can be.

Mickey Dolenz — drummer, singer, comic and all around noisemaker left a Los Angeles technical trade school to become lead singer in a pop-rock group called the Missing Links.

Between appearances with the Missing Links, Micky took odd acting jobs which included segments of "Peyton Place" and "Mr. Novak." Being sort of a jack-of-all-trades, when singing and acting dates were scarce, Micky worked as a mechanic.

Actor's Son

Micky was born in Los Angeles on March 8, 1945, the son of an actor—the late George Dolenz. At ten, Micky began a three year run as television's "Circus Boy." When the series folded, Micky returned to school in the San Fernando Valley. Upon graduation from Grant High, he entered Valley College but transferred in his second semester to L.A. Tech-Trade. It was then that he made his first serious move toward music.

Like Davy Jones, Mike Nesmith and Peter Tork, Micky responded to an ad in *Variety* a year ago calling for "insane boys" to audition for roles in a comedy series for today's teens. And like the others, he was tested and signed because he was indeed a "Monkee," whether he knew it or not.

Although giving the appearance of being much smaller, Micky stands an even six feet and is frequently described as "athletic and restless." He shares an apartment with Davy Jones in West L.A. and drives around on a motorcycle.

David Jones, now known as Davy, left his home in Manchester, England to "become something," when he was fourteen and a half. He left with the full blessings of his father, a railroad fitter.

Davy was born December 30, 1945 with a great will to succeed. His dad knew it then and he knows it now. The tough, compact Davy headed for England's Newmarket Racetrack to become a jockey trainee. Between riding jobs, he discovered life among England's young set and explored places from which the great new musical sounds were coming. Eventually, he became part of the scene at The Cellar.

Davy's first acting job resulted from an audition at the BBC where he played a juvenile delinquent in a radio drama. This led to a steady job on a daytime series called "Morning Story."

However, he still continued at the racetrack and ironically enough it was through the racetrack that he met London theatrical executives who helped him land a leading role in the musical hit, "Oliver," in which Davy played the Artful Dodger.

From "Oliver" Davy proceeded on to "Pickwick" and won special acclaim from the American critics. Both plays were, of course, extremely successful on Broadway and were the reasons that the young Mr. Jones initially made the trip to America where he has been living for the past four years.

Not Quite

When "Pickwick" closed its Broadway run, the Colpix Record people spotted Davy's potential and signed him to a recording contract. He cut a record called "Dream Girl" which was a bomb—but not entirely because it brought him to California in time to read that ad in *Variety* and become a Monkee.

Peter Tork was playing guitar, ukelele, five-string banjo and bass before his voice changed. Later he picked up piano, French horn and other various instruments. All of which he learned to play well.

Born in Washington, D.C., February 13, 1944, Peter was raised in Connecticut. His father, H. J. Torkelson, is Associate Professor of Economics at the University of Connecticut. On two traumatic occasions, Peter himself enrolled in college with the highly respectable goal of becoming an English professor. When Peter's first try at college (Carleton College in Minnesota) failed, he returned to New England and worked for 14 months in a thread mill. When his second attempt at college turned out to be equally ill-fated, he decided to select another line of work in self-defense.

Therefore, Peter began his musical career in New York's Greenwich Village, performing as singer-musician in various pass-the-hat hideaways where the music was, at least, always new. But when money became something of a necessity, he toured with the Phoenix Singers as accompanist. He stayed with the Singers for six months, during which time he continually kept one goal in mind—to reach California.

Being rather strong-willed, Peter did come to California and was here only two months when he read the ad which made him a Monkee.

Mike Nesmith is a guitar-playing, song-writing Texan with a college degree, a solid interest in Renaissance music and the ability to shift gears to rock and roll with apparent ease. His hair rides rather long, his accent is definitely Texas-inspired and his guitar-playing is distinctively professional.

Born in Dallas, Texas on December 30, 1942, Mike traveled next to San Antonio where he attended college and expanded his knowledge of folk singing and guitar playing. When he became bored with singing the same songs, he wrote his own and upon graduation decided to seek his fortune as a folk singer in Hollywood.

Three

Arriving in Hollywood, Mike met up with a bass player named John Lundgren and the two of them set out on a road tour which had them booked for five shows a day. Upon their return, seasoned but far from wealthy, they added a third member—Bill. And the three of them traded in their folk for rock 'n roll. Mike wrote all their material and just as fame and fortune was about to descend (or so they say) the draft board arrived and Mike went back to being a single act.

His first job as a single act was at Ledbetter's, a well-known Los Angeles folk club, where he met with a tidy amount of success. It was along about this time that Mike was doing his weekly reading and ran across the famous ad.

And so, a mechanic, a jockey and two folk singers have become the hottest new group in the nation. Thanks to an ad.

Wipe Out Woebegone Hair

Get with Shontex Dandrid Shampoo
Big FREE SAMPLE DEAL... NOW!

Like the price is right! Send for a freebee of the one shampoo guaranteed to give the go-go to woebegone hair, or your money back. Makes flaked-up limp, lifeless hair wake up, shape up! Or else. Mail coupon. Get free sample, plus certificate worth 50c off on purchase of Dandrid Shampoo at any store. This deal gets better and better! Do it!

Mail to: **Shontex Dandrid Shampoo Deal**
922 N. Vine St., Hollywood 90038

Send me my free sample of Dandrid Shampoo and my 50c-off certificate for when I go to buy some at the store. I enclose 10c to cover cost of packaging and mailing, which is only fair for such a good deal.

Name: _____

Address: _____

City: _____ State _____ Zip _____

KRLA ARCHIVES

Tallulah Reed Wins L.A. Teenage Title

A beautiful, brown-eyed UCLA freshman recently won out over 10 other finalists for the coveted title of Miss Teenage Los Angeles. Miss Tallulah Reed, 17, was crowned this city's youngest queen by Casey Kasem on his afternoon TV show, "Shebang."

Miss Reed now goes to Dallas, Texas as the Los Angeles entree in the Miss Teenage America pageant held Oct. 29 through Nov. 5. The winner of the national pageant receives a $10,000 scholarship and numerous other top prizes.

Miss Reed, the first Negro ever to win the local title, is studying writing and acting at UCLA. She is the daughter of David and Anne Reed of Los Angeles.

In Dallas, Miss Reed will be judged on the same qualities that established her the winner of the Los Angeles contest: personality, poise, intelligence, appearance and talent.

Besides the scholarship, the national winner will receive a guaranteed $5,000 in personal appearance fees, a 1967 Mercury Cougar, 50 shares of stock in the Dr. Pepper Co., and other prizes.

CASEY KASEM congratulates Miss Tallulah Reed after she was crowned Miss Teenage Los Angeles. Miss Reed, a 17-year-old freshman at UCLA, now goes to Dallas, Tex. to compete for Miss Teenage America.

> "You may hate yourself in the morning, but you are going to enjoy 'Alfie' very much. 'Alfie' uses people—mainly women—and throws them away like tissues."
> — LIFE Magazine

> ★★★★ (Highest Rating)
> "People are going to stop talking about 'Virginia Woolf' and start talking about 'Alfie'."
> — Wanda Hale, N.Y. DAILY NEWS

> "UNREELS MORE LIKE A SCORE CARD THAN A SCENARIO."
> — TIME Magazine

PARAMOUNT PICTURES presents

ALFIE
(RECOMMENDED FOR MATURE AUDIENCES)

MICHAEL CAINE IS ALFIE
MILLICENT MARTIN • JULIA FOSTER • JANE ASHER
SHIRLEY ANNE FIELD • VIVIEN MERCHANT • ELEANOR BRON
WITH SHELLEY WINTERS AS RUBY   TECHNICOLOR® TECHNISCOPE®   A PARAMOUNT PICTURE
A LEWIS GILBERT PRODUCTION   SCREENPLAY BY BILL NAUGHTON BASED ON THE PLAY 'ALFIE' BY BILL NAUGHTON
MUSIC BY SONNY ROLLINS • PRODUCED AND DIRECTED BY LEWIS GILBERT

Winner of the Special Jury Award at the Cannes Film Festival

NOW PLAYING — CREST THEATRE, WESTWOOD BLVD.

ATTENTION!!!
High Schools, Colleges, Universities and Clubs:

CASEY KASEM MAY BE ABLE TO SERVE YOU!

Let Casey HELP You Put On A Show Or Dance
Contact Casey at:
HO 2-7253

Tony Curtis • Virna Lisi • George C. Scott

Not with my wife, you don't!

A NORMAN PANAMA PRODUCTION
CO-STARRING CARROLL O'CONNOR GEORGE TYNE EDDIE RYDER
TECHNICOLOR® FROM WARNER BROS.

EXCLUSIVE ENGAGEMENT
NOW PLAYING!
DAILY AT: 1:45 • 4:00 • 6:15 • 8:30 • 10:45 PM

PACIFIC'S HOLLYWOOD
PANTAGES
HOLLYWOOD BLVD. at VINE
'Crossroad of the Stars'
HO. 9-7161

KRLA ARCHIVES

Top 40 Requests

1. MELLOW MELLOW .... Donovan
2. I WANTA BE FREE .... The Monkees
3. GOOD VIBRATIONS .... Beach Boys
4. 96 TEARS .... ? And The Mysterians
5. LADY GODIVA .... Peter & Gordon
6. DANDY .... Herman's Hermits
7. HURRAH FOR HAZEL .... Tommy Roe
8. WALK AWAY RENEE .... The Left Banke
9. CHERISH .... Association
10. RAIN ON THE ROOF .... Lovin' Spoonful
11. TALK TALK .... Music Machine
12. 7:00 O'CLOCK NEWS .... Simon & Garfunkel
13. WHY PICK ON ME? .... Standells
14. STOP, STOP, STOP .... Hollies
15. CAN I GET TO KNOW YOU BETTER? .... Turtles
16. WINCHESTER CATHEDRAL .... The New Vaudeville Band
17. PSYCHOTIC REACTION .... Count Five
18. YOU ARE SHE .... Chad & Jeremy
19. LAST TRAIN TO CLARKSVILLE .... The Monkees
20. NEXT TIME YOU SEE ME .... Robbs
21. I'M YOUR PUPPET .... James & Bobby Purify
22. POOR SIDE OF TOWN .... Johnny Rivers
23. HAVE YOU SEEN YOUR MOTHER, BABY,
    STANDING IN THE SHADOW? .... The Rolling Stones
24. OUT OF TIME .... Chris Farlowe
25. YOU KEEP ME HANGIN' ON .... Supremes
26. CHERRY, CHERRY .... Neil Diamond
27. LOVE IS A HURTIN' THING .... Lou Rawls
28. I JUST DON'T KNOW WHAT TO DO .... Dionne Warwick
29. SEE SEE RIDER .... Eric Burdon & The Animals
30. BABY .... Carla Thomas
31. LOOK THROUGH MY WINDOW .... The Mama's & Papa's
32. IF I WERE A CARPENTER .... Bobby Darin
33. PAINT ME A PICTURE .... Gary Lewis & The Playboys
34. WHO AM I? .... Petula Clark
35. REACH OUT, I'LL BE THERE .... Four Tops
36. THE GREAT AIRPLANE STRIKE .... Paul Revere & The Raiders
37. SATISFIED MIND .... Bobby Hebb
38. MR. SPACEMAN .... The Byrds
39. SHE COMES TO ME .... Chicago Loop
40. DEVIL WITH A BLUE DRESS ON .... Mitch Ryder & The Detroit Wheels

FUNTEEN BONUS COUPON OFFERINGS

All the Bonus Coupons printed in the back section of the Go-Guide are listed below:

NOW AVAILABLE TO MEMBERS ONLY:

A Supplement containing 30 additional coupons. Send 25c (for handling) plus a stamped, self-addressed envelope to

SUPPLEMENT
P.O. Box 1235, Beverly Hills, Calif.

A. DISCOTEEN CLUB, 5136 No. Citrus, Covina
 • $1 off admission anytime with Go-Card
 • 2 for 1 admission with Go-Book
C. SAN FERNANDO TEEN CENTER, 17400 Victory Blvd., Van Nuys
 • 2 for 1 admission with Go-Book
D. DRUM CITY — GUITAR TOWN, 15525 Sherman Way, Van Nuys; 5611 Jumilla, Woodland Hills; 6226 Santa Monica Blvd.
 • 2 "crazy fit" book covers—nothing to buy — Go-Book
 • $6 gift certificate with $15 purchase — Go-Book
E. HOBBYLAND, 1626 So. Robertson, Los Angeles
 • Free gift — nothing to buy — Go-Book
 • 20% off any purchase with Go-Card
F. ORANGE JULIUS, 6767 Santa Monica Blvd., Los Angeles
 • Free Orange Julius with any purchase — Go-Book
G. GAZZARRI'S, 319 No. La Cienega
 • 2 for 1 admission with Go-Book
J. MICHAEL'S JEWELERS, 7510 Woodman, Van Nuys
 • Free Beatle jewelry piece with Go-Book
K. KOOKIE KAPERS, 7840 Santa Monica Blvd., Los Angeles
 • $5 gift certificate with $15 purchase — Go-Book
L. DUNDEE DONUTS, 6322 W. 3rd., Los Angeles
 • Free Donuts — nothing to buy — Go-Book
M. NORTHRIDGE VALLEY SKATELAND, 18140 Parthenia, Northridge
 • 2 for 1 admission with Go-Book
N. EZRA'S OASIS, 316 No. La Cienega, Los Angeles
 • 2 for 1 food or drink with Go-Book
O. ORANGE JULIUS, 6001 W. Pico, Los Angeles
 • Free Orange Julius with any purchase — Go-Book
P. PASADENA CIVIC AUDITORIUM DANCE, 300 Green St., Pasadena
 • Free admission for two with Go-Book
Q. ORANGE JULIUS, 1715 W. Pico Blvd., Santa Monica
 • Free Orange Julius with any purchase — Go-Book
R. VALLEY ICE SKATING CENTER, 18361 Ventura Blvd., Tarzana
 • 2 for 1 admission with Go-Book
S. SHIRT SHACK, 19000 Lincoln Blvd., Santa Monica
 • $5 gift certificate with $15 purchase — Go-Book
T. ICE HOUSE PASADENA, 24 No. Mentor, Pasadena
 • 2 for 1 admission with Go-Book
U. ICE HOUSE GLENDALE, 234 So. Brand, Glendale
 • 2 for 1 admission with Go-Book
V. DE WALD'S BALLROOM, 831 W. Las Tunas Drive, San Gabriel
 Extra-Book • Free admission for 2 with Extra Book
W. CAFE DANSSA, 11533 W. Pico, L.A.
 Extra-Book • 2 for 1 admission Sundays only with Go-Card
X. SWINGING YOUNG ADULTS CLUB, Guys & Dolls A Go Go, 3617 Crenshaw, L.A.
 Extra-Book • Discount admission anytime with Go-Card
Z. ORANGE JULIUS, 5734 Santa Monica Blvd., L.A.
 Extra-Book • Free Orange Julius anytime with Go-Card
AA. INTERNATIONAL TEEN WORLD FESTIVAL—Dec. 26th thru Jan 2nd
 Extra-Book • 2 for 1 admission with Extra-Book
BB. CINNAMON CINDER, 11345 Ventura Blvd., No. Hollywood
 Extra-Book • 2 for 1 admission with Extra-Book
CC. CINNAMON CINDER, 4401 Pacific Coast Highway, Long Beach
 Extra-Book • 2 for 1 admission with Extra-Book

ICE HOUSE GLENDALE
234 So. Brand
Reservations: 245-5043

NOV. 1-6

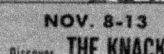

Eddie Brown
formerly of Joe & Eddie

NOV. 8-13
Discover **THE KNACK**

You'll Be Sorry If You Don't

ICE HOUSE PASADENA
24 No. Mentor Ave.
Reservations: 681-9942

NOV. 1-27
BOB LIND

"Elusive Butterfly"
— plus —
David-Troy & The Slippery Rock String Band

Former member of Vejtables & Preachers seeks good bass player and lead guitarist. Must sing good harmony. 19 or over. Bill or Don (213) 882-2225.

...NO ONE BELIEVED THEY EXISTED — so we're proving it with a pix of your friendly Norsemen! Do you still doubt our good word???

Inside KRLA
By Eden

All right—howcum none of you have staked out a claim on those $10,000 smackers KRLA is offering each week in the Football Sweepstakes? I'm ashamed of you gang; I mean, *I* wouldn't be that slow to lay my greedy little paws on ten grand! If I were *eligible*, that is, but the KRLA Contest officials have declared me ineligible on the grounds of heresy (I'm part *witch*, you know) — but if you are eligible (which you are) the word is *charge*!

As a matter of fact, you just can't *help* winning something if you listen to KRLA — which we all do! Every single day on the old Scuzzabalooer's show, for example, you can win the top ten requested singles just by sending in your name and address on a post card now.

And here's another brand new giveaway from KRLA: every Saturday night from now on is a Bonus Bash on the Dick Biondi show where you can *win* the record you call in to request.

And of course, I know you haven't forgotten the '67 Car Sweepstakes. Who — and I mean *who* — else but KRLA would offer you the car of *your* choice?! Well, all right — I mean, I didn't get up at 5:00 o'clock this morning to pick blueberries in Scotland — I got up to tell you about these contests, so *get in there and enter away*, people!!!

Speaking of people, did you all see the KRLA Freak Out at the Great Western Exhibit Fair? Woooooooo! With unbelievable-types like that outside, who *cares* about the legend of the Great Pumpkin?! Not I, says I! (P.S. Did you notice that the Freak Out seemed to be patterned loosely (as in, *very*!) after the Hullabalooer's daily radio fiasco? Well, we freaks *do* have to hang together, you know!)

WARREN BEATTY
SUSANNAH YORK

From London to the Riviera, a hair-raising tale of gallant love and truly desperate adventure!

KALEIDOSCOPE

the switched-on thriller!!!

A GERSHWIN-KASTNER PRODUCTION   CLIVE REVILL ERIC PORTER
Written by ROBERT & JANE HOWARD CARRINGTON · Produced by ELLIOTT KASTNER · Directed by JACK SMIGHT
TECHNICOLOR® FROM WARNER BROS.

SOON! AT A THEATER OR DRIVE-IN NEAR YOU

KRLA ARCHIVES

DISCussion
By Eden

One of the prettiest songs from the brilliant pen of poet-singer Paul Simon is the brand new Simon and Garfunkel release, "A Hazy Shade of Winter."

There's a very present sound about the voices, and a good solid beat to back them up and satisfy the popsters, and an entire tuneful of great lyrics to reassure us of the talents of young Mr. Simon.

A definite Top Ten chart item.

★ ★ ★

And speaking of talented writers, the unbelievably great Motown team of Holland-Dozier-Holland has come up with another smash vehicle in "(Come 'Round Here) I'm The One You Need" for the Miracles.

Smokey Robinson and Co. have done a great job on this uptempo rocker, and it will probably remind many of some of their early recordings, brought up to date with a taste of the current Motown Sound.

★ ★ ★

This week's award for the most unbelievable song title, and possibly the most ridiculous group name goes to Dr. West's Medicine Show and Junk Band with their first release, "The Eggplant That Ate Chicago."

Geez, Ranger Bob... I like that one *almost* as much as The W.C. Fields Memorial Electric String Band!

Nope! On second thought, I think I like *The Peanut Butter Conspiracy* better!!! (You're welcome, Russ!)

★ ★ ★

A song which should be receiving more attention is the new one by Brenda Lee, "Coming On Strong." This is one of the best and most commercial chart entries from the petite songstress in a long time and really deserves a spot in the Top 20.

★ ★ ★

Three really *outtasite* (all due apologies to Fang!) R&B tunes to hit the pop charts this week are "But It's Alright," by J.J. Jackson; "Don't Be A Drop-Out," by the King, James Brown; and "Knock On Wood," by Eddie Floyd. Throw these three discs on your turntables at home and grab an earful of soul for yourselves, there.

★ ★ ★

*Oh*kay, gang—the McCoy's new discertation is "Don't Worry Mother, Your Son's Heart Is Pure." Need we say more??!!!!

Really feel awfully sorry for Herb Alpert, don't you? Poor thing was only making a few million—a *day!*—with his own recordings with the TJ Brass, so now he has about three other groups on his A&M label to go out and earn those lil ol' pesos for him.

Sandpipers have a hit with their unbelievably beautiful rendition of "Louie, Louie" (there were a number of Dirty-Old-Men-types who never thought they'd hear *this* one done this way!); and the newest by Sergio Mendes and Brazil '66, "Mas Que Nada," which incidentally was produced by none other than Israel's favorite Mariachi!!

Some Things are Nice to Have Around...

things you feel "at home" with

...the Utility™ ball pen

A good, practical pen for students. Fashionable, too.
There are twelve brilliant colors.
The color of the pen is the color of the ink.

Lots of students buy two or three at a time. Maybe because it's only 39¢
Maybe because it writes nice.
Or maybe they just like to have two or three or twelve around.

Lindy®

 manufactured by LINDY PEN CO., no. hollywood, calif. 91605, u.s.a.

KRLA ARCHIVES

Association Set Tour, Book, Album And Movie

By Louise Criscione

If the totally insane idea ever runs through your head, even for a second, do yourself a favor and get rid of it. Fast. Because it's a losing cause—The Association is never going to tell you the truth regarding their formation. At least, not the *whole* truth. One will inform you of a group called the Men. Another will mention an avocado. And still another will admit that it all began with a house. Perhaps if you pieced it all together like a puzzle, you could emerge with some sort of a composite picture. But only if you have about a hundred years to devote to the problem.

Those who call themselves wise will ignore the question completely because it is, after all, rather anticlimatic. The future always means more than the past and the future for The Association promises a million-watt spotlight. The past only offers a darkened, smoke-filled room.

Pandora's What??

November marks the beginning of a cross-country tour, the release of "Pandora's Golden Heebe Jeebees" and the Association's second album. And all things remaining equal, it could bring with it the certification of "And Then Along Comes The Association" as a million-selling album. That out of the way, if luck holds out and the presses continue to operate "Crank Your Spreaders" stands a magnificent chance of changing the world.

Andy Williams and Ed "Pop" Sullivan are currently standing in line for an opportunity to have The Association on their television shows and if negotiations don't take on the aura of the U.N debating the admittance of Red China, it won't be too long before six Associates make their debut on the movie screen.

With the unquenchable enthusiasm of first-row fans, we've managed to get a bit carried away and have unexcusably rambled on with one-liner notes instead of full-fledged Association facts. So . . . back to the beginning—not the past, mind you, but the beginning of the future.

Tour Dates

On November 12, the group leaves on their second nation-wide tour. They'll be gone a month and will hit 19 cities. In order of their appearance, the chosen cities are Honolulu, Hawaii; Val Priso, Indiana; Lansing, Michigan; Madison, Wisconsin; Chicago, Illinois; Kansas City, Missouri; Urbana, Illinois (University of Illinois); Indianapolis, Indiana; Fort Wayne, Indiana; South Bend, Indiana; Pittsburgh, Pennsylvania; Detroit, Michigan; Cleveland, Ohio; Cincinnatti, Ohio; and Toronto, Canada.

Fourteen of the tour dates will be with the Lovin' Spoonful sharing the bill as well as a chartered plane. The Toronto gig will be played on December 11 and as soon as the curtain falls and the screaming dies, The Association will wing their way back to Calif.

During their absence (sometime around mid-November) the second Association album will be released. As we go to press, they're administering the finishing touches to it in a small studio down the street. All six Associates are convinced that this second long-play effort is much better than their first and since that debut album is soon expected to be declared a million-seller, The Association had to go some to top it. Of course, with six creative (as well as literary) minds in the group, it's much easier for them to keep from slipping into one bag or to be content with one static sound.

Believe it or not, "Crank Your Spreaders" will be the name of a book. If you know The Association, you'll believe it and if you aren't acquainted with them you'll just have to trust us—and we'll just have to hope that no one changes the title.

"Crank Your Spreaders" is *naturally*, an Association book. Its release date could be in November or December (would you believe next October?) but according to Russ "just say it will be out soon." "Soon" is, however, a word which is definitely open for debate.

Movie Stars

And the movie? It's all in the negotiation stages at the moment—but it has to happen, eventually. Can't you just see it? They could throw people into bathtubs full of Crisco, drive reporters out of their minds, man the movie cameras themselves, coast along on the wrong side of the street, go in the "out" doors, play their instruments in waste baskets and pin the world together with a giant "purify button."

And best of all—it wouldn't require any acting ability whatsoever! Because Association ala' natural has been known to blow your mind.

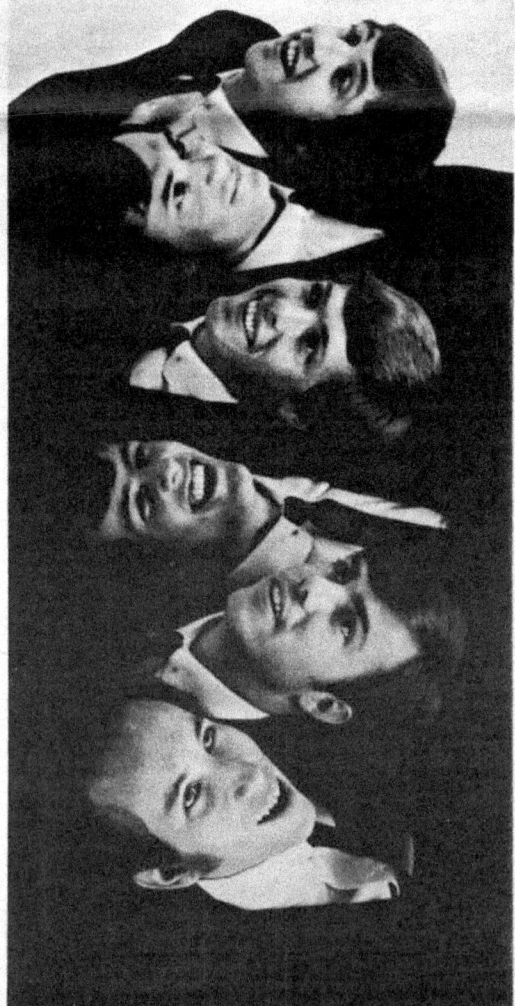

KRLA ARCHIVES

The Adventures of Robin Boyd

©1965 By Shirley Poston

At the crack of dawn, Robin Boyd gave a loud moan and flang the covers to the floor.

She had been lying upon her bed of pain since midnight, trying her best to sleep tight (hic) in preparation for the ordeal she was to face the following morn, but had succeeded only in coming down with the "Big Eye" (known in less colorful circles as insomnia.)

Four Inches

As far as she could see (which was usually about four inches because she refused to wear her glasses out of the house) (not to mention out of vanity), there was no point in continuing to wrootch about in her trundle. So, stuffing a kangaroo into each pocket, she set off for a brisk walk through the city (har) of East Pitchfork.

(No, you aren't seeing things. Yes, the above paragraph did say that Robin stuffed a kangaroo in each pocket. Oddly enough, she did this because the kangaroos she stuffed in each pocket were called "pocket kangaroos." At least that's what George had called them when he'd given them to her as a going-away present.

Ten minutes later, having completed her brisk walk through the aforementioned city (ho) (as in hum), Robin sagged onto the front stairs of her new home-on-the-range and contemplated her navel through seventeen sweaters.

"This am-day place is for the birds," she twitted peevishly, addressing these sentiments to Popsicle and Momsicle, who had ventured out of her pockets.

As the sound of her voice carried across the endless prairie which surrounded the city (cough), an antelope and a deer at play paused to nudge each other sardonically and snarl "*I'll* say."

Meanwhile, back at the raunch . . . er . . . ranch (style-house, that is), Robin rained a few more choice comments upon the astonished ears of the Sicle family (who had taken one look at the icy ground and were now venturing back *into* her pockets at an approximate speed of four thousand miles per hour) and fell into a deep silence. (At this moment, she would have preferred a *well*.)

Never in her wildest dreams had she imagined that she would one day find herself feezing into an embittered lump on a doorstep in South Dakota, talking not only to herself, but to *kangaroos*.

And, to make things worse (were that possible), she was not only minus her magic powers. She was also without one luvely Liverpudlian genie.

The night before the Boyds had left California for this A-D place, Robin had tried to bid George a rational, non-melodramatic goodbye, and had eneded up playing a farewell scene that made "Romeo & Juliet" look like a situation comedy.

Vanished

The evening hadn't been *all* stark tragedy, of course. George had gone all out to take her mind off her problems (in *his* own inimitable fashion), and there had been several moments (would you believe *hours?*) when Robin had figured this was *worth* going to South Dakota for. (Would you, in fact, believe South *Africa?*)

But she changed her mind the next morning, when after being rudely awakened by her weeping (not as in willow) (as in redwood) sister, she found that George's tea pot had vanished from the living room mantel.

He'd cautioned her to expect this, as it was going to take time for him to get some silly am-day transfer, but Robin was still horrified by his disappearance, and she joined the sturdy Ringo (as in Boyd) in a series of caterwauls that had the entire neighborhood up in time to witness the exit of the century.

(If the truth were known, the neighbors were already up anyway, having synchronized alarm clocks the night before. It was hardly any secret that Mrs. Boyd and her two daughters were in a perfectly marvelous snit about having to move to South Dakota, and no one wanted to miss out on any of the fun.)

Just then, Robin heard the sound of something stirring inside the house (trouble, no doubt), and she stalked into same and started getting ready for the aforementioned ordeal. Namely, her first day of school at John Q. Obnoxious High. (Actually, it was called John Q. Onassis, but her own version seemed more appropos.)

After taking a luke-warm bath (which she had read was supposed to make one pleasantly pink) (which turned her a rather barfy shade of blue instead), Robin dragged on the outfit she had carefully selected for this great (as in grate) occasion and stomped into the kitchen.

The rest of the family was clustered about the breakfast table. Mr. Boyd was well-hidden behind a copy of the Pitchfork Tines (get it?) (*forget* it!), which protected him from the hostile glances of his wife and progeny, and as Robin hurled herself into a chair, she couldn't resist poking Ringo's droomstick through the society (oh, *sure*) page. (This would have been a less messy move had she bothered to remove the droomstick from around Ringo's neck *prior* to said poking, but Robin was in *no* mood for *details*.)

After a few moments of staring waspishly into her bowl of Soggies, Robin reached over and drank her father's coffee. Then she took Ringo in hand (no small task in itself) and fled.

As they left the house, bundled in the furry coats they'd bought to protect themselves from the elements (and to confuse the coyotes who would undoubtedly come prowling around their lunchbuckets), Mr. Boyd came out from behind the newspaper long enough to offer them a ride to school.

Robin longed to say yes, but couldn't. They had sent their father to Coventry the day they left California (that's British for not speaking to people who send *you* to *South Dakota*) and the sound barrier (which Mr. Boyd secretly found to be the most blissful experience of his entire life) was still in effect.

Remembering that a love of exercise was not among her sister's few virtues, Robin clamped a hand over Ringo's flannel-mouth and propelled the rotund 12-year-old out the door.

When Robin had first learned that she and Ringo would be going to the same school, she had been utterly *outraged*. The very *idea*, having a junior and senior high in the same building. It was almost *unsanitary*.

(When she had learned that at the aforementioned John Q. Obnoxious, grades *one* through *twelve* were quartered in the same building, she had been utterly *outradeoud*.)

Still, on this particular morning, she was grateful for Ringo's company. It gave her someone to mutter to as she lurched along, warming her hands on Mom and Pop Sicle. It also gave her someone to lean on when she kicked vengefully at a clump of dirt only to find it, like herself, was frozen solid.

The school was located in Pitchfork, which was an exhausting five-block walk from the suburb (burp) of East Pitchfork. They arrived on the scene just after the final warning bell had rung, and the only signs of life were dark billows of smoke belching from the rooftop.

Holy Smoke

Certain that with *her* luck, the smoke indicated a chimney instead of a four-alarm fire, Robin ground Ringo to a halt and peered anxiously at John Q.

Accustomed to the bright, rambling campus of her alma mater back in California, Robin paled at the sight of this huge, three-story, red-brick hulk of a building.

Had she been in possession of her magic powers (not to mention her marbles), this Boyd (as in boid) would have returned to Capistrano. But there was nothing she could do except swallow the urge to flap off into the sunrise and sog off into the school.

When they reached the front door, Robin stopped again to smooth the icy strands of her long red hair and push aside her bangs so that at least one blue eye was visible. As a final gesture, she took one of her famous deep breaths.

After she recovered from her coughing fit (all that fresh air was just too much of a shock for her smog-oriented lungs), they made their grand entrance.

Robin soon discovered, however, that *grand* was not the *word*.

Them being strangers and all, Robin wouldn't have minded if passing students had stared and said "who's that?"

But she *did* mind them saying "*WHAT's* that?"

(*To Be Continued Next Issue*)

...HERMAN AND TIPPY IN SCENE FROM "CANTERVILLE GHOST."

HERMAN IS SMASH IN THE GHOST

Peter Noone, alias Herman, has turned into quite an actor with his television debut on "The Canterville Ghost," an ABC-TV "Stage 67" segment.

Sir Michael Redgrave, in a dual role, portrayed the contemporary Lord Canterville and the three-centuries-old ghost of Sir Simon de Canterville, both inhabitants of the ancient castle, Canterville Hall. When the castle is rented and occupied by the American ambassador to the Court of St. James (Douglas Fairbanks, Jr.), and his wife (Natalie Schafer), his daughter (Tippy Walker) and sons (David Charkham and Mark Colleano) the ghost finds the tenants insensitive to this most grizzly gavottes, and the Ambassador's daughter is persistently wooed in prose and song by a young mod Duke (Peter Noone.)

...HERMAN READS OVER THE SHOULDER OF DOUG FAIRBANKS JR.

KRLA ARCHIVES

Tommy Roe Invites The Beat To His New Home

By Carol Deck

California has Disneyland, the Golden Gate, the only Major League baseball team to make three errors in one inning of a World Series Game, and, now Tommy Roe.

Tommy—sexy Southerner supreme—has been being sexy and Southern in Atlanta, Ga. for some time now and has finally decided with the aid of a couple of chicks called "Sweet Pea" and "Hazel," to try being sexy and Southern in Southern California, Hollywood, to be exact.

Invites World

Somehow squeezing time out between tours, recording sessions and being a regular on "Where The Action Is," Tommy recently moved to Hollywood and promptly invited the whole world, via The BEAT, to come visit his new home.

After collecting this reporter and a photographer in his gold Lincoln Continental, he took off up a winding road in the Hollywood hills for his new home, stopping only to pick up practically his entire wardrobe from a laundry (where he illegally parked said Lincoln, but got away without a ticket).

Climbing out from under all the clothes he had perched atop us, we followed Tommy into the living room where we at once got the feeling we weren't alone.

Actually it was just that one whole wall of the living room is a mirror covered with gold antiquing.

After hanging up his clothes in the huge walk-in closet in the downstairs bedroom (the living room is on street level and the bedroom is below it—the house kind of hangs off the hill) Tommy personally conducted us on a tour of his new home.

He was still in the process of moving and, at that point, was missing several things, such as dishes and linen, but he had his color TV with his and hers remote controls, so he was happy.

He's a bit of a TV nut—actually it isn't the TV that fascinates him but the remote controls. He loves changing stations every time a commercial comes on. And he says he's looking for a "her" to play with the other remote control goody.

During the tour, Tommy pointed out the TV, upper and lower patios, his stamp collection (yes, he actually collects stamps) his gun collection including a WWI Lueger and his lack of a can opener (a terrible condition in this world of canned everything—thank heaven for pop tops!).

But of more interest were the things he didn't point out. Like the silver record for "Shelia" and the citations of achievement for "Shelia" and "Everybody" and most of all the 1966 Ray Petersen Humaniatrian Award with the engraving "To Tommy Roe—A Warm, Sincere, Devoted Human Being."

TDR

We also noted his luggage with the initials TDR and asked what the "D" stood for.

"My mother named me Thomas David Roe because David killed a giant and she hoped that while I was a teenager I'd kill a giant." Did he? "No."

Back to the house, he says he bought it because it was owned by an interior decorator and was well decorated and because of the neighbors, one in particular. "Ooh, is she groovy," gleamed Tommy.

Before leaving Tommy to his moving in chores we had a few moments to talk and he told us that although "Shelia" had been written about a specific girl (who's name was actually Frida) neither "Sweet Pea" nor "Hurray For Hazel" was.

"No, I'm getting too old for that now," he said at the grand old age of 24.

...TOMMY POSES IN HIS GOLD LINCOLN CONTINENTAL

...TOMMY RELAXES WITH GUITAR AND GOLD RECORD.

BEAT Photo: Chuck Boyd

CL2563 CS9363

Catch up on the NOW Sound.

Simon and Garfunkel's new single

"HAZY SHADE OF WINTER"

On COLUMBIA RECORDS

For Girls Only

By Shirley Poston

Will the class please come to order?

On second thought, will the class just please come *to*? If you don't, you're going to miss out on something really fascinating. (This column, for instance?) (You should live so long).

Anylane, it seems I received a letter from a girl named Karen who told me about a "language" called "Liverpole Backslang." (I think maybe she meant Liver*pool* instead of pole, but am probably out of mind). (As usual).

You're Kidding!

Here's how it goes . . . you put the syllable "ag" before the first vowel in every word. The example Karen used was "Gageorge lagoves Shagirley!" Which, of course, says *George loves Shirley!* (*I* should live so long). (And am planning to).

Karen says backslang is very conspicious (parddon?) in handwritty, but fabulous when spoken.

I've been trying it out ever since, and it's really neat. The funniest word I've come up with yet is *Ragingo*. (Sorry about that, Mr. Starkey). (You angel).

Really, it is great fun, and I can see (a nice change) that if a person really worked at it, you could learn to speak it fluently.

So far, all I can say is "Shagirley lagoves Gageorge, tagoo!" (*Tagoo?*) But I swear (often) that I'm really going to learn it, and I hope you will too because then I'm going to teach it to Robin Irene Boyd (who could teach me a thing or two herself if the truth were known) (and it is).

Just in case you already know how to speak it and I'm the only person in the entire world who hasn't heard of bagackslang (hey, I did it!), just consider the source and remember that I haven't been well lately. (Then cross out the lately).

Speaking Of . . .

Speaking of Robin Irene (refooldyah), I do hate to bore you with dull, tiresome stories of my uneventful life, but something reasonably humorous happened the other day.

I was wandering around in the produce section of a market near our house (I have this thing for wandering around in produce sections) (we vegetables must stick together), and I ran into a friend of my mom's.

Said friend is a writer and I always get so am-day embarassed I can't even think (nothing new) when she asks me about how my writty is coming.

Naturally, she asked me the fateful question, and I mumbled something remarkably intelligent like "dandy."

Then, while I was staring redfaced at the fruit counter, hoping she'd drop the subject, she didn't drop the subject. Instead, she said: "what's the title of that fiction story you've been writing?"

You aren't going to *believe* what I said. Still staring at the fruit counter, I re-mumbled: "The Adventures Of *Banana Boyd*."

I give up. I simply cannot carry on a conversation with a sane, rational individual. (Remember the time I was trying to be so profound and said "Which came first, the chicken or the *horse*?") (Gawd).

Speaking of George . . . don't forget to S.S.F.M., kiddo! (Has anyone figured out what that means yet?) (I hope not). (I don't mind being collected by the netflingers every so often, but the county jail is quite another story).

What I was really going to say was speaking of conversations, I've heard of another funny thingy that sends strangers scrambling toward the exits. What you do is make an imaginary companion, and talk to him a lot. This is especially effective when you're walking down the street along—would you believe *alone*? (If you read this column, you'll believe *anything*). Or when you go into a restaurant, make sure your companion has his own place at the table. (If you have a spare farthing, order a coke for him. The results are fantastic!) (But boy, are those bars hard to saw through).

Georgia?

Thanks to everyone who replied about the search for a copy of the Beatles' "My Bonnie." I've passed yer letters on to the person who was looking for this record! However, another problem has arisen.

Cher can wear a dress! The occasion? An audience with Pope Paul VI.

(Arose?) (By any other name would . . . oh never *mind*). One of your letters mentioned something about a Beatle song called "Georgia Brown?" Huh???? This is the first I've heard of it (and I'm usually the last to know). Is there such a record? Help!

Did you hear what Ragingo . . . sorry, Ringo suggested as a possible title when they were trying to find a name for their "Revolver" album? He thought they should call it "After Geometry." You know, sort of a play on the Stones' "Aftermath?" (Well, *I* think it's funny). (And *I* would).

Oh, before I forget, the "pocket kangaroos" mentioned in this chapter of R.I.B. actually do exist. I mean, there are such things. They only cost about five dollars each, and although they do look sorfto (if that doesn't work, try sortof) (which reminds me of the time one of your wrote and asked if the initials S.P. stand for Soft Poston) (why would that remind me of *that*?) (how should I know?) . . . what on earth was I blithering about before that last seizure? Oh, kangaroos. (She said nonchalantly as they came for her).

Hmmm

Anyparth (hmmm, not bad) (hmmm, not good, either), you can buy such animules in some pet shops and they're really rather groovy, even if they do look sortof (if that doesn't work, try sorfto) like mice. Someone tried to tell me they come in assorted *colors*, but it's going to be awhile before I'm far enough gone to believe *that* one. (Fifteen minutes at least).

Did you know that if you really dig someone, your pulse starts going faster at the mention of his name? Weird, but true. Several of us conducted an experiment along these lines last adamandevening (down, girl), and it works! All you do is have someone take your pulse and start naming off names. My pulse plodded along through Frank, Bill and Fred, but when she said "George!," I started ticking like a time bomb. It worked for the other members of the herd (well, it's more colorful than *crowd*), too.

Great idea! If you suspect that a friend of yours has a secret lech for someone who belongs to y-o-u (or else), don't tell her the details of the pulse bit. Just say you're thing equally clever (as in cleaver), and then throw his name in and see what happens. If *she* starts ticking, well . . . speak of time bombs. going to "play a game" or some-

Another interesting goodie is to take a tablet (yeah, yeah, yeah) (merely another attempt at humor, mom) and pencil and go off into a corner by yourself. First you think the name of your big hang-up (as in George) (as in Pant Harrison) over and over. If no men in white are lurking nearby, mutter the name a few times for good measure. Then just let your mind (choke) wander (unhook its leash first) and write down every word or phrase the George-ro-whomever brings to mind (re-choke).

When you run out (of the door and race screaming in the direction of Surrey) (with the fringe-benefits on top) (re-down, girl), you can either show your stream-of-(un)consciousness to your friends, or fling it hurriedly into the nearest fireplace. (Providing, of course, that it doesn't ignite under its own steam). (Well said, girl).

Truly an interesting thingy, and very self-revealing if you have a tendency to get carried away (in a covered basket).

While I'm on this subject, I would love to tell you about a marvelous trick that's played with a sugar cube (*mother*, it's *not* what you're *thinking*) (I ask you, what kind of girl does she think I *am*?) (I would appreciate it deeply if none of you would ever answer that question). Howsomever, there are too many details and you know how I am about explaining things. I shall endeavor to condense it into a few (thousand) well chosen words, and print it at a later date.

Speaking of later, lagater!

DINO, DESI & BILLY

GIANT SOUVENIR BOOK

Regular $1.25

ONLY $1.00

(including postage)

Includes all the facts about Dino, Desi & Billy—

- getting the full treatment in Hawaii—leis, lipstick and showers
- what their famous parents think of their success
- the type of girls they like and DISLIKE
- their first TV show and how it happened
- their favorite cars
- their musical backgrounds
- pictures of their family and fans
- and much, much more

Just fill in the coupon below, enclose $1.00 and it's all yours.

SOUVENIR BOOK
6290 Sunset Blvd., Suite 504
Hollywood 28, Calif.

Name_____
Address_____
City_____ State_____ Zip_____

Enclosed find $1.00 cash ☐ . . . check ☐ . . . money order ☐

KRLA ARCHIVES

THE HARD TIMES will sing wherever a crowd gathers to hear them.

Hard Times Come Into Pop World

By Jamie McCluskey III

HARD TIMES HAS COME! And I, for one, hope they're here to stay! And why not? Hard Times never looked better! I mean, how can you argue with five talented, handsome, fun-loving teases? Right!

Just the other day for example, HARD TIMES came to our offices, and I'm sure we'll never be quite the same again! They invaded in a large group composed of Paul Wheatbread, the 20-year-old drummer for the group; Bob Morris, bass player and 23-year-old "senior citizen" of the tribe; 19-year-old lead singer, Rudy Romero; Lee Keefer—also a venerable 23, and a self-taught musician; and, Bill Richardson, 21, guitarist with a Flamenco background.

When they are not busily involved in creating general havoic in The BEAT offices, the boys explain that they "would like to do HARD TIME music, that we write and compose, and arrange, ourselves."

I asked Rudy to describe HARD TIME music for us, and he began: "HARD TIME music is . . ." "Outta*site!!*" finished Bill. "It has a strong beat usually," Rudy continued, "and we usually sing about love. Not necessarily the love of . . . " "of the girls," offered Bob, "but love in general," added Lee. "Right," agreed Rudy, "domestic tranquility!" Bill laughed and added, "We love bananas, pears, buildings, streets, *anything!*"

In the middle of Lee's comments, Rudy decided that he would like to play reporter, and grabbing the mike he demanded, "Tell us about your $2,500 dollar ring!" Lee immediately replied: "It was given to me by a mystery friend who thought I would look good in it!"

Rudy followed rapidly with another question, "Are you a born leader?" to which Lee promptly replied, "That's what my *mother* says!"

All five of the HARD TIMES enjoy *good* music—music which is well-performed, and Bill seemed to be speaking for the majority of the guys as he explained: "Psychedelic music? If I'm in the mood for it, I like it sometimes. But, as a whole, it's kind of monotonous and boring.

"It's not something that I really appreciate. I appreciate music for *music*—something that's enjoyable to listen to."

Frequently very quiet and thoughtful as he observes closely everything going on about him, blond-and-blue-eyed Lee Keefer spoke up then to explain: "*Psychedelic* is an over-used word to begin with; as far as psychedelic, or electronic, music—or *whatever* it is—only *real* music is going to win in the end, and only real music is going to last. I think the rest of it is pretty synthetic."

I asked about the group's humor, and all five answered in unison: "Sick!!" After a couple minutes of thought, Bill related one of their best practical jokes on one another.

"Bob and Rudy each took one valuable thing from each of us and went climbing up in the mountains and hid them under rocks and things like that, and then came back with maps. They'd left little signs on the trees and stuff for our next clue, and that night . . . it *rained*, and all the little maps got washed away! So, we've got valuables hidden all over the mountains!"

Ambitions? Yes, the HARD TIMES are very ambitious. They hope to be able to someday get involved in movies, possibly playing their own characters on screen. For right now, they are all very much concerned with the music which they are presenting to the public and the *way* in which they are presenting it.

Yes, HARD TIMES *have* come . . . at last! . . . and you can believe your boots when we tell you that they're here to stay. If you don't believe us—well, just tune them in on "Where The Action Is" some afternoon (they are the newest addition to the "Action" family) and find out for yourself just how wonderful HARD TIMES can be!

The Left Banke Pulling Away From Commercialism

By Rick Johnson

"People expect a lot out of a pop group," Steve Martin said, "they expect you to continually pour out witty little answers they think are cute.

It's almost like they want you to be something other than human. We can't—and don't even try—to do that. We just say what we feel and don't try to put on any fronts."

Steve's evaluation came after a lengthy interview of his group, the Left Banke, and we were inclined to agree with him. All afternoon the five New Yorkers had spared us the little absurdities associated with some pop groups.

The Left Banke are new on the pop scene, but they have some very definite—if not brash—ideas on their music and pop music in general.

"I don't suppose you could put our music in any particular classification," said Mike Brown, who composed "Walk Away Rene." "We try to get away from commercial aspects in our music.

"Away From Us"

"Better yet," he continued, "I think commerciality gets away from us."

The Left Banke probably take as much commerciality out of their music as can be taken out. They don't like traveling and don't particularly relish gigs. They don't like follow up records and don't look for a certain image.

They don't even seem to mind releasing a "bomb" occasionally. "I get a certain satisfaction out of recording the song anyway," said Jeff Winfield.

Mostly, they are just interested in turning out "real music."

"We would never record anything written by someone else, either," said George Cameron, who writes much of his group's music. "We do all of our own writing. Right now we have about 30 songs of our own."

Polite

All five of the Left Banke are 18 years old. At first, they are polite and rather reserved—until the conversation turns to their feelings on their music.

Then it's hard to get a word in edgewise.

"How was the party at Cass' house last night?" I finally queried.

"How did you find out about that?" asked a startled Tom Finn.

"The word's out. Now would you like to give your version?"

Finally realizing the intended jest, George Cameron explained. "It was nothing really . . . just a little gathering.

"Several of us just went up to her home to take in the view. She has a beautiful home. It was really a gas."

The heavy demand placed on the Left Banke after their first record has created an almost new life for them, but they have accepted it with grace.

"I suppose each of us had a bit of a swelled head at first," admitted Steve, "but it was nothing serious."

They are now touring the country promoting their record, and it was their first trip to California. While Tom and George were mildly extolling its virtues, Mike disagreed.

"I still like New York," he said stubbornly. "I don't feel really comfortable when I'm away from it."

"But New York is dirty and grubby," Mike countered, "but I still love it."

Until about eight months ago, the group had never been exposed to the public eye. They spent a lot of time rehearsing and knocking about New York recording studios, but as a group had never even performed a local gig.

Now they have one of the biggest records in the country and are playing some of the top entertainment spots, but it's hard to imagine they really changed after their overnight success.

They dress a little wilder and keep a little busier, but those are probably the only differences.

When they return to New York they plan to record their first album. But it will be a little different from most entertainers' first album.

"One thing we will never do on an album," Mike said emphatically, "is put, like, 'Walk Away Rene' in real big letters and then under that put 'The Left Banke.'

All Good Ones

"We feel every song on our album will be a good one, not just one certain one."

"I suppose we'll release a single off the album," said Steve, "but it won't be anything like 'Walk Away Rene.' One thing we'll never do is release two songs that sound just alike."

The Left Banke are refreshing for their originality. A lot of groups talk about defying trends but few mean it. You get the impression the Left Banke really mean it.

THE LEFT BANKE (l. to r.-front) Steve Martin, Jeff Winfield, (rear) Mike Brown, Tom Finn, George Cameron.

KRLA ARCHIVES

KRLA ARCHIVES

America's Largest Teen NEWSpaper 25¢

KRLA Edition BEAT
DECEMBER 3, 1966

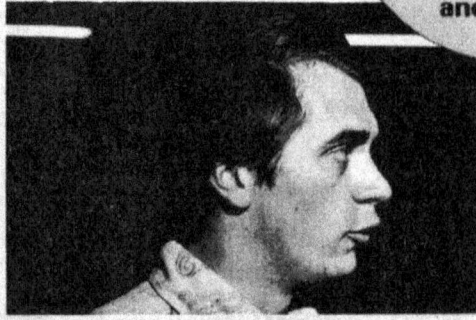

THE ASSOCIATION IS UNNECESSARY like WATER SLEEP FOOD and LOVE

KRLA BEAT

Volume 2, Number 29 — December 3, 1966

Beach Boys Rate Riots On Their English Tour

The way English crowds were reacting, you'd think the year was 1965 and the Beatles were in the vicinity.

But it's almost 1967, the Beatles have probably forgotten each other's names, and the world—England, at least—appears to have a new set of heroes.

Those heroes are America's Beach Boys—and they're receiving as riotous a welcome in England as the Beatles ever witnessed. Sources in London say the six Californians have all but replaced the Beatles as England's favorite group.

The Beach Boys, even without the presence of Brian Wilson, were assured of a sell-out tour before they left America.

Beatles Split? . . . Epstein Mum

Three years after instigating an entire era, the Beatles are breaking up.

At least, that's the concensus among London music observers and those close to the princes of pop. The word came as a whisper at first, but subsequent statements by Brian Epstein and the Beatles themselves have given the speculation certainty.

National wire services broke the story last week, and when no one in the Beatles' organization denied it, more than 200 angry Beatles' fans picketed Epstein's London home in protest.

But not even the Beatles' manager, who probably hasn't seen his group en masse in nearly four months, could deny the story.

Instead, he pointed to the Beatles' forthcoming film as an indication the foursome would remain intact. John and Paul are writing the entire music score for the 1967 film, he pointed out.

But even the film will have a strange irony to it. Not once do all four Beatles appear simultaneously in the film.

Asked bluntly if the Beatles are breaking up, Epstein was quoted by an English newspaper as saying he'd have to call a special meeting with the Beatles to discuss their futures.

"That's silly," said a press spokesman, "he sees them all the time, he doesn't need to have a special meeting to discuss their future."

Epstein's ambiguous statements suddenly bore new significance as speculations of a Beatles break-up increased. His strangely worded refusal of an invitation for the Beatles to appear in a two-hour television spectacular to aid victims of the Aberfan slag-heap disaster was seen in a new light.

Although everyone from the Rolling Stones to Richard Burton and Elizabeth Taylor agreed to appear, Epstein refused, saying: "I know without consulting them the boys would feel unable to make an appearance of this sort for too many reasons to enumerate."

The following day, Epstein twisted out another ambigious statement to the press. "The Beatles have changed their thoughts as their career has been

(Turn to Page 5)

...THE BEATLES IN THE GOOD OLD DAYS WHEN THEY STILL WORKED TOGETHER!

Turners Draw English Fire

Ike and Tina Turner, in England on a goodwill promotional tour, recently came across a note of disharmony when singer Jimmy James levied a harsh verbal blast against the popular American duo.

James, leader of a group called the Vagabonds, made a series of heated accusations against Ike and Tina as the Americans prepared to return to the States.

The conflict began when Ike and Tina were asked by an English music magazine to review a selection of new records that would soon be released in Britain.

The Californians gave the new Vagabond single, "Ain't Love Good, Ain't Love Proud," a highly unfavorable review. Outspoken Tina said there was "nothing professional about the record," adding that James "has a terrible voice."

Ike said the new single "sounded like it's been done on a home recorder."

James countered with an attack of his own. Two of his more printable views were that the duo's analysis was "vicious" and "unwarranted."

As for the quality and precision of recording techniques, Vagabond manager Peter Meaden was insistent it wasn't "done on a home recorder." He said the group put more than $4,500 into the recording, which featured "14 tracks for an LP with strings, brass and top session men."

But James wasn't satisfied with merely a defence of his new record. He launched into a severe personal attack of Ike and Tina.

"Tell Tina that screaming isn't singing and we've got one James Brown already," he said angrily. "And I hope they find Phil Spector's phone number soon—they need him."

IKE AND TINA DREW HEATED VERBAL COMMENT FROM ENGLAND

Inside the BEAT

ERIC TO CHANGE AGAIN	3
ASSOCIATION DAZE	6-7
JAGGER'S FARLOWE	10
JOHNNY RIVER'S DECEPTION	11
YARDBIRD QUALITY	13
SOUL OF RYDER	14
VAUDEVILLE TAKING OVER	15

The BEAT is published bi-weekly by BEAT Publications, Inc., editorial and advertising offices at 6290 Sunset Blvd., Suite 504, Hollywood, California 90028. U.S. bureaus in Hollywood, San Francisco, New York, Chicago and Nashville; overseas correspondents in London, Liverpool and Manchester, England. Sale price 25 cents. Subscription price: U.S. and possessions, $5 per year; Canada and foreign rates, $9 per year. Second class postage prepaid at Los Angeles, California.

MONKEES AWARDED TWO GOLD RECORDS

The Monkees, those assembly line products who have created a new concept in TV programming, are now just part of a great big happy family. The family tree reads: RCA Victor, proud father; Colgems, healthy infant; and the Monkees, healthy infant's favorite toy.

The Monkees were assigned to the new Colgems label, a division of RCA, only two months ago but already everything has come up roses for RCA, Colgems and the Monkees.

Only several weeks after the release of the Monkees' first single, "Last Train To Clarksville," and their new album, "The Monkees," both discs were at the top of their respective categories on the charts.

And now both have been certified as million-sellers.

The success of the Monkees has solidified the relationship between Colgems and RCA. Commenting on the liason, RCA vice president Steve Sholes stated, "This is the first time in the history of the RIAA that a newly formed label has achieved such success with its debut releases, and we are delighted with our affiliation with Colgems."

The Monkees' single was released four weeks in advance of the group's debut on TV this fall. The record has been number one in the nation for the past two weeks.

The group's first LP was released at the same time their TV debut was aired. It was the country's top selling LP less than a month after its release.

Don Kirshner, Colgems president, is the music supervisor for all the group's recordings and music score for their TV series. Kirshner is now working on material for the Monkees' next single and LP.

The ironic part of the Monkees' disc success is the fact that the studio musicians, not the Monkees themselves, were used on both "The Last Train To Clarksville" and their album. But, apparently, Monkee fans consider it "part of the game" and continued to rush to their record stores to purchase anything with the Monkee name attached to it.

KRLA ARCHIVES

Letters TO THE EDITOR

ARE BEATLES LAZY?

Dear BEAT:
The letter from Jill Ann Powell, printed in the November 5 issue of The BEAT, was exactly true! The Beatles are nothing but four lazy slobs! Jill Ann said the Beatles came to San Francisco, did a 33 minute performance and left. Well, of all the nerve.

After the Beatles finished singing, they should have walked out into the audience and shaken the hands of all 25 thousand!

They would have probably gotten ripped to shreds, but that was the tour's last show, so it wouldn't have mattered. They should have invited the whole audience to a party after the show instead of returning to Los Angeles. A demolished hotel wouldn't have mattered if all those people were happy.

I know all of that sounds ridiculous but no more ridiculous than the complaints from "Beatle fans" about never seeing the guys. I agree with those of you who say the Beatles should tour more, but they stay in hiding when they do tour for everyone's protection.

The Beatles are *not* stuck-up and snobbish. I met them briefly in August of 1965 and they were quite nice. Maybe that was because I didn't try to tear their clothes off.

Just what do "Beatle fans" expect? I'm sure John, Paul, George and Ringo would be interested in knowing.

Jill, you're *not* a Beatle fan. Now crown me!
Marcia Baker

MONKEES

Dear BEAT:
Last night we heard on the radio that the Monkees were going to be taken off the air. Is this true? If so, why?

All us Monkee luvers want to know, so please tell us.
Candi & Friends

Relax, Candi, the Monkees are not going off the air—at least, not for awhile. Their ratings have been rather low, however, but backers of the show are going to give it every possible chance to remain on the air.
The Editor

BRIAN OUT?

Dear BEAT:
What ever happened to Brian Wilson of the Beach Boys? I saw a picture in The BEAT recently and someone had replaced him.
R.V.R.

For personal appearance dates, Brian has been replaced by Bruce Johnson.
The Editor

AUSTRALIAN REPORT

Dear BEAT:
First, I'd like to thank you for a great publication, The BEAT. It's absolutely great! We came to Australia from California and what I really missed was The BEAT, so I decided to subscribe. There are around 30 American teenagers here in Gladstone. Most of us are here because of the Kaiser Aluminum Plant here.

I have a complaint to make. Why doesn't America pay any attention to Australia? Everyone's so hung up on England. Sure, England has become the swinginest place in the world but Australia is pretty hip too. The top group here is the Easybeats. At the moment, they're in England and seem to be doing pretty well. They all live in P.J. Proby's old house in St. John's Wood. Two of them are Dutch and the other three are Aussies. Their first record in England, "Friday On My Mind," has just made the charts this week.

Everyone here and in England is pretty sure that the Easybeats are headed for the top. And if they make it, everyone in the States will hear of them and find out how great the Easybeats are.

Australian radio stations are good, though the DJ's seem pretty dead to me after listening to California disc jockeys. They play all of the new records and keep everyone up-to-date.

Thanks for listening.
Julie Hendrickson

SICK & TIRED

Dear BEAT:
I have had it! I'm sick and tired of all these English groups. I have been in bed all summer long with a broken leg and I have kept a close track on all of the groups.

All I ever read about is how the English groups come over here and take all the money from us teens and then turn around and cut down America and us boys and girls. It just makes me sick.

The Beatles are one group that is like this. They are forever putting us and America down but without us where would they be?

The Mindbenders are one group that is nothing but mouth. They do more talking about how dumb we are than they do singing! I'd like to know what makes them think they are so good. Give me Paul Revere and the Raiders any day.

So come on all of you kids, let's do something about it.
John Rose

ASSOCIATION HAS CLASS

Dear BEAT:
My favorite group is the Association. I think they're the greatest! They are on their way to the top and it proves one thing—they've got talent!

I am thankful to The BEAT for featuring them as often as you do. I have only found one article featuring them in any of the "popular" magazines, while The BEAT has had articles on them many times.

Thanks again for your great newspaper and please feature the Association as often as possible because I think they've got class!
Susan Reetz

BEATLES

Dear BEAT:
I do not mind whether you print this or not but I felt I just had to write and tell you what a wonderful paper you do. I have a pen-pal in California who sent me a copy of BEAT and although I have only received one copy, I just had to put pen to paper and tell you how wonderful you are.

I find it very interesting and amusing to compare pop in England to pop in the States. Unlike five or six years back, most U.S. pop stars are little known here.

For most people, though I am sure a few would disagree, the Beatles are no longer "in" over here. Yet groups like the Monkees—well, I certainly (and I'm sure many others) have never heard of them before—seem, from your paper anyhow, to be one of the best up and coming new groups on the scene.
Sylvia Roberts
Bedford, England

READER REBUTTAL

Dear BEAT:
In your October 22 issue of the fabulous BEAT, there was a letter I'd like to comment about. The title was "Dare Ya To Print It" by a Peggy Langlands. This letter was so, so, well heaven only knows the word for it (stupid might do very nicely) that I got out the handiest scrap of paper and pen and wrote this letter of contradiction to you.

(1) She said the only letters ever printed in The BEAT about The BEAT are good ones. Well, natch! Those are the only ones ever written and sent. Even then, they printed your letter, didn't they? There may be letters of suggestions but never an actual bad word about this absolutely "in" paper. Let me say there are also many, many (try 100) more good articles in this paper than just a mere few.

(2) There is a larger variety of articles in this paper than you'll find in other teen papers—anywhere. Length of hair has nothing to do with talent either. Peggy, if the Association had long hair would you still like them? Smolder on that one awhile.

(3) You can't please everyone all of the time so why not sit tight and wait till an article on your fave(s) come out? (Read all the other neat and tripple articles while you are at it.)

(4) I am afraid that the printing of one full page article on the Robbs (who are very new, but good) would never in a lifetime of decades *kill The BEAT*.

(5) And last but not least, the Association isn't the only talented group around, long or short hair, that's for sure! The Beatles, Beach Boys, Sonny & Cher, Supremes (look at their hair!), Monkees, Raiders and Yardbirds just to name a lot of long-haired, talented groups.

Don't get me wrong, Peggy or anyone, I have nothing against the Association (I think they are as neat as I do many, many others), nor am I saying nobody has a right to their own opinion, but what I am saying is "hair has no bearing on talent." People will like the songs before they even *see* the group in many cases.

Thank you, BEAT and everyone having to do with this newspaper and a half (and three quarters) for listening to me. I only hope I have done some good as far as altering some people's attitudes.
Jeanette Wahl

MORE KINKS

Dear BEAT:
I think that you have a very groovy newspaper and I thoroughly enjoy everything that's in it. But there is something missing. You are always publishing big sections on the Beatles and the Stones and other such groups but what about the Kinks?

Surely they are one of the least talked about and one of the better groups in pop music. I realize that you do print about them occasionally but only to tell about Peter being unable to rejoin the group (which is too bad) or other such things.

I wish you would please print this letter for I feel that it's very important for people to take more notice of this wonderful group. So please, BEAT, print lots more on the Kinks and if you can, would you please print a picture of Dave. He's simply the grooviest!
Chris Owens

MARRIED?

Dear BEAT:
I would like to have something cleared up, okay? Everyone is saying that the Monkees are all single, right? Wrong! Today in the Chronicle Examiner it said that Mike Nesmith is married and has a 20 month old son. Really?

I would appreciate finding out either who is lying or who has made a mistake. Please print this letter because I am sure that a few individuals would like to know besides me. Thank you.
Pam Howe

Mike Nesmith is indeed married and does have a young son.
The Editor

HOLLIES

Dear BEAT:
There are a few Hollies-lovers out this way and we'd like to know if there is a fan club for the five somewhere that we could join. If you know of one, please print it so that we can join immediately. We're desperate!

Also, is Allan Clarke married?
Barb Niebaum

You may write to the Hollies at 126 Princess Street, Stockport, Cheshire, England. They'll be able to tell you exactly who to contact regarding fan club information. Yes, Allan is married.
The Editor

'NOT TRUE'

Dear BEAT:
Today as I got home from school, I opened the newspaper and began to read. I came to one of those columns where they tell you about what's going on in the city and what happens at social events and business meetings, things like that and others. Well, I looked at it and the word "Beatle" caught my eye.

It said: "The Beatles have informed Capitol Records, their U.S. waxworks, that they will record one more album and then that's it, period."

This same writer said two weeks ago that the Beatles will break up within six months. I have but one question—is it all true? Please print this letter or send me back a quick letter. But please answer it.
Steve Cribari

A spokesman for Capitol says: "Not true." We agree.
The Editor

KRLA ARCHIVES

On the BEAT
By Louise Criscione

Leave it to the Monkees to make a joke out of that which everyone else considers close to sacred. Their latest feat took place when the group was awarded two Gold Records—one for "Last Train To Clarksville" and the other for their debut album, "The Monkees." Upon receiving the two Gold Records, they tore their gold album right out of its frame to make sure that the Goldie would actually fit inside an album jacket! Satisfied that it would, they placed the coveted disc back into its frame and announced that "you can't play a Gold Record anyway!" No, but you can sure spend the money it represents.

Surprisingly enough, their television show has so far received rather low ratings causing panic among their many fans. Afraid that the show will be dropped, Monkee fans are busy writing letters to the network, the sponsors and anyone else they can think of. However, the Monkees aren't sweating it—with the amount of money already spent on promotion Screen Gems can't afford to axe the show!

Johnny Too

Speaking of Gold Records, Johnny Rivers has just collected one on his 24th birthday for his million-selling "Poor Side Of Town." A self-penned song, it marked a drastic change of pace for Johnny but one which the record-buying public seemed to find a million dollars to their liking. Johnny's next single, "Phoenix," is possibly even better than "Poor Side Of Town"—would you believe two million at the cash registers?

The Lovin' Spoonful chalked up another credit when they were signed to compose the musical score for "You're A Big Boy Now" which stars Elizabeth Harman, Julie Harris and Geraldine Page.

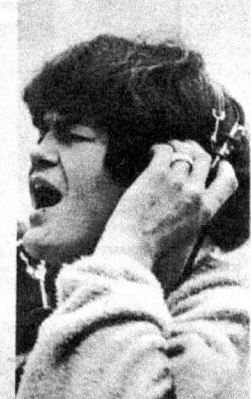
... MICKEY DOLENZ

The Spoonful have finally decided to move themselves out of the state of New York to join part of the Association tour which is scheduled to wind itself up on December 11. Although complaints have been made to the effect that the Spoonful are neglecting the rest of the Fifty in favor of New York, the majority of their fans don't seem to mind the snub as "Rain On The Roof" continues to climb up the charts. Perhaps absence *does* make the heart grow fonder?

Herbie's World

Herbie Alpert is not satisfied with being the hottest item in music, now he's out to take over the whole world! A&M Records, the Alpert Moss Company, announced its purchase of the Davon Music catalogue—thereby gaining copyrights on "Along Comes Mary," "Green Back Dollar" and "The World I Used To Know." In addition to the copyrights, former Davon writers, Tandyn Almer and Mason Williams, will be penning hits for Irving Music (an affiliate of A&M.) About the only thing those in the business are asking is: "What now, Herbie?"

The biggest question mark on the pop scene is the deepening Beatle mystery. No album, no single, no movie, no annual Christmas tour of England. Indications are running hot and heavy that as far as the U.S. is concerned we've seen the Beatles "live" for the last time. Perhaps the movie will eventually be made and if they can find the time to get themselves altogether in a recording studio, there will be more records—but as far as personal appearances are concerned there will be no more.

... JOHN LENNON

Past Tense

Of course, no one will give an official statement to that effect but the second-guessers seem to be convinced. And John Lennon didn't help matters when he said: "For the past six years I have been a Beatle. It's been a jolly good life and we've had a good many laughs but it can't go on forever." He then went on to admit that his fellow Beatles are also concerned with what to do in the future. "From time to time," said the Chief Beatle, "we gather and speak about it." And that is exactly how it stands—nothing confirmed, nothing denied. Just a lot of rumors and second-guesses.

Rascals Win Court Plea— Temporarily

With most groups fighting to get their names on albums today, the Young Rascals have filed suit to keep their name and picture off a forthcoming LP.

The Rascals and Atlantic Records obtained a temporary injunction against Pickwick International, Design Records and the Keel Manufacturing Corp., prohibiting the manufacture, sales or distribution of the album "The Young Rascals—The Isley Brothers."

The Rascals demand the withdrawal of the album from the market on the grounds that the performances on the album designated as the Young Rascals were actually by another group.

The New York-based group won the injunction last week in New York State Supreme Court. The temporary injunction remains in effect until the case is brought to trial.

Judge Nathaniel T. Helman, who issued the temporary injunction, prohibited Pickwick and the other two defendants from "stating, claiming, implying or inferring . . . in advertisements or advertising materials . . . that the performances reproduced on Design Records DLP 253 entitled 'The Young Rascals—The Isley Brothers' were by the plaintiffs."

Judge Helman also prohibited Pickwick from selling any copies to wholesalers, record dealers or the general public.

... FELIX CAVALIERE (Head Rascal) smiles at court victory.

'Hip' Burdon Talking Split

Eric Burdon has had his new Animals only a few weeks, and believe it or not, he's already talking about a split. The littlest Animal revealed last week that only three members of his present group are likely to remain with him.

Burdon said he would revamp the personnel of the Animals for the second time at the end of his present tour with Georgie Fame.

Burdon has a new kick these days—psychedelic music—and it appears, a similar interest is almost a prerequisite for the musicians who accompany him. Danny McCullough, John Weidner and Barry Jenkins share Burdon's interest in what was originally an American craze.

Hippy Talk

As for Burdon, psychedelic "hippy" language is already finding its place in his vocabulary. He describes the three musicians who are likely to remain with him in a fashion that would befit the truest Sunset Strip "freak."

"23-year-old Danny is a kind of Irish navy I found digging a hole in the road outside the Scotch of St. James," he said. "He was formerly with the 'McAlpines' group. He's sufficiently off his head to fit in with the crowd and does a great impression of Ken Dodd. He's written a song for 'Doddy,' entitled 'Hello Choochie Face!'

"John Weider is an 18-year-old Cockney character, and he and Danny are working on some new compositions for the group—bluesy based. Weird guy—he dances about all by himself. He goes to clubs, looks around to see if anyone is watching, then 'freaks out' on the floor.

"Barry Jenkins, otherwise known as Polly Perkins, is still with me because he cares about his music the same way I do.

"My ex-lead guitarist, Hilton Valentine, is now one of the world's great religious leaders—he only steps down to communicate with mortals occasionally. At present, he's helping with my management and doing a grand job."

Burdon's psychedelic notions appear to be more than just a passing fancy. In his last trip to the United States, Burdon recorded some material with Frank Zappa—the leader of the Mothers of Invention and foremost musician in the psychedelic field.

Burdon predicts a hit for the single, "Another Side Of Life," to be released in the States soon. He doesn't, however, expect either his psychedelic records of the psychedelic scene in general to spread to England.

"I don't think it will catch on as a musical form in England because the humor and language used in the lyrics of 'freak-out' music are a very 'in' thing closely tied to the U.S. scene," he said.

He appears to be right in his evaluation. Neither his exportation of psychedelic music nor his frequent change of partners has particularly appealed to English audiences.

On his opening night of a recent tour he was barely audible over the chants and yelling from hecklers sprinkled throughout the audience. How had other audiences received him?

"About the same," he said. "People don't like changes, and at present I'm supposed to be the villain who broke up the Animals. I didn't break up anything. WE broke up.

Resentment

"Also I think there's some resentment that I've been spending so much time in America. The man who deserted Britain, that's me! Boo, boo!

"I go on stage to chants of 'We want Geno!' which doesn't help too much. But that guy's got a great act.

"As soon as this tour finishes, I'm going to get an act together which will set the stage on fire. At present, we're still working up the musical side."

Burdon intends to air his own brand of psychedelic music on the American stage on his next tour here. Until then, he couldn't resist one parting invitation to the whole freaky, psychedlic world.

"Freaks of the world unite!" he said triumphantly. "Zoot Money is trying to take over and God help America when Jenkins, McCullough and Weider hit there next year!"

KRLA ARCHIVES

PICTURES in the NEWS

ELVIS PRESLEY WAS RECENTLY AWARDED the first annual Sigma Chi Fraternity Youth Leadership Award on the set of his movie, "Easy Come, Easy Go." John Romain (left) presented plaques to Elvis as "the public figure who has set the highest standard for the nation's youth to follow." Also representing the Alpha Upsilon Chapter, USC, were Pat Larkin and Bill Brown.

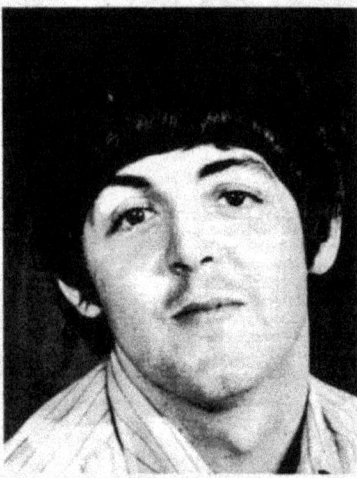

PAUL McCARTNEY AND HIS FELLOW BEATLES haven't been doing any group work since their last U.S. tour but individually all but Ringo are keeping themselves quite busy. John is, of course, making a movie; George is growing a mustache and learning to play sitar; Ringo is playing with his baby boy. And Paul? Rumor has it he is the voice behind Donovan in "Mellow Yellow."

DUSTY SPRINGFIELD HAS BEEN trying for months to reach the U.S. but has faced all sorts of hang-ups, including the airline strike. However, she is now here and has just opened a three-week stint at New York's famous Basin Street East. Dusty opened to a sell-out audience and was the recipient of rave reviews from everyone who attended.

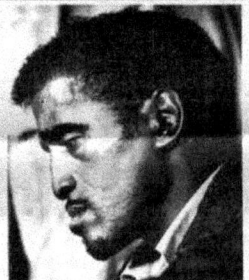

SAMMY DAVIS, JR. HAS BEEN GIVEN the green light by Vice President Hubert Humphrey on the entertainer's long-awaited chance to visit Viet Nam and perform for our servicemen. Davis had been seeking permission to tour the strife-torn country for more than a year but it took a call to the Vice President before clearances were made.

FOR THE FIRST TIME in the history of Philips Records, an entire month is being set aside in tribute to the 4 Seasons. Therefore, the month of November is officially "The 4 Seasons' Month"—at least, as far as Philips is concerned. During the past five years, the 4 Seasons have managed to come up with a consistent string of hit singles and albums. Their first single, "Sherry," reached the peak of its popularity exactly five years ago.

'in' people are talking about...

Donovan really being blue—not yellow... Whether or not Rudy Valee records will make a comeback since we're in the middle of vaudeville again... What Robinson did with Friday on Saturday night... How upset Sir Douglas was about the article written by an agent but signed with his name... Dandy really being a fink... Herbie taking over the world and how sweet it is to have a Jewish South of the Border man at the top... The feeling Neil has and how many females wish he'd feel nicely toward them... Why Question Mark is making like a secret agent man.

PEOPLE ARE TALKING ABOUT whether or not the Stones will actually make that movie and wondering if they're trying to pull a Beatle on us... Why George has grown that mass of hair on his face... Eric using the Clara Ward singers as a back-up group... Mike Nesmith discarding his cap in favor of hair... How the Peanut Butter Conspiracy is spreading all over the city and how totally out of sight it is when a slice of banana is added (you're welcome, Russ)... Berry keepin' Diana hangin' on... The M&P hit which isn't really... Why the devil was wearing a blue dress when everyone thought he was a guy... How satisfied Bobby's mind is—also his wallet.

PEOPLE ARE TALKING ABOUT how nice it is that Johnny's record is such a hit 'cause he can move out of the poor side of town... Why Bobby would ever want to be a carpenter and deciding it was probably because he was over-charged when they built his house... Whether or not Simon and Garfunkel are out to start a new trend—one which will feature a 24 hour news report... How long it's going to take before Renee finally gets that "walk away" message through her head... Why the fantastic Miracles cancelled... How everyone is trying to tell Dionne what to do... Tommy's version of the Wild Thing and how totally different it becomes with a Southern accent.

PEOPLE ARE TALKING ABOUT the Spoonful capturing their inspiration from nature—what with the city in the summer and the wet roof—and wondering when they'll release snow on the freeway... Whether or not it will be Elvis or Elvis' guitar making that appearance at the World's Fair and coming to the obvious conclusion that it will be his guitar... The gigantic Kwella hoax which goes to prove that there is a camp in Africa too... Lee's holy cow, Martha being ready and Hymn #5... What really happened to Dylan because he hasn't been seen since that motorcycle accident... The Kingsmen putting out "Guantanamera" which is only fair after "Louie, Louie" by the Sandpipers... How freaky the West Coast scene is getting and how hilarious the rest of the nation thinks the whole thing is.

PEOPLE ARE TALKING ABOUT starting a giant "Stop The Hollies" campaign... Scott's "Go Electric" literature... Tokens of Happenings and how hard it is to tell which group is which... What's going on in the pop world and deciding that nothing is and that's the whole problem... The Beatles being "out" but possibly coming back "in" if they'd only do something together... The Monkees and the Association definitely being "in" while most English groups are "out"... Soul being "in" but straight folk "out"... Bill Cosby and Lou Rawls being very "in" while Batman and the Green Hornet are "out" but vaudeville being "in"... Mini skirts being "in" but bell-bottoms being "out"... Gregorian chants possibly making a return and after that "Swing Low, Sweet Chariot" by the Byrds... The Righteous Brothers being currently "out" while the Purify Brothers are "in"... Light shows being a gigantic drag while psychedelic music is even worse than a drag—it's dead.

PEOPLE ARE TALKING ABOUT America being "in" again and scoring two for our side... How positively groovy it would be if Davy was really six feet tall but had everyone fooled.. What would happen if Mick switched sisters... Cass having little talent but a whole lot of beauty... What a talker Johnny is... How long it will take before there are no more Kinks left in pop... Herman speaking straight and blowing the whole pop scene wide open... What a groove it would be if Frankie Avalon, Fabian and Bobby Rydell all came back to us—perhaps as a trio... Yardbird rumors being "in" while Stone rumors are a thing of the past.

KRLA ARCHIVES

Censorship Hits!

American censorship lashed out at another British record recently, so rather than risk the loss of U.S. radio air play, Dave Dee, Dozy, Beaky, Mick and Tich re-taped their controversial single, "Bend It."

The Britons flew copies of the altered disc with modified lyrics to U.S. radio stations last week. The song was originally banned here because the lyrics were allegedly "suggestive."

In an open letter to U.S. deejays, the group defends the lyrics but apologizes for "unwittingly" offending deejays.

"Our two countries are so close in most things that it is always surprising to find the exception cases where meanings and innuendo differ between us," the boys said.

"This time (with the new version), we feel confident, the exhortation to 'Bend It' can only be construed as an invitation to a dance!"

DINO, DESI & BILLY
GIANT SOUVENIR BOOK
Regular $1.25
ONLY $1.00
(including postage)

Includes all the facts about Dino, Desi & Billy —
- getting the full treatment in Hawaii — leis, lipstick and showers
- what their famous parents think of their success
- the type of girls they like and DISLIKE
- their first TV show and how it happened
- their favorite cars
- their musical backgrounds
- pictures of their family and fans
- and much, much more

Just fill in the coupon below, enclose $1.00 and it's all yours.

SOUVENIR BOOK
6290 Sunset Blvd., Suite 504
Hollywood 28, Calif.

Name_____
Address_____
City_____ State_____ Zip____
Enclosed find $1.00 cash ☐ ... check ☐ ... money order ☐

...BOBBY DARIN INTENDS TO MAKE HIS "COMEBACK" COMPLETE.

BEATLES SPLIT..?

(Continued from Page 1)
altered by their attitudes in the past," he said. "Naturally, this pattern will continue.

"I'd be a fool to forecast exactly how it will be."

To anyone familiar with the Beatles' schedule during the past four months, the alleged break up will come as no surprise.

John has been in Spain filming his first effort without the other three Beatles. George was in India learning to play the sitar, his favorite instrument now. Ringo has been in and out of London and Paul is now taking a vacation abroad.

The four have kept it no secret in the last few months that they were disenchanted with group work and wanted to expand their individual talents. None of the Beatles would apparently be without a new field when the group splits.

John expresses distaste for the Beatles earlier, harder recordings. "Songs like 'Eight Days A Week' and 'She Loves You' sound like big drags to me now," he told an interviewer recently.

BEATLE COMMENTS:

JOHN LENNON: "I suppose we've got to go on being the four mop-tops. We've no intention of splitting up. We will go on recording."

GEORGE HARRISON: "We've had four years of doing what everybody else wants us to do. Everything the Beatles have done so far has been rubbish as I see it today. We're not kidding ourselves."

IAN WHITCOMB IS positive proof that being a pop star is not all it's cracked up to be. On tour with the Raiders, Ian was involved in some frightening moments. "In Greenville, South Carolina," reveals Ian, "we were nearly killed! Some local hooligans decided that they didn't like our long hair and came after us with knives. The police intervened several times but to no avail. Finally we had to defend ourselves. The whole thing turned into a huge free-for-all! It ended with our being told to lock ourselves in our rooms."

Bob Darin Inks Long Contract

After nearly four years of disc dormancy, Bobby Darin has found the winning combination—and he doesn't intend to lose it again.

The actor-singer has signed a long-term agreement with Charles Koppelman and Don Rubin, the two producers responsible for "If I Were A Carpenter." Darin's "comback" single soared to number two in the nation and was a hit abroad.

The Koppelman and Rubin associates have established a notable ledger of hit records. In their 15 months together they have been responsible for eight records in the top 10.

Darin's forthcoming LP, "If I Were A Carpenter," was also produced by Koppelman and Rubin. The album will be released in November.

Darin is currently in England, where he has a starring role in a major film. The forthcoming film is "Stranger In A House" and co-stars Geraldine Chapman and James Mason.

WALKER BROS. LEAVE STAGE UNEXPECTEDLY

The Walker Brothers, long noted as outspoken rebels of the pop music world, walked off stage at a sell-out concert in Bristol last week in protest of the lights being off during their act.

The 2,000 ticket holders constituted a full scale riot as Bristol's Colston Hall's entertainment manager pleaded with the Walkers to go back onstage.

But the trio refused, leaving the theatre without performing a single song.

Ken Cowley, entertainment manager, said the Walkers were within their rights to leave the stage but said sponsors of the performance reserved the right to turn off the lights when it became necessary.

"It was a very young audience," said Cowley. "They had reached a state of high excitement by the time the Walkers came on.

In Rome, Do As The Romans Do Believes George

"In Rome," they say, "do as the Romans do."

Both George Harrison and his Indian sitar teacher, Ravi Shankar, are avid subscribers to this timeless adage—and that was what caused all the commotion at London International Airport last week.

Harrison, sporting a mustache and cloaked in traditional Indian garb, was on hand to greet his teacher as a mass of reporters and onlookers gathered around.

But when the Indian visitor stepped from the jet airliner, he was dressed in stylish European apparel!

KRLA ARCHIVES

..."IT'S A BIRD, IT'S A PLANE"

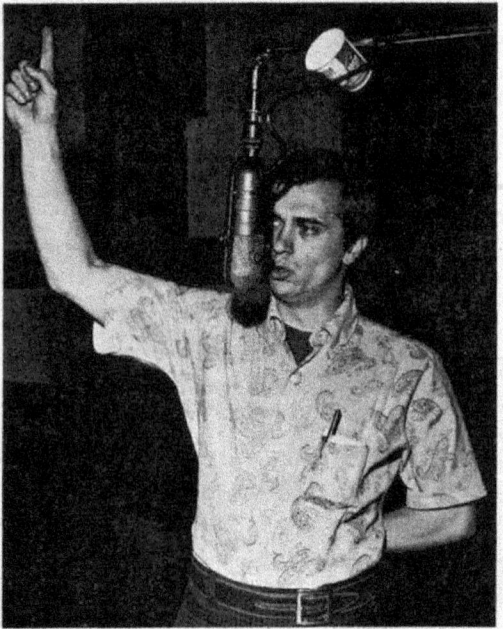

..."NO, IT'S ME—BRIAN ASSOCIATED!"

A Daze Worth Of Association

HOLLYWOOD—It's an ordinary street. Busy but otherwise like any other street in a big city. Its the buildings which surround the street that make it so special. Recording studios, movie studios, famous restaurants and "in" clubs. Tourists tend to flock to the restaurants and clubs which is quite a shame because the recording studios are where the happening people congregate. Practically any day of the week you can find at least one top group or artist utilizing the facilities of a Sunset recording studio. Beach Boys, Mama's & Papa's, Rolling Stones, Raiders. They're all to be found, at one time or another, recording hits inside the sheltered buildings on Sunset Blvd.

Seen It All

Today in Studio Two at Western Recorders you find the Association. You've seen them before, of course. A year ago at a local club, several months later at a sell-out concert, yesterday on a national television show. You've seen the whole thing. The hype, the polite applause, the hit which wasn't, the in-born talent which needed developing, the potentially powerful act which lacked tightness.

And then the line of reporters asking, begging, demanding interviews, pictures, information, *anything*. The thunderous ovations, the encores, the million-selling single, the mature creativeness which people call talent, the professionally tight act.

A year can be as short as it is long; the months as alike as they are different. A year ago you couldn't care less. Today you kick yourself for being so blind. Invitations to Association recording sessions and appearances were politely declined as you decided that it wouldn't be worth the bother. Today you watch in amazement as people queue up just to be introduced to the six members of the group you once classified as "talented but without a prayer of being nationally popular." And you wonder why you never saw it before, why you had no faith.

As you sit in the semi-darkness of Studio Two watching the Association create another hit, the months of the past year fade into one another and it's easy to remember how it all happened. An anxious agent interrupting your coffee break to play "One Too Many Mornings" by some group called the Association. Your opinion? It's okay. How about driving out to the Ice House to see them, maybe an interview? Well, this week is pretty busy, maybe some other time.

Persistence is usually rewarded and in the case of the Association it was the cause of an interview. Of course, *you* didn't do it. You were supposed to, but being basically clever (stupid might be more truthful) you got out of it and someone else made the "sacrifice" of wasting an evening attempting to interview six Associates.

Not You

An interview, a picture, now the whole staff is hung on them. Except you. Good looking? Sure, but so what? Talented? Possibly, but so are a lot of other people.

You shut them out of your mind, probably a bunch of swell-heads anyway. Then one day you make the mistake of arriving early. All alone in the office and the phone refuses to stop ringing. And right in the midst of the confusion an unfamiliar head pops into the office. Selling something? No, looking for someone. Not here. So, he scribbles a message on a scrap of paper and starts to leave. Wait, you forgot to write down your name. Russ Giguere of the Association.

Hmm. Not too bad, rather friendly. Perhaps they're not *all* stuck-up. More days, more weeks. Terry, Gary, Jim, Ted, Brian. They all took to the habit of dropping by and within a month you had met them all. Have a little change of heart? Not really. True, none of them are swell-headed. Fact is, they're all quite friendly—crazy, but a nice sort of crazy. Which automatically eliminates them since *everyone* knows nice guys never make it.

As People

More months. You still find it a little hard keeping the right names with the right faces. But it's getting easier. "Along Comes Mary." A hit. Maybe you'll change your mind now. Not on your life, baby, hundreds of groups have one hit and then zero. You had, admittedly, made a slight turn-about by this time. You dug 'em. Plain and simple. But you dug them as people—as entertainers you still had your doubts. Due mainly to the fact that you had only seen them perform once—way back when you couldn't tell one from the other.

A debut album. Perhaps you've been entirely wrong. They are talented, very. Maybe nice guys *do* occasionally make it. So, you mysteriously found yourself on the other side of the fence, crossing your fingers that the Association would not be a one-hit wonder.

"Cherish." Number one in the nation. A top group, fan mail, sell-outs, a Gold Record. And ugly talk. It seems to be a standing rule. Whenever somebody makes it big, hundreds of jealous mouths get their kicks out of "gossip" (lies might be a more appropriate word). Sometimes that gossip becomes fact. You've seen it happen before.

It's almost impossible to count the number of entertainers who have been nice to you when they were struggling to get that hit. Then when they got it, they lost the memory part of their brain and suddenly forgot they had ever known you. They're "stars" and they take great pleasure out of stomping on those who helped them up that ladder.

The Association weren't like that. No one could make you believe that they'd actually forget, though a lot of people tried to. "They'll kick you right in the teeth, just watch." No! *They* won't. They're different. They'll still come by; they'll still be the nutty, nice guys they've always been.

Pride In What?

And for once in your life, you were right. They didn't change. Not at all. A year meant success but basically nothing else was different. Except you. Now you accept their invitations to "come out and see us." Now you take tremendous pride in the group you'd predicted would never make it.

Of course, your reasoning is totally off. You had nothing to do with their success. Besides a few pictures, an occasional mention and a few pots of coffee you did nothing for them. Yet, you get this strange tingle when you sit in a sell-out audience and listen to the waves of deafening applause and the screams of "more, more" which go hand-in-hand with their appearance. The whole thing is like a movie—only it isn't.

Ted's crashing cymbals rudely wake you up, bring you back to today. "Good one, let's hear it," says Jerry Yester (Jim's brother and the group's producer). The playback blares out and you notice the intent concentration on the faces of all six Associates. It's probably the first time you've seen them all so serious. But then, recording is serious business to the Association and they've been at it since nine o'clock this morning.

Anyone else would have been worn out. But anyone else is *not* the Association. The playback ends and they revert back to their old selves. Tossing jokes back and forth, pushing coins into vending machines, teasing, laughing, making plans and then changing plans. Cut a few radio promos and then everyone can split.

So, back into the studio troop the big six. Gathered around the mike, they go through one of the promos. Halfway through, Brian makes a mistake and his cohorts break into uncontrollable laughter and then decide to leave the "mistake" in. Funnier that way. More promos, a playback on all of them and then the word: "Everybody can split, meet at Terry's house at 5:30."

Late

But at 5:30 even Terry isn't at his house! Punctuality is not everyone's virtue. Fifteen minutes later, Terry rushes inside to get ready. Directly across the hall, Jim is *contemplating* getting ready and Russ is down the street at an art gallery purchasing yet another painting. One more and he'll have to buy a house just to hang them in! And the rest of the group? On their way—*maybe*.

Sometime after six, the "group wagon" makes its appearance and with it Gary, Brian and Ted are accounted for. A quick count is made and the wagon's lights split the now-darkened street as the Association procession winds its way through the rush hour traffic toward its destination—the Pauly Pavilion at UCLA.

Destination reached, six Associates make a running leap down a flight of stairs and into the arena-type building. Looks of stark terror appear on the faces of the officials inside as the door bursts open and full-speed ahead the Associa-

KRLA ARCHIVES

...RUSS AND BRIAN TRY OUT A MIKE AT UCLA.

...WHILE GARY AND JIM "BOP-DO-BA."

...AND TERRY YELLS "AH."

...TED ADJUSTS HIS DRUMS AS THE "TUNING UP" CONTINUES.

...THE SHOW OVER, RUSS TAKES TIME TO SIGN AUTOGRAPHS.

tion make a beeline for their equipment which had been resting peacefully on the floor. Guitars in hand, the business of "tuning up" begins—and lasts for close to an hour.

Tuning Business

"Put the mikes up higher, please." "Can you hear our voices?" "Well, I can't hear a thing I'm singing." "This mike is off." "Everyone except us off the floor." Guitars are picked up, tuned, laid down. "Let's do one." The sound of "Enter The Young." "Hold it, I can't hear." "Can we have the mikes higher?" "How much longer do we have?" "Seven minutes." "Don't let anyone in, we're not ready yet." One verse into "Blistered" and Russ calls out: "That's okay. Good."

Everyone satisfied, the instruments are discarded as the six Associates spread out in six different directions. Russ gathers up his jacket, Terry hunts for his shoe, Brian heads for the dressing rooms but doesn't quite make it as several fans who have managed to get inside ask for autographs.

The doors open, ticket holders pour in and scramble for seats as the Association rush into the dressing rooms, discuss last minute changes and climb into their stage suits. Once dressed and ready to go on, they all head into the showers for a couple of choruses of "Silent Night."

Then it's lights down and "ladies and gentlemen, we're proud to present..." And there they are—running on stage, instigating a string of witty remarks, evoking laughter and applause as easily and smoothly as a waiter pouring a cup of coffee without spilling a drop. They finish, take the last bow and disappear into the dressing room, the house lights come on but the applause refuses to stop—so back they come for "Pandora's Golden Heebie Jeebies."

This time it definitely is finis, an exodus begins toward the doors and pandemonium is running rampant in the dressing rooms. A uniformed guard stands at the dressing room door but, judging from the number of people milling around the group's particular dressing room, he's on the losing end of the game.

A shower, a change and one by one they make their way out. They are asked to step outside and sign autographs for the throngs who are patiently waiting for that final glimpse of their favorite group. You really expect them to decline. After all, they've been at it since nine in the morning with no break to speak of. Unless they're super-human, they have to be tired by now. But to your surprise, they nod in the affirmative and make their way past the guard and are immediately engulfed in a mass of humanity. All with one goal. To get a name on a piece of paper, maybe even to shake a hand.

You watch as wave upon wave arrive with autograph books, programs, scraps of paper. And again you wonder why it took you so long to see it. Manners are pushed out of your mind as you wearily squeeze your way through the fans and out into the cold night air.

But Today

Tomorrow, noon, United Airlines. Keep repeating those words and maybe you won't forget to get yourself up in time to make it to the airport. They're going to Hawaii. Yesterday you would have cursed your luck at drawing an assignment which not only fell on a Saturday but which had you yelling aloha to the Association as they boarded a plane. But today it doesn't seem quite so bad. Today you're still trying to make up for the year before when you said they'd never make it.

Today, after all, is groovy. Much better than yesterday when you were being a hot-shot know-it-all and the Association wasn't on top of the world.

...TED AND JIM (BACKGROUND) OBLIGE BY SIGNING PROGRAMS.

KRLA ARCHIVES

KRLA TO PRESENT JOAN BAEZ

Joan Baez, who has not given a concert in the Los Angeles area in more than two years, will conduct two benefit shows at the Santa Monica Civic Auditorium, Dec. 16.

KRLA and Doug Weston of the Troubadour will sponsor the two performances. Miss Baez will appear at 7:30 p.m. and later at 10.

Miss Baez is donating her talents to benefit the Delano farm workers. Funds raised will be used for food, housing, medical care, education programs and self-help projects, according to Cesar Chavez, founder and director of the National Farm Workers Association.

Sell-out audiences for both shows are expected to see Miss Baez make her first singing appearance in California since late 1964. Seven thousand tickets are now on sale at the Santa Monica Civic Auditorium box office and at Mutual ticket agencies.

Ticket prices are $5, $4, $3, and $2.50.

Miss Baez, considered by many to be the foremost folk singer in the country, has devoted most of her time recently toward the foundation and development of a peace school in Southern California. During this time she has made numerous TV appearances and has been the object of several feature articles in national magazines.

Miss Baez is currently on the nation's LP charts with her Christmas album, "Noel."

JOAN BAEZ GETS READY FOR HER KRLA APPEARANCE ON DEC. 16

Inside KRLA
By Eden

'Tis the season to be jolly, fa la la la la, la la la la..' it's OK everyone, I'm just getting in practice for the annual KRLA Caroling Crusade, to be led this year by Golden Larynx himself, Bill Slater.

Have you noticed how many more contests you get per minute on KRLA than anywhere else in the world? I mean, we have even *more* contests than the *gas stations*...with the notable exception of Valhalla, of course!

We've only just finished the ever-exciting Beat the Bird contest, in which hundreds of lucky KRLA listeners plucked themselves a free Thanksgiving turkey. And just before that, we gave away a brand new, 1967 fully-equipped-with-*everything*. Mustang to a lucky young lady by the name of Marilyn Dare, from Gatewood Street, in Los Angeles. Marilyn *Dared* to drop us a post card telling us that she'd like to have a Mustang—and now it's hers!

This month, we've contacted world-famous car designer, George Barris, who has agreed to custom design a brand new 1967 Chevrolet Camaro for another lucky KRLA listener. We had over 70,000 entries in the '67 New Car Contest, and if this contest appeals to you... better start listening closely *now* for more details.

Most of you are probably already aware of the nightly Biondi Bash, in which the World's Ugliest and Skinniest DJ gives away the record *you* call in and request. But, now we've started something new. From now on (beginning on last Veteran's Day), every school holiday will be celebrated with a day-long Bonus Bash on *all* the shows. So stay close to your radio *and* your *phone*!

Speaking of giveaways, if you'd like to have the Top Ten Requested singles between the hours of 3:00 and 6:00 on KRLA, just send your name and address in on a post card to Dave Hull's Top Ten Requested Singles and Dave might send you all ten discs tomorrow. As a matter of fact, he's giving away the Top Ten Requested Records on his show *every*day, so how can you lose?

Be sure and keep your radios with you on Friday and Saturday nights, as well, no matter what you're doing—going to a show, rioting on the Sunset Strip, dancing in your favorite discotheque, or *whatever*, 'cause the Man Who Knows The Score—KRLA's own Danny Baxter, and Dick Biondi will be keeping you informed on all the up-to-the-minute reports on all the football scores, just as soon as they come in from the high schools and colleges all over the Southland.

One more thing for you to do this week—call KRLA at 681-2376 anytime during the hours of 8:00 A.M. and 12 Midnight and volunteer your services for the Danny Thomas St. Jude's Teen March. It's for a very worthy cause, and this is your chance to really help.

While I'm thinking about it, I have a few handy hints for marvelous Christmas gift items for all your friends and whatevers this Yuletide. Why not send a life-sized, full-color, stuffed with 100% pure cotton replica of our own Prancing Vikings from Valhalla to your loved ones back East? (We even have one model which *cries* when you pull its *horns*!).

I've been considering having Bob Eubanks bronzed, sequined, and tagged "Granny Goose" and sending him to my cousin who grows *provocative potatoes* back in Idaho.

Or, perhaps I could interest you in a small replica of the Hullabalooer's famous horn—perfect for those friends who are fond of blowing their *own* horns!

I'm also sending Batman a life-sized portrait (in living Bat-color) of our own Bat Manager, J.B. (the one we affectionately call John-John, remember him?) and to Robin, a plaster bust of Robin Hill, our favorite engineer.

If it's **"ORIGINAL BRITISH GROUPS"** you want, on L'P's, E'P's or Singles, **WE HAVE THEM.**

also
introducing the new L.P. by
"ROUVAUN"
"THE WORLD'S GREATEST SINGER"
singing
"LOVE SONGS"
on Kalome Label

Lewin Record Paradise
6507 Hollywood Blvd. (at Wilcox)
HO. 4-8088   L.A. 90028

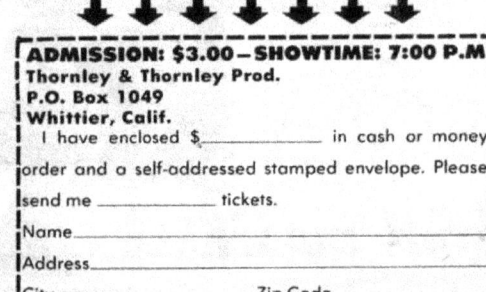

NOV. 22 — DEC. 4

FOLK, FUN AND SATIRE
OF

THE MITCHELL TRIO

PLUS

JOHN DENVER HORE
NEW ZEALAND'S FINEST ENTERTAINER

AT DOUG WESTON'S
Troubadour
9081 SANTA MONICA BLVD.
L.A. NEAR DOHENY

RESERVATIONS
CR 6-6168

KRLA ARCHIVES

ATTENTION!!!
High Schools, Colleges, Universities and Clubs:

CASEY KASEM MAY BE ABLE TO SERVE YOU!

Let Casey HELP You Put On A Show Or Dance

Contact Casey at:
HO 2-7253

Top 40 Requests

1	LADY GODIVA	Peter & Gordon
2	I WANTA BE FREE	The Monkees
3	MELLOW YELLOW	Donovan
4	GOOD VIBRATIONS	The Beach Boys
5	PUSHING TOO HARD	The Seeds
6	WHERE DID ROBINSON CRUSOE GO	Ian Whitcomb
7	THE BEAR	Fastest Group Alive
8	HAPPENINGS TEN YEARS TIME AGO	The Yardbirds
9	96 TEARS	? And The Mysterians
10	HURRAH FOR HAZEL	Tommy Roe
11	RAIN ON THE ROOF	Lovin' Spoonful
12	CHERISH	The Association
13	TALK TALK	Music Machine
14	DANDY	Herman's Hermits
15	WINCHESTER CATHEDRAL	New Vaudeville Band
16	WALK AWAY RENEE	Left Banke
17	WHY PICK ON ME	The Standells
18	CAN I GET TO KNOW YOU BETTER	The Turtles
19	STOP STOP STOP	The Hollies
20	I GOT THE FEELING	Neil Diamond
21	I'M YOUR PUPPET	James & Bobby Purify
22	YOU KEEP ME HANGIN' ON	The Supremes
23	POOR SIDE OF TOWN	Johnny Rivers
24	B-A-B-Y	Carla Thomas
25	LOVE IS A HURTIN' THING	Lou Rawls
26	HAZY SHADE OF WINTER	Simon & Garfunkel
27	HAVE YOU SEEN YOUR MOTHER, BABY, STANDING IN THE SHADOW?	Rolling Stones
28	SATISFIED MIND	Bobby Hebb
29	WHO AM I	Petula Clark
30	LOOK THROUGH MY WINDOW	Mama's & Papa's
31	OUT OF TIME	Chris Farlowe
32	DEVIL WITH A BLUE DRESS ON	Mitch Ryder
33	PSYCHOTIC REACTION	Count Five
34	SEE SEE RIDER	Eric Burdon & The Animals
35	PAINT ME A PICTURE	Gary Lewis
36	ON THIS SIDE OF GOODBYE	Righteous Brothers
37	I'M READY FOR LOVE	Martha & The Vandellas
38	HEAVEN MUST HAVE SENT YOU	The Elgins
39	REACH OUT I'LL BE THERE	Four Tops
40	BUT IT'S ALRIGHT	J.J. Jackson

ANN-MARGRET STARTS TO SWING THE DAY BEFORE THANKSGIVING ALL OVER TOWN!

KRLA GIVES A MUSTANG

KRLA had to sift through 70,000 entries to find a winner of its new car contest, but when the grand drawing was finally held, Marilyn Dare of Los Angeles was a little leary of accepting the 1967 Mustang.

Marilyn admitted later that when station officials first notified her she had won the automobile she thought it was a joke. When it was delivered, however, she laughed at her earlier skepticism.

Marilyn chose a Mustang because "Mustangs are so pretty." The car is equipped with every conceivable option offered by the Ford Motor Company.

Marilyn was chosen winner from around 500 finalists. KRLA's new car contest lasted from Oct. 1 to Nov. 9, with an average of 25 finalists chosen daily.

Chevrolet's Camaro, which was the predominant choice among entrants of the contest, has inspired a new contest held by KRLA. The station is now in the process of giving away a 1967 Camaro, completely customized by famed auto designer George Barris.

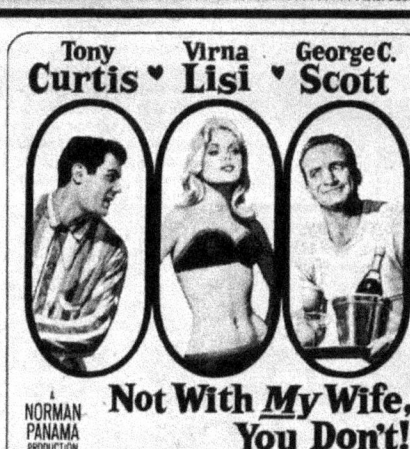

THE NEW CLUB TROPICANA
247 E. MANCHESTER, L.A.

NOW APPEARING

HUGH MASEKELA

TEENAGERS WELCOME

For Reservations—758-7615

KRLA ARCHIVES

...CHRIS

Farlowe—Soul And Gravel And No. 1

In England, people knew about Chris Farlowe and his gravel voice long before his "Out Of Time" established him here. For more than two years he has been rated that country's top soul singer.

His recording manager is Mick Jagger, and Jagger, with pride and possibly a trace of presumptuousness calls Farlowe his "protege." Others don't take that liberty. Eric Burdon, Georgie Fame, Alan Price and Spencer Davis have all lauded Farlowe as England's best.

But fame is one thing; monitary success is something else. You don't amass a fortune simply on your reputation with the public and respect from your peers.

Not Buying

For a long time, this was the story of Chris Farlowe. While everybody was admiring Farlowe's talents they were insignificantly forgetting to buy his records.

He turned out three records, "The Fool," "Farlowe In The Midnight Hours" and "Think." None of them really overpowered he selling market.

Then under the watchful eye of Mick Jagger, Farlowe recorded "Out Of Time," and had his first real chart smash. For a month the disc was No. 1 in England. And although it didn't make America's most coveted spot, it actually sold more copies here.

Farlowe's voice gives him an edge on his soul singing contemporaries. It broke when he was ten, and has developed a rasping, knife-edged quality that makes it an ideal tool for what he wants to sing.

"I don't think I could sing pop'," says Chris. "I've got a 'soul' voice and I feel it; and if they give me a straight pop tune to sing I would turn it into something else."

Chris Farlowe is unusually quiet —almost sullen. He isn't really a good talker, and if an interviewer gets off the subject of music with Chris the conversation ends up pretty one-sided. With the interviewer having to supply the verbal power.

Chris was born John Henry Deighton. The Deighton family moved from Chris's birthplace "somewhere in Essex" when he was a baby, and went to live in Islington, North London.

Chris's father took a job with the Daily Mirror as a printer. When he was 11 Chris went to Sir William Collins Technical College and studied engineering.

In his last year, they had finished their course early, and Chris took a joiner's course to finish the term. He liked it so much he decided to become a joiner instead of an engineer.

He was associated with a small instrumental-singing group during this time, however, and he later decided to go into singing professionally.

Farlowe met Rik Gunnell, who runs the Flamingo and Ram Jam Clubs and who became his manager.

In October, 1965, Gunnell bumped into Andrew Oldham, who used to work for Rik in the Flamingo Club as a washer-up and hot dog fryer. Andy told Rik of his plans to start an independent record company called Immediate Records.

Oldham

"I'd been following Andy Oldham's career with interest for a long time," said Rik. "Everything he did, he did so whole-heartedly and well—from frying hot dogs to managing the Rolling Stones. I knew right away that Immediate Records was going to be a success and I offered Andy two of my artists."

One of those artists was Chris Farlowe. Farlowe's reputation began to grow and Mick Jagger took an immediate interest in him. And on the pair's fourth record effort together, the producer-singer team hit it big.

For Girls only
by shirley poston

Usually, when I'm trying to express something that means a lot to me, I get all nervous and think I have to write it and re-write it and re-*re*-write it until it's letter perfect (which it never is.)

I'm not going to do that this time. I'm just going to say what I feel inside. Once. And if I don't get it out right, I guess that'll be because it wasn't ready to come out yet. Oh well, at least I'll have tried.

It's been exactly twenty-four hours since I heard the news or the rumor or whatever-it-is that the Beatles are going to break up soon. When I did hear this, I felt almost the same way I did that morning when I turned on a radio and heard that George was married.

Panic

I don't know if there are any words for that kind of feeling. But the word *panic* comes close. Anyway, that's the way I felt all day yesterday. I kept finding myself thinking *please don't let it be true*.

Last night I did the same thing I always do when I'm really shook up about something concerning the Beatles. I piled all of their albums on the phonograph and just listened.

I can see right now, just from reading what I've written so far, that I'm not going to be able to say all this the way I want to. It's not coming out right. But I still have to try, so bear with me.

What I'm trying to say is this... little by little, as I kept listening to those dear songs and those dear voices (forgive me for getting out the violins, I just can't help it), I felt the panic beginning to subside. Then, when I was finally calm enough to think, I spent the next few hours really working at trying to understand the situation. (The Beatles call this "sorting it out" – a wonderful way of putting it.)

I was still very muddled and miserable when I finally did go to sleep, but when I woke up this morning, I had the strangest, most beautiful feeling I've ever experienced in my life.

To me, loving the Beatles has always been an odd mixture of emotions. They've made me happy in so many ways, and sad in others because I couldn't be with them or belong to him. But there's always been an undercurrent of fear in that mixture. That something would happen to them during one of their tours. That all of their records wouldn't hit the number one spot. That their lack of pretense would get them into trouble with this phoney world. That they wouldn't always stay on top where they belong because so many of their fans are growing up now and having to go on to other things.

If you love them, too, I'm sure you've felt this same feeling, and been terrified of ever having to see the day when someone would say "The Beatles? Oh, yeah. Whatever happened to them?"

I think that strange, beautiful feeling I'm experiencing is taking place because, for the first time in almost three years, I'm not afraid for them.

The Beatles are The Beatles. They don't need adjectives to describe them, because the word Beatle has become sysnonomous with talent and success and love. And now, if this rumored decision to disband is true, it always will be.

Oh, God, if I could just get this out on paper. Things change. That's just the way life is. But the Beatles will never change. What they've given us is finally safe from harm. Nothing can change it or take it away now. Because there's one thing you can't change or erase, and that's a beautiful memory.

Yesterday I wondered how we could possibly give them up. Today I realize we're only giving a part of them *back*. To *them*. So they can stop being a phenomenon and have their chance to be people.

I also wondered how I could possibly live without them. I know better than that now. Without them? I'll never be without them until the day I die. None of us will be. We'll have their music and their movies and their everything to remember them by. And we'll also have the people they'll become when The Beatles become George Harrison, John Lennon, Paul McCartney and Richard Starkey.

Not Dying

They aren't dying. They're living, and growing up and going on to other things, like us. But that doesn't mean we won't still have a lot of each other to keep and use to keep growing.

They're doing the same thing we are. They gave us so much, and now we're using what they gave us to make better lives for ourselves. Well, we gave to them, too. The Beatles' music has gone from fun to brilliant. So have they. Sure, they had this much talent all the time, but they didn't realize it or put it to work until we gave them the confidence and the drive to progress. Now they want to progress even more, in many directions.

It gives me a wonderful feeling to know that they're always going to be part of me and I'm always going to be part of them.

But there's something even more wonderful. Like I said before, Beatlemania will always remain intact. Three years suspended forever, out of the reach of anyone or anything that might have destroyed it, because it's suspended inside millions of people.

I feel lucky to be one of those people. I want to die when I think I may never see George Harrison stand on a stage again, and stamp his foot to Ringo's beat and laugh with John and share a microphone with Paul. But the memory of the times I have seen him is so much sweeter now.

I also want to die when I think there'll be a time when there won't be any new Beatle records to look forward to. But now the records they've already made are so much dearer to me.

Live On

Mostly, I want to live and I want them to live, and if they feel they can do it better as individuals instead of Beatles, then that's what they should do.

Please don't think I want them to break up. I want it to go on the way it is now, and never stop. But I also want me to go on the way I am now, writing ridiculous columns and being in love with a beautiful boy from Liverpool. And I guess that isn't possible either. We're all changing, and always changing. That's life, too. But it's so good to know that the Beatles and us are changing because of each other.

Someday I'll try to put this into better words. For the moment, I just want to say, for the millionth time, that I love them. Whatever they decide to do is okay with me, because they proved to me a long time ago that everything they do is beautiful.

Vaudevilles Plan First USA Visit

Representatives of Vaudeville are coming to the U.S.—via England!

The New Vaudeville Band, who dipped into America's musical past for "Winchester Cathedral" and a world-wide hit, will arrive here in late November for an extensive tour that includes at least one TV appearance.

The group's first city-by-city tour of the U.S. will be highlighted by a guest appearance on the Ed Sullivan Show. Their promotion trip ends Dec. 10.

The tour was arranged between Jackie Green of Joe Glazer's office here and Tito Burns of the Harold Davidson office in England.

The group's single is number seven in the U.S.—the second week it has held the position.

BB Disc Gets Fast Getaway

"Good Vibrations" is apparently the fastest breaking record in the history of the Beach Boys—or Capitol Records, for that matter.

The disc has allegedly broken all sales records for a one-week period. Capitol said the single racked up sales of 293,000 in four days, with an additional 100,000 copies back-ordered from customers.

KRLA ARCHIVES

Great Rivers' Deception

By Eden

Yes, it's true. As the vast listening public, you have been deceived; *lied to*. And now we must make amends and present you with the truth. Johnny Rivers does *not* live on the "*Poor* Side Of Town."

As a point in fact, Johnny lives in a very large and beautiful home located in the hills of the exclusive Trousdale Estates in Beverly Hills. He is not on relief, or even tottering on he brink of destitution. If the truth must be told—Johnny Rivers is, indeed, a very wealthy young man.

Once A Week

Johnny and I have spoken many times, and now we even refer jokingly to our Annual Once-A-Week interview for *The BEAT*. So, on a windy day just recently, when Johnny invited *The BEAT* to pay him a visit in his home, it was sort of like a class reunion! We sat comfortably in the large, golden-lighted living room and talked about many things.

Things like rumors, for example. There have been many Grape Vine-type whispers of late that a movie is being written around Johnny. True or false, Mr. R? "No ... in *front* of me! Not really. I'm just studying with Jeff Corey, and I'm waiting till something comes along that I dig."

I asked if he would be interested in doing a musical, but Johnny insisted that "I'd like to try a dramatic thing first."

Something else about which Johnny has always been quite serious is his songwriting. Many people were pleasantly surprised then they discovered that Johnny had written his nationwide smash, "Poor Side Of Town."

Johnny has always expressed a desire to develop his songwriting abilities, but unlike so many more commercial-crazy writers, Johnny remains an *artist* about his craft, and staunchly refuses to release anything to the public unless he fully believes in its value. It was this way with "Poor Side Of Town," and it will be so with all the records to come.

"I've been trying to write a follow-up and I haven't come up with anything yet that really knocked me out. I'm just the kind of writer that, just every once in a while an idea will hit me that is really strong—like 'Poor Side Of Town' —and then I'll write it."

Another serious topic of conversation for Johnny concerns Viet Nam. *The BEAT* reported to you several months ago that Johnny was taking a show over to the war-torn Asian country to entertain our fighting troops there.

Now Johnny is making plans for a return visit, probably at the end of January or the beginning of February and from there Johnny will probably tour Europe before his return to Uncle Samland.

"Poor Side Of Town" was quite a change of pace in material for Johnny, and although he believed in its quality, he admits that there were a few moments of worry as to the public reaction to the record before it was released.

As for a continuation of this style, Johnny refuses to cut another record which will sound exactly like this one, simply because this one was a hit. Each individual record must be able to stand on its own merits.

Johnny applied that to what he considers to be a change now going on in the pop world, as well. He explained that it is like a message which is passed down a long line of people, and usually winds up being greatly distorted by the time it reaches the end of the line.

"I think that the Beatles *did* come up with a good thing, but it's gotten to where it just went down the line, and everybody tried to do it, and it just got so way out, so far from what it really was that it was distorted.

"Everybody suddenly came out with the long hair, and everybody suddenly had a group and cut a record. That's why I've noticed on the charts, especially in the last few weeks, that some of the artists who haven't been around in quite a while have got hit records on the charts. Bobby Darin and even Eddie Fisher's got a hit record on the charts. I think people are getting a little tired of the other thing, and they're starting to go back to talent, which is sort of a good thing.

Complaint

Johnny has gone on record as being a regular reader of *The BEAT*, but his one complaint this afternoon was that we didn't have comments on the current record scene from the likes of people like The Chairman of The Board, Frank Sinatra. Therefore, since Johnny was planning on flying up to Las Vegas to catch Mr. Sinatra's show that night, he decided that he was going to tell The Leader all about the wonderfulness of *The BEAT* and how Frank should definitely do an interview with us.

When last seen, Johnny was planning on cornering the Blue-Eyed-Leader-of-the-Clan in the *steam room* with his questions. Now *you* know, and *we* know, that Johnny can do a disappearing act on a high *stool* when he performs, so lets just hope that he and Mr. S. don't decide to have a very lengthy conversation in that steam room, on account of the fact that if they aren't a pair of Drip Dry Human Beings, we may be speaking to Johnny *next* week from the *Short*(er) Side of Town!

... JOHNNY PLANS RETURN TO VIETNAM.

J. J. JACKSON:
'Not All Peaches'

By Walt Syers

"Do I dig soul? Man, I eat, sleep and breathe hog jowls and chitlins.

"Why, when I have a recording session I put a big pot of gravy in the middle of the floor so everybody can get a little."

The speaker was a hulking, bowling ball of a man with a sly grin and round, rolling eyeballs. He had the impish appearance of a dark, overgrown character out of "Snow White and the Seven Dwarfs."

J. J. Jackson looks like any minute his third grade teacher is about to come in, grip him by an enlarged ear, and lead him back to class. All 285 pounds of him.

J.J. is a one-man show—whether he's in front of 2,000 spectators or a single reporter. He tells a joke, rolls his eyeballs around and laughs from way down deep. It's a kind of soul laughter ... and it's contagious.

There is an old adage to the effect that "the fatter the happier." J.J. Jackson is a happy man. A very happy man.

When you get past his immensity the next thing you notice is his flashy attire. Last week he was wearing a shiny maroon suit and matching cufflinks that were of such size they would have restricted the arm movement of most men.

It is rumored his suits are a completely new dimension in men's clothing. They are wrap-around.

He looks scrubbed and sharp, and he has a ready-made explanation for his good grooming. "My mamma always said nottin' looks better 'n a fat little boy that can DRESS."

J.J.'s verbal intonements are actually exaggerations. He is an intelligent man, three years of college and an English major behind him. But when he gets wound up— and he generally stays that way— he uses "soul" language.

J.J. wears an almost constant grin. He has reason for it, too. His current record, "But It's Alright," is at the number 26 spot nationally, hitting both pop and R&B charts.

The record, his first big one, demonstrates not only his singing talents, but also his writing, composing and producing skills. It also establishes him as a singer— not just a studio man.

J.J. hit it big early this year when he was "discovered" by his present manager, Peter Paul. Since then, J.J. has written a handful of songs for the Shangri-las, Mary Wells, and Inez Foxx.

When he played the Appollo Theatre in New York recently, he was rewarded by a standing ovation—a feat not easily accomplished before calloused Appollo audiences.

But perhaps the biggest compliment of the entire show came from Sam, half of the Sam and Dave team.

"When everything started Sam was downstairs in the dressing room," J.J. explained. "Then I saw him come runnin' upstairs to see what was happening."

At this point his broad face brightened and was enveloped by a massive grin. He chuckled, and continued: "After the show he told me, 'I ain't never met a fool who can make me come upstairs and then make me come out there and sweat.'"

Any conversation with J.J. is just naturally sparked with little stories like this one. He's fat and happy and propelled by what seems to be an endless energy.

... J.J. JACKSON — HUMAN BOWLING BALL.

KRLA ARCHIVES

DISCUSSION
By Eden

"Happenings Ten Years Time Time Ago"—it's by the Yardbirds and it is great! Never ceases to be a source of amazement when these talented boys come up with so much class in an area in which it is so easy to fail.

Their music was labeled *electronic* when they first came out, and a whole new trend was developed from that, which eventually led to an even larger distortion commonly labeled in this country "psychedelic."

The difference with the Yardbirds' music is that theirs is the *real* thing—not just the attempt at commercialized electronic noise which we have been flooded with of late.

Listen closely to this disc—the elements of melody and rhythm remain constant and at a level of perfection and listenability throughout the record. And that instrumental break in the middle of the record is beyond belief! Jeff has got his guitar *talking* now! A tipping of The *BEAT* cap to producer Simon Napier-Bell is in order here, too.

* * *

Another new British group on the scene is John's Children, and their first release is a weird thing entitled "Smashed! Blocked!" This one takes a lot of listening to, but it's actually quite good.

Plus points to listen for are guitar work 'a la Brian Wilson, a pretty melody, Yardbird-type instrumentation in the beginning, Beatle-inspired horns and a huge production. By the time the disc is over, it is an emotional experience—but it takes a while. This one might be a hit here.

* * *

Frank Sinatra (you remember him; he's the guy who finally married the girl from Peyton Place!) has another hit on his wealthy little hands with "That's Life." This is a blues-rocker that swings as only Sinatra can make it swing, and it's a hit.

Definitely not the best record The Leader-type has ever waxed, and it obviously doesn't do a lot for his voice — but who cares? Sinatra is *Sinatra*, and we should *all* have hits that sound as *bad* as his!

* * *

Females of the pop world . . . brace yourselves! Your ever-loving, Prince Charming, here of the pop scene has done the *undoable!* Yes, it's true . . . Herbie is *singing* on his newest record!

If you can pull your poor selves together long enough, you'll note that all the rest of the Brass are singing on this one, too.

Oh, yes—the record is entitled "Mame," and it's going to be a hit. (Did you have any doubts???) Hmmmmm—I wonder if all this Mexican music Herbie is cutting is completely *kosher??!!!!!!*

* * *

Great, great R&B release from Wilson Pickett is his newest, "Mustang Sally." Whole lotta soulful talent here. And more R&B class comes to us from the always soulful, ever classy Motown representatives—The Temptations. Temptin' the nation's charts this time around with "(I Know) I'm Losing You."

Some Things are Nice to Have Around...

things you feel "at home" with

...the Utility™ ball pen

A good, practical pen for students. Fashionable, too.
There are twelve brilliant colors.
The color of the pen is the color of the ink.

Lots of students buy two or three at a time. Maybe because it's only 39¢
Maybe because it writes nice.
Or maybe they just like to have two or three or twelve around.

Lindy®

 manufactured by LINDY PEN CO., no. hollywood, calif. 91605, u.s.a.

KRLA ARCHIVES

Yardbirds: 'Kids Want More Quality'

By Eden

The problem in the world of popular music seems to be that we have finally reached a point of saturation, a very dangerous point, indeed. There are too many groups to listen to; too many groups to see. Too many groups of three guitars, a drum, and lots of hair.

Too often the music sounds all alike, the faces fade into one vast, familiar blur—the only result a blinding, deafening, unintelligible carcophony of noise.

The only refuge seems to be the rare and hard-to-find groups of truly talented individuals who are offering something more than mere commercialism to the increasingly-nauseated public.

Influence

One such group, impossible to overlook, five talented musicians who cannot be allowed to go unmentioned, the Yardbirds certainly are a group of musicians who have had an enormous influence on popular music in the last year and a half.

Over an early morning cup of coffee in The BEAT offices, we spoke of popular music—its failures and successes. Jimmy Paige, the newest Yardbird, spoke of the ever-changing structure of pop music.

"In my personal opinion, I think it's starting to get prettier again; in England, it is, anyway. And more precise. This seems to happen every three years. You get to this stage where it gets pretty stagnant, and everything's getting pretty again. And then, I suppose in another six months, some group is going to start happening with the big beat again, and it'll go right back to very earthy stuff."

Just about a year ago, the American pop-conscious public became aware of the Yardbirds and of the unique and original music which they were playing. We became acquainted with them through their first two hit records, "For Your Love," and "Heart Full of Soul," but it wasn't until they released "I'm A Man," that the entire country discovered their genius and trend-setting talents.

This third Yardbird hit created a sensation throughout the entire American pop scene, and the new sound was labeled everything from "electronic," to "psychedelic;" a whole new area of musical communication had been created.

At first, it might have seemed to inexperienced observers that this brand new kind of sound was inherently electronic, and watching the masterful way in which Jeff Beck worked with his guitar and amplifier only reinforced this initial impression.

Electronic

Jim explained, "Pop music can be psychedelic but not necessarily electronic. Electronic music *helps*—it's a much easier way of getting a psychedelic theme. But you can do this—get over a psychedelic point—without being necessarily electronic."

At this point, Jimmy Paige raised his own question, "What do you term 'psychedelic'?" Then offered his own possible answer: "If you're terming it as something which is bringing an image to the mind, then it will obviously happen with electronic music, because that is basically *all* that, isn't it. You just get sensations from the music."

Psychedelic

Jimmy was also interrupted here by the other members of the group whose diverse opinions were eventually summed up by Keith's statement on the psychedelic type of music: "Dylan's lyrics are psychedelic; he's *lyrically* psychedelic. And *our* sound is psychedelic. There are just several mediums of putting it across. I mean, you could be psychedelic and have a brass band playing."

Keith explained further: "What we're trying to do with our music is trying to induce the same thing in the audience, the same feeling, the same sort of experiences that LSD does—it's very hard to do!"

What is that sort of experience? "Well, to induce a state of timelessness and destroy the awareness of where you are. You just go inside your head—blow-your-mind, sort of thing!"

Although they originally began at the Crawdaddy Club in Richmond, England playing their own brand of R&B-oriented music, the Yardbirds spent many months of intensive practice and experimentation perfecting the revolutionary new sound which they fianlly presented to the public.

In the beginning, their goals, their original conceptions of the music they were developing were, as Chris explains, pretty much the same.

"The idea was to make the people listening to us become directly involved with the music and us and get lost in it. None of our music has ever been sort of to the point of every note *planned*—the idea was to have large patches of free form and things like that, so people in the audience could really get lost in the music. That was one of the original ideas."

Abstract Sounds

Keith added to this, "Right from the offset we did imply *abstract sounds*. To go as far as calling it 'electronic' is, well . . . it's electronic guitars going through amplifiers, so *that* makes it sound electronic. But, we just plumped for the *sounds* and the *abstract sounds*, more or less right from the beginning of the group."

Keith also took time to consider the changes now occurring in popular music, explaining, "Scenes are changing now where kids aren't really buying a record 50% for the group, like they used to. It *was* 50% buying the image of the group and 50% the noise on the record.

"It's now changing to a situation where the kids want more quality for the money they pay for their records, therefore the *production* has *got* to go up, the quality's got to be *much* better. And, Brian Wilson is definitely doing this; his production on his records is fantastic!"

Weird

The situation in which the Yardbirds now find themselves has also changed over the last year or so, and is quite definitely fantastic. Their brand new record—"Happenings Ten Years' Time Ago"—was released on November 2 and is further testimonial of their extraordinary creative talents. Even Chris, in speaking of the record, describes the 30-second instrumental break in the middle of the record as being "weird and quite advanced for us."

Just recently the group filmed a motion picture for the noted Italian director, Antonioni, entitled "Blow Up." Susannah York is one of the stars of the film—in which the Yardbirds will be portraying themselves—and it shows every indication of going to the Film Festival upon its release.

Unusual, highly intelligent, and uniquely talented—these are the characteristics of the Yardbirds which will keep them at the top of their profession. Keep them on a high plateau where they won't get wet, even though so many are being "saturated!"

BEAT SHOWCASE
(spotlighting new talent on the pop scene)

THE SPIKE DRIVERS—This East Coast group says "we communicate" with young people, adding that they are going to raise the standard of folk-rock. A big assignment, **BEAT** things, but the all-married (sorry!) group intends to try!

THE PEANUT BUTTER CONSPIRACY—"The Peanut Butter Conspiracy Is Spreading" say bumper stickers all over Southern California, much to the consternation of adults and little kids. However, this group means not the brown, sticky, chunky kind but a musical version. Left to right, they are Sandy, John, Jim, Lance and Al. "They're spreading," Russ of the Association whispers conspiratorially.

KRLA ARCHIVES

The Soul Of Ryder

By Louise Criscione

Many try but few white entertainers really succeed in singing the blues as they should be sung. The blues which come from deep inside seem to be born—not made. Perhaps that is why you can count the number of true white blues singers on the fingers of one hand.

Every so often one does come along. And one such person who not only came along but made a big-money name for himself is Mitch Ryder.

Mitch and his Detroit Wheels have forsaken the element of the music business which is commonly referred to as "commercial" blues in favor of "the straight stuff."

"I think that the exciting thing about the present day scene is the excitement itself. It is marvelous to be on stage and feel the audience reacting. I can't understand the performer who is satisfied with polite applause. The greatest thing in the world is to have the audience right there every step of the way . . . there has to be this give and take so that the performer and the audience experience the same thing at the same time. That's why they are in the same place."

The history of Mitch and the Detroit Wheels begins, quite naturally, with Mitch himself. He was raised in that part of the U.S. which has been nicknamed "Soul Country" – Detroit. His father was a part time radio singer and Mitch grew up in an atmosphere where music was as ordinary as combing your hair. According to Mitch, his first most exciting experience was hearing Little Richard sing "Keep A Knockin'" because it was then that Mitch and the world of beat were introduced.

"I sang semi-classical and standard while at school in the day and worked singing blues with a Negro group at night." The sight of Mitch singing lead with a Negro group caused people to stare. In fact, says Mitch: "A few people snickered, but they don't anymore."

However, it wasn't until the Beatles arrived on the Stateside musical scene that Mitch made a move to establish his own group. He named his infant group "Billy Lee & The Rivieras" but due to the fact that they did not have their own sound but merely imitated what was currently "in" the group as it then stood never reached maturity.

Billy Lee and the Rivieras did eventually evolve into Mitch Ryder and the Detroit Wheels when their manager saw that the group was unique when they were just being themselves. He put a sudden and definite stop to the group singing songs that had been made popular by other groups. A complete turn-about was thus put into motion and because of it Mitch and the Wheels came up with a song called "Jenny Takes A Ride." And she did – all the way to the top.

It's rather ironic that Mitch and the Wheels were big-drawers when they had received no radio play on their records. Their popularity was strictly by word-of-mouth proving how far the spoken word can go and how fast it can travel. In Mitch's case, it preceeded him to such an extent that he was able to demand top money for personal appearances – despite the fact that he lacked a record on the charts.

Mitch need not rely on "mouth" reporting now that "Jenny" is behind him and "Devil With A Blue Dress On/Good Golly Miss Molly" is scurrying up the nation's charts. And just as there was Beatlemania – there is now an illness known as "Mitch Ryder Fever." It's prevalent on the East Coast but according to record sales, the West Coast had better arm itself. The fever is most definitely spreading.

...MITCH RYDER — DIRECT FROM THE SOUL COUNTRY.

The Adventures of Robin Boyd

©1965 By Shirley Poston

Robin Boyd was seated hotly (I'll say) on the radiator in the 2nd-Floor girls' washroom ripping at her dress when Ringo (as in Boyd, as in Boyd) slammed tearfully through the door.

"What are you *doing?*" her sturdy sister stopped blithering long enough to inquire.

Robin re-ripped. "Letting down my hem," she growled savagely. "I'm tired of those . . . those *hillbillies* gawking at me like they've never seen a pair of *knees* before. Now, what are *you* blubbering about?"

"This!"

"*This!*" Ringo blubbered. And tearing the Ludwig droomstick off her neck, she flang it, chain and all, into the nearest commode and flushed bitterly.

"Ringo!" Robin cried, leaping up from the radiator out of consternation (not to mention necessity) (hotly is not the *word*). "What's *wrong?*"

"What *isn't?*" sobbed Ringo. "Everybody laughed at my *droomstick* and they don't even know who the Beatles *are* because they aren't allowed to play Beatle *records* at school dances which they don't even *have* and two boys said my new coat looks like a *panda* and my teacher says I have to use my *real* name instead of Ringo and I forgot what it *is!* (Whew.)"

"It's Beverly," Robin said helpfully. "Beverly Lou Boyd."

"My *Gawd*," Ringo wailed. "You've gotta be *kidding!*"

Robin shook her aching head. "I wish I were," she muttered grimly, glaring at herself in the full-

She had tried so hard to dress simply for her first day of school at John Q. Obnoxious High, and she had certainly succeeded.

Sane-Set

After an hour of being stared at by the skirt-and-sweater sane-set, and leered at by their plaid-flannel-shirted (not to mention mouthed) male counterparts, Robin had raced for the nearest throne-room and yanked off the lace stockings which she thought went sooo nicely with her brown suede dress. And, in her next class, her fellow students had gaped openly as her legs turned from tan to a shiver-some shade of frostbite-purple.

And her most recent attempt at Conformity-A-La-Pitchfork had been another miserable failure. The hem of her dress was now dangling raggedly just above her now-famous (make that *infamous*) knee-caps, and with her Just-A-Touch of mascara blearily smeared from blithering, she looked *very* simply dressed.

Well, at least it was lunch time which everyone else called "dinner" (stupe) and she could go home and change into something practical(ly unbelievable) like the rest of the hilly-billies or whatever they were wore.

Going to their lockers, Robin and Ringo flang on their pandaser-coats. As they waddled down the hall, they were apprehended by a stout teacher who had, not unappropriately, tried to cram the larger portion of her anatomy into a whale-bone corset.

The robust instructor tried her best (which certainly made one wary of her *worst*) to propel them into the school lunchroom.

Taking one glance at the display of floppy jello salads flanked by a vat of sloppy-joe mixture that looked more like Fricasse Of Toad, Ringo and Robin exchanged gags and chorused "let's split-as-in-go."

"Furriners"

They did just that, and the teacher stared after them as though she were expecting them to split-as-in-paramecium (amobea?) (forget it.) "Furriners," she muttered (again, not unappropriately), as they re-waddled furrily out of the building, and vowed to keep her eye on this twosome just as soon as it was returned from the glass-polishers.

The first word uttered when said twosome trooped angrily into the Boyd house (never *mind* about the ones uttered on the *way* to the Boyd house) was a full-volume blast from Ringo.

"Who in the ell-hay named a nice kid like meself *Beverly Lou Boyd?*" she demanded hysterically.

"That *person* did," replied their mother, hiding the raw hot dog she'd been munching and starting to prepare a nutritious luncheon of dandelion greens and poached eggs.

"That person who's in Coventry because we're in South Dakota?" asked Robin, referring to their former father. (They hadn't spoken to him since the day they left California, and in his opinion, Coventry was not only a nice place to visit, he would also like to live there.)

Floyd??

"The same," Mrs. Boyd said fiendishly. "And I think it's high time you girls knew the truth. *His* name is *not* F.A. Boyd as he would have the world believe. It is *Floyd Boyd.*"

"*Floyd-Boyd?*" they shrieked in unison. And then the three of them cackled so loudly, Mrs. Boyd lost her head, dumped the aforementioned nutritious luncheon into the garbage disposal (the Boyd dog) and passed out raw hot dogs all round.

If it hadn't been for the sudden appearance of the aforementioned Floyd-Boyd, Robin and Ringo might never have gone back to school that afternoon. But when he walked into the kitchen at ten-of-one, carrying a rifle, the girls didn't wait around to see if he was *really* just going to "do a little hunting."

The second half of her first day was always to remain a blur to Robin (who just wouldn't have it any other way.) Everyone was probably still whispering and pointing as she moped from class to class, but she was totally unaware of their presence. On the way back to school, she'd seen a tea pot in the window of a harness store (??) and that had done it.

Since there wasn't even a touch of Just-A-Touch left after the scrubbing she'd given her ex-face, she felt free to slobber secretly into a sodden kleenex whenever the memory of her georgeous genie was too mutch (which it had never failed to be yet) for her.

Promptly at four, she sped out of John Q. and nearly ran down olde Beverly-Lou-Boyd who was waiting plumply on the front steps.

They were nearly home when it happened. Robin had just said that she'd give twenty years of her life to see just one *human being* who wasn't wearing *saddle* shoes.

Suddenly, Ringo grabbed her wildly (which made it even wilder.) "Don't look now," she hissed, "but I think you're going to die young."

Robin's gaze followed Ringo's pudgy and pointing finger. Then she gasped. Just ahead of them, a mirage was loping along the crumbling sidewalk. A tall, thin, semi-long-haired mirage clad in bell bottoms, boots and other rational, sensible items of apparel.

And it was then that Robin knew what she must do.

Mirage!

Leaping seventeen feet into the air, she caught up with the mirage and grabbed it by a leather-jacketed arm. It whirled around to face her wordlessly (which couldn't think of a thing to say as usual.)

Finally, after what seemed like six years of peering into a sharp pair of shades, Robin laughed so loud they heard her all the way to Sioux City, Iowa (wherever *that* was) (not to mention *whatever*.)

"Are you a boy or are you a girl?" she giggled.

The mirage then grinned and spoke four beautiful words which were sheer poetry to Robin's ears . . .

"You might well arsk!"

(To Be Continued Next Issue)

KRLA ARCHIVES

The BEAT Goes To The Movies

'THE SWINGER'

Beautiful, young and ambitious, Kelly Olsson (Ann-Margret) tries to have her stories published in Girl-Lure Magazine, a publication mainly devoted to the undraped female form. However, the senior editor of the magazine, Ric Colby (Tony Franciosa) not only rejects Kelly's stories but practically has her thrown out of his office when she becomes too insistent.

Bright Idea

Furious about being turned down because her stories are too "clean," Kelly gets a bright idea about getting up a sure-sale story. Accordingly, Kelly purchases a stack of sexy paperback books and pilfering lines and situations from all of them manages to come up with a story which she attempts to pass off as her autobiography.

Sir Hubert

Ric doesn't buy it but the magazine's publisher, Sir Hubert Charles (Robert Coote), decides to publish Kelly's "autobiography." Ric, in the meantime, sets out to make a "nice girl" out of Kelly who, in reality, is *already* a nice girl.

Some of the mishaps in Ric's campaign to play Pygmalion and Kelly's attempt to portray a "bad girl" are hilarious. It's not until the end of the movie, of course, that the real truth comes out and Kelly and Ric admit to having fallen in love with each other.

No Message

"The Swinger," a Paramount production, really does swing. It's a romantic comedy which, thankfully enough, offers no "message"—just laughs. Says George Sidney, the producer: "If laughs are what the public is looking for in these tension-ridden times, then this film should be just what the doctor ordered to make them forget their troubles for awhile."

And "The Swinger" does just that.

ANN-MARGRET in scene from Paramount's "The Swinger."

...ANN-MARGRET ACTS as a human paint brush for bizarre drawing.

Grandma's Vaudeville Sound Starts Pop Music Trend

By Rochelle Reed

Movies, some say, killed Vaudeville but apparently pop music is bringing it back to life.

Today's scene has Vaudeville music dotting the charts from both big names and newcomers. With the spotlight on Mod, which in turn emphasizes the intricate designs and jewelry of Yesterday, Vaudeville music could be the only follow-up to paisley, kaleidoscopes and boutiques.

Main proponents of Grandma's music are six Englishmen known as the New Vaudeville Band, whose "Winchester Cathedral" is topping charts both here and in the Mother Country. Grandpa, with an aggravated nasal condition, could have sung the vocal himself.

"I'm not saying we're really offering anything new, but it's a change," understates "Winchester" composer Geoff (pronounced Jeff) Stephens who also sang lead on the recording.

And now, safely out of the first three paragraphs, BEAT will let you in on a secret that a few people wish WAS a secret: the New Vaudeville Band, just rounding up a big U.S. tour, DIDN'T record "Winchester Cathedral." Composer-singer Geoff Stephens recorded the song, backed by London session musicians. When they refused to join into a band to promote the disc, Stephens gathered the present New Vaudeville Band for the bi-continental tour rounds.

That's why the Vaudeville six won't talk about "Winchester" but concentrate on detouring the conversation to their next, or really first, recording—"Shirl." Penned by Geoff Stephens-Jon Carter, the tune reportedly retains the Vaudeville sound according to vocalist Mick Wilsher but then again 'it'll be different."

The New Vaudeville Band would like to wrap up the whole trend into the catch-all, Good Time Music. But in America, this naturally smacks of Lovin' Spoonful, an upsetting thought to the Band (they hate the term 'group') and they steadily insist their band wasn't influenced by anyone.

This brings up another artist on the charts with the Vaudeville—Good Time Sound. Donovan's "Mellow Yellow" is a U.S. smash and will no doubt enjoy the same success in England. And saffron, or deep orange, is a throw-back to radio days and Grandma's cooking.

Oddly enough, "Winchester" composer Geoff Stephens is Donovan's ex-manager. Donovan wrote "Mellow Yellow" himself and Stephens alone penned "Winchester." But the two came up with a similar Good Time sound.

This really isn't unusual. Two people at opposite ends of the earth invariably work on similar inventions, unaware of the other. And without fail, two books on the same subject are simultaneously released—by different publishers. So too in music.

The catch-all phrase, Good Time Music, has spawned a third—Peter and Gordon's "Lady Godiva," a groovy tune which

Ian Whitcomb—Mod Mod Music

reminds today's youth that Grandma's day wasn't all that dull, nor was mother's for that matter.

The P and G duo wanted their song to be something different, which indeed it would have been if "Winchester" and "Yellow" hadn't been pressed at the same time.

There is no indication that any of the Good-Time, Vaudeville proponents pulled a Phil Spector and rushed their discs off the presses in a day or so when the first

Donovan—Mellow Good Time

Vaudeville song began to break, but all did manage to market the discs at the same time.

Ian Whitcomb was next on the vaudeville scene with "Where Did Robinson Crusoe Go?" Record-buyers reaction to the disc? Very good.

Musicians of bags other than the Good Time sound have a tendency to classify the Vaudeville influence as just another put-on, similar to "They're Coming To Take Me Away, Ha Ha."

PETER AND GORDON—Something very different in "Lady Godiva" turned very normal with the advent of the great new vaudeville sound.

KRLA ARCHIVES

KRLA ARCHIVES

America's Pop Music NEWSpaper 25¢

KRLA Edition
BEAT
DECEMBER 17, 1966

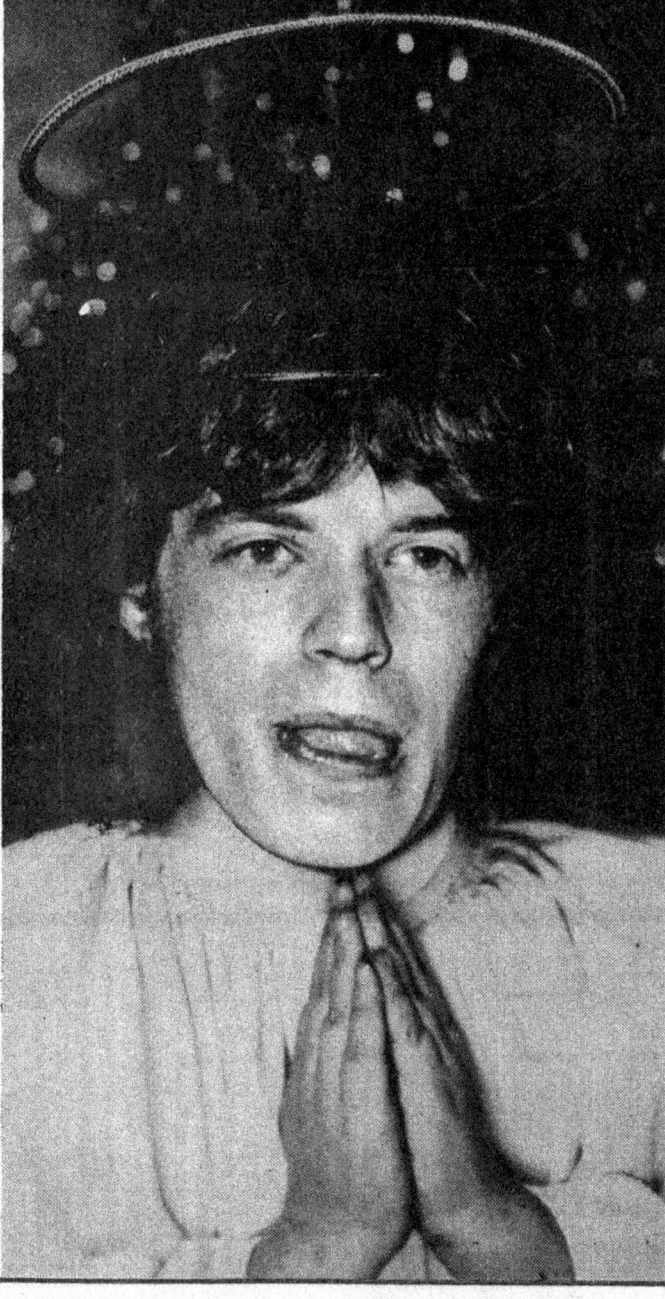

MERRY CHRISTMAS

KRLA ARCHIVES

KRLA BEAT
MERRY CHRISTMAS

Volume 2, Number 30   December 17, 1966

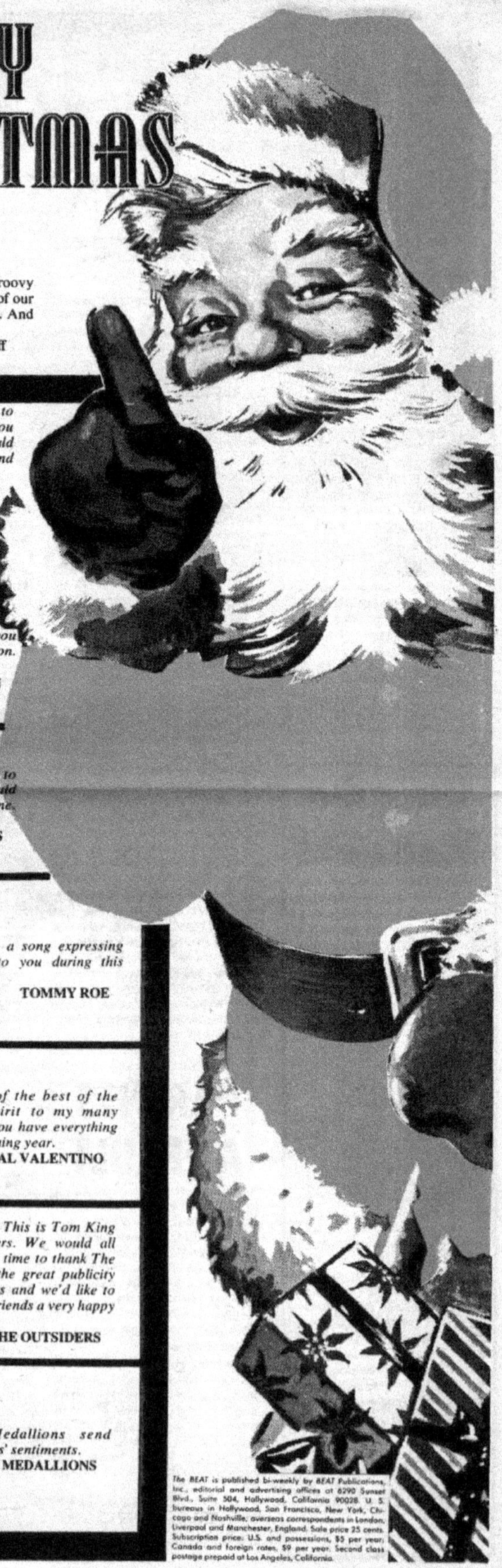

We at *The BEAT* would like to take this opportunity to thank all of you for making 1966 such a groovy year for us. During this Christmas season we've received phone calls, letters and telegrams from many of our pop friends and we'd like to share some of them with you as sort of a Christmas card from *The BEAT*. And once again — Merry Christmas to all of you and our very best wishes for the new year.

The BEAT Staff

We have a favor to ask. We would like to enlist your help in promoting The BEAT's Christmas issue. During Christmas week, we'd like you to go naked. When you see others in offices, on the streets and in restaurants without their clothes, you will instinctively know that they are wishing you a Merry Christmas from The BEAT. We intend to be touring during the holidays. Without clothes it will be a cold but cool Christmas.

THE MONKEES

To all you BEAT readers we would like to take this time to thank you for all the support you have given us during the past year and we would like to wish you all a very Merry Christmas and a happy New Year.

THE BEATLES

This is your old buddy, Bill Cosby, taking an opportunity to wish you a very Merry Christmas and the best for the coming year. You know what the best is . . . that's when your Christmas stocking is filled with something besides a foot.

BILL COSBY

May all the good thoughts and things you cherish be multiplied during this holiday season. Warmth and thanks from the Association.

THE ASSOCIATION

While we'll be home in England this season, we all hope to spend Christmas some year with our many friends in America. Our warmest regards.

THE YARDBIRDS

Hello you soulin' people! This is Lou Rawls to say you have been a groovy bunch and I would like to thank you for all the help you've given me. I wish all of you the best for the coming year.

LOU RAWLS

Have a healthy Christmas.
BRIAN WILSON

Peace on earth, good will to teenagers and may the unconstituional 10 o'clock curfew be lifted.
JOHNNY RIVERS

I've written a song expressing my feelings to you during this joyous season.
TOMMY ROE

We wish all of you BEAT readers a monstrously Merry Christmas and the hope that over the holidays you will eat the fat and check the collestoral count.
THE TURTLES

I wish all the readers of The BEAT a Christmas filled with happiness as thick as the hair on Santa Claus' beard.
BRENDA LEE

I wish all of the best of the Christmas spirit to my many friends. May you have everything good in the coming year.
SAL VALENTINO

We would like to say thanks to The BEAT for all their help during the past year. And to all you BEAT readers we would like to extend our best wishes for a happy holiday season and a wonderful new year.
PETER & GORDON

I wish a warm and cozy season to all my friends — both old and new.
SANDY POSEY

Hi everyone. This is Tom King of the Outsiders. We would all like to take this time to thank The BEAT for all the great publicity they've given us and we'd like to wish all of our friends a very happy holiday season.
THE OUTSIDERS

I wish you could all go camping with me this Christmas — even if there's no snow, no trees, no reindeer, etc.
TIM MORGAN

I wish you all could spend the Christmas holidays with me in the South this year. To all my friends and neighbors no matter how far away you live, Merry Christmas.
BILLY JOE ROYAL

Swinging Medallions send swinging seasons' sentiments.
SWINGING MEDALLIONS

The BEAT is published bi-weekly by BEAT Publications, Inc., editorial and advertising offices at 6290 Sunset Blvd., Suite 504, Hollywood, California 90028. U.S. bureaus in Hollywood, San Francisco, New York, Chicago and Nashville; overseas correspondents in London, Liverpool and Manchester, England. Sale price 25 cents. Subscription price: U.S. and possessions, $5 per year; Canada and foreign rates, $9 per year. Second class postage prepaid at Los Angeles, California.

Letters TO THE EDITOR

DISCUSSION

Dear *BEAT*:
After reading Discussion in the November 19 issue, I would like to express my opinion to what Eden has said.

I really dig Simon & Garfunkel's "A Hazy Shade Of Winter," also their "Seven O'Clock News/Silent Night." As for "Coming On Strong," I'll be disappointed if it doesn't make the top ten. In regards to R&B singers, how can you call James Brown "The King?" Personally, I cannot stomach his records!

For my money, Chris Farlowe is far better than Brown will ever be. To go a step further, Mitch Ryder and the Detroit Wheels are probably the greatest R&B performers since Little Richard and Jerry Lee Lewis. At best, James Brown is "mediocre."

Last but not least, was the background music for the Monkees theme song also provided by studio musicians? How phony can you get!

In closing, keep up the fine newspaper.
Dave Therianelt

Yes, Dave, studio musicians were used for the Monkees' theme.
The Editor

Quiz On Monkees

Dear *BEAT*:
Is it really true that the Monkees don't play the instruments themselves for their records? If it is, I just can't believe it! On their TV show, they sure do a good imitation of playing.

One question which has been bothering me is, if they don't play for their records, why not? If they know how to play the instruments or are learning, why can't and don't they play them? I won't believe it! None of my friends do either.

We all think you're putting us on! Actually, I think it is all a publicity stunt. You know, *The BEAT* is not always right! I wish all these singing groups would stop doing such ridiculous publicity stunts. They're all silly and stupid and they never do help much anyway!

Thank you for letting me have my say!
Joyce Damante

The Monkees used session musicians on their first single and album because when these records were cut they (Micky and Davy in particular) were just learning how to play. It was not a publicity stunt. The practice of using session musicians in recording is certainly not new—it has been going on and will continue as long as records are made. Some groups use them and some don't. The Monkees did; however, it's safe to say that they won't for long.
The Editor

Down With Associates

Dear *BEAT*:
I am writing this letter in protest of the group The Association whom I regard as very commercial and very repetitious. I have recently seen The Association perform, they are not only sickening but they sound quite bad musically and vocally.

Their new record, "Pandora's Golden Hebee Jeebees," is a copy of a very good record by Terry Knight and the Pack, "A Change Is On The Way." I was very pleased to have been able to see Terry Knight and the Pack at a local club. Terry, I consider, is a very excellent singer and the group I regard as fair. I know that Terry Knight copied the Yardbirds on his first attempt, "Better Man Than I," but I feel his "Change Is On The Way" has emerged he and his group into their own.

"Change" is a little reminiscent of "Still I'm Sad" but at least it's original.

That's not what I can say for the Association with all the publicity for them in teen magazines and in your paper no wonder they are popular. I think you have neglected to point out the faults of this group. Since they were the group who didn't like long hair for their image was of short hair.

I hope you will listen to The Association's record of "Pandora's Golden Heebee Jeebees" and Terry Knight and the Packs' record "A Change Is On The Way." If you'll listen closely you will find the comparison quite the same.

Thank you for letting me speak my mind. And I only hope this letter is printed so other people will understand the point I'm trying to make.
Shawn Walker

PARENTS AT FAULT

Dear *BEAT*:
I'm sick of adults knocking the teenage generation. They claim that the teenagers of today are all dirty, disrespectful, delinquent and lazy. Adults also claim that the "bums" who hang-out on the Sunset Strip are a bunch of "filthy, bearded slobs" and "cheap, immoral girls." (I'll admit that there *is* some truth to this.)

The thing that really kills me is that they ridicule and blame the younger generation yet they can't seem to understand that it is their generation who brought up the teenagers! The adults of today are 99% at fault for the "dirty, disrespectful, rebellious" teens of today.

Thank you for letting me get this off my chest. I hope you agree with me.
Karen Altman

THE BEATLE IMITATORS

Dear *BEAT*:
I cannot understand what is so tremendously special about the Monkees. They are imitators. Their style on television is simply a copy of the Beatles and not even a very good one. They are a bit corny.

Individually none of them have the great humor, originality, and the beautiful carefree attitude toward life that the Beatles have. They neither write nor play their music. And all their lines on the show are taken from scriptwriters. All they do is sing—many people who haven't had the money to back them up can sing. The Monkees cannot even sing that well. Their harmony is a combination of the Beatles and the Byrds. Again, they are imitating.

They really have nothing unique about them which distinguishes them enough to have the radio stations plugging them constantly. I really do hope they do not become a top group such as the Beatles, Stones, Lovin' Spoonful, Beach Boys, the Who and all the other popular groups who have talent because there would be no reason for it.

This just goes to show what happens to four boys who are a little bit cute, have no talent to speak of, but do have money and backing. Oh well, Nancy Sinatra made it.
A Beatle fan

SUGGESTIONS

Dear *BEAT*:
(1) Shirley Poston forever! I wish she would make "The Adventures of Robin Boyd" into a book.
(2) To the Count Five: I was never so proud. I was a number one fan of theirs but now I'm number one plus.
(3) The Association, the Left Banke and the Hard Times rule!
(4) Teen Panel is the finest thing that has happened to The *BEAT*.
Glenda Wobig

THE BEST EVER READ

Dear *BEAT*:
I'm one of the biggest Association fans in the world and I hunt down every article and picture printed of them and paste them into my Association scrapbook. Anyway, I'm writing to tell you that the article in your December 3 issue, "A Daze Worth Of The Association," was THE best article I have ever read—about anybody!

It is going into a place of honor in my scrapbook. I do have one question to ask you, though. Who wrote the article? Whoever it is is to be congratulated on a really excellent piece of journalism.
Brenda Blackwell

Louise Criscione was the anonymous author of the Association article.
The Editor

'UP WITH ADULTS'

Dear *BEAT*:
Up with adults! Not "down with kids" but "up with adults." Granted, some of the adults deserve the declining respect they are getting—just as some teens deserve the stereotyped teen image—but I think it's time someone spoke up for the adults; someone other than the adults, that is.

A lot of us see the problems of the world and instead of rolling up our sleeves and working toward eventual absolvement of these problems, would rather sit back and blame them on our parents.

Our general "they caused it, let them fix it" attitude too often seems to be the philosophy. Sure, there are a lot of things wrong with the world—a lot of things to change—but that's what youth is for! To carry torches and start fires—fires of change.

The fact that world society is troubled is not new, you know. Our parents weren't handed a perfect world either. They've had their chance at it—and now it's our turn to make of it the best we can. They made mistakes, sure, but which of us hasn't? We should remember that our parents have lived through two wars and a depression.

We're living through affluence. Both generations have their problems and both must rise to face them. Let's stop laughing at the adults for mistakes and start learning from those mistakes—and thinking how we can avoid similar situations.

In one of his songs, Sonny Bono said: "I'll make that other cheek mine." How 'bout it, kids?
Billie Jo Heltne

A SONG LETTER

Dear *BEAT*:
If I Were A Carpenter I would be Born Free but I'm Your Puppet and you Keep Me Hangin' On. If you See See Rider just Walk Away Renee because Love Is A Hurtin' Thing.

Have You Seen Your Mother, Baby, Standing In The Shadow because she's having a Psychotic Reaction over Dandy. Look Through My Window In The Midnight Hour and you can Cherish me because I'm Ready For Love.

Meet me at the Bus Stop when the Wedding Bell Blues start playing at the Winchester Cathedral and we will take the Last Train To Clarksville because there is a Great Airplane Strike going on.

If you were Born A Woman on the Poor Side Of Town just Reach Out I'll Be There because I've Got You Under My Skin but don't worry Beauty Is Only Skin Deep so you don't have to cry 96 Tears, Baby.

Hey, Joe, Open The Door To Your Heart because It Hurts Me. Black Is Black just like Cherry Cherry who fell in the Rain On The Roof.
John Rose

SOME SEEDS

Dear *BEAT*:
I was wondering if it is possible that you could run a few items on Love and the Seeds. Both groups are really good and deserve a few words of mention.
Dubby

BEATLES

Dear *BEAT*:
Would you please print the enclosed open letter to the Beatles? Thank you very much for your help. I really enjoy The *BEAT*, keep up the excellent work.

Dear Beatles:
I very sincerely hope that you are not going to split up, but if you must, you must. You have just as much right as anyone else to be individuals and live your lives the way you want to.

Nothing will ever begin to fill the gap you would leave if you split up.

I want to thank you for all the happiness you have given me. I only regret that I never saw you in concert. I hope that as you go through life you will find all the happiness you have been able to give me.
Linda Green

MORE ON SPOONFUL

Dear *BEAT*:
As subscribers to The *BEAT* we'd like to compliment you for presenting the best in the field of pop music. However, we feel that you haven't had nearly enough on one of the most original and talented groups around, the Lovin' Spoonful.

In the past year or so, American groups have regained a hold on the pop music charts—thanks to groups such as the Association, the Byrds, the Mama's and Papa's and the Spoonful. Not that we have anything against English groups, but their sound is no longer rare. The individuality of the above mentioned groups push them ahead of their time, unable to be duplicated. We feel that *The BEAT* should concentrate on the sounds of tomorrow happening today, not the sounds of yesterday, overdone today.

The Spoonful sing of happiness and love, so lacking in the world today. One Spoonful album can do more for you than any high from any drug.

Also, we think *The BEAT* should spotlight the writers of today, for they will be known as the greatest artists of our generation. Lennon and McCartney and Dylan are probably our best contemporary composers. Given a few years, John Sebastian and John Phillips will rank among them.

Now let's work on keeping U.S. groups on the top of the pop music charts. In the words of John Sebastian: "It had to happen."
Gail, Melly, Louise & Timmi

KRLA ARCHIVES

On the BEAT
By Louise Criscione

Sonny and Cher really maneuvered a cool move when they found themselves ten non-professional young people from the junior choir of the First Baptist Church of Van Nuys to act as background singers for Cher's latest recording, a Sonny Bono composition titled "Mama." Sonny, acting as producer, also used 22 strings and 7 percussion-rhythm men for the record.

Looks as if Neil Diamond is back writing hits for artists other than himself. He penned "I'm A Believer" for the Monkees. The record received one of the largest advance orders in the history of the record business and is expected to reach the nation's top ten on the strength of discs which have been pre-sold.

Neil's own career is going nowhere but up with his "I Got The Feelin'" making a large dent in the charts. Movie and television people are not overlooking Neil's potential either. He's currently up for a lead role in a motion picture and is also being considered for a television series. If Neil gets either or both parts, he will write the theme music and score as well as acting.

Quaife Returns

In a surprise move, Pete Quaife has rejoined his old buddies, the Kinks. Pete, who was injuried in an automobile accident nearly six months ago, has not been able to perform due to the injuries he received. So, a couple of months ago Pete announced that he was leaving the Kinks in favor of a non-professional job in Denmark. But now it has been revealed that Pete went to Denmark for an operation. When the operation was successfully completed and Pete had recuperated, he asked to rejoin the Kinks and was, naturally, welcomed back into the group.

... NEIL DIAMOND

The Four Tops not only received a royal reception from their English fans but from the world of British pop as well when Brian Epstein threw a huge party to honor the American chart-toppers. Guests at the party included John Lennon, George Harrison, Mick Jagger, Keith Richard, Charlie Watts, Eric Burdon and Donovan.

Despite the fact that John Lennon has finished up his movie and returned to England, the four Beatles have yet to get together. George is in London (complete with mustache) but Ringo has journeyed off to Liverpool for a visit and Paul is enjoying himself "somewhere in Europe." However, if all goes as planned, the four Beatles should congregate in London sometime this month to record a single.

Sinatra Giggle

Western Recorders was really swinging last week what with the Mama's and Papa's, Brian Wilson, the Association and Frank Sinatra all utilizing the recording studio's facilities. Surprisingly enough, the one getting all the giggles was Sinatra. His appearance was reminiscent of the D-Day landing what with his entire entourage marching into the studio behind Sinatra. Of course, his personal guards manned the doors and a prerequisite for men in his party seemed to be an expensive suit, white (starched) shirt and tie. Sitting in the "spectator seats" they certainly presented quite a contrast to the studio's other "guests."

What Sinatra was even *doing* recording at Western is anybody's guess but rumor has it that the Chairman would like very much to keep turning out records which appeal to teen record-buyers and was, therefore, at Western to capture a "young sound." True or false, it makes interesting speculation any way you look at it.

It's nice to see that Mick, Keith and Charlie made it to the Tops' party—most people thought they had dropped off the face of the earth! They certainly haven't been making much noise since they left the U.S. in August. Even the usually talkative Mick has been silent, which is quite a shame because he can always be depended upon to offend *someone* by what he says—therefore, keeping things from becoming too terribly dull.

Before I forget—Merry Christmas and thanks to everyone for making it such a swinging year.

... MICK JAGGER

The Association Report From Their U.S. Tour

Dear *BEAT*, up, down, back and dead:

Well, we are now in an airplane unable to land because of fog, so we can't play Davenport with the Spoonful tonight. Instead we will have to fly to Minneapolis and land there. Oh well, we need an extra night of rest anyway!

The tour is really going well, the people we run into are almost always warm and friendly and the crowds have been good. This tour is going a little smoother than the others but it is still exhausting.

We worked with the new Vaudeville Band in Madison, Wisconsin. They were really good. They really are neat to watch, a really fine group of really fine reallies. I hope we have the opportunity to work with them again.

Chicago was really neat too. They have a lot of groovy shops and clubs and their auditorium (McCormick Place) is a beautiful place to perform, fine acoustics, professional lighting and just generally groovy.

I still miss Los Angeles and the rest of California and, of course, love to everyone.

Soon,
Love,
Russ

'Action' Is Picked Up By ABC-TV

With television shows being dropped all over the country, Dick Clark's "Where the Action Is" has been picked up by ABC-TV for thirteen more weeks. Thus, Clark has the only two national pop music shows on the air. His other is the famous perennial, "American Bandstand."

The cast of "Where The Action Is" includes Steve Alaimo, Paul Revere and the Raiders, Keith Allison, Tina Mson, The Hardtimes and Tommy Roe.

Beach Boys Latest To Earn Goldie

The Beach Boys were greeted with some nice news when they made their triumphant return from England this weekend. Their latest single, "Good Vibrations," has surpassed the 925,000 mark in sales and has thus become the biggest-selling single in Beach Boy history.

"Good Vibrations" has now outsold such big Beach Boy hits as "Help Me, Rhonda," "I Get Around" and "Sloop John B.," all of which were in the 900,000 category. If "Vibrations" continues its sales pace it will become the first million-selling single for the group.

... ASSOCIATION (l. to r.) Gary, Russ, Jim, Ted, Brian, Terry.

RINGO FOLLOWS JOHN: BEATLES TO NEW YORK?

Apparently Ringo Starr would like to follow in John Lennon's footsteps and go the movie route alone. According to the Beatle drummer, their third movie venture has been postponed again and while John, Paul and George seem to have things to occupy them during the long wait, Ringo does not.

"So, it would be very nice if the right film part came along. Brian gets offers for all of us every week, but none of them have suited me as yet.

"I'd rather the four of us filmed together," added Ringo, "but if there is going to be a long wait I'd be happy with something to do in the meantime.

And even if we do go ahead early in the new year I could do something on my own later."

So, Brian Epstein is reportedly on the lookout for a suitable movie role for Ringo.

As you know, the Beatles have announced that they will do no more personal appearances. But there is a gentleman in New York who is doing his upmost to change the Beatles' minds. Sid Bernstein, who promoted the Beatles twice in Shea Stadium in New York, has offered the Beatles $500,000 to return to the United States for two back-to-back appearances at Shea.

The Beatles received $320,000 for their two performances at Shea during 1965 and 1966. In return for his $500,000 offer,

Bernstein wants the Beatles' Shea date to be their only performance in the U.S. "so I can get all of the kids from Chicago, Philadelphia, Boston and Washington as well as the New York area." Bernstein lost $680 on the Beatles' 1966 show but declares that "it wasn't really a loss because the experience was so rich."

No word has been forthcoming from the Beatles as to whether they will accept or decline Bernstein's offer.

... RINGO WANTS FILM PART

BEAT Photo: Howard L. Bingham

KRLA ARCHIVES

GIFT SUGGESTIONS FOR POP PEOPLE...

...A GIRLFRIEND for Herman

...SOME NEW CLOTHES for the Supremes

...MORE MONEY so Johnny can move

...A CAR like James Bond has

TOGETHERNESS

...DRAFT DEFERMENT for Gary

BIRTH CERTIFICATE so Pet knows who she is

...A JUICY CARROT for Brian

...A SON for Bill Cosby

'in' people are talking about...

Sinatra and the Association meeting head-on and wishing like crazy that they would've been there to see it happen... The fact that with his mustache and hair about the only thing visible on George Harrison's face is his nose—and he's the wrong Beatle to feature a nose... The trouble on the Strip being blown up like that and whether or not press is a four-letter word... Brian Wilson turning vegetarian and wondering if he has himself confused with Gary Alexander... The funny way the Kitchen Cinq spell sink and deciding that they must have been influenced by the Cyrkle... Rudy Vallee honestly trying to make a comeback... How people would rather hear about the hazy winter than how silent the night is... The Eggplant that ate Chicago and what it all has to do with Dr. West's Medicine Show and Junk Band... The conversation piece in the middle of "Happenings"... The sudden run on Bears.

PEOPLE ARE TALKING ABOUT the Beatles "no more personal appearance" announcement and how important it really is now... What Bill Cosby thinks is best in your Christmas stocking... Rhythm 'n' Blues completely taking over and deciding that it would probably be a groovy change... Whether or not the big K will enter the movies or television and hoping that he does 'cause what a pity it would be to lose him altogether... What makes Sullivan bring back the DC5 every other week and how Dave goofed it good the last time around with his "sympathy" remark... Whatever happened to Chuck Berry... Andy perhaps going over to Sinatra to get that million a year guarantee for the next five years... Lou leaving what he started.

PEOPLE ARE TALKING ABOUT having a freak out for Christmas... Otis drawing 8,000 on a rainy Sunday in England and what it all means to people like Herman and the Walkers... Sal going solo and how sweet it is... Tommy switching bags — finally... Papa John showering everybody at the recording session with confetti... Donovan not making it too huge in his native land and wondering if he's trying to pull a Herman on us... Whether or not Joan Baez refuses that part of her paycheck which is derived from military installations, etc.... How horrible it is that Shane is being dropped since he's the only really long-hair representative who rides a horse.

PEOPLE ARE TALKING ABOUT what a giggle Jeff must have gotten out of that story about him having a nervous breakdown and being in a London hospital when he was right here in California all the time... Beach Boys purchasing four Rolls Royces and Brian emerging with Lou's old one which formerly belonged to one Ringo Starr... What's happened to Tom Jones... Lesley trying to look like Pet but not succeeding... How much of Hollywood is owned by Trini... When the Spoonful are going to get their fill of New York... What's behind the "Beatles to leave Epstein" rumor... Inter-group squabbles taking their toll on a popular group's stage performance and how long they think they can hide their "differences" from audiences... Whether or not Elvis is alive and living in Argentina... The unexcusable antics of Buddy and wondering what he has against Dusty.

PEOPLE ARE TALKING ABOUT the Seeds' hard work beginning to pay off... The knack of catching the Knack... The Hardly-Worthit Report and how hilarious the thing is... The big spread with Eric Burdon's by-line in this month's Ebony... Lou's intro to "Tobacco Road" being like it really is and, therefore, causing people to laugh 'cause it hits too close to home and the only other thing they could do is think... Noel having a particularly happy and prosperous one this time around... How perennial the Seasons are going to be... How big the Beach Boys went over in England and wondering if the British are just now discovering surfing and striped shirts too... Whether or not Mick is suffering from acute lockjaw... How funny Rick Nelson looks with long hair... The Monkees turning into believers and how sweet it is to Screen Gems, Colgems, RCA and Neil Diamond—just to name a few.

PEOPLE ARE TALKING ABOUT being born free and making a mint out of the fact... How well Mitch sells his soul... The Turtles allowing their soup to cool... Cass moving out of the A-frame... Smashed, bombed and John's Children wanting awfully badly to come Stateside... How it all has to do with numbers—at least, that's what Brian said... The state of things when if the draft doesn't get you, the curfew does... The fact that if the Beatles decide to drop recording what will happen to innovations in album covers... December being Bill Cosby month and furiously trying to come up with some sort of celebration for the occasion and deciding that they'll settle for an autograph if they can be assured of a handshake as well... The Who "live" sounding quite a bit like breaking dishes with a little rattle of silverware thrown in for good measure.

KRLA ARCHIVES

THIS Christmas... GIVE YOUR FRIENDS BEAT

Order BEAT now... in time for Christmas... at special low rates.

ONLY $3 FOR YOUR FIRST SUBSCRIPTION... $1 FOR EACH ADDITIONAL GIFT SUBSCRIPTION... WE SEND YOU GIFT CARDS TO GIVE YOUR FRIENDS.

BEAT... America's largest teen NEWSpaper... bringing you exclusive stories, interviews and pictures on all your favorite stars... BEAT is accurate... entertaining... educational... covering musical talent in both the U.S. and Europe... BEAT is the *only* way to stay informed about the fast-moving world of pop!

FOREIGN SUBSCRIPTIONS — $9.00 PER YEAR.

MAIL TO: BEAT SUBSCRIPTIONS, 6290 Sunset Blvd., Hollywood 90028.

My name is _____
Address _____
City _____ State _____ Zip _____

☐ Send BEAT for Xmas (names listed below).
☐ I also want a BEAT subscription.
Total enclosed $_____ for _____ subscriptions.
I enclose ☐ cash ☐ check ☐ money order.

Coupon
Name _____
Address _____
City _____ State _____ Zip _____

Coupon
Name _____
Address _____
City _____ State _____ Zip _____

Coupon
Name _____
Address _____
City _____ State _____ Zip _____

Coupon
Name _____
Address _____
City _____ State _____ Zip _____

Coupon
Name _____
Address _____
City _____ State _____ Zip _____

Coupon
Name _____
Address _____
City _____ State _____ Zip _____

KRLA ARCHIVES

BEAT Exclusive

Vibrations—Brian Wilson Style

MIKE "SPINACH," DAVID "CARROT," BRIAN "GEMINI" AND BRIAN'S COUSIN, BARRY. YOU MAY BELIEVE IT IF YOU WANT TO!
BEAT Photo: Guy Webster

(EDITOR'S NOTE: Every so often we turn The BEAT typewriters over to the entertainers themselves. This time around, Brian Wilson has written an exclusive story for us. What's it all about? Only Brian knows for sure!)

By Brian Wilson

PART I

It was a sunny day outside, but Brian Gemini was unable to appreciate the beauty of nature as he stumbled through the Vegetable Forest, choking with ill health.

Suddenly, in the midst of a violent nasal attack, Brian fell into a giant tomato, and tumbled down, down, *down*, to the very seedy bottom. There were large bagpipes under Brian's eyes, but even those didn't prevent him from seeing many grotesque and frightening seeds on his way down through the tomato.

He landed at the bottom—SPLAT!—and looking back up to the top, he saw a carrot floating down toward him. Grasping firmly onto the carrot, Brian ate it quickly, and, *lo and behold!*—it gave him some very out-of-sight vision, of a very out-of-sight world.

Now, Brian Gemini was a very quick-witted sort of soul, and he perceived instantly that he would need a great deal of out-of-sight energy to be able to cope with this brand new out-of-sight world which he had just seen with his new-found out-of-sight vision.

Shortly after this enlightening perception, a large glob of very green spinach quite fortuitously splatted down upon Brian's knee. What luck! But then, the glob of spinach—who's given name was Michael—began to speak: "Now, I'm *really* mad," he said, said he. "There is a Roving Radish reporter who wants to change my name to Sidney Spinach. I will not bend to the wishes of the teen-oriented Reporter Establishment," Michael Spinach-Glob globbled firmly.

"Hmmmph!" retorted Brian Gemini. "Why don't you let yourself get eaten up, just once?"

"Well," hesitated the Green Glob, "If I don't have to be called *Sidney*; I will if you will call me Michael."

Brian Gemini agreed immediately and enthusiastically ate the spinach, which gave him instant energy. Just then, Brian saw the Jolly Jewish Carrot (who had escaped from the Chicken Soup) floating down toward him. Watching the Carrot's descent, Brian G. said loud enough for everyone to hear: "That carrot is much too big to eat."

At that precise moment in tomato history, the Carrot landed and introduced himself: "I'm the Jolly Jewish Carrot, and I've just escaped from the Chicken Soup. Hello! I've just come down from Carrot Heaven to help you see just *Where It's At*, and tell you that the world is really *Out-Of-Sight!*" Thus spake the Jolly Jewish Carrot.

Pulling himself up to his full carrot-top height, Jolly J. continued: "I see you've just devoured Spinach, and with that energy—you are now going to explore the out-of-sight world."

Inspired by J.J.'s pep talk, Brian Gemini, filled with new-found vegetable vigor, jumped to his feet and was red as a beet and then said with great emotion: "David Carrot—we'll soon be in the pink!" "That's what *you* think," poetically retorted the carrot, with somewhat less emotion than Brian.

Just then Brian exclaimed: "Oh! Here comes the celery now!" "Ouch!" he added emphatically as he was smashed upon the heady by a stringy stalk of impertinent celery that didn't seem to know just whose head it had smashed.

Well . . . Brian blew his cool and chucked it as far as he could. To which David Carrot immediately reproached: "That's not very nice Brian! Don't be so up-tight. You've got to use the strength that the spinach gave you for *good things*," he instructed.

(Turn to Page 14)

BEAT SHOWCASE
(spotlighting new talent on the pop scene)

THE KIT KATS are Philadelphia's hottest group with hopes of duplicating their success nationwide. From their varied former occupations—classical musician, drummer in a burlesque house—the foursome switched to rock 'n roll. The Kit Kats are Carl Hausman, Ron Cichonski, Kit Stewart, "Big John" Bradley.

THE BALLROOM are the latest thing out of Our Productions, which is in the process of launching a number of new singers on the pop scene. Their sound, one BEAT staffer says, is sort of Mama and Papa-ish. Top (left to right) Curt Boettcher, Michele O'Malley. Bottom (left to right) Jim Bell and Sandy Salisbury.

JOHN'S CHILDREN have just released "Smashed! Blocked!" in Europe and the U.S. The disc, which is receiving good listener reaction, is a musical plea to the "new wave generation." John's Children, actually children of English aristocrats, appear on stage in white high-necked sweaters and mystical medallions. Their main audience may be the U.S. which they hope to visit the first of the year. Currently, the guys are touring Europe, under the managership of Simon Napier-Bell, who also manages the Yardbirds. From left to right, John's Children are John Melvin Hewlett, Christopher Townson, Andrew Anthony Ellison and Geoffrey Hugh Robert McCleland.

KRLA ARCHIVES

...JEFF BECK ENTERING THE "BEAT" DOOR.

Jeff Beck: Alone In The Yardbirds

By Eden

A young man named Jeff Beck—a very important and integral part of a group called The Yardbirds—nearly always stands alone.

He is possibly the most revered guitar player on the pop scene today. Rock and roll musicians worship him; the highest compliment they can receive is to be called "the Jeff Beck of the group."

What does Jeff Beck, leader of pop music, think about the developments occuring in the field today?

"The main thing about it is that the quality of musicianship has gotten better and the songs have gotten stronger. The meanings of the words have gotten better.

"The introduction of weird instruments shows a strong sign of musical interest—more than just a bit of *moneymaking*."

What does Jeff think about the exchange of ideas between popular groups?

"The main influence is the Beatles, isn't it? It's *got* to be, because without the Beatles, there wouldn't be *half* the groups there are today. And without half the groups today—there wouldn't be any musical ideas going around. Because groups give ideas to one another—or *steal* an idea might be more like it!

"It *is*, in a way, an *exchange* because what we've 'stolen' from other people, they don't know about. We prefer to take the credit for what we do like any other person."

Although there were sounds of people all around us—jingling of water glasses, clanging of silverware—Jeff sat quite still, moving only to pick up his sandwich or emphasize a point in his conversation. But suddenly he came alive to rebel against the label of "electronic" so often tagged on his music.

"The original concept of our music was to just play what was inside us, and the best way of putting it over was by making 'electronic' sounds.

"You see, it's not like electronic music—if anybody thinks it is, go out and buy an album of electronic music and see how much different it is. I mean, one or two bits might remind them of electronic music, but it really isn't—the idea isn't. It's just a means of using a guitar to put over a different sound, a different feel.

"We don't like people tagging our music but if they're going to make a tag, then obviously we're going to have to fall in line with what they want to call it. We'd just like to be recognized for the things we do.

"I've heard an example of 'psychedelic' music, but it was just *rubbish*. It was just a noise—it was somebody just having what they call a 'freak-out.' It sounded like *me* giving my guitar to *Mum* and saying Mum—play it! It's just musically *rubbish*. But I'm not going to say that that matters nowadays!"

What would Jeff like to do with his future?

"I'd like to do record producing, but only by myself—and only my own music because I have no idea of record production on any other thing, like strings and brass, and all that.

"I'd like to produce our records—but I'm not going to try, because it would ruin the Yardbirds' sound. It wouldn't ruin it, but it would alter it—and therefore, perhaps lose some of the individualism.

"That's because each of our records isn't produced by anybody—it just happens. The record is built up from the ground and no *one* person can take the credit for it at the end. It's everybody's combined efforts.

"I've got an example of my production together with Jimmy Paige and it's an instrumental. It's very stirring and its got an intensive, pulsating beat, which goes on and on and on, and it just explodes at the end. We designed it to affect a man's mind—or, to make it sound as if the man was affected when he wrote it. I think we'll release it in an album, but it's going to be put out as a single by me. It's been finished three months, and there's no name for it!"

Did Jeff ever set out to make Jeff Beck what he is today, or did it just happen?

"I never wished to be where I am—status wise. When I was at home, I was quite content to be myself and just go on out and play to anybody. I'd play my heart out, even if there were only ten people in the audience, because I really wasn't aware of all this.

"But now, I've been placed up, really, on a pedestal, without even wishing it, where as if the kids hear that, they'll think; 'Only give *me* a chance! I spent my last cent buying a guitar—just give me a chance!' But, believe me, if they ever had the chance, and they got up and did as much work as we've done, they'd be regretting it!"

Open Letter On Alleged Split Between Beatles

Dear *BEAT*:

I've just finished reading your "Beatles Split?" story, and would like to send along some information that might help clear up this new controversy.

When the Beatles appeared in my city this summer, my father attended the press conference. He taped the entire conference for me, and I wouldn't part with this tape for anything, but I will have a copy made and send it to you if you require proof of what I'm going to tell you.

This is the portion of the conference which applies to the subject at hand, and I repeat it verbatim.

A Possibility

Reporter: "Recently, have you seriously thought of breaking up?"

Paul: "What do you mean by breaking up? We haven't thought that the time has come for us to break up, but we've realized the possibility that breaking up is a natural progression because we can't go on forever like this. We have to think about it and prepare for it in case it did happen, which it should, you know. It's got to sometime."

Reporter: "Then you consider breaking up a natural progression?"

John: "Yes, you never know..."

Paul: "Well, we don't know, but we've got to think about it now, so we're not at a loss if it does happen."

This is exactly what the Beatles said, and I think their comments are proof enough that the recent developments are not evidence of any "sudden decision." They are more evidence of "indecision," and not the "sudden" kind.

If they were already willing to discuss the possibility of breaking up way back in August, they must have been thinking about this for a long time. I feel they're *still* just thinking about it.

Comparing their statements in Washington with what they've said on the breaking up subject since, I feel they're thinking about it *less* seriously than they were three months ago. It just seems more serious now because everyone is printing what they're saying.

I hope I'm making myself clear. If their Washington comments had been printed all over the country at the time they were made, the big Beatle-Break-Up scare would have happened then. And probably with more reason than it's happening now. Since they returned to England, they've said nothing this definite. As a matter of fact, they haven't said much of anything.

I think the whole thing is nothing but another attempt, by adult publications (newspapers, etc.) to keep cashing in on the way the Beatles sell more copies for them. Until the trouble in Manila, nothing was said about the Beatles for a long time. But that controversy, and then John's bit about religion sold a lot of newspapers, and now everyone is just trying to keep the ball rolling.

Unfair?

I don't think this is fair, to the Beatles or to their fans. It's making them apprehensive, like they've got to make up their minds right away, and it's making us terrified that they might make a decision we'll find hard to accept.

The possibility of breaking up does exist in the Beatles' minds, or they wouldn't have mentioned it last summer. And they probably wouldn't have mentioned it or felt quite so strongly about it then if they hadn't been under all the pressures that come with a Beatle tour.

I think it is imperative that all publications (including The *BEAT*) drop the subject. If this doesn't happen, the Beatles might be pressured into doing something they had no intention of doing this early in the game. Surely everyone must realize that their eventual break-up as a group is *inevitable*. Much as we love them, even *we* know they can't go on as they are *forever*. But with all the rumors and hysteria, they might just start thinking, "Well, we're going to have to do it someday, and since the trouble has already started, why not get it over with now?"

Premature Burial

If the Beatles do decide to break up within the very near future, I'll always believe it was a premature burial of the group, caused by this latest controversy. But whenever they break up—this year or ten years from now—I hope everyone realizes that we will still have them as individuals.

Paul and George will undoubtedly remain in the music field, while John may divide his time between music and writing (maybe even acting). And if people don't stop speculating on "what on earth Ringo will do with himself," I'm going to start screaming. He's my favorite, and everyone seems to have forgotten that during the first year or so of Beatlemania, Ringo was considered to be the "most likely to succeed" on his own. There were even a lot of rumors about him receiving multi-million dollar offers to star in comedy films.

There are many things Ringo can do when and if he's minus his Beatle-status. And if all else fails, he can always run for President again. Only this time, maybe we'd be fortunate enough for him to win!

Name Withheld By Request
Washington, D. C.

BEATLES (RINGO, JOHN, PAUL, GEORGE) ON WHAT MAY TURN OUT TO BE LAST U.S. VISIT AS A GROUP.

BEAT Photo: Howard L. Bingham

KRLA ARCHIVES

Top 40 Requests

1. I'M A BELIEVER .... The Monkees
2. BORN FREE .... Roger Williams
3. LADY GODIVA .... Peter & Gordon
4. I WANTA BE FREE .... The Monkees
5. GOOD THING .... Paul Revere & Raiders
6. HELP ME GIRL .... Eric Burdon & The Animals
7. YOU'RE PUSHING TOO HARD .... Seeds
8. GOOD VIBRATIONS .... Beach Boys
9. 96 TEARS .... ? & Mysterians
10. MELLOW YELLOW .... Donovan
11. SMASHED, BLOCKED .... John's Children
12. HOORAY FOR HAZEL .... Tommy Roe
13. PANDORA'S GOLDEN HEEBEE JEEBEES .... Association
14. HAPPENINGS 10 YEAR'S TIME AGO .... Yardbirds
15. WHERE DID ROBINSON CRUSOE GO? .... Ian Whitcomb
16. I NEED SOMEONE .... ? & Mysterians
17. THE BEARS .... Fastest Group Alive
18. S.O.S. .... Terry Randall
19. SNOOPY VS. THE RED BARON .... Royal Guardsmen
20. IN A DUSTY OLD ROOM .... Noel Harrison
21. DEVIL WITH A BLUE DRESS ON/GOOD GOLLY MISS MOLLY .... Mitch Ryder & Detroit Wheels
22. WINCHESTER CATHEDRAL .... New Vaudeville Band
23. YOU KEEP ME HANGING ON .... The Supremes
24. BUT IT'S ALRIGHT .... J.J. Jackson
25. HEAVEN MUST HAVE SENT YOU .... Elgins
26. I GOT THE FEELING .... Neil Diamond
27. I'M YOUR PUPPET .... James and Bobby Purify
28. BABY .... Carla Thomas
29. KNOCK ON WOOD .... Eddie Floyd
30. FULL MEASURE .... Lovin' Spoonful
31. TALK, TALK .... Music Machine
32. MAME .... Herb Alpert & Tijuana Brass
33. A HAZY SHADE OF WINTER .... Simon & Garfunkel
34. THAT'S LIFE .... Frank Sinatra
35. I'M READY FOR LOVE .... Martha & Vandellas
36. WHY PICK ON ME? .... Standells
37. COME ROUND HERE, I'M THE ONE YOU NEED .... Miracles
38. TOGETHER FOREVER .... Viola Wills
39. STOP, STOP, STOP .... Hollies
40. I'LL MAKE IT EASY .... Incredibles

Inside KRLA
By Eden

Specially made for all of you KRLA Sweethearts out there is the brand new Sweetheart Tree feature of Casey's Sunday afternoon get-together. Be sure to listen in and perhaps you will year *your* Sweetheart on the tree.

What do you think about the recent happenings on the Sunset Strip? Do you have an opinion about the controversy which you would like to voice? If so, why not drop me a line and perhaps we can print some of *your* ideas and thoughts on the subject.

By the way, in answer to the many questions which have come pouring in, no—the Bob Dylan wig has *not* yet been fitted over the top of the station... but that's 'cause we couldn't find *half* a wig to fit! However, we are looking forward to the Grand *Fitting* Ceremonies sometime in the near future!

Even though you've only just gotten over the initial indigestion of Thanksgiving, I think it's only fair to remind you that Christmas *is* just around the corner. And you *know* what that means! At any rate, since I will have neither "time nor *money* enough" to buy all the gifties which I would like to this year, I will take this opportunity to *wish* my gifts to one and all.

To Charlie O'Donnell, I wish one "Happy Time," non-toxic set of water colors. To Bob Eubanks, a year's supply of Granny Goose potato chips—and a pale blue, 30-gallon hat to match his eyes.

For Dave Hull, I wish the world's largest horn, the "Herbie Alpert Songbook of old Mexican Favorites for the Passover Service."

For Dick Biondi—a set of ear muffs and a year's supply of vitamin B supplements. For Pat Moore, an Identification Card and a Weather Room. For Bill Slater—one morefree weekday, a new janitor, and a nauseous green sweater to go along with the dinner he owes us at La Scala. For Robin Hill, peace and joy at this festive time and throughout the coming year, and one jar of Super Duper Beatle-do Hair Cream.

To Terry M. — some Jiffy Freckle Remover; and someone with a lot of patience. For Mark L. —a bell, book, candle, and Captain Kid's legacy. To Brian W.— a giant tomato personally autographed by Vic Tanny. To Carol D.—a 12-foot pussy cat fully equipped with 32 tons of exquisite imported Siberian tea. For Louise C.—a left-hand Jewish ball player who can play Mexican folk songs on the tambourine in the keys of C, H, and K Minor while he's in the shower. To Howard Turtle—Nush! To Chip Turtle—happiness. To Sean Connery — ME!!! (Oooopppps!)

For Lou Adler—a month's supply of razor blades, and an autographed copy of the 42nd Psalm. For John Phillips—a cowboy hat. For Papa Denny—a rag doll who will understand. For Tommy Roe—blue eyes and Southern Love.

Tim Morgan Goes Folk-Rock For Baez Concert

Tim Morgan, a legend in himself as well as one of the most popular singing talents working the West Coast, goes folk-rock for the first time as the special guest star for the Joan Baez concerts, Friday, Dec. 16, 7:30 and 10 p.m. at the Santa Monica Civic Auditorium.

The benefit concerts, produced by Radio Station KRLA and Doug Weston of The Troubadour, will aid the Delano Farm Workers.

Tim Morgon, heretofore, has been principally a folk performer, accompanying himself on an acoustical guitar. In his rock debut, the legendary singer will perform several songs backed by Your Gang, Mercury recording artists, including "2:10 Train" and "I'm Just A Boy," written for Tim by Bobby Jameson.

At 23, Tim Morgon holds a record for having appeared in concert at more high schools and colleges in Southern California than any other single artist or group. He has recorded five albums which sold over 200,000 in California alone.

Tickets for the Baez concert, at $5, $4, $3 and $2.50 are going quickly and it is suggested the remaining be bought as soon as possible.

...TIM MORGON

...JOAN BAEZ

ATTENTION!!!
High Schools, Colleges, Universities and Clubs:

CASEY KASEM MAY BE ABLE TO SERVE YOU!

Let Casey HELP You Put On A Show Or Dance
Contact Casey at:
HO 2-7253

The ICE HOUSE GLENDALE
folk music in concert
234 South Brand Blvd.
Glendale, California 91204

Reservations: 245-5043

DEEP SIX
Nov. 29 – Dec. 4
Dec. 20-25

The KNACK
Dec. 6-18
– plus –
LEE MALLORY
Dec. 6-18

Also
THE BIG BROTHERS
Nov. 29 – Dec. 4
Dec. 20-31

DEEP SIX

THE KNACK

LEE MALLORY

ICE HOUSE PASADENA
24 No. Mentor — Reservations: 681-9942

Paul (Sykes)
Maffitt & Davies
Pat Paulsen

Nov. 29 – Jan. 21

KRLA ARCHIVES

Chaos On The Sunset Strip

Teens Demonstrate For Dance Rights

By Mike Tuck

Still stinging from more than two weeks of violence and protests, the Sunset Strip quieted this week as irate teens and law officials held fast by their original positions concerning the controversial 10 p.m. curfew.

The truce appeared only temporary, however, as grim-faced policemen were still needed to quell gatherings of youths who refused to lessen their stronghold along the famed section of Sunset Blvd.

Yet unresolved was any sort of satisfactory agreement between law officials and teenagers, who, if anything, grew even more bitter at giving up dancing privileges and being forced off the street promptly at 10 o'clock.

Teens and Sunset Strip club owners resolved they would continue their fight to return the Strip to its former condition.

"Where do they expect us to go?" asked a long-haired protester during a recent march. "Hollywood Blvd. used to be the scene but everybody objected to that so we came here. But where do we go from here?"

Club owners, already showing financial losses since the enactment of the curfew and withdrawal of youth permits, were equally forceful in denouncing the tactics of the police department and County Supervisors.

Elmer Valentine, owner of the Whiskey A-Go-Go, called the new measures "stupid" and "insane."

"These laws don't just affect the Strip," he said, "but under certain conditions they now make dancing illegal in the entire county."

Valentine fired a telgram to Sen. George Murphy, an elevated song and dance man himself, asking if dancing is really that dangerous.

To compensate for the loss of his youth permit, Valentine immediately terminated the sale of alcoholic beverages at his club. The Whiskey was thus enabled to continue allowing anyone over 18 to dance without the accompaniment of a parent or guardian.

Clubs in other parts of the county were hit equally hard by the loss of their youth permits. Dick Maddalena, owner of the Discoteen in West Covina, said unless revisions are made his club may be forced out of business.

The Discoteen caters largely to youths under 18, meaning it is unlawful for them to dance without a legal guardian present.

Enforcement of the curfew, which touched off the initial backlash, combined with the later decision by the County Supervisors to withdraw youth permits. Teen rioting along the Strip then became a national focal point.

The measure, the county's final, drastic effort to end youth dominance of Sunset, ended teen entrance and dancing in many of the clubs.

Without youth permits, the following changes have been made in clubs catering to teens:

• No one under 21 is allowed in any establishment serving alcoholic beverages and not credited as a certified restaurant.

• Persons 18 to 21 are allowed to enter establishments serving alcoholic beverages so long as the establishment is also a certified restaurant. They are not allowed to dance, however, if the establishment does serve liquor.

• Persons under 18 may enter any establishment not serving alcoholic beverages but they cannot dance unless accompanied by a legal guardian.

Enforcement of the laws has taken a concentrated effort by the police department. As many as 250 patrolmen have been dispatched to the troubled area during recent rioting.

TEENS MASS ON THE SUNSET STRIP to protest curfew laws and dance regulations.

Their number couldn't match that of the protesters, however, who numbered up to 1,300 at times.

The rioting began rather insignificantly Nov. 11 when police first began enforcing the curfew law. Only a handful of teens protested that night, but their cause gained increased momentum the following weekend.

Massive sidewalk marches were organized as placard-carrying youths paraded down the Strip.

Despite an overall picture of non-violence, there were several beatings and cases of vandalism. Several automobiles were pelted with rocks and eggs and a city bus was seized and held by a mob for more than an hour.

Scores of teenagers were hauled to jail as a caravan of police paddy wagons patrolled the area. In all, more than 250 youths have been arrested.

Most, however, were released without reprimand.

On the fourth consecutive night of rioting, patrolmen successfully employed new tactics to disperse gatherings. Of the 1,200 participating teens, all but a handful had left the Strip shortly after 10 o'clock.

After 10:00, pedestrians were warned to "move on" any time a gathering occurred. Traffic, likewise, moved at a faster clip as motorcycle policemen directed the flow.

At 10:03 a police sound truck weaved through the congestion and broadcast:

"Attention! Attention! It is now past 10 p.m. The curfew law is now in effect. Anyone under the age of 18 years remaining in this area will be arrested!"

Nineteen arrests were made that night—cutting the total for the previous evening in half.

More recent protest marches have been free from violence, but have continued to garner large numbers of participants.

Should violence occur again this week, police fear the proceedings might get out of hand. Councilman Eugene Debs summed up the fears of the police department when he warned Sunset Strip is "a dangerous powderkeg—ready to explode."

LEE MALLORY, Valiant recording artist who recently released his first single, "That's The Way It's Going To Be," is appearing at the Ice House in Glendale with the Knack Dec. 6-18. You shouldn't miss it!

THE NEW CLUB TROPICANA
247 E. MANCHESTER, L.A.

For Reservations – 758-7615
TEENAGERS WELCOME

NOW APPEARING
THE GENIUS OF
CHET BAKER
- also -
THE INCOMPARABLE
RAY BRYANT TRIO

KRLA ARCHIVES

Simon And Garfunkel Selling Intellectualism

By Carol Deck

Intellectualism has always been an underground movement in America. It is something that the majority of people view as just a fad—like swallowing goldfish or wearing bell bottoms.

The small group of people who consider themselves or are considered "intellectuals" are a selfish lot with no desire to let the rest of the world in on what they've found. They just want to sit and look down their noses at the poor, uninformed masses.

And one thing is very certain about intellectualism—you can't package it and sell it commercially.

At least that's what they thought. But then two young men emerged from the New York folk scene and quietly set about disproving them.

Megapolis Life

Using their own unlikely names —Simon and Garfunkel—they grew into a singing and writing duo and began producing some unique thoughts on the trials and joys of life in the megapolis.

Their songs were not the laments of adolescent love and rejection, but their songs sold to the same kids.

Their songs were about man's inability to communicate with man and they sold to teenagers who cry "nobody understands us." Their songs were about the alienation and loneliness of the Big City and they sold to kids from New York to Mule Shoe, Texas.

And in their personalities they lived up to their music. They showed themselves to be rather intense, though hardly solemn young men with extensive educations and literary interests ranging from James Joyce to "kids who write on subway walls."

Paul Simon graduated from Queens College in New York with a degree in English literature and started making jaunts to Europe, becoming known over there as a singer and song writer of much merit.

Finding Time

Art Garfunkel continued in graduate work at Columbia University but found time between exams, term papers and other demands of student life, to join Paul periodically.

But it wasn't until the release of "Sounds Of Silence" that America began to take notice of the two young men who were to prove that you can sell deep, intense intellectualism to the masses.

Suddenly, Paul Simon was right up there with Bob Dylan and people began to quote him almost as much, perhaps more some time, for whereas, many people feel that Dylan's gone into himself and is writing very introspectively, Paul writes outside of himself.

Latest sample of their work is "Hazy Shade Of Winter." Although the title sounds very Lovin' Spoonfulish the lyrics are definitely Paul Simon.

But the song that is being listened to and talked about is on their latest album, "Parsley, Sage, Rosemary and Thyme."

It's titled "7 O'Clock News/ Silent Night" and it's simply a very beautiful rendition of "Silent Night" sung by the duo with a somewhat typical newscast over it.

The newscast is done by Charlie O'Donnell, Southern California disc jockey and announcer for "American Bandstand."

The effect of the newscast, including the murder of the nine nurses in Chicago, and the ever beautiful Christmas carol is stunning and chilling.

Many people, hearing the song on the radio for the first time, reach to adjust the radio dial thinking they're getting interference. By the time they realize that the interference is deliberate they become aware of what's happening on the record and are jarred out of it only when the D.J. must come in with his trivia.

The somewhat brutality of the record is unusual for Simon and Garfunkel but the simplicity of it is definitely their style.

Their songs are complete short stories and poems set to music.

... PAUL SIMON AND ART GARFUNKEL — INTELLECTUALS OF POP.

They aren't pop idols in the sense that young girls don't scream or faint at their appearance and they don't do many personal appearances because of Garfunkel's continuing studies and Simon's continuing search for material. It's almost as though Simon doesn't have time to stop and perform what he's already written because he's already on to new ideas and realities.

Paul Simon and Art Garfunkel have added a bit of class, a bit of depth, a bit of intelligence to the pop scene, and for that they deserve the respect so often denied people in the pop scene.

The Adventures of Robin Boyd

©1965 By Shirley Poston

Still not knowing whether the stranger was a boy or a girl, Robin flang her arms around he-she-and/ or-it and wept.

"I can't *believe* it," she blubbered thankfully. "A human being who wears bell bottoms and reads John Lennon books! *Here*, in the wilds of the hills!"

"Plains," corrected the stranger. Robin grimaced. "Would you believe plains without the *L*?"

The stranger larfed. "Otherwise known as getting the L out of the plains?"

"Amen"

"Amen," Robin breathed reverently. Suddenly she sobered (not as in up) (one can't have everything.) "I don't think I should be hugging you if you're a girl." Then she thought of George (of jealous Genie fame). "And I *know* I hadn't *better* be hugging you if you're a *boy*."

The stranger relaxed again. "Relax, I'm a girl. I just don't look like one because I wear my hair like Ringo, except for the sidies, of course. And also because I'm skinny and flagat chagested."

"*Hah?*" Robin inquired politely.

"That's Liverpool backslang," the stranger explained. "I'll teach it to you lagater. Anyway, my name's Budgie. What's yours?"

"*Budgie?*" Robin roared. "As in *big-fat-yellow?*"

"The same," grinned Budgie. "It's really Francine, but never mind about that."

"I know just what you mean," said Robin Irene.

Within two minutes, R. and B. were fast (I'll say) friends, and they were soon loping down the street, trading life histories while Ringo (as in Boyd) brought up the rear. (No comment.) (There are times when I don't trust meself.) (I should join a large and disorderly crowd.)

Budgie's past didn't take much telling. She'd lived *(lived?)* in Pitchfork all her life, and had admittedly been "a real saddle-shoe" until the summer of 1965. That was when she'd run away from home. She had made it all the way to Minneapolis, and before her parents had come for her with a long rope, she'd managed to sneak into a Beatle concert.

Toward Mecca

"And I've never been the same," Budgie finished, clicking her boot heels together and bowing gratefully toward the Mecca. (Actually, not having a very good sense of direction, she really bowed toward Crab Grass, Iowa, but that's another story.) (You hope.)

Robin then launched into *her* fascinating (as in *zzzzzzz*) saga. Course, she couldn't tell everything. If she started babbling on about her magic powers, she'd *never* get them back.

Dying to tell all about George, she exercised her will power (which sure *needed* the exercise) and settled for relating that she had a boyfriend back home who looked just like George Harrison.

Marched

After she had revived Budgie (although Pauley was *her* fave Beatle, Budgie felt obligated to honor the other three with an occasional faint), they marched on over to the Boyd house (literally, that is, while singing "Yellow Submarine" at the top of their ex-lungs) (try it sometime) (it can't hurt anything, you know—they've already decided to come for you.)

For the next two hours, they listened to Beatle records. Then Mrs. Boyd took off her galvanized ear muffs and asked Budgie to stay for dinner.

When her kind (of unavoidable) invitation had been accepted, Robin's mother went to the telephone to dial "Chicken Delight," but since the nearest location was in Cincinatti, and the food would probably be cold before it arrived, they ended up having more hot dogs.

After din-dins, Robin and Budgie went for a long walk in the country. (The town itself wasn't long enough to take a *short* walk in.) (But it should only take one of the same, off an even *shorter* pier.)

This was the first time Robin had ventured (not as in ad) outside the house in the evening, and she was amazed by the deserted streets.

"Where *is* everyone?" she wailed. "It's only eight o'clock!"

Budgie shrugged. "Home weaving samplers, probably."

"Creeps," Robin muttered.

"Not really," Budgie said after they'd trudged a few more miles. "Most of them are pretty nice. They're just out-of-it. I've tried to get through to them, but it's too big a job for one person."

Robin's ears stood straight up (which saved her the trouble of lecturing them about their terrible posture), and her eyes took on a familiar and fiendish glint. "I'll bet the *two* of us could . . ." she began.

". . . *liven them up!*" Budgie interrupted hysterically.

Only Alleged

"Liven Forest *Lawn* up if we put our alleged minds to it!" Robin added gleefully, not to mention modestly.

"*Crazzzzy!*" blared The Budge. "When do we start?"

"*Immediately*," Robin blithered. "As in forward *harch!*"

As the strains (I'll say) of "Yellow Submarine" once again carried across the endless prairie, a shivering deer and a half-frozen antelope paused at play. They couldn't be *sure* it was a discouraging word they were hearing, but it was sure close *enough*, so they decided to overlook their differences and honeymoon in Miami.

When R. and B. got back to R's house, B. called her folks and whined a lot until they agreed to let her sleep over that night. (Would you believe that *year?*)

Emancipation

Adjourning to Robin's room, they started making plans for the Emancipation of Pitchfork, but they were so tired from their frostbitten safari, they fell asleep instead.

Robin was deep in a perfectly marvelous dream about George when Budgie gave her a poke.

"Hey, Rob?"

"Yeah, Budge?"

"I don't wish to alarm you, but there's a Beatle in this bedroom."

Robin moaned sleepily. "The kind of bugs they have around *here*, it wouldn't surprise me if there was a *tarantula* in this bedroom."

Budgie started to explain that she didn't mean Beatle-as-in-beetle, but she needn't have bothered. Robin sort of got the general idea when she felt her arm being yanked clean out of the socket.

(To Be Continued Next Issue)

KRLA ARCHIVES

Americans Regain Pop Throne!

By Tammy Hitchcock

Say anything you want about the music business. Call it any name in the book. And no matter what you say, you'll probably be at least partially correct. But never call it predictable. Because it is not.

It's short hair, Frankie Avalon, buck shoes, Danny and the Juniors, the bop, the Kingston Trio, look alike stage outfits, "Puff The Magic Dragon," and the Twist. Then it's a long span of zero when nothing happens and slowly it shrivels up until something has to give. And suddenly it's long hair, Beatles, accents, "come as you are," and "watch out, world, the British are coming."

And come they did. The skeptical said it was a "fad." You can call it that—but it's a fad which has taken almost three years to kill. Today, only nine survive the British triumph. Only nine English artists today are on the nation's record charts.

Wide Open

Americans have broken the music scene wide open. The Four Tops made number one in England and the Beach Boys have knocked the Beatles from their British throne. New faces and old names have become neighbors on the charts. The Monkees, the Left Banke, Question Mark and the Mysterians have moved in next to the Four Seasons, Bobby Darin, the Supremes and Johnny Rivers.

The whole musical spectrum has spread itself out so that one no longer has to live in a specific bag to make it. Mitch Ryder is selling colored soul to a white audience; Johnny Rivers is selling pretty music to the jet set; Tommy Roe is selling Mickey Mouse songs to somebody; the Association sold harmony to everyone and then switched to Gregorian chants; The Mothers smell bad but have a loyal following and a booster in the form of Eric Burdon. Electronic music sells but then so does "Born Free."

The ratio of long hair to popularity has narrowed so that ears are safe to show again. Long hair is still most definitely "in" but it is no longer a prerequisite to record sales. American audiences have matured sufficiently to judge records and entertainers on talent rather than appearance. The general attitude is "wear what you want, look grubby or clean—but have talent to back you up."

Rhythm 'n' blues, be it "commercial" or "straight," is now an integral part of the pop scene. Performers other than those from the Motown stable are appearing on the pop charts. James and Bobby Purify, J.J. Jackson and Lou Rawls ride next to the Supremes, Four Tops, Miracles and the Temptations.

Andy Warhol's Plastic Inevitable was a marvelous idea but turned out to be an experience rather than a habit. The curious flocked to see the light shows and underground movies and having satisfied their curiousity never returned. But their psychedelic musical counterparts have remained in a limited capacity. They probably won't take over the world but they'll rack up impressive sales at cash registers while they last.

It is only fitting that the four men who launched the British attack have announced that they will no longer make personal appearances. With the Beatles officially declaring themselves out, speculation turns to the Stones who have been strangely silent these past months. While the Stones' American visits have been naturally limited, up until now, they have managed to keep themselves in the news by simply allowing Mick Jagger to open his mouth. Tact was never his virtue but his lack of it was an effective way to make sure the Stones were on the controversial side of the fence. The Mouth has not uttered a controversial statement since he left the U.S. last summer.

The third part of the triumverate, Herman, never was too controversial but he offset his lack of headlines by making frequent visits to the U.S. . . . Herman obviously does not intend to sink with the ship and is, therefore, currently touring Stateside again.

Eric Burdon has emerged as a star in his own right by weathering his "Animal storm" on the sheer strength and determination of his own personality. He took his professional life into his own hands by dumping his group but won the gamble when "Help Me Girl" was released. Ironically enough, the record promises to be one of his biggest sellers despite the fact that it followed immediately on the heels of his announcement that he was turning hippy and would soon be dumping his "second Animal brigade."

Broken Rules

Everywhere you look, rules are being broken and dissenters are coming out ahead. The Lovin' Spoonful are nationally popular despite themselves. Their total disregard for convention causes people to shudder and yet they turn out hit after hit. The law of the music business decrees that in order to be successful one must not stagnate in one part of the country. Move out and conquer new lands. The Spoonful don't believe it for a minute. They practically hibernate in New York, leaving for a tour only when they are forced to. Their fans are hardput to remember exactly when they last saw the group "live." Yet, the rain keeps falling on the roof.

However, "stay at home" is not the order of the day for all performers. The Raiders tried staying put and that is exactly where their careers stayed. They took to the road and now they're a top group.

With new groups and single artists coming on strong, oldies refuse to be left out. And comebacks are officially "in," especially with Bobby Darin and Tommy Roe. Darin is, admittedly, an extremely talented performer. He broke into the business via the teen market, then moved on to capture the adult audiences. He spent a good many years raking in the money in the nation's top adult clubs. Then "If I Were A Carpenter" and Bobby's back selling records to the teens.

Tommy Roe dates back to "Shelia," "Everybody," and then a lot of years of nothing. He was all but forgotten when out of nowhere came "Sweet Pea." A catchy but definitely Mickey Mouse sound. Tommy knew the hazards involved in falling into a Mickey Mouse bag but he took his chances with a girl named "Hazel" and made it two hits in a row.

Anything Goes

And so goes today's scene. It's as mixed and wide-open as it can possibly be. It's the long hair and "wear anything" Mama's and Papa's; the studio made, session-musician-aided Monkees; the suit and tie, harmony conscious Association; Frank Sinatra's "Life;" the surf, hot-rod, vibrations of the Beach Boys; the cool soul of Lou Rawls; the strings of Johnny Rivers; the old vaudeville sound; the psychedelic world of Frank Zappa; and the good time of the Lovin' Spoonful.

What's to come tomorrow? A change. But a change to what no one knows for sure.

...GOOD TIME SPOONFUL

...STRINGS OF RIVERS

...HIP MAMA'S & PAPA'S

...MICKEY MOUSE OF ROE

...MUSICIAN HELPED MONKEES

KRLA ARCHIVES

PICTURES in the NEWS

BILL COSBY has been awarded an entire month by Warner Brothers' Records in honor of Bill's recent great achievement for winning four Gold Records.

JOHN LENNON'S FINISHED his solo movie stint and is now back in London.

SONNY AND CHER ARE spearheading an innovation in recording techniques by hiring ten non-professional young people to sing background for Cher's latest single, "Mama."

HERB ALPERT grossed $221,685 in a seven-performance concert tour but played during halftime at USC-Notre Dame game for nothing.

RAY CHARLES was fined $10,000 and given a five year suspended sentence on a narcotic charge to which Charles pleaded guilty. He was place on four year probabtion.

TEEN PANEL
Unidentified Flying Objects: Yes Or No?

In this issue, teenagers talk about what everyone else seems to be discussing these days — the possibility that UFO's may actually be visitors from outer space.

The following is a number of teen opinions on this subject, gathered by a roving BEAT reporter. Stay tuned to The BEAT for a teen panel session on this same subject soon.

If you would like to participate on this or other future panels, or would like to suggest a possible topic of group conversation, please send a postcard to The BEAT.

* * *

P.L. (15) — "It would be easier for me to believe this if it weren't for the type of person who goes around saying there's life on other planets. Most of these people are nuts, I hate to be classed with them."

Not Probable

W.H. (18) — "It's possible that 'flying saucers' are space ships from other worlds, but it's not probable."

D.S. (17) — "I just heard about a group of people from California who went out into the desert and actually 'communicated' with space ships. They couldn't see or hear them, but they just 'knew' they were out there, and were able to communicate. Not with words, with thoughts. Hundreds of people went. It was some kind of convention. I'm beginning to wonder. Maybe something *is* out there. How could that many people be crazy?"

J.P.(15) — "We're making a joke of UFO's and we shouldn't. It really burned me when I read that the Byrds took out an insurance policy just in case someone out there took them up on their invitation in the song "Mr. Spaceman." It makes the whole thing sound like a joke and it's not. It's not funny. Who are we to say there couldn't be other civilizations or cultures? If there are, they must really be laughing at us. We just don't know, that's why we have to joke. Underneath, a lot of people are really worried."

L.H. (14) — "I used to wonder about flying saucers until I saw a TV program that showed new inventions like planes that rise straight into the air and wild-looking contraptions that really look like something from another world. If I'd seen one of those things in the sky instead of on television, I'd have started yelling 'flying saucer!' I'd have started running, too. Everyone should see these films. It's the people who don't know about the latest advances who get all shook up."

T.G. (19) — "I saw a flying saucer, or a flying *something*, when we were on vacation in the Mid-West a few years ago. It was at night and a very bright light crossed the sky from horizon to horizon in just a matter of seconds. It was followed by a weird sound and a sudden burst of wind. I called the airport and they admitted there hadn't been any scheduled planes in the area, but they hadn't seen what I saw, and they just laughed. I didn't laugh and I'm still not laughing."

W.M.(16) — "There's so much government hush-hush about UFO's, no one really knows the whole story. They're afraid people would panic, and they probably would. If the objects are from other planets, then they're far more advanced than we are, and should have enough sense to stay home. I wouldn't blame them for coming around, though. It must be interesting for them to watch us destroying ourselves."

Friendly

F.W. (16) — "If they're out there, they're friendly, or at least peaceful. They've proved that by not attacking us. I don't think they exist, but if they do, I'm not afraid of them. They're centuries ahead of us scientifically, so they must be as far ahead personally and aware that war and fighting solves nothing."

D.D. (15) — "I'd give *anything* if a space ship would land right on my front lawn. The whole thing just fascinates me, and I'd love to see it with my own eyes. I think more people are feeling this way — more curious instead of terrified. If life does exist on other planets, I don't think they'll land on earth until enough people calm down. If they didn't wait, a big hysterical scene would develop. But when they do, I sure hope they land at my house. I feel the same way about nuclear warfare. If they drop a bomb, I hope it falls on me because I don't want to live in the kind of world that would let a thing like that happen."

G.Y. (18) — "The saucer scare is nothing but a farce. It's a way for people to amuse themselves and occupy themselves so they won't have to cope with reality. Look at TV — many of the popular shows are fantasies. It's just a way of adding a little color and excitement. It's easier than trying to change their dull little lives on their own."

R.K. (17) — "I'd rather not even discuss the subject. If enough kids say they don't discount the possibility of visitors from outer space, people are going to start equating flying-saucer-nuts with teenagers, and that'll give them another reason to put us down. They forget that this generation is actively involved in science at school, and that we're more aware of the subject. It's something new to them and it's just a part of life to us. Sure there might be life on other planets, but you say that and you're immediately branded as a kook by people who are too set in their ways to let new ideas penetrate."

Space Pilot

J.S. (16) — "My father is interested in UFO's, but he doesn't go overboard about it. He has a friend who swears he's actually seen a transcript of a conversation that the government had with a space ship 'pilot' years ago. He says — my dad's friend — that this information hasn't been released to the public for obvious reasons. Everyone would get into a panic, and we have enough problems already. Other things like this have happened, but we never get to hear about them. This particular conversation wasn't very informative because it was so hard to hear what was being said, and the person (or whatever) could speak only a few words of English. But communication was made, *verbal* communication, and the person didn't speak with an accent that was recognizable from any language or dialect we have on earth. I know this sounds completely ridiculous, but this man has a doctorate in the space field and he knows what he's talking about. He's not a weirdo, either. I'm getting very interested in all this myself."

R.J. (15) — "This subject is just like religion. No one can prove there's a God and no one can

Like Religion

prove there isn't. It's the same with UFO's. Unidentified Flying Objects do exist, but no one can prove they are or aren't from outer space."

T.N. (19) — "I read where people have almost destroyed the property owned by some man who says a space ship landed near his home. To me, that's a lot crazier than believing in little green men. I hope there is life on other planets. Maybe they can give us a few pointers."

G.L. (17) — "Some of my best friends are from outer space."

KRLA ARCHIVES

...MUSIC MACHINE TALKING ALL THE WAY TO THE BANK!

Music Machine: Grim Or Grinning?

By Rochelle Reed

They're a grim-looking group. They dress in all-black, wear one glove apiece and their dark hair is cut in similar bowl-like styles. They've yet to give a toothy grin.

But the Music Machine, who sing that "my name is really Mud," have that pie-in-the-eye smile and for a good reason! Their recording of "Talk Talk," until now just a California coast hit, is growing into a nationally popular disc.

Just this week, "Talk Talk" debuted at 100 on U.S. music charts. Reminiscent of Stones-Yardbirds-Who, the recording might very well hit the top 10 if California tastes are an indication of national trends.

So now that the Machine is starting to make it really big, BEAT has been receiving anxious inquiries saying "tell us more!" And here goes:

Sean Bonniwell is the lead vocalist and master of singing "Oh ...ooohhh...OOOOHHHH" at opportune moments. Born Thomas Sean Bonniwell on a Friday morning in 1942, he is a native of San Francisco. Sean is the leader of the Machine as well as writer of the group's material. He plays rhythm guitar, organ, trumpet and bass. If this seems like a heavy load, Sean disagrees. He loves activity and says, "the more you have to do, the less trouble you get into."

Keith Olsen entered rock 'n roll via the Jimmy Rogers bag, for whom he used to play bass. Through Rogers, he met Chad and Jeremy who in turn introduced him to Gale Garnett. She hired him on the spot.

Unfulfilled

Keith says he enjoyed his early years with Rogers and Gale but felt unfulfilled as an entertainer and musician. He found his notch, with the Machine he says and adds, "the group's standards are so high it takes all the dedication and hard work in me to keep up with the high ideals that make the Music Machine."

Though Keith's statement may sound a little syrupy in print, the Minneapolis-born musician (1943) really means it.

Ron Edgar, like Keith, was born in Minneapolis but a year later (1944). Ron sarted out playing drums in the jazz bag and spent several years studying percussion techniques and playing with jazz bands around Minneapolis. He met Sean in 1962 and decided to join the Machine.

"I thought I had found my direction in jazz drums," he says, "but something was missing. I know now that that something was belonging to a unit with a direction. In the Machine, I find a sense of contribution, dedication and a feeling that's kind of like being the axle of a wheel. That wheel works hard, and I'm happy to be a part of it."

Mark Landon, 22, shares Ron and Keith's regard for the Machine. "I've played lead guitar before, or thought I did anyway," he says. "When I joined the group though it wasn't long before I discovered what was expected of me. For the first time in my life I knew what dedication meant. I found out what it means to feel pride in my work. The Machine has changed my life, and it's great."

Unusual Life

Mark has an unusual life to change. Born Mark Zarret Landon, he is of Russian descent but came into the world (of all places) in China. Possibly because of his background, Mark has many varying pleasures and dislikes. He always has something to say, and usually knows what he's talking about. An excellent drummer, he's also fairly easy-going, something which attracted Sean. Mark was only in Los Angeles a short time before Sean drafted him into the Machine.

Doug Rhodes, born in Palo Alto in 1945, is sometimes called "Dusty." You name an instrument and he can play it. He concentrates on organ, harmonica and flute for the Music Machine, but occasionally pulls out guitar and bass as well.

The rest of the group call Doug "The Old Chord Master," a nickname Sean pinned on him after he began dissecting Sean's chord changes.

"It can't be done," he says, "I never know what's coming next." As for the Machine, he adds, "musically it's refreshing, and the demanding standards are challenging and rewarding."

Though Sean, Keith, Ron, Mark and Doug may think of themselves as a Machine, it's in name only. Like a tree, they have the internal unity it takes to make a hit.

Rawls 'Live' At Tahitian Recalls 'Death' In Florida

By Louise Criscione

Lou Rawls was definitely "live" on the floor of the Royal Tahitian as he opened a week-long stand at the famous Polynesian night spot. He had only a piano, a bass and a set of drums to back him up—but that was all he needed as he cleverly induced his audience to applaud, to laugh and to clap along with the "blues" singer who spent five years in the "up and coming" category.

"I don't ever want to get too far away from the blues," Rawls told his standing-room-only audience so no one was surprised when his cool soul burst into "St. James Infirmary." But when he easily switched to "On A Clear Day" and then into a beautiful rendition of "The Shadow Of Your Smile" he set the capacity crowd into frenzied applause.

Encore

For well over an hour, Rawls entertained with his boyish charm, his quick wit and his tremendous voice. It was only natural, then, that the audience refused to let Lou leave the stage—so, with deafening applause and shouts of "more, more" Rawls returned for an encore and immediately launched into his famous "Tobacco Road" monologue. It was then that the audience had a hard time deciding if it should laugh or cry.

If you've never heard it, Lou does at least fifteen minutes on the "Tobacco Road" which is situated in Chicago. It's where Lou was raised and the "Road" that he knows the best. When he speaks of the poverty located on Chicago's South Side, he does it in such a way that your natural instinct is to laugh. But what he is saying is not funny—and if you were to analyze it you can almost hear Rawls say: "Let my people go."

During the press conference following the show, Lou was asked whether or not he was bothered by people laughing at the satire in his "Tobacco" monologue. "It doesn't bother me because people who accept it as a comedy skit really don't want to accept it as reality.

"They look at you like this," continued Lou, wrinkling his nose and appearing about nineteen, "then they pick up the papers in the morning and see it all over the front page. And they still ask me, 'Hey, man, is that true?'"

"Dead"

Before coming into the solo spotlight, Lou spent time working with the Pilgrim Travelers, a famed gospel group. In November, 1958, he was leaving a gig in St. Louis at 3 a.m. when he was seriously injured in an auto accident which left him "dead for five days."

When Lou was released from the hospital, he had no memory at all but his manager, J.W. Alexander, insisted that he continue performing. "I was on stage in Hollandale, Florida, singing 'Over And Over' when I came to my sense," recalled Lou. "That was weird! I had a bandage on my head and my hair had all been shaved off."

After listening to Rawls on record and then seeing him perform "live" the question was presented as to why he chose a small back-up group for his performances. "I personally prefer a small band," answered Lou. "It gives me more freedom. With a big band you lock yourself in—too much freedom then leaves you completely outside."

Not Talking

Lou was every bit as impressive at the press conference as he was on stage. It was something of a special night at the Tahitian as roughly 20 high school editors and reporters were invited to Lou's opening. At the press conference, they were, perhaps, a little awed at being so close to Lou or perhaps it marked the first real press conference for many. At any rate, they seemed unable to find many questions to ask Lou—so he did a turn-about and questioned them!

In fact, Lou became so enthralled in talking to the teenagers that he had to almost be physically dragged away for the second show! Even as he was leaving, Lou kept turning back to talk to the students in an attempt to thank each one of them personally for coming. Over and over, he was heard to say: "Thanks for coming; I hope you enjoyed the show."

He had to be kidding, of course. How could anyone help but enjoy the kind of show Lou Rawls puts on? Unless you were blind and deaf, that is.

...LOU RAWLS — COOL SOUL OF "ST. JAMES INFIRMARY."

BEAT Photo: Earl Fowler

KRLA ARCHIVES

DISCussion
By Eden

My pick of the week this column has got to be the new rendition of "Hey Joe," recorded by Tim Rose. He sounds like a cross between Hoyt Axton and Barry McGuire (if you're ready for that!), although it is entirely possible that behind this gravel-voiced balladeer lies a beautiful voice.

The lyrics to this song have never been outstanding representatives of thought or communication, the tune is certainly not one of the most beautiful – but this new version is absolutely great. The record has a great "feel," and there is a definite emotional appeal in the arrangement as well as an excellent drum background. This one has to be a hit.

* * *

Another surprise hit this week comes to us from the Monkees. These boys are not reknowned for their true music abilities or creative talents, however they have come up with their best release to date.

"I'm A Believer" is, first of all, a great song – thanks to composer, Neil Diamond – and the Monkees have a very good arrangement going for them, as well as some excellent A&R work (compliments of Dave Hassinger) aiding their efforts. Most surprising thing of all is that they have even managed to get a little bit of *soul* into the disc.

My only regret is that it wasn't recorded first by the Beatles, who could have really taken care of business, or perhaps even its author, Neil Diamond, who's in charge of the corporation in the first place!

* * *

Have to admit that there are a lot of *"Good Things"* going on this week, and aside from the Raiders' hit of the same name, watch out for a beautiful tune called "Miranda," written by Phil Ochs, recorded by the Gentle Soul.

'VIBRATIONS'
(Continued from Page 6)

Immediately seeing the error of his youthful ways, Brian G. agreed and said: "C'mon David Carrot, let's go find that celery!" And suddenly from deep within, Michael Spinach encouraged: "Hurry up, man – find that celery and eat it. I'm *lonely* in here!"

Brian burped compassionately and exclaimed: "We've got to get *out* of this tomato!"

PART II

Brian uttered, "Ooops – I just fell into your swimming pool, and the fact that I have on a Super Face Mask and a pair of Pro Swim Fins is merely *happenstance!*"

Just then, Hal Blaine vigorously beat a blue-eyed path to the swimming pool and pointing doggedly at Brian Gemini screamed: *"Get out* of my Chicken Soup before I get sore and call the cops!"

So, watching the nice looking young man (whose hair was always combed neatly in place) Brian thoughtfully went like this: "OK – let's hear that one more time, but a little bit *louder* this time. And, hold it *right there* while I call Guy Webster!"

PART III

– THE END –

Some Things are Nice to Have Around...

things you feel "at home" with

...the Utility™ ball pen

A good, practical pen for students. Fashionable, too.

There are twelve brilliant colors.

The color of the pen is the color of the ink.

Lots of students buy two or three at a time. Maybe because it's only 39¢

Maybe because it writes nice.

Or maybe they just like to have two or three or twelve around.

Lindy®

 manufactured by LINDY PEN CO., no. hollywood, calif. 91605, u.s.a.

KRLA ARCHIVES

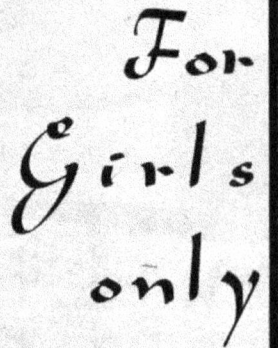

For Girls only

by shirley poston

Welcome to Blither Junction. Before I start raving on (I've ever *stopped?*), must tell you that Judy Mancz has done it again! If you recall, some time ago she illustrated a whole chapter of Robin Irene Boyd. Well, she's done it again! (Oh, I already said that.) (Which figures.)

Two problems ensue. How to ever thank her for sending me these fabulous goodies. How to manage it so all of you can have a look at them. Will start working on solving both instantaneously!

Another thank you. To the girl who sent me the poem she wrote about "Mortie The Camel." I hope you won't mind, but it was so hilarious, I just had to send a copy of it to someone who seems to have "influenced" your writing (not to mention mine.) Namely, Big John. (As in Lennon.)

Unfortunately

I think I mentioned previously that I know someone who knows him quite well, and since that someone just left for England, I sent "Mortie" with him. Unfortunately, I can't print the poem here. It isn't bad or anything. It just discusses another of the many subjects adults don't think we know about, and why shatter our C.C. (as in cool, calm) image, I always say.

Oh, more thanks. This time to everyone who answered my question about whether there is or isn't a Beatle record called "Sweet Georgia Brown." There is! It's on a British album (one I've never even heard of) (do you ever get the feeling that I just got off the boat?) (as in, what's up, dock?) (Gawd) ... anyway, the album is called "The Amazing Young Beatles." Just as soon as my keeper will let me out, I'll see if it's possible to buy the album in this country, and let you know.

Re-Help!

There's another Beatle song I've been meaning to ask you about for centuries. Several times on the radio (guess what station) (plug, plug) I *swear* (I'll say) I've heard the Beatles singing "Shout!" Am I obviously out of my mind (never answer that question), or is this maybe a track from the same album or what? Has anyone else heard it? *Re*-help!

Speaking of the Beatles (which I hardly ever do) (not), I'm naturally a little embarrassed about the way I blithered in the last issue, but I did mean what I said, so I guess it's worth getting a little red around the gills when I think about it.

I shouldn't say this, but I'm going to. Not too long ago, I got about half mad at George P. Harrison. (Would you believe one-*fourth* mad?) I read one of his comments (in *The BEAT*) (*re*-plug, plug) where he said something about everything they (the Beatles) have done so far being "rubbish."

At first I thought, "thanks a lot, fella," on account of this doesn't say much for his opinion of my taste in music and/or men (as in him.) But I got to thinking about it, and I feel I know why he said it. Just from talking to a few people who traveled with the Beatles this summer, I've found out that George wasn't in what you'd call an ecstatic mood during the tour, and I can't say I blame him. At the time it's happening, a tour probably seems like a horrible drag, except for those few moments when they finally get to a stage and can do what they came for.

He was probably in a bad humor when he made the remark, and there's something else I'd never even thought of. Have you ever realized that none of the Beatles understand what they've accomplished? Sure, they know they've become huge stars and had hit after hit, but the accomplishments I'm refering (referring?) (I am an excelent speler) to is the difference they've made in *people*.

Feel It

In order to realize and understand that impact, you almost have to have felt it yourself. It isn't something you can explain, and it's too far inside for it to show on the outside. The Beatles know we scream for them, but I don't think they know the real reason why we scream. They couldn't possibly, because every scream has a different meaning, because it's coming from a different person.

Someday, for the Beatles' sake, I hope someone will put their impact into words, and explain to them how they not only changed us, but started something new that could change the whole world. So many of you put something like this on your letters to me ... "The Beatles Equal Love" or "The Beatles Are Love."

"I Wonder"

Well, I know what that means, and how it feels, and so do you or you wouldn't say it. But do *they* know what it means and how it feels? I really wonder. I don't think they do.

God, I hope someone will be able to tell them someday. Not just how *she* was effected. How *all* of us were. I think it would matter to them terribly.

Oh, Shirley, for crying in a pail, will you *stop* awready?

Remember the "stream of consciousness" games I was babbling about a few columns back? Well, here's a brand new one. I've already tried it and ... *zap!*

Say you're a George fan (I'LL SAY). Well, what you do is get yourself into a George mood. Then, while you're still thinking of him very intensely, think of a color. Then write down what flashes through your mind (alleged.)

To give you an idea, the following is what a friend of mine wrote down while thinking of John Lennon and the color red: "Two cigarettes glowing in the dark ... a small boy watching in wonder as the first sunset he's ever noticed scrubs a dirty city ... a shirt he wore once ... a color my mind sees when they won't let him speak his."

Man, how poetic can you get? My stream of consciousness thingies seem rather puny by comparison, but then, is anyone perfect? (I ask you.) (But, once again, do not answer!)

Anygoat?

Anygoat (just *kidding*) (oh, good *gagrief*), it's a fun game to play. If I ever get up the nerve, I'll tell you some of the stuff I wrote down about Gageorge (as in gageorgeous). I'm sure you're just *dying to hear them*. So, no doubt, are the postal inspectors.

Since I have been warned to keep this column down to sensible (by all means) proportions, and not gabble on for seven thousand pages, I'd better end this mess for now.

Yours for bigger and better heavy-duty jungle-weave nets!

...THE YOUNGBLOODS

The Youngbloods—Hair, Hunger And Harmonicas

They call themselves the Youngbloods and they have out a ridiculously original song called "Grizzly Bear," but when you get to know them you can't imagine how they ever got together much less stayed together.

There's Jesse Colin Young, dark haired and kind of off-hand handsome. The group collected around Jesse, but he says he is not their leader—they don't have one.

Jesse was a moderately successful folk singer and song writer, appearing in a Boston coffee house when a lean young man with a long mane of hair strolled in.

He was Jerry Corbitt and he gradually began backing Jesse on guitar and harmonica and even did a little singing with him.

"Jerry lives in a dream," says Jesse. "He *always* leaves his harmonicas on stage, and somebody *always* takes them and he *always* comes back and says, 'Hey, somebody took my harmonicas,' and he's *always* surprised."

The idea of the Youngbloods came nearer to reality when they met Joe Bauer, their polite and mysterious drummer.

"This little short-haired character from Memphis had just come to Boston looking for work," Jerry recalls. "He was hungry and we were hungry and that's how we got Joe."

But Joe was a jazz drummer, while the group was developing in a rock and roll direction with tinges of rhythm and blues. So Joe practically re-learned to play drums. "He sure learned good," says Jerry.

The group was completed with the addition of Banana (yes, Banana) who was originally a bluegrass banjo player but had lead his own rock group as guitarist and vocalist.

With the Youngbloods he took up another new instrument, the electric piano that has now become a major factor in the Youngblood's sound.

For six months the four worked and experimented together, then, with the aid and encouragement of their manager, Herbert S. Gart, and executives at RCA, they came forth with their first single, and started on that long, grueling road to success.

How Well Do You Know The Field Of Popular Music??

Test your pop knowledge by seeing how many of these questions you can answer correctly. Then brag a lot.

1. Jim Valley, now a member of the Raiders, was formerly a member of which of the following groups? (a) Dan & The Goodtimes, (b) Don & The Goodtimes, (c) The Syndicate of Sound.
2. There's quite a substantial rumor going around that the "voice" that appears behind Donovan on "Mellow Yellow" is actually (a) Eric Burdon, (b) John Lennon, (c) Paul McCartney.
3. The composer of "If I Were A Carpenter" is using this song as the back-up side on his own record (titled "Hang On To A Dream.") His name is (a) Bob Lind, (b) Tim Hardin, (c) P.F. Sloan.
4. Keith, the singer with no last name is actually (a) Barry Keefer, (b) Keith Allison, (c) Barry Keith.
5. Which of the following groups is now back together again? (a) The Dovells, (b) Dion & The Belmonts (c) M.F.Q.
6. Which of the following groups just had their first number one single in England? (a) Beach Boys, (b) Mitch Ryder & The Detroit Wheels, (c) The Four Tops.
7. What pop group warbles in Woody Allen's zany movie "What's Up, Tiger Lily?"? (a) Revere's Raiders, (b) Lovin' Spoonful, (c) The Left Banke.
8. Which of these groups now has the number one record album in the country? (a) Beatles, (b) Rolling Stones, (c) Monkees.
9. Tony Hatch produces Petula Clark's records and also helps her write many of her numbers. What relation are Tony and Pet? (a) Husband and wife, (b) brother and sister, (c) none.
10. Which of the following pop stars has been drafted and leaves for UncleSamsVille soon? (a) Johnny Rivers, (b) Neil Diamond, (c) Gary Lewis.

QUIZ ANSWERS

1–b (Don & The Goodtimes are now in Hollywood and should have a record out soon), 2–c (and the folks who are saying it's Paul in the background are people who should know), 3–b, 4–a (at least that's what his bio says, but he jokes about the name so much, we're beginning to wonder if it's for real after all), 5–b (Dion was with a group called the Wanderers a few months back, but is now back with the Belmonts of olde), 6–c (The Four Tops' "Reach Out I'll Be There" was number one in America, as well.) 7–b, 8–c, 9–a, 10–c.

KRLA ARCHIVES

KRLA ARCHIVES

America's Pop Music NEWSpaper

KRLA Edition BEAT

DECEMBER 31, 1966

25¢

happy new year!

KRLA BEAT

Volume 2, Number 31 — December 31, 1966

PROPOSED BEATLE FILM 'NOT ABOUT POP GROUP'

Don't look for the Beatles' forthcoming movie to change their new image.

Because, once again, the Beatles won't be acting like Beatles.

Film Producer Walter Shenson arrived in California last week and though reluctant to talk about the long-awaited flick, admitted "it's not about a pop group."

"For over a year I've looked at ideas from distinguished writers and playwrights, but Owen Holder's two-page idea was the only one I — and the boys — liked," Shenson said.

Shenson said filming would "hopefully" begin in February.

Jagger, Richard Sign For Million

STONES' MOVIE OFF?

Individual members of the Rolling Stones scored big financial victories last week but it now appears the group has suffered a final setback on its long-awaited movie.

While Mick Jagger and Keith Richard were signing a new $1,000,000 American writing deal, London sources were speculating on plans for "Only Lovers Left Alive" to be junked.

No Reason

The Stones were due to start work on the film last month, but no one could give an official concrete explanation for the delay. "As far as we know," said a spokesman for the British Film Institute, "the film has not gotten past the project stage yet."

Stones manager Andrew Oldham was unavailable for comment last week but a spokesman for Decca Records said: "The whole matter is surrounded by legalities. As far as we know, there have been no new developments."

If the movie has not been scrapped, it will probably be the middle of next year before filming begins.

Jagger and Richard, meanwhile, have continued to remain successful on their own. Their $1,000,000 contract, negotiated by Allen Klein, ties up the popular songwriting team for the next three years.

The guarantee against royalties was set through the Gideon Music firm in America. The Stones retain their British publishing firm, Mirage Music, which they own with Oldham.

Responsible for the bulk of the Rolling Stones major hits, Jagger and Richard will control all of future copyrights under the new deal. The guaranteed $1,000,000 comes in the form of advances.

Contrast

This procedure is in direct contrast to at least one other prominent case in which the writers involved, though obtaining the same guarantee figure of $1,000,000, actually surrendered the rights to their songs.

Jagger and Richard have been highly successful with material not only for the Stones but for other artists as well.

MICK JAGGER AND KEITH RICHARD are obviously happy over just signing a one million dollar writer's deal.

Beach Boys Lift Beatles' World Crown

Indications of the approach of an entirely new era were revealed when the Beach Boys replaced the Beatles as the world's most outstanding group in an annual poll taken by an English magazine.

The Beach Boys' victory marked the first time in three years the Beatles have failed to win the top position — and furthered America's claim as the pop citadel of the world.

The Beach Boys' drew 5,321 votes compared to the Beatles' 5,221. Despite losing their world crown, the Beatles drew an easy victory over the Rolling Stones for the most outstanding group in England.

The Beach Boys' victory wasn't entirely unexpected. The reaction they received on their recent tour of England was remindful of the furore caused by the Beatles several years ago.

But the Beatles haven't toured England for nearly a year and it has been months since their last release. The Beach Boys, meanwhile, sold more than 300,000 copies of "Good Vibrations" in England alone.

Had their emergence as the world's top group affected the six Californians? "The group was in good shape for what happened to them in England," said leader Brian Wilson, who didn't make the recent English tour.

"It is very inspring," he added. "It's a great lift to the group."

Brian said the award would possibly affect the respect the group commands, but probably would not alter their recording and stage performances.

"But," Brian concluded, "the guys are getting stronger and stronger."

Inside the BEAT

Monkees Win Third Goldie 3
'In' People Are Talking About 6
Beat Predictions for '67 7
Robin Boyd 10
Bill Cosby Shocks 'Em 13
World Of Brian Hyland 14
Four Tops In Action 15

Movie Script Big Decision For Monkees

The Monkees were already discussing plans for their first movie last week as they arrived back in California from their smash personal appearance tour of Hawaii.

Still in search of a suitable script, the boys agreed that after their unique TV series they would have to be highly selective.

"We want it to be as different a movie," said Micky Dolenz, "as the series was to TV. And we want to bring back a lot of the old Hollywood glamour and excitement with it."

The foursome first realized their national popularity when they were greeted by a mob scene on their first outing in Hawaii.

Back in California, however, Mike Nesmith admits the Monkees still have a way to go. He was refused admittance at Martoni's in Hollywood.

"I agree I looked kinda scruffy in a blue jean jacket and with this long hair," he said. "That's why I asked if we could come in. When they said no, we went to the Villa Capri!"

BEACH BOYS Mike Love and Carl Wilson meet the 4 Tops in London where both groups were on a smash tour

KRLA ARCHIVES

Letters TO THE EDITOR

BEATLE RIGHT TO MOVE

Dear BEAT:
Of late, there has been much controversy over the Beatles... are they lazy, arrogant, splitting up and so forth ad nauseum. I speak in defense of the Beatles and I speak for their right to choose the way of life that will make them happiest.

The impact of the Beatles on our new music has been, to say the least, profound. They ushered in a new sound and helped to pioneer and develop it. They have more than satisfied their fans and followers with one of the finest sets of records ever produced.

It is my belief that their latest album, "Revolver," was truly one of the great musical accomplishments of history, ranking with such as Orff's "Carmna Burana," Beethovan's "Ninth Symphony," the Congolese Mass "Missa Luba" and the glorious achievements of the Baroque and High Renaissance periods. Many people consider the record truly holy and beautiful. Many feel that the only way that the Beatles can excel their performance is with the production of a symphony or an opera.

In order to do this, they must have a chance to work in the media necessary for their own satisfaction. The Beatles have transcended the pop-rock world and have taken to themselves true stature as artists.

While the artist is bound to his public and to the spirit of his times, he is bound just as strongly to his artistic vision. And the truly visionary Beatles have as much right to the development of their art for their own fulfillment as have any of us.

I say that if the Beatles choose to part, to progress in the arts or in their personal lives as they will, the choice is theirs' and well-earned.

We owe them much, for they have brought joy and a new vitality to the music and literature of our age, and now is the time to salute them, wishing them well in whatever undertakings they may pursue.

Sebastopol James
Asst. Director of Festivals

THAT'S LIFE

Dear BEAT:
I, like everyone else in their right mind, am an Association fan. It was a year ago December that I first saw them. And for all their success I am happy to say that they are today still just as wonderful as they were that Wednesday when I first spoke with them.

Due to circumstances beyond my control, I must sadly state that they wouldn't remember me if they all fell over me at the same time. However, that's life.

I would also appreciate it if you would give a little public recognition to two people that are very close to the magnificent six. They are Gaye Beacom (fan club president) and Pete (their "band boy"). Gaye and Pete are two of the grooviest people in the world and it's about time that tribute was paid to the "behind the scenes" people.

Thank you and keep up the good work.
Maureen Sullivan

HAPPENINGS

Dear BEAT:
We would just like to let you know how great your paper is. When we hear rumors or stories about anyone (especially the Beatles) we don't worry – we simply wait until our copy of The BEAT arrives. Then we know for sure what's happening.

Although the whole paper is filled with interesting news of the pop world, the best feature is still Robin Boyd. Please give Shirley Poston our congratulations and tell her to keep up the good work.
Teresa & Mary Connor

STILL 'IN'

Dear BEAT:
I hope you print this letter for all the Beatle fans who think they are losing their popularity. I live in England and know for a fact that the Beatles are still the number one "in" group (and I think the stupid bloke that said they aren't should have her head examined.)

Shirley Poston's article (For Girls Only) was very touching and she really expressed the same feelings that I have for the fabulous Beatles and their breaking up.

When my American pen pal heard how popular the Beach Boys are over here, she said: "How could they be so crazy over such creeps?" I agree.

In my mind, as far as I'm concerned the Beatles will always be the number one group and no one can ever take their place.
Sally Jean Watts
London, England

P.A.T.A. MONKEES

Dear BEAT:
Once again I take pen in hand (which is certainly better than taking pen in foot) to write you with still more suggestions for P.A.T.A. – Monkee style.

People are talking about how differently people treat Davy from that time he came to California to promote "Pickwick" and only Tom Frandsen noticed him... How much Micky's changed since his days as Mike Swain, Missing Link, when he used to be "quiet" and admitted the type of girl he likes (college girl, 5'2", shoulder length blonde hair)... Mike's real opinion of wool hats... Saving old thread because Peter might have had a part in making it... How funny it is that a certain magazine spent four pages telling the world that The Monkees would never be as big as the Beatles ("synthetic") and then had an advice column called "Dear Monkees" in the same issue... Other people worrying about whether or not "The Monkees" would be cancelled when the show has sponsors until May and NBC never having been that stupid... Whether or not Peter is the real Midnight Skulker.

Please keep printing more things on the Monkees. They're groovy.
Linda Delker

BEAUTIFUL JOB

Dear BEAT:
It's hard for any true Beatle fan to realize and believe that they are really breaking up. I think Shirley Poston did a beautiful job of expressing her, and millions of other fans feelings, toward them and I'd like to thank her for writing it.

We used to think no one understood us, but I guess they do.
Candy & Friends

SUMMATION OF PROTEST

Dear BEAT:
I would like to get my two cents in about Simon and Garfunkel's new song, "Seven O'Clock News/Silent Night." I think this song sums up all of the protest songs. It is not loud and brassy like those of Barry McGuire and Bob Dylan and others. It very calmly places its points on the table, so to speak, so that you can come to your own conclusions. I think people get more out of this than those others.
Ken Moore

THANKS FOR...

Dear BEAT:
I love your groovy paper. Thanks for the fab stories and pix on the Association and Herman.

Please print some stories about my faves, Paul Revere and the Raiders, Joey Paige, Steve Alaimo, the Seeds and how about a feature on the Action Kids?

About the Beatles breaking up: if this is what will make them happy then their fans have no right to expect them to do anything else.

Keep up the good work and thanks.
Carl Janowitz

ASSOCIATION ANNIVERSARY

Dear BEAT:
First, I want to thank you for all of the groovy Association fans you have accumulated over the past year. It all started out approximately one year ago when you printed an article on the Association entitled, "Meet The Association – Agents of G.R.O.O.V.E." This, in my opinion, was a very good feature article, especially when the guys weren't even known, much less discovered!

I'm not on this to praise your paper or to write a bunch of rubbish just to get this printed – as it doesn't work that way. You have to be sincere and dedicated to get anywhere.

I do want to say that if you give a group of hard-working, honest, intelligent and, above all, talented guys (like the Association) a chance they are going to come up and be a group to be looked up to by people instead of looked down upon. You did this and did it by being sincere and dedicated.

They've come a long way since their high school dance and Ice Housing days. They deserve every bit of credit that they are getting. You're doing everything you can to see to this. I'm grateful and can vouch for all the rest of their Associated followers.

We love them for what they are. Their music and talent is just as much a part of them as their inevitably wonderful personalities. They're groovy and, let's face it, there will never be another group to compare with them and their ultrally warm sincereness toward their fans. They've got the integrity, intelligence and class that's going to keep them on top for a long time.

But mostly, I'd like to say to them: Success has changed a lot of people but I've spoken to you since then and it hasn't changed you in the least. Keep on grooving and don't let anything stand in your way. Russ or Terry in particular, if you by some chance happen to read this please remember me, I was at the Goldstreet that nite.
Barbra

ARE THEM THEM?

Dear BEAT:
Are Them Them or are they the Belfast Gipsies? I would like to know who really sings "Gloria's Dream." It's a very groovy song.

The teenagers here in Hanford had the pleasure of seeing Them perform in person. It was a very exciting show; Jim Armstrong even gave my sister his guitar pick. Van really belted out all the songs, he has real soul in his voice. There was no pushing or shoving – everyone behaved.

At the end of the show the boys were nice enough to stop and sign autographs on pictures of THEMselves which were in The BEAT. That's one issue of The BEAT that I'll treasure for the rest of my life. Here's hoping that THEM come back again.
Gloria Lopez

Them and the Belfast Gipsies are two different groups. However, three ex-members of Them are featured on "Gloria's Dream."
The Editor

FOR THE DEFENSE

Dear BEAT:
There have been many times I've wanted to write but I just never got around to it. Now I am mad – I feel I have to say something or I'll blow my mind!

My letter is actually to one Shawn Walker who wrote a letter entitled "Down With Associates." I would like to ask a question – Who is she (he) to judge anyone? I have seen the Association in concert many times and I feel they are fantastically talented.

I would like to ask another question – Did she (he) go into the concert with an open mind or did she dislike them before she even sat down?

It seems to me that the group, Terry Knight and the Pack, that she seemed to be endorsing, can't be too swift – I've only heard about them from letters in The BEAT. Their record can't be too fabulous, I've never heard it.

The Association, to my knowledge, has never said or implied that they "didn't like long hair." If you look closely, Shawn, you'll notice that three of the members have rather long hair – not terribly long but not short either.

Shawn, I understand the point you tried to make and it's terribly ridiculous. If you've ever met and talked to those six men you'd realize you can't help but love them. You don't feel like a fan, you feel like a friend.

They're very friendly, very talented and very original. Shawn, do you know any other group who has comedy, poetry and wears matching suits in their act – I don't. Also, do you know any group who stays after each and every performance to sign autographs for anyone who wants them? I don't.

Shawn, I sincerely hope that your favorite group, Terry Knight and the Pack, can make it as well as my favorite group, the Association, has. But I don't feel that you should judge and ridicule someone else to make your preference seem better.

Thank you, BEAT. I hope very much that you'll print this so that people will see my point of view and also in defense of the Association.
Linda Fergus

Linda, you'll be happy to hear that you were one of many who wrote in to defend the Association against Shawn's charge of "unoriginality." However, we do not have the space to print all the letters but we would like to thank you all for writing and assure you that each and every letter received is read.
The Editor

On the Beat

By Louise Criscione

Well, it finally happened. The Beatles are back together again in a recording studio in St. John's Wood cutting a new single and album! John's hair has grown back, Ringo has done away with his beard and George has shaved off his moustache. However, Paul McCartney is still hanging onto the moustache he picked up while on a safari in Kenya, Africa.

What a sense of humor Bill Cosby has. Disguised as a nun for an "I Spy" segment, Cosby wore the outfit over to the commissary and walked up to Sidney Poitier wearing a sign saying "If Sidney Can Win The Award, So Can I." Of course, Bill was going a step further than Poitier. In "Lilies Of The Field" Poitier only *helped* the nuns, he didn't *dress* like one!

Bill has been given a guarantee of $250,000 for a ten day concert tour and his stint at Harrah's in Lake Tahoe has been extended another week because the first two weeks have already been sold out. Too bad the man's so unpopular.

Scott "Thinking"

Scott Engle of the Walker Brothers has been having his share of personal problems lately (one of which almost cost him his life) so he checked into a monastery on the Isle of Wright to spend ten days "thinking and sorting out my life."

If all goes as planned, the Monkees will soon be as big in England as they are here in the U.S. At least, Decca Records is set to give them the same kind of build-up they received in the States. The Monkees' television show starts beaming in Britain the first of the year and, if at all possible, Decca hopes to get the English-born Davy Jones over for a British visit.

The quote of the week came from Lou Rawls. Said the man: "Don't worry about Sandy Koufax, he and Gabby (John Roseboro) can write a book called 'Kosher Soul.'" Not a bad idea — if not interesting, at least it would be original.

On the personal appearance side of the Rawls' picture, he's just been signed to play the Cocoanut Grove during April. The Grove would like to present the Supremes as well but the contract has not yet been signed.

...GEORGE HARRISON.

Elvis 'Til 1974

Those of you who consider Elvis Presley professionally dead will be interested in hearing that RCA has picked up their option on Elvis as an exclusive recording artist until December 31, 1974. Elvis, who has been recording for the RCA label since 1955, has continued to sell an amazing number of records during those eleven years and, surprisingly enough, his sales reached their peak during 1965.

Though Presley marriage rumors have been making the rounds since Elvis first wriggled his hips on national television, this is the first year that Elvis left himself wide open for rumor-mongers by signing his Christmas cards "Elvis Presley and Family." Of course, you can interpret that to mean his father, step-mother and step-sister but you can bet that those rumor people will have a hey-day with it.

The Spoonful and the Association should join forces more often. In a joint appearance in Chicago, the two groups pulled in a neat $47,000. Not at all bad for one stop on a cross-country tour, is it?

It's interesting to track down the performers who were teen idols before the Beatles came along. Frankie Avalon just opened in Vegas, Bobby Rydell just closed in Vegas, Dick Chamberlain is set for a stint on Broadway in the old "Breakfast At Tiffanys" which is now "Holly Golightly" starring Mary Tyler Moore, and Bobby Darin is right back selling singles to teens. What a difference a few years makes.

The Rolling Stones have forsaken Hollywood to cut their latest album in England. It marks the first time in a long while that the Stones have recorded in England and it leaves a nice question mark as to why they've decided to go back to the British studios which they describe as "inferior" to American studios.

...DICK CHAMBERLAIN.

Ho-Hum... Third Goldie For The Singing Monkees

When the Monkees go panning for gold it doesn't take them long to strike it rich.

They have a sort of ridiculous Midas touch when it comes to million-selling records. Their latest release, "I'm A Believer," has already been awarded a gold disc after only three weeks of sales.

If the Monkees ever release a single that amasses only 900,000 sales — and they haven't so far — it will be a catastrophe. Their first single and album were assured of gold awards with a record brevity.

Their first album sold so well, in fact, that RCA decided to withdraw all single copies of "Last Train To Clarksville" from the market. It didn't matter, because the disc had already sold 1,000,000 copies and the LP was selling more like a single than an album.

The album, "The Monkees," has been No. 1 in the nation since late October.

The monetary success of The Monkees' initial album prompted RCA to set back the release date on the group's second single. The response to "I'm a Believer" has been the warmest given a RCA disc since the peak of the Elvis Presley era.

And that would make a believer out of anyone.

MONKEES (l. to r.) Peter, Davy, Micky, Mike collect another one!

Hermits Edge Beach Boys For Top Disc

Herman's Hermits surprised a lot of people when their "No Milk Today" was voted the top pop song of Europe in a six-country pop jury. The Hermits' recording edged the Beach Boys' "Good Vibrations" for top honors.

The poll was taken on a European pop radio program that was broadcast into the six countries. The radio series called 1,200 voters in Britain, Scandinavia, Belgium and Spain.

Each of the participating countries presented several entries for the top award. "No Milk Today," which drew 391 votes, was one of Norway's entries while "Good Vibrations" was submitted by the Beach Boys' stronghold, England.

The top seven winning records were all English-language discs.

Rascals Take Quick Jaunt To England

The Young Rascals have just returned from a quick trip to England and France, where they performed on television and made several personal appearances.

The group also released their new single, "Too Many Fish In The Sea."

Government Wins 'Pirate' Opener

By Mike Tuck

In the first war between England and the pirates since Long John Silver terrorized the seas, the British government has won the opening battle.

No ships were sunk and no skull and crossbone flags were taken as souvenirs, but two pirate ships were ordered to exit British waters. The pirates, infuriated, say they'll be back to fight another day.

Mod Pirates

Modern pirates, as any hip Englishman will tell you, are the independent radio stations that operate from galleons just off the English coast. With only one state radio station in England, pirate stations offer the only pop music presentation in that country.

And that's why the majority of English youths are pulling for the pirates — not the British government — to win the current court battle.

The government holds the pirates operate illegally — that even though they aren't located in England proper they invade England's exclusive territorial broadcasting rights.

The courts took the side of the British government in the opening round of the confrontation. Radio 390 and Radio Essex were fined $280 each and ordered to shut down operations.

A plea by the prosecution asking for confiscation of the two stations' equipment, however, was denied. The court ruled it would still be too easy for the two stations to purchase new equipment and resume operations.

Subsequent statements by station officials confirmed the speculation.

Radio 390 station boss Ted Allbeury stopped transmissions but, said he will seek a high court order to overrule the first verdict. And even if this fails, he says he will resume alternate plans for broadcasting.

Until now, pirates could escape English jurisdiction by operating in international waters three miles offshore. The court's initial verdict, however, made this illegal.

If the appeals of 390 and Essex fail, the government should have no difficulty banning other ship-based stations operating in territorial waters.

The pirates own a large portion of the English listening audience. Radio 390 claims an audience of 4.8 million, while Essex is estimated to amass three million listeners.

Listener Response

The immediate court decision will give government officials a chance to see listener response — and the effect it has on England's lone legal station, BBC.

The station, long a rub with teens and pop musicians, is based on an easy music format. To lure teens, BBC officials have promised an all-music wave length, primarily pop oriented, to replace the pirates before Christmas.

But neither the pirates, teens nor the musicians union have endorsed the proposal yet. The war may be only beginning.

KRLA ARCHIVES

'66 WAS THE

...THE BEATLES ALMOST MADE A MOVIE

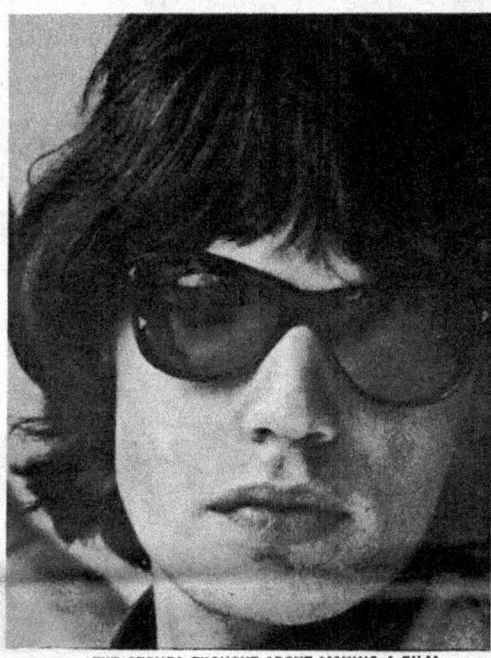

...THE STONES THOUGHT ABOUT MAKING A FILM

...THE BEACH BOYS CAME BACK—WITH WIVES

...THE MONKEES WERE CREATED TO THE DELIGHT OF MILLIONS

...ERIC DUMPED THE ANIMALS

KRLA ARCHIVES

YEAR THAT...

...THE MAMA'S AND PAPA'S OFFICIALLY ARRIVED ON THE POP SCENE

...SINATRA TURNED TEENY-BOPPER

...LENNON TALKED ABOUT JESUS

...GENE CLARK WENT SOLO

...NOEL HARRISON & STEPHANIE POWERS BECAME SPIES

...LEN ENDED A CAREER

...S/SGT. BARRY SADLER PROTESTED THE ANTI-PROTESTERS

...FREAK OUTS MADE THE POP SCENE

KRLA ARCHIVES

Band Plays, But Didn't Cut 'Cathedral'

RUDY VALLEE IS MAKING A MUSICAL COMEBACK, thanks to the New Vaudeville Band who have dusted off Vallee's sound. Standing (left to right) are Mick, Hugh, Neil and Henry. Bob "Pops" and Ian are sitting.

By Rochelle Reed

Did you see the New Vaudeville Band on television? Or maybe catch a personal appearance?

If you did, prepare to be heartbroken. The New Vaudeville Band that you saw did not record the number 1 disc, "Winchester Cathedral."

The number was actually cut in Britain by a group of studio musicians assembled by writer, producer and lead singer Geoff Stephens. But when "Winchester Cathedral" became successful, Stephens hastily collected what is now the New Vaudeville Band to take care of appearances and tours.

Actually, the result wasn't too bad and the band is definitely planning to issue their own release. In the meantime, raking in money from their tour isn't exactly unpleasant for the English lads.

Then too, having the nerve to admit you didn't cut a record when you're playing it far and wide is admirable, so maybe the whole "Cathedral" episode will turn out for the best.

Former Teacher

At least, Geoff Stephens is convinced that it will. A former teacher turned manager-producer, he was at one time manager to Donovan and has written songs for Peter and Gordon, Brenda Lee and the Spencer Davis Group.

Part of the reason for the conception of a song like "Winchester Cathedral" and its old-style "new beat" sound, was Geoff's own personal hang-up with exploring old junk shops. He reportedly has rambled around old record shops for years, seeking out obscure "junk" records from the 1920's and 30's.

His home in Southend, Essex, is also a tribute to his love for the Rudy Vallee era. It is brimming over with his "junk" collection, complete with an old wind-up phonograph from the period.

Stephens explained that when he cut "Winchester Cathedral," he just thought it was a "good time" sound but the success of the record has proven that his predilections about the musical style have been borne out by public acclaim for the "happy" sound.

Now that he has an actual New Vaudeville Band, Stephens says, "the public seems to like the Vaudeville kind of thing, so we'll probably do more and more of that."

Good Time

"We are aiming basically to do what I call modern good time numbers and some really old numbers," he added.

The New Vaudeville Band records on Fontana Records. Members are Mick Wilsher, Hugh Watts, Neil Korner, Henry Harrison, Bob "Pops" Kerr and Ian Green. All hail from England.

Vaudevilles Strike Gold

Vaudeville may have gone out with high button shoes but you'll have a hard time convincing that to the RIAA, the New Vaudeville Band or more than 1,000,000 people who bought "Winchester Cathedral."

The England export — the first for Geoff Stephens and crew — was certified a gold disc less than two months after it was released here. Fontana Records, which achieved its first million seller with the single, predicts a total sales figure of 1,500,000.

The "Winchester Cathedral" album has passed the 250,000 sales totals, with Fontana manager Lou Dennis optimistically speculating about the album's chances of reaching the $1,000,000 sales mark.

Dennis flew to Madison, Wisc., after hearing of the single sales mark and personally awarded the seven Britons the gold record.

'in' people are talking about...

How long it's taken the Beach Boys to earn a Gold Record when groups like the Monkees and ? and The Mysterians accomplished the feat their first time out . . . What the signature on Presley's Christmas cards was really supposed to mean . . . The Jagger rumor which made the rounds last week . . . Humbug buttons taking over the world or at least beating out the "Go Naked" buttons . . . How sick the "Bye Bye Gary" bit was . . . The Four Tops new one sounding like "Reach Out I'll Be There" revisited but being great anyway.

PEOPLE ARE TALKING ABOUT how long it's going to be before Herman says something really controversial and deciding the time is definitely drawing near . . . Whether or not the Beatles will stick to their "no more personal appearance" decision . . . How long it will be before England is officially "out" and thinking that, from the looks of things, it will be soon . . . Who is buying all those DC5 records and why . . . How well the Association came across on the "Andy Williams" show . . . The poor quality of some of the discs being released and wondering if the pendulum is finally beginning to swing the other way.

PEOPLE ARE TALKING ABOUT Mitch Ryder's offer to play the famous Apollo and how unfortunate it was that he couldn't do it . . . Why the Chairman thinks he must stick that trivia onto the end of every otherwise groovy record he puts out and trying to decide if he's insulting the teens or trying to pick up the adults . . . How much alike Mame and Dolly are . . . The communication breakdown with Roy and the Emperor's karate chop . . . Don Ho being suddenly "in" on the Mainland and Hawaiians are wondering what took us so long . . . Bringing Lou all their heartaches since he's on record asking for them . . . How much a full measure really means to the Spoonful . . . Tommy's recent obsession with the snow . . . Finally catching the knack and deciding it was a pleasant surprise except for the remark about Lee which was definitely in the poorest of taste . . . The family dog and wondering when there are going to be nationwide puppies.

PEOPLE ARE TALKING ABOUT what a renaissance the Association just turned out and how sweet it is . . . Now that we have Mustang Sally when we're going to get Camaro Sue . . . Peanuts, Snoopy and the sunshine Superman and thinking it's about time Beetle Bailey got into the act . . . How many groups are going to split before '68 makes its appearance . . . Blocked being the British term for the American high . . . Ray thinking that he doesn't need a doctor but the court thinking that he does . . . Trying to get some questions and answers . . . When the Happenings are going to record some new material and coming to the conclusion that as long as they continue to sell the old ones why should they turn hippy . . . What it takes to get a hit single nowadays and deciding that from some of the records on the charts today it doesn't take a whole heck of a lot.

PEOPLE ARE TALKING ABOUT how many promotion men are billing their up-and-coming groups as "the next Beatles" and how hilarious their cheek is . . . When the Grammy people are going to decide that rock 'n roll is music . . . Georgy not catching on like the Seekers hoped she would . . . What would happen if Arthur, Dink, Banana and an Electric Purne joined forces . . . Who the girl was who stood behind Bobby when he checked into the mirror yesterday . . . Money making the rounds yet again . . . What performer is finally going to make the break that he's been rumored to have made six months ago . . . Otis mixing in a little tenderness with his soul and possibly getting a smash . . . Monkee fans being, above all, believers.

PEOPLE ARE TALKING ABOUT what the Stones will pull to get back in the news — perhaps a cross-Atlantic swimming contest? . . . Question Mark and the Mysterians admitting that they need somebody . . . Whether or not Mark would lose his power if someone cut off his hair and deciding that it might be worth the risk . . . Knocking on wood and getting a hit record . . . Whether or not Tom Jones will join Motown and how groovy it will be if he does . . . Dylan making his presence known within the next month or giving it up altogether . . . What the hold-up is with Johnny . . . The Mama's and Papa's losing a bit of their instant impact and wondering if they'll come back in full force or move to the Carribean again.

KRLA ARCHIVES

The Beat Predicts
In 1967

- Sonny and Cher's movie, "Good Times," will finally be released and will spell either the beginning of a new phase or the end for the duo.
- The Beach Boys will continue to be influential.
- The Beatles will make no personal appearances in 1967, not even the fabulous offer from Sid Bernstein to play Shea Stadium.
- The psychedelic music fad will end but will be replaced by something almost as ridiculous.
- The new TV season will include at least a dozen imitations of "The Monkees," which will be dropped.
- Eric Burdon will change members of his group several more times before he finally realizes that he's a solo artist.
- Paul McCartney will reveal that he's married.
- There'll be personnel changes in the Yardbirds and Turtles.
- Dylan will come out of hiding and begin a new phase in his career.
- Motown will go towards good music, particularly with the Supremes and Stevie Wonder.
- Groups will start thinning out and solo artists will return.
- Rhythm and Blues will be *the* one big influence on pop music.
- The following groups will disappear from the scene after a short-lived success: Seeds, Music Machine, ? & Mysterians, Buffalo Springfield, Love, and the Count Five.
- Longer-lived groups who will vanish include the Byrds and Mamas and Papas.
- 1966 will be the last year of personal appearances by Herman's Hermits.
- Major hits will be put out by Mitch Ryder, Johnny Rivers, Eric Burdon, the Association, Sam the Sham and at least one all-girl group.
- The Sunset Strip in Hollywood will die for teenagers and will go back to an over-21 hangout.
- The real story behind Bobby Fuller's death will not be revealed, this year or any.
- Paul Simon will get married as will one of the Raiders.
- A tragic death will spell the end for one popular group and the draft will catch many American groups.
- Lennon-McCartney, Burt Bacharach, Bob Lind, Paul Simon, Neil Diamond and, of course, Dylan will be the major writing influences of the year.
- A member of a top female singing group will want to get married but won't.
- The Stones will severely cut back the number of personal appearances they do but will find some way of staying in the news.
- The Walker Brothers will return to America as they left — broke and unnoticed.
- And America will continue to ignore the great talents of the Everly Brothers, Roy Orbison and Gene Pitney.

FINAL DEATH for the Byrds

A MARRIAGE for Paul?   THE BEGINNING or the end?

STILL NO RECOGNITION from America for the Everly Brothers

IS THIS THE YEAR that Paul reveals that he's married?

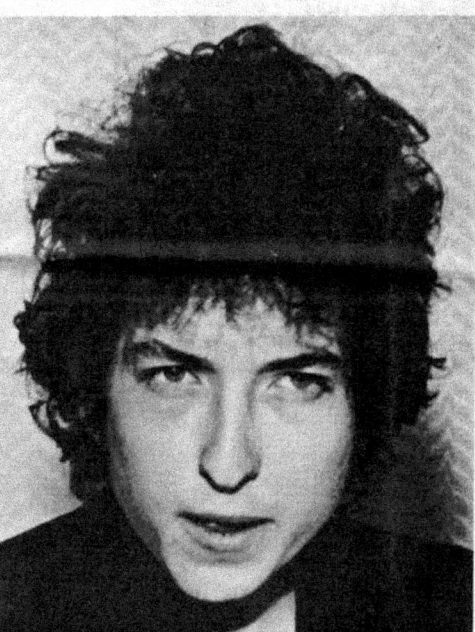

ANOTHER COMEBACK and another new phase for Dylan in '67

THE MIGHTY RIVERS will go on and on making hit records.

KRLA ARCHIVES

Top 40 Requests

1	I'M A BELIEVER/STEPPING STONE	Monkees
2	SNOOPY VS. THE RED BARON	Royal Guardsmen
3	THERE'S GOT TO BE A WORD	Innocents
4	BORN FREE	Roger Williams
5	LADY GODIVA	Peter and Gordon
6	I WANTA BE FREE	Monkees
7	FULL MEASURE	Lovin' Spoonful
8	GOOD THING	Paul Revere & Raiders
9	HELP ME GIRL	Eric Burdon & Animals
10	S.O.S.	Terry Randall
11	GOOD VIBRATIONS	Beach Boys
12	ECHOES	Gene Clark
13	PANDORA'S GOLDEN HEEBEE JEEBEES	Association
14	PUSHING TOO HARD	Seeds
15	DEVIL WITH THE BLUE DRESS ON	Mitch Ryder & Detroit Wheels
16	96 TEARS	? & Mysterians
17	HAPPENINGS 10 YEARS TIME AGO	Yardbirds
18	MELLOW YELLOW	Donovan
19	SMASHED, BLOCKED	John's Children
20	I NEED SOMEBODY	? & Mysterians
21	WINCHESTER CATHEDRAL	New Vaudeville Band
22	KNOCK ON WOOD	Eddie Floyd
23	YOU KEEP ME HANGING ON	Supremes
24	BUT IT'S ALRIGHT	J. J. Jackson
25	I GOT A FEELING	Neil Diamond
26	I'M YOUR PUPPET	James and Bobby Purify
27	HEAVEN MUST HAVE SENT YOU	Elgins
28	B-A-B-Y	Carla Thomas
29	THAT'S LIFE	Frank Sinatra
30	COME ROUND, I'M THE ONE YOU NEED	Miracles
31	MAME	Herb Alpert & Tijuana Brass
32	TOGETHER FOREVER	Viola Wills
33	I'LL MAKE IT EASY	Incredibles
34	STANDING IN THE SHADOW OF LOVE	Four Tops
35	TELL IT LIKE IT IS	Aaron Neville
36	EAST, WEST	Herman's Hermits
37	I KNOW I'M LOSING YOU	Temptations
38	WHERE DID ROBINSON CRUSOE GO?	Ian Whitcomb
39	WEDDING BELL BLUES	Laura Nyro
40	COMING ON STRONG	Brenda Lee

Inside KRLA
By Eden

Happy New Year, everyone, and may this year be the very best year ever for everyone in all of KRLA Land.

Everyone here at the station has been busy making resolutions for this brand new year, in addition to wishing their friends a Happy, and some of them are pretty impressive. The resolutions, that is.

Pat Moore resolved to get out into the sun a little more often, and maybe come up with a tan by January 7; Charlio resolved to be the Number One Blues Shouter and Soul Singer in all of the Land of 1110.

Bob Eubanks has resolved to give up potato chips and take up bare-backed bull riding, while the Caser has promised to go into toothpaste commercials as the All-American smile.

The Scuzzabalooer has resolved to toot on key from now on, and Johnny Hayes has sworn to have a fire in his fireplace at least five nights out of seven.

And Dick Biondi? Well, he's resolved to stay out of the glove compartments of Camaro's from now on! Happy New Year fellas!

There have been many guests to the station in recent weeks, including Sonny and Cher and Ian Whitcomb. Sonny and Cher have a brand new hit record out – written and produced by Sonny, as usual – and sung by Cher. Entitled "Mama" it is one of the most beautiful, and touching songs on the pop charts right now, and certainly one of the best ever from the sensational duo.

Speaking of Cher, by the way, I would like to ease your fears and reassure you that the station's management has definitely decided *not* to place a "Cher Wig" atop the proud head of KRLA.

Instead, we have succeeded in turning our "Sonny Bono Page Boy" into a "Bob Dylan Fright Wig" and everyone seems quite pleased with the results thus far.

Predictions for this Brand New Year Ahead? Well, I'll stick my neck out and say that it'll probably be pretty long (as years go!) at least 365 days' worth, anyway.

Charlio will sign an agreement to paint a frescoe of the Beatles on the inside ceiling of the DJ booth. And our favorite Bat Manager, John-John, will get a cape and learn to fly.

This year will probably see the wane and final death of the Byrds, along with at least a dozen groups of far lesser name and stature. Topping the talent and popularity polls by the end of the year will be The Beatles, The Stones, and The Yardbirds. On this side of the foam, Top Spots will be filled by the Beach Boys (watch out for the fabulous quintet; '67 is said to be "their year!"), Paul Revere and the Raiders (no stopping these talented nuts now!), and the Lovin' Spoonful.

Contemporary music will continue to grow and expand in scope and value during this next year, and so will the artists and performers involved in its creation.

In the very near future, for those of you who are sports-minded, the KRLApes will travel to John Glenn High School on January 4, at 8:00, and to Thousand Oaks High School on January 11, at 8:30. See you there.

For everyone in the Land of 1110 (and even those who are "out of it!") – thank you for making 1966 such a great year for all of us on The *BEAT* staff, and may 1967 return the gift to you tenfold. HAPPY NEW YEAR EVERYONE!!!

CHER — In, not on KRLA

WHAT A CRAZY WORLD — The Lovin' Spoonful's "Full Measure" is a large size hit in Los Angeles, but most of the rest of the world, including England, is playing the other side, "Nashville Cats," which hasn't even been heard much here. "Nashville Cats" is the side that's on the national charts too. If you've got the record, flip it over and hear what everyone else is listening to.

ATTENTION!!!
High Schools, Colleges, Universities and Clubs:

CASEY KASEM MAY BE ABLE TO SERVE YOU!

Let Casey HELP You Put On A Show Or Dance

Contact Casey at: HO 2-7253

KRLA ARCHIVES

Strip Of No Man's Land

The following is the first half of an opinion poll where teenagers give their views on the Sunset Strip controversy. Part II of this series will appear in the next issue.

The BEAT wishes to thank all of the teens who expressed their feelings to our roving reporter.

* * *

S.M. (17) – "The whole thing is stupid, and most people don't even know why it's happening. They think it all started because of the traffic problem. Well, most of the kids who hang around the Strip regularly don't even have cars. If there was a traffic problem, any more so than there is any place else on week-end nights, it was caused by kids coming in from other towns to cruise up and down — the way they used to on Hollywood Blvd. That and the droves of adults who came to have a peek at the freaks. It's happening because the big powerful property-owners on the Strip don't want the kids around any more, and figured that police harrassment would get rid of them."

Invited

T.W. (15) – "Kids didn't 'take over the Strip.' It died because adults stopped going to the high-priced clubs. So the club-owners tried something new and turned their places into teenage spots, and kids started going to the Strip. But, they were 'invited' to do so, and at first they were welcomed with open arms. The trouble didn't start until people realized these kids didn't have a lot of money to spend. I don't blame them for revolting against the way they've been treated. It's a pretty revolting situation."

R.B. (19) – "If the public knew some of the things the police or sheriffs or whatever they are have done to teenagers who've been picked up on the Strip, *everyone* would be out there carrying signs. The kids shouldn't have had to do the protesting. Their parents should have done it for them."

F.L. (19) – "Every time there's a controversy involving teenagers, the same thing happens. The whole thing is blown out of proportion and pretty soon the real issues get lost in the shuffle. This is what's happened with the Strip. The cops and the papers are trying to make it look like 'long hair' and 'narcotics' are the issues, and they aren't. You have to be up there to know what's *really* going on, and *why* it's going on. But if you *are* up there, you're automatically branded a kook and what you have to say doesn't matter. I could tell you a lot of things, but what good would it do? Who'd listen?"

H.K. (16) – "I think all this is proving something important. The police on the Strip are armed, and the kids aren't, but little by little, the kids are winning. This proves that words and non-violence are stronger weapons than guns and night-sticks. It takes longer to win that way, but it's worth it."

C.M. (15) – "I really don't know what I think about all the commotion. My folks won't let me go near the Strip, so I only know what I've read in the paper and seen on TV. I've only seen one side of the story. I'd have to hear the other side from the kids before I'd feel qualified to arrive at an opinion."

S.A. (18) – "The teenagers on the Strip are just being used as pawns in a power play. And public officials are using the situation to create more powerful images for themselves. If someone could only get all the kids together and show them how they could use the situation to *their* advantage for a change. The best thing they could do would be say 'forget it' and completely boycott the Strip. That would sure leave a lot of people standing around with egg on their faces."

E.F. (17) – "Teenagers have every right to be on the Strip, and I'm glad they're standing up to anyone who tries to take away that right. But I think they're going about it the wrong way. Demonstrations and marches don't help, because the American middle class, otherwise known as the majority, equates demonstrations and marches with nuts and kooks. They should protest in some way that might have a chance of swaying public opinion to their side. What way that would be, I don't know. I can't think of one. But as long as public opinion is on the side of the cops, the kids don't have a chance. And the more people the cops have behind them, the more carried away they'll get."

R.E. (14) – "These teenagers are acting ridiculous, but I don't much blame them. The other side is just as out of hand."

T.J. (17) – "Police harrassment on the Strip has been going on for months. I went there with my older sister quite a few times, and we were asked for I.D.'s every three steps. I got a kick out of it though, because my sister looks about 18 and is actually 24. Most of the times she was stopped, she was older than the deputy who'd stopped her. I think there are two reasons why everything erupted. The police went too far, and instead of trying to calm things down, certain people just stirred it up worse for their own personal gains. Don't forget, it isn't that long until the next election."

Ignorance?

R.V. (18) – "The 'controversy' is mostly just a lot of people talking about something they know very little about, which is usually the case with controversies. It's not really their fault, though. They should go and look for themselves, so they would know the facts, but most people either can't or won't do that. All they see are biased accounts in the papers. Very few writers are reporting the scene objectively."

T.H. (17) – "I was in a restaurant the other night and a guy at the next table was spouting off about the Strip and how they should lock up all the kids and throw away the key. He kept saying how different teenagers were in his day, and how much smarter and better, etc. Well, when he said 'We had *gentle* things in our lives,' I just couldn't resist. I leaned over and said 'yes, and we're celebrating the 25th anniversary of one of them tonight.' That sure shut him up. The date was December 7th."

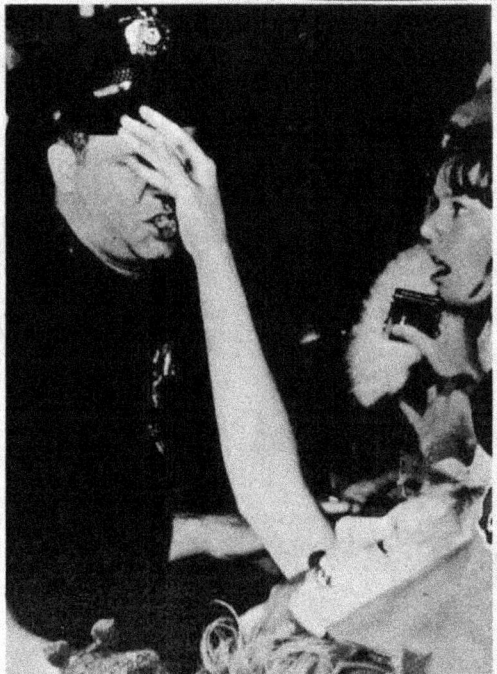
VIOLENCE DOES SOMETIMES break out between teenagers and police officers when teens feel their rights are being taken away.

THINGS ARE NOT ALL BAD — There are times when law enforcement officers and teenagers are on friendly terms as shown by this photo.

The girl with the most co-operative apartment in town **Any Wednesday**
An hilarious bed-time story.
(but not exactly for the kiddies!)
Starring JANE FONDA · JASON ROBARDS · DEAN JONES
Also Starring ROSEMARY MURPHY
TECHNICOLOR® FROM WARNER BROS.
EXCLUSIVE ENGAGEMENT
NOW PLAYING! PACIFIC'S HOLLYWOOD **PANTAGES**
Hollywood Blvd. at Vine
Crossroad of the Stars!
HO. 6-7161

THE NEW CLUB TROPICANA
247 E. MANCHESTER, L.A.

STARTING DEC. 16 **WES MONTGOMERY** **Limited Engagement**

TEENAGERS WELCOME *"Bumpin"* **For Reservations—758-7615**

KRLA ARCHIVES

The Sandpipers Are Following Herb Alpert's Good Example

By Carol Deck

1966 was a big year for three young men who are a rarity in the entertainment world, particularly the pop portion of that world.

Jim Brady, Mike Piano and Richard Schoff all have rather short hair, dress in suits, sports jackets or maybe a sharp sweater at their casualest, can carry a tune in 11 different languages and (or should I say but, in spite of all this) have had two hit records.

To look at them you'd never even place them in show business much less the top 40 field, but they are the Sandpipers.

They have a sort of novelty act—they can sing very well and have proven it with their first hit, "Guantanamera," an album by the same name and their second release, that highly unusual arrangement of "Louie Louie."

The three have known each other for over 10 years. They met in the Mitchell Boys Choir, to which they attribute all they have learned about singing, discipline, poise and every other phase of entertaining

Sopranos?

All three were boy sopranos in The Mitchell choir but as their voices deepened they began singing harmony and finally had to leave the choir in 1960 when they were all 16 and had developed their present voices.

A year after leaving the choir they joined together with a friend of Richard's, a songwriter named Nick Cahuernga, and decided to record some of Nick's songs under the name "The Four Seasons."

"But then the present Four Seasons came out with a few hits and that ended that," recalls Mike.

Nick decided to stick to songwriting then and Mike, Jim and Richard became the Grads.

Almost

They remained the Grads for almost five years and came close to having a hit with a song called "Their Hearts Were Full of Spring" in 1963.

In November of 1965 they decided to go back and visit Herb Alpert who had been interested in the group before but at that time his A&M records was just getting started and wasn't really ready to sign the Grads.

Herb was ready this time. He signed the boys and a search for material began. Their first recording for the label, like many _rst recordings, wasn't exactly a hit. It was titled "Everything in the Garden."

But A&M's producer, Tommy Li Puma, found a thing called "Guantanamera" on an album that Pete Seeger cut live at Carnegie Hall that Tommy thought might be right for the group.

The song was written in 1891 in Cuba and is of the Guahira type—songs workers sing in the fields.

But A&M then decided the group needed a new name. "How would it look if 10 years from now we're still the Grads," said Mike.

"About 15 minutes before the record went to the printing firm we picked the Sandpipers," they remember.

If you've seen them lip syncing the song on TV you realize that something is missing—like the female voices on the record.

There were four girls on the record and the guys now carry two girls with them on the road so they can reproduce the sound.

They followed "Guantanamera" with "Louie Louie," an old R&B standard, but they did it a new way—slow and pretty.

"We did it as a joke but everyone took it as just a nice pretty song," says Mike.

"Yeah, a lot of people don't know what we're singing when we sing it," adds Jim.

New Single

They're cutting a new single this week that should be out sometime this month or next.

The Sandpipers have worked hard at training their voices and learning the ropes of show business. They've had some great teachers and you can be sure these guys aren't just one or two hit wonders. They're talented guys and they're going to be around for a while.

"We're just following the good example of Herb," says Jim.

... JIM, RICHARD AND MIKE

The Adventures of Robin Boyd

©1965 By Shirley Poston

"George!" screeched Robin, as before Budgie's horrified eyes, the luvley (not to mention livid) Liverpudlian genie yanked his master - er - mistress - urp - client out of her trundle. "What are you doing here?" she added, retrieving her ex-self from the rug.

George glowered handsomely. "To coin a phrase, YOU MIGHT WELL ARSK!"

Snowbank!

With this, he gave an angry snap of the olde finger and the next thing Robin knew, the two of them were standing up to their respective eyebrows in a snowbank.

"George!" Robin repeated repetitiously (guess who knows what still rules), her teeth clacking out the finale of Ringo's (as in Boyd) fave droom solo. "I'm freezing!"

George snarled, re-snapped, and they were immediately swathed in Indian blankets which featured the Crazy Horse design (not to mention aroma).

"Hey!" Robin gasped. "I thought your magic powers didn't work in South Dakota! Did you get your transfer already? Didyah, huh? Didyah?"

George re-yanked. "I had to get another power loan, you twit-nit! And what's more, I had to take a bus from the border."

Robin suddenly fell senseless into the aforementioned snowbank. George was really here! Her George! But, where being without him had been a terrible problem, being with him was going to make things even worse. On account of because his arrival hadn't exactly gone what one might call unnoticed.

"The Budge!" Robin wailed hysterically. "The Budge saw you! How will I ever explain it?"

George hauled her to her feet (not to mention his). "Robin Irene Boyd! Forget about explaining it to The Budge . . . the whattttt? . . . and worry about explaining it to me!"

But Robin wasn't listening. "A dream, that's it, a dream," she rattled. "I'll say it was only a dream. No . . . she'll never buy that one."

"What did you just say?" George thundered. (Shortly thereafter, a nearby clump of cottonwoods was struck by lightning.) (Robin failed to pale as she was used to George's tantrums by now, but the situation sure shook the ell-hay out of the Lone Ranger and Tonto.)

"I said 'a dream, that's it, a dream'," Robin replied patiently. "Then I said 'I'll say it was only a dream,' After that, I went on to say 'no . . .'"

"SHURRUPPPP!" George interrupted. "I mean did you say SHE?"

Robin shrugged. "Sure, why?" "Do you mean to tell me that person is a girl?"

Robin puffed up defensively (not to mention offensively). "Of course she's a girl. What did you think she was, a . . . a . . ."

But she never got to finish the sentence (which was just as well because she couldn't think of anything clever to say) because she was too busy trying to pick up George (this is a newsflash?), who was now taking his turn in the snowbank.

Suddenly, Robin saw the light and flang her larfing genie back into same. "You wretch!" she shrieked. "You thought . . . you had the audacity to think . . . what kind of a girl do you think I am?"

Hysterical

Fortunately, George was still too hysterical to answer her question with a rousing "I don't think, I KNOW!" But that didn't stop Robin from pouncing on him furiously. (For those interested, him furiously is located very near him . . . oh, never mind.)

"I couldn't see you clearly because this am-day place is so far away," he panted as Robin rolled him furiously (I said never mind) in the snow. "So I made a mistake! So kill me!"

"An excellent suggestion," Robin seethed, flinging flakes down the back of his former neck. Then something stopped her short. (Or was it her long?) (Whatever.)

"Lots of people make that same mistake," she admitted grudgingly. "It's because of the way The Budge dresses, and her being sort of skinny and flagat-chagested . . . that's Liverpool backslang," she added helpfully.

"No kidding." (George did not say this kindly.) (Nor, if the truth were known, did he say kidding.)

"Oh, George," Robin simpered. "Even if you did spy on me like a suspicious sneak, and even if you do have a thoroughly vile mind, I'm sooooo glad to see you!"

George gave her one of his (in) famous looks. "How glad?"

Robin returned the look. "This glad," she answered, re-pouncing. and, within seconds, the snowbank had melted.

When Robin got back to her trundle, which was all too soon because George had to return to California before his power loan ran out, The Budge was snoring blissfully. But Robin didn't join her friend in Sand-Man-Land (oh comma barf) for quite some time. Instead, she stayed awake thinking about something George had come up with.

When she'd told him of the problem in Pitchfork (as in square is not the word) and bellowed that the town didn't even have one single rock-and-roll band, George hadn't been the slightest bit sympathetic and had made this simple suggestion: "So, start your own."

Well, simple WAS the word. Not only was Robin's musical talent somewhat limited. (There were times when she had trouble playing the radio.) So was the supply of music instruments. (Would you believe Ringo's collection of oatmeal cartons?) (Whoops . . . set of drooms, set of drooms.)

Ripping Idea

Still, aside from these minor details, it was a positively ripping idea! And when Robin finally did drift off, she dreamed she was the star performer in a huge band.

Suddenly, it was morning, and someone was shaking her.

"Oh, Rob-in," Budgie sing-songed, not without a trace of sarcasm. "Wake up and tell me I dreamed it."

Robin groggily opened one eye. "You dreamed it," she groaned. Then she fell back to sleep.

"Oh, Rob-in," Budgie re-sing-songed (re-sing-sang?) (re-songsinged?) (get the nets). "Now wake up and tell me I'm dreaming that too!"

Robin groggily opened another eye. "You're dreaming that, too," she re-groaned obligingly. Then she fell out of bed.

(To Be Continued Next Issue)

KRLA ARCHIVES

THIS Christmas... GIVE YOUR FRIENDS BEAT

Order BEAT now... in time for Christmas... at special low rates.

ONLY $3 FOR YOUR FIRST SUBSCRIPTION... $1 FOR EACH ADDITIONAL GIFT SUBSCRIPTION... WE SEND YOU GIFT CARDS TO GIVE YOUR FRIENDS.

BEAT... America's largest teen NEWSpaper... bringing you exclusive stories, interviews and pictures on all your favorite stars... *BEAT* is accurate... entertaining... educational... covering musical talent in both the U.S. and Europe... *BEAT* is the only way to stay informed about the fast-moving world of pop!

FOREIGN SUBSCRIPTIONS—$9.00 PER YEAR.

MAIL TO: *BEAT* SUBSCRIPTIONS, 6290 Sunset Blvd., Hollywood 90028.

My name is_____
Address_____
City_____ State_____ Zip_____

☐ Send BEAT for Xmas (names listed below).
☐ I also want a BEAT subscription.
Total enclosed $_____ for_____ subscriptions.
I enclose ☐ cash ☐ check ☐ money order.

Coupon
Name_____
Address_____
City_____ State_____ Zip_____

Coupon
Name_____
Address_____
City_____ State_____ Zip_____

Coupon
Name_____
Address_____
City_____ State_____ Zip_____

Coupon
Name_____
Address_____
City_____ State_____ Zip_____

Coupon
Name_____
Address_____
City_____ State_____ Zip_____

Coupon
Name_____
Address_____
City_____ State_____ Zip_____

KRLA ARCHIVES

DISCussion By Eden

One of the prettiest records to date from Cher is her newest, "Mama." This one is another Sonny Bono composition, and it really is a tear-jerker.

The consensus of opinion nowadays seems to indicate that Sonny will be doing a lot more behind-the-scenes work and letting his beautiful wife hold the spotlight alone from now on.

* * *

Gene Clark has gone from group (Byrds) to group (Gene Clark) to solo singer (himself.) His first solo effort is a beautiful ballad entitled "Echoes."

A beautiful, thought-provoking lyric and a lush string arrangement add up to a possible First Hit Total for Gene.

* * *

Written in about ten minutes, recorded almost immediately, and now well on its way up the charts is the Buffalo Springfield's second release, "For What It's Worth." You'll have to listen to this one for a while before you really feel it, but it is definitely "worthy" of the Top 20 lists.

* * *

One of the best records to be released this week has been "Georgy Girl," by the Seekers. This talented trio has always had a beautiful vocal blend, and they use it to its best advantage in their discing of this sparkling movie theme.

* * *

The Lovin' Spoonful have yet to release two records which sound at all alike—or even slightly *related!* And that's not the easiest feat to accomplish in this Popsy Turvy Record World!

The latest release from the Spoonful is "Full Measure," and though it might not seem as "revolutionary" or inventive as some of their others at first, listen a little more closely.

The arrangement, production, and use of lyrics in this record are excellent and succeed in blending together in a beautiful tapestry of sound. Another hit for the "Spoons."

* * *

On the brand new Animal's album, "Animalization," there is a cut entitled "Hey, Gyp," written by Donovan and "souled" by Eric Burdon. It is one of the greatest ever from Eric and should definitely be released as a single.

Sen. Dirksen Next Beatle?

One of the best selling Christmas albums for 1966 was cut by someone whose hair style resembles Bob Dylan's but whose era dates back farther than the New Vaudeville Band.

U.S. Sen. Dirksen's first LP, "Gallant Men," had as many advance orders as the first Beatle album, and Sen. Dirksen doesn't even sing!

Does this mean Sen. Dirksen may replace the Beatles? "I sort of doubt that, but he's making a good start," said one Capitol records official.

Can you imagine Sen. Dirksen and Mrs. Miller on the same bill?

Some Things are Nice to Have Around...

things you feel "at home" with

...the Utility™ ball pen

A good, practical pen for students. Fashionable, too.
There are twelve brilliant colors.
The color of the pen is the color of the ink.

Lots of students buy two or three at a time. Maybe because it's only 39¢
Maybe because it writes nice.
Or maybe they just like to have two or three or twelve around.

Lindy®

 manufactured by LINDY PEN CO., no. hollywood, calif. 91605, u.s.a.

KRLA ARCHIVES

Why Mitch Ryder Sells His 'Soul'

(Editor's note: Mitch Ryder is probably the foremost American exponent of white soul. Rhythm 'n blues is one of the toughest musical fields for a Caucasian to enter and succeed in. And yet, Mitch Ryder and his Detroit Wheels have managed to do just that. So, we've asked Mitch to explain why he chose soul and what makes him tick when he's on stage.)

By Mitch Ryder

One of the most difficult things to do is to try to explain my philosophy of life or of work. It always seems to come out stuffy and phony. I usually like to think that my work explains itself — but anyway, here goes.

In America, there are, we might say, two "sounds." One we call "soul" music; the other is smoother, slicker. I prefer soul music because it is more personal and more rewarding. It is difficult and really calls for self-discipline because it expresses emotion and you can't fake it — at least I can't.

I think there is nothing more easily spotted than a false emotion and performers who try to create this false emotion and excitement are only kidding themselves. A performer who breaks a guitar string or splits his trousers purposely every performance is just taking the easy way out and isn't kidding his audience. I believe that if a performer really feels what he is saying or doing, then this feeling communicates itself without resorting to tricks.

I think that the exciting thing about the present day scene is the excitement itself. It is marvelous to be on stage and feel the audience reacting. I can't understand the performer who is satisfied with polite applause. The greatest thing in the world is to have the audience right there every step of the way. There has to be this give and take so that the performer and the audience experience the same things at the same time. That's why they are in the same place.

The big thing is to understand yourself. You can't express an emotion you never felt. The Detroit Wheels and I are working hard at this and we hope we are growing with this knowledge.

Bill Cosby Shocks 'Em With Ad Libbed Humor

By Louise Criscione

If Bill Cosby is not the naturally funniest man alive, he runs a very close second. Listen to his million-selling albums, watch him on "I Spy" and the image he projects is not an image at all — it's the man himself. An intelligent, friendly, funny guy — period. No put on, no phoniness. Just Bill Cosby, person, and you can take him or leave him.

And last night the people upstairs at Martoni's were taking him — gladly. Warner Brothers Records hosted a party for Bill in honor of the certification of his four albums as million sellers.

He and his beautiful wife, Camille, arrived *early* and Bill, who has to be the extrovert of all time, strolled up to every single guest, shook hands and introduced himself. Those who had never before met Bill found themselves with mouths open and eyes bugging out. A person of Bill's stature being *that* friendly — must be a mirage.

Stands Alone

And the biggest shock was still to come. It's a well-known fact that many comedians are not naturally funny. They rely on writers to come up with jokes that will make people laugh. The technique is their own but the words are borrowed. And that's where Bill Cosby stands alone. He himself is funny. Not physically funny, not standard catch-line funny. You might call it creatively funny for lack of a better definition because he writes all of his own material. But ironically enough, Bill doesn't even *have* to write down his material — he can ad lib like no other personality alive!

Dressed in sort of a semi-Mod suit, Bill mounted the small platform while the President of Warner Brothers Records, J.K. Maitland, attempted to make the presentation. "I think this is the first time that four albums have been certified as million sellers within the span of 30 days," began Mr. Maitland. "Yes, I think it is," quipped Bill, perfectly deadpan. "And this is the first time in the history of the record business that a comedian has won four Gold records," continued Maitland. "I believe it is," piped Bill. "I got a look at Shelly Berman's and his are mostly silver. Mine are *all* silver!"

Wrong Places

"'Bill Cosby Is A Very Funny Fellow, Right?' was Bill's first album," said Maitland, handing the Gold mounted disc to Cosby. "'Bill Cosby Is A Very Funny Fellow, Right?' was my first album," repeated Bill, "which was cut 'live' at the Bitter End in New York. Then we handed the tapes to 'em, all nice and wrinkled, and they put the canned laughter in... all the wrong places. That way, people listen to the album and hear 'em laughing, so they laugh too and then they say: 'Wait a minute, what's so funny?' It's beautiful."

"Anyway, my first record sold three...copies. They walked me all over New York to introduce me. 'Course, we didn't go into any record stores or radio stations — just into people's homes. They'd say: 'This is Bill Cosby!' 'Yeah, right, Bill *who*???' Why don't you try singing, Bill?'

"Then there was the time I first met Lou Rawls. He looked down and saw the album and he said: 'Hey, man, did you write all those songs?' I tried to sell Lou Rawls and the Mama's and Papa's to Moe Austin but he told me to take a hike. So, I brought him Lena Horne, Diahann Carroll and Nancy Wilson as The New Supremes!"

Right

"Bill's next album was 'I Started Out As A Child,'" continued Maitland, passing along the second Goldie to Bill. "Right," confirmed Bill, "'I Started Out As A Child' was my second album. It was cut 'live' at Mr. Kelly's in Chicago and then we handed them the tapes and they put in the canned laughter," and Bill was off and running on the "history" of his second album.

Five minutes later, history lesson on L.P. number two completed, Bill was handed his third Gold Record along with the question, "Why Is There Air?" "Why Is There Air?" mimicked Bill. "You know, that one was funny because we handed them the tapes and they said: 'What's this? A fifteen minute cut?!! The disc jockeys will never play that, it's too long.' But they did. They liked it. They'd play part of it and then say: 'Tune in next week, folks, to find out why there is air.'"

Bill's fourth Gold Record was for his "Wonderfulness" album. "Yes, we took the picture for this one and went through the whole bit. Ed Thrasher spends weeks hunting me down and then we go out and take the picture and stick it on the album and old Ed's never won an award. So, for my next album, 'Take A Hike,' I'm gonna stand against a wall like you do in high school, you know with the whole graduation outfit, and maybe Ed'll get an award for that!

"I'd like to thank you all for showing up tonight. The food was bad but you got freebies on the booze. I'd like to thank all the disc jockeys for playing my records. They're wonderful. They come on: 'This is Bill Cosby' (uttered in a deep baritone) and then I come on: "I started out as a child" (mimed in a high alto). It's wonderful.

"And I'd like to have you thank your children. I love the children for introducing me to the parents. You know, it's the kids, man, they come home with my record, put it on the record player and the parents hear it and say: 'That guy's funny.' I love the kids; they're beautiful."

The thing about Bill Cosby is that he's so natural. And in the age of the great phonies, that's rare. He's strictly himself. And himself smokes cigars, wears glasses and makes jokes which aren't really jokes but are hilarious anyway because he says it like it is. Himself is about as genuinely nice and down to earth as a person can be. And what elese is there?

...BILL COSBY — NO IMAGE, JUST HIMSELF

KRLA ARCHIVES

Brian Joins The Hip Set And Things Are A 'Gas'

...BRIAN EVEN DIGS CALIFORNIA AIR!

By Tom Tully

"We're going mountain climbing tomorrow," Brian Hyland announced, glancing out the window of his fifth floor suite and inspecting the hills surrounding Hollywood.

"Ya know," he concluded, "California is a gas."

A heavy rain the previous day had washed the atmosphere of all smog and now the late afternoon sun painted deep red patches on the hills. The colorful spectrum had a sedate effect as Brian reflected on his new home in Southern California.

"I even like the way the air smells out here," he said. "It's terrible in New York."

Domination

"New York used to be the center of things but I think California is now. What I really like about California is the way young people dominate everything ... fashions, trends, and especially the record industry. Young people just seem to have more to say.

"New York has gotten kind of stagnant. The older generation is still in control there."

Lately, Brian has taken control himself. By leaving New York's jet set and joining California's hip set, he has come up with his first two hit records in nearly four years.

Although he only reached legal voting age this year, "The Joker Went Wild" and "Run Run, Look and See" marks the biggest "comeback" since teenagers re-discovered Frank Sinatra.

"I wasn't having too much recording success in New York," he admitted. "I wanted to work with Snuff Garret, who is a great producer, so I came to California. The idea of moving out here appealed to me anyway.

Today, Brian Hyland is a big name again. "Last week Jimmy Clanton recorded one of my songs and this morning Rudy Vallee shook my hand," he laughed.

Brian's career has been on a crazy roller coaster ride since it began in 1960. He has produced everything from novelty songs to pretty ballads to medium-paced rockers, and his own classification of "young music" is about the only label you can put on his recordings.

He first hit it big in 1960 with "Itsy Bitsy Teeny Weeny Yellow Polka Dot Bikini," a song that sold nearly two million copies despite the fact that the lyrics were as unfortunate as the title.

It should have come as no surprise to Brian when the RIAA, after suffering through the tongue twisting title, misspelled his first name on the gold record.

His songs could only get better after that, and they did. "Let Me Belong To You," "Ginny Come Lately" and "Sealed With A Kiss," all big successes, followed.

After 1962, however, a long drought began.

"Even when I didn't have a hit record I continued to tour a lot," Brian said. "I suppose the response was pretty good. I went on several tours with Dick Clark here, but I spent a lot of my time touring abroad.

"I got the best receptions in places like Buenos Aires. A lot of times a record doesn't break in other countries for two or three years after it's released here.

"Gratifying"

"Lately, the response I've been getting in the U.S. has really been gratifying. It makes a lot of difference if you've had a record on the charts recently. I guess U.S. fans are kind of fickle in that way, but that's the way it should be. It inspires you to put out better records."

Brian has made it back to the top even though he had a lot against him. He dresses with a collegiate flair, has relatively short hair and is a soloist.

He has made one concession — he is in the process of forming a back-up group. "They'll be called the Jokers," he said. "I'm only forming a group for convenience. It gets hectic playing with a different group every day and rehearsing the same things over and over."

 ## For Girls Only

By Shirley Poston

I'd like to say a few (thousand) words about vespers.

Rather than try to explain (in my own inimitable – thank Gawd – fashion) what I mean by *that*, I shall quote from a letter which was sent to me by one of both of my many readers.

"I started reading your column as soon as it started. It was amusing and I enjoyed your cute stories. I noticed an odd similarity tho. You sounded just like me! And you sort of let on that you were a Beatle fan (duh!)

Spooky Deals

"Well, time went on and it got worse. My friends and I would be on some kick one week, and the next week we'd *read it in your column!!* Talk about spooky deals and E.S.P.! We also noticed it in Robin Boyd.

"Anyroad, the vespers (spooky deals) were getting worse all the time, and they weren't just coincidences!

"One day, I was reading Robin quietly on the couch amidst my mates who were watching TV. I was squirming in excitement as it was one of the chapters where she was 'attacking' him. Anyroad, I read the sentence where you said he held her closely and then went on to add that the closely is located just beneath the farley.

"DEAD, DEAD, DEAD!! I was literally DEAD all over the room! You see, *farley* is one of our fave descriptions of a certain part of the bod!

"It's even been worse lately. One other major vesper is you and I are APE (you bet!!!!!) over GEORGE - PANT - MOAN HARRISON!"

At this point in the letter, she related a perfectly marvtastic (spoken like a true spaz, Shirl) story about the time her pen pal journeyed to the Harrison (gasp) abode in Surrey and met George (rasp!) Hopefully, I will have both the good sense and the room to elaborate on that subject next column (I get tired of saying pillar.)

Howlever (hah?), for the marmot, let's get back to vespers-ville.

Shortly before I read the thingy I just quoted, I swore (no doubt) that the next time I received that kind of letter, I was going to crouch in the nearest corner and twitch.

Not that I don't *like* getting said sort of letter. It's just that I've been getting so many of them lately, I was beginning to fear for my sanity. Not just letters that say "we sound like each other." Letters citing actual examples of things I've written about that I couldn't possibly have known about it.

Not only that, either. Also letters where you tell me about stuff you've done that I've done *too*, and not even mentioned in my ravings.

I was honestly beginning to wonder if I was a witch (as in Wanda) or something! Or if maybe I was writing all those letters to *myself!* (Stranger things haven't happened yet, but stick around, because in this crowd, they're bound to.)

Well, needless to say, the aforementioned letter really set me off (as in the straw that broke the chicken's back) (no . . . that isn't quite it) and true to my word, I crouched in the nearest corner and twitched.

"Why Is . . ."

Unfortunelately (I barg your parddon), we had company at the time (a friend of me dad's), and it wasn't long before said friend got around to asking: "Why is that poor girl crouched in a corner twitching?"

Much to my parents' dismay, I was only too happy to tell him. Not just about the letter. The whole story. And I shall now relate his opinion of same.

First of all, he poo-poohed the witch-E.S.P. theory. "Pure coincidence," said he.

"Impossible," said I (and I usually am.)

"You're crazy," he replied (as my folks nodded fervently.) "Coincidences happen because people have a great deal in common. But, generally, people don't learn to communicate outside of their own circle, so they never discover the similarities."

Well, after I'd disagreed some more (I kindof *like* the thought of being a witch) (spelled with an ee-bay), he went on to say that this vesper-type-thingy is typical of the younger generation. Irrationality and fantasy are a big part of every person's life, but heretofore, people wouldn't admit to having a zany side, except to close friends, for fear of having others think they'd dropped one or two.

He thinks we're just the opposite, and that we don't give a ding-dong-am-day *what* people think. Therefore, we're not only able to be more our real selves, but are able to communicate said self to others, even people we don't even know.

I've just read all this over, and I see that I've explained this in my usual dull, boring way. Sorry about that. And I really mean that, because it's a fascinating subject.

Anygeorge

Anygeorge (salivate), he ended the conversation with a remark that made me want to fling myself at his feet and rain kisses upon his up-turned face (my sense of direction leaves something to be desired) (it should join the crowd.) It not only proved he'd seen "Help." It was also a mouthful.

First he stared at me. Then he stared at the batch of letters I was clutching. Then he larfed and said: "One of these days, you characters are going to – dare I say it – rule the world. I wonder if you won't do a better job than we did."

Fling, fling, and kissie-kissies! That really made me feel good. Course, it still doesn't completely answer the vesper question as far as I'm concerned, but I do think he's right about the communication bit. And we just probably *will* do a better job of – dare I say it – ruling the world (our generation, I mean, not *us*) because we won't be constantly bent out of shape from trying to be someone on the outside that we aren't on the inside.

I swear to God, I am really blithering today. I think I'm going to give up writing (it gave *me* up long ago) and take up taxidermy. Say, that's not a bad idea. I could start by stuffing George. (Into the back seat of a car headed in the direction of Mexico, that is.)

In closing (my tiresome yap), I'll let you in on my dad's P.S. to the conversation. Said he, after a long and very wary look in my direction: "Of course, we mustn't disregard the possibility that all of you are hopelessly insane."

I refrained from saying that this sort of thing has been known to run in the family. But I intend to mention said possibility (would you believe *probability?*) soon.

Would you believe the day after Christmas?

KRLA ARCHIVES

EPSTEIN BOOKS TOUR
Four Tops Spin Thru Britain

By Rochelle Reed

"You've GOT to be kidding!" everyone usually says borrowing the phrase from Monkee Davy Jones for the occasion.

But it really is true. Four guys far on the other side of their teens can sing louder than the Yardbirds, smile more than Herman and jump around more than the Raiders. In fact, they do it all the time, here and abroad, in clubs and concert, for both fun and profit.

The "older" foursome is the Four Tops, currently sitting securely on the musical charts with "Standing In The Shadow Of Love," a sound-alike to "Reach Out, I'll Be There!"

Though firmly implanted in the Motown corporation for all their U.S. musical needs, the Tops are being booked in England by Brian Epstein. He handled their SRO November tour and was reportedly negotiating a Christmas tour for them with the Beatles until the "no more personal appearances" edict by the pop kings.

To prove there were no hard feelings, both John and Paul showed up at the party Epstein threw for the Tops, which also featured noted guests such as Mick Jagger, Keith Richard, Donovan, Eric Burdon, Charlie Watts, and Georgie Fame.

Later that night the party moved to the Saville Theatre, were Mick Jagger reportedly jumped around like a teeny bopper fan while the Tops were onstage.

In fact, Jagger's reaction mirrored all of England's feelings towards the Tops—they want more, more, more. Levi, Lawrence, Renaldo and Abdul were plastered throughout the English trades in features, columns, record reviews, critiques, and appeared on magazine covers and television shows.

The American apostles of rhythm and blues are being worshipped by the English record buying set. It took a Beach Boys' disc, "Good Vibrations" to displace "Reach Out" from its number one spot on the charts.

A new disc by the Tops—or any Motown artist—is awaited with almost the same excitement the U.S. reserves for Beatle albums. Britain is in the throes of an R&B period, which should get even more powerful according to English sources.

Some of the most ardent fans of American Negro jazz hail from the U.K., as well as fans of little known American R & B singers. Even the Beatles and Stones admit that they stole their ideas from people like Chuck Berry, John Hurt and Fats Domino. Eric Burdon, in fact, penned an article for the latest edition of Ebony mentioning how he had been influenced by R & B and blues singers.

The English are counting off the days until the January tour of the Tops, when concert halls will be filled with sell-out audiences crying for just one more number. This is a dramatic change from the earlier tour of the Supremes, when the British trades panned their performance and their sound. At the time, the opinion was that the Supremes were too polished, too restrained and too well-produced to call themselves R & B artists.

But this can't, and indeed isn't said, about the Tops. Devastating is the word more usually applied to their wild, gyrating performance. Among all the concert reviews run in England, not one nixed the group.

The Tops have been together since 1954, when they all lived in the same town but attended different high schools. They signed with Motown in 1964 and since then have issued a number of best selling discs on both rock 'n roll and R & B charts.

...LEVI STUBBS

THREE TOPS (L TO R) Lawrence Payton, Abdul Fakir and Renaldo Benson tell Levi what they think when he suggests they stand in the shadows.

BEAT SHOWCASE
(spotlighting new talent on the pop scene)

THE PURPLE GANG

The Purple Gang's first booking was at a Southern California gas station, where they were supposed to "make lots of noise and attract people." Among what the Gang attracted was an MGM recording contract, resulting in their first disc, "Bring Your Own Self Down."

JOHN D'ANDREA & THE YOUNG GYANTS

This group is beginning the big way—an album called "John d'Andrea and The Young Gyants at the Chez." A mixture of the big band sound and pop, the seven Young Gyants are led, naturally, by John D'Andrea pictured above.

THE MANDALA

The Mandala hail from Canada but take their name from the ancient Hindu-Buddhist culture (Mandala means universe.) The group puts on a stirring 'soul' show complete with a headlong dive into the audience by leader George Olliver.

KRLA ARCHIVES

KRLA ARCHIVES

America's Pop Music NEWSpaper 25¢

KRLA Edition BEAT

JANUARY 14, 1967

The Great Gem Take-Over of NEIL'S DIAMONDS & MICK'S STONES

BEAT Photo: Dorie Damewood

BEAT Photo: Robert Young

KRLA BEAT

Volume 2, Number 32 — January 14, 1967

Stones—No. One Sellers Of Year

Britain's Rolling Stones have won an honor for their nation by being named the top American record sellers during 1966, according to a tabulation of the leading American trade-paper annual polls.

Results of the polls were released this week with the five Rolling Stones showing up as the number one attraction in each of the three top album polls. In addition, they were voted into three second places in the top singles polls. No other act achieved a comparable combined rating.

Other than these year-end honors, the Stones have managed to come up with four consecutive gold records, with a fifth, "Got Live If You Want It," nearing the million-selling mark.

The four Stones' gold records were "Out Of Our Heads," "December's Children," "Big Hits—High Tide And Green Grass" and "Aftermath." Both "Big Hits" and "Aftermath" were released during 1966.

Their latest album, "Got Live If You Want It," was almost assured of a gold record by advance orders which totalled close to the necessary million.

On the singles front, the Stones chalked up four number one records, one number three and two number five discs. The four chart-toppers were "Get Off My Cloud," "19th Nervous Breakdown," "Paint It Black" and "Mother's Little Helper b/w "Lady Jane." The Stones' single which checked into the number three slot was "As Tears Go By" and "Have You Seen Your Mother, Baby, Standing In The Shadow" reached the national number five spot.

All the Stones' hit singles, as well as the majority of their album cuts, were written by group members, Mick Jagger and Keith Richard. In fact, the Jagger/Richard team has been so successful during the past two years that they recently signed a new three-year publishing deal which will guarantee them at least one million dollars.

Meanwhile, there is still no word on whether the Stones will go ahead with their proposed debut film, "Only Lover's Left Alive."

...THE YARDBIRDS AS THEY WERE BEFORE JEFF BECK (CENTER) LEFT THE GROUP.

BEAT EXCLUSIVE
Beck Exits 'Birds

According to a reliable source closely connected with the Yardbirds, The BEAT has learned in an exclusive interview that Jeff Beck is no longer a member of the Yardbirds.

"Jeff Beck is definitely not coming back with the group," reported our source. "The Yardbirds will continue with just the four boys—Keith Relf, Chris Dreja, Jim McCarty and Jimmy Page. In fact, Jeff has formed a group of his own."

The official announcement came as no shock since Beck was rumored to have been considering leaving the group for the past six months. He did not appear with the Yardbirds in their last U.S. tour and was not set to fly to America with the group for their current tour.

Simon Napier-Bell indicated last week that Jeff would shortly be leaving the group but refused to give a definite statement to the press until he could return to England and talk to the entire group.

Jeff's split with the Yardbirds was by mutual consent. "The Yardbirds just disagreed with him (Beck) because they felt that while he had mental and physical problems 'the show must go on.' That sort of thing. The other members of the group put their personal problems aside and they felt that Jeff was not holding up his side of it," continued The BEAT source.

"So, they kind of agreed to disagree. Jeff had made up his mind that he was not going back with the group. It's definitely a split." Admittedly, Jeff's guitar work was an integral part of the total Yardbird sound. His use of the feedback has been widely imitated in the field of pop music. What will happen to the Yardbirds minus the guitar of Jeff Beck?

"I don't think it will make any difference to the success of the group," answered our source. "For the last four months they've been doing their concerts without Jeff. I think it will continue on to bigger and better things for the Yardbirds. They're carrying the name 'Yardbirds' with them and in many ways Jimmy Page is just as good as Jeff. It's ironic that Jeff was instrumental in bringin Jimmy into the group in the first place."

Jeff's new group is, alledgedly, far from the recording stage as neither a name nor all the group members have yet been chosen.

BOBBY GOLDSBORO IN ALABAMA HOSPITAL

The BEAT has learned that recording artist, Bobby Goldsboro, succumbed to an enforced rest last week when a strep throat landed him in the hospital in his hometown, Dothan, Alabama.

At press time, Goldsboro was reported responding well to treatment and is expected to be back in action well before his scheduled engagements next month in Europe. Bobby's European dates include his first appearance at the San Remo Song Festival, preceded by television appearances in England and France.

Bobby's latest single, "Blue Autumn," hit the national charts almost immediately upon its release and appears to be the biggest hit single for Bobby in quite a few months.

Bobby became ill in Nashville and was unable to carry out a scheduled date to produce a debut single for a new group, The Boys Next Door.

Inside the BEAT

LETTERS TO THE EDITOR	2
SONNY & CHER SIGNED FOR MOVIE	3
'IN' PEOPLE ARE TALKING ABOUT	4
COSBY, DILLER WIN GOLDEN APPLES	5
PICS IN THE NEWS	6
IN THE NEIL DIAMOND BAG	7
PHONE CALL FROM JOHN'S CHILDREN	10
FORMULA FOR POP SUCCESS	11
JOAN BAEZ SPEAKS OUT	12
RAIDERS ON THE RUN	13
FOR GIRLS ONLY	14
CARL WILSON DISCUSSES BEACH BOYS	15

Alpert, TJB World Tour

Herb Alpert and his Tijuana Brass, who have made a habit during the past year of smashing attendance records across the nation, are packing their suitcases to break some more!

They're set for a series of appearances which will take them half-way around the world, beginning in Chicago in January and ending up in Hawaii on April 17.

First date is January 12-18 at McCormick Place, Chicago to be followed on January 19 at Cobo Hall, Detroit; January 20, Public Auditorium, Cleveland; January 21, Convention Hall, Philadelphia; February 8, Kiel Auditorium, St. Louis.

Herbie and the TJB will begin a Far Eastern tour on March 26.

...JAGGER AND COHORTS named top U.S. record sellers

KRLA ARCHIVES

Letters TO THE EDITOR

SILENCE THE BRITISHERS!

Dear BEAT:
I'm in complete agreement with John Rose's recent letter which you printed in The BEAT. Now that England's groups have met success, they seem to think that American groups will steal it from them.

The Beatles have continually put down American fans after being polite while Stateside. Mick Jagger says he "hates America." The Hollies "will not tour the U.S. unless the money's right."

If it wasn't for America, most of these groups wouldn't have made it as they have. There is plenty of U.S. talent in America to put down the English, such as the Byrds, Young Rascals, Standells, Mama's and Papa's, Bob Dylan, the Association, and not to forget the Beach Boys who are drawing a gigantic following in England right now!

The list of American talent could go on and on. So, why can't the English, who literally inherited R&B and rock 'n' roll from the U.S., see this and shut up?
Trent Rollow

HERMITS

Dear BEAT:
Why is it that they don't talk about the other Hermits? Why aren't the other Hermits given a chance? They always have articles on Herman, Herman, Herman... but not Karl, Keith, Lek or Barry!

Only every now and then they'll have an article on the Hermits but never much. I think the other Hermits work just as hard, are just as well dressed, are just as talented and, last but not least, are just as cute as Herman! Especially Karl. You see, I like him the best.

So, please print more stuff on the other Hermits as well.
Edith Eskridge

ASSOCIATION CORNER

Dear BEAT:
In your December 17 issue, you published a letter from one Shawn Walker expressing her dislike (to put it mildly) of the Association. You (the staff) should be commended for allowing the Association non-fans to be heard; it shows that you are not a one-sided operation. So perhaps you will allow me also to air my views to the pulbic and to answer Shawn's opinions with a few of my own.

Shawn states that "Pandora's Golden Heebee Jeebee," written by Gary Alexander of the Association, is a copy of "A Change Is On The Way" by Terry Knight and the Pack. There are two points to be made on this subject: 1) Gary Alexander has enough songwriting talent on his own; he doesn't need to copy from ANYONE. 2) To quote Shawn's letter: "... 'A Change Is On The Way' may be reminiscent of Still I'm Sad' but at least it's original." WHAT?????

Shawn further states that The Association sounds bad on stage. Recently, The BEAT had an article called "A Daze Worth of Association." This article said that the Association worked all day at a recording session and then had to play a concert that night. Anyone who was at that concert will tell you that the guys sounded absolutely great. Either Shawn caught the Association on one of their bad days, or she caught them on one of HER bad days.

Shawn goes on to say that the Association became popular merely through good press coverage. Anyone with common sense knows that a paper or magazine doesn't back a group unless the group has talent and/or class, as does the Association. Horror of horrors—they can actually sing! Shock of all shocks—they are all accomplished musicians! (Terry plays 23 instruments). Wonder of wonders—they write great songs too! (Their first album is well on its way to becoming a million-seller and eight of the songs on that album were written by the Association. Their new album, "Renaissance," contains only songs written by the Association.) Surprise of all surprises—one can actually see their faces instead of a waterfall of hair, and they actually dress neatly! How's THAT for talent and class? Perhaps talent and class makes the difference between the success of the Association and the success of Terry Knight and the Pack (WHO??????).

Well, this is it from the soapbox. I hope that Shawn Walker will go to see the Association again and this time with an open mind. I'll go to see Terry Knight and the Pack, as soon as I find out who they are.
Gerrie Morgan

DIAMOND PRAISE

Dear BEAT:
I'd like to throw a little praise someone's way. He's one of the most warm-hearted, witty and talented persons I know in show business. He's had three solid hits, written countless songs for others including the Monkees' smash new hit, "I'm A Believer."

There was a benefit show in San Francisco, sponsored by KYA. He flew in all the way from New York at his own expense and did part of the show. This is how I met Neil Diamond.

I was lucky enough to meet Neil again on "Where The Action Is" and do a concert in Houston, Texas with him which enabled me to get to know him better. Fame means nothing to Neil, money means even less. Neil loves people and music and he devotes quantities of time to both. I hope we get to read a lot more about Neil in The BEAT. "I'm A Believer" in Neil Diamond.
John Sharhey
Syndicate of Sound

SPY REPORT

Dear BEAT:
Anonymous spy wishes to inform you of the whereabouts of the now defunct Grassroots. No longer even the Unquenchable Thirst. They cancelled their engagement at the Whiskey and split up.

Lead guitarist Bill Fulton was going to India (to follow G.H.) but he's now got something cooking with Sal Valentino. Rhythm guitarist Denny Ellis is looking for a band or will o to the San Francisco Art Institute. Dave Stensen, bass, is also looking for a band. Joe Larson, former drummer, has signed a new group with A&M. And the more recent drummer, Bill Schoppe, has gone home.
You Are Welcome
P.S. Anyone wanting to get in touch with Dave or Denny can write to 553 Francisco Street, North Beach, San Francisco and they'll get it.

ON THE WAY

Dear BEAT:
This letter is concerning many letters in your December 17 issue. First of all, to Dave T.—you sure are a quack that doesn't know his music. The day that James Brown isn't king of us all, we need tolay down and die. James has soul to give away.

Also, to the chicken who signed "A Beatle Fan"—what right do you have to be down on the Monkees? They were new and fresh and everybody liked them. They also have their own sound. As for being a top group, they're already on their way! Besides all of this, they are cute and have a great sense of humor. And they're a bunch of great guys!
Cyndi Patton

THE ENGLISH EYE VIEW

Dear BEAT:
We realize that you won't print this because you receive so many other letters but we've wanted to comment on a few things we've read. You have a great newspaper, yeah great! Very worthwhile reading and buying. The other mags and such seem to be pure rubbish.

We're from Britain and just recently came to the States to look at all that's happening in your pop culture. It's very exciting. San Francisco is an especially beautiful place and the groups there are great, gear, fab and all the rest of those "pimply hyperboles!" We agree that it's the "Liverpool of America."

But the Monkees? Someone must be joking. They have no talent whatsoever—where's the appeal? They neither write their own music nor play a lot of it. We've even heard that on one side of their album, they couldn't do it so they got another group to sing it. They're corny and imitative of the Beatles. We agree with a well-known jazz and pop music critic who says: "They may well be the biggest press agent put-on in the history of entertainment!" Can such a contrived, untalented group with only television, press and money behind them presently have the number one album in the country, on which they neither wrote, played nor sang the songs? Apparently so. And being fellows, we are not impressed by the fact that Davy Jones is cute.

By the way, in a recent issue of The BEAT a girl, apparently from Britain, wrote in and said that the Beatles are "out" in England. This is not so. Despite the fact that we dislike people always saying who and what's "in" or "out" the Beatles are definitely "in" back home. "Revolver" is the greatest. It's a real shame that they are breaking up—they who started it all. But it seems to be true. Things won't be the same without the Beatles and their "filthy Eastern ways."

Shirley Poston is marvelous. We luv her dearly. And before we go back to Merry Olde England we'd like to see a photo of her—so could you print one? Thank you.

We do like your country in spite of Vietnam and the Monkees.
David Huntington   Terrance White
Jeff Hammond   Richard Bailey
Keith Chandler   Jonathan Campbell
And Others

THREE YEARS FOR DC5

Dear BEAT:
The Dave Clark Five are three years old! After three years and many hits, the DC5 are still the same well mannered English gentlemen who first came to America in 1964.

In three years they've released 17 songs; all of which were hits. They've made appearances before the Queen, once in '65 and again this year.

All in all it's been a very successful three years for the "Glad All Over" boys. The future is even brighter. They were rated 8th in sales through the month of November 1966 in Britain. They've done even better in the States!

Their continued success is assured by their great talent, unlimited energy and their love of their fans. They've never disappointed their fans without just cause. Consequently, their fans remain loyal.

It's been a great three years filled with joys, tears and excitement—both for the boys and for their fans.
Dawn Lee

LIKE FINE OLD WINE

Dear BEAT:
Ever since the rumor started that the Beatles were breaking up I have been trying to formulate in my mind a letter to The BEAT expressing my feelings about it. Never have had any trouble before when it came to putting it into words but somehow this time the words elude me.

I know the reason why now, after reading the December 3 BEAT. Shirley Poston had all the words I wanted to use. Everything she said about all they have given us in their wonderful music, their movies, the fabulous, thrilling, exciting concerts, this will always be with us and like fine old wine, mellow as the years fade the memory in our hearts.

The thought of never seeing them again in person is a cold, chilling realization, but like the death of a very loved one, we know the grief will subside in time and maybe with the unpredictable Beatles we will have a wonderful surprise in store if they decided to make a "comeback" someday.

All I would add to Shirley's column is that I am thankful that they are still good friends and are finally getting the chance to do what makes them happy. There will never be anyone to equal their impact and they are retiring as a group while they are on top of the world. My heart is heavy because the void they leave in my life will be a long time closing, but I wish them well and end with eternal gratitude for having had them while we did.
"Mom"
P.S. I sign this way because once The BEAT printed one of my letters under the headline "Mom Defends John."

KRLA ARCHIVES

On the BEAT
By Louise Criscione

Speculation is running rampant as to what the five Rolling Stones are up to. Since they last departed the U.S. in July, they've cut one album, "Got Live If You Want It," and have done little else. Their debut film, "Only Lover's Left Alive," has allegedly been shelved and there has been no word when, or if, the Stones will again tour Stateside.

But what's even more startling is the fact that Mick Jagger, who always has something to say, has not said anything newsworthy in months! Jagger's silence even lead to rumors that the Mighty Mick was dead but the rumors, of course, were totally untrue. What, then, is keeping Jagger from talking? Perhaps he's turned conservative in his old age which, if true, will be a terrible blow to the pop press which has learned to rely on Mick to stir up a large dose of controversy by merely commenting on the state of the weather. Oh well, long live Jagger and may he soon re-open his mouth.

Donovan Surprise

Surprise announcement from Donovan, thus far Britain's number one protester. "I've got nothing very controversial or frank to say. I'm not a rebel any more. All that ban-the-bomb stuff is behind me. These days I don't want to protest or put anybody down. I just want to please." Poor Joan Baez—who is going to march with her in London now that Donovan has left the cause?

It's practically impossible to name all the entertainers who have recorded Dylan material. But the latest tribute to the curly-haired singer/composer/poet has to be the wildest yet. Sebastian Cabot has cut an entire album which includes narratives of Dylan lyrics. The title of the album? "Sebastian Cabot, Actor, Performs the Works of Bob Dylan, Poet." What else?

QUICK ONES: Add to your list of singers turning actors—the Righteous Brothers guesting on "Please Don't Eat The Daisies" and Bob Goulet appearing in the "Brother Love" segment of "The Big Valley" . . . Bobby Darin is set to direct his first television show for Rediffusion in London . . . Capitol not overjoyed because the Beatles were unable to furnish them with material for an album in time for the brisk Christmas business . . . Sonny & Cher's debut movie title changed from "Good Times" to "New Times, Happy Times" . . . Young Rascals a smash on their long-planned British visit . . . Brian Epstein unlikely to accept Sid Bernstein's fabulous offer for the Beatles to play Shea Stadium this year.

Nix On Holly

Sometimes I definitely think the Powers That Be are working dilligently against me. I had no sooner finished printing that Dick Chamberlain (alias "Dr. Kildare") was set for Broadway in "Holly Golightly" when David Merrick, the show's producer, announced that the show will close before it ever reaches Broadway. Merrick pronounced the show "a bore" and set about refunding a million dollars worth of advance ticket money.

Law suits are the "in" thing of the day and, accordingly, two of the Four Seasons, Bob Gaudio and Nick Massi, have filed a six million dollar suit against Premier Albums and Coronet Records for alleged use of their "name and likenesses" on an album called "At The Hop." The complaint states that in 1962, without written or oral consent, Premier and Coronet used the pictures and name on an album which was recorded by the Four Lovers

It looks as if Herman and his Hermits may tour the Orient immediately following their American tour which winds up in January. Negotiations are currently underway to send the popular British group to Australia and the Far East, where they were a gigantic smash on their first visit a year ago. Meanwhile, the group's first movie under their new MGM contract, "Mrs. Brown You've Got A Lovely Daughter," is scheduled to go before the cameras in April.

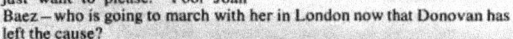
...MICK JAGGER
BEAT Photo: Robert Young

...HERMAN

Sonny And Cher Set For Second Starring Movie

Although Sonny and Cher's first feature film will not be released until May, they've already been signed for their second movie by Steve Broidy. Broidy, exercising his option on the famous duo under an original two-picture contract, stated that the second film will be a musical-comedy to be filmed in color and scheduled to begin shooting in April.

An Original

The original story, tentatively titled "Ignaz," is being written directly for the screen by Jack Guss, who recently completed the screenplay titled, "Doris Day's Guide to Crime, Gambling and Other Illicit Pleasures." Guss has also written a play, "No Deposit, No Return," which is scheduled for Broadway in May starring Red Buttons and Lee Grant.

Sonny and Cher's film debut, "Good Times," has been pushed back repeatedly and was finally sold to ABC-Paramount who are scheduled to finally release the film through Columbia Pictures sometime in May.

Set Records

On the personal appearance side of the Sonny and Cher picture, they recently set new gross records on their three latest concert dates with figures topping the $100,000 mark.

Sonny and Cher found themselves smack in the middle of a new controversy a couple of weeks ago when the city council of Monterey Park, California voted to revoke their invitation to the duo to

DESPITE FACT THAT their first movie has not been released, Sonny and Cher have already been signed for their second movie.

appear on that city's float in the New Year's Rose Parade. The action came about after the city council members saw a newspaper picture of Sonny and Cher amid teens on the troubled Sunset Strip.

At a press conference, Sonny said: "I am hurt and shocked but not angry. We went down to the Strip to observe the teenagers. This, primarily, is my business. The youngsters are my business. The Strip is the breeding ground of the new sounds. If the alleged brutality is there I want to know it, although I am opposed to violence in any form. I do sympathize with what is going on up at the Strip and I am surprised at the apathy of many people."

Sonny did admit that while on the Strip the night the photo was taken he did speak to a group of teens but he said that there were also ministers and many adults present.

Sonny declared that while police brutality is one of the issues on the Strip, he "did not witness any police brutality there and I never have witnessed it."

Cher remained relatively quiet throughout the press conference because "Sonny has said it all."

GENE PITNEY TO LAUNCH FILM CAREER

Gene Pitney, who hasn't had much success lately on this side of the Atlantic but who is a gigantic international star, has announced plans to produce a 90 minute film in Italy immediately following his appearance there in January at the San Remo Festival.

Pitney's appearance at San Remo marks his return after three recent consecutive monthly television engagements in Italy. Last January Pitney's performance earned him second place which, to date, has been the highest finish accomplished by an American performer in the Festival.

M&P's Notch Gold Album

The Mama's and Papa's collected their second gold album last week when the Record Industry Association of America certified "The Mama's And The Papa's as a million seller.

SENATOR DIRKSEN—THE NEXT RECORDING IDOL?

"Gallant Men," the first album recorded by Senator Everett Dirksen (R., Ill.) and the first album ever recorded by a United States Senator, has proven itself a pre-release smash by passing the million dollar mark in sales to retailers prior to its general release to the public.

W.B. Tallant, Jr., Capitol Records Vice President and National Sales Manager, revealed that the company has already received orders for over a million dollars' worth of the album, plus more than 300,000 copies of the singles, "Gallant Men/The New Colossus," which was taken from the album.

"We haven't seen anything like the demand for the Dirksen LP since we introduced the first Beatles album in January, 1964," stated Tallant. "Airplay on the single record has been very heavy in almost all parts of the country and the Senator's appearance on Johnny Carson's "Tonight" show has produced a phenomenal deluge of phone calls and orders. Our biggest problem now is to supply stock on the LP. Five different manufacturing plants are pressing the LP and we hope to supply most of the demand within the next two weeks."

The Senator's album is an historical/documentary, which chronicles the "American Adventure"—from the Pilgrim's arrival and the signing of the Declaration of Independence to the War of 1812 and the arrival of the Statue of Liberty.

Senator Dirksen narrates throughout the album and recites such historic works as "Lincoln's Gettysburg Address," "The Pledge of Allegiance," "The Mayflower Compact" and "The Star Spangled Banner."

It's only fair that a politician is making a huge splash in the entertainment industry what with the state of California owning a Governor who is a former actor and a U.S. Senator who was once a song and dance man as well as an actor. About the only thing left now is for Mrs. Miller to run for the presidency in '68.

KRLA ARCHIVES

Petula Named Top Female Vocalist

Petula Clark, who has won more awards than just about any female vocalist on the pop scene, was named Number One Female Vocalist of 1966 by *Cash Box*. The award was presented to Petula at Caesars Palace where she was making her Las Vegas debut. Immediately following her stint at Caesars, Pet moved on to Harold's Club in Reno for a SRO stand at the famed night spot.

Petula holds the distinction of being a top recording artist and box office draw not only in the U.S. but all over Europe as well. The British born artist, who now makes her home in France, will return to America in March for a tour of Eastern and Western universities and colleges. She will also spend most of her summer "vacation" in the U.S. headlining a series of state fairs.

Petula will also make return guest appearances on practically every major variety show on the air.

Dave Clark Five: 14 Gold Discs, Fine Future

By Rochelle Reed

The Dave Clark Five, easily recognizable by their neatly cropped hair, immaculate suits and cheery smiles, have emerged as the true princes of pop. The reason? Fourteen—that's right—fourteen gold records!

In other words, the number of gold discs held by the Five are equal to the number of performances they've made on the Ed Sullivan Show—another whopping fourteen!

Started Trend

"Glad All Over" started the trend for the DC Five, who were then busy trying to raise money so Dave's soccer team could travel to Holland for competition. But once it became obvious that Dave could compete much better in the music business, he shelved his white socks and grabbed his drumsticks for good.

As originators of the "Tottenham Sound" and contemporaries of the Beatles, the DC Five started traveling all over the world and still do. But starting this month, they will limit their appearances to a total of three months per year.

Dave, unlike many pop singers, is the true "brain" behind the group. He retains complete control of his career as manager, producer, director, designer, inventor, actor, and owner of many varied properties including apartments and stores.

Dave has an infallible sense of timing for personal appearances, keeping tight control of both under and over-exposure of the group. He produces almost all masters of DC Five's recordings, then leases them to record companies.

But Dave does much more—and most of it unknown to his fans.

He's an actor—often seen as an extra in well-known films (one was "The VIP's). These appearances in over 30 movies have taught him much about film-making, which leads to Dave's next enterprise.

He's recently formed a company to produce films like those seen on the Ed Sullivan show where the guys drove their XKE's and rode horseback. He has more of these shorts in the works, as well as a color special to be shown on both American and English television sometime this spring.

Plus, Dave has film rights on several books and scripts, which he hopes to produce as full length movies.

Dave is also an inventor, with a patent on a microphone which attached to a saxophone eliminates feedback.

Many of the fashions currently displayed on Carnaby Street were designed by Dave, but he refuses to have his name on them simply for commercial value. (The shirts worn by the Monkees are very reminiscent of those originally worn by the DC Five.)

The rest of the group—Rick, Lenny, Dennis and Mike—are also sharp businessmen, each owning their own corporations plus a wealth of commercial properties.

More Exposure

Though the DC Five are indeed limiting personal appearances to three months a year, the move is designed in order to work on films and projects which will give fans more exposure to the group as personalities, or "as themselves" as Dave says.

The DC Five, which have silently stayed at the top of the record industry the past four years, are emerging, under Dave's leadership, as much more than just a pop group.

DAVE CLARK has formed his own production company and is seen here directing one of the shorts he has filmed on the DC Five. More movies are set for the near future as well as a color television special for TV.

'in' people are talking about...

Sonny and Cher's latest controversy... How banana wonderful got in with all those bop-do-wahs and how funny it is that no one noticed it... Tommy's painting and how he made sure it was worth something by smearing paint over the money... Paul McCartney catching the Young Rascals in London—not once but twice... Now that Herman has the East and West if he could only get the North and South he'd have a world monopoly... Why they're making such a fuss over Gary doing his duty.

PEOPLE ARE TALKING ABOUT Georgy getting to be a really popular girl and wondering what took so long... The Bagdad Blues which turned into a Kaleidoscope... How there has to be a word for the innocence... That eggplant which devoured Chicago and threatens to eat the rest of the country too... How come Sandy was born a woman to remain a single girl and deciding it was probably so she could have two hits in a row... How the Monkees could have three records on the nation's charts and not pick up huge ratings for their television show... How *Time* can't be all bad since it put a picture of Keith Richard between it's covers.

PEOPLE ARE TALKING ABOUT Screaming Chicken being a Midwestern happening—at least, that's what Russ says while Zollie proclaims he's "the world's skinniest and greatest blues singer;" we thought it was a new way of fixing chicken... The dry hole singers possibly getting another hit even though it is very reminiscent of the We Five who have long since vanished... Lee Mallory's potential and wondering how he manages to stay so skinny when he eats plenty and deciding that it's that key which weighs him down... Which "Action" group will disappear since Don and the Goodtimes have been signed as regulars on the show.

PEOPLE ARE TALKING ABOUT how ironic it would be if Drake outsells his former group mates... Black really being black for the Los Bravos... How Neil must really be cool if even his fellow entertainers think so... The cat in a new group who sounds like Dylan with a voice... Sinatra possibly getting a number one despite the ending... Whatever happened to the Ronnettes... Whether or not Sen. Dirksen will be the next Dylan and deciding that he definitely has the hair for it... How Bobby Vinton could be a coming home soldier... When the Mighty Mick is going to re-open his mouth and hoping that it's soon because things are becoming unbearably dull.

PEOPLE ARE TALKING ABOUT why Teddy's dad had to get into the act and mess things up like that... Blue turning to grey and how long it's been in the can... Which group the girl is going to help — Animals or Outsiders... How ironic the title on Ray's single is... Stevie finally finding his place in the sun... Aron telling it like it is and Ronnie crying... Rodney being the stand-in for Davy... How long the Supremes are going to keep hanging on and conservatively estimating another 25 years... Why Gene can't come up with a smash in his own native country... Ditto for the Everly Brothers.

PEOPLE ARE TALKING ABOUT whether or not the Beatles will ever make that ill-fated third movie and deciding that if they haven't found a script in all this time they probably won't ever find one... The Association joining forces with the Smothers Brothers and what a happening *that's* going to be... How the Hollies should put out a record called "Stop The Stop Stop Stop"... The farce of a trade paper's announcement that Gary Lewis is the top male vocalist of the year... Bob getting a lot like his butterfly—elusive... Fans forcing Scott out of the monastary... Paul finishing up the score for Haley's movie without any help from John... How the Monkees are making believers out of quite a few skeptics.

PEOPLE ARE TALKING ABOUT how the New Vaudeville Band got away with it when the T-Bones didn't... When Mitch is going to settle for one song on each side and deciding that maybe he's trying to bring back EP's... Laura having the swingingest blues on record in a long time and wondering why it isn't happening coast to coast... How Terry can be original when he's reminiscent of the Yardbirds... Tommy Roe using "Mickey Mouse" to describe his sound—we had nothing to do with it... When the Peanut Butter Conspiracy is going to spread 'round the country... How certain property owners figure that it's better to have heavies on the Strip than long-haired kids and deciding that maybe they've forgotten what it was like to have Mickey Cohen sitting in a restaurant with bullets flying through the windows.

KRLA ARCHIVES

Cosby And Diller Chosen Golden Apples By Press

Bill Cosby, winner of four gold records and star of the popular "I Spy" television series, and Phyllis Diller, perfectly coiffured star of TV's "Pruitts Of Southhampton," were named winners of this year's Golden Apple awards given annually by the Hollywood Women's Press Club.

Elvis Presley and Natalie Wood received the dubious honor of being chosen the Sour Apples of 1966.

The Golden Apples are given to the two stars who have proven themselves to be highly co-operative with the members of the press while the Sour Apples go to the entertainers who have, in the opinion of the Hollywood Women's Press Club, been most unco-operative with the press.

Our congratulations to Bill and Phyllis and better luck next year to Mr. Presley and Miss Wood!

... BILL COSBY named a Golden Apple by Hollywood Women's Press.

The Seekers Set Tri-Country Gigs

The Seekers have waited a long time for another smash on the U.S. charts and it looks as if "Georgy Girl" just might be lucky number two for the group which set the pop world on its ears with "I'll Never Find Another You."

The Seekers are originally from Australia but have spent most of their time in England where they've met with considerable chart success. However, they're set to leave England in March for what could be termed a world tour since they will tour in Australia, America and Canada.

"We're looking forward to going home," admits the group's lone female, Judith. "It's been a year since we were last there. We're going to do a huge charity concert in Melbourne called 'Music For The People.' We played it last year to an audience of 110,000 which was tremendously thrilling."

While in Australia, the Seekers will also make a documentary and will then journey to Canada to appear in the "Expo-67" world fair. "We're very proud because it's the first time we've been asked to represent our country and this is a great honor," said Judith in regard to their Canadian appearance.

ELVIS WAS CHOSEN SOUR APPLE

... PHILLIS DILLER registers surprise at winning Golden Apple.

ANOTHER ONE FOR DONOVAN

Donovan has received his second gold record for his chart-topping "Mellow Yellow," on which Paul McCartney allegedly provided some of the background. Donovan's first goldie was for his equally successful "Sunshine Superman."

New Deal

England's answer to our Bob Dylan has also signed a new writer's deal with Southern Music whereby Donovan will receive substantially increased earnings over his former contract. Donovan and Southern are now equal partners in a new publishing firm, Donovan Ltd., which already includes his two most recent hit singles as well as all of his former songs, such as "Catch The Wind." Donovan will receive all writer's royalties and 50 percent of the publisher's share of royalties.

Problems Resolved

The problems which developed in Britain over the release of Donovan's "Sunshine Superman" have now been resolved and the disc is in current release in England. Donovan will return to the U.S. in February for a tour and an appearance on "Ed Sullivan."

... DONOVAN WINS number two

Bobby's 'Sunny' Marks 46

It's small wonder that Bobby Hebb has a "Satisfied Mind." His chart-topping, million-selling, self-penned "Sunny" now boasts 46 cover versions! "At least, there were that many versions we knew of a week ago," explained Bobby. "Of course, that's the version I know of. There could be some more versions we haven't heard about yet!"

Bobby, who is currently on the Dick Clark national tour, received a gold record for his "Sunny" which sold more than a million singles by the first of October and which reached the coveted number one spot in the nation.

Twenty-five year old Bobby, who has been composing since 1958 and has more than 3,000 songs to his credit said that he has no objections to artists covering his songs.

"Cover versions of my record? Why should I mind? It draws attention to my own version of 'Sunny' and don't forget I'm the composer too. So, the more people that sing it, the more satisfying it is to me."

Bobby recently completed a smash tour of England (which is now in the throes of an R&B revolution) and his current Stateside single is "Love Me."

BEAT Photo: Howard L. Bingham
... BOBBY DOESN'T MIND the 46 cover versions of 'Sunny.'

KRLA ARCHIVES

PICTURES in the NEWS

THE DAVE CLARK FIVE pose happily with the fourteen gold records which the group has earned during their three successful years in show business. The latest million-seller for the DC5 was "The Dave Clark Five's Greatest Hits." The boys set another sort of record by appearing on the "Ed Sullivan Show" fourteen times.

ROY ORBISON recently flew to London to star in the first show of the New Year for British television's "Sunday At The Palladium." Orbison will return to England in late February for another appearance on "Palladium" and will remain in England for a five-week series of personal appearances. Between his "Palladium" dates, Roy will venture to Australia and New Zealand.

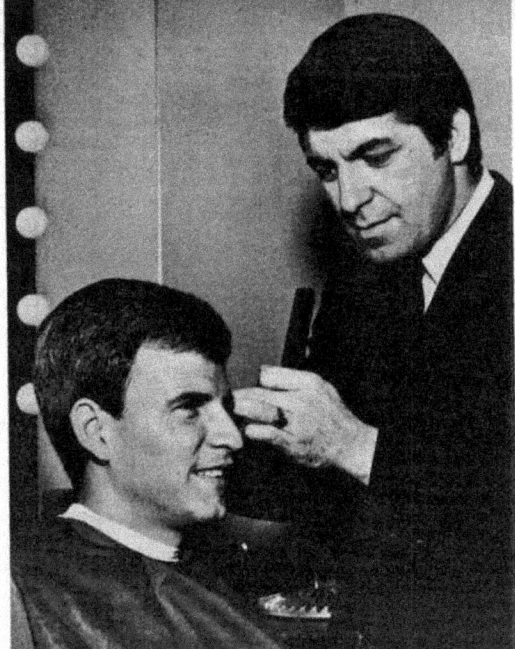

BOBBY RYDELL just might start a whole new trend in hair styles. He's pictured above in his "Wilde Californian" hair style which was created by the gentleman to his right in the above photo, Darrell Wilde. Wilde created it for Rydell to enable Bobby to go as long as three weeks between hair cuts. Wilde believes the hair style will "become a popular cut for entertainers because of its quiet elegance and ease of handling." But Bobby's ears and part of his forehead show.

SENATOR EVERETT DIRKSEN is shown here with his disc producing team during a reception in Washington, D.C. Background music for the Senator's "Gallant Men" was composed, arranged and conducted by John Cacavas (left) while Arch Lustberg (right) produced the Senator's readings of the text. The single is moving rapidly up the nation's charts and the album is already assured of a million dollars worth of sales.

KRLA ARCHIVES

Strictly In The Diamond Bag

By Louise Criscione

For one reason or another, most people tend to throw Neil Diamond into the "serious, loner, angry young man" bag. Which is something like terming President Johnson an introvert. Neil is, admittedly, serious about a lot of things—his music and writing in particular—and he is something of a loner—he moves without the aid of five publicists, three managers, two road managers and a photographer—but an angry young man? Not on your life.

Writers are a curious breed, a breed which divides itself into two parts. Those who follow trends and those who remain, for the most part, original. Although Neil is probably opposed to classification, he fits neatly into the latter category. But it's not easy. "It's very difficult to have a certain amount of individuality in writing and I will go out of my way to avoid trends. If you're creative, you can write creative songs.

"If I wanted to go along with trends, I would've made the Monkees' song just like 'Last Train To Clarksville.' But I just wrote a song I liked that I felt the Monkees could do a good job on."

Ironic

The fact that Neil wrote "I'm A Believer" for the Monkees was in itself rather ironic since Neil started out in the music business by writing songs for other artists. At the time he said he felt "like a speech-writer" having his songs, the things he believed in, recorded by other artists. And, yet, today with three consecutive hit records of his own he turns around and writes a song for the Monkees. A change of heart?

"It's only when you're writing *strictly* for other people that it gets on you but occasionally I will write for other artists. Right now I'm writing a song for Jay and the Americans because I like their sound. Before, everything was for other people. Now it's comfortable for me to let other people use my songs.

"The range I can write in is much greater than what I can perform in and, so, I couldn't perform all the songs I've written. All the people I know thought I was crazy to let the Monkees have 'I'm A Believer' but I felt it was more for the Monkees than for myself. It might've been a hit record if I had recorded it but it wouldn't have sold two million!"

Two At Once

"I'm A Believer" is, naturally, one of the biggest singles currently on the market. It was assured of a gold record before it was even released and, therefore, went almost immediately to the top of the nation's charts by-passing Neil's own "I've Got The Feeling," on its way to number one.

How did Neil feel when a song he had written, but which was recorded by someone else, leap-frogged over his own disc? "Let's see, how did I feel? I felt kinda good because it was selling so well and I had written it."

No one can deny the fact that Neil is a highly successful pop writer but, true to form, he's not satisfied with remaining in one place. "I'd like to write movie themes," admitted Neil. "It's very difficult because if you approach a movie producer and tell him you'll write him a theme which will be a big hit as a single, he'll look at you and then take Sam Shultz. It's funny, they cry that there isn't any freshness but on the other hand while they say that they deny pop pop writers their chance to show freshness. But just as the Beatles opened up a whole new image for pop music, I think pop writers will open up a whole new world by writing movie themes."

There are certain entertainers who enjoy the respect of their fellow performers. Others do not—they claim it's unnecessary because it is the fans who buy records, not people already in the business. Neil is one man who possesses the respect of just about everyone in the music business but how important does he honestly feel this respect is?

"It's definitely important because the people in any business are more aware of what's happning in that business. The kids know who recorded what song but they're probably not as hip to what's actually going on within the business, so when people in the business offer opinions it means that much more because what they say holds more weight. It's very nice to get that kind of criticism. But, of course, if it's bad criticism, it means nothing!" laughed Neil.

Pop In Russia

When he first walked into our offices, some seven months ago, Neil admitted that his big ambition was to take a rock show to Russia. He still holds that ambition. "I sent out about half a dozen letters to just about everybody but they probably ended up in wastebaskets all over the country!

"People get into ruts. They'd much rather send Louis Armstrong, who is great, to Russia than some pop singer. But pop is big business, so why deny it? It's like a whole new world over there (Russia). They keep people in their own pegs; they don't want them to move. They want to keep the status quo. Sending a pop show over to Russia for the kids would be like getting a foot in the door which is probably why the Russian government wouldn't be too happy to let a pop artist in. But the sad thing is that I've never gotten a serious reply to any of my letters."

Controversial is a world usually reserved for foreign pop artists. For some reason, the American artists tend to stay on the safe side of the fence, probably because their publicity man is always there to make sure of it. Neil Diamond, however, says exactly what he pleases—and managers per se do not please him.

"I think most managers don't know what they're talking about but they get away with it because the talent is so young today that it's easier to hand them a line and get away with it. Everyone from taxi cab drivers to salesmen are trying to become managers and they just don't belong.

...**NEIL DIAMOND:** "All the people I know thought I was crazy to let the Monkees have 'I'm A Believer'."

"The sad thing is that these kids are so very intense and sincere about their music—they want so much to be successful—that they're very easy pickings for people. I was signed for a seven year contract for 50% of my earnings only because I wanted so much to be successful and have people record my songs that it ended up that my father had to take most of his earnings, which weren't much, out of the bank to get me out of my contract. It was a very bitter experience," recalled Neil shaking his head.

"Of course, there are good managers and the good ones are great. And the kids who can get a good manager are lucky. But I'd say 99.9% of the people who are managers today don't know what they're doing. The point I made was that there is good and bad in everything but the bad managers are like leeches. They sign a half-dozen acts a night.

"This is probably the only one single topic I could get into a fight, a fist fight, over."

The news leaked out that Neil was up for a lead in a motion picture and also a possible television series for next season. "We have secret', " admitted Neil. "I have a number of things that are coming through but they don't want me to say anything about them. I'd definitely like to go into acting. But I'd never give up my writing and singing—it's so much a part of me."

Up front for Neil is a possible tour of England with Herman in February. "It's there if I want it," said Neil, "but I haven't decided yet if I'll go."

For sure, Neil will move into an area where he's never traveled before—the world of colleges. It's a strange world, devoid of screaming and hysterical crowds. It's a world where your audience sits silently and listens to what you're saying—applause comes only if you're accepted and you're only accepted if you have something to say.

The college circuit literally "scares the hell" out of many entertainers. But Neil is looking forward to it. "It's where I belong," he says. "When you do nothing but rock 'n' roll concerts it's kind of like having shortcake with every meal. I want to get to people. But I hope that my music and what I'd like to say has a broad appeal. Which means that it appeals to a lot of broads," he laughed.

And on the record scene? "I should be cutting a new album next month, mostly of new things I've written and some old ones that I love. I'd like to use only my own material on this album."

Strolling towards the door, Neil turned to make one final comment.

"Love — there should be much more of it."

Neil Diamond—there should be at least ten more of him. One is not nearly enough to go around.

KRLA ARCHIVES

Top 40 Requests

1. I'M A BELIEVER .... The Monkees
2. THE BEAT GOES ON .... Sonny & Cher
3. SNOOPY VS. THE RED BARON .... Royal Guardsmen
4. GEORGY GIRL .... The Seekers
5. THERE'S GOT TO BE A WORD .... The Innocence
6. KNIGHT IN RUSTY ARMOR .... Peter & Gordon
7. HELLO, HELLO .... Sopwith Camel
8. FOR WHAT IT'S WORTH .... Buffalo Springfield
9. FULL MEASURE .... Lovin' Spoonful
10. BORN FREE .... Roger Williams
11. EAST WEST .... Herman's Hermits
12. PUSHIN' TOO HARD .... The Seeds
13. GOOD THING .... Paul Revere & Raiders
14. LADY GODIVA .... Peter & Gordon
15. HELP ME, GIRL .... Eric Burdon & The Animals
16. I WANNA BE FREE .... The Monkees
17. THE EGGPLANT THAT ATE CHICAGO ..... Dr. West's Medicine Show & Junk Band
18. PLEASE .... The Kaleidoscope
19. ECHOES .... Gene Clark
20. GOOD VIBRATIONS .... The Beach Boys
21. WEDDING BELL BLUES .... Laura Nyro
22. TELL IT LIKE IT IS .... Aaron Neville
23. WINCHESTER CATHEDRAL .... New Vaudeville Band
24. IT MAY BE WINTER .... Felice Taylor
25. WORDS OF LOVE .... Mama's & Papa's
26. STANDING IN THE SHADOWS OF LOVE .. 4 Tops
27. DEVIL WITH A BLUE DRESS ON/GOOD GOLLY MISS MOLLY ..... Mitch Ryder
28. SMASHED, BLOCKED .... John's Children
29. THAT'S LIFE .... Frank Sinatra
30. KNOCK ON WOOD .... Eddie Floyd
31. I NEED SOMEBODY .... ? And The Mysterians
32. SUGAR TOWN .... Nancy Sinatra
33. LOOK WHAT YOU'VE DONE .... The Pozo Seco Singers
34. SINGLE GIRL .... Sandy Posey
35. TOGETHER FOREVER .... Viola Wills
36. CRY .... Ronnie Dove
37. 96.8 .... Keith
38. TELL IT TO THE RAIN .... Four Seasons
39. MUSIC TO WATCH GIRLS BY .... The Bob Crewe Generation
40. WHACK, WHACK .... The Young-Holt Trio

...DON AND THE GOODTIMES SIGNED AS "ACTION" REGULARS.

The girl with the most co-operative apartment in town **Any Wednesday**
An hilarious bed-time story.
(but not exactly for the kiddies!)

JaNE FONDA · JaSON ROBaRDS · DEAN JONES
Also Starring ROSEMARY MURPHY
TECHNICOLOR® · FROM WARNER BROS.

EXCLUSIVE ENGAGEMENT
NOW PLAYING!
PANTAGES
PACIFIC'S HOLLYWOOD
Hollywood Blvd. at Vine
Crossroad of the Stars!
HO. 6-7161

KRLA DISC JOCKEY DICK BIONDI drops by the Paramount set of "Chucka" to collect donations from Ernest Borgnine and Luciana Paluzzi for the American Campaign for Italian Flood Relief.

ICE HOUSE GLENDALE
234 So. Brand Ave.
Reservations 245-5043
Thru Jan. 14
THE NITTY GRITTY DIRT BAND

ATTENTION!!!
High Schools, Colleges, Universities and Clubs:

CASEY KASEM MAY BE ABLE TO SERVE YOU!

Let Casey HELP You Put On A Show Or Dance
Contact Casey at: HO 2-7253

KRLA ARCHIVES

A Simple Math Lesson:

America's Pop Music NEWSpaper 25¢

KRLA Edition BEAT

24 issues per yr.
x .25 each copy
$6.00

But

NOW—$5.00 a year Subscription
Limited Offer!!

One full year—Only $3.00

KRLA BEAT

Mail to:
The BEAT #504
6290 Sunset Blvd.
Hollywood, Calif. 90028

Name_____
Address_____
City_____ State_____ Zip_____

I want ☐ BEAT for one year — only $3.00
I enclose ☐ cash ☐ check ☐ money order.

Strip Of No Man's Land

This is the second half of *The BEAT's* opinion poll where teens express their feelings about the Sunset Strip controversy. Part I appeared in the last issue.

Only ages and initials appear with the opinions, which were gathered by a roving *BEAT* reporter, to ensure the privacy of the teenagers who exercised their freedom of speech.

★ ★ ★

Q.O. (18)—"There was no trouble on the Strip until the cops started it. No more trouble than there is any other place in the city. It was crowded, but there wasn't any trouble. Everything got started when the cops started. It got so you couldn't walk five steps without getting stopped."

R.W. (16)—"It burns me to hear people asking why the kids keep going to the Strip when they know they'll just get in trouble. That's *why* they keep going. You go up there and you can find yourself in jail for no reason, when you haven't done one thing wrong. Teenagers' rights are being violated, and they go back for more because they're mad. If they stopped going, the other side would have won, and it doesn't deserve to. We at least have to fight back that much, by continuing to be on the Strip."

A.V. (16)—"Why doesn't anyone print what's going on in other parts of Los Angeles? Police getting after teenagers isn't confined to the Strip. It's starting to happen all over town. Getting after them when they aren't doing anything wrong, I mean. I should know. I was stopped on the way out of a movie theater. It was just after ten o'clock, and they made me show them my I.D. When they saw how old I was, they said I'd better get home fast. I admire the kids on the Strip for not taking this kind of treatment."

E.L. (15)—"We didn't get violent until the cops got violent. If they can do it, why can't we? We have a right to defend ourselves, don't we?"

W.S. (19)—"It's about time someone found out why they want the kids out of the Strip area so bad. It's almost like someone ordered the police to get rid of the teenage element no matter what they had to do to accomplish this. There's more to this than we know about. I think they want to convert the Strip into something that wouldn't be successful unless they were able to keep kids out of the area. But first they have to get them out.

If this is true, and it could be, they probably want to make the Strip into something controversial, or they'd come out and say what their plans are."

D.K. (17)—"I don't get any of this, especially the part about the National Guard being on alert. The *National Guard?* Someone has got to be kidding. No, they aren't kidding, they're trying to make the situation sound like a full-scale riot. It isn't that way at all. Something is going on in this town."

O.C. (16)—"I was there the night things got kind of wild and the bit happened with the buses. It wasn't written up in the paper the way it happened. It was made to sound like there were thousands of dollars worth of damage. The total damage done was a hundred and fifty-eight dollars, including towing charges for the buses. I'm against violence, but when somebody pushes you too far for too long, you get too mad to think clearly."

F.L. (18)—"You wouldn't believe some of the people who have been arrested on the Strip, just because they happened to be there. People everyone knows. The police really change their tune when they find out they've dragged in somebody important for no reason. I think the whole thing is a big game, not being played by the kids, being played *with* them."

M.M. (18)—"More and more people are coming over to the kids' side. Quite a few adults were beaten up by police a few Saturday nights ago. They were yelling across the street at the kids at Pandora's and the police moved in on them instead of the kids. That wasn't in the paper. I don't know why it wasn't, but I never saw it. It should have been printed. Even more people might realize it isn't just teenagers who are getting kicked around. They talk about kids taking drugs. The police are the ones who are acting like they're on something."

J.H. (16)—"It's unbelievable. All of it. That thing about Sonny & Cher not getting to be in the Rose Parade because they happened to be on the Strip and a photographer took a picture of them. I live in the town (Monterey Park) that voted not to let them be in the parade. I'm ashamed to live there. Why are people so narrow? I just can't believe any of this could happen in this country."

B.N. (15)—"I think the whole business is hilarious. It shows how dumb most kids are. The Strip is no big deal. It isn't even fun. But they're putting up this big fight to stay there, and that's giving the cops an excuse to have a field day. These kids are either too young or too dumb to know where the real fun is. They'd rather march and carry signs instead of picking up on the action in places the cops don't even know about."

...**HERE THEY COME**—for better or worse they're on their way

KRLA ARCHIVES

John's Children At $3.00 A Minute

By Rochelle Reed

The ingredients for a typical day of work at *The BEAT* usually consists of six jabbering PR men, five screaming reporters, four clicking typewriters, three ringing telephones, two playful poodles, one blaring radio and no composure what-so-ever.

Consequently, it came as no surprise when I picked up the phone to hear a nasal voice announce, "London, England calling," followed by "Hello, Hallo, Hell!OOOOO, Hi!"

John's Children had met Alexander Graham Bell.

First In Line

First on the line was manager Simon Napier-Bell, who does similar duties for the Yardbirds. There was a peculiar tinge to his speech, as though he'd just finished devouring his air mail edition of the paper, stamps and all. Diabolical delight does that to some people.

"Here's Chris," he said innocently.

After a momentary pause, drummer Chris plugged into the line.

"Hello!"
"Hi!"
"Hi!"
"Hello!"
"This is Chris..."

After we finished introducing ourselves, I got down to business.

"How did John's Children first get together?"

"Well... I don't know... we just sort of... had a group... and..."

Leapfrogging through my head, I remembered that the group had just finished a tour in France. So, I switched to Method #2.

"How did Paris audiences react to your performances?"

"Paris audiences? They like *wild* stuff... we let ourselves go. Sometimes we were half carried off the stage!"

About this time, bass guitarist John broke into the conversation.

"What's happening on the pop scene in England?" I questioned.

"I think it's died down a lot," John answered. "We've completely broken with the scene. We're very unconventional."

"How did you arrive at that?"

"We just started doing it. We never followed anyone or anything else...we just started realizing it."

Which is precisely how it all happened for the British lads who, for once, weren't born poor and footloose.

John's Children have had very good educations at private schools and universities before turning to music fulltime. Simon Napier-Bell describes their personal performances a message of the "English new wave generation." "Andrew, who sings lead on "Smashed! Blocked!", usually gets into a trance, as if he were at a seance," he says.

Other members of John's Children — John, Chris and Geoffrey — often work on lead singer Andrew to provoke him into a state of submission or manipulate him like a puppet. Eventually, Andrew is hyped into a state of sublimity to the point where he collapses on stage before the set is complete.

"When are you coming to the U.S.?" I asked Andy, knowing full well that the date is set for sometime this month. "And by the way," I asked innocently, "How's the weather?"

"COOOOOOOOLD!" boomed through the receiver, as though London was only six blocks, rather than six thousand miles away.

I leaned back in my chair, opened the curtains, and described California weather. "It's about 80 degrees," I said for a starter.

"Ohhhhhhh..."

"And we can see all the way to the ocean."

DESPITE THE USUAL VISA TROUBLE, John's Children are hoping to hit the U.S. later this month. Seen from left to right are, John Hewlett, Chris Townson, and Andrew Ellison and Geoffrey McCleland.

"AHHHHHHHHH..."

"There's a girl walking down Vine Street in shorts."

"You're kidding????"

"How do you feel about coming to the U.S.?"

"We're looking forward to it!" exclaimed Andy excitedly.

Not to leave out Geoffrey, lead guitarist, I asked to talk to him.

"Describe the rest of the guys," I ordered him.

Description?

He gulped several times and launched into his version of John's Children.

"Well, John's very ugly. He's sort of short, has three legs and walks on his head. Chris, well, he's a big egotist, always trying to boost his personality. Andy? Andy's lovely and has blond hair..."

The five-way connection suddenly exploded: "Egotist? Egotist? Ugly? Short!... wait a minute! What do you look like?"

"Me?" I asked.

"Yes, you. We're doing a little article on you for an English paper, you see, and the weather here is cold and it's just fine and there's people walking down the street in swimsuits but there's snow on the mountains and they have three legs and John, well, he wears a white crew neck sweater and sometimes they have to pull Andrew off the stage and it has snow on it and you sound far away and hello? hallo? hi? Well, hi there and you don't say and quite, quite and you have long hair? and say, my name's Andrew, I'm Chris, say Geoffrey, how's the weather...?"

I spent the rest of the day playing with the two poodles. It wasn't as much fun as talking to John's Children, but it was much saner.

The Adventures of Robin Boyd

©1965 By Shirley Poston

Robin's jaw dropped a distance of approximately seven feet, revealing not only her surprise, but the fact that her group *hadn't* had 34% fewer cavities.

"I repeat," repeated The Budge. "Tell me I'm dreaming *that!*"

"You're dreaming *that*," Robin twittered, in one of her rare(ly successful) attempts at humor. But it wasn't foony.

The Budge stamped her foot (Robin's, that is.) "You tell me where that *came* from," she demanded hoarsely. "And you tell me where that came from RIGHT NOW!"

"Can't Imagine"

Robin smiled hysterically. "I can't imagine what you're talking about."

"I'm talking about *THAT!*" blithered The Budge.

"Oh," Robin shrieked nonchalantly. "Do you happen to be referring to the two new guitars, the two new amps, and the set of drums which happen to be stacked in the corner of my room?"

"Thank Gawd... she sees them, too." With this, The Budge swooned senseless to the carpet.

Feeling like joining her, Robin controlled herself (a pleasant change.) The Budge's average Standard-Faint usually lasted about ten seconds. But, this was a Super-Snit, which meant Robin had at least half-a-mo to come up with an answer.

The motor in Robin's alleged head went into high gear, and although she could swear she heard a rod knocking, she was ready when The Budge began to stir (using the spoon she always kept handy for... oh, let's not start *that* again.)

"I will now tell you where that came from," Robin announced as her friend's eyes crept warily open. "I don't honestly *know* where it came from."

The Budge checked her watch. "Fast, but not good," she said, not without a touch of sarcasm.

"Hah?" Robin inquired politely.

"I mean that's one of the fastest whoppers I've ever heard anyone make up, but it's not good *enough*, you *twit!*"

"But... but..." Robin butted. "It's *not* a whopper."

And, in a way, it wasn't. George had been there just hours ago. During his visit, Robin had wailed that there wasn't one single (or, for that matter, *married*) rock and roll band in the city (argh) of Pitchfork.

When George had suggested *she* start one, she had re-wailed about her lack of musical instruments (not to mention her lack of talent). Now, after having put two and two together (and coming up with five, as usual), Robin assumed George was responsible for all this. But she wasn't really telling Budgie a whopper. Maybe she *dishonestly* knew, but she didn't *honestly* know! Re-hah?)

"Robin *Boyd*," spat The Budge. "Gerroff it and explain those drums and those..."

"DROOMS?" Ringo (as in Boyd, as in Boyd) interrupted in a bellow from the other side of the closed door. "Did I hear someone say *drooms?*" she re-bellowed, bursting (and I kid you not) into the room.

Then she set eyes on the shiny set of same. "LOODWIGS," she boomed. Falling to her knees, she embraced the bass and kissed the cymbal so hard its teeth rattled.

It was several moments (and it seemed like *years*) before she stopped long enough to address Robin and Budgie, who were staring at her aghast. (Located, for those interested, near her aghastly.)

Anyparth???

"Where did all this stuff come from, anyparth?"

"It belongs to The Budge," Robin lied, nearly severaing a rather necessary portion of her friend's anatomy with a pinch that came directly to the point. "We're going to start our own group!"

"Groovesville!" shouted Ringo. With this, she flang a guitar at Robin and recommenced blamming.

"Not in *here*, stupid," Robin snapped, and Ringo immediately ran out of the room, clutching the brass drum.

The minute she left, Budgie returned the pinch. "Why did you say *that?*"

"I *had* to," Robin hissed. "I don't want to start a big hysterical bit about where the stuff came from until we find *out* where it came from!"

The Budge gave her a look that would have shattered glass. "Okay, Robin *Irene* Boyd. I'll believe you about dreaming the Beatle in the bedroom. And I'll *pretend* to believe you about the instruments. But if ONE MORE unbelievable thingy happens, I am going to stagger off toward the horizon, *drooling!*"

"But *mother*," they heard Ringo wail. "We're starting our own group! Budge has guitars, too, and amps and everything! We have to start *practicing!*"

"Not in *here*, stupid," replied Mrs. Boyd, addressing this comment to the bass drum instead of her sturdy daughter. (It was difficult to tell, difficult to tell.)

"But *where?*" Ringo re-wailed. Mrs. Boyd pointed out the window at the endless South Dakota prairie. "Out there," she said firmly. "*Way* out there."

Some time later, after the instruments had been set up in the middle of nowhere (I'll say), and plugged in (thanks to the thirty-six extension cords Mrs. Boyd was only *too* happy to provide), the girls were ready for their first try.

Robin picked up a frosty guitar. She looked at The Budge. "This is going to be gross," she warned. "I've never played one of these things before."

The Budge picked up a frosty guitar. She looked at Robin. "I have a feeling *gross* is not the word. I don't even know which end you blow into."

"Oh, well," Robin shrugged. "We can learn." Then she turned to Ringo, who was carefully adjusting her tam. "So hit it already, Beverly Lou."

Ringo started to hit it. Suddenly the three of them burst into hysterical laughter.

"Does this remind you of anything?" Robin croaked.

"As in shivering on the plains?" Budgie roared.

Which Plains?

"As in Salisbury?" Ringo wheezed.

"*We look just like the Beatles!*" they burbled in unison.

Continuing to burble, Robin took aim and struck the first chord (fully expecting it to strike her back.)

They made it half-way through "The Night Before" before they realized what was happening. And it was then that Robin knew what she must do.

She must run after Budgie, who had just staggered off toward the horizon, *drooling!* And, by the time she caught up with her, she must have dreamed up the whopper of all *time*. On account of because they didn't just *look* like the Beatles. They also *sounded* like them!

(To Be Continued Next Issue)

KRLA ARCHIVES

Formula For Pop Success

By Carol Deck

Ever notice how most of the successful pop groups fall into a pattern? It's almost as though there's a formula for creating a successful group.

Like, for instance, there's the genius — every group (and I'm only talking about the groups that make it — forget those that don't) has at least one genius at it's core (a John Lennon, Eric Burdon or Brian Wilson.) Some groups are lucky and have more than one genius, but it's essential that you have at least one.

Musician

Then too, you've got to have a top rated musician, someone who's mastered at least one instrument to such an extent that he's recognized by his peers as tops for that instrument (a George Harrison or a Jeff Beck.)

It's also essential that you have at least one very good looking member whom fans can point out to their parents as proof that not all rock and roll singers are ugly. You've got to have a Paul McCartney (keep calm kids, I know there's a lot more to Paul than just his looks), a Mark Lindsay or a Davy Jones. Even the Stones, who aren't exactly world reknowned for their beauty, have Keith Richard.

And every group has a quiet member — someone who says absolutely nothing during interviews and generally refuses to express his opinions on the world (Charlie Watts, Chris Dreja and Peter Tork.) These are the ones that worry reporters for we know that usually the less they say the more they think and often have great insights into the world about them but getting it out of them is like pulling teeth. These are also the ones the fans tend to want to mother.

Combinations

Well, those four are the basic essentials for a group, but there's one more that really shouldn't be left out and that is the clown. A successful group usually has one member who is a fun loving, outgoing, extroverted character who generally keeps everyone's spirits up. There's Micky Dolenz, Dennis Wilson, Zollie Yanovsky, Phil Volk. A clown may not be totally necessary, but he sure helps.

And of course you can have any combinations of the above. There's the quiet genius (John Sebastian, Jim McGuinn), the good looking genius (Herb Alpert), and the good looking clown (Herman.) And there are many top rated quiet musicians, for people who dedicate their lives to an instrument tend to be a little on the quiet side with society.

This formula, and variations of it, have proved successful with numerous groups. Look at the Beatles. They're almost a prototype of it. They've got a genius (Lennon), a musician (Harrison), a good looker (McCartney) (I know, I know there's more to Paul than just what meets the eye) and a combination clown and quiet one (Ringo — he's not the extroverted kind of clown, but he has a natural sense of comedy that may put him in the Buster Keaton category some day).

But then there's the Stones. They've got a little bit of everything, as every top group does, but they've also got the mighty mouth — Jagger — who never has played by the rules. Jagger is likely to be, at any point in the game, all or none of these all by himself.

Then There's . . .

And then there's the Association, who can't be anything but tops just because they have so much of everything. All six of them are capable of genius, they've got a couple of really top musicians and when it comes to clowning, they're all out-right idiots. I suppose if you're looking for great looks, Ted will stand out and when it comes to being the quiet type, theoretically all six are capable, but Brian probably would get the credit in that department.

So you see it really isn't that hard to create a good group. You just find one member in each category, or any combinations thereof, add a lot of luck and you're on your way to your first million seller.

BEATLES have all components for success — Bob Vaughn has UNCLE.

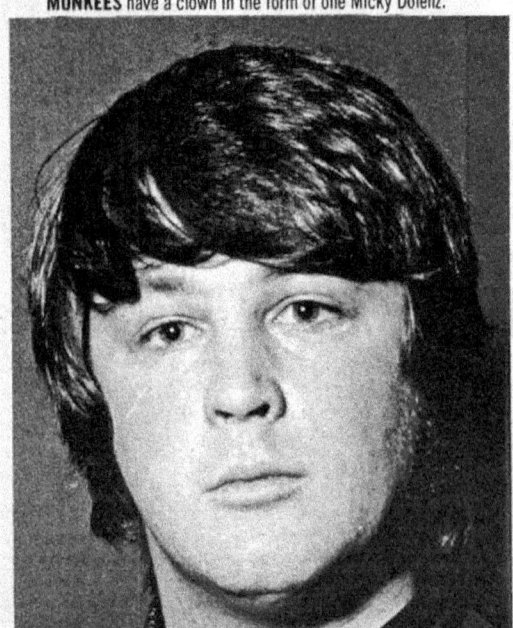

MONKEES have a clown in the form of one Micky Dolenz.

STONES have a non-conformist.

BEACH BOYS have the "genius" of Brian Wilson.

RAIDERS have pony-tailed Mark.

ASSOCIATION number six but wish Elke Summer was lucky seven.

KRLA ARCHIVES

Joan Baez: A Study In Protest

By Rochelle Reed

When the curtains draw back and the spotlight silhouettes her against an empty stage, it's difficult to believe that slight, dark-haired Joan Baez is standing in opposition to the entire United States government.

Each year, Joan (she refuses to be called Miss Baez) withholds 60 percent of her taxes from the Internal Revenue Service, and when the percentage going towards the military is increased to 75 percent in April, she will withhold that amount.

The reason is that though her voice carries messages of emptiness, hunger and sorrow, Joan believes that another life exists beneath the surface of the wars, violence and mass corruption about which she sings. Because of this innate belief, the girl with the sound of a songbird has remained silent for nearly a year, devoting her time instead to "growing up" and operating her Institute for the Study of Non-violence in Carmel, California.

Last month, Joan came out of her voluntary withdrawal to perform at a Los Angeles concert, with proceeds going to striking Delano, Calif. farm workers. Beforehand, she held a press conference, explaining to anxious newspaper and wire service reporters why she has adopted her highly unpopular philosophy and how she is attempting to convert others.

Joan first began withholding the majority of her taxes three years ago, when she returned her partial payment with a note to the effect that she refused to support the military.

"Some Game"

"After they realized this wasn't just some little game I was playing," she says, "they began to get worried." Until now, the government has proceeded to get the money out of the bank, she explained to the press, but conceivably the day may come when there is no money to withdraw. Then the government would begin by attaching her house, school and other material possessions.

"I won't pay the 60 percent," she says, "not only because of Viet Nam but any war," adding that "of course," she would go to jail in support of her beliefs.

Though most of the press conference was confined to social-political observations, BEAT managed to question Joan about some of the present day developments on the music and youth scene.

Upon hearing that Sonny and Cher were kicked off a Rose Parade float after they were photographed observing a demonstration on Sunset Strip, she commented, "Offhand, it sounds like a pretty dumb thing for (Monterey Park) to do."

As for the Sunset Strip, Joan paraphrased Mahatma Gandi, Indian social reformer and advocate of non-violence. "Gandhi said hoodlums were not dropped out of the sky. The curfew or lack of one isn't really going to stop anyone. It's hard to know what to do. These kids are lost, confused. What, really, have we shown them that's better?"

Joan cuts all her recordings either in concert or at New York studios. She plans to complete a rock and roll album soon, although she adds that she has "no taste for most of it." She has completed some songs that she classifies as "rank" and says "the rank stuff I'll drop and fill it in with things I think are nice."

But the life of Joan Baez is no longer limited to music. Instead, she yearns to be much more than a singer – a scholar, writer and student.

Joan's main concern is the advocation of non-violence, and her philosophy is summed up by the contradiction she finds in the phrase, "God and Country." This, she says, is a paradox: it must be either one or the other, not both. The reason is that God says "Thou shalt not kill" and Country says "Thou shalt not kill, except for enemies"—which change, according to Joan, every five years. She cites the fact that in the last twenty years, enemies of the United States have included the Germany, Russia, Communist Satellites, Japanese, Red Chinese and Viet Cong.

Realistic?

"I'm trying to be realistic," she offers. "There's no chance at all for us to survive more than 10 or 20 years at the rate we're going. All the Presidents say so. Somehow," she continues, "the world must come to a complete stop and reverse directions."

Joan hopes to realize a "world where it's no longer fair to bump off someone because he's an enemy. We say it's wrong to kill, then we start making excuses. Eventually, if we're to survive, we have to deal with the 'enemy' without having to drop napalm all over him."

Meanwhile, Joan plans to concentrate her efforts on her school, and says that if she turns out one pacifist a year, she's satisfied.

Gazing out to the press, the corners of her mouth turned up in a smile, Joan declared, "I just wish they'd try to draft 25-year-old ladies."

JOAN BAEZ... TAKING TIME OUT TO "GROW UP."

BEAT SHOWCASE
(spotlighting new talent on the pop scene)

THE BOYS NEXT DOOR
An Indiana BEAT subscriber clued us in on this group, currently sweeping the Midwest scene. They've performed with the Beach Boys (whom they slightly resemble), Lovin' Spoonful, Herman and others. Back, (left to right), The Boys Next Door (we wish!) are Skeet Bushor, Jim Koss; middle, Steve Drybread, Steve Lester; and in front, Jim Adams.

THE KITCHEN CINQ
"Everything but the kitchen sink," people always say about a woman's handbag. Now Suzie Jane Kokum has found herself a Kitchen Cinq, which she is producing for LHI Records. Counterclock-wise, the Cinq include Dallas Smith, Dale Gardner, Jim Parker, Mark Creamer and Johnny Stark.

THE PAPERHANGERS
Another of our readers wrote us about The Paperhangers, a Southern California group who "sound naturally like the Association." The guys range in age from 17 to 19 and will soon release a single on Capitol, "Guess What I See" c/w "Time Will Tell." Left to right, The Paperhangers are Pete Berggquist, Ron Anello, Vito Giovannelli, Brent Maglia.

KRLA ARCHIVES

...DR. VON MEIER pictured during one of his UCLA classes.

Professor Of Pop Requires *The BEAT*

We heard through the grapevine that BEAT is required reading at the University of California at Los Angeles but we didn't really believe it until last week, when suddenly our office was swamped with college students asking to see our files.

We happily obliged, since it turned out the students were working on term papers for the art history class in which BEAT really is required reading. Their assignment was to document a particular record from its conception in the artists' mind to its final drop from the music charts.

We thought the unique class was interesting enough to warrant a story so we asked UCLA student Ron Koslow to tell us more about his class and the professor who teaches it.

By Ron Koslow

He stands at the lectern wearing an orange shirt, flowered Carnaby street tie, checked pants and a striped jacket. The sounds of the Stones or Supremes fill the lecture hall as over four hundred UCLA students anxiously await the words of Dr. Kurt Von Meier, professor of pop and authority on rock 'n roll, past and present.

At 32, with a Ph.D. in Art History from Princeton University, Kurt Von Meier is becoming widely acknowledged as one of the true experts on the history and development of rock 'n roll.

"Let's face it," Dr. Von Meier says, "pop music as we know it today is the most widespread, influential musical form the world has ever known. It offers something for everyone, combining many different sounds and ideas from many different places.

Best Blues

"For example, we have some of the best blues music coming to us via England from the Stones and Animals, in addition to the great continuing tradition of singers like Otis Redding or Bobby "Blue" Bland, not to mention the ever present soul of James Brown.

"Here at home," he continues, "we have some of the most meaningful poetry of the 20th century, put to music by Bob Dylan and Chuck Berry. It's also amazing to see how the Beatles continue to revolutionize the industry—their genius cannot be denied."

As for the groups of the future, the professor points to the Velvet Underground (who he convinced to visit a Hollywood club, The Trip, last May). He also cites the Who, a brilliant young English group and the City Lights, an underground L.A. group. These groups specialize in experimental sounds, often with experimental instrumentation and must be both heard and seen to be appreciated.

Book

Dr. Von Meier, along with Dr. Carl Belz of Mills College in Oakland, is in the process of completing the first substantial book ever written on the history and development of the rock 'n roll/pop music scene.

"We hope the book will help young people to appreciate their music more, and give adults a better understanding of why it should be appreciated," he concludes.

Anita Bryant Honored By USO Council

Anita Bryant has been elected to the USO National Council by action of the National Board of Governors. Long active in numerous phases of USO activities, Miss Bryant has been honored by Chicago's USO with the 25th anniversary Silver Medallion Award and is the recipient of the Gold 25th Anniversary charm presented at the 1966 National Council dinner in Washington, D.C.

Anita spent the Christmas holidays with Bob Hope and his troupe entertaining our servicemen in Vietnam. It marked Anita's seventy consecutive holiday tour overseas for USO, as well as her fourth to entertain troops stationed in Vietnam.

The Raiders On The Run

By Eden

They're running...running... RUNNING *faster* every day; *longer* every night; *farther* with each week and month; and *still* they go on *running*.

Running to the waiting plane... running for a taxicab...running for the concert stage...running to the dressing rooms...running from the frenzied fans...running to another plane.

The Raider's world is a *running* world; a world of non-stop activity and motion, one which never, ever stands still or stops to catch its breath...*or theirs!*

Inside Glimpses

But sometimes...just *sometimes*, they slow down just enough that you can catch a *glimpse* of what goes on *inside* the Raider world, behind the running which surrounds it. And then you will see five highly intelligent, distinctly different individuals involved in five very special "running" worlds of their own.

You might find a dazzling smile, set off by two of the world's most distinguished front teeth and that would have to be The Fang. Phil Volk—of bass guitars, and cowboy hats; of smiles, and laughs, and practical jokes, of artist's brushes, and writer's pens; of singer's notes of happy songs.

Although he fairly bursts with noise and happy motion most of the time, he, too, can be a man of quiet, sitting off to one side for just a moment to contemplate the world around him. He gathers precious, favorite things around him; and his collection includes close friends and family, a fairy tale childhood, and fond memories of happy days spent in schools back home.

Not far away there *has* to be another smile, a horn of laughter, and Phillip's "twin" onstage— Harpo. Blue eyes which meet you head on with honesty; a smile that says "I love you!"; and a personality which *no one* could resist! This Raider is, perhaps, the most consistent, almost never seen without a smile, and seldom found in moods of sadness.

Only moments snatched from running times are given over to solitary moods of pensive obserbation—but those unusual moments of isolation are quite extraordinary, and seldom seen by others. The deeper thoughts of sensitivity and compassion are kept quietly within him, and find their release only in the physical expression of his actions.

"The Wizard" — the mad-scientist of the group—the question mark who sits behind the drums...that's Smitty. Perhaps the quietest Raider, the one who keeps the most unsaid, Smitty is *always* one of the most *astounding* individuals in the world.

Onstage—an excellent drummer, a master of good timing and comic actions. Off-stage, away from cameras...there is too much of the serious side of life to distract him from his laughter. He smiles a very bright and shiny smile—one which can light up his face as well as everything around him. But that smile is much more strictly rationed when the world is temporarily *not* tuned-in.

Worries

He worries about his fellow man, and about the dangers of war and fighting. He thinks about the problems as they exist now—but most importantly, he *goes on* to think of possible *solutions*. No, he's not the complaining kind. If there is a problem to be dealt with—Smitty will be the first to roll up his sleeves and pitch in; he can't content himself with simply sitting on the sidelines and grumbling disgruntled gripes of "life and times."

"Uncle Paul"—the perennial parent to just about *everyone*. The man who counsels friends and children, Raiders and fans, and anyone else who comes to him for advice.

One of the most talented comedians in the world, "Uncle Paul" is a master of subtle humor, the art of understatement, the all-important element of timing. A very funny man—onstage.

But when he isn't *running* frantically 'round a stage, you will find a very different Blue-Eyed Leader beneath that feathered Raider hat. His shoulders may be stooped just slightly, but if you look a little closer, you will see that they are weighted-down by the burden of responsibility which Paul has taken unto himself.

He is the one who must worry about four other Raiders; about each performance, and the direction in which all five careers will go at once from here; he is the one who worries about the money, and protects the interests of the group.

He is the one who is sought after for advice, and he is the one who must be father-brother-friend-adviser-baby sitter-guardian-performer-Leader and even *human being*. Not an *easy* task for *anyone!* But he is still the Fearless Leader of us all, and though he may assume all the responsibilities of his "family"—he never forgets to turn around and smile. Thank you, Uncle Paul.

One more—another Raider—the one who stands, perhaps, as a *symbol* of the Raiders—the one who stands....*alone*. And that is the only one-word way to speak of Mark Lindsay, a man who requires so *many* words that it is difficult to speak of him *at all!*

For the cameras, for the people—smiling, happy, dashing, gallant, laughing, care-free and outgoing. But even Mark's running must run slower sometimes, and then you see the torment and confusion of a young man searching for his name and meaning in a very *nameless* world of labels.

People

The first to be most deeply affected by other people, he is sometimes the last to show it, and *always* the last to forget it; people and their thoughts and problems stay with him a very long, long time.

And still, he is *alone*, and running...to his future, to a new world, and someday...to *himself*.

RAIDERS...running to another stage...running to a waiting crowd...running from the world behind them...*RAIDERS RUNNING TO SUCCESS*.

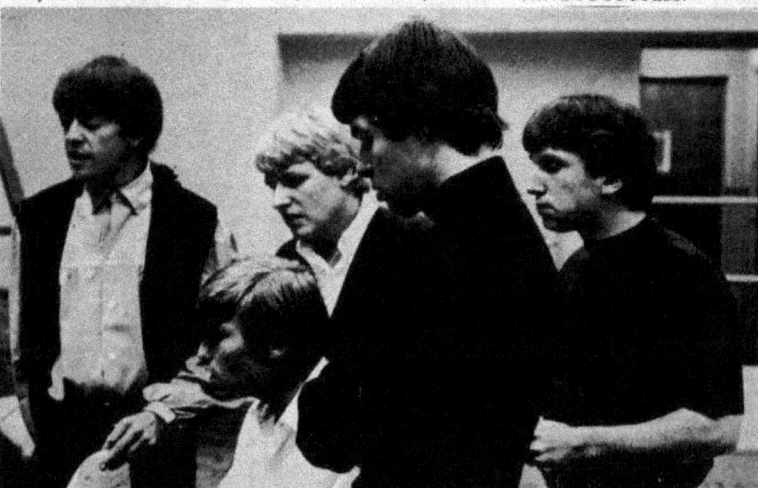

...THE RAIDERS IRON OUT the kinks in a new song with their producer, Terry Melcher.

KRLA ARCHIVES

Sandy Baron—Man Of Every Media

By Carol Deck

Sanfred Beresofsky never became a comedian. He always was one.

But it wasn't until he shortened his name to Sandy Baron, taking the Baron from the name of a bookstore in Brooklyn, and began making noise in practically every media of the entertainment industry that the *world* realized that he was a comedian, and a very good one.

During a break in the filming of his TV series, "Hey Landlord," Sandy explained a few of his ideas on the show, teenagers, his past and his future.

At the age of 28 Sandy's a little passed the teenage stage, but he's written several successful rock and roll songs and personally respects teens immensely.

"I hate calling them teens, though. I call them people."

A short while back Sandy was working off Broadway and supplementing his salary by writing songs. His most successful were, "I See The Writing On The Wall" and "Take Good Care of Her," both recorded by Adam Wade and "Let True Love Begin" the next to the last song Nat "King" Cole recorded.

Something New

Now he's working on something new. "I'm writing a contemporary musical about what happens in America to young satirists who poke fun at things people don't want to poke fun at."

It's still in the idea stage but the idea includes musical arrangements by someone like Burt Bacharach and music by someone like the Spoonful. It's to be similar to the story of Lenny Bruce.

Meanwhile he's working hard on the TV show. Sandy's performed in practically every media — records, Broadway, off Broadway, movies, nightclubs and television — but says he feels most comfortable in TV, particularly on "Hey Landlord" because it's one of the few TV series filmed in front of a live audience.

"TV combines the best of all of them. You gotta be honest and know who you are like on Broadway. You know you're not the whole ball game like in the movies. You're in front of a live audience so you've got the excitement of night clubs."

The one other field he really digs is college tours. "They explode your head. They love the same sense of danger that I do and I can break in new material with them."

About the show he says, "We've got the single toughest time slot on the air — against 'Ed Sullivan' and 'The F.B.I.'. But it's better than the other one they offered us — against the Star Spangled Banner and Let Us Pray."

But he's got great hopes for the show anyway. "It's gonna be a hit, although the title of the show doesn't help us at all."

No Trap

It's often said that there's nothing like a TV series to destroy a comedian but Sandy has no fear of being trapped in "Hey Landlord" for years to come.

"It won't be on for 10 or 12 years because Woody and I will outgrow it. And the audience will demand that we eventually get married. They'll sense that we're mature enough to get married and won't accept it anymore."

As far as marriage goes, Sandy already is, and very happily so. His wife, Ger, was once a dancer on "Hullabaloo" and he describes her as "getting groovier every day." Their friends call them Sandy and Ger and Sandy says, "We're the Sonny and Cher of comedy."

And comedy, Sandy realized early in life, is here to stay.

"I can't remember a day in my life when I didn't realize that people are absolutely insane.

"Comedy is one thing that ain't never going out of style. The one thing that mankind will always want to do is to laugh at mankind."

For Girls only

by shirley poston

I really hate to do a thingy like this to you, but do you happen to recall my last column? Yes, yes, I know...you had just finally succeeded in forgetting it and here I go bringing it up (as in chuck) again.

Still, the reference to my most recent scrambled mess of writty is necessary. On account of because this is sort of a continuation of same.

No, no, I'm not going to start vabbling (?) about vespers again. But this column (shirley I jest) is the second part of the letter which you read the first part of last week. (WHATTTTT?)

You remember. The part where the letter-writer's pen pal went to visit...dare I gasp it...GEORGE!

And away we go.

"I have this pen pal who lives in Herts, England and to make a long story short, she and her friend (both Beatle lovers) went to Surrey (aaah...just the sound of the place where he B-r-e-a-t-h-e-s!) for the day to see if they could find J.G. and R's homes. Well, neither John or Ringo were home. However, they did manage to see Zak with his nanny.

"So on they walked to Esher. (EEEK! They're closer!) They had a hard time finding the place, but suddenly *there it was*. A huge wall! It was George's home, and the electric gate was *OPEN!*

"They tried peeking around and saw HIM walking around near the window. (Oh, that sweet bouncin' walk.) Anywindow, they waited around outside and this man (Indian) came out in a car. He said that George had bought some Persien (spelling) rugs from him and he showed them the signed check!

"After he left, Pattie came racing out (in a car). They realized that this was their chance to talk to him without anyone around. So they walked in and went toward the door. (They had made him a cat and mouse out of black felt and wanted him to have them.)

"As they neared the door, they saw him scowl out at them. Suddenly, before they knocked, the door burst open and THERE HE WAS! (OH DIE!)

"He wasn't mad at all. He was larfing and grinning all over the place. His hair was very long and dark and sort of fluffy. He had on white pants and a blue-and-white striped shirt. The shirt was all open at the neck and his adamsapple was sooo sexy.

"I'll try and relate the conversation which followed...

G. — "We've got something for you!"

George — "What's this? Let's see."

K. — "It's a cat, but we forgot his tail."

At this point, G. smelled something coming from the house and asked if George had been using Dettol.

George — "Yeah, the cat's been _____ all over the carpet again." (No, he didn't say what you're thinking.)

All of them laughed and then they asked for his autograph. When he said "sure, luvs", they asked for an autograph for me, too.

"They talked a bit more and then left. They sent me the autograph and some gravel and leaves from his house. I think I must have been in shock for hours! I'm surprised the neighbors didn't think I was being murdered the way I was spazing around the house!"

Well, I can't say I *blame* her for spazing around. I'm afraid to even *think* of what I'd do if I received something like that in the mail. (In other words, re-get out the Dettol, whatever that is.)

I see I've been up to my usual confusing tricks. I never know how to get it across that I'm printing what someone else said. You're supposed to start each paragraph with one of those "thingies," but I don't believe I quite made it, as usual.

Oh well, I'd promise to get my grammar straightened out (not to mention my gramper), but I have a feeling it would be all in vain. By the time I had it all figured out, they would have come for me anynet.

Speaking of Goerge...I haven't said that for so long, I've forgotten how to spel it... speaking of coming-for-me, before they do, I must tell you about something that is truly the wildest thingy in the entire. (As in world, as in world.)

It is undoubtedly the mind-blower of the century when a person is...aheam...rather *interested* in someone who has the same first name as your fave. (As in George.) (Re-spaz.)

I say "rather interested" because if you're totally sprung over the name-alike, you think of him instead of Harrison when you're murmuring "Oh, *George*" at appropriate moments.

Really, it is a blast. So much of a blast, it's almost worth going out and conducting a *search* for your own George, John, Mark, Pauley, Richie, and what-have-you. (What have I? A problem.)

If you succeed, you'll also find yourself using his name constantly when you're talking to him (not to mention when you aren't).

That sounds moronic, but will try to explain. Like, my name is Shirley (when it isn't Mud), but if you were talking to me, you wouldn't start every sentence with my name. Think about it. You really don't use a person's name that often.

Howsomever, when it's a case of same-name, you say it practically every other breath. And considering the fact that my breath goes out for track every time I even think of George Hilton Harrison (that's an inn joke) (Gawd), that's saying a lot.

Speaking of saying a lot, it would be nice if I would at least start saying *something* in this... this...oh, *you* know...again. But I've been in such a blithery mood lately, I've really been foaming at the typewriter.

Oh, well...maybe you need the sleep.

DISCussion

There seems to have been a rash of recent releases from Sonny and Cher, but the very latest duo-disking from the pair is one of the best.

Cher's solo effort was the beautiful "Mama," but now Sonny and Cher have recorded together once again and the result is a very timely, well-performed, well-produced record entitled "The Beat Goes On." This should be their biggest national hit in many months.

* * *

P.J. Proby confided to *The BEAT*, in an exclusive interview some months ago when he first returned to this country, that he would be doing no more recording for at least three years, due to some legal hang-ups with his record company.

Apparently those "hang-ups" have straightened themselves out, however, because P.J. has returned to the pop chart race with a very strong R&B-type entry, "Niki Hoeky." The title-tag doesn't make a lot of sense, and the lyrics aren't too much more profound, but the record is about as funky as Mr. Proby can get... and that's pretty *funky*!

R&B seems to be the dominant trend — or one of them — in the pop field right now, and certainly it is one direction in which many pop people are heading. So, watch for a hit with this new one.

* * *

There has been quite a promotion campaign launched for a new young singer named simply "Keith." Since most huge promotion campaigns usually turn out to be just another boring type campaign, they are frequently ignored.

Only accidentally having heard his first record, "(98.6)" did I discover that there might just be something to this one after all. It's actually a very good, slightly unusual, slightly pretty, slightly original disc and with enough "promotion" — he might have a hit. P.S. Flip side is entitled "The Teeny Bopper Song."

* * *

Many complimentations to Mr. Tom Jones for "The Green, Green Grass of Home." Beautiful song and poignant lyrics are gonna propel this one to the top for Tiger Tom.

By the way, next time someone tells you that Eric Burdon is England's greatest (and perhaps *only*) soul singer, tell them to turn their ears on to Tom-Tom. He may be of Welsh descent, but that's part of the British Isles!

KRLA ARCHIVES

The BEAT Goes To The Movies

'ANY WEDNESDAY'

The actors can't be pinned down in "Any Wednesday"—because Warner Bros.' new Technicolor comedy boasts one of the most unusual optical effects ever attempted in a motion picture.

Stars Jane Fonda, Jason Robards, Dean Jones and Rosemary Murphy are shifted about various settings by director Robert Ellis Miller, via a complicated split-screen effect. During a single scene, Robards appears and disappears thrice on screen, being "wiped out" each time by the movement of another actor, in another place.

It's all part of the frantic action in the zany comedy of romantic errors, based on Muriel Resnik's hit Broadway play.

Julius J. Epstein produced "Any Wednesday" from his own screenplay. The motion picture was filmed partly on location in New York City, on the fashionable upper East Side.

...HAPPINESS IS A BIRTHDAY CAKE?

...HAPPINESS FOR DEAN IS A PAIR OF KEYS.

...RAINY DAY BLUES FOR JANE AND JASON.

...DEAN JONES PORTRAYS A HAPPY ARRIVAL FROM AKRON, OHIO.

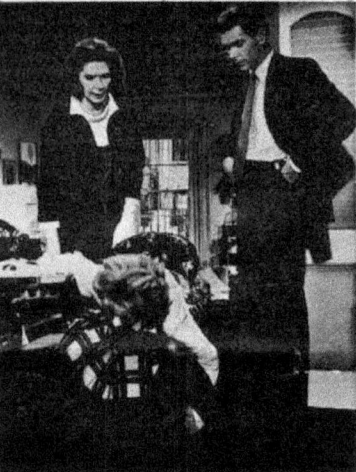
...ONE OF THE MORE GRACEFUL SCENES!

CARL WILSON:
'Weird Sounds Don't Blow My Mind'

By Eden

There are three Wilson brothers, a cousin, and a friend. Brian, Carl, Dennis, Mike and Al. Collectively, they are The Beach Boys. There are five of them, but they are seldom "collected" into the same place at the same time unless they are on tour, or performing.

You will find them dropping in on one another at home, or racing their cars, or riding their motorcycles, or writing a new song, or re-recording a track until it "feels" just right, or just "getting away from it all" down by the beach.

Unusual Trio

The Wilsons Three are a most unusual trio of brothers. Brian and Carl are the two most alike; apart from the obvious physical resemblance, Brian—the eldest—and Carl—the "baby" of the family—think and speak and even act very much along the same lines. They are very much interested in thinking; in the various thought processes, in the spiritual and emotional concepts of the mind, and with the various powers—both *known* and as yet undiscovered, which are possessed by the mind.

Dennis—the middle Wilson brother—is the "nature boy" as brother Brian describes him. He is the young man so sensitive that he can communicate with the creatures and creations of nature. He loves all things concerned with the outdoors, and is an avid enthusiast of nearly all outdoor sports.

Racer

He is also the driving expert in the family, and is well-known for his expert racing.

As human beings, the Wilsons are all warm and generous people. They have a talent for more-or-less "adopting" you and making *you* feel like a member of the family. Which might, at times, be easier than it sounds, for it quickly seems as though the *whole world* is a part of the Wilson family! There are a vast number of cousins and other assorted Wilson-type relatives to be found in the near vicinity of any one of the Beach Boys.

All five of the Beach Boys (except Bruce Johnson) are married now, but this has in no way hurt their popularity. Perhaps that is because their fans are able to pick up the warm family-vibrations from the group, and can feel somehow included in that family.

Carl is the most recent departee from the bachelor ranks, and his beautiful bride is the sister of Billy Hinsche, of Dino, Desi, and Billy.

I stopped in to visit Carl and Annie in their beautiful Beverly Hills home and was immediately greeted with the usual warmth and hospitality which is so characteristic of the Wilsons.

Carl studied guitar briefly for about three months once when he took lessons from a studio. Then, a friend—John Maus, of the successful Walker Brothers—taught him a great deal about the guitar.

Harmony

This was the only formal musical education which Carl has had, yet he is a member of a group whose music has had a very widespread affect on the very structure of popular music. Like his talented brother, Carl is very much interested in harmony—always one of the most important factors in the unique Beach Boys' sounds, and for a moment he considered the possible meanings of harmony.

He called it a "love vibration"—a really strong emotion or feeling. And "vibrations" are very important to both Carl and Brian. Each record must have exactly the "right sound," the "right feeling." It must give very good vibrations before they will release it.

Emotions

He explained that, "I don't think people would be as emotional listening to a one-note solo instead of a beautiful harmony passage. Harmony carries a vibration that, I think a single note just doesn't have."

Carl feels that "vibrations" are important to everyone, though everyone is not consciously aware of them. Trying to relate his concept of these vibrations to others, Carl tried to sum his ideas up by explaining that "Vibrations are just another plane, or plateau of sensitivity. It's just another *feeling*; you *feel* vibrations."

Carl has a fine appreciation of good music—music which is well-written and well-executed. And though he enjoys different and interesting instrumentations, he doesn't necessarily go for the ultra-weird. "Weird sounds don't blow my mind—*great* ones do!"

He hasn't yet begun to involve himself in the writing and producing area of record production, but agrees that he would be interested in someday giving it a try. He greatly admires the work and talents of Brian, but feels that he hasn't yet become interested enough in these things to be able to work in this area. Philosophically, he concludes that, "If it will come—it will come."

New Album

Motion pictures hold a very strong attraction for Carl, and he hopes to be able to become involved in that medium of entertainment as soon as possible. The immediate future holds the creation of a new album—an LP which is very important to all of the Beach Boys—and a European tour in October.

As for the future after that... well, it is undoubtedly full of very good vibrations for the Beach Boys.

KRLA ARCHIVES

RECORDS FREE FROM RC®
You'll Flip at the ZZZIP in RC® Cola

while you swing to your favorite stars! RC and music, perfect partners for the perfect lift

TAKE 1 ALBUM FREE

For everyone you buy... with 6 cork liners or seals from R.C. bottle caps over 100 Capitol LP's available. Order as often as you wish. Nothing to join. Look for this display at your favorite store.

Here's your best way yet to save *more* on the records you want. In dollars-and-cents terms you get two albums that the Capitol Record Club sells for $3.98 each time you buy one. The savings are even bigger on stereo records! And there are no shipping charges to pay, nothing else to join or buy.

What's more, you choose from top albums by today's biggest stars, including the Beatles, David McCallum, Frank Sinatra, Lou Rawls, Buck Owens, Petula Clark, the Outsiders, Nancy Wilson, Dean Martin, Sonny James, the Beach Boys and many others.

OTHER FINE BRANDS: DIET-RITE®COLA, NEHI®BEVERAGES, PART-T-PAK®BEVERAGES, UPPER 10®
"ROYAL CROWN" AND "RC" REG. U.S. PAT. OFF., ©1966 ROYAL CROWN COLA CO.

KRLA ARCHIVES

America's Pop Music NEWSpaper

KRLA Edition BEAT

JANUARY 28, 1967

25¢

MONKEES SURPASS BEATLE SALES!
See Page 1

KRLA BEAT

Volume 2, Number 33   January 28, 1967

TOM JONES AWARDED GOLD RECORD; FIRST IN HISTORY OF DISC LABEL

Tom Jones became the first British artist in the history of Decca Records to receive a Gold Record for British sales when his "Green Green Grass Of Home" passed the million mark last week.

While Gold Records are admittedly hard to come by in the States, they are almost impossible to win in England. In fact, the popular Mr. Jones was the *only* British artist to win a Gold Record (for English sales) during 1966!

Following Tom's South American tour, he flies to New York where he is tentatively set for an appearance on the "Ed Sullivan Show" before winging back to England to headline the bill on "London Paddadium."

Monkees Top Beatle Record!

The Monkees are one up on the Beatles. The four Monkees have broken the existing Beatle record by selling over three million copies of their first album, "The Monkees," — more than *any* previous Beatle album has sold!

"Last Train To Clarksville" has sold well over the one million mark and "I'm A Believer" has already passed the two and half million point. Meanwhile, advance orders on the Monkees' second album, "More Of The Monkees," indicate that it will, in all probability, outsell their first LP.

Controversy

Ever since the Monkees first graced the nation's airwaves, they've been the object of heated controversy with one side claiming the Monkees are nothing but Beatle imitators while the other side stoutly proclaims the Monkees are *not* imitators but an original, talented group.

Perhaps the only objective way to decipher who is the world's top group is through the number of discs sold and the number of attendance records set. Judging popularity on that basis, the Beatles are still the number one group. However, in the span of only four months, the Monkees have already topped the Beatles in the number of albums sold — leaving only single records and personal appearances to go before they officially take-over the Beatle crown.

With two and half million copies of "I'm A Believer" sold in the U.S. alone, the Monkees are not even near the all-time Beatle record of five million copies of "I Want To Hold Your Hand."

Monkee personal appearances have been necessarily limited due to the filming of their television show. However, they have managed to break away for short tours — their last grossing $159,753 in only four concerts. They still have quite a way to go before they top the Beatle records of selling-out such places as Shea Stadium in New York and the Hollywood Bowl.

The Monkees have managed, though, to cause the same sort of wild hysteria which goes hand-in-hand with a Beatle concert. Their first personal appearance, in Hawaii, saw the Monkees playing before a packed audience while wave upon wave of anxious Monkee fans hurled themselves bodily at the stage.

Mob Scene

"Fifty cops were fighting them off with clubs," said Davy Jones, recalling the mob scene in Hawaii. "I don't want any part of that. But I suppose they have to do it. If the girls got to us they would tear us apart."

Up until December 31, the Monkees belonged exclusively to the U.S. but now their television show is being aired over the BBC and "I'm A Believer" sold over 400,000 in the first week of British release.

(Turn To Page 5)

... MONKEES READ fairy tales and sell over three million albums!

MITCH RYDER LEAVES WHEELS — FORMS SHOW

... MITCH RYDER

Mitch Ryder, who has been termed "the white man's James Brown," is now set to give Brown a run for his money by forming the Mitch Ryder Show, which will include a ten-piece orchestra to back Mitch.

"It seems more like a Broadway production," said Alan Stroh, Ryder's manager. "The total investment will be in the area of $30,000 with some of the best talent around guiding us because we decided that since we are taking this giant step, we should do it right.

"Jamie Rodgers of 'Golden Boy' is directing choreography and Hutch Davie is doing the arrangements. Special lighting and electronic systems have been designed and Mitch's costumes by Charles Lisenby will cost $3,000."

The Detroit Wheels will no longer travel with Mitch but are still signed to New Voice Records and will continue to release discs.

Bob Dylan For Films

Bob Dylan, who has not been seen since his accident, has reportedly left Columbia Records for MGM.

The MGM deal supposedly gives Dylan full control of the production of his records and also gives the leader of folk a chance to enter movies via the label's father, Metro-Goldwyn-Mayer.

The new deal certainly puts an end to the recent round of "Dylan is really dead" rumors which have been floating around since his "disappearance."

Inside the BEAT

LETTERS TO THE EDITOR 2
MICK DENIES DEATH RUMORS 3
HAPPENINGS IN POP 4
'IN' PEOPLE ARE TALKING ABOUT 4
LEFT BANKE SPEAK OUT 5
THE LEFT-BEHIND SPOONFUL 6
BEATLES NOT SPLITTING 7
PICS IN THE NEWS 10
CAPTURING NOEL HARRISON 11
ADVENTURES OF ROBIN BOYD 12
RUSS GIGUERE'S SCENE 13
MARVIN GAYE'S MUSIC 14
SAN FRANCISCO'S MOJO MEN 15

HERMAN, HOLLIES SPECIAL

Herman's Hermits and the Hollies were joined by a CBS-TV crew during their concerts in Green Bay, Wis.; Charlotte, N.C.; Fort Worth and El Paso, Texas; Albuquerque, N.M.; Indianapolis and Chicago.

During the concerts and airport mob scenes, the television crew shot valuable footage which will form the basis of an hour-long television special to be shown on April 11 over CBS.

KRLA ARCHIVES

Letters TO THE EDITOR

VICTORY

Dear BEAT:
Noted in your Pics In The News feature of the December 17 issue the photo of Ray Charles with the caption underneath "Ray Charles was fined $10,000 and given a four year suspended sentence on a narcotics charge to which Charles pleaded guilty. He was placed on four years probation." This is exactly what did happen but beyond that there is an extremely interesting story.

The real significance of what happened in Boston was the decision by the court, after hearing testimony by doctors and psychiatrists, that Ray had truly cured himself of drug addiction and is now able to take his place in society once again, subject only to semi-annual check-ups during the four years' probation period. This victory by Ray is as inspiring a story of personal triumph as I have ever encountered.
Best regards,
Dick Gersh

JEFF BECK WRITES US

Dear BEAT:
Merry Christmas — even though it's a bit late!
As I expect you know, I have left the Yardbirds and am recording with my own group tomorrow. So, I'll be keeping in touch with you and be letting you know what's happening for me.
Happy New Year.
Jeff Beck
England

KINGSTON TRIO TOO

Dear BEAT:
In the December 31 issue of The BEAT, you published a letter from Linda Fergus. She says that she does not know of a group other than the Association that has "comedy, poetry and wears matching suits in their act." Obviously, she has never been to a Kingston Trio concert.

The Trio stays after every performance to sign autographs and give interviews with their fans. The Trio is really a great bunch of guys and Nick, John and Bob will always be my "faves" (to use a teeny-bopper cliche.) Their road manager, George Yanok, and bass player, Dean "Mad Dog" Reilly, are really groovy too.

Thank you for the Trio articles which The BEAT has published in the past but I hope that you print many more in the future. Thank you for listening and I hope that you see my point of view.
Beth Mason

DOWN WITH CRITICISM

Dear BEAT:
I've read so many comments in your Letters To The Editor, some for, some against the pop groups today. There are many groups I like and even more that I don't like but I would never write in putting one down.

I know that somewhere there is someone who practically lives just for one of those groups I don't like. Everyone is different, we all like certain groups and that's the way it should be. It's enough for me to know that everyone does have their own group, what if they didn't?

I feel sorry for someone who just doesn't go in for any group. They are missing something beautiful, wonderful. So, if I know a person who likes someone I don't, I don't say anything, why should I? I want everyone to be happy and I don't think it should be by my rules and likes.
Thank you very much.
Kay Thompson

SEEDS

Dear BEAT:
How about printing some pictures of the fabulous Seeds? They've been on a tour so you should have something on them. I've seen them perform quite often and they are the best thing since the Rolling Stones—I think. They have a different sound and they also have Shy.

So, please let's have some pictures on the Seeds.
Karen

PLEASING 'EM

Dear BEAT:
Why do you keep knocking the Dave Clark Five? Why don't you pick on some bums like the Stones? I've met the Dave Clark Five and they love their fans just as much as we love them. They're a fantastic group!
Agnes Miko

You might be interested in knowing that we received a letter the same day your's was delivered which demanded to know why we always pick on the Stones and why we don't pick on someone like the DC5. "You can't please all the people all of the time," is the truest statement ever made!
The Editor

PREDICTION AFTERMATH

Dear BEAT:
Bought your December 31 issue and read all those "wise" predictions you made. I must say, I've never seen a bigger bunch of half-witted, asinine statements in my life. You guys have finally revealed yourselves for what you are, a bunch of anti-long hair, 1959-type bourgies. If any of those predictions come true, it'll be because of an out-and-out effort by people like you to make them come true.

The most ridiculous of your "predictions" was the impending death of Love. I saw them last nite and must say that they were great. All those rumors of them falling apart are completely wrong. Of course, they'll never be another Association or other such fine group, but, then, we can't have everything, can we? I guess we'll just have to be satisfied with the fact that Love is great and give up any hopes of them ever being the wholesome, clean-cut, All-American, antiseptic-type group as the Association and their like.

As far as I'm concerned, you people on The BEAT can lock yourselves up in a closet with your Everly Brothers' records and stay there. The BEAT has changed and died.
Andy Rodriquez

The only thing we'd like to say, Andy, is that all members of The BEAT staff are under 21 and among four of us we total 80 inches of hair!
The Editor

GOTTA START SOMEWHERE

Dear BEAT:
Can you please print the enclosed poem for me? A lot of my friends have told me that I should send it in.

Wow! I have so much to say that I hardly know where to begin but I must start somewhere.

(1) To Shawn Walker: The Association are not sickening! They are one of the best groups around. I've seen them "live" and luv them. Before the concert I didn't like them either but after seeing them I realized how wrong I was! They're really a good (as in fab) group.

(2) To Russ of the Association: Remember the other night at Santa Monica Civic? You're groovy.

(3) The Monkees are not copying the Beatles! The Beatles have made their money so why put down the fab Monkees? Keep up the good work and print lots more on them! Monkees rule.

(4) Please (with a Lovin' Spoonful on top) print more on the Lovin' Spoonful. Next to the Monkees they're my favorite group and I know a lot of other people besides myself would like to see more on them!

(5) To Mark of the Turtles: I love you!
Thank you for letting me say all this.
Audrey Fulton

A Poem
Among the grass roots the turtles play
Up in the leaves the monkees stay
But what is that up in the sky?
Why it's the byrds, they're eight miles high!

Under the left banke are the beatles' homes
But they'd better watch out for rolling stones
They'd better beware of yardbirds too
Or else they'll end up in a stew.

Animals are scared of shadows of knight
They really get a count V fright
And when they hear the wailers tones
It chills them to their very bones.

A band of raiders comes out at night
And robbs from everything in sight
They make their fortunes from music machines
But they must keep away from searchers scenes!

In Greenwich Village the critters stay
And forget the hard times of the day
In caverns do dwell the hermits and troggs
Far away from the London fog.

Of course, the spoonful are really quite lovin'
So, what can be said after all this ... nothin'!
Audrey Fulton

OPEN LETTER TO BEATLES

Dear BEAT:
Please print my humble letter in your great paper. It is an open letter to the Beatles.

Dear Beatles:
I hope the coming year brings you what you want out of life. In the meantime, I have a few presents for each of you.

For Mr. Lennon: I hope that you can "stay as slim as you are," and that the world will someday satisfy you.

For Mr. McCartney: I have — me, and a set of rubber teeth.

For Mr. Harrison: First, a plea that you are never photographed in your swim trunks again (your body breaks my heart!) Also, a gold-plated sitar so you can stand out from all your imitators and, of course, a mustache cup.

For Mr. Starr: Since the greatest gift in life is love, you are truly the man who has everything.

These things are the least I can give you in return for what you have given me.
Mari Anzar

WHAT ABOUT MOTOWN?

Dear BEAT:
We are writing this concerning your 1967 predictions. You stated that "Motown will go toward good music, particularly with the Supremes and Stevie Wonder." Have you forgotten about such great hits as "My Girl," "Get Ready" and "My Baby" by the Temptations? Along with "Baby, I Need Your Loving" and "Reach Out I'll Be There" by the Four Tops. Plus, hit songs put out by such great Motown artists as the Miracles, Marvelettes, Jr. Walker and the All-Stars, The Elgins, Jimmy Ruffin, Marvin Gaye, Isley Brothers, Chris Clark and Martha and the Vandellas.

How can they go toward "good music" when this is great music?

Also, you stated that "Lennon-McCartney, Burt Bacharach, Bob Lind, Paul Simon, Neil Diamond and, of course, Dylan will be the major writing influences of the year." You surely forgot, "the dynamic trio" of Holland, Dozier and Holland. To least mention Smoky Robinson.

With people like this working as a team, how could you forget them?
Steve & Brad Rice

When we were using the term "good music" we were doing so in the sense in which it is used in the music business to describe the type of music which artists such as Nancy Wilson, Vic Damone, John Gary, etc. use. Naturally, "good music" occasionally finds its way onto the pop charts. A perfect example is "Born Free," which is definitely "good music" but which is played on pop stations. However, the term "good music" was not used as a synonym for "great music" and was not meant to imply that pop music or rhythm 'n' blues is not good music. To the charge of neglecting Holland, Dozier and Holland, we plead guilty.
The Editor

KRLA ARCHIVES

On the BEAT

By Louise Criscione

Whether you like it or not, the Monkees are very big business. On their just-completed U.S. tour, the boys grossed a neat $159,753 in just four cities. Davy Jones took time off before the tour to visit England, where "The Monkees" is now being aired on the BBC, and left his native country in the wake of all sorts of predictions that England would soon follow America in proclaiming the Monkees one of the biggest groups on the scene.

However, being a Monkee is not *entirely* peaches and cream—though about 90% of it is! While certainly a popular show, "The Monkees" ran into early rating problems but recently picked up enough ratings to virtually assure it of another season on television.

But the four Monkees find themselves in the position of being the objects of some rather heated jealousy from other pop groups. Davy admits that the Monkees take quite a bit of chopping from groups who have had to work long and hard in all sorts of dives in order to make it big and, therefore, resent the fact that the Monkees had it all made for them. What the other groups *don't* realize, according to Davy, is that: "We're not a group, we're an *act*." A popular act, Mr. Jones, a *popular* act. And that, in essence, is the difference.

... PETER TORK

Electrifying Stones

Whoever thought up the phrase "the electrifying Rolling Stones" didn't know how absolutely right the Stones were going to prove him to be. It was concrete fact on several occasions, especially the one in which Keith Richard was knocked unconscious when his guitar made contact with a microphone. But the latest to get in on the act was the Mighty Mick. Last week in London, the Stones' lead singer extraordinaire fell to the stage after being on the receiving end of an electric shock from a hand mike. Mick was not harmed and stage hands attributed the accident to the static electricity from so much long hair, combined with the heat in the auditorium.

Paul McCartney has given the reason behind the Beatles' decision to do no more personal appearances. Apparently, the reason boils down to the fact that there is so much screaming during a Beatle concert that they feel they are no longer being heard or listened to by their audiences. And secondly, says Paul, the Beatles' stage act has not improved at all during the past four years while their records have progressed unbelievably from "Meet The Beatles" to "Revolver."

Limitations on stage have been a thorn in the Beatles' sides for quite sometime. Quite frankly, with only three guitars and a set of drums the Beatles have been unable to reproduce their later records which utilize many instruments. Both Paul and Ringo agree that if the Beatles were to attempt to reproduce their records "live" they would have to work up a brand new stage act, perhaps using a back-up band. This they are not about to do—so that's that.

"Rubbish"

Anyway, the Beatles would like you to know that their decision to nix all tours as well as their individual ambitions do *not* mean that the Beatles are splitting up. In fact, Paul calls the break-up rumors "rubbish" and Ringo adds that these rumors are definitely the outcome of "jealousy."

QUICK ONES: Tom Jones is assured of a gold record for his fantastic "Green Green Grass Of Home," making it the biggest selling British single of 1966 ... Add the Hollies to the list of pop entertainers appearing in the San Remo Song Festival ... The Stones will appear on "London Palladium" with Andy Oldham in charge of the show's sound system, which is the first time someone outside of the show's crew has operated its sound system ... Georgie Fame is set for a stint at New York's Basin Street East in March ... Ringo says all four Beatles are Beach Boy fans and, therefore, were not in the least bit hurt by the beating the BB's gave the Beatles in the English polls ... Look for the Kinks to make their screen debut in a script written by the group's leader, Ray Davies ... Donovan likely to make his film debut in '67 ... Music Machine's fans up-in-arms over *BEAT*'s prediction that they will not be a major group during '67.

... TOM JONES

Stones' Film Set To Roll; Mick Denies 'Death' Rumors

Despite rumors and statements by certain Stone-officials, the Rolling Stones' first motion picture is set to roll "within the next very few months," according to Allen Klein, the Stones' business manager.

Emphatically denying the reports that the film was to be dropped, Klein stated: "We have had some problems with the screen play but these are the only problems we've ever had and they are being sorted out. We have signed contracts and have already been advanced 90,000 pounds," continued Klein. "Does that sound as though there was any doubt about the picture?"

Partial Script

Klein added that 80 pages of script material from writers, Keith Waterhouse and Willis Hall, have already been received. Waterhouse and Hall are adapting the Dave Wallace novel for the movie version of "Only Lover's Left Alive."

"The pages are coming to us by airmail as they are completed. As soon as we have a finished script, we'll set out the production schedule. We firmly expect filming to start within the next few months," said Klein.

Rumor-Mongers

Klein took issue with "rumor-mongers who seem to delight in grasping at any straw to put the Stones down" and said he was particularly concerned that "certain official sources have contributed to the doubt factor by their public statements. When they know well enough that the picture is going ahead, it seems strange indeed to read statements from spokesmen about legalities. I repeat, contracts are signed and the film *will* be put into production."

During the last month rumors that Mick Jagger was dead spread like wild-fire throughout the U.S. However, Les Perrin, Stones' Press Officer, declared: "Mr. Jagger wishes to deny that he is dead and say that the rumors have been grossly exaggerated."

WALKERS IN EXILE

The Walker Brothers have been forced out of England by the expiration of their British work permits. Accordingly, the Walkers have been set for a world-wide tour.

The Walkers head out for Singapore, Australia and New Zealand, winding up in Auckland on February 2. Next stop is set to be in Japan, followed by concerts in Manila and Hong Kong.

Then it's back to Europe for the Walkers with appearances in Germany, Holland and Austria. European countries to be visited by the Walkers for the first time will be Italy, Spain, Yugoslavia and Belgium.

This will bring the Walkers up until May 19 when their work permits once again become valid in Britain.

... "NOT DEAD" SAYS JAGGER — who is obviously alive!

'CONTROVERSY' FIRST PROOF OF VALIDITY?

With everyone writing books concerning the assassination of President John F. Kennedy, Capitol Records has decided to get into the act by releasing an album entitled "The Controversy."

According to Capitol, the album is an in-depth audio study of the late President's assassination, the Warren Report and the subsequent controversy.

Alan W. Livingston, the president of Capitol, announced at a press conference that the album contains a number of news "firsts" not previously presented via any other communications media. Included will be:

(1) The actual voices and statements of eye-witnesses to the assassination who support the "second assassin" theory;

(2) Critics and advocates of the Warren Report heard face-to-face for the first time;

(3) Participants in the shooting of Lee Harvey Oswald are heard publicly for the first time;

(4) Personal descriptions of the assassination and its aftermath by members of the late President's Dallas motorcade.

Livingston went on to explain the behind-the-scenes work on the album. "A number of months ago, we at Capitol determined to apply the techniques of audio journalism to the most controversial news event of our day, the assassination of President Kennedy. Journalist Lawrence Shiller, was assigned as producer. He traveled over eleven thousand miles to tape interviews with many different participants in the tragic events of November, 1963. The results of Mr. Schiller's work have gone far beyond our original expectations. In my opinion, the album constitutes perhaps the most startling and dramatic audio documentary ever produced.

"The album is not only a fascinating listening experience, but it is proof, I think, that recordings can be as valid a medium of contemporary news coverage as any newspaper, magazine or TV report. In our view, the album itself is a **news** event, a capsule of living history."

"The Controversy" has been issued on Capitol's Probe label and will include the voices of John F. Kennedy, Jack Ruby and Lee Harvey Oswald.

KRLA ARCHIVES

DAVE CLARK DELAYS FILM

The Dave Clark Five have joined the ranks of the Beatles and Stones in the "movie problem" category. The Beatles are having script trouble, the Stones are having screen play trouble and now the DC5 are having director trouble!

"The Dave Clark Five movie, "You'll Never Get Away With It," was scheduled to go into production this month but has been set back because Dave can't find a suitable director for the film. He wanted Tony Miles and Brian Forbes but neither director could work the movie into their tight schedules.

Clark is now negotiating with a French director but has announced that the movie will be canned until later in the year, at which time he hopes to have his director problem solved.

VAUDEVILLES TO TOUR U.S.

The New Vaudeville Band is set to pack up their "Winchester Cathedral" and return to the United States for a tour beginning on February 14 and winding up on March 22.

Following the tour, the Band is tentatively set to play a two-week stint at the Rainbow Room in New York beginning on March 27.

Television-wise, the New Vaudeville Band will appear on "Hollywood Palace" on February 24 and are likely to pay a return visit to "Ed Sullivan" on March 19.

The group has also been offered a week-stand at the Michigan State Fair in August but have not yet decided whether or not to accept the engagement.

HAPPENING

STANDELLS FOR 'RIOT'

The Standells have been signed by MGM to appear in the upcoming MGM movie, "Riot On Sunset Strip." The Standells will sing the title song as well as several songs to be used in the movie. The group will also take care of some acting chores in the film.

"Riot On Sunset Strip" is being produced by Sam Katzman and began production during the latter part of December.

The Standells have completed filming a one-hour special CBS-TV News Documentary.

SPRINGFIELD SET FOR COPA

Dusty Springfield has been tentatively set to play New York's famous Copacabana in June and the Sands Hotel in Las Vegas in July. Dusty is also discussing offers to appear in Japan and Italy as well as a proposed offer for a return engagement at New York's Basin Street East.

England's BBC would like Dusty to film a new television series for them to be shown during the summer. Dusty is already set to make her major club debut when she opens for a month long engagement at London's Talk Of The Town during the first part of April.

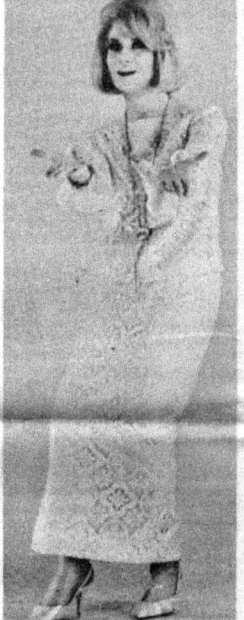

'in' people are talking about...

The Monkees graduating to the Cow Palace... The reasons for the Beatles nix on personal appearances being quite logical but wondering why they omitted the fact that they no longer need the bread *or* the exposure... What would happen if the Buckinghams joined forces with the Palace Guard... How low is action going to go and deciding that with some of the regulars it's about as low as it can be but, of course, without any competition what else can be expected?

PEOPLE ARE TALKING ABOUT who started those Jagger rumors and how stupid he (she) must have felt when Mick showed up–obviously alive... The real Senator Bobby thinking that his imitation "Wild Thing" is quite a giggle, which it is... What a coup it would be if "Georgy Girl" won an Oscar since apparently neither the motion picture industry nor those responsible for the Grammy Awards admit that the pop scene exists... The constant rumors that both the Four Tops and Jr. Walker have departed Motown... Paul thinking the Supremes are just a carbon copy of their records.

PEOPLE ARE TALKING ABOUT the vehement denials from the Knack that they ever said what "in" people understood them to say–so may the matter die... The picture of John, Ringo and Uncle George holding John Julian and commenting on how proud John looked of his cute son... Tom Jones shopping for a set of trains to gift his son with but they're really for the senior Jones to play with... How unbelievably popular Bob Vaughn is in Japan due, in some measure, to the fact that the Japanese take "U.N.C.L.E." so seriously that they checked through Vaughn's luggage in search of those "weapons" which all good UNCLE agents possess and were bitterly disappointed when they failed to find any! Manila then jumped into the act by awarding Vaughn a 50 man motorcycle escort–second only to LBJ's... Paul's admittance that he was not approached to write Hayley's music – it was the other way around.

PEOPLE ARE TALKING ABOUT why the Mama's and Papa's are in hiding–especially since they have a hit record... The scholarship fund which the Wonderfullness man set up... Dusty returning despite the shabby treatment she received last time around... Whether or not Jeff is going to emerge the winner... What a tight fan following the DC5 possess in Phoenix... What happened to Eric's proposed book and deciding that no publisher was brave enough to print it... The Mothers taking over New York and the Cheetah arriving on the West Coast... The potential of the Yellow Payges and wondering how many other talented groups are wandering around virtually unnoticed.

PEOPLE ARE TALKING ABOUT the fantastic emmigration to the West and deciding that it must be because you can almost get rundown by Steve McQueen and his "bike", ride the elevator with Dean Jones, watch Mick Jagger pick out clothes at DeVos, spot Peter Duel maneuvering his car down the street, see P.J. Proby munching a hot dog, catch the look on David Carrdine's face when the sales lady informs him the price of a plastic chess set, or take a helicopter over to the Beatle hideaway... Capitol having the best timing in the world–or else the best luck... How it's kind of a drag to have body temperature and an eggplant the subjects of hits.

PEOPLE ARE TALKING ABOUT how only the Stones could get away with a title like that... The claims that the Monkees second album has already sold two million probably being true, or soon will be... Lou getting a month off his own, belated though it is... How the beat does go on despite the criticism from all sorts of "experts" on the subject... The sweet victory of being named *Time's* Man Of The Year... How much the 5th Dimension sounds like the M's & P's... Sebastian penning a possible hit for Darin, proving yet again how much Bobby would like to comeback to the lucrative teen market... Those rumors about the big Mama and wondering whether or not they're true.

PEOPLE ARE TALKING ABOUT the Sinatras being back to back and wondering when the rest of 'em are going to get in there... Noel Harrison being mobbed on his recent U.S. promotion tour and what power these UNCLES have since Bob and David have captured the East and Noel and aunt Stephanie have taken care of the West... How since Evie didn't quite make it, Patti's now doing her best with it... Most guys not needing music to watch girls by... Whether or not the Kinks have really come to a dead end street and hoping they haven't ...'67 being a spiritual year?

KRLA ARCHIVES

Tips For Aspiring Pop Free-Lancers

**By Joanne McPortland
Jill Wiechman**

With the frightening numbers of teenagers who are making pop-music journalism their hobby—either working for a certain publication or freelancing—we feel that it's timely to submit a few choice hints for those would-be Brenda Starrs. Gleaned from our experiences as the two most terrified freelance reporters in the business, they are guaranteed to help anyone avoid the myriad pitfalls one encounters in the interview situation. Of course, they don't cover everything, but half the fun of interviewing your favorite people is the unbelievably weird mistakes you're bound to make.

Partnership

1. If possible, form a partnership. There's safety in numbers, especially if the prospect of carrying on a lucid conversation with one of your favorite performers threatens to completely unhinge you. After all, your companion can always be trusted to kick you in the ankle if you start to say something you'll regret later. We've found the perfect balance—when frightened, one of us babbles endlessly and unintelligably, and the other remains absolutely silent.

2. Approach it seriously (After you've approached, you can have all the fun you want.) It's not an easy business to get into. If you've found a staff position with a publication, a major portion of your problem is solved. If, however, you decide to freelance (that's what it's called when you don't have a job and you have to beg a magazine to print your article) you're going to have major difficulties obtaining an interview. First of all, make sure you've got a publication to at least consider your mat'rial. Then, besiege your subject's press agent. If you've always considered yourself the courageous type, you can do this in person: otherwise your best bet is the phone. One thing to remember here is to sound confident; if you talk to the agent as an equal you'll have a greater chance than if you giggle, stutter, or otherwise inferiorize yourself.

Worry

3. Okay, you've got the interview. After the indecent interval of sheer hysteria, you can settle down and start worrying again. Have you got questions prepared? If so, are they intelligent questions? There's nothing more boring—both for you and the subject — than an interview that consists of the usual like-and-dislike inanities. To make a good impression, try "personalizing" your questions—read up on your subject and ask him technical questions that will allow him to answer with more than one word. Are you sure of the time and place of the interview? DON'T be late. (Unless you have to come fifteen miles on a bus: then it's excusable —but not very.)

4. During the interview: We can't tell you anything, because every situation varies. Just play it by ear.

5. Miscellaneous hints: Dress simply; nothing's more embarrassing than showing up overdressed —especially if there are other girls present. Have an Alka-Seltzer for breakfast the day of the interview —if you don't need it when you take it, you will later. Don't stay any longer than you're wanted; many times stars are in a rush, and you're lucky to be getting even a little of their time. (This, of course, means to stick around until whoever-it-is starts giving you hints, like "Are you still here?") And most of all, remember that stars are people, too. We were frozen with fear during our first interview, until we realized that the people we were interviewing were as frightened as we were! If you just relax and be yourself, you'll not only have an interview to your credit; you'll have some pretty fantastic memories, too.

Most Sets Film Debut

Mickey Most, one of the most successful independent record producers today, is branching out into films and is currently in the United States negotiating with several Hollywood movie companies.

Most has already completed the script for his first film venture, "Dandy," which he will produce and direct.

His reputation as a film director and producer, however, will have a difficult time matching his reputation for disc success. Most has had an almost relentless string of top hits since his arrival here from South Africa two years ago.

With 51 million records to his credit, Most has been responsible for establishing such groups as the Animals, Herman's Hermits, Donovan and the Nashville Teens.

Most's first joint disc effort with Donovan produced the English folk singers' first number one hit with "Sunshine Superman."

Although Most will now devote the majority of his time to films, he will continue to produce records for Donovan and Herman's Hermits.

MONKEES

(Continued From Page 1)

The Monkees intend to insure their already snow-balling English popularity by flying over around the first of February for a ten day visit aimed, primarily, at radio and television promotion.

If all goes as planned, the Monkees will make a three week return visit to England on a tour with the Troggs during August. However, this tour is still in the negotiation stage.

Whether the Monkees manage to overthrow the Beatles or not, at least they have the satisfaction of knowing they've come the closest yet.

...THE LEFT BANKE (front) Steve, Rick, Tom (rear) Mike and George.

The Left Banke: People Expect A Lot Of A Group

By Rochelle Reed

"People expect a lot out of a pop group," commented Steve Martin recently. "They expect you to continually pour out witty little answers they think are cute."

This slice of cynacism toward the pop singer's dilemma of always being "on stage" isn't derogatory, coming from the Left Banke. Rather it denotes one of the highest accolades a rock 'n roll group can pay to fans—the desire for constant improvement rather than banking to compacency in the idolatry of admirers.

After the Manhatten-based Left Banke watched their first disc, "Walk Away Renee," climb up and down the charts, they were faced with the decision of what to put out next.

"Pretty Ballerina" was the answer. A simple theme embellished with chamber strings and a subtle, insinuating drumbeat, the single is an excellent representative of baroque pop. It is also a fitting follow-up to the hauntingly beautiful "Walk Away Renee."

The group, though, has trouble categorizing their music. "I don't suppose you could put our music in any particular classification," said Mike Brown, the writer of "Walk Away Renee."—"But we do try to get away from commercial aspects in our music.

"Better yet, I think commerciality gets away from us," he added.

The Left Banke don't relish travel and can't stand "gigs." They prefer to concentrate all their efforts on turning out "real music," with as much of it as possible written by the guys themselves.

Mike explains that to create an original and unique sound, the group "has to produce" its own material. Their new LP will contain all-original material.

"We'd like to eventually play concerts where people come to sit and just listen . . . we're definitely not aspiring to be a 'dance' group.

"Of course, we hope to combine our being a concert-type group with the production of hit material."

In that regard, the Left Banke has not changed their view since their beginning about a year ago. Their view of the music they produced at that time was serious. It still is.

"People occasionally ask about the kind of music we play," Mike said, "but I think we'll have to be better known before they really begin to think of us as that serious a group."

Mike plays piano, harpsichord, organ and claivichord. For a time, he searched desperately to find a clavinet, an 18th century keyboard instrument, because he liked the tone. "But I found out that it wasn't substantial enough to take on the road. So now I use an electric piano."

The newest member of the Left Banke ensemble is 19-year-old Rick Brand who is now the lead guitarist with the group. Like the other members of the group today, Rick calls Manhattan home base.

Bass player Tom Finn, 18, once wanted to become a railroad engineer, but when he and Mike met and discovered each other's musical interests, they immediately began writing songs together. They were, in effect, the original nucleus of the Left Banke.

Vocalist Steve Martin is the "idol" of the group. His vocals are responsible for a lot of the excitement the group generates on live dates. Steve's background is quite cosmopolitan since he has traveled through all parts of the world and once attended school in Madrid, Spain.

Finally, there's drummer George Cameron, also 19. George provides that distinctive crisp and subtle rhythm backing that characterizes the Left Banke arrangements.

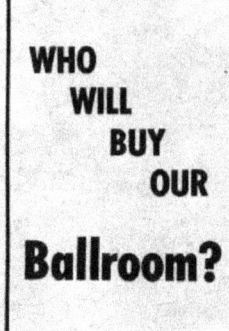

WHO WILL BUY OUR Ballroom?

KRLA ARCHIVES

Keith Obtains A Hit Disc With Body Temperature!

By Tammy Hitchcock

His real name is James Barry Keefer but to the world of pop he is known only as Keith. He's been from Degas to Dylan, from Rembrandt to Ringo, from art school to "98.6." Keith's urge to flee has lead him to what he calls "today." But if prodded he will explain what "today" is. "Dylan, the Stones, England—all that. That's what's happening. That's me, too, and I have to go with it."

Along the way, Keith has managed to pick up a mop of long, rather unruly hair—hair which once resembled Dylan's to a terribly uncanny degree. The styles of Carnaby Street have an avid devotee in Keith who is seen only in bell-bottomed hip-huggers, which he keeps up with the aid of the widest belts he can find. His ensemble is topped by a Carnaby coat of wide whale corduroy and ended with high-heeled, pointed-toe boots.

Search

Ask what he's looking for and instead of answering "a hit record" Keith will reply: "I'm looking for things that are free and unrestrained." His search took root in the Spring of 1945 in Philadelphia but really started to mature when Keith reached the mighty age of 13.

That's when he first tried out his vocal chords in a seventh grade operetta. His debut was followed by a succession of school plays which, in turn, solidified his addiction to pleasing audiences and winning public approval. However, according to Keith his search for recognition is not totally the kind which involves signing autographs and finding his name at the top of the groupie list. But rather the kind that says "job well done" whether it is spoken or silenty implied.

Keith is a self-taught guitar and harmonica player. A performer who writes as well as he sings. An individual whose biggest ambition is to get to England "to see the scene."

Lost In Jersey

Actually, it's sort of a wonder that Keith is even on wax. Driving from Philadelphia to New York for the session which produced his first release, "Ain't Gonna Lie," Keith made a wrong turn in Jersey and arrived in New York some three hours late. Luckily, when Keith finally did make his presence he found the producer, engineer, musicians et al., still waiting around the studio and the session came off—late, but at least it came off.

However, shortly after "Ain't Gonna Lie" was released Keith disappeared. He had moved but had failed to notify his record label, so Mercury spent countless hours trying to hunt him down. But all to no avail. Then one day, quite by accident, Keith heard his record on the radio and phoned Mercury's distributor to see how the disc was selling. But all Keith heard on the other end of the line was a screaming "Keith come home!"

And come home he didn't quite do. Instead he invested his record royalties in a small, but smart, apartment on the upper East side of Manhattan. His move from Philadelphia to New York was not his idea. "I had to move to New York primarily for business reasons," says Keith. "My mentor, Jerry Ross, the Philadelphia A&R man who discovered me and gave me my first chance advised me to try to reside in New York City. At first, it seemed like a hang-up. Here I was working on a hit record that was building. I didn't have much time, but I was advised by Jerry Ross to make the move to New York, so I did."

Although the move required taking time out from personal appearances, etc., Keith is now quite happy that he found his "pad," as he refers to it, because now he's closer to "where the action is."

Comfort

Keith's "pad" is located in a new high-rise apartment not far from the East River bank. Upon entering his apartment, you are immediately hit with the impression of comfortable living—but the apartment definitely has a "lived-in" look, not a trace of "museum-like" atmosphere is to be found within Keith's "mansion."

The first physical object which hits your eye is a wild collage in which the artist has used everything from crayon to charcoal to bits of paper to create a surrealistic impression of an ageless woman. Gold is the predominant color throughout the apartment and you wonder how long Keith will have to wait until he can add a gold record to the decor. Not long if "98.6" keeps up its swift sales-pace!

If you didn't know Keith was a pop singer, you'd swear that he was a definite school-boy "bookworm" for his apartment features 30 shelves which are lined with books and inexpensive art objects. His longest wall is hung with shelf-like furniture which interior decorators refer to as "suspension furniture." Twenty-eight feet of such furniture hangs suspended from the walls in Keith's "pad."

Failure

Keith is something of a complete failure in the cooking department. But he's tried! He even went out and purchased all kinds of cook books, so that when the hot dogs, hamburgers and frozen dinners take their toll he can try cooking by manual. "So far," he says with a grin, "I've goofed on trying things in those recipe books that are a bit complicated, but I'm learning!" Which is comforting to know.

Sandwiched in between his cooking lessons and house cleaning, Keith runs all over the country making appearances and attempting to explain the significance of "98.6"—which is, according to Keith, body temperature. And that's all he has to say on the subject! But for what it's worth, 98.6 with quotes around it is a nationwide smash for Keith—alias James Barry Keefer.

...KEITH (far right) entertains some of his friends in his apartment.

...FROM A CELLAR to a full measure equals Spoonful's success.

How Did Spoonful Become Left Out?

By Louise Criscione

The Lovin' Spoonful have taken over a large segment of pop music but except for their fans, hardly anyone was aware of the coup. "Winchester Cathedral" came along, sold over a million and was hailed as the return of "good time music."

People spoke of the comeback of Rudy Vallee, an eggplant supposedly ate Chicago and the Sop-with Camel got into the good time act with "Hello, Hello." But what about the Lovin' Spoonful?

Obviously overlooked by those anxious to write novels on the return of happy, uncomplicated lyrics, the Spoonful have been singing their own brand of "good time" for well over a year. It's true that a number of national news magazines have included the Spoonful between their covers, but since they are able to move around without the aid of a dozen security guards and since instances of girls scaling 24 stories in order to obtain a Spoonful autograph are rare, the press tends to overlook the group which has unobtrusively gone about their way selling records, breaking records and, in general, being highly successful.

Eastern-Bred

The Spoonful were born in New York City and so it is without much surprise that they spend the majority of their time among the skyscrapers and Village hippies. The West Coast hasn't seen them in ages and the Midwest receives only an occasional glimpse of the Spoonful. New York bred 'em and New York is going to keep 'em—yet their records are nationwide smashes. A rather novel love affair since "out of sight, out of mind" is the rule by which most fans abide. But obviously, most fans are not Spoonful fans.

Perhaps the most human fact about the Spoonful is that they didn't make it right away. The story goes that the Spoonful presented themselves to the owner of the Night Owl Cafe in Greenwich Village, went through their repertoire and instead of being hired on the spot were informed that "these guys don't make it."

Undaunted, the infant group beat a path to the freight elevator down to the basement of the Albert Hotel and there, in the midst of a huge water pool filled with bugs and insects, they practiced for two months. Vibrations from their amps caused the ceiling to drop flakes of paint and other such delightful things on their heads. Enter the now-famous Spoonful hats—used then only to keep their hair from acquiring bits and pieces of unwanted particles.

Balloon Style

Their two-month rehearsal completed, the Spoonful once more journeyed to the Night Owl and on the second time around managed to so impress the club's owner that he immediately hired them and pulled out his wallet to the tune of having 1,000 balloons printed up with the slogan: "I Love You—The Lovin' Spoonful."

And, so were born the Lovin' Spoonful. Word spread around the city that a "fantastic new group" was playing at the Night Owl. Entertainers took to dropping in, fans were made and, finally record companies came through with offers. Kama Sutra won the label battle and "Do You Believe In Magic" led the way for "You Didn't Have To Be So Nice," "Did You Ever Have To Make Up Your Mind?," "Daydream," "Summer In The City" and "Full Measure."

The Spoonful have always been the exponents of their own kind of "good time"—a brand which has the approval of the entire nation. You can't fight it because their record of six hits in a row speaks for itself. So, the next time you get into a discussion of the Great Good Time Comeback don't forget to add the Lovin' Spoonful to the top of the list. After all, if Rudy Vallee originated it—the Spoonful certainly brought it back to life.

KRLA ARCHIVES

Beatles Are Not Breaking Up!

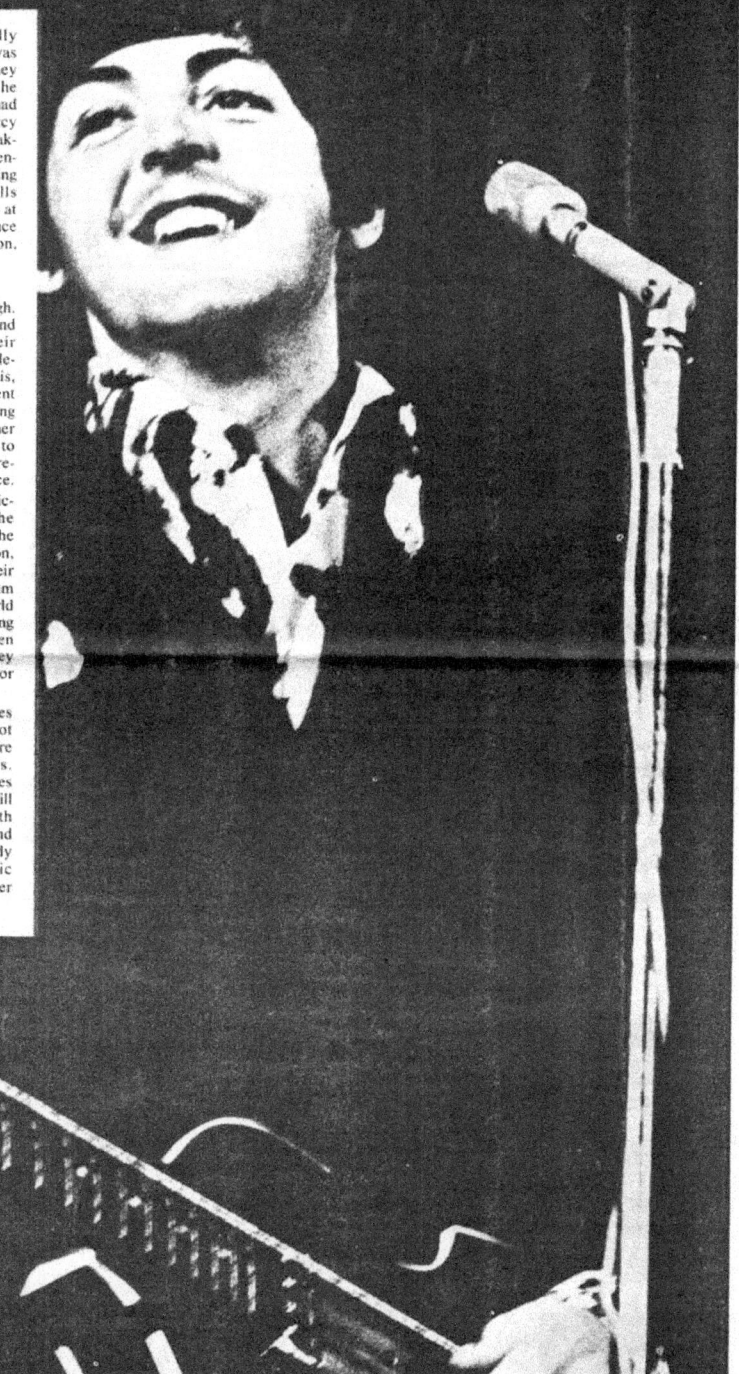

By Louise Criscione

Let's cut out the hysteria and the sobbing and the rumors. The Beatles are not splitting up! At least, not literally. It's true that individually each Beatle is pursuing his own goals and, in time, a break-up will inevitably rear its head. But right now, today, both Paul McCartney and Ringo Starr have emphatically denied that a split is anywhere near imminent.

Naturally, when the announcement of no more personal appearances was handed down, speculation spread that it was finis for the Beatles as a group. And John Lennon didn't help matters much when he told a reporter that his years as a Beatle "had been fun." By using the past tense, John's statement was taken to mean that those Beatle years were over.

The End?

And, at the time, those years certainly appeared to be coming to a definite end. John was off filming his movie, Paul was busy writing the music for "The Family Way," George was in India learning sitar techniques and Ringo was getting bored and looking around for a solo movie stint for himself. "Revolver" was the newest piece of Beatle material issued and there was no official word on a script for the Beatles third movie.

During this lull in group activity, reporters and gossips, who for lack of anything better to occupy their time and available space, began a long string of rumors and insinuations. None of which were flattering to the Beatles and none of which caused rejoicing in their fans' ranks.

Probably the most popular "news" was the hot rumor that jealousy existed between the Beatles. Reporters claiming a "scoop" added wood to the already burning fire by gleefully pointing to the fact that Ringo was jealous of the others because they collected writer's royalties and he didn't . . . that George was mad because John picked off a juicy movie role . . . that Paul was breaking the famous and successful Lennon-McCartney team by writing the music for a Hayley Mills movie . . . that John was furious at Paul for not asking his assistance in composing the music. And on, and on and on.

"Isn't Any"

Until enough was just enough. Tired of picking up papers and magazines to read about their alleged jealousy, Paul finally declared: "There isn't any." Fact is, continued Paul, by doing different things each Beatle can pass along his new information to the other three. Thus, allowing the group to progress and maintain their tremendous popularity and influence.

Remaining delightfully unpredictable, in the very midst of the break-up and jealousy rumors, the Beatles congregated in London, cut a Christmas message for their fans, started work on a new album and a new single and told the world that, while they were still having script difficulties, a story had been selected and if all went well they would begin filming in March or April.

So, with personal appearances definitely out and a third movie not definitely in, what *is* in the future for the Beatles? Better records. Without the pressure of tour dates to confine them, the Beatles will be able to progress musically with no trouble at all. And they intend to do just that. They are not ready to be counted out of the music business just yet—and you better bet your life they won't be!

KRLA ARCHIVES

Top 40 Requests

1. I'M A BELIEVER .... Monkees
2. SNOOPY VS. RED BARON .... Royal Guardsmen
3. RUBY TUESDAY .... Rolling Stones
4. PRETTY BALLERINA .... The Left Banke
5. FOR WHAT IT'S WORTH .... Buffalo Springfield
6. HELLO, HELLO .... Sopwith Camel
7. 96.6 .... Keith
8. THE BEAT GOES ON .... Sonny & Cher
9. GEORGY GIRL .... The Seekers
10. MR. FARMER .... The Seeds
11. PUSHIN' TOO HARD .... The Seeds
12. I WANNA BE FREE .... The Monkees
13. KNIGHT IN RUSTY ARMOR .... Peter & Gordon
14. THERE'S GOT TO BE A WORD .... The Innocence
15. BORN FREE .... Roger Williams
16. EAST, WEST .... Herman's Hermits
17. FULL MEASURE .... Lovin' Spoonful
18. KIND OF A DRAG .... Buckinghams
19. SINGLE GIRL .... Sandy Posey
20. LADY GODIVA .... Peter & Gordon
21. IT MAY BE WINTER OUTSIDE .... Felice Taylor
22. WEDDING BELL BLUES .... Laura Nyro
23. HELP ME GIRL .... Eric Burdon & Animals
24. SUGAR TOWN .... Nancy Sinatra
25. TELL IT LIKE IT IS .... Aaron Neville
26. WINCHESTER CATHEDRAL .... New Vaudeville Band
27. STANDING IN THE SHADOWS OF LOVE .... Four Tops
28. GOOD VIBRATIONS .... Beach Boys
29. KNOCK ON WOOD .... Eddie Floyd
30. WORDS OF LOVE .... Mama's & Papa's
31. GOOD THING .... Paul Revere & Raiders
32. WACK WACK .... Young-Holt Trio
33. TELL IT TO THE RAIN .... Four Seasons
34. THAT'S LIFE .... Frank Sinatra
35. COLOR MY WORLD .... Petula Clark
36. I NEED SOMEBODY .... ? & The Mysterians
37. MUSIC TO WATCH GIRLS BY .... Bob Crewe Generation
38. DEVIL WITH A BLUE DRESS ON/GOOD GOLLY MISS MOLLY .... Mitch Ryder
39. NO FAIR AT ALL .... The Association
40. YOU GOT TO ME .... Neil Diamond

Inside KRLA
By Eden

For those of you who have requested it, this week I am printing the top ten most requested songs from the Top 100 list of most requested tunes from 1966.

The songs are, Number One through Ten: "I Want To Be Free," "Cherish," "Paperback Writer," "Fortune Teller," "Groovy Kind of Love," "Hey Joe," "96 Tears," "California Dreaming," "Little Red Riding Hood," and "Yellow Submarine."

Beatles hold down two of the top ten positions, while the Stones captured only one. Making first time appearances on the year-end top ten were new groups like the Association, Monkees, and Question Mark and the Mysterians.

For all those who have asked for a complete listing, we will print the Top 100 list of most requested tunes in its entirety in the next issue of *The BEAT*.

Oh, yes — if there are any loyal sports fans who are up-in-arms out there in the Land of 1110 over the nastiness of the Super Bowl predicament, please breathe easier as KRLA has once again come to your rescue.

Yes, KRLA — the Mr. Neat of the radio world — has done it again, even if it *is* sort of an "underground" kind of done-it! If you would like to see the telecast of the Super Bowl (and *whooooo wouldn't*???) just look to KRLA, for we have a complete set of instructions all made up on how you can construct your very own receiver, and these instructions are available upon request.

ATTENTION!!!
High Schools, Colleges, Universities and Clubs:

CASEY KASEM MAY BE ABLE TO SERVE YOU!

Let Casey HELP You Put On A Show Or Dance
Contact Casey at:
HO 2-7253

ICE HOUSE GLENDALE
234 So. Brand Ave. — Reservations 245-5043

Rock 'n Roll Gypsies
b/w Road To Nowhere
(5829 Capitol)
By HEARTS & FLOWERS
at the Ice House thru
JAN. 29

This is the hit song that was written about the happenings on the Sunset Strip long before they ever happened.

— PLUS —

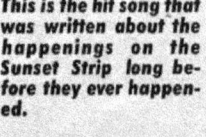

Tim Morgan   Travelers Three
Jan. 15-22   Jan. 22-29

The girl with the most co-operative apartment in town

Any Wednesday

An hilarious bed-time story.
(but not exactly for the kiddies!)

Starring **JANE FONDA · JASON ROBARDS · DEAN JONES**
Also Starring **ROSEMARY MURPHY**

TECHNICOLOR® — FROM WARNER BROS.

STARTS JAN. 25th   AT A THEATRE OR DRIVE-IN NEAR YOU!

KRLA ARCHIVES

Sonny and Cher Answer The KRLA Request Lines

CHER APPEARS studious while signing autographs in the station lobby

SONNY PAUSES to light up a cigarette on the steps to KRLA before going in to answer phones.

SONNY LEAVES the station to the strains of "The Beat Goes On."

A Simple Math Lesson:

America's Pop Music NEWSpaper 25¢

THE BEAT

24 issues per yr.
x .25 each copy
_____
$6.00

But

NOW—$5.00 a year Subscription
Limited Offer!!

One full year—Only $3.00

THE BEAT

Mail to:
The BEAT #504
6290 Sunset Blvd.
Hollywood, Calif. 90028

Name_____
Address_____
City_____ State_____ Zip_____

I want ☐ BEAT for one year—only $3.00
I enclose ☐ cash ☐ check ☐ money order.

PICTURES in the NEWS

THE MONKEES (left to right) Mike, Micky, Peter and Davy took a three week hiatus from their television show to play a cross-country tour which grossed $159,753 in four gigs. Davy paid a visit to England, where "The Monkees" is now being aired over the BBC, and commented that the British censors may crop the show slightly because "I've been using a lot of things which don't mean anything in America but certainly do in England."

DON AND THE GOODTIMES, newest regulars on "Where The Action Is," thoroughly confused David Ketchum, Agent 13 on "Get Smart," during an off-camera visit. Ketchum may have been asking which of the other "Action" regulars will soon depart the show, since it's inconceivable that all three groups can sandwich into the half-hour program. Other regulars on the show are Paul Revere and the Raiders and the Hard Times.

JEFF BECK finally out of the Yardbirds after months of rumors, has just signed a recording contract with Mickie Most, independent producer for Herman, Donovan and other big names. Jeff will solo as a singer and guitarist under the managership of Simon Napier-Bell (Yardbird manager) and Most's partner, Peter Grant. Unconfirmed rumors from London are currently hinting that Jeff has just married aspiring actress, Mary Hughes.

THE BEACH BOYS are the stars of a 24 minute color film entitled "The Beach Boys In London." The film, which as yet is only scheduled for British release, spotlights the singers during their November English tour with clips of both interviews and performances. It is being released by Immediate Music, the company which publishes Beach Boys' compositions in England.

KRLA ARCHIVES

The Fine Art Of Catching Noel

The all-new resounding sound of the Jordan "Boss" Amplifier ...

☐ YES, I want professional sound, too! If the new Jordan Boss amps back up the top pop groups, then they're worth looking into. So send me full info on the resounding sound of Jordan —the Ultimate for total vocal/instrumental amplification! And better send me the name of my nearest Jordan dealer, too—after all, hearing is believing!

Mail this coupon to:
JORDAN ELECTRONICS
a division of Victoreen Instrument Co.
121 So. Palm Avenue
Alhambra, California 91803

NAME
ADDRESS
CITY   STATE
The instrument I play is

By Carol Deck

Ring—"Greene-Stone Productions, may I help you?"

"Yes, I'm from *The BEAT* and we'd like to interview Noel Harrison."

"Oh, well we just produced his last record. You'll have to talk to his manager about an interview."

"Thanks."

Ring—"Mr. Winkler's office, may I help you?"

"Yes, I'm from *The BEAT* and we'd like to interview Noel Harrison."

"Of course, I'll check with Mr. Winkler and call you back."

"Thanks."

Ring—BEAT Publications, may I help you?"

"This is Erwin Winkler's secretary. We understand you want Mr. Harrison Saturday night to present an award on your TV show."

We'll Take Him

"Well, we *would* like Mr. Harrison any time but we're a newspaper and we don't have either a TV show or an award for him to present, however if you'll give us a little time..."

"Oh, we must have you confused with someone else."

"Good thinkin', still, if you'll just give us a little time..."

Ring—"Mr. Winkler's office..."

"Yes, you can help me, I'm from *The BEAT* and we'd *still* like to interview Noel Harrison."

"I think I have it straight now. Mr. Winkler says its OK, but I'll have to find out what time is convenient for Mr. Harrison and call you back."

"Thanks."

Ring—"BEAT Publications, may I help you?"

"This is Dorothy from the UNCLE set. I got a message to call you about David's tickets."

"David who? Tickets to what?"

"David McCallum..."

"But that's the wrong UNCLE. We wanted the *girl* from UNCLE, I mean the guy on the "Girl from UNCLE," I mean . . . tickets to what?"

"I don't know, I just got this message."

"Gad, well we don't have any tickets for David but could you possibly know how we can get to Noel Harrison?"

"But he's the wrong UNCLE agent. We only handle the men from UNCLE, I mean . . . why don't you try Greene-Stone, they produced his last record."

"Thanks."

Ring—"Mr. Winkler's office, may I help you?"

"I sure hope so."

"Oh hello again, Mr. Harrison says lunch tomorrow would be fine but you'll have to check with Miss Ivy, she handles his publicity."

(Gronk, why didn't someone tell us that 3 hours ago?)

Ring—"Miss Ivy, may I help you?"

"I doubt it, no one else seems to be able to. Anyway I'm from *The BEAT* and we'd like..."

"To interview Noel, I thought that was all set for lunch tomorrow. Was there some problem?"

(Some problem, she asks, some problem?!!!!)

"I'm glad you asked about that car," Noel said at lunch the next day, referring to the UNCLE car that's just been introduced on "The Girl From UNCLE."

"I tried to run it into a wall but failed. It was produced by a toy manufacturer to sell toys, which is fine for the toy company, but if you're going to do it, do it right."

Uncle On Fire

"The first time I got in it, it caught fire and there's no fire wall between the driver and the engine, which is a legal requirement on all cars.

"And when you get in it, *if* you can get the door open, that is, you close the door and knock yourself out.

"It's a Corvair frame and they usually move the engine from behind the wheels to in front of them but they didn't with this one and all it takes is three people leaning on the back and the thing stands on end.

"And it really does everything it's supposed to, shoots rockets, creates a smoke screen and even has a bullet proof screen that comes up behind the driver. It's really ridiculous, because nothing else on the whole show actually does what it's supposed to.

"Stephanie drove it once and said 'you can drive it.' I tried very hard to smash it up. And I hear I have to do a love scene in it, too."

Is it possible the car doesn't like Noel either?

"After what I've said about it, I don't doubt it."

If Noel could take a half dozen or so artists and erase them from the scene he says he would take the fakes. He specifically mentions the Shangri-Las.

"I resent them particularly because when I had out "A Young Girl," they also had a death song out and we were grouped together."

He can also do without James and Bobby Purify and Mitch Ryder.

As for his favorites he lists the Beatles, Donovan ("Would you believe I actually copied down the entire lyrics to 'The Trip' from the album because I couldn't find the sheet music.") Lovin' Spoonful, Buffalo Springfield, Animals, Kinks, Bobby Hebb and the Supremes.

He also likes the Monkees— "Although it may be commercial fakery, they've got a thing going." —And Sonny and Cher, although he doesn't really dig their latest record, "The Beat Goes On."

"The first time I heard it I thought it was the best thing they'd ever done, but the lyrics are incomplete and it doesn't compare with Dylan or Lind. Sonny's done better."

He kind of feels the same way about the Rolling Stones, who he thinks are "heading up a blind alley."

"I really liked their stuff up until about the middle of last year, until after 'Aftermath.' What they're doing now is untidy. My favorite of theirs is 'Last Time.' It's got beautiful figures in it. When it first came out and I'd hear it in the car, I'd roll down the windows and turn it up full blast."

...NOEL HARRISON takes a breather from "U.N.C.L.E." shooting.

...THE DAILY FLASH give Noel and run for his uncle in the "Drublegratz Affair."

KRLA ARCHIVES

The Adventures of Robin Boyd

©1965 By Shirley Poston

Several weeks had passed since the day of Salisbury-Plains-Fame when Robin, The Budge and Ringo (as in Boyd, as in Boyd) had discovered their mysterious talents.

They had been quite a shock at first. Especially to The Budge, who, prior to the arrival of Robin Irene Boyd, had led a sheltered life (on a *leash*, to hear *her* tell it.) And it was quite a shock with good reason.

Just Like...

First the two new guitars, the amps, and the set of drooms had appeared out of nowhere. Then, to their re-amazement, they'd found their formerly talentless selves able to play the instruments beautifully. What's more, they could warble like angels. In other words, they sounded just like the *Beatles!*

When they realized this, Budgie had raced toward the horizon, drooling, with a distraught Robin Irene hot on her heels.

When Robin managed to catch up with her blithering friend, she couldn't very well reveal that George of Genie fame (not to mention frame) (and let's do) was obviously behind all the mysterious surprises. So she had to settle for giving Budgie the following sensible explanation.

Sensible Explanation: "There are thingys about me that I can't tell you so don't ask because if I answer there *won't* be thingys about me that I can't tell you. Is that clear?"

Sensible Reply: "As mud."

However, as mud will do, it covered the ground, and although The Budge continued to cast hysterical sidelong glances at Robin from time to time, she stopped asking questions.

The sturdy Ringo neither requested nor required an explanation. She was so deliriously happy over having Loodwigs to blam on instead of oatmeal cartons, she couldn't have cared less *where* her drooms and/or her talents came from. Besides, she knew better than to ask.

Only Snarl

If she did, Robin would probably only snarl and say "the stork brought them." At which time Ringo would have to remind her sister that it would be somewhat difficult for a stork to carry a set of Loodwigs. At which time Robin would undoubtedly re-snarl and say "well, he carried *you*, didn't he?"

Rather than have to answer this question with a smug "that's what *you* think, kiddo," and shatter her un-cool image, Ringo, as they say in the droom trade, kept her trap shut.

When the initial amazement had worn off and the practice session re-begun, the girls had two more enormous shocks.

Shock #1 — They discovered they could sound like not only the Beatles, but the stars of their choice!

Shock #2 — It started snowing and their amps got wet. (Otherwise known as an electrifying experience.)

From then on, they practiced faithfully every day, and after awhile even Mrs. Boyd admitted they weren't bad and allowed them to rehearse in the basement rumpus (I'll say) room.

Debut?

But they soon tired of just rehearsing and began moaning around for something to rehearse *for*. Like their debut, for instance. And, *again* with good reason. (Repetition — dare I say it — rules the world!) Besides all their imitations, they'd developed an ear-shattering but immensely groovy (if they did say so themselves) (which they did) sound of their own. They'd even selected appropriate (though I'm not saying to *what*) costumes. And they were getting am-day tired of being all dressed up with no place to go-go.

In later years, when they were looking back on it all (from various hilltop sanitariums), they never could quite remember exactly who came up with the zingwhammer, so they each continued to claim it was *their* idea. (At which times their respective keepers nodded patiently.)

Actually, it was Mrs. Boyd who suggested that since there were no clubs for them to play in, they should start their own! (Her galvanized ear-muffs were beginning to chafe, and she thought this might be a good way to get the trio out of her basement.) (Not to mention her life.)

Whatever, she soon lived to regret the suggestion. Because, after the town (har) of Pitchfork had been scoured in a search for a suitable (as in *free*) location for the club, it began to look that the only possible place for same *was* the basement.

When approached about this possibility, Mrs. Boyd really threw the threesome. Drawing herself up somewhat haughtily, she replied: "Do I look like Pete Best's mother?"

Rawther!

Since that sort of settled *that* (raw*ther*), they continued to look elsewhere, and got nowhere at the rapidest (?) of rates.

It was during one of these hunts that they finally agreed on a name for their group. For days, Ringo had been insisting they call themselves *The Wash-And-Wear-wolves*, and The Budge had battled fiercely for *The Inverted Mordent*. Robin was thoroughly appalled by the former (the title, not her sister) (come to think of it, *both*), and thought the latter sounded dirty. (The Budge swore (I'll say) up and down it was merely a musical term, merely a musical term.)

The Budge, incidentally, was by now so caught up in it all, she had stopped casting hysterical sidelong glances at Robin. In fact, she had started shrieking an occasional "I CAN *SING!*" thereupon bursting into an aria from "Rigoletto." (Or was it a rigoletto from "Aria?")

Anyname, rather than fight for her own idea for a group tag (would you believe *Robin And The Hoods?*) (leave us hope not), Robin re-thought and feebly made one final offering.

"Would you believe *The Mockingbirds?*", she arsked, and she might well, because it was perfect, what with them being birds who did imitations and all that-there stuff.

Mockingbirds

They became The Mockingbirds by unanimous decision. However, there were still bigger and better traumas to solve. Said birds still didn't have a pit to hiss in - er - a nest to mock in.

Just when Robin was beginning to think all was lost, it happened. She and The Budge were trudging home from school one afternoon. (Ringo had stayed home that day with a crick in her neck.) (Sleeping with a snare drum under one's pillow may be a mite uncomfortable, but baby, that's *loyalty!*)

On their weary way, they paused to sulk in front of a marvelously hideous building they'd been ogling to no avail (the sign out front clearly stated FOR SALE OR RENT.)

Suddenly, Robin fell to her knees and began blubbering gratefully. For, as you may have guessed, it was then that she knew what she must do.

(To Be Continued Next Issue)

BEAT SHOWCASE
(spotlighting new talent on the pop scene)

THE KALEIDOSCOPE
A real live Turkish gypsy and a couple of college professors sound like what Dylan wishes he could sound like on their first single, "Please." Already way up on Southern California charts, "Please" seems destined for nationwide acclaim. Left to right (top) David Lindley, Fenrus Epp, John Vidican and (bottom) Sol (that's all) and Chris Darrow.

THE CRYAN' SHAMES
This Chicago-based group is planning to tear up airways with their disk, "I Wanna Meet You" c/w "We Could Be Happy." After all, anyone with the names Denny, Toad, Jim, J.C. Hooke, Grape and Stonehenge have to do well! Left to right (top) Denny, Stonehenge, Grape and (bottom) J.C. Hooke, Jim.

KRLA ARCHIVES

TEEN PANEL
The Use Of Drugs By American Teens

In this issue, The BEAT's Teen Panel discusses another of the hottest subjects of the day—the use of drugs by teenagers.

Participating are Bill (18), Keith (17), Diane (17) and Cynthia (16).

If you would like to participate in a future Teen Panel, or suggest a topic, please send a postcard to The BEAT.

* * *

Keith—"Before we get started, someone had better clarify exactly what is meant by the word 'drugs.' It could mean anything from aspirin to LSD."

Cynthia—"I think most people consider 'drugs' to be something that's used for kicks."

Bill—"That doesn't make the description fit. A lot of things used for 'kicks' aren't drugs. Marijuana certainly isn't. It's a weed."

Diane—"We could sit here all day and try to categorize what is a drug and what isn't, but I don't think that's what we're here for. We're here to discuss just how widespread the use of drugs is among teenagers. 'Drugs' in this case, meaning anything that is synonomous with narcotics in the eyes of society."

Bill—"Practically everything is synonomous with narcotics in the eyes of society, at this particular time anyway. Teenagers are synonomous with narcotics. Five years ago, if you mentioned narcotics, people immediately thought 'dope fiends.' Now you say the word, and people think 'teenagers.' It isn't this way. They're making it sound like every kid in the world is walking around stoned out of his mind most of the time."

Diane—"Anyone *with* a mind knows better than that. The question is, how *many* kids are? You seem to know a lot about the subject. What's your estimate of how many?"

Bill—"Very few, if you're referring to walking around stoned most of the time. Not just very few teens, very few anyone. The big majority of people don't have that kind of time. I would say maybe forty percent of the U.S. population under the age of 25 has tried some kind of 'drug.' Marijuana, probably, or pep pills. They're the easiest to get ahold of. I've tried both. I didn't like the pills because I got nervous. The other was fine, but I wouldn't want to do it all the time. It's like having a drink. That isn't something you do all the time either, not unless you've really got problems."

Keith—"I agree with that. Most of the teenagers who do try the milder stuff don't do it constantly. There are too many other things to do. But I don't think they feel they're doing something horrible when they do try it, or use it occasionally. I don't know about pills or LSD but there are a lot of medical reports that say pot is harmless. I can't see why they don't just legalize it."

Cynthia—"I can see why they don't. There's no way to control it. Control it socially, is what I mean. They once banned alcohol for this same reason, and it took a lot of doing to bring that under control. They had to make laws for when and how it could be sold, and laws to keep people from driving when they've been drinking. A lot break the laws, but I don't suppose most do. They're for your own protection. They'd have to put the same kind of restrictions on marijuana. It probably will be legalized someday. I don't think the stronger drugs will be, though, and I don't think they should be. Doctors should be able to use say, LSD, when they know it will help, but it's too unpredictable for social use."

Diane—"Does anyone here know anyone who's ever tried LSD or actual drugs? I don't."

Bill—"I don't either, not personally. LSD is popular with college students, I know that, and if I wanted to try it myself, I'd know where to get it, but I don't especially care to try it. I'm sure a lot of teenagers have tried it, but nowhere near the forty percent who have probably experimented with pot or pills. If you care about yourself, and have any brains, you realized that LSD is a big step and not just a 12-hour trip. That stuff can backfire."

Keith—"Have you noticed that there's very little mention made of the 'hard stuff'? I doubt if there's much of a problem with that. Getting involved with heroin or something like that takes a special kind of person. Someone who *really* doesn't give a damn. When you start that, you know you aren't going to be able to stop. You go that route only when you have nothing to lose, and most teenagers have plenty to lose. To answer Diane's question, I don't know anyone who's taken LSD or the 'hard stuff.' I know several who've tried pot, but none of them made a habit of it."

Cynthia—"I don't even know anyone who's tried marijuana, but several kids I know well enough to discuss it with are curious about it. I used to think it was something really terrible until I read more about it. I know it isn't now and sometimes I get curious myself. But terrible things can happen to you if you get caught. That I can't understand. If they legalize it, they have to legalize it for everyone, so I can see why control of some sort is a necessity. But why such *stiff* penalties for something that's actually harmless?"

Bill—"I read an article where someone suggested—I think it was Allen Ginsburg—that they have to keep it illegal or the Narcotics Bureau would be put out of commission. I may not even have the name of the 'Bureau' right, but there's this special section of law enforcement devoted just to the apprehension of people who sell or use the 'lesser drugs.' If this weren't illegal, a lot of people would be out of a job."

(The second half of this panel discussion will appear in the next issue of The BEAT.)

BEAT EXCLUSIVE
Russ & His Scene

By Rochelle Reed

(This is the first in a series of exclusive interviews with all members of the Association.)

Russ is a fast mover. He doesn't walk, he rushes. He doesn't talk, he thrusts out thoughts, moods, emotions and the urgent nowness that is characteristic of him. All at a speed of 78 rpm in our 33 rpm world.

Like this week. Russ rushed into our office, fell into a chair, stuck an apple in his mouth and challenged, "Go ahead, ask me why I'm growing a mustache."

The explanation for the light brown 5 day growth adorning his upper lip was simple: "I've never had a mustache before."

Directness

Simplicity isn't the keynote to Russ Giguere, one of six Associates, but directness definitely is. He understands himself as few people ever do. "I have more control over my life than most people have over theirs," he says willingly. "I try to live as spontaneously as possible... I follow my feelings.

"I'm happy almost all the time. I'm seldom depressed. Oh, once in awhile my career depresses me. Occasionally, it's not moving as fast as I'd like it to, but I'm young, anxious...

"Everything works out just as I want it," he says, but Russ is far from being Voltaire's Candide, even in his private life. "No," he denies, "I'm not a Candide, but I'm able, through manipulation, to have a large amount of good and little bad in my life."

A fan of science fiction writer Ray Bradbury, Russ feels that "the good in people has to win out" in future generations. "If people would relax and just let what has to come, come out, then the good has to win out. I know it."

Russ finds many of his truths in the world through intuition, or "just knowing it." For instance, he "believes" in flying saucers, though he hates to say "believes." "I just 'know' it," he prefers to say, "I've got no facts to back me up, I just know it."

Russ dropped out of high school after completing the 10th grade, and from San Diego, he traveled to Los Angeles. He sang with various groups, none too successful, before launching the Association with the other five members. Meanwhile, he worked as everything from a dishwasher to background singer to support himself. When the Association was still a young group doing local gigs, Russ walked from one end of Los Angeles to the other. He used to maintain that no one needs a car because they can walk anywhere they want to go. But finally success turned his head—to a "racy" 1959 Volkswagon convertible.

Art Major

An art major while he was in school, Russ still dabbles in it, mostly buying paintings. He reads widely, attends movies constantly and is fond of all types of music from classical to Indian.

He listens to very little pop music. "The majority of pop music is worthless, and you can quote me on that, rather, say I find no merit in most of it. There's an awfully lot of good to make up for the larger percentage of bad, however."

Russ doesn't go for music fads, either. "Pop baroque is as important to my daily life as psychedelic music," he says in mock seriousness, then flashing a smile.

Though Russ composed "I'll Be Your Man" and "I'm The One," he denies that he's a songwriter. "Take 'I'll Be Your Man.' I'm not really a writer. One day I got up and sat down in a chair and started playing my guitar and Blah! out it came. It was the same way with the other one. Actually, I'm just lucky those came out."

Though not active politically, Russ says he only becomes so when he's in jeaporty of "being stepped on."

"I'm afraid the government might take over too much. Human rights are slowly being taken away. I don't smoke or drink, because I think it's poison to the system, but that doesn't mean other people don't have the right to."

Let Live

The controlling factor in Russ' life seems to be an overwhelming 'live and let live' attitude, his ability to say, "Fine. That's your scene." It's an admirable quality in the highly complex, detailed, ruleized world of today.

The Associate who "knows" things is as a violin, with different strings of his nature wound to varying degrees of tightness. He thinks as he speaks, and finds many of his ideas as he verbalizes. If he has a problem, he talks about it until finally, he works around to a solution.

It takes a race-horse constitution to keep up with Russ. It is especially difficult to take several sentences from the many he pours out and call it an interview. For Russ pours out words as fast as Jim sings "Along Comes Mary." Which, if you've listened to the song, is pretty fast indeed.

KRLA ARCHIVES

'The Music Really Saves Me'—Gaye

By Eden

There are some performers who succeed in escaping the boundaries and restrictions normally imposed upon their profession. They somehow manage to go "above and beyond the realm of ordinary performance." They exude a very special quality, one which attracts and endears their many enthusiastic fans: the quality is *class*, and a man who has *a lot* of it is Marvin Gaye.

Truth

He is spoken of as a "total professional," the "performer's performer." And when *he* speaks, it is in a voice of thoughtfulness and sincerity. "The one basic thing in a performance, or the first fundamental I would say, should be *truth*. And when I use that word, I would like to take in sincerity, love, duty, and a very truthful and un-negative approach to people and audiences. Be a *truthful* performer, that's most important."

There are many performers who are simply "doing a job." They have set out to earn a living and the fact that they chose this particular profession in which to do so is only incidental. Not so with Marvin Gaye, however. He is not only devoted to his profession, but he is a *part* of it, and he *lives* the music he makes all his life.

"Happiness, is . . . my mother and father; my family in Detroit, Motown, and *golf*! And, my love — last, but definitely *not* least — my love for music. It's really my salvation.

Sensitive

"When I'm in the dumps or when I don't feel like I should feel, music really saves me. I can really feel very low — I'm a very sensitive person — I get extremely depressed at times, and I find that music really perks me up and makes me very, very happy."

Not a man of static existence, Marvin Gaye is on the move. He is interested in growing and expanding his own talents and abilities, and he is also interested in the growth of the industry in which he is working.

"That's what music needs nowadays — it needs a whole new *difference*; a complete overhauling. The blues is basic; you need to take the whole blues scope and re-arrange it. Maybe start backward, and come forward! Music is very tired, I think.

"Rhythm and blues has been around for years and is a completely Negro-oriented heritage, going back to when my great-grandfather was a slave. Through the ages, it has not been an accepted thing, socially, for American whites to feel that Negro folklore should be an accepted social type music; it was strictly for Negroes, and that was the end of that!

Anybody

"Through the years, it takes foreigners, English folk, and Australian people — *anybody* but Americans! — to recognize the great music potential of Negro folklore. As soon as they decide that this music has merit and this is good music, they record it.

"Well, if *they* record it and sing it, then it becomes socially accepted by Americans. Negroes only represent so much buying power, and a lot of white people have to buy your records, because there are only so many Negroes who are going to buy your records, before you become very popular in the pop field.

"Since the English people have been flooding this country with their records and their sounds — and they all revert back to our Negro folklore and all our basic blues songs — then it becomes 'pop.' So, now a Negro can sing the same things he's been singing for years and attain popularity, because it's an accepted social music now.

"In fact, it's the greatest thing that could ever happen to Negroes; it's done tremendous things for the race, because our music is going to become *art* now. I think American pop music is art, and now that people are singing rhythm and blues it is establishing Negro folklore as a basic and acceptable art. I'm very happy for it."

For Girls only.
by shirley poston

This may be my last column. Because when a certain someone sees what I'm going to print, this may also be my last breath.

You see, I heard some very good (as in SPAZ) news today, and although I didn't ask if I could print it, I didn't promise *not* to, and besides, I've GOT to.

Passed-Down

Here's what happened. A friend of mine told me that a friend of hers saw, with her very own peepers, a letter written (and very recently) by someone who is *extremely* related to one of the Beatles.

And, there was a certain paragraph in that letter which read, and I---blither---quote: "The Beatles will NEVER EVER break up. That is on the level!"

I realize that the way I came by this information has a distinct "I-said-that-he-said-you-said-I-said-huh?" ring to it. I also realize that in many cases, one can't exactly swear (ho) by news received under such circumstances. *But*, in this case, the people involved are completely trustworthy, so I'm inclined to believe every beautiful word.

Not that I know exactly what they mean. I'd like to think it means the Beatles may tour again after all, but that's probably just wishful thinking on my part. Whatever, I think this is a ultra-firm indication that they will stay together as a group, always.

Rubbed Out

Now, if my friend would like to kill me, I'm available. Hopefully, since I didn't come out and say who said what, said friend will only rub it in a little, as opposed to having me rubbed out.

Re-whatever, the news was too beautiful to keep to myself, and I'm willing to pay the consequences if necessary. (She said bravely as she left town on the next bus).

Now, if I can get my mind (A.I.A.) (As In Alleged) off George (as in *Pant*), I have something reasonably humorous to related.

We've talked before about how much fun it is to come up with a totally ridiculous comment right in the middle of a conversation. Particularly when you've been sitting quietly (weaving a sampler, no doubt), listening to other people talk.

The more ridiculous and the less the comment has to do with the subject at hand, the better. And it's really super ool-cay if your "contribution" has absolutely nothing to do with *anything*.

Anynut, I heard what I consider to be the wildest such comment ever. Right in the middle of a long, boring conversation, a certain person turned to me and said: "Neat but not gaudy, the devil said as he painted his tail green."

You probably had to be there to fully understand why it broke everyone up into seven million pieces, because it doesn't make a whit of sense. So, give it a try and you'll see what I mean. I tried it out the next day, during a lull at the dinner table.

Previous to that, the family had been fearful of my sanity. Now they're just fearful, *period*.

Speaking of—no, I don't dare say it—speaking of families, I've found a great way to keep your folks from sending you to boarding school (you know, the kind with bars) (and not the kind of bars you're thinking either). If your folks are really teed off because they've asked you to do something at least four million times, and they finally reach the "you get up and do it this *instant* if you care to live long," here's a good way to get them back into a better mood.

Stand up and toddle slowly away, mumuring "I am moving my left leg, I am moving my right leg, etc." If it doesn't get a laugh, maybe they at least won't hit you *quite* so hard.

Cool Moves

At this time, I would like to thank my dog for another in a long series of cool moves. Someone sent me a package, but unfortunately, the aforementioned canine individual got to it before I did. Among the remnants, I found a can-opener with the following note attached: "You mentioned that George was a knight in shining armor . . . well . . . ."

The rest of the goddies . . . sorry, goodies were scattered all over the house, and should I ever get them (not to mention my wits) collected, I'll tell you about the remainder. Judging from the one thingy I did find intact, I'd better find the rest before my mother gets her hands on them (not to mention me).

This isn't the first time this has happened. If I could just teach that dog to have a little couth and stop opening presents with her teeth. The least she could do is be mannerly and open them the way I do. (With my feet).

By the road, I realize I say this after every holiday, but I do the same thing during every holiday, and may as well admit it. What am I garbling about? Food, that's what. Tons and tons and acres and acres of wonderful food, food, food.

I'm still going around with unbuttoned waistbands as a result of having piled it in by the truckloads during Christmas. I don't know why they bothered stuffing the turkey this year. They could have just stuffed same into me and saved a lot of trouble, because that's where most of the din-dins ended up.

Funny bit. We had company during Stuffing Season and I kept using the word din-dins. He thought I was saying *ding-dings*!

Speaking of ding-a-lings, will someone please answer that phone?

More Blubber

Back to the subject of blubber for a moment. Right after New Year's, I got out the "Hard Day's Night" album and started the toe-touching, hut-two-three-four bit again. I think it's finally starting to work. I got into some of my clothes this morning without having to use a shoe horn.

If you're having similar problems, remember that this album is the world's greatest for exercising to. Among other things.

One more bit of fascinating (as in zzzzzzz) info before I go. I got a letter from a pen pal who said she'd had a perfectly horrible time on New Year's Eve because "Kim was wearing his bat suit again."

I instantly wrote back and demanded to know what *that* meant. (Kim is her boyfriend). She replied that in her gang (crowd?) (bunch?) (of idiots?) (forget it), that means someone is acting up and doing snarly bat-type thingies.

Well, I have to go now. If I ever hope to get into *my* bat suit tonight (when I fling a tantrum in hopes of getting to use the car), I'd better get back to "Hard Day's Night."

Groan.

NY FIRM SETS BEATLE BOOK

Another Beatle book will soon hit newstands — this one published by an American firm.

Simon & Schuster, New York based publishers, have commissioned a full length book on the rise of the Beatles and the accompanying Beatlemania. The book will contain a detailed study of their careers from Liverpool days to the present.

The work, as yet untitled, will also offer interviews, personal observations by entertainment writers and those close to the Beatles, plus reviews of both records and performances.

The book is not financed in any way by the Beatles themselves, unlike other handbooks on the foursome.

Dusty Booked Around World

Dusty Springfield will spend the spring and summer flying around the world for her various performances. Presently singing in English clubs, she will soon leave for a European tour.

In May, she will visit Switzerland, Belgium and Holland. In June, she will play a club in Majorca, Spain. She will also make another appearance at New York's Basin Street East, as well as appearing at the Sands Hotel in Las Vegas in July. During August, the busy singer flies to Japan for a two day stint in Tokyo.

KRLA ARCHIVES

The Wizardry Of Mojo Men

By Connie Storm

San Francisco contains a veritable stockpile of pop talent. It's the Liverpool of America for psychedelic sounds, the U.S. base for Crawdaddys and Caverns.

To date, the Jefferson Airplane, We Five and Beau Brummels have come out of the Bay city, made hits and gone back in. Now groups like the Sopwith Camel ("Hello, Hello") and Mojo Men are replacing them.

"Sit Down I Think I Love You" is the latest San Francisco export to the pop scene. Written by Steve Stills of the Buffalo Springfield, it fell into the hands of The Mojo Men and through various witchcraft practices of their own, is now well on the way up national charts.

"Mojo" is the voodoo term for good magic, though The Mojo Men prefer to think of it as wizardry in music. Actually, The Mojo Men actually aren't all men—one outstanding member is a female drummer by the name of Jan.

The 5 foot tall Jan Errico, who is really a "Mojo Girl," gives The Mojo Men a distinctive sound through the use of her unique voice. She also gives them a unique asset as a female drummer.

Jan achieved popularity in another, now defunct, San Francisco group, The Vejtables. Picking up both drummer and lead vocalist chores, she had two area hits, "I Still Love You" and "The Last Thing On My Mind."

Jan replaced Dennis DeCarr, the original drummer for the group, when he left for Florida to continue his art studies. Otherwise, the group remains the same as when it formed in early 1965. Jim Alaimo, 23, is bass guitarist and vocalist Paul (Buddy) Curcio, 21, is featured on lead guitar. Don Metchick, 22, doubles on organ and harmonica.

Always a very popular San Francisco group, they produced two area hits, "Dance With Me" and "She's My Baby."

"Sit Down I Think I Love You" is the first disc cut by the three Mojo Men and one Mojo Girl. A catchy song, Jim, Buddy, Don and Jan reportedly have that top ten feeling about the recording.

Very possibly, it might be true. San Francisco columnist Herb Caen used one prominent word to describe the group: "fantastic."

DISCussion

Seems as though the Monkees are improving these days. True, we *have* said a few seemingly uncomplimentary things about this quartet, but most of them have been—believe it or not!—quite valid.

We have printed, as have other publications, that the Monkees were not recording their own material, and in some cases were not even singing it.

One irate Monkee fan protested my December 17 column regarding this subject: "I think you're being totally *unfair*. The Monkees are just as good if not better than the Beatles ever will be or were. As for being 'helped' by session musicians—phooey. I don't and won't believe it."

Dear "Just An Opinion": You are very definitely entitled to your own opinion, and I certainly won't argue with your personal preferences. But valid criticism goes far beyond our individual tastes in music. It is for this reason that musicians, musicologists, performers, and other talented and qualified people have gone on record praising the Beatles: not just because *they*, individually, like them, but for the musical achievements of the Beatles and for the phenomenal effect and influence they have had on the entire structure of contemporary music.

I think it will be readily agreed that, as yet, the Monkees are a long, long way from setting trends or developing new concepts in music.

Although you say you have read in "other publications" that the Monkees do, indeed, sing and play on their sessions, we would like to clarify this matter—honestly and in a straight-forward manner—once and for all.

A gigantic search was conducted looking for the right four boys to portray the Monkees on the TV series which was then on the drawing boards, and when they were found—only *two* of them were musicians in any sense of the word... and this is a self-admission, as well. Mike Nesmith has been playing guitar, and writing and singing songs in coffee houses for years. In fact, The BEAT staff had the pleasure of meeting him and seeing him perform for the first time before he was ever connected with this pop group, and he is a very talented young man.

Peter Tork is also a folksinger, who has been playing and singing for some time. Apart from these two, however, the group was not a musician's dream when they began. Although Micky supposedly *can* play the guitar, the powers-that-be put him on drums—which he could *not* play. And then there is Davy Jones, who plays no instrument, save the tambourine or maraccas, cannot read music, and even has difficulty in "hearing" the right sound when he listens to it.

However, Davy *is* trying to improve and is currently studying the guitar. Ditto for Micky and his tom-toms. All four boys will be the first to admit to you that they were not the best when they began, and they are well aware of the low-esteem in which they are currently held by other groups who claim they had to *work* their way (the *hard* way) up to the top and a hit record, while the Monkees had their path *bought* for them.

Davy defends the group by explaining that, "We're *not* a group, we're an act." Onstage, the boys put in more time than a regular singing group and even reappear individually to perform various skits, etc.

Although it may, at first, be difficult to accept if you have not been a part of this industry, it is not in the slightest unusual to use session musicians in order to achieve better musical quality; it's been done for years... and by some of the biggest groups. The main objection to the Monkees has been the *extent* to which they did it.

However—all is not yet lost for you devout Monkee fans. They are, indeed, studying their new craft and making a serious attempt to improve. An excellent example of that effort is their very latest release, "Mary, Mary"—written, sung and produced by Mike Nesmith. It is probably one of the best things the Monkees have released to date and is a definite sign of progress.

Their brand new album is also supposed to be quite good, and though I have not yet heard the LP in its entirety, the few cuts I have heard show a greater degree of originality and an improvement in quality over the first album.

They aren't yet Beatles (or whatever standard of excellence you choose), but give them time. They may have a few Monkee-shines in store for us yet.

BEAT Photo: Chuck Boyd

JOHNNY RIVERS has signed for the San Remo Song Festival.

KRLA ARCHIVES

KRLA ARCHIVES

America's Pop Music NEWSpaper 25¢

KRLA Edition BEAT
February 11, 1967

Conspiracy To 'Kill' Monkees

Is Baez The 'Phoanie?'

Beatles Holding On

Stones And Sex

War Between The Generations

BEAT Art: Henri Munsford

KRLA ARCHIVES

Letters TO THE EDITOR

THE MONKEE REBUTTAL

Dear BEAT:

This letter is a rebuttal of the letter you got from some English (?) boys in the January 14 edition of The BEAT. They said they liked almost everything in the United States of America, except the Monkees and Vietnam. Good for them! That's their point of view.

Now, I'd like to share my point of view with them and others. First off, I like the Monkees not just because "Davy Jones is cute," but because I like their new, refreshing, fast-moving TV show. I also dig their great sound! The boys wrote in and said that "they neither write their own music nor play a lot of it," which has just a particle of truth in it. Mike Nesmith wrote two of the songs on their first album. As for not playing their own music, they used studio musicians for recordings but they can play the guitars and Micky is learning to play the drums.

By the way, there are some other groups who don't write their own songs like Peter and Gordon. And as for playing their own music, look at Sonny and Cher—they don't play their own but does that make them not good, hey fellows? The boys also said that the Monkees were not talented. Man! They must be nuts! Oh, sorry that's just my own opinion (and several others I might add.)

As for Viet Nam, I'm not qualified to speak on the subject, but I'm sure it's being handled with care by qualified people and sooner or later the right will come out and show its colors!

Valerie MacMillan

P.S. The BEAT rules!

HELP REPEAT BEATLES

Dear BEAT:

First of all I would like to say what a great newspaper you have. Secondly, is what I really want to say. I have just finished watching the show "Beatles At Shea Stadium" and it has done something to me. First to hear that the Beatles aren't going to make any more appearances came as a blow to me.

On that day a little of my world was dropped beneath me. I guess only a Beatle fan can even try to express this feeling. Shirley Poston put it beautifully but I feel I must add my bit. Tonight my little bit of world was restored. Sure I cried, just like millions of others did tonight. But I cried for a different reason, not because Paul was so handsome, not because Ringo was adorable, not because George was silent, not because John was so sexy, but because they were the Beatles—four fabulous guys together again, together doing what makes the world happy.

Don't get me wrong, I'm glad the Beatles are pursuing what makes them the most happy. Tonight my world was restored with a small bit of film. That's why I want to ask all the Beatles' fans, who the Beatles mean something to, to write to the sponsors of the program and urge them to repeat the show. You can write to ABC-TV in your area and ask them. You can write to Clairol Hair Dressing and plead with them to sponsor it again and what a great show it was.

And the big one is to write to the U.S.A. Beatles' Fan Club and the English Fan Club to have the Beatles appear one more time in the U.S. I'm sure if all of us here try our best with letters, petitions, etc., we can have the Beatles' show and a live concert. That would mean a lot to all the fans all over the U.S. So, please, please try.

Lynn Williams

SPOONFUL AND RAIDERS

Dear BEAT:

I am writing this letter for two reasons. The first is to congratulate you for such a groovy newspaper. The BEAT is most certainly bigger and better than ever! Shirley Poston is simply great! One of my favorite articles is entitled "In People Are Talking About." Not only is it funny, truthful and fabulous—it is also anonymous! I am sure that many people would like to know just WHO is doing the fine work, please. Speaking of fine work, keep it up!

Now I come to my second reason. I have noticed that although The BEAT prints many articles on many groups, you have not printed nearly anything on two of the best and most acclaimed groups around — the Lovin' Spoonful and Paul Revere and the Raiders. C'mon, now, it's not like you to ignore talent! These are groups who keep a stronghold of American music on the pop charts and are as great, if not greater, than many of the British singers. I hope you will listen to all of the Spoonful and Raider fans who are asking for a fair chance for their faves.

Laurie Shapiro

SUPREMES FORGOTTEN?

Dear BEAT:

I am writing this letter after long considering whether or not I would have enough courage to write it—so now here I go.

For a long time I have been a fan of the English groups and there has never been any doubt in my mind about who reigns in that category (the Beatles and Stones, of course.) But, I also have been a fan of our own American groups. But the one thing that never fails to upset me is how everyone (well, maybe not everyone) seems to overlook the Supremes.

In American music, comparatively the groups, there is no doubt about who has sold more records and albums—of course, the Supremes. Secondly, their past three singles have all reached number one in America, besides other countries. What other American group or any other group, really, can say this?

Whenever you, or any other magazine or newspaper, does mention them it is hardly never in comparison or on equal status with the Monkees, Beach Boys, Mama's and Papa's, Lovin' Spoonful, Association, etc. So, I slowly began to think about this and it grew more in my mind until I had to say something about it. Please accept my thanks for taking time to read this and I sincerely hope you print it so maybe others will see the light as I did. Thank you.

Norman Myers

THANKS

Dear BEAT:

We would like to extend our thanks for the presentation you have given us in the BEAT Showcase. We would also like to thank all of our fans, through you, for being the toughest.

To all our fans—we hope to meet each and every one of you personally. We will be as you want us to be and do as you wish us to do. We are yours and we belong to you.

The Paperhangers

IS IT PAUL?

Dear BEAT:

I am writing this letter to inform you of the regrettable error which has been made on the Beatles' "Revolver" album. I am very surprised that it has not been called to your attention sooner.

The "Revolver" album states that the song "Here, There and Everywhere" was sung by Paul McCartney. Yet, if you listen carefully, it is unmistakably the voice of John Lennon. My friends and I are certain of this fact. Especially if you compare this song to "Girl," the similarity in voice would be extraordinary if these two songs were indeed sung by two different people.

I wish you would look into this matter. If I am wrong, I am very sorry and stand corrected.

Jullian McIntyre

Paul sings "Here, There and Everywhere."

The Editor

NEIL DIAMOND—THAT ONE MAGICAL 'SOLITARY MAN'

Dear BEAT:

I can't say how really, truly overjoyed I was by the article you did in your January 14 issue—"Strictly In The Diamond Bag."

When I heard his first song ("Solitary Man"), I didn't really like it. Then came "Cherry, Cherry." That song really awakened me to his talent. He's fantastic!

How any person can be so very talented and yet not affected by all his fame and have such a wonderful view of life is hard for me to understand. Not to mention his fantastic looks!

He's concerned with what's going on around him. He's not a selfish, self-centered person. For instance, the effort he's put into his idea for a pop show in Russia. What other entertainer as great as he has tried to spread his good will?

Neil Diamond has, undoubtedly, had to leave some part of himself to the world before he passes on (dread the thought!) He is the type of person who will contribute something to the betterment of humanity. In my eyes, Neil Diamond will leave some type of effect on this group of teenagers. Why? Because we want him to. He's that certain, magical "Solitary Man."

If I had one goal in my life, it would be to meet Neil Diamond and be able to know what he thinks deep inside.

This will probably get filed away and forgotten but I just want to say that Louise's story was really an ideal inside picture of a great star and I envy her so much for being able to talk to him and with him.

Please, please have more stories like that in your future issues — it was fabulous. More on him, too!

Andrea Ruiz

P.S. I agree "there should be at least 10 more of him" but I'd rather like to meet the real one! He's really "Got To Me."

DAVY JONES SAYS TO FORGET THE RUMORS

Dear BEAT:

I am from Pittsburgh and I received a subscription to BEAT for Christmas from my girlfriend. I think the articles are great, especially "In" People and Robin Boyd. I read one article entitled "The British Eye View" in which some boys were cutting up the Monkees. To quote the letter, these boys said: "We've even heard that on one side of their album, they couldn't do it so they got another group to sing it."

I would like to know where they heard this because I have learned from a very factual magazine that they do sing all the songs on both sides of the album and I know also who sings what on both sides of the album in case those boys would be interested in knowing this.

To quote Davy Jones: "Forget those rumors that we don't work on our own records. I can assure you that we do and dig doing it—and we work hard."

These boys also said: "They're corny and imitative of the Beatles." Personally, I think that these boys are afraid that the Monkees are going to rule out the Beatles. Even though I like the Beatles, they are dropping out of sight and I am positive that after the Monkees finish their tour they will be number one in America.

Donne Michaelson

THE YOUNG RASCALS ARE REALLY LIVING

Dear BEAT:

In a recent "In" People Are Talking About column you have the nerve to ask the question "What happened to the Young Rascals?" What's wrong with you people anyway?

The Rascals aren't dead old men so why can't you print anything on them? I saw them twice in person and believe me they put on a better show than anyone else I've seen and that includes the Stones, Raiders, DC5, Hermits, etc.

Don't get me wrong, I love BEAT. You have terrific news on great groups like the Stones, Spoonful, Byrds, etc., but never on the Rascals. And then you have the nerve to ask what happened to them. I dare you to print this letter from an unsatisfied BEAT fan.

Faith Daley

Sorry you're unsatisfied, Faith, but we're great fans of the Rascals and we'd like nothing better than to see them get another national number one hit. We're well aware of the fact that the Rascals are not "dead old men." Eddie was up here a couple of days ago and there is no one more alive than he is! Anyway, maybe you'll be satisfied when you see the next issue of BEAT.

The Editor

KRLA ARCHIVES

On the BEAT
By Louise Criscione

The Beatles have won the lawsuit filed against them by United Press photographer, Joseph Bodnar. The photographer alleged that he was beaten by a guard employed by Globe Protection, Inc. during the Beatles' 1965 concert at the Hollywood Bowl and asked for $10,000 in punitive damages from each of the defendents (which included Capitol Records and Globe Protection as well as the Beatles), plus $1,000 each for compensatory damages.

However, Superior Judge Richard Wells awarded judgment in favor of the Beatles with no decision yet reached regarding Globe and Capitol Records.

Stone Controversy

As always, the Rolling Stones caused considerable controversy and chaos when they flew into New York for the "Ed Sullivan Show." The controversy, of course, surrounded the change in lyrics of "Let's Spend The Night Together" for the Sullivan stint as well as the fact that the majority of U.S. radio stations are refusing to play that side in favor of "Ruby Tuesday," which was originally the "B" side.

Part of the chaos occurred at Kennedy International when the Stones landed. The limousines taking them to their hotel were involved in a near-accident when one of the cars pulling off the runway almost collided with a moving jet. The rest of the chaos took place outside the CBS studios when the Stones arrived for the Sullivan rehearsals and fans assembled for a glimpse of the group broke into something of a riot—ending with Mick cutting his hand. None of the other Stones were injured but the melee was much too close for comfort.

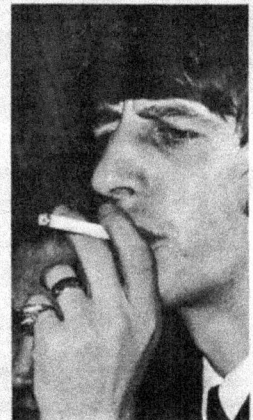

... RINGO STARR

The debut of "The Monkees" on British television was met with the same uproar as greeted the show and the group when they aired on American television. People are lining up on both sides of the Atlantic either for or against the Monkees. And, of course, the ever-present knockers have finally given up the project of destroying the Beatles and are now happily engaged in attempting to "kill" the Monkees. Which is, in itself, something of a major accomplishment since these knockers only go for those in the "big time."

Jealousy High

Jealousy is at its peak with groups who have not made it busily crying in their beer—not to mention, dreaming up new ways of putting-down Micky, Mike, Peter and Davy. But Monkee fans are happy—rightly so, since everything with the name "Monkees" on it is selling like nothing since the Beatles arrived on U.S. soil.

Eric Burdon best typified the feeling of most mature people when he said: "They (The Monkees) make very good records and I can't understand how people get upset about them." Eric went on to add that he digs the Monkee discs "no matter how people scream" and ended with the sound advice to "just enjoy the records" and never mind the soul-searching behind the Monkees' success. Ditto for their TV show.

Keith Relf believes that the Yardbirds are stale to the British fans. However, Keith states that the Yardbirds are not alone in their predicament. "Unless you get to the level of the Beatles or Stones," said Keith, "you all become stale to the kids after a year or two."

Both Keith and Jimmy Page agree that musically it's all happening Stateside "with the Monkees at the commercial end of the product and at the other end the Mothers of Invention. And we are in the middle trying to bridge the gap."

... KEITH RELF

QUICK ONES: Johnny Rivers has been chosen to sing the title for "Casino Royale" ... Cher came down with the flu, causing a set-back in the duo's appearance on "Man From U.N.C.L.E." ... The New Vaudeville Band is set to tape a "Hollywood Palace" on February 24 for an April 15 airing ... Herb Alpert and the TJB were all set to play McCormick Place in Chicago but it burned down the night they arrived in town.

Simon & Garfunkel In Philharmonic Opening

Simon and Garfunkel made their first major New York concert appearance when they played the Philharmonic Hall last Sunday. The duo launched to immediate fame when their "Sounds Of Silence," a commentary on lack of communication, became the country's chart-topper. Since then, a series of other hit singles and innumerable concerts throughout the U.S. advanced their career with accelerating momentum.

Paul Simon and Art Garfunkel are hailed as leaders in a school of popular music which sees the pop lyric as a vehicle for intelligent statements concerning the world we live in. Their specific concerns are with problems peculiar to an increasingly complex society—loneliness, alienation, lack of communication. What has brought the duo serious critical attention as well as popularity is the uncluttered but highly poetic imagery of their lyrics and the quality of their understated vocal style.

Simon and Garfunkel have been singing together since they were thirteen but their professional efforts were in the coffee houses of Greenwich Village. Plans are now underway for a tour covering Australia, Hawaii, the Philippines and Japan.

... ART GARFUNKEL AND PAUL SIMON listen to session playback.

THE BLUES MAGOOS—FROM 'UNDER' TO PSYCHEDELIC

The Blues Magoos whose "Nothing Yet" is currently breaking out nationwide are set to take off on a unique promotion campaign. The group leaves on a chartered special executive airliner for a two to three week tour covering twenty major markets.

"The full impact of the Blues Magoos," says Alan Mink, Mercury National Product Manager, "is realized only when the visual quality of the group is demonstrated. It was for that reason that Mercury and the group's management undertook the widespread tour exposure. We think that the Blues Magoos represent an entirely new concept in pop music. For that reason, they must be seen as well as heard in as many areas as possible."

The Blues Magoos are being billed as a "psychedelic rock group" but before their debut single, "Nothing Yet," they were known as an "underground" group in Greenwich Village.

... THE BLUES MAGOOS "must be seen as well as heard."

THE WHO STATESIDE IN APRIL

The Who are definitely coming Stateside on April 16. The British group who enjoyed smashing success with "My Generation" will play gigs in Detroit, New York and California.

Confirmed television dates for The Who include "Action," "Ed Sullivan," "Tonight," "Mike Douglas" and Clay Cole's New York show.

Pet Clark, Davis, Jr. Attendants

One of the wildest entertainment weddings of the new year took place in Las Vegas when French singer Charles Aznavour married Swedish ex-model Ulla Thorssell.

The bride wore a silver-threaded lace miniskirt and the already twice wed Aznavour announced that "this is her first and last marriage."

Petula Clark was matron of honor at the wedding and Sammy Davis Jr. took over the chores as best man.

KRLA ARCHIVES

"YOU!" Micky, Davy and Peter tell Mike while the crew looks on.

... REST COMES TO THE MONKEES wherever they can find it and they find it here in front of the cameras.

The Monkees Amid Controlled Confusion

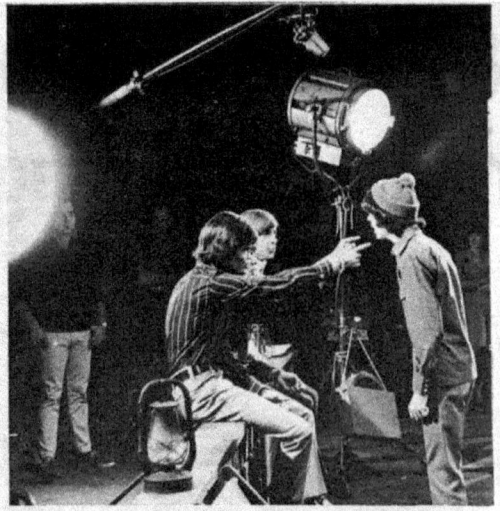

... MIKE AND MICKY turn on serious faces to listen to the director.

By Louise Criscione

What is this, Knock The Monkees Year? Some sort of a giant conspiracy to destroy, devour and flush four people down the drain to wallow in the mud of thrumpted-up controversy?

From the definitely-slanted and certainly-twisted press coming out from California to London on the Monkees, one is almost forced to conclude that *someone somewhere* is working at fever pitch to feed angles and author stories in such a way as to insure that Davy, Mike, Peter and Micky emerge smelling very much like four talentless puppets whose strings are pulled by some almighty studio power constantly hovering over them.

Chosen For

The first fact hungrily seized upon by the ever-expanding horde of Knockers was that Micky Dolenz, Mike Nesmith, Peter Tork and Davy Jones were hand-picked out of 437 applicants to be television's "Monkees." Big deal. You don't for one minute cling to the naive belief that Bill Cosby was the only man considered for "I Spy" or that David McCallum was the sole aspirant to the role of Illya Kuryakin, do you? Cosby was handpicked by Sheldon Leonard because he felt Cosby was the best man for the role of Alexander Scott.

And so were Mike, Peter, Davy and Micky chosen by Burt Schneider and Bob Rafelson to be the Monkees because they felt these four were best suited for the job.

Yet, that an ad was placed and that 437 young men turned up in answer to that ad has been the basis for slams, knocks and, in essence, made to appear as some sort of a completely bizarre method of casting a television show. If anything, that today's Monkees were chosen out of so many is nothing short of a major accomplishment proving that they were better than 434 others. Face it, the larger the field the harder to win.

Yet, that Davy, Micky, Mike and Peter came out winners has been met with nothing but ridicule! How strange this logic.

Nevertheless, whether applauded or jeered, "The Monkees" made it on the air and "The Last Train to Clarksville" began a ride which ended on top of the national charts with over one million passengers eagerly purchasing tickets for the accelerated Monkee ride.

Then all hell broke loose with the "news" that session musicians were used on the Monkees' first album. Stories were slanted to make an uninformed public believe that session musicians were a never-before-used commodity. Charges of "public deception" were hurled at the Monkees. Even national news magazines joined in the fun and those who had never been to a recording session and have absolutely no *true* conception of how a record is made were led to believe that the Monkees were the only group in the world who utilized the talents of others besides themselves to achieve the best sound on record.

When, in fact, session musicians have been, and are being used (in part or in whole) by practically *every* group or artist today.

You don't have to take anyone's word for it — just read the credits on some of your albums. You may be shattered to discover that a string quartet was used to back Paul McCartney on "Yesterday," that George Martin played piano on "In My Life" and that Organ Evans was the one playing organ on "You Won't See Me."

Stones Too

Perhaps you're a Rolling Stones' fan who is laboring under the misconception that only Stone talent is used on their albums. Just check some credits and you'll find that Gene Pitney played piano on "Little By Little" and that Phil Spector — not Mick Jagger — handled the maracas on that track.

Still not satisfied? Well, then how about the fact that Jack Nitzche, Ian Stewart and J. W. Alexander were used on "Out of Our Heads?" And on down the list it goes. Why, then, have there been no headlines slashing into the Beatles and Stones for the use of other musicians on their records?

Understand, this is in no way an attempt to knock the Beatles, the Stones or anyone else but merely proof that the use of other musicians while recording is a common occurance. And what's so horrible about it anyway? The public is entitled to the best possible sound on a record and what real difference does it make whether you get that sound out of a session musician or out of an idiot beating a scrubboard?

As for the Monkees, you obviously dug the end result or sales would never have climbed over the 3 million mark for the album. You wanted something you could enjoy — you got it. So why all the garbage about their records?

And plenty being written about the Monkees is just that — garbage. One national magazine in describing a Monkee session pointed out the fact that after the instrumental track was finished each Monkee put on earphones and faced the microphone to add the vocals while their instruments lay on the studio floor.

Farce!

What did you think, each Monkee turned his *back* on the mike? Or that after the instrumental track is complete you're supposed to keep right on playing? What total farce!

In any case, whether or not you still doubt the honesty of Monkee records, you had better believe that from seven in the morning until seven at night Davy, Micky, Peter and Mike work on something which is very much a part of them — their television show.

Arriving on the Monkee set around ten o'clock, you'll find Micky and Davy performing an impromptu duet on "She," Peter catching 40 winks on a couch while props are shoved around him and Mike answering the phone.

The props and lighting set for a scene and the call goes out: "Okay, let's have the first team in."

Mike, Micky, Peter and Davy collectively assembled, the scene is shot, changes made and re-shot. The off-camera antics of the Monkees are roughly those you see on-

KRLA ARCHIVES

...DAVY STARES in disbelief as Rosemarie and Mike emote!

...PETER AND FRIEND can't believe it either.

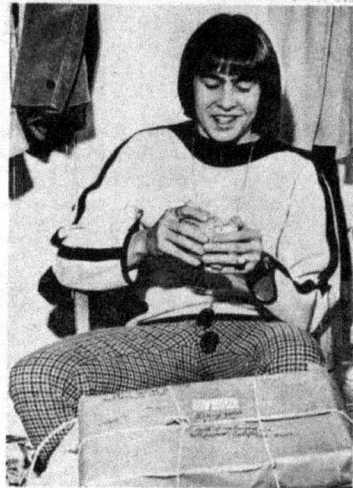

DAVY OPENS gifts from fans in his dressing room.

...MIKE AND PETER go over music for the next scene.

...MICKY heads for the door.

BUT DAVY JONES sticks around to chat with Louise Criscione about Monkee personal appearances.

screen, with lines tossed back and forth, ideas exchanged, opinions voiced and faces twisted into all sorts of contortions.

The scene shot to satisfaction, Davy rushes off to his dressing room for a wardrobe change and Peter hails a passerby: "Can I have a swig of your milk, man?" Micky appears with a half-eaten sandwich and a can of Hawaiian punch and Mike strolls in with Sally (the hairdresser) and her everpresent comb trailing behind him to give each of the Monkees the once-over before another scene is shot.

Trouble

This one gives the Monkees a little trouble and is done several times before the director nods: "Print that one." And again the Monkees fan out in four different directions. You follow Davy into his dressing room where he's surrounded by bags full of gifts which arrived in the morning mail.

"You have to answer them, 'cause like these cufflinks," Davy says holding up a set, "you know they must have cost at least four bucks. So, you have to answer." More packages are opened—more cufflinks, a shirt, a key chain, flowers from Hawaii.

"David Jones!" "They're always yelling at me," Davy laughs as he shifts one sack of mail out of his way and hurries out of the dressing room just in time to hear "David Jones!" ring out again.

In a corner about as far away from the confusion as it is possible to get, Mike and Peter with guitars in hand are going over the music they're set to play in the next scene and Micky has claimed the couch for his turn at catching a few winks while he can. But no one's rest lasts long as the "first team" is called in for the next scene.

At one thirty, a lunch break is called and three Monkees make their way towards the door. "Hey, Davy," yells Mike, "don't forget lunch."

"I'm going to the doctor."

"Yeah, that's what I said, don't forget to go to the doctor."

Lunch break over, the cast and crew re-assembles and the visitors grow in number as four or five different groups of fans are admitted onto the set. Davy and Peter sing "Don't Let The Sun Catch You Crying" for their visitors and Mama Cass pops her head in and is soon in the midst of conversation with Peter. And so it goes. Scenes are set up, shot, reshot and sent on their way to be printed.

Six o'clock arrives and with it most of the visitors, photographers and everyone else not essential for the rest of the day's shooting beat a hasty path for the door. The Monkees stay behind with a good hour's shooting still to be done. Hopefully by seven they'll have it wrapped up and will be able to leave stage seven behind them—until tomorrow.

KRLA ARCHIVES

MAMA'S AND PAPA'S SET BRITISH TV

The Mama's and Papa's left at the end of January for a visit to England and the Continent.

While in Britain, the Mama's and Papa's will appear on "Top Of The Pops," the "Rolf Harris Show," "London Palladium" and will also film their own television spectacular to be aired on BBC-2.

After several European dates, the group returns to England for a concert at London's Royal Albert Hall on February 16. Following that appearance, the group is not scheduled to work until early May.

...MAMA'S AND PAPA'S
BEAT Photo: Chuck Boyd

Italians Pick Sinatra As Best Singer

Frank Sinatra has been selected the "Best Singer In The World" for 1966 by Italy's official recording industry trade organization, the wordy Organizzazione Nazionale per l'Assegnzatione del Disco d'Oro.

The selection was made in an annual poll of Italian newspaper, magazine and trade publication music critics.

Sinatra was notified of the honor when he received an official cablegram inviting him to accept the award at the group's annual presentation, held this year in Piacenza, south of Milan.

HAPPENING

Donovan Tells Of Trade-Out With Beatles

Donovan has finally cemented rumor into fact by revealing that Paul McCartney's voice *is* featured on "Mellow Yellow" as something of a trade-out between Donovan and the Beatles.

When the Beatles were cutting "Yellow Submarine," Donovan "helped a little with the lyrics." Therefore, Paul returned the favor by appearing at Donovan's session and whispering "Mellow Yellow" at the appropriate time!

Donovan is firmly convinced that the success of the disc in the U.S. is due to the fact that "it is a driving song. A great many of the discs are heard on car radios and if the music is not sympathetic to the driver, one push of the button and he's on another station."

...CHER
BEAT Photo: Robert Young

BONOS ARE OFF FOR SAN REMO

Before leaving for Italy and the San Remo Song Festival, Sonny and Cher hosted a foreign press screening of their first motion picture, "Good Times," in New York.

Immediately following the screening, the duo took off for the Festival as one of the U.S. entrys (Johnny Rivers and Dionne Warwick also competed in the San Remo Festival.)

Sonny and Cher are set for several personal appearances while in Europe, with stop-offs scheduled for Paris, Milan, West Berlin and London.

This Spring, the husband and wife team will start work on their second movie. "Good Times" will be released on Memorial Day.

...NANCY & FRANK SINATRA
BEAT Photo: Robert Caster

'in' people are talking about...

Davy's obsession with pool and how he plays it almost every night at a spot on Sunset... The possibility of the Beatles coming to California in March for a television show... The Roaring 20's cartoon on the Beatles' album... Bob Mitchum cutting an album... The rumors about Cass apparently being true... How great the Stones looked on Sullivan and what a showman Mick really is and how sad that most radio stations have refused to play "Let's Spend The Night Together" because it's "obscene"... Davy Jones sporting a shorter haircut... Whether or not Aaron Neville really exists.

PEOPLE ARE TALKING ABOUT how really great the Miracles are and how many pop groups could learn quite a few things by watching the fantastic Smokey Robinson... The Raven Madd making it big—if their first session is any indication of things to come... The middle-aged editor who has most pop groups putting her down behind her back because they're afraid to say it to her face and what a sad situation that is... The happening people in San Francisco and where it is all going to end... How unpopular the new Governor of California has made himself with the state's youth... How much better Dino looks with his long hair—very reminiscent of Paul McCartney, which definitely is not bad.

PEOPLE ARE TALKING ABOUT the Electric Prunes... Don and the Goodtimes being exactly that — good... How sad it is that certain teen publications have given Bill Cosby a bad taste in his mouth and how the rest of us would like to hang them in effigy for making it so hard for us... A new "Shindig" type show being hoped-for next season and how much we could use one... John's fantastic sense of humor by showing up at Georgie Fame's costume party dressed as a priest!... The same party featuring Paul as a general, Ringo as an Arab, Jane Asher as an angel and Brian Epstein as a clown... Monkees being number one in England by the time you read this and the British censors having to work overtime to eliminate some of Davy's antics.

PEOPLE ARE TALKING ABOUT the Walkers possibly coming Stateside and Sonny and Cher visiting England... For what it's worth, just about everyone digs the Springfields' latest... How it's about time Chris had a follow-up... What the lyrics to "Niki Hokey" really mean... Cass possibly remaining in England after the M's & P's British tour... The Yardbirds in "Blow-Up"... How many performers turned up for the Miracles opening at the Whisky and stayed 'till the club closed... Mark Lindsay's contribution to *The BEAT*... How far up you can go before you come down... How well Mitch is going to do without his Wheels... What you have to do to be a rock 'n' roll star... Kind of a drag being anything but that... What Diana thinks of Felice — or better yet, what Motown thinks about the situation.

PEOPLE ARE TALKING ABOUT how really funny it would be to see the real Senator Bobby doing "Wild Thing" on "Ed Sullivan" or perhaps Ronald Reagan singing "Please, Please, Please"... Herbie Alpert flying to Chicago to play the McCormick Place only to find that it had burned down... Beatles turning down Bernstein's million dollar offer—just like we said they would... "Hi, what's happening? Anybody going toward Canter's?"... Knocking out the red baron... The fact that we happen to dig the Beatles, Stones and the Monkees—So what do you think of that?... The uproar over the Monkees' admission that they've used session musicians on their records when those inside the business happen to know that practically all of the top groups use, or have used, session musicians.

PEOPLE ARE TALKING ABOUT Bobby Hebb getting married because he collects pennys and how overwhelmed he was at the small cars and big trucks in England... The increased number of pop artists in this year's San Remo Song Festival... How groovy Neil would be in the movies and hoping that it won't take movie studios long to recognize that fact... Monkees taking over the top spot from Tom Jones after Tom's seven week stand at number one in England... Nancy maybe not being able to sing but sure looking good on the cover... How much Andy Warhol looks like Adam Faith... How crowded that address on Wimpole Street is... Whether Peter and Gordon can expand it to three consecutive hits in a row.

KRLA ARCHIVES

WAR BETWEEN THE GENERATIONS

'This Thing Can't Be Stopped'

Or Beware The Postage Stamps You Lick!

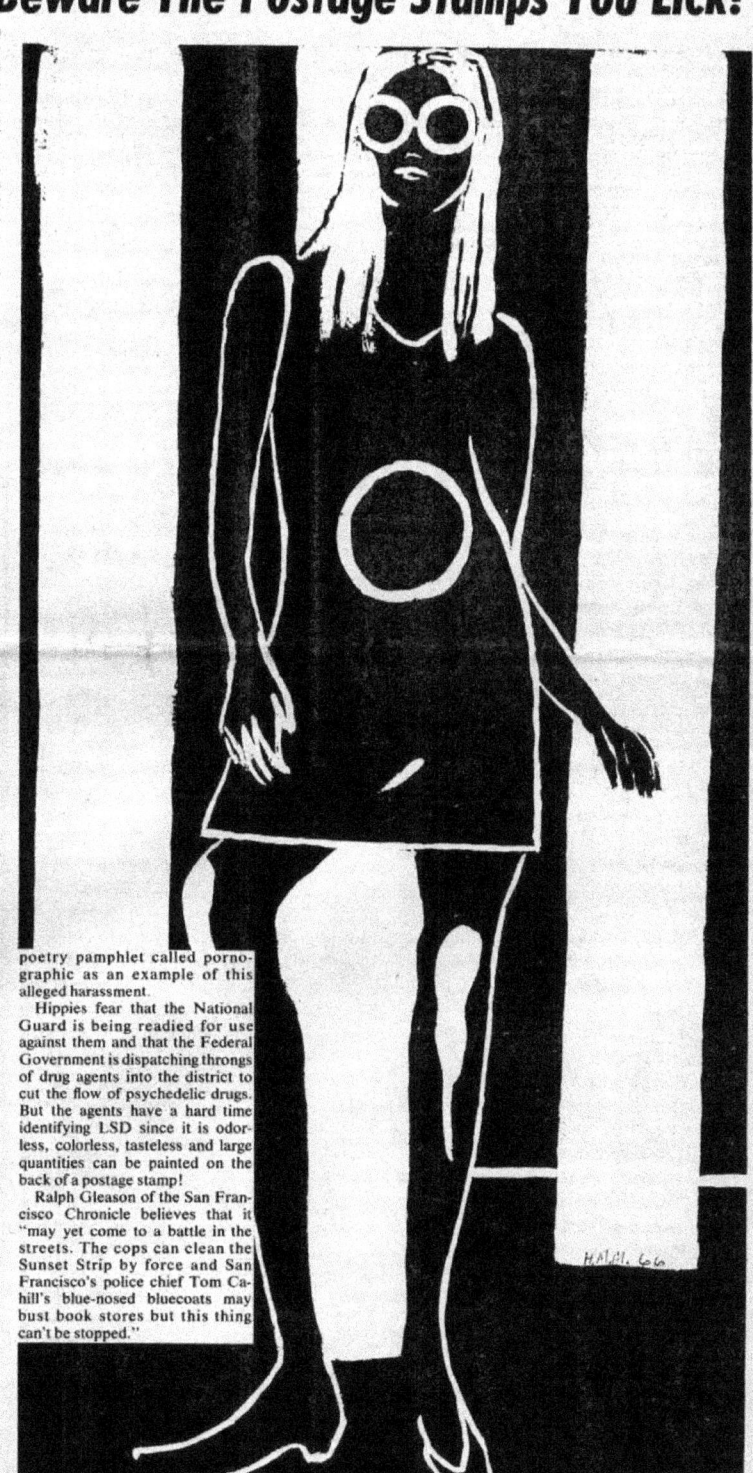

BEAT ART: Henri Munsford

"In the war between the generations, the kids are right and they will win." — Ralph Gleason

If you're under 25 you're one of the kids who will win. You make up half of the American population, were named *Time's* Man of the Year, influence all segments of mass media and spend millions of dollars annually. You march on the Strip, protest the war in Vietnam, catch a Cong bullet in your belly, dig the Monkees, join the Peace Corps., believe in love, frown on prejudice, dab in politics and fight for what you believe in.

You forsake taboo for honesty, will speak out on any subject, attend light shows, buy Motown, favor personality over appearance, go to school, scoff at the charge that you're sheep, laugh at matrons on the dance floor, cringe when you're called a child, drive a car, feel pop music belongs to you and are preparing for your take-over as policy makers of the country.

Haight-Ashbury

You've been called the Generation of Protest but the handle doesn't especially fit. Protest has been around too long—you think you're ideas are fresh. Your parents protested the law on alcohol, over 5,000 under-25's call the Haight-Ashbury section of San Francisco home and protest the illegality of psychedelic drugs. The word "beatnik" is out since beat was previously used to mean uninvolved in emotion, politics or much of anything else. The Haight-Ashbury dwellers are very much involved.

They're called "hippies" or "happeners," seek intense sensual and emotional experiences as a way of widening their awareness of themselves, believe in "consciousness expansion" by way of LSD or marijuana—though not all hippies use drugs. Other methods include yoga breathing, special diets, electronic music, light shows and sauna baths.

Chet Helms is a 24-year-old dance promoter with a $250,000 a year business. He is also an influential member of the Haight-Ashbury hippies. Helms' dances are "happenings" and the music is now known as "San Francisco Acid Rock." Says Helms: "We (the hippies) are assuming the role of taste-makers. The next step, as the number of young voters escalates, may be political."

The hippies are against the war in Vietnam and the draft. They deplore racial segregation and laws against psychedelic drugs. They do not believe in chastity, thrift or cleanliness. Parents, say the hippies, are "half-persons," hypocrites and are constantly threatening to blow up the world with a bomb.

LSD

In Haight-Ashbury, LSD sells for $2 a capsule and word has filtered out that five grams (100,000 doses) is moved in San Francisco each week. Special pipes for marijuana are sold in stores and hippies congregate outside the Psychedelic Book Shop singing, dancing and playing guitars.

San Francisco bred the beatnik. It's only fair the city should sire the hippie. But San Francisco's older generation finds the hippie anything but welcome. The Haight Street Merchants Association refuses to admit the hippie businessmen into their organization. So the hippies, who own approximately 25 shops, have formed their own group—H.I.P.

Alcoholics Anonymous and the Salvation Army have nothing on the Haight-Ashbury hippies. There are phone numbers to call in case of police brutality or a bad "trip." The Artists Liberation Front provides free public entertainment and the Diggers offer free food and clothing with no questions asked. "Our function," say the Diggers, "is to remove people's need to work for food. There's plenty available." The Diggers gather rejected vegetables in the market and stale bread from the bakeries.

The hippies charge the police "harass" them daily with "illegal searches," using the arrests in The Psychedelic Shop for sale of a poetry pamphlet called pornographic as an example of this alleged harassment.

Hippies fear that the National Guard is being readied for use against them and that the Federal Government is dispatching throngs of drug agents into the district to cut the flow of psychedelic drugs. But the agents have a hard time identifying LSD since it is odorless, colorless, tasteless and large quantities can be painted on the back of a postage stamp!

Ralph Gleason of the San Francisco Chronicle believes that it "may yet come to a battle in the streets. The cops can clean the Sunset Strip by force and San Francisco's police chief Tom Cahill's blue-nosed bluecoats may bust book stores but this thing can't be stopped."

HULLABALOO
ROCK & ROLL SHOWPLACE OF THE WORLD

presents

Friday & Saturday — Jan. 27 & 28

BUFFALO SPRINGFIELD

PLUS ALL-STAR SHOW

Friday only — Feb. 3

THE SEEDS

PLUS ALL STAR SHOW

6230 SUNSET BLVD., HOLLYWOOD — HO. 6-8281

KRLA ARCHIVES

KRLA Comes To Rescue Of Local Football Fans

Pete Rozzelle stood his ground. "Absolutely no change will be made," he said, "in my decision to black out the Super Bowl game in this area."

And you know what? Pete-baby is a man of his word!

Even in the face of a Superior Court suit, the football commissioner insisted that the player's share of money might be "affected" if people could see it on TV. Noting the $12.00 price for tickets, the *Defender of Faith*, that *Champion of Right*, KRLA, decided to *sabotage* the plans for such a blackout. The answer was lying just 130 miles to the south, in San Diego, where Channels 8 and 10 would carry the game. Ordering the engineering department into overtime work, Station Manager John Barret put a whole team on 'round-the-clock, developing a special high-gain antenna.

The result: *The KRLA Simple S-B Antenna!* This amazing do-it-yourself electronic marvel was a special design that actually pulled in the distant San Diego stations clearly!

Plans were offered free to all who asked. The equipment required: five coat hangers (straightened) and an old broom stick (6 feet long) and some TV lead-in wire.

Following instructions, happy Southlanders were busily constructing their own outdoor antenna. Yes, a few hapless weekenders slipped off the roof and smashed up potted plants and femurs, but some of us *just are not technically minded,* have you noticed?

There were some who grumbled about law suits when the contraption didn't pull in anything more than louder static, but these soreheads were just bad losers.

Many reported unusual success. One sports fan had gone halfway through a lecture on Tse-Tse flies before he realized his amazing antenna was pulling in a UHF station in Vancouver. When he turned the antenna around, he caught the wire in his coat, and, well, he lived on a hill that was too high anyway.

Tens of thousands of requests were filled by KRLA, in this unparalleled public service, in which engineering science triumphed over Dark Ages thinking.

KRLA still has a few thousand copies of the plans left, and we're sure they'd come in handy the NEXT time somebody tries to pull a fast one on LA sports fans! Just send a self-addressed stamped envelope to KRLA Pasadena. You, too, will hail the Simple S-B!

Warner Bros. unlocks all the doors of the sensation-filled best seller.

It's like you're running a big city... a unique empire... a private world with a do-not-disturb sign on every door...

HOTEL

Starring ROD TAYLOR
CATHERINE SPAAK · KARL MALDEN · MELVYN DOUGLAS · RICHARD CONTE · MICHAEL RENNIE
KEVIN McCARTHY and MERLE OBERON as "The Duchess"   Original Music by Johnny Keating
Based on the novel by Arthur Hailey · Written for the Screen and Produced by WENDELL MAYES
Directed by RICHARD QUINE   TECHNICOLOR® FROM WARNER BROS.

EXCLUSIVE ENGAGEMENT STARTS
WEDNESDAY, FEB. 8th
CALL THEATRE FOR SHOW TIMES

WORLD FAMOUS GRAUMAN'S
CHINESE
HOLLYWOOD BLVD. · HO 4-8111

Top 40 Requests

1	I'M A BELIEVER	Monkees
2	RUBY TUESDAY	Rolling Stones
3	I HAD TOO MUCH TO DREAM LAST NIGHT	Electric Prunes
4	SIT DOWN, I THINK I LOVE YOU	Mojo Men
5	HAPPY TOGETHER	The Turtles
6	SNOOPY VS. THE RED BARON	Royal Guardsmen
7	KIND OF A DRAG	Buckinghams
8	MR. FARMER	The Seeds
9	PRETTY BALLERINA	The Left Banke
10	GEORGY GIRL	The Seekers
11	WE AIN'T GOT NOTHIN' YET	Blue Magoos
12	BORN FREE	Roger Williams
13	NO FAIR AT ALL	The Association
14	98.6	Keith
15	FOR WHAT IT'S WORTH	Buffalo Springfield
16	SINGLE GIRL	Sandy Posey
17	HELLO, HELLO	Sopwith Camel
18	THE BEAT GOES ON	Sonny & Cher
19	KNIGHT IN SHINING ARMOR	Peter & Gordon
20	SUGAR TOWN	Nancy Sinatra
21	FULL MEASURE	Lovin' Spoonful
22	LOVE IS HERE, NOW YOU'RE GONE	Supremes
23	TELL IT LIKE IT IS	Aaron Neville
24	WEDDING BELL BLUES	Laura Nyro
25	MUSIC TO WATCH GIRLS BY	Bob Crewe Generation
26	YOU GOT TO ME	Neil Diamond
27	IT MAY BE WINTER OUTSIDE	Felice Taylor
28	STANDING IN THE SHADOWS OF LOVE	Four Tops
29	WORDS OF LOVE/DANCING IN THE STREETS	The Mama's & Papa's
30	THERE'S GOT TO BE A WORD	The Innocence
31	GIVE ME SOME LOVIN'	Spencer Davis Group
32	GREEN, GREEN GRASS OF HOME	Tom Jones
33	MERCY, MERCY, MERCY	Cannonball Aderly
34	WILD THING	Senator Bobby
35	NIKI HOKEY	P. J. Proby
36	I'VE PASSED THIS WAY BEFORE	Jimmy Ruffin
37	SO YOU WANT TO BE A ROCK 'N ROLL STAR	The Byrds
38	LONELY TOO LONG	The Young Rascals
39	HELP ME GIRL	Eric Burdon & Animals
40	EPISTLE TO DIPPY	Donovan

FOR SALE

Private collection of custom cartridge tapes 4 track — for car Stereo-Pbk.
Only the very best of the "Rolling Stones," "Supremes," "Beatles," "The Motown Groups" and all the top hits of 1965-66.
If interested, please call Paul Arthur at: HO 4-5045.
Reasonably priced.

WANTED

Lead guitarist and bass guitarist for Beatle-type music. Must be able to sing GOOD harmony. Draft exempt and single, nineteen and over and free to travel. Promoters have many excellent opportunities for the right people. Call Mr. Schaefer or Mr. Magers at
882-2225
883-3203
341-6897

8528 De Soto Ave. No. 3, Canoga Park

ATTENTION!!!

High Schools, Colleges, Universities and Clubs:

CASEY KASEM MAY BE ABLE TO SERVE YOU!

Let Casey HELP You Put On A Show Or Dance
Contact Casey at:
HO 2-7253

KRLA ARCHIVES

KRLA Launches New Educational Division

Radio KRLA has created a new educational division within the station to examine and report on the problems and issues found on Southern California's many and varied college and university campuses it was announced by KRLA station manager John R. Barrett.

At the same time, Barrett disclosed that the new division would be headed by Dr. Averell Burman, who received his Doctorate in history at USC and is a broadcasting instructor at Long Beach State.

In accepting the post, Dr. Burman said, "The 'good old days', which may never have existed, are long gone. Today's student will not put up with playing a passive role. The student is determined to take part in affairs on and off campus and it is from the student that the expression 'participatory government' has arisen. It is our hope that KRLA's educational division can achieve total involvement with the students of Southern California."

Dr. Burman's first assignment for KRLA was to probe campus reaction to Governor Ronald Reagan's proposal to institute a tuition fee of $200.00 at California State colleges. Dr. Burman and his staff, backed up by KRLA's news department, visited campuses interviewing students and educators on this and other vital questions. The reports were aired hourly during news broadcasts on KRLA.

Nationally recognized for its biting documentary studies of contemporary social problems, KRLA launches its drive into this new area with the hope that students will be candid with Dr. Burman and his staff and look to KRLA for communications and information heretofore unavailable on radio or television.

NANCY WILSON and her show, featuring Maynard Ferguson, his band, and the Bola Sete Trio, will be presented at the Shrine Auditorium February 4.

...CASEY KASEM.

Casey's 'Shebang' Returns

Pop music TV shows have been dying all over the place but KTLA's, "Shebang" is being reborn, the only one of its type to be canceled and then rescheduled.

The show, hosted by KRLA's Casey Kasem, will return as a weekly series beginning Jan. 30 from 7:30 to 8:30 Monday nights.

The show will be bucking The Monkees, which is shown at the same time on another channel.

Inside KRLA
By Eden

Welcome back to KRLA is the message going out to The Rebel, Reb Foster, this week, as he returns to the Land of 1110. The Rebel and his good friend, Maude Skidmore, will be taking over the 9:00 to noon spot from Bob Eubanks from now on.

Bob has many obligations outside of his chores as a DJ, including hosting-duties on his successful TV show, "The Newlywed Game," and he will continue to be a part-time and weekend DJ only for KRLA in order to devote more time to his other activities.

Funny rumor going around this week is that blue-eyed Bob is trying to do a little matchmaking of his own in an attempt to get Maude and The Rebel to the "hitching post" so that they can come on his TV show as contestants!

Well, children—once again we find that Valentine's Day is just around the next heart-shaped corner, and once again that center of Southland culture, KRLA, is conducting an art contest to select the greatest artist in the Southland, and also to establish Pasadena as the Los Angeles Art Center for all of the Los Angeles County.

As in the last five successful years, the top prize being offered is $1,000 and all entries will be cheerfully accepted—although none of them can be returned. Although nothing has been definitely set as yet, there is a possibility that the Coliseum will be rented to store the thousands of entries in this year as the Bat Cave is still more than overflowing from last year's entries.

Send your Valentine entry to KRLA before midnight, February 13, and who knows—you might be the Sweetheart of KRLA this February 14.

Actually, I have many fond memories of KRLA Valentine Contests of the past few years. For example, there were a couple of rather outstanding entries last year which gained a certain amount of fame around the Hallowed Halls of KRLA.

One entry was a gigantic heart-shaped *pizza*—which, unfortunately, was one of the *early* entries and therefore had to sit in one of the entry rooms for quite some time. The "aroma" of that entry was just delightful... not to mention *very long-lasting*!!!

Most of the people in KRLA Kountry still haven't quite recovered from the ten day engagement of Smokey Robinson and the Miracles at the Whisky A Go Go. These boys are definitely one of the most fantastic groups in the country (have been for many years) and Smokey is not only a genius, but one of the nicest, warmest, most modest individuals I've ever met. (P.S. Anyone wishing to join my brand new Smokey Robinson Fan Club *loses*, due to the fact that I'm extremely prone to intense attacks of *jealousy*!!!)

Reminder for Bill Slater: Two members of *The BEAT* staff are *still* waiting for you to get your airplane revved up.

KRLA ARCHIVES

Scene From The British Side
Sex, Stones & Sullivan

"I'm not superstitious" remarked Mick Jagger at London Airport on Friday, January 13. And to prove his point he marched jauntily beneath a couple of ladders before boarding his aircraft for New York.

He should never have flown on Friday the 13th. Clearly, Ed Sullivan would have let The Rolling Stones sing "Let's Spend The Night Together" had Mick played it cool and flown on Thursday, the 12th.

To me, the most curious part of the Sullivan banning is the fact that all the other lyrics in the song got an "O.K. to broadcast" stamp from the production people. If Sullivan had refused to allow the group to perform in part or whole the troublesome number I would have appreciated his line of thinking whether or not I agreed with it.

But all that had to go was one insignificant phrase, "The Night," so the revised and O.K. line would become "Let's Spend SOME TIME Together." As though the real objection was to the specific hours involved and not the "togetherness" bit at all!

Two Points

Leaving aside for a moment the rights and wrongs of the lyrics-change ultimatum, consider two other points. (1) Does an appearance on "The Ed Sullivan Show" (or any other network production for that matter) play a truly important part in promoting the popularity of any given record? (2) Does the very fact that the Sullivan incident gained worldwide press publicity draw valuable attention to the latest release by The Rolling Stones?

Look down your current Top 40 list. I don't think you'll find too many Ed Sullivan TV guests among the names. It must be true that a lesser-known artist has a lot to gain if a big TV appearance coincides with the issue of a record. But in the case of The Stones or anybody else with a large and long-standing army of followers, a TV performance can not be expected to boost disc sales or push a record way up when it wouldn't have gone way up in any case.

On my second point I'm sure there must be at least a few thousand folk who rushed out to find themselves copies of the original "Let's Spend The Night Together" because they were convinced they'd find much more than those two words "The Night" on the record!

Censorship?

Of course the real issue involved here is just how much censorship any form of art from theater to painting, from sculpture to lieterature should be called upon to tolerate. And that's not an argument you can cut and dry in a column of paragraphs. If people are going to chop up song lyrics to look for double meanings I guess they could put up a case for banning most best-sellers. I mean poor old Sandy's "Single Girl" would go right out of the window for a start.

Before, we go any further let me turn the argument over to you. Should The Stones have been allowed to perform "Let's Spend The Night Together" without any change of title? Were they wise to agree to the change and stay in the show—or should they have walked out and skipped the appearance altogether? We've entered an era, a decade, of freer expression applying to every segment of life from politics and religion to sex and sin. Is it or is it not ludicrous that "The Night" should cause such an uproar in 1967?

U.K. POP NEWS ROUND-UP — BY TONY BARROW

First of many '67 U.S. pop visitors to London are THE FOUR TOPS, in for a nine-city series of 18 shows at the head of a bill which also features THE MERSEYS, New Jersey songstress MADELINE BELL and Liverpool's REMO FOUR who used to back Tommy Quickly before he quit the business.

Obie, Duke, Levi and Larry left a wonderful impression with everyone they met in London last November. Fans and business experts were equally pleased by the utter professionalism of the Four on and off stage.

If THE MONKEES will move over to let them in, The Four Tops will have another Number One hit in the U.K. with "Standing In The Shadows Of Love" while they're with us on tour.

THE TROGGS are coming out with their second U.K. album, the first to be released thru Page One Records, this week. Title is "Trogglodynamite" which includes Reg Presley's "I Want You To Come Into My Life," the title likely to go on the top deck of their February single in America. That will be issued to coincide with the group's U.S. promotion trip via which they plan to look in on 22 key cities in ten days using their own charter aircraft.

After three installments of their weekly show had been screened by BBC Television, THE MONKEES went to Number One in the U.K. charts with "I'm A Believer" which sold a quarter of a million copies within ten days of release.

Then came the inevitable "exposure" stories slamming The Monkees for not playing very much of the music heard on their records.

Jack Bentley, showbiz page writer in London's Sunday Mirror ran the headline THE MONKEES—AND A SPOOF THAT PAID OFF. A DISGRACE TO THE POP WORLD. He calls the success of "a gigantic Hollywood TV publicity campaign—an insult to pop fans, a threat to the pop business as a whole and a deterrent to any youngster who has a musical future in mind."

At another part of his page Bentley suggests that "Americans never forgave the Beatles for not being born there so they decided to create their own."

Meanwhile, in the days immediately following the publication of the Bentley report, "I'm A Believer" sold in constantly fantastic quantities and vast advance orders started to pour in for the just-released album which shows every indication of hitting the jackpot as the fastest-selling U.K. album since "Rubber Soul!"

BEAT Art: Henri Munsford

The Beatles' Plans For '67: Records, TV Specials And . . . ?

By Tony Barrow

Newspaper reporters and magazine editors on both sides of the Atlantic seem to have had a thoroughly enjoyable time over the past couple of months moulding an astonishing variety of make-believe futures for THE BEATLES. If any of their prolific predictions should grow from guesswork into fact it will be little more than fortunate coincidence for the writers concerned.

The truth is that The Beatles themselves haven't mapped out a future for the group. They've never been strong for planning ahead and now that their schedule isn't sewn up with contracted touring timetables, they're free to think about next month when next month comes, next year when 1968 comes.

Beatle Workshop

They've been recording together at the E.M.I. studios near Paul's home in St. John's Wood since the first week of December. By the middle of January they'd completed three tracks. If that doesn't sound too healthy a product from something over 100 hours of studio time it's only fair to remember that they use sessions for much more than just recording. The studio has become their workshop for writing, arranging, rehearsing. They scrap as many as four out of five tapes. They wait while specialist musicians are fetched in to augment their backings.

With breaks when they run out of material and have to start from scratch on new words and tunes, The Beatles will go on recording until the time comes to start work on their third much-delayed motion picture.

They are not expected to make guest-star appearances on any television shows in London or abroad this year BUT they like the idea of making their own TV specials and are hoping to build a complete program around the new songs now being recorded for their first 1967 album.

Remain A Group

For recording, filming and a limited amount of television activity they'll stay together as a group. There's no question of The Beatles splitting up or ceasing to exist. At the same time there's every reason to believe that Ringo will follow John and make his solo screen debut and that the other two would be prepared to do the same thing if ideal scripts come into their hands.

On Friday, January 13 an unusperstitious JANE ASHER flew out from London Airport at the beginning of a four-and-a-half month American tour in which she'll play Juliet with the Old Vic Company. On the eve of her departure she confirmed that she loved Paul very deeply and that "he feels the same." She denied that there was any possibility of their wedding taking place in America but Jane will have several weeks during the Old Vic touring season when she could easily return home to London to see her family. And, of course, Paul.

All The Beatles—plus their two road managers—have grown mustaches. Chronoligically speaking, the whisker cultivation project went like this:—GOERGE let a small crop of hairs cover his upper lip before he left for India. PAUL produced a sort of inverted 'U' shape of hair around his mouth in preparation for his France/Spain/Kenya vacation.

RINGO started his mustache and decided to spread it into a beard as long ago as October when he and Maureen visited John and Cyn on the "How I Won The War" movie set in Spain.

GEORGE came home and had a shave.

JOHN'S healthy luxurious of mustache-with-accessories (hair all down each side of his face from ears to the jaw joints, long line across the upper lip and drooping clusters of hair running straight down towards the chin) took effect once the boys started recording in December.

GEORGE had a re-think about the whole thing and re-grew a mustache with beard before Christmas.

MAL EVANS has the most powerful-looking mustache of all —but he's had three months to work on it.

NEIL ASPINALL claims that his mustache will not be truly presentable before Easter although it has been under cultivation since early November.

BRIAN EPSTEIN has neither beard nor mustache.

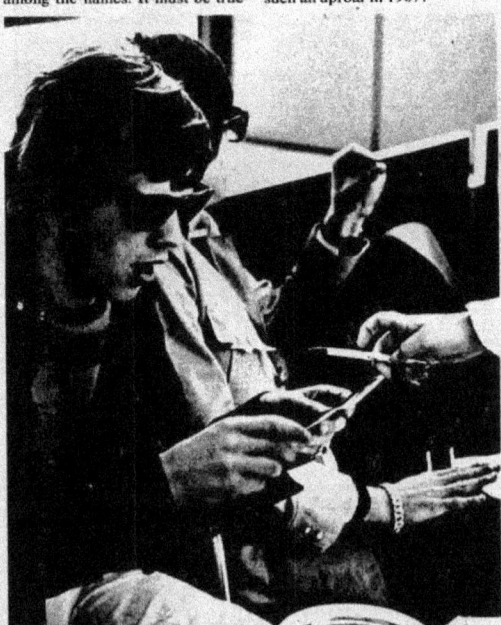

... MICK AND KEITH sign autographs at the airport.
BEAT Photo: Robert Young

KRLA ARCHIVES

...**STUDENTS AT UCLA GATHER** to listen and debate Gov. Reagan's tuition proposal—one which has caused him to be hung in effigy at several universities throughout the state.

STUDENT VIEW OF TUITION PROPOSAL

'We're Not Going To Let Them Destroy Us'
'Why Worry, We'll All Be Drafted Anyway'

By Ron Koslow

As newly elected Governor Ronald Reagan makes himself comfortable in the Governor's chair, California is divided in controversy over his recent proposals.

In an attempt to cut back the state budget, Gov. Reagan has proposed tuitions of $400 for the University of California and $200 for all state colleges; heretofore these institutions have been tuition-free to all residents of the state. It is the youth of California that will be most affected should these proposals be adopted. Already the enrollment for state colleges has "frozen" for next September, offering no openings for new students, and the various campuses of the University are preparing themselves for similar "emergency moves."

Consequences

All over the state, students are considering the personal consequences. Many will be unable to meet the proposed tuition demands, and thus will be deprived of an education. Others will be forced to cut down their study loads in order to devote time to earning money for their school expenses, while still others will be totally unaffected knowing that whatever the tuition, it will be provided by their parents.

What seems most unfortunate though, is the effect these stunning proposals have had on high school students who are now preparing to enter college. Many seem discouraged and disillusioned, realizing that the adoption of these proposals could alter their futures.

Greatest Threat

On the other hand, a large number of wage earning adults in the state favor Gov. Reagan's position, anxious to avoid any extra tax increase, and eager to stamp out the elements of protest and free speech which have proven to be an integral part of the academic atmosphere. It is this group that poses the greatest threat to the academic future of the state: they are indeed among the most vocal in expressing their opinions, yet ironically they are the furthest removed from the academic scene.

In order to get a more immediate response to the problem, this reporter plunged into the eye of the hurricane, visiting several campuses for some first hand opinions and reactions.

D.S. (20)—*a junior at the Berkeley campus*—"All over the world, people look to Berkeley as a center of 'learning' in the United States. It's happening here! At this point there is no other atmosphere in the country that is as stimulating or exciting. This is because individual expression and personal freedom have been encouraged both by the faculty and the student body. This is what makes Berkeley great.

Naturally there are those who think of us as a group of 'kooks and nuts'; the Governor is one of them. They think they can shut us up by cutting us off financially, by hitting us in our pocket books. They believe a student who must worry about money can't afford to worry about personal freedoms. They couldn't be more wrong! If the proposal is passed, we will work even harder for our beliefs. We're not going to let them destroy us. What Mr. Reagan has failed to consider is the coming of age of an enormous population of War Babies; the very group he's discriminating against will be voting in the next election, and believe me, they won't forget."

T.G. (21)—*a senior at U.C.L.A.*—"The University of California was established in 1868, and has since worked to become one of the finest state universities in the country. Attaining this reputation was no easy job. It took a lot of money and time to bring the U.C. to where it is today, and it seems senseless to risk doing permanent damage to an institution that is just now fulfilling its original goals. Is it really worth it? I'm sure there are other areas in the state government that could be cut back without risking serious damage; let the officials trim down their expense paid 'business trips' and other 'fringe benefits.'

The trouble has just begun, top-notch teachers will be leaving their jobs, classes will be over-crowded, and many worthy students will be deprived of an education.

"A Shame"

P.M.-(18)—*a senior at University High School*—"Luckily the proposed increase won't affect me, as my father is helping me with my education. It's a shame though that certain kids who have done good work throughout high school, will now have to worry about financing their education. I think the college years should be a time for new experiences—all kinds—not only book learning; there will be many students who will not have the opportunity to get full benefit from their college years due to financial burdens.

It seems to me that Gov. Reagan would want to encourage all people to get a higher education. After all, successful people pay higher taxes."

B.A.—(17)—*a junior at Grant High School*—"Why is everyone worried about it? By the time it's passed, we'll all be drafted anyway.

Seriously though I think California is going insane and the rest of the country is following in our footsteps. Well, back to 'Death Valley Days'!"

Going Insane

R.S.—(18)—*a senior at Los Angeles High School*—"There are six children in my family. So far, two of my brothers and one sister have received their educations at California state colleges. We have always felt fortunate that it was possible to get a good college education, without paying a large tuition. My father will not be able to afford the new proposed tuition and I'll probably have to postpone college until I have earned enough money to pay my way through.

I am planning to become a teacher, and I'm sure there are others who are planning a career in education or research who will be discouraged from their goals. This could mean that the state would be deprived of many teachers, scientists, and doctors."

KRLA ARCHIVES

TEEN PANEL:
Teenagers And Drugs: Part II

This is the second half of The BEAT's Teen Panel discussion on the subject of "drugs." Part One appeared in the last issue.

Participating are Bill (18), Keith (17), Diane (17) and Cynthia (16).

If you would like to participate in a future Teen Panel, or suggest a topic, please send a postcard to The BEAT.

★ ★ ★

Cynthia — "Here's a question I've always wanted to ask someone. If you wanted to buy marijuana, how do you go about it? Not that I intend to rush out and buy some. But, if I did, how would I? Just stand around on a street corner and wait until someone offered to sell me some?"

Bill — "As far as I know, that only happens in the movies. It could happen in a really bad section of town, maybe, but no one stands around on corners in those areas unless they're tired of living. You just ask around, and find someone who knows someone who knows where to get it. You'd be surprised the people who do know."

Gangsters?

Cynthia — "Another thing. What *kind* of people sell it? For some reason I imagine them to be gangsters. Are they?"

Keith — "They might be, on a high level — bad choice of words there, sorry about that. I mean, the people who control the major sources of large amounts of pot could easily be a crime syndicate. There's a lot of money in this, and you always find 'gangsters' wherever there's money. But I think the average person who sells it is probably just that — an average person. They sell just enough of it to make a living or for extra money if they have another job. I suppose most of them do have other jobs. It's very risky to sell enough of it to make a living. It's a lot of work, too. You don't just pick it off the vine and smoke it. You have to go through a whole cleaning process and all that."

Diane — "Something I've always wondered is if teenagers buy more marijuana than adults. I would think teenagers would buy more. Not LSD or that other horrible stuff, but the other, yes. Does anyone know if there are actual statistics about this?"

Bill — "There are statistics to show the percentage of adults and teenagers *caught* with marijuana, but other than that — and I don't know what the percentages are — how could there be statistics? Who'd dare admit they bought it or who they sold it to. By the way, *why* would you think teenagers would buy more than adults. I agree, but I want to know why you base that opinion."

Diane — "Well, not *teenagers* necessarily. I'd say young people more than older people. Adults have spent a whole lifetime having it drummed into them that one marijuana cigarette means you'll end up a dope addict. They've heard it's habit-forming, which doctors now say it isn't, although regular cigarettes are. They've been told it's a narcotic, which it isn't. They're not nearly as apt to try it as people who have heard both sides of the story. And it's a terrible chance to take, legally. An adult has more to lose than a teenager, like a job or even worse, going to jail and ruining your life's work and your reputation."

Bill — "There's another reason. It's a lot more difficult for an adult to come by. A young person can ask friends without worrying he's going to become a social outcast for having asked. But an adult whose social circle is on the typical middle-class level isn't about to pop over to the tract house next door and ask Mrs. Jones if she knows where he can buy a joint or two. Mrs. Jones might be the biggest pot-head in town, but adults are much less open about this than younger people. They have to be. For all Mrs. Jones knows, the guy next door may be on the vice squad."

Cynthia — "Bill is the only one who's said he's actually tried pot — I feel dumb saying that — no, I feel like I sound like a dope fiend, and I know better than that. It's weird — oh never mind. What I want to know is, has anyone else here tried it?"

Keith — "I wasn't going to say anything, but yes I did try it one time. It wasn't much. Just a nice feeling."

Diane — "I've had the chance to, but I haven't. I don't think I will either, not for a few years anyway. It's too big a chance. Maybe you think a teenager has less to lose than an adult, and that's true in ways, but what about what it would do to your family if you got caught? It would kill my folks. They don't understand what it is, not really. It would just kill them. If I ever try it, I'll do it when I'm on my own, so no one would get hurt but me if anything happened."

Bill — "Are you sure you aren't scared that it might become a hang-up?"

Diane — "That never even occurred to me. You don't get physically addicted to marijuana. If you get addicted at all, it's mental and all in your mind. I have better things to do with my mind."

Cynthia — "You know what they should do? Since so many people do use it, someone should have the courage to come out and say how to use it right. Some big national magazine should run this kind of article so everyone would read it. We never talk about this sort of thing. We just try to pretend it doesn't exist, but it does exist. They should come out and tell when it should be used and how much and tell what to do if it makes you sick or afraid. If I tried it, I'd have no idea what to expect, or how to handle it. But that won't stop me or anyone from trying it, so people should be told the truth."

Keith — "That would actually be the first step to the 'social control' you were talking about awhile back. It's very powerful in large quantities. It doesn't leave a lasting effect — although I have heard it's dangerous to use if you're upset or have mental or emotional problems — but you can get so far up you don't know or care what you're doing. That isn't safe to do unless you're in the middle of the desert. I don't think it's too smart wherever you are. That's like using alcohol to get plastered out of your mind instead of having a few to relax and enjoy yourself more."

Handle Yourself

Bill — "This is really the whole crux of the matter. You *have* to know how to handle it or you can go off the deep end just out of inexperience. I don't recommend it to *anyone*, but I don't put it down either. It's up to each person, but you have to be able to handle yourself first before you can handle it. Like drinking. Some people go ape and fall off bar-stools. Others can sit and drink all night. It's a thing between you and yourself. All of us will probably see it legalized in our lifetime, but that doesn't mean it's anything to play around with. If everything isn't cool, including you, you're asking for trouble and you'll probably get it."

BEAT Photos: Chuck Boyd

IN TO CATCH MIRACLES ON OPENING NIGHT WERE . . .

. . . PAPA JOHN AND MAMA MICHELLE.

. . . MIRACLES ON STAGE AT Whisky souling out "Mickey's Monkey"

MAMA CASS & TERRY MELCHER diggin' Miracles.

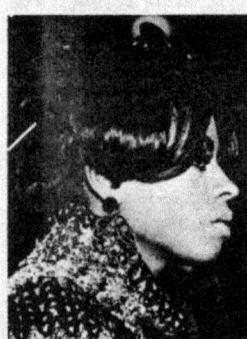
. . . SUPREME DIANA ROSS

. . . RASCAL DINO DANELLI and Louise Criscione observe Rascal Gene

. . . JOHNNY RIVERS

BOB HATFIELD grins at Smokey.

KRLA ARCHIVES

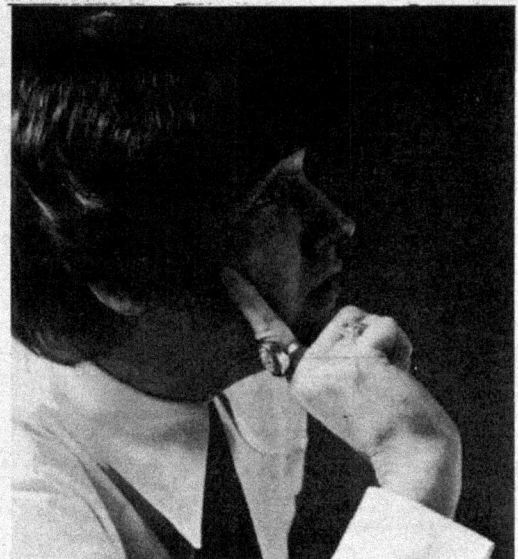

"MY ACT WAS BASED on physical contact with the audience."

Proby

..."THEY HAD TO TOUCH ME."

POPDOM'S TRAGIC FIGURE

By Ron Koslow

It was a case of great American Possibilities, in the true tradition of Ben Franklin and Horatio Algier. He was tall and dark and good looking and with a great deal of hard work and honesty (his father had told him), he would succeed; he couldn't miss. So Jimmy Smith stood on the corner of Hollywood and Vine late one afternoon in 1955 and watched his father's car head back to Houston.

Jimmy had come to Hollywood to "Become," to realize his conception of himself. He wanted to be a star — from the day he won the Carnation Milk talent contest in Hitching Post, Texas at the age of ten — he wanted to be a star.

Becoming

His father was right: "Becoming" was hard work. But he stuck to it, playing small parts in the early teenage "dragstrip" movies and making demo discs for Elvis Presley. He named himself Jet Powers ("I was searching for a name that suited my personality.") In 1960, in hopes of breaking a "dry spell" in his career he again changed his name; this time he was P. J. Proby ("Something with a little class.") But it was not until 1963 that his luck changed, and the wait during those three years was lonely. His time was running out; he was then twenty-five, almost too old for a teenage idol.

And suddenly it happened — Ben Franklin/Horatio Algier style; it all payed off. A guy, named Jack Good had "seem him around" and invited him to perform on the pilot of a new T.V. rock-and-roll show, "Shindig." The original show would be broadcast from London and features the Beatles. In April of 1964, Proby was introduced to the world, via telstar, by the Beatles. Now if the Beatles say it's good, Baby, you better believe it's better than good. So when Mr. P.J. Proby woke up the next morning, he was a star; he was in demand.

Things began happening quickly — by July of 1964, his first record, "Hold Me" was number three on the charts. By October, his second record, "Together" was number eight on the charts. In January of 1965, his third disc, "Somewhere" was number four.

Meanwhile, he developed one of the most exciting stage personalities England has ever known. He manifested his admittedly romantic personality ("If I were a chick, I'd marry Walt Disney") in his stage presence and dress. His hair, tied in a pony-tail a la Tom Jones, his special costume of stretch velvet consisted of a loose fitting shirt ("to hide my beer belly") and tight fitting pants ("I wanted to make sure the kids sitting far back could see all of my movements.") His movements couldn't be missed; wildly provocative in a pseudo-effeminate style, he explains, "my whole act is made up from different girls I've known. I took the walk from a girl in Hollywood, the body movements from a dancer in the Ed Sullivan show, and the pout from Chrissie Shrimpton (Jean's sister and Rolling Stone Mick Jagger's "fiance.")

His act geared to underage girls would drive them beserk; he embodied all the passion and sex that he thought they dreamed of. He packed them in. It was due to his tremendous concert appeal, the fact that he could draw above and beyond capacity crowds, that he was led to commit his first error.

The ABC Theater chain owns a majority of the theaters in England. They are a big concern; in America, they might be called a monopoly. In any case, they are not to be reckoned with lightly. Proby performed frequently in the ABC theaters until he began accusing the promoters of "jamming up" the gate receipts. Proby claimed that promoters were packing 6,000 people into a hall that normally held 5,000 and not reporting the added revenue.

He attempted to publicly expose this alleged dishonesty on the part of the promoters and for this, and no doubt many other reasons, he was branded a "trouble-maker," the "Union Organizer of Pop Stars." From then on, Proby felt that his "powerful enemies" were waiting for him to make just one mistake, one slip.

It happened on the night of January 31 at the Ritz Cinema, Luton. The stretch velvet pants stretched a bit too much and split down the middle. The following morning it was announced that Proby was to be banned from the ABC theaters on charges of obscenity. On February 8, ABC-TV followed suit. By February 24, he had been banned from the great Drome Concert Hall in Brighton and the all-powerful BBC. Proby claims that these actions against him involved over $200,000 (Proby's figures) in cancelled engagements.

His one hope was the promised three "Shindig" shows he had contracted to do during a brief Hollywood visit. It was then that he had hoped to launch a full-scale American campaign.

Proby maintains that Jack Good, the producer of "Shindig" had promised him top billing and a special introduction to U.S. audiences. It was only after the successful first show that Proby discovered Jack Good was leaving the show and a new producer then took over.

Disillusioned

At rehearsals for the second show, Proby felt that he was neither getting the top billing nor the special exposure he had expected. Proby also claimed that he was expected to stand behind the featured artist during the finale. (Editor's note: The BEAT staff cannot remember an instance where the "Shindig" finale was staged in such a way that one artist was expected to stand behind another artist. This, however, is Proby's contention.)

"I had no choice, it was a matter of principle. I had to walk off. I realized they would try to ruin me if I did, but I refused to stand behind another performer."

So he walked off the show, consequently, he feels, to be blackballed from U.S. TV and cutting off his channel to success in the United States. He returned to England in September only to be notified that his work permit had expired and he would have to return to the States for at least six months. Now he was caught in a cross-fire.

Weakening

He returned to the U.S. and opened at a club in Hollywood that April. Since that time, he has been waiting, trying to find a way to break into the U.S. market. Meanwhile, his position in Europe is weakening.

"I can go back to England now, but I know a performer hasn't really made it until he cracks the U.S. scene."

His time now is occupied with putting together a new album for Liberty Records and lounging around his Benedict Canyon house doing nothing.

"Sometimes I get frustrated and lonely and start feeling sorry for myself. I know I made several mistakes, but I had no choice. I knew at the time that I'd probably get burned, but I had no choice. I've got confidence, though, I know I've got talent and I know that I'll bounce back — if not as a teenage idol, then as an adult appeal singer — thank God I'm not limited."

As this article goes to press, P.J. Proby is in the process of "bouncing back." His new record "Niki Hokey" is now on the charts and moving well; and he is booked for several T.V. appearances. With his pony-tail shorn, his new image is that of a slightly decadent choir boy, natural, with no gimmicks.

EARLY '66, the lowest ebb of his career, playing cheap Australian music halls. "At that time I was living like an animal," he recalls.

BEAT Photos: Courtesy of Liberty Records

KRLA ARCHIVES

BRIAN COLE—ASSOCIATE WITH A FACE LIKE A LINE DRAWING.

BEAT EXCLUSIVE

Unquiet Brian

By Rochelle Reed

(This is the second in a series of exclusive BEAT interviews with all members of the Association.)

"HEY!" the voice bellowed across the recording studio. "What do you mean by 'the quiet one' . . . 'THE QUIET ONE'?"

Outright yelling was The BEAT-labeled "quiet" singer, Brian Cole of the Association, who earned his title for being silently unsmiling onstage and certainly not offstage, where he is one of the greatest talkers of all time.

Screaming?

Putting down his guitar on a nearby chair, Brian continued shouting his defense, meanwhile maneuvering us through the maze of doors leading out of the room.

We journeyed out of the studio and over to the commissary, where we indulged in a glass of milk (it helps Brian's voice) and a quiet interview.

"I never say what I'm thinking but I talk 200 percent as much as the other guys in the group, say 10 percent as much and know . . ." but he wouldn't let me print the rest.

"Basically, I'm an introvert," Brian continued. "I come on so loud everyone thinks I'm extroverted. Actually, I'm very shy but I overcome it."

Brian has managed to overcome it so well that he recently played professor-for-a-day at a San Francisco high school, taking over several English and History classes.

"What I found surprising is that the kids actually listened to me . . . I mean really listened. The kids know where it's at, but they grow up into adults."

Born in Tacoma, Wash., 23 year old Brian is a man of many moods. In one sentence, he can go from elation to anger, joy to sadness, and back again without realizing his face has charted every word like a fine line drawing.

Matching Brian's many moods are the 38 jobs he's held to date. From advertising to upholstery, Brian has voluntarily left all but one of the jobs because they bored him. "I have so many interests I go from one to the next," he says, which could sound like the Association is only a temporary occupation for this transient personality. That would be roughly a correct statement, but there is more to the story.

"Music I love!" he states emphatically. "I can't play necessarily that well though. Put it this way . . . it's not what I started out to do and it's not what I'll wind up doing."

Acting, the irresistible occupation that whispers to many hopefuls, also beckons to Brian. He's caught up with the stage and spends many of his free hours thinking up one-act plays.

This touch of intellectualism must surprise a few of Brian's former instructors. "In all of high school," he confesses, "I studied 6 hours, and that was to write a term paper, 'I.Q. and It's Relation to Psychology,' which I wrote purposely to blow the teacher's mind. (It did.)

Lousy Grades

"I used to get lousy grades in school, but I got 99's for three years in a row on the Iowa tests (I.Q. measurement exams)," he continues.

Then Brian relates a bizarre story about a school psychologist who couldn't believe his scores, a year or so of examinations and the final verdict that there wasn't a thing in the world wrong with Brian, so why didn't they start on his parents? Brian sums up the story with a simple, "Nothing changed." Youth, however, is changing all the time, according to Brian.

"The younger generation—my generation—scares me. Some want to be different for any reason. What they don't understand is that they've being classified and nullified. They're losing their realization of reality.

"I can't understand it. They fight for individual rights but condone practices that take away those very rights. They want to be free but become bigots by limiting others. They're almost as dogmatic as their elders. Really, there are few people over about 28 with any processes of free thought," he continued.

"Lots of people come on strong and bitter. But you don't change things by force. You must be insane to fight!

"Someone once asked me in an interview to name the most stupid question I was ever asked. I answered, 'Do you want to fight?'"

"I was once a devout coward, but not any more," the Associate went on. After an accident that everyone thought would leave him permanently blind, Brian bounced back with a fighting spirit. "I was learning Braille within two weeks," he says.

Decidedly an individualist, Brian is an outgoing person who seldom lets anyone inside his personality. A rapid, restless talker, he sometimes gives the impression of being the rabbit in Alice In Wonderland. In fact, when Terry walked into the session a half-hour late, it was "quiet" Brian who yelled the recitation,

"I'm late, I'm late,
For a very important date.
No time to say 'hello,'
No time to say 'goodbye,'
I'm late, I'm late, I'm late!"

The Adventures of Robin Boyd...

©1965 By Shirley Poston

Robin sat blearily at her desk, surrounded by seven thousand crumples of paper. But she was smiling.

Earlier that day, when she and The Budge had been lurking about, looking for an inexpensive (as in free) location for their club, a certain name on the for-sale-or-rent sign on a certain building had fallen into place.

Since moving to Pitchfork, Robin had endeavored to familiarize herself with the folk-lore of the region. In other words, she'd been listening to nasty gossip over the back fence. And, in the process, she had learned plenty about Archibald Neville.

The aforementioned, it seems, was the Mayor of the town (gag.) Every other term, that is. Due to a clause in the city (moop) charter, a mayor could not hold office for two consecutive terms.

Every other two years, Mr. Neville (who was fondly known as Baldy The Crook) took what he had saved from his modest salary as Mayor and went to live in the Fountainbleu Hotel in Miami. Two years later he came back, and was re-elected (or else.)

This had been going on for years. However, there was a rumor going around that when he returned from Florida next fall and started all that baby-kissing ap-cray again, not one single person was going to vote for old (censored.) (Nor were any of the married persons.)

Perfectly Vicious

Mr. Neville had gotten wind of the rumor (when the wind blows in South Dakota, the wind doesn't kid around) and labeled it "perfectly vicious." "What do those (re-censored) yokels know anyway?" he had added.

And when Robin realized this was the same Neville who owned the building they were ogling, it didn't take her long to dream up the fiendish thingy of all time.

For the past several hours, she'd been at her desk, going out of her drawer trying to compose just the right letter to Baldy. And she had finally succeeded.

Dear Mr. Neville:
I am pleased to announce that plans are being made to construct a youth center in Pitchfork. This badly needed recreation facility will be named after the town's leading citizen. Namely, yourself.
A fund-raising campaign is now in progress. Since the center is to be constructed in your honor, we cannot possibly accept a donation from Your Honor. However, knowing you will insist on contributing, we have found a way to make this possible.
We notice that your building on State Street (that great street) is unoccupied at present and would like to use it this next month to present a series of musical entertainments. The proceeds will go toward the construction of the center.
This would help the project greatly, and we would make every effort to return the favor. Please let us hear from you soon.
R. Boyd, Chairman
South Dakota Young People's Committee To Elect Mayor And/Or Governor Neville

Well, *soon* was not the *word*. Four days after she'd mailed this missive, Robin happened to run into the postman (literally, having seen too many old Dagwood movies on the telly), who delivered a suntanned letter into her shaking mitts.

That noon, Robin grabbed The Budge bodily and dragged her into the school cafeteria, that being the only place Beverly Lou Boyd (as in Ringo, as in Ringo) wouldn't dream of looking for them.

Budgie battled bravely at first, but agreed to have a bite there (a *cockroach* bite, no doubt) when she realized something was in an elevated position (as in up, as in up.)

First Robin handed her friend a carbon of the letter to Baldy. Then she quietly placed a door-key between them on the table. (She was afraid to show her the simpering note his (dis)Honor had sent with the Key. Budgie was having enough trouble keeping her lunch down as it was, not to mention as it were.)

First The Budge turned white as six sheets. Then she belched so loud they heard her in Brooklyn.

"You *liar*," she breathed, ignoring the hysterical silence of the surrounding students. "You marvelous, *beautiful* liar."

"I am *not*," Robin hissed, bristling (or was it brissed, histling?). We *will* put the money toward a youth center. Gawd knows this place *needs* one, or will after we liven *up* these cadavers."

The Budge thought this over and finally nodded. "You may have a point there."

And, Robin did (in addition to the one atop her head.) She had the fiendish thingy even further figured out. After the first month, they'd send another letter to Baldy. By then they'd have made enough money to actually rent his building for the next month, as a temporary site for the center. Since he wouldn't (dare) dream of accepting the full amount (and might give it to them free if she played her cards right) (the ones up her sleeve), most of the mon could be put in Center building fund. (Hopefully, they'd be able to use a few farthings to make improvements on the temporary center.) (Rent a gun and shoot some of the rats, for instance.)

Pitching In

If the gendarmes didn't clap them in irons, the plan would probably work until Baldy came home, and by then they'd have enough money to build their own center! Especially if other Pitchforkians (*hah?*) pitched in (whew) and helped!

They'd get nothing out of it personally except a place for the Mockingbirds to perform and the satisfaction of proving to this am-day urg-bay that there was more to life than crocheting doilies. But that was enough reward. The cause was worthwhile, and besides it would also keep one's mind off the fact that one was still minus one's magic powers and georgeous genie (climb-a-wall) (take off your shoes first, those heel marks are rough to explain.)

After Robin had explained all this (not the last part, not the last part), Budgie nodded even more agreeably. But she still wasn't quite convinced.

"Two questions," she said firmly. "How do you intend to explain there's *Four* members," she added, providing that the Boyd dog wasn't in one of its non-partisan snits again.

"Five," re-added The Budge. (Her cat could care less about politics except when the issue at hand involved the tuna industry.) "Next question. Am I to believe we are *really* going to call it the *Archibald Neville Youth Center?* That is utterly *vagomitsville!*"

Robin smiled somewhat superciliously (she was sorta smug about it, as well.) "Wellllll," she drawled. "Would you believe *The Neville Club?*"

(To Be Continued Next Issue)

KRLA ARCHIVES

Paulrey Vear, Radishes—Mark Unravels (?) Tale

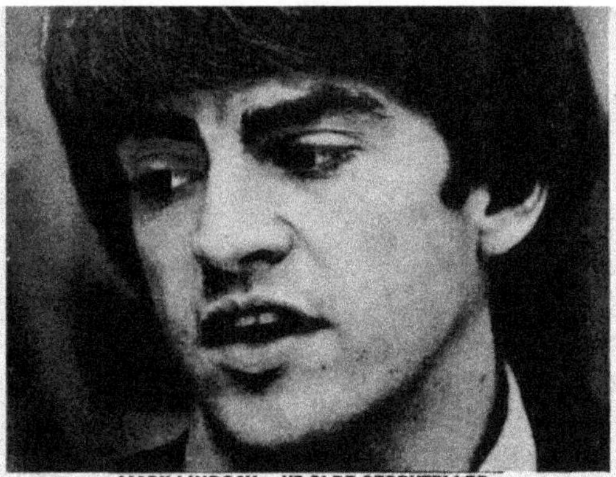

MARK LINDSAY—YE OLDE STORYTELLER.

"The Undisputed and Original Origin of Paulrey Vear and the Radishes—or How to Secede From Business Without Really Trying."

By Mark Lindsay

Once upon a time, approximately the 14th century to be exact, in they tiny kingdom of Purdubia (near Syria on the Sea of Dreams), on a narrow, winding street in the heart of the city, Basbah (on the wrong side of the tracks), lived a poor struggling tent-maker, called by friend and foe alike, Paulrey Vear.

Every morning, bright and early (about 11 or 12:00), Paulrey would stagger to his stall in the market place and half-heartedly with great vigor would begin his daily task of tent-making.

Poor Paulrey

Poor Paulrey, he hardly had room in his stall to sew. His finished merchandise—circus tents, Boy Scout tents, camping tents, sheep herder tents, and even pup tents—filled every available nook and cranny of his stall, because everyone in the city of Basbah lived in stone houses. Stones were very plentiful in Basbah (it was the Basbahnian farmers' main crop). And besides, ever since the great fire of '69 (1369) people *had* to live in stone houses by Royal Decree (and you don't mess with the *King*, baby).

One smoggy day, Paulrey (who had run out of canvas anyway) was fed up. He casually flicked his last cigarette (smoking was not against the law) into the great pile of unsold tents and without a backward glance ("forge ahead slowly" was his motto) he strolled through the market place, seemingly unaware of the smoke and flames roaring skyward behind him, until he reached the (Square of the Unsquare Ones), where he observed his longtime friend, Marc Lintworthy, squatting in front of a large wicker basket, his cheeks puffing, his face red, and in his mouth a strange instrument resembling an Albanian water pipe.

"What is *that* thing?" nosily inquired Paulrey. "*That thing*," said Marc, removing the mouthpiece from his mouth (clever move) and rolling his eyes, "is called a 'Sack-of-Foam' and it is a new-type instrument I instantaneously invented just a few minutes ago when I was inspired by a sudden cloud of smoke in the sky."

"What do it do?" asked Paul, noisily sucking on the mouthpiece. "Just watch!" So saying, Marc grabbed the Sac-of-Foam and proceeded to finger the keys and blow vast quantities of air into the small end of the instrument. A hideous, wailing, moaning sound was produced and a large black snake, which had been hiding in the wicker basket, suddenly reared up on its hind legs, coughed twice and galloped away through the crowd which had gathered 'round the pair, attracted by the noise.

"That ain't half bad," said Paul sickly, and silently turning off the light bulb which had appeared above his head, he quickly hustled his friend into a nearby alley where he proceeded to explain in warm, maple syrupy tones his Plan, which he had been working on constantly for the past 15 seconds. His Plan, which he assured Marc was sure-fire (a quality Paulrey seemed to have down pat) was to form a musical group, or Rock and Roll Banned, as he called it, and entertain the King, thereby gaining great favor in the eyes of the King, with the end result of being put on a Royal Pension and living happily ever after.

"I don't know," said Marc reflectively scratching his left sideburn. "What if the King doesn't like my playing or your dancing? Maybe we should organize a larger group. Perhaps if we had some sort of rhythm section..." "Hark!" said Paulrey, who had suddenly become all ears. "What is it?" inquired Marc who was gaining in wonder at the hundreds of ears protruding from all parts of Paulrey's body.

Listening closely, they both became aware of a steady *thump thump* coming from around a bend in the alley. "That," said Paulrey with an authoritative bedside manner, "is either a Hindu elephant with an enlarged heart, or else we've found our rhythm section!"

Peering cautiously around the corner, they observed Black-Smith the chimney-sweep, who derived his name from the thick, black soot that covered his entire body like a huge licorice blanket (licorice blanket??).

Black-Smith was in the act of cleaning himself—a process that required him to throw his body smartly against the alley wall—thereby producing the aforementioned thumping sound.

"Stop!"

"Hold it! Stop! Wait-a-minum! By-Jove-I-think-you've-got-it!" So screaming, Paulrey rushed forward and, aided by his faithful Indian companion, Marc, they rushed forward, and rushing forward they grabbed Black-Smith and rushed him forward and tied him to a weeping willow tree growing on the Banks of the River Charles, and started washing his brain with the idea of joining a rock and roll Banned as a rock and roll drummer.

"But first," said Paulrey, "you must improve your grooming." Quickly, they (Paulrey and Marc) began stripping huge strips of black soot from his (Black-Smith's) body.

Hastily, they began pasting the strips back again when it became apparent that under all that soot Black-Smith was as naked as a jaywalker.

"Maybe if we glued a few gold buttons on his front, we could fake everyone into believing he is wearing a black velvet double-breasted," said Marc, tackily. "No sooner done than said!" and quickly reaching into his right pants cuff, Paulrey produced a handful of brass coins, which he deftly attached to the front of Black-Smith's soot-coat.

"Don't tread on me!" gleefully shouted the three, and marched into the sunset towards the King's castle.

After a full day's travel in the direction of the North Star, which gave the lustre of midday to objects below, the Kingward trio decided to camp for the night in a clearing in the forest which had suddenly appeared in the trees.

(What will happen to Paulrey Vear, Marc Lintworthy and Black-Smith? See next issue of BEAT to find out!)

SHIRLEY You Jest!

By Shirley Poston

Meep, spaz and other expressions of inner merriment! Not to mention noisy thank-yous to Mary Ann S., who sent me George's (don't I wish) autograph!

Course, I had to mail it right back to her or she would have appeared on my doorstep, rattling a long chain. It was great having a look at his real-type hand-writty. Before I sent the photo back (with the autygrap on it), I actually slept with it under my pillow! (Speaking of long chains...)

Mary Ann received the writty from George's mum, and even sent along the envelope it arrived in. I'd love to write her myself and ask for one, but I'm embarrassed to after the way I've talked about her georgeous, beautiful, tall, thin, exy-say son. (Getting a bit warm in here all of a suddy, isn't it?)

Oh, well, one day I'll turn over a new leash (otherwise known as a new leash on life) and elevate my mind.

Looslier?

Speaking of my mind (and using the term looslier than usual), I would like to give a piece of same to whoever's responsible for the expert splicing job in a certain print of a certain movie. It seems that one of the few prints of "Help" in circulation these days really *needs* help.

One of the best parts in the film (where John sings "You've Got To Hide Your Love Away" and George flirts with Ahme and then faints when she takes out the needle) (a long story if you haven't seen the movie, and if you haven't, *you* need help)... what was I saying ... oh, this whole part is chopped to ribbons. I suppose the film broke and instead of getting another copy, they just elmered (as in glued) it back together. (Good show.)

I've heard more people complaining about this and I hereby join them. I went to see "Help" again (and again) recently, and guess what! It was that gnarled-up print!

Must admit that what happened in the theater was almost worth missing this grrrrr-oovy part. Everyone rared back in their seats and yelled fabulous thingies at the poor projectionist.

Seriously, this is inexcuseable, and if it happens to you, go find the manager and demand your money back. (This will be especially profitable if you sneaked-in in the first place.) Don't think *I* didn't tell him a thing or two (because I didn't). (I did frown rather darkly and make fists in my pockets, though.)

Speaking of—you guessed it—I've had another of my rare realie dreams (not to be confused with the whoppers I make up) (I wish you could see me in the morning after a particularly spectacular wishful-thinky) (but *you* don't wish you could see me). Anydream, here's what my sick, sick subconscious came up with.

I was in a restaurant or some such and noticed that John Lennon was standing at the bar. I didn't get shook or anything because in my dream I seemed to know him.

Sauntering over, I said: "Hi, John. What's become of George? I haven't seen him around lately."

John shrugged. "He's been busy with protest marches for the Delano farm workers."

I shrugged. "Oh, yeah, I forgot."

The end. Isn't that a weirdie? Whaddyahmean I made it all up? If I'm gonna make up dreams about George (which I am, tonight for instance) I can do better than *that*. (You should hear the one about the time we were locked in a dumb-waiter.) (I'm not as dumb as I look, you know.)

In case any of you are planning a trip (and aren't we all, aren't we all), here's a wise word from a weary traveler.

A pen pal of mine spent the holidays in the British West Indies and she sent me the following advice.

A Bang

If you happen to go for a long walk in the dark of night when everyone in town is snozzing peacefully in their trundles, and you should happen to find a very large firecracker left over from the New Year's Eve celebrations, do not suppose it is a dud and feel you are safe in lighting it just for a lark.

As she so sagely put it: "They heard the blank-of-a-blank in *Cuba!*"

Wow, I really got a bang out of that! (Puns upon a time...)

If the name of this column (I get tired of saying pillar) hasn't already been changed, it soon will be. *The BEAT* asked me to come up with some possible titles, but I rather doubt that they'll go for "The Spastic Shirley Poston". (I still think it should be titled "For Gawd's Sake", don't you?) (Never answer that question.)

Before I forget, here's another good way to annoy the rest of the world. Find out the English translation of the names of great people in history, and refer to them in that impolite but thoroughly maddening manner. Frinstance, Enrico is Italian for Henry. I've already experimented with that one. Some rational adult was giving me the business about my taste in music (it used to be vanilla but is now moving along toward strawberry), and I said waspishly, "well, we can't *all* be Henry Caruso." Oooh, did that get his goat, and I kid you not. (Boy, am I killing me.)

Georgy Girl

Hey, there, Georgy-Gril (whoops), there's another Georgy deep inside ... sorry about that. I was thinking about that song and got carried away (in a padlocked basket). I think that one is a real car-faller (as in fall out of the car, what else)? One of these eons, I'm going to have that put on an I.D. bracelet.

I'm also going to take another Georgy up on the kind offer he made in "Love You To". (Sweet of him to be so generous, with him so busy and all.) (Success really *hasn't* gone to his head one jot, has it?)

Down, gril.

Before I go (aper than usual) I must apoligize to Glenna and Roccie for being very late in picking up my mail. Too late to be of any help on a report they were doing for school. Still, I wouldn't have been of any help anyway. They had to interview a journalist, and although I've been called a number of thingies in me time, that's never been one of them.

Kissies and thankys to Jennie Vodka and Soupbone Jones (would I lie to you?) (Quiet!) (Not to mention *Quite!*) for sending me a memo pad (and Shirley pen) with the initials S.H. (For Shirley Harrison, I hearly *hope*) ... To C.D. of Merced for the beautiful pix and further adventures ... To Helen for the SIPNUM doll (and never *mind* what *that* means).

KRLA ARCHIVES

RECORDS FREE FROM RC®
You'll Flip at the ZZZIP in RC® Cola

while you swing to your favorite stars! RC and music, perfect partners for the perfect lift

TAKE 1 ALBUM FREE

For everyone you buy... with 6 cork liners or seals from R.C. bottle caps over 100 Capitol LP's available. Order as often as you wish. Nothing to join. Look for this display at your favorite store.

Here's your best way yet to save *more* on the records you want. In dollars-and-cents terms you get *two* albums that the Capitol Record Club sells for $3.98 each time you buy *one*. The savings are even bigger on stereo records! And there are no shipping charges to pay, nothing else to join or buy.

What's more, you choose from top albums by today's biggest stars, including the Beatles, David McCallum, Frank Sinatra, Lou Rawls, Buck Owens, Petula Clark, the Outsiders, Nancy Wilson, Dean Martin, Sonny James, the Beach Boys and many others.

OTHER FINE BRANDS: DIET-RITE®COLA, NEHI®BEVERAGES, PART-T-PAK®BEVERAGES, UPPER 10® "ROYAL CROWN" AND "RC" REG. U.S. PAT. OFF.; ©1966 ROYAL CROWN COLA CO.

KRLA ARCHIVES

America's Pop Music NEWSpaper 25¢

KRLA Edition BEAT

February 25, 1967

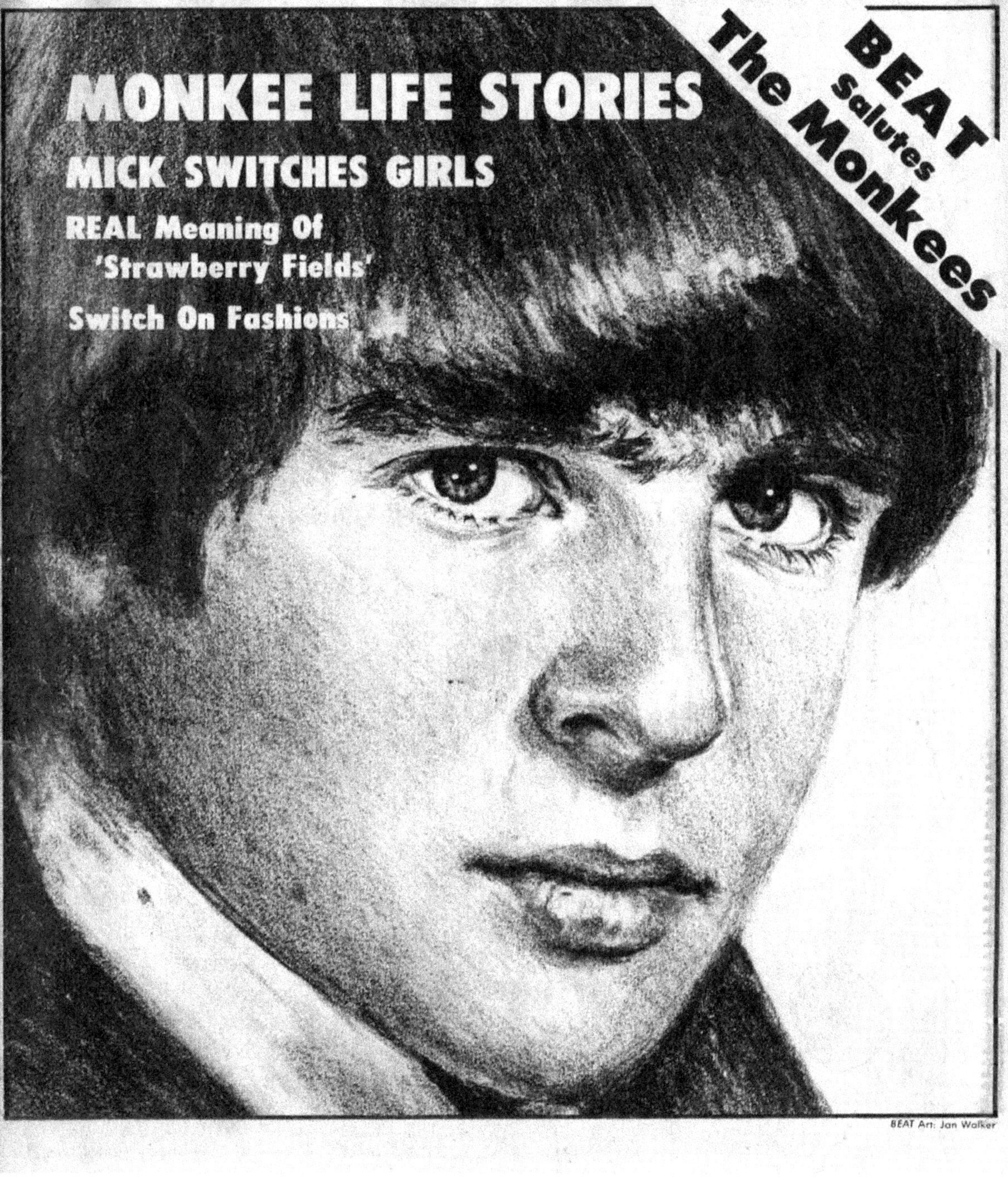

MONKEE LIFE STORIES

MICK SWITCHES GIRLS

REAL Meaning Of 'Strawberry Fields'

Switch On Fashions

BEAT Salutes The Monkees

BEAT Art: Jan Walker

KRLA BEAT

Volume 2, Number 35 — February 25, 1967

SALUTES The Monkees

KRLA ARCHIVES

Page 2 — THE BEAT — February 25, 1967

KINGSTONS BREAK UP!

The Kingston Trio, a favorite among college audiences since 1957, will break up as a group on June 1. The Trio signed a five-year contract with Decca Records last year and will honor that contract by continuing to record for the next four years. However, when the Trio winds up their stint at San Francisco's hungry i on June 1 they will make no more personal appearances.

The reason for the split is quite simple — working as a group has become "restricting artistically." John Stewart, who replaced Dave Guard in 1961, is the only member of the Trio who has definite plans for the future. He will start a group of his own.

Bob Shane and Nick Reynolds, who have been part of the Kingston Trio since its conception, have no immediate plans for their futures.

The Kingston Trio's biggest hit was, of course, their famous "Tom Dooly" which hit the nation's charts in 1958. Since then, they've cut 27 albums — the first eight of which were gold record winners.

They were something of a show business tradition. They're great and we're sure everyone will be sorry to see them break up.

RAIDERS WIN FIRST GOLDIE

Paul Revere and the Raiders have won a gold record for their million-selling album, "Just Like Us." Although the group has had numerous hits, this is the first time they've won a gold record.

The Raiders are regulars on "Where The Action Is" and make frequent guest appearances on the nation's top variety shows. They are constantly touring the U.S. and in 1966, at the request of the U.S. government, the Raiders made a tour of a number of Job Corps Camps throughout the country and also appeared in Santo Domingo, capital of the Dominican Republic.

HAPPENING

WATTS ADDS CARTOONS TO HIS CREDITS

Charlie Watts, the soft-spoken Rolling Stone, has more artistic talent than most people give him credit for. In addition to drumming for the Stones, the versatile Mr. Watts provided the cartoon illustrations and captions which are on the back of the new Stone album. "Between The Buttons."

This latest project adds a new dimension to Charlie's literary career, which began in England with the publication of two books written by him. The first book, "Ode To A Highflying Bird," is a touching treatise on a subject close to Charlie's heart, the late Charlie "Bird" Parker.

Picturing the "Bird" as a real cartoon bird bursting forth from an egg in a nest, the story traces the career of Bird Parker from the moment he cracked his egg in Kansas City to his unhappy demise in New York City.

Another Watts' effort, his second book, is titled "The Zoo Of Flags." The 48 page book contains color drawings of animals from countries all over the world.

$76 MILLION FOR ELVIS

While the Beatles, Stones and Dave Clark Five find nothing but hitches in their movie plans, Elvis Presley rolls along making film after film.

Two MGM movies are up-coming for Elvis this year. The first will be "Pot Luck," and his second will be "Bumble Bee, O' Bumble Bee."

MGM has announced that Elvis' first seven pictures for them, including his currently released "Spinout," have grossed more then 76 million dollars!

"Double Trouble," is completed and awaiting its release this summer. Presley's first MGM movie venture, "Jailhouse Rock," is still in re-issue after already playing more than 30,000 dates.

Following his "Bumble Bee" movie, Elvis has three more pictures to make for MGM before his longterm contract runs out. However, having already grossed in excess of $76 million for the studio, it's safe to say that MGM will do anything in its power to get Presley's signature on another long-term contract!

GARY LEWIS TO MARRY

Mr. and Mrs. Jerry Lewis have announced the engagement of their son, Gary Lewis, to Sara Jane Suzara, 22, of Manila.

Gary is, of course, the leader of the Playboys and is currently serving in the Army. His fiancee is the daughter of Captain and Mrs. Andres Suzara. Her father is chief pilot of Manila Harbor and president of the Philippine Islands Pilot Association.

Sara is now in the United States living with Gary's parents in their Bel Air, California home. No date has yet been set for the wedding.

New Guitarist For Standells

After auditioning 163 new applicants, the Standells have selected John Fleck to replace their former bass guitarist, Dave Burke, who is exchanging show business life for Army life.

John Fleck was a former member of Love and is able to play an assortment of instruments including bass guitar, trumpet, flugle horn and harmonica.

Other members of the Standells are Larry Tamblyn, Dick Dodd and Tony Valentino. The group is currently featured in "Riot On Sunset Strip," which, ironically enough, is also the title of their latest single!

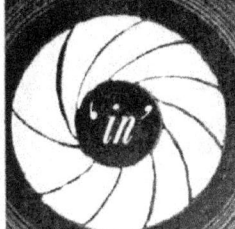

people are talking about...

Steve Marriott of the Small Faces allegedly taking over with Chrissie Shrimpton where Mick Jagger left off . . . how excited the Monkees were at gaining the top spot on the British charts and how simply hilarious it is that Brian Epstein is grooming The Who to be "Britain's answer to the Monkees". They have to be kidding! But apparently they're not as the pilot for The Who's television show is set to go . . . how really great Bobby and Billy are and how terrible it will be if the Righteous Brothers decide to stick exclusively to the lucrative adult night club circuit. . . . the Yardbirds trying to bridge that gap but postponing their U.S. tour until May . . . Dusty joining Johnny in the Casino Royale . . . Wyman stepping solidly into the producing bag with Hamilton and the Movement . . . Bill Cosby signing up to 800 autographs a night at the Flamingo and completely destroying the hotel's help by being sooo nice — the staff didn't believe genuinely nice stars existed . . . what it really takes to be a rock 'n' roll star . . . why Diana Ross insists upon wearing the wig that hides half her face . . . whether "dream" is really "drink."

. . . Ted Bluechel and his five pet rats and the couch he had to get rid of because of them . . . the Cyrkle getting fatter . . . the Springfield saying it like it is . . . when Tom Jones is going to get his own television show in America . . . whatever happened to the Syndicate of Sound . . . whether or not the rumors that Jagger wishes to go solo are true or merely a topic rerun . . . how happy the Turtles were to finally record something they really dug and how nice that it paid off . . . Boyce and Hart probably getting tired of talking about nothing but Monkees . . . those in the know who say that the Beatles will leave Epstein for Bernstein the second their contract runs out . . . the phoniness of some teen magazines and wondering if the teens see through it.

. . . Wilson recording the Stones' theme song . . . "night" being a four letter word while "time" is apparently a five-letter word and marveling at how some TV executives figure . . . moustaches being very "in" since the Beatles, Russ Giguere, Sal Valentino, John Philips, etc. all sport them . . . what a sad joke the Mama's and Papa's new album title is . . . the Blue Magoos ain't getting nothin' yet — except a hit record . . . the accident Davy Jones had with the studio gate and the fact that he's not overjoyed at the idea of having a picture of his apartment building printed in a magazine since he now gets a steady stream of fans pounding at his door at ridiculous hours.

. . . Paul McCartney being the only Arab at the party — according to Mick Jagger . . . whether or not Brian Wilson is really a genius . . . the decision to re-cut "No Fair At All" being a bad one — we think . . . the rumors hitting everywhere that Paul and Jane have definitely called it quits.

Meeting 'Em Monkee By Monkee

...MICKY DOLENZ — and his dog, You.

MICKY DOLENZ was born in Los Angeles, California on March 8, 1945, the son of an actor, the late George Dolenz. Micky first entered show business at the grand old age of ten when he became television's "Circus Boy." His stint as the young Circus traveler with the pet elephant, Bimbo, lasted for three years. When the show folded, Micky returned to public school in the San Fernando Valley.

After graduating from Grant High School, Micky entered Valley College but transferred in his second semester to Los Angeles Trade Tech. His stay at Trade Tech did not last too long, however, as Micky left school to become the lead singer in a rock group called the Missing Links.

Between his jobs with the Missing Links, Micky went back to occasional acting, appearing in such television shows as "Peyton Place" and "Mr. Novak." When Micky could find neither acting nor singing jobs, he worked as a mechanic.

Like the other Monkees, Micky, of course, saw that now-famous ad in *Variety*, applied and was chosen to be one of television's Monkees. "Right now, I'm doing exactly what I want to be doing," says Micky but for his years-from-now future Micky has plenty of ambitions. He's like to go back to school, perhaps be a teacher. He'd like to produce, direct and act in his own shows. He's thought about being an architectural draftsman or an electronic engineer.

As a hobby, Micky lists photography and as for his tastes in girls — he likes girls with long hair and girls with short hair. His taste in clothes runs to double-breasted tee shirts, casual and dressy. He drives a Pontiac and digs Motown.

Micky played guitar before he ever joined the Monkees but the powers that be decided that Micky should be the group's drummer — so he took to learning the fine art of drumming.

Micky stands six-feet, is definitely on the lean side, is athletic and tends to be quite restless.

...PETER TORK — formerly of the Village.

MIKE NESMITH was born in Dallas, Texas on December 30, 1942. He was never too popular in school, due, Mike thinks, to the fact that he loved pulling pranks. Although he didn't graduate from high school, Mike entered San Antonio College which is where he met his wife, Phyllis.

Mike got a guitar for Christmas when he was 19 and immediately set about learning how to play. He couldn't read notes, so he wrote his own material. While still in college, Mike began making personal appearances, first as a country/western singer and guitarist and later as a performer of "today's sound." After college, Mike left Texas for Southern California where he teamed up with John Lundgren, a bass player, and the duo played gigs around the area. They added a drummer and became a rock group but it was very short-lived as the draft board came into the action and split up the group.

Mike joined the Air Force but as soon as his time was up he returned to the Southern California music scene at the Ledbetter's and Troubadour as a solo folk act.

Roughly a year ago, his friends urged him to answer the *Variety* ad. "I don't know why they chose me," says Mike, "but I'm glad they did because I am really enjoying everything that's happening to me."

Mike stands at six-foot one, weighs 155 pounds, has dark brown hair and eyes and is constantly seen wearing a wool hat on screen but not off. He enjoys stripping down cars, hotrodding and riding skate boards. He has a small son named Christian.

PETER TORK was born in Washington, D.C. on February 13, 1942 and raised in Connecticut. His father, H.J. Torkelson, is now an Associate Professor of Economics at the University of Connecticut. Peter's father was a First Lieutenant in the Army and was stationed in Berlin, which is where Peter spent the early part of his life.

Upon the family's return to America, they settled in Madison, Wisconsin. Since children start to school in Germany when they're five, Peter was always younger than his classmates when he returned to school in the U.S. This caused Peter to be unhappy in school and unable to make many friends because of his age.

Peter became interested in drama during high school but never played a leading role in a school play because he was too small. He worked on the campus humor magazine with his brother, Nick, but didn't become interested in popular music until he entered Carleton College with the goal of becoming an English professor. His first try at college life failed and Peter spent the next year working in a thread factory. Peter tried college again after the thread factory but flunked out at the beginning of his junior year.

Although he had played French horn in the school bands, Peter did not really go professional until he hit Greenwich Village. He performed as a singer/musician in various pass-the-hat spots in the Village and eventually landed a job accompanying the Phoenix Singers.

Peter was in Los Angeles only two months (playing local clubs) when he read the ad, applied and was made a Monkee.

...MIKE NESMITH — from Texas with love.

DAVY JONES was born on December 30, 1945 in Manchester, England. His father was a railroad fitter and while certainly not destitute the Jones family *was* on the poor side. Davy's favorite game as a child was playing doctor and because his father didn't have enough money to buy many toys, Davy made his own.

Davy remembers going to church with his family but not liking it much "because I had to sit still." He wanted to join the church choir but was rejected because everyone thought he had a terrible voice! To make up for the choir rejection, Davy would go to the hospitals and sing to the patients.

He was definitely sports-minded and when he was 13 he played on all three school football teams. Davy's mother was a pianist, his three sisters sang and Davy performed in the school plays — though he seldom captured a leading role because he was so small. One role he *did* get and loved was that of Tom Sawyer.

Davy's mother died when he was 14 and it was during that same year that he left home with his father's blessing to become a jockey. During his training at the Newmarket Racetrack, Davy acted between his riding jobs. His first acting job resulted from an audition at the BBC where he played a juvenile delinquent in a radio drama. This, in turn, lead to a stady job on a daytime series called "Morning Story."

Davy still continued at the racetrack and it was through his riding that he met London theatrical executives who helped him land a leading role in the musical hit, "Oliver." Davy played the Artful Dodger and came to the U.S. with the company when "Oliver" opened Stateside. He was then 16.

Following "Oliver," Davy stepped into "Pickwick" and it was this show which brought him to Hollywood. While here he did guest spots on several television series, his most remembered being that of a glue-sniffer on "Ben Casey."

Not many people remember, but Davy gave the singing business a try during this period, signing with Colpix and releasing a single, "What Are We Going To Do," which subsequently bombed.

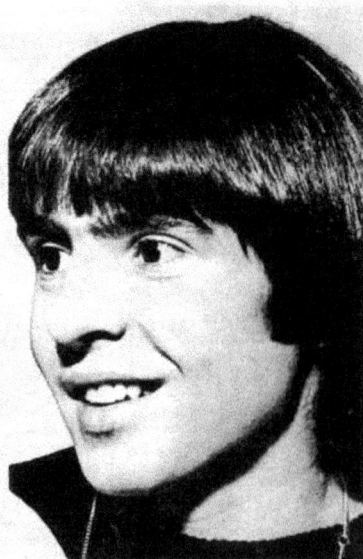

...DAVY JONES — from horses to Monkees.

KRLA ARCHIVES

SHOOTING THE MONKEES
Is Like Riding A Roller Coaster

..."SURE YOU LOOK like Tarzan."

..."OH, YEAH!"

..."OH, NO!"

..."THE BETTER TO eat you with, my dear."

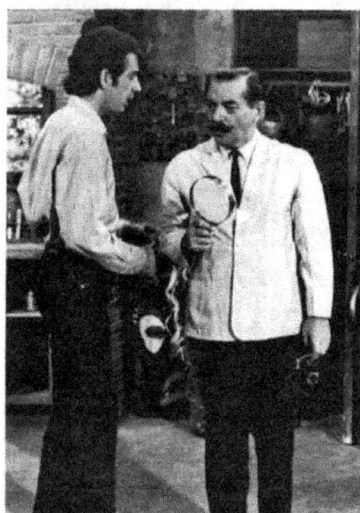
..."BUT there are no Monkees here."

..."I AM TOO Super Frog!"

February 25, 1967 — THE BEAT — Page 5

Getting Down To MONKEE Business

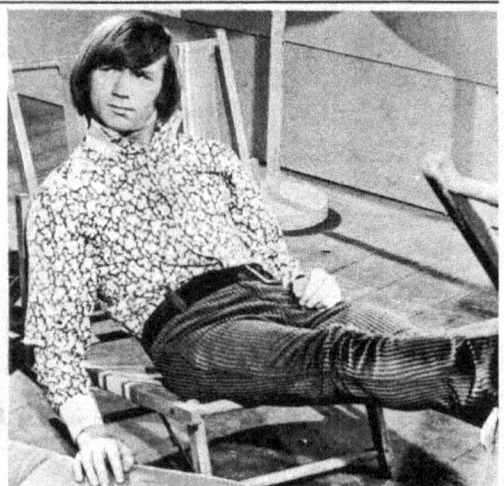

Opens Exclusive Engagement
CREST THEATRE—February 15

It's all about a typical everyday American family consisting of a mother, two man-eating piranhas, several Venus fly-traps, her baby son, age 25, his luscious baby sitter and Dad, who of course just hangs around the house.

SEVEN ARTS / RAY STARK in Association with PARAMOUNT PICTURES Presents

Oh Dad, Poor Dad
Mamma's Hung You In The Closet And I'm Feelin' So Sad

A RICHARD QUINE PRODUCTION starring
Rosalind Russell
Robert Morse • Barbara Harris • Hugh Griffith • Jonathan Winters As The Commodore

Produced by RAY STARK and STANLEY RUBIN Directed by RICHARD QUINE Screenplay by IAN BERNARD From the Stage Play by ARTHUR L. KOPIT Music by NEAL HEFTI TECHNICOLOR® A PARAMOUNT Picture

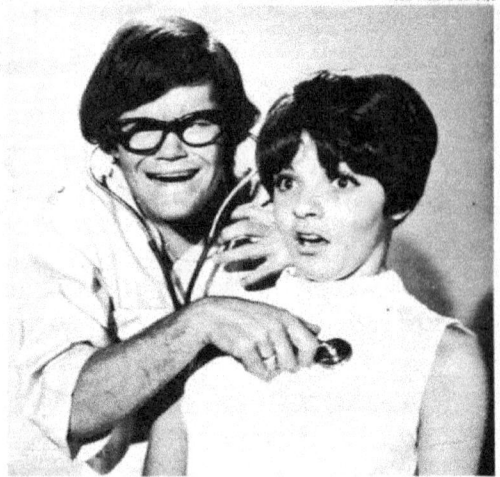

Tailoring For The Monkees

By Rochelle Reed

Outfitting the Monkees is a big business! Davy, Mike, Peter and Micky own 250 pairs of pants for screen wear alone, and the sewing machines are whirring every day.

Since they began filming, the Monkees have collected some 1800 sets of clothes, and that's just a start — so says Gene Ashman, who assumes the mammoth, but fascinating task of clothing all four guys.

An expert in the field, Gene has clothed major movie stars for over 16 years, but that doesn't make him uncool — Gene knows a groovy outfit when he sees it. Or designs it, as the case may be.

Gene and a Hollywood clothier, Lenny Able, collaborated on the design of the double button shirts which have become almost a trademark for the group, and Lenny sewed them up.

Plasterin front

Lenny wound up making numerous sets of the shirts, which have a "Plasterin front" and not double breasted front, Gene explained. The guys own them in four different colors — burgundy, Navy blue, gold and cream.

With the shirts, the Monkees generally wear Herringbone or Gambler's Stripe (larger than pin stripe) pants and, of course, boots. Their trousers, tapered and fitted especially for each Monkee, are cut about two inches higher than the usual hip-hugger design but give the appearance of being the real thing.

The Monkees are seldom forced to go through tiring fittings. Early in their careers, they were measured by the studio tailor shop and the shop presents each haberdasher with exact figures from which he cuts the clothes. The Monkees themselves drop by only if special tailoring is needed.

Gene describes Monkee clothes as the "Mod-Western look." An appropriate tag, it sums up the slightly English clothes Davy wears, the Western garb favored by Mike and the in-between styles worn by Micky and Peter.

Different Styles

Though the Monkees' clothes usually look identical on television, closer examination reveals they are cut differently for each member of the group. While Davy wears his modified English style suits, Mike's may be three button, Peter's one button and Micky's double-breasted.

"We wanted something not strictly Carnaby Street," Gene explained, adding that many Carnaby costumes are "absolute plagiarism of old period costumes."

The main idea, he went on, is to "complement the Monkees rather than make them unique." In other words, Screen Gems wants the Monkees easily identifiable to everyone, and not freaks or clothes horses. They also want each Monkee to be an individual, and wear clothes fitting his personality.

Future Monkee shows will hold changes and additions to the Monkee wardrobe. New shirts have just been completed, and are a distinct departure from the double button style. The basic front design this time is a V-shape, designed to make the shoulders appear wide and then narrow down at the waist.

..."MOD-WESTERN"

... GAMBLER'S STRIPE PANTS

... MODIFIED ENGLISH

... TIE-SCARF COMING UP

The shirts, made in a cotton Chambray material, have been sewn up in three colors.

Gene has also designed a "tie-scarf" for the Monkees. Somewhere between an ascot and a tie, it is worn close to the neck like an ascot or can be draped underneath the collar, like a scarf or tie.

Both Lenny and Gene agreed that "the guys have great taste." Davy and Mike especially are noted for knowing when they try on a suit whether it looks right or not. "They are 99 per cent right," Lenny added.

But can you ever imagine the Monkees getting their clothes dirty? Happens all the time, says Gene. And each night after filming stops, all the Monkees clothes are dry cleaned and returned to the set by the next morning.

In their private lives, the Monkees dress very much as they do on screen. Davy just recently, purchased some modified bell-bottom trousers for his vacation, along with several shirts.

Though Monkee styles are less extreme than many worn by pop groups, they are definitely trend setters. In fact, Gene predicts that within several months, people all all over the world will be switching on with the "Mod-Western Look."

THE ASSOCIATION
NO FAIR AT ALL
V 758

From
Their Album

RENAISSANCE

Valiant RECORDS

KRLA ARCHIVES

BOYCE AND HART:
What It's Like Cutting The Monkees

By Eden

"We've had many, many funny experiences with the Monkees in the studio, beginning with the first session we ever had with them. We *met* them at the studio for the first time after we'd written the first three songs for the pilot, which hadn't been made yet. The guys had just been picked—in fact, we sat through about 97 interviews when they were picking the guys."

The young man speaking was Bobby Hart—one half of the successful Boyce-Hart songwriting team that has become internationally famous for their work with the Monkees as writers and producers.

Seated in a conference room down the hall from their Hollywood offices, the boys were reminiscing about some of their early experiences with the phenomenal young quartet. Bobby continued:

Bad Quartet

"We finally met the four of them in the studio and they decided they were going to try to sing our song, the Monkee theme—except, they had *never* rehearsed it—I don't think they ever saw the song until that time! They weren't really that enthused! It sounded like a *bad* barber shop quartet at that time!"

"They hadn't been together too much and they were just getting to know each other, so they were nervous too," Tommy injected. "Right," agreed Bobby, "it was a new thing for all of us." "We were kind of nervous that night too; and *we sounded like bad barbers!*" concluded Tommy.

"And then we all got into a wrestling match on the floor," Bobby remembered. "It was kind of a *disaster*—it lasted about an hour and then we all gave in!"

Tommy took over the story here and explained that: "Recording with the boys is very interesting; we look forward to it. They're sort of relaxed now, so when we go to a recording session, it's not like a regular recording session where everybody's up-tight and real nervous; we just get very, very relaxed and we always have fun.

"Micky's a comedian and he cracks a lot of jokes and does a lot of imitations—like Jonathan Winters and stuff like that. They're *all* funny — Peter and Mike and Davy."

Both Tommy and Bobby agreed that one of their funniest experiences was cutting the "Gonna Buy Me A Dog" track on the first album. Tommy remembered: "Most of that song was like an ad-lib, all this talking—it was Davy and Micky just sort of ad-libbing because they really dig each other, and they just started ad-libbing throughout that song. Davy started saying things back to Micky, and Micky kept saying things back to Davy during the song and it was so funny that we decided that we should leave that in. That's the way they were on television and that's the way they *are*; they're very funny."

Bobby added that: "If you've heard that cut on the album—well, *every* song that we recorded with them started out that way. They have fun with everything they do."

At this point, Tommy and Bobby decided to sing *their* version of the tune for me, and in an attempt to find the right note (K minor, I think!); Bobby suddenly got up from the table and very quietly walked over to the corner of the room and stood on his head, humming the note of C, and looking much like an inverted human *pitch fork!* The Monkees are not the only comedians in this group!

"They're On"

Once he managed to return himself to an upright position, Bobby continued to speak about his four zany friends: "They're funny constantly; they're *on* all the time, just as long as there is anyone around to watch, they're *on!* From the first time we met them until now, they've always been *on*. It's like continual unbelievably funny things, one after another. They're always doing something funny!"

Tommy and Bobby have spent some time on tour with The Monkees, and Tommy recalled one funny incident which occurred on the road recently. "We went with them to Phoenix and after the show, there were about 15,000 people there running and screaming; Bobby and I were in a limousine trying to get out of the crowd, and about 40 of them jumped on top of the limousine. They were sitting on top of the car, and the guy was driving down the street and there were girls' feet and arms hanging off the top and we were going about 30 miles an hour; there were people hanging all over the top and they were crushing the top in—they pulled out the aerial and broke the air conditioning and the radio—and we rolled down the window and said, 'Hey girls—we're going on the *freeway* in a minute and you'd better jump off!' And we were riding right down the *middle of town* and there were *30 girls* all over the car! They were just hanging on and it was a very wild thing; but, they finally jumped off and nobody was hurt."

Hysterical Girls

Bobby picked up from there: "There were always girls backstage who fainted, and they were carried out on stretchers and ambulances—some of them were hysterical and some of them just wanted to meet the Monkees. But many times I saw, mostly Micky—sometimes Davy, and sometimes one of the others—go over and put his arm around a girl who was particularly overcome and comfort her. Micky's very good with the kids—if there were a choice, he'd go out into the crowd and associate with the kids rather than running."

Tommy and Bobby both feel that the images which the public has of the four Monkees are actually quite close to what they are as human beings; they really are warm, generous, funny, fun-loving guys "when they are at home." Most importantly, both boys agree that the Monkees are four of the best friends they have—and four of the grooviest guys *anywhere.*

BOBBY HART
TOMMY BOYCE

..."WE MET THEM after we'd written the first three songs."

..."THEY'RE FUNNY constantly."

..."THERE WERE always girls backstage."

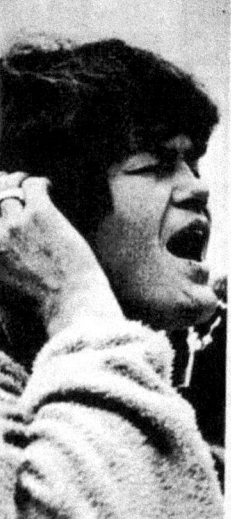
..."MICKY'S A comedian."

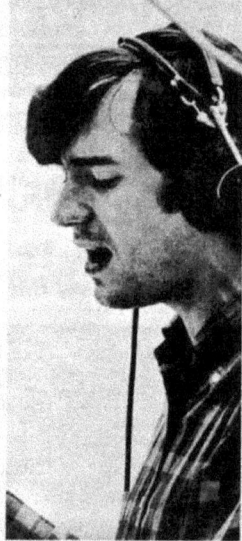
"WRESTLING on the floor."

KRLA ARCHIVES

Top 40 Requests

1. PENNY LANE/STRAWBERRY FIELDS FOREVER .... Beatles
2. HAPPY TOGETHER .... Turtles
3. SHE .... Monkees
4. RUBY TUESDAY .... Rolling Stones
5. I HAD TOO MUCH TO DREAM LAST NIGHT .... Electric Prunes
6. SIT DOWN I THINK I LOVE YOU .... Mojo Men
7. UPS AND DOWNS .... Paul Revere and Raiders
8. GEORGY GIRL .... Seekers
9. PRETTY BALLERINA .... Left Banke
10. MISTER FARMER .... Seeds
11. FOR WHAT IT'S WORTH .... Buffalo Springfield
12. SNOOPY VS. THE RED BARON .... Royal Guardsmen
13. NO FAIR AT ALL .... Association
14. LITTLE BLACK EGG .... Night Crawlers
15. KIND OF A DRAG .... Buckinghams
16. WE AIN'T GOT NOTHING YET .... Blues Magoos
17. EPISTLE TO DIPPY .... Donovan
18. THE BEAT GOES ON .... Sonny and Cher
19. 98.6 .... Keith
20. DARLING, BE HOME SOON .... Lovin' Spoonful
21. LOVE IS HERE AND NOW YOU'RE GONE .... Supremes
22. I'M A BELIEVER .... Monkees
23. MUSIC TO WATCH GIRLS BY .... Bob Crewe Generation
24. YOU GOT TO ME .... Neil Diamond
25. SO YOU WANT TO BE A ROCK AND ROLL STAR .... Birds
26. GIVE ME SOME LOVING .... Spencer Davis Group
27. TELL IT LIKE IT IS .... Aaron Neville
28. HELLO HELLO .... Sophwith Camel
29. WEDDING BELL BLUES .... Laura Nyro
30. IT MAY BE WINTER OUTSIDE .... Felice Taylor
31. THEN YOU CAN SAY GOODBY .... Casinos
32. LONELY TOO LONG .... Young Rascals
33. GREEN GREEN GRASS OF HOME .... Tom Jones
34. BABY, I NEED YOUR LOVING .... Johnny Rivers
35. KNIGHT IN RUSTY ARMOR .... Peter and Gordon
36. NIKI HOEKY .... P.J. Proby
37. I'VE PASSED THIS WAY BEFORE .... Jimmy Ruffin
38. STANDING IN THE SHADOWS OF LOVE .... Four Tops
39. LETS FALL IN LOVE .... Peaches and Herb
40. DON'T DO IT .... Mickey Dolenz

By Pen

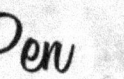

Can you imagine a meeting of over 598,700 people sitting down and picking the records that they want to hear on KRLA?

Well, this is what happens every week at KRLA... using a combination of methods to select a final list of records to be played on the air.

KRLA's music staff, headed by Dick Moreland, KRLA's Program Director, and Terry Reece, KRLA's Music Director and former Cal State College student, sifts through over 50,000 requests per week taken on our phone lines selecting the most requested songs.

KRLA's staff attends filming and rehearsal sessions premiering various artists. For example, Dick Moreland attended sessions for "The Monkees" months before the show went on the air to determine whether the group would be to the liking of our listening audience. The result being that Dick voted the Monkees a smash even before the record buying public had even heard of the group!

KRLA's survey of southland music sales covers record stores from Santa Barbara to San Diego indicating what records listeners are actually buying.

Then, after all of the weekly results have been compiled, the final programming decisions rest with Dick Moreland and Terry... and the work behind these decisions has paid off. When a record is played on KRLA it's recognized as a mark of success.

GAZZARRI'S
Hollywood A Go Go
319 North La Cienega, L.A.

FEB. 14-19

Closing Feb. 12 — TEDDY NEELY FIVE

Dancing — 18 and over
Alcoholic beverages not served to anyone under 21

THE STANDELLS

8 p.m. 'til 2 a.m. — Continuous Entertainment
For Reservations CALL OL 2-9498 Closed Mondays

ICE HOUSE — GLENDALE
234 So. Brand Ave.   Reservations: 245-5043

The Standells
"Riot On Sunset Strip"
ends
Sun. Feb. 12
3 Shows Sunday nite
(Monday is a legal holiday)

The new sound of the legendary
Tim Morgon
Feb. 14-19

Hearts & Flowers
thru Feb. 12
and again
Feb. 21-26
"Rock 'n Roll Gypsies"

plus Comedian **Pat Paulsen**
(See him on the Smothers' Bros. Comedy Hour.)

Warner Bros. unlocks all the doors of the sensation-filled best seller.

It's like you're running a big city... a unique empire... a private world with a do-not-disturb sign on every door...

HOTEL

Starring ROD TAYLOR
CATHERINE SPAAK · KARL MALDEN · MELVYN DOUGLAS · RICHARD CONTE · MICHAEL RENNIE
KEVIN McCARTHY and MERLE OBERON as "The Duchess"   Original Music by Johnny Keating
Based on the novel by Arthur Hailey · Written for the Screen and Produced by WENDELL MAYES
Directed by RICHARD QUINE   TECHNICOLOR® FROM WARNER BROS.

EXCLUSIVE ENGAGEMENT
NOW PLAYING!   PACIFIC'S HOLLYWOOD **PANTAGES**

KRLA ARCHIVES

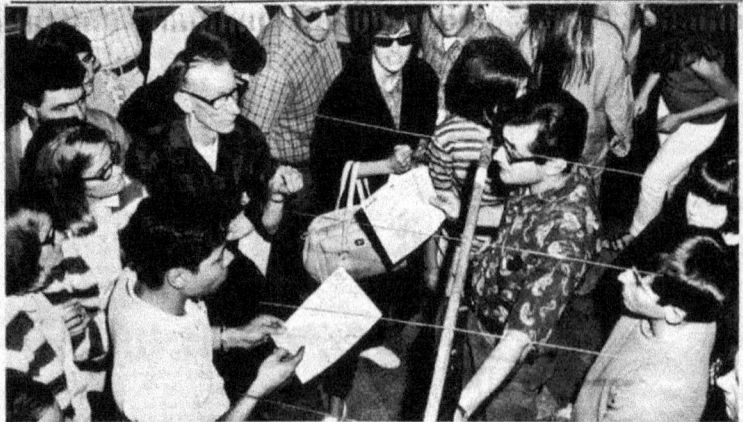

KRLA SHOWED HOW TO BEAT the blackout and tune in the Super Bowl with the simple SB antenna made from five coat hangers, a broomstick and some TV lead-in wire, and the idea became so popular that many people are still using their antenna to tune in all their favorite programs from San Diego. Dave Hull is shown demonstrating positioning of the antenna in the KRLA lobby.

WILLIAM MARSHALL, deputy director of Douglass House in Watts presents Mayor Yorty with tickets to the recent world premiere of Otto Preminger's "Hurry Sundown" at Grauman's Chinese Theatre. Total box office receipts go to Watts Writers' Workshop at Douglass House, founded and directed by famed author Budd Shulberg—and Otto Preminger matches every $3.00 ticket purchase with an equal contribution. KRLA Radio has purchased twenty pairs of tickets.

KRLA Welcomes Back The Wild One—Rebel Foster

By Jamie McClusky III

Welcome Home, Rebel! Yes—it's true; the Rebel is back on 1110 and in answer to all your questions, here's the low-down on the Wild One with the Rebel Yell.

He is six feet tall, has brownish-looking hair—"it turns blonde in the summer!"—weighs in at 160 pounds, has green eyes, and explains that: "I'm *beautiful!*"

Reb began his career in radio while he was in college in Texas. At one time, he had the only rock and roll radio program on the air in Fort Worth, Texas on the 9:00 to midnight show.

Since that time Reb has worked in radio stations all across the United States, and his ambition remains the same now as it was when he began back in Fort Worth: "Just to please as many people as I can!"

On and off the air, Reb enjoys listening to *all* kinds of music, especially that which he prefers to call "contemporary music" which is his description of pop music today. His favorite artists are still the Beatles, and he very enthusiastically exclaims: "I've been a Beatle fan for *years!*" Right now he prefers the "Penny Lane" side of the new Beatle record, but insists that the other side is also a groove.

Definitely a member of the "in" set (whoever *they* are!), The Rebel explains: "I like the way people's heads are right now—I'm with them 100% and I'm doing everything I can to help them out!"

Inside KRLA
By Eden

Once again KRLA was out in front and leading the pack by a mile as the old Scuzzabalooer introduced the brand new Beatles' single to the Southland first on his program. Our request Lines have been burning up 24 hours a day for both sides, and we're still wondering if one side will come out ahead. Which is your favorite—"Penny Lane" or "Strawberry Fields Forever?" Let us know what you think.

Guests at the station in the last couple of weeks have included the Turtles who currently have one of the hottest records in the Land of 1110—"Happy Together"—which has been one of the most requested songs nearly every hour, being knocked down only by the Beatles.

The Buffalo Springfield—another local group currently riding high on the charts with their single, "For What It's Worth," also paid us a visit and answered our request lines.

The Valentine Contest will be just about over as you read this column and we will have the results for you just as soon as possible. (Hope the winner isn't another *pizza* this year!) Hope your Valentine's Day is a real sweetheart.

Have a hot new rumor for you this week: it's been whispered on the local fig-vine that Dick Moreland is actually *alive, alive* and living in a canteen in Argentina. We'll check that one out for you.

Also, a brand new female trio—KRLA's answer to the Supremes—is being formed. Group members under consideration include: Mrs. Miller (in screaming color!), and Maude Skidmore (who is just *in!*). Their first release will be a remake of the old standard, "Rock Around the Clock" b/w "Strangers in the Night."

At this point we would like to pause just long enough to inform Bill Slater that if he doesn't get his little old airplane up to the *BEAT* offices immediately we are going to defect to the local helicopter service! C'mon Bill—the sky might fall down before we get the ride!

ATTENTION!!

High Schools, Colleges, Universities and Clubs:

CASEY KASEM MAY BE ABLE TO SERVE YOU!

Let Casey HELP You Put On A Show Or Dance

Contact Casey at: **HO 2-7253**

VALLEY MUSIC THEATRE
AIR CONDITIONED
20600 VENTURA BOULEVARD, WOODLAND HILLS

Sherman Enterprises Presents...

•• ONE NIGHT ONLY ••

LOVE

plus
CANNED HEAT Blues Band
Iron Butterfly Direct from The Galaxy
East Side Kids
Morning Glory

FEB 18

SAT. EVE. 8 P.M.

$2.50 - $3.50

CALL NOW
883-9900

Reserve Tickets NOW ON SALE At Box Office

FEB. 21 – MAR. 5

HOYT AXTON
AND
GALE GARNETT

MAR. 7-19 – ODETTA
MAR. 21-26 – GLENN YARBROUGH

RESERVATIONS
276-6168

AT DOUG WESTON'S
Troubadour
9081 SANTA MONICA BLVD.
L.A. NEAR DOHENY

KRLA ARCHIVES

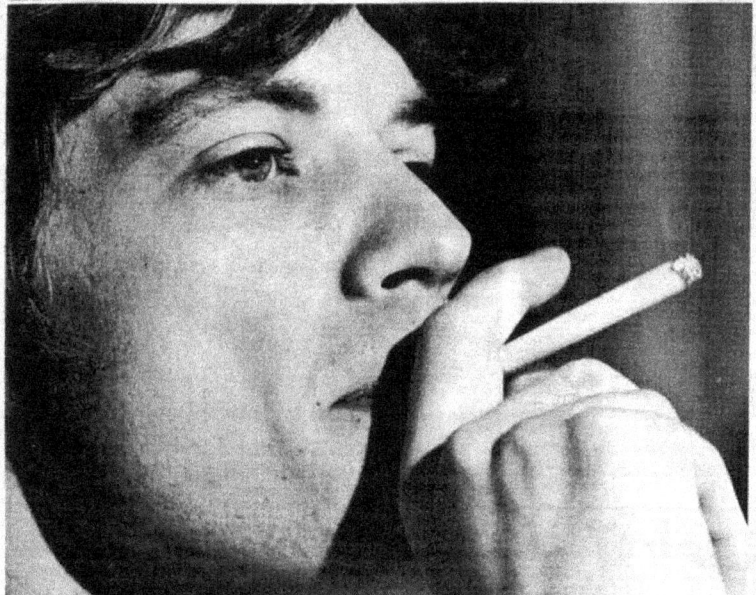

MICK JAGGER
Leader Of Revolt Against Mother Love And Morality?

By Louise Criscione

Mick Jagger, head Rolling Stone, can at times become the image of everything that causes parents to shudder in utter disbelief and shock at what they feel is a youth rebellion against mother love, morality and all else which is held sacred.

"I'm not leading the revolt," says the pop singer who first made headlines under the dubious banner: "would you want your daughter to marry a Rolling Stone?"

Dressed in a green velvet jacket, deep-red shirt and grey pants, Mick warmed to the subject of old versus young — '67 style.

Blame

"If the family unit is breaking down, if there is more illegitimacy around," said Mick, "parents might consider whether *they* went wrong instead of blaming their children — or the lyrics of pop songs. As for me, well, I guess I can stand the abuse."

Abuse is something which Jagger knows plenty about. He never attempted to don the mask of a clean-cut, God-fearing, yes ma'am ing individual which is so readily accepted by everyone over 30. Instead he remained his outspoken self, saying exactly what he felt in spite of the fact that his opinions were quite often given headline treatment and blown up all out of proportion. His hair has stayed long and preferably unkempt and his movements on stage have been termed "obscene" — though, in fact, they are not.

It has become a favorite pasttime to read double-meanings into Jagger/Richard compositions. The Stones have hardly appeared on a television show where at least one line of "Satisfaction" has not been edited out.

Mick calls the whole furor over double-meanings in pop songs "hypocritical." "You can find a dirty meaning in any song. The British don't have any objections to 'Let's Spend The Night Together,' which simply means 'why not spend the evening together.' So, why should the Americans," challenged Mick.

"On the Sullivan Show, they were only worried about the sponsors. Let's think of the lyrics of some old song. How about, 'If A Body Meet A Body Comin' Thru The Rye?' Yeah, what does that mean?" grinned Jagger.

Informed that many American disc jockeys were banning "Let's Spend The Night Together," Mick shook his now-famous head. "I can't believe most disc jockeys would do so. Maybe some of those horrible 21-year-old all-Americans who call themselves disc jockeys would."

Ever since the Rolling Stones came into the pop light, those who relish making predictions have been busily telling the world that eventually Mick Jagger would leave the Rolling Stones to go solo. For the past three years, it hasn't happened but perhaps that "eventually" is now just around the corner.

Jagger Move

"I can understand the Beatles," said Mick in reference to their decision to do no more personal appearances. "I don't like working either. I've been in a group for three years and it's time to make a move. The thing is to make the right move. That's what's on the Beatles' minds — and mine.

"I never wanted to be an entertainer," admitted Jagger. "If you stay as an entertainer, you wind up doing night club dates, at least, in the United States. And that's a horrible fate."

Mick would not elaborate on whether or not he's made definite plans for his future but movies loom in his mind. "Though, as everyone knows, good film scripts are hard to find."

A self-made millionaire, Mick lives like one and thinks nothing of spending five or six thousand dollars a year on clothes. There is no financial pressure on Mick. He need not make a hasty decision. "I've got a songwriting contract worth more than a million dollars for the next three years. I also produce records, which the Beatles do not, and I can wait for the right things to come along. But touring again — I think not."

Since many believe that all pop singers are idiots who never made it past the third grade, they'd be very surprised to discover that Mick Jagger, whether he wiggles obscenely on stage or not, is an intelligent, well-educated young man who attended the London School of Economics and who talks easily about the problems facing the youth of today.

Insight

He believes that the current crop of parents blame the pop groups and everyone else they can think of for the problems and attitudes of their children in a desperate attempt to avoid looking at themselves.

"They (parents) call the illegitimacy figures shocking," said Mick, "but, frankly, how many parents do anything to prevent it?"

The use of drugs by teens is another problem which Mick feels parents are avoiding. "They should say 'why do our children take drugs?' And try to understand the reasons. Believe me, parents are worrying about the wrong things these days. They ought to be worrying about themselves and *their* problems and that might resolve some of their childrens."

WHERE IT IS --- IS WHERE YOU FIND IT!
---IF YOUR OUT LOOKIN'
---IF YOUR NOT DON'T CALL US!

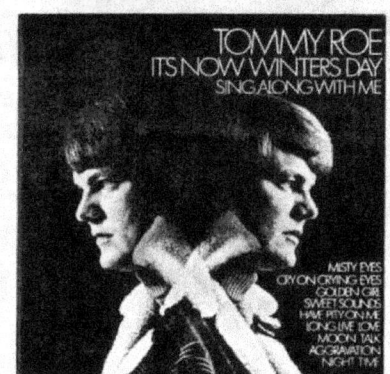

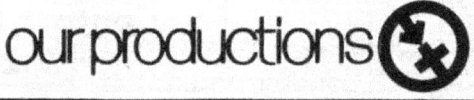

KRLA ARCHIVES

On the BEAT

By Louise Criscione

First off, I'd like to remind you that starting with the next issue of *BEAT* we'll be running a classified section. It'll cost 20 cents a word for classified ads and 10 cents a word for personals. It ought to be a gas 'cause you can sell, swap, or finagle anything you like as well as send personal messages to your friends (or enemies) all over the world via *The BEAT*. I think I'll start it off by swiping Shirley's Beatle collection and selling it to the highest bidder!

Practically the whole staff drove to Las Vegas between last issue and this one (how's that for exact date) to see Bill Cosby and the Righteous Brothers. Fantastic, beautiful, out of sight. What can you say about those two acts? A little hype—if you ever get the chance to see either Bill or the Righteous Brothers "live" you'd better do it. The Righteous Brothers had the Blossoms singing background for them and, of course, they were their usual talented selves. Bill Cosby had only Bill Cosby backing him—but that, love, is all that's needed. He *has* to be the greatest natural comedian of all time.

Nazi Trouble

Brian Jones ran into a little trouble by posing in a Nazi uniform. It was strictly satirical, declares Brian. "With all that long hair in a Nazi uniform, couldn't people see that it was a satirical thing?" Apparently, they couldn't as those other than Stone fans worked themselves up into a real fever, calling Brian a Nazi sympathizer—which, by the way, he is not. Brian pointed out that right after his "Nazi picture" Peter O'Toole was photographed wearing a German uniform for a movie he's making and no one objected—but, of course, he's not a Rolling Stone. Which means a lot to some people. On the happy side, the Stones' "Got Live If You Want It" has been certified as a million seller—making it five gold records for the Stones.

...BILL COSBY

The Young Rascals are back on top again. It's taken a while for them to come back with a really strong song to follow-up their "Good Lovin'" but it looks as if "Lonely Too Long" is going to do it for them. Of course, their new album, "Collections," isn't hindering them either! They just finished playing two sell-out nights at Action City in New York where they set a house record by grossing $32,000.

Now on to some new groups — David McCallum recently introduced the Knack at a party thrown by Capitol Records. High school editors were invited as well as the working press — a great idea and a perfect opportunity for teens to meet entertainers. David posed for pictures with the editors as well as signing autographs for everyone. A charming man, not to mention a popular and talented performer.

Knack Of...

Capitol is putting big money behind the Knack and there is no doubt about the fact that they're good. They have an amazing amount of stage presence for such a young group and I wouldn't be at all surprised if they make it quite a big way.

Another group to keep your eyes on is Don and the Goodtimes. Of course, they're now regulars on "Action" but if you really want to see what they're made of catch them "live." You can't help but keep your eyes glued to little Don because it's hard to believe that he's really playing organ, dancing and thumping the tambourine all at the same time!

BEAT Photo: Chuck Boyd
...DAVID McCALLUM

CLASSIFIEDS

BEAT is beginning a classified column, designed to buy, sell, find, lose, trade, give, announce, notify, warn, or say whatever you wish.

Ads will be accepted for just about anything, including

- for sale — wanted — pen pals
- fan clubs — announcements — personals
- lost guys and gals — special notices — everything else

Prices are cheap! Only 20¢ a word for classifieds and a mere 10¢ a word for personal messages (from you to someone else without an item for sale, trade, etc. involved).

Now, what's a word? Well, it's the usual thing plus two exceptions: the city and the state count as only one word (Hollywood, California) and the number and street (6290 Sunset Blvd.) are only one word.

Send all advertisements (clearly printed or typed) along with the correct amount of money to:

Classifieds
BEAT Publications
6290 Sunset Blvd. Suite 504
Hollywood, California 90028

Paul Revere and the Raiders Strike Again!
with

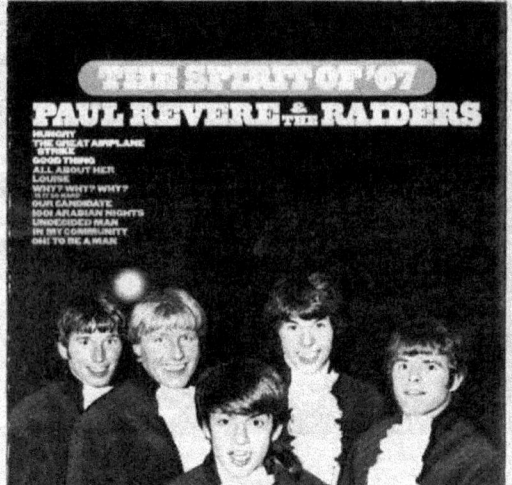

The Spirit of '67
CL 2595   CS 9395

JUST LIKE US
CL 2451   CS 9351

MIDNIGHT RIDE   **HERE THEY COME**
CL 2508   CS 9305   CL 2307   CS 9107

Be Sure To Get Their New Single—
"Ups and Downs" 4-44018

the NOW Sound on COLUMBIA RECORDS

Available at your favorite record shop.

KRLA ARCHIVES

'We'll Protest In Suits And Ties'—Terry

(Editor's Note: This is the third in a series of interviews with all members of the Association. Next issue—Ted).

If Terry could, he'd have a ten second delay on his life, much like radio talk programs delay their telephone caller's words.

He'd use the time to check exactly what he said and did, because to Association singer Terry Kirkman, the all important thing in life is to "check your motivations."

Sneaking in just under the wire as a member of the celebrated "Generation 25 and Under," 25-year-old Terry parks his Mustang on the edge of today's mainstream and only starts it up occasionally to offer comments and sometimes, action.

"I see kids who are becoming actionists on Sunset or in Berkeley," he says, "or at least, many of them think of themselves as actionists. But 50 percent is hanky panky. I don't see enough people checking their own motivations.

"A couple of years ago, about three or four, I went on a couple of CORE marches. But I was disappointed because the majority of people there were hanger-oners.

"I've often wondered—this is my big plan—what would happen if one day all Sunset Strip stopped and said, 'All right, for the next six months, we won't present ourselves in any way that might be offensive. We'll protest in suits and ties.'"

He stopped momentarily to let the entire image sink in, nodding his head at the thought of it all. "In a sense, they are defeating their purpose," he continued. "I've always wondered about the kid who walks around with 10,000 buttons stuck on him and really grubby dress. And I don't mean long hair!"

Terry, obviously, would have to be one of the last people to dislike long hair. Sideburns down his cheeks and hair in his eyes, he's hardly a candidate for the college look, though at one time he was indeed wrapped up in the student image.

"I majored in journalism in college, but I never had any intention of getting a degree. I still write, when I can get my mind free—usually prose and poetry."

After leaving college, the Associate spent his first years of professional singing in coffee houses and wherever the folk and jazz crowd congregated, meeting and singing with people like Frank Zappa, who Terry describes as "a genius with a strange and valid perspective—I guess you might say Zappa is a rebel with a cause."

Zappa, hairy leader to the frank Mothers of Invention, seems like an unlikely candidate for genius, coming from Terry, until you realize that to Terry, it's the person that counts.

"The individual is in danger of being crushed by the mass. A person leaves school and is swallowed up by the corporate image. In fact, one of the most often asked questions to prospective employees is 'What are your plans for retirement?'

"There's a big gap between the guy making it on his own efforts and the corporate man," he emphasizes.

With several hit disks and two successful albums beneath his pillow, Terry doesn't consider himself as having "made it."

"But I've made it to the opportunity of making it," he explains. "If I do something now, it will be observed. Now I have a market where I didn't a year ago."

Terry chose to bet his success on a group, rather than going solo, because "there are more possibilities, sound-wise. It's virtually impossible to be a single act. Your chances of success are limited."

Happy with the Association and his "one-sixth say-so," he finds that respect from fellow performers "means an awfully lot to me. From a performance standpoint, if you're good enough for other performers to appreciate what you're doing, then you've really created something."

This "creating something," along with "checking motivations" is probably the major emphasis in Terry's life. But the creative element in a person often is accompanied by the inability to get along with anything or anyone. Terry, however, manages to be remarkably objective and a bit humorous towards himself and others.

"More often than not, I make myself laugh," says Terry, who always wears the comical look of a beagle who just woke up. "But I guess it's innocence that really makes me laugh . . . a puppy or a baby . . . that feeling in people in general. It's the same thing that makes me cry or get angry.

"I've got a lot more control over my temper than I used to. Now I'm fairly even tempered. But I'm given to sudden outbursts. I'll sit on something and let it bother me and then, whammm!"

Terry remains even tempered around *BEAT* offices, enough for the staff to tease him about being a "teen idol." And how does he feel when he looks at himself in the mirror and sees what very well might be a Birdie image.

"I consider it very carefully. I take it seriously, I really do. I've got to check what I say and do," he says.

In other words, he uses that ten second delay to "check my motivations," then proceeds to make it, with the help of the Association, on his own merits.

...TERRY KIRKMAN—Standing back to "Check My Motivations."

Eschew socks.

Great look, great feel. That's the whole idea behind new Bare/Foot/Gear **leather** sneakers. They're the first sockless shoes ever made.

What makes them sockless is their design and special leather. The design you can see. The leather comes from a secret process. It's top-grain **steerhide**, nothing less. Even the insoles are this leather. Our special process makes this steerhide tough, yet soft; meaty yet supple.

(Added advantage: Bare/Foot/Gear sockless sneakers will outlast those cloth sneakers of yours two to three times.)

Take a closer look. All the good stores named below, and other good stores, too, carry Bare/Foot/Gear.

Go there.

Berkeley, Don/Dave; La Jolla, Lion's; Long Beach, Buffums'; Los Angeles, Bullock's, Campbell's, Mr. Guy, Phelps-Wilger; West L.A. Lew Ritter, Mark's Boot Shop; Pasadena, Atkinson's, Phelps-Wilger; San Diego, Lion's; San Francisco, The Town Squire; San Jose, New Englander; Santa Ana, Buffums', Bullock's; Tempe, Ariz., Oxford Shop.

BARE FOOT GEAR
Original Sockless Shoes.

If no store is listed in your area, write Bare/Foot/Gear, 522 Veteran, L.A., Cal. 90024. ©1967, Willie Loman & Sons, Inc.

KRLA ARCHIVES

"SHE'S THE ONE," points out Chrissie, Mick's long-time girlfriend.

...MARIANNE FAITHFULL is the new Jagger girlfriend, though "marriage is a drag" according to Mick.

Mick Sheds Chrissie For Faithfull

By Tony Barrow

Ever since he confirmed publically that he was no longer dating Chrissie Shrimpton it has been fairly common knowledge in London that MICK JAGGER spends plenty of time in the company of songstress MARIANNE FAITHFULL.

At the end of January, Marianne, looking slimmer and lovelier than ever in knee-high boots and a French zip-front mini-dress, took off for the Italian Riviera to sing "The One Who Hopes" in the San Remo Song Festival.

The following Thursday Mick followed her and booked himself into a stylish suite at the plushy Rocca del Capo Hotel just outside San Remo. When her song failed to make the Festival finals Mick was on hand to offer sympathy and in no time press boys were poised to write their romance reports!

"We have only been going out regularly for the last three months" Mick told them. "My friendship with Marianne is an old one. She felt a bit lonely and phoned me to come over. I thought it was a good idea to come and keep her company."

The couple were seen together in several of San Remo's best bars but Marianne obviously sad at her lack of success in the Festival, insisted upon saying as little as possible to those who tried to get near them.

Before returning to London, Mick and Marianne rented a boat and went for a sail in the watery winter sunshine.

"Our friendship is not likely to get serious," declared Mick, "marriage is a drag."

Marianne, 20, is the mother of a 14-month-old son, Nicholas. She is separated from her husband, London art gallery man John Dunbar.

MEANWHILE back in London ...19-year-old model and trainee actress CHRISSIE SHRIMPTON'S current town-and-around escort is STEVE MARRIOTT of THE SMALL FACES. Says Steve: "I'm very fond of her." Says Chrissie: "Marriage isn't for me. I'm not rushing into anything."

The group's London representative, Tito Burns, hopeful MAMA'S AND PAPA'S will undertake lengthy British tour this summer... WALKER BROTHERS new U.K. single is "Stay With Me Baby"... In Britain the CBS label issues single, "Echoes," by GENE CLARK, the Byrd who flew so high he found himself all alone... CILLA BLACK started work on location in Birmingham as co-star with DAVID WARNER in the comedy movie "WORK... Is A Four Letter Word." In colour, the picture is based on the highly successful 1965 West End play "Eh?"

Cilla has a non-singing role. Warner is the man who hit the headlines in the title role of the movie "Morgan, A Suitable Case For Treatment."

At ATV's "London Palladium Show" MICK JAGGER introduced THE STONES' current hit with the announcement: "And now here's the dirty one!" Palladium TV people let him sing the original lyrics of "Let's Spend The ____ Together"... Songstress SHANI WALLIS signed to play Nancy in the screen version of Lionel Bart's musical "Oliver!"

Paul's Penny And Lennon's Strawberry —From The Inside

By Tony Barrow

It's been six months since The Beatles brought out a single. Now as ultimate evidence for all those split-up rumour-builders here comes the group's first new record for '67! There are no 'A' and 'B' sides so far as John, Paul, George and Ringo are concerned. Just two contrasting titles — "PENNY LANE" and "STRAWBERRY FIELDS FOREVER" — which are linked with The Beatles' Liverpool past.

So you want to know the secret of PENNY LANE for a start. Maybe you imagined that Penny must be some fondly-remembered bird from Paul's teeny-boppin' days. Yes, they'd believe that in Iowa — but not in Liverpool. Any Merseysider could tell you about Penny Lane. It's a well-known suburban street to the south side of Liverpool's city centre. It's the meeting point of five different streets — and five thousand different residents who live in that thickly populated neighbourhood. On a Saturday morning at Penny Lane you might easily spot Paul's poppy-selling nurse standing on the traffic island near the corner. Or his bloke with a picture of the Queen tucked away in a waistcoat pocket.

"PENNY LANE," sung by Paul and John contains (for the most part) Paul's own ideas. It is a happy-go-beat number with a busy street-scene atmosphere in the arrangement and the sort of simple, infectious tune you remember after a single spin of the record.

STRAWBERRY FIELDS? Yes, they really do exist but you couldn't grow strawberries there in a decade of Beatle Birthdays! John did most of the composing work on this — so he's the one who solos on the record. He roughed out the first basic lyrics last October when he was filming "How I Won The War" in Almeria, Spain. Liverpool street maps don't mark out Strawberry Fields. That's the name given to a dull-green expanse of grass and a bit of a pond located just down the street from John's original home in Menlove Avenue, Woolton, Liverpool 25.

"STRAWBERRY FIELDS FOREVER," playing for just five seconds more than four minutes, is the longest track ever recorded by The Beatles. As far as John's vocal technique is concerned you might describe it as a further extension of the style he created for "Tomorrow Never Knows." After something like 3-1/2 minutes — the final segment building into a fantastic barrage of percussion during which George and Paul play bongos and tympani, Mal Evans plays tambourine and John thumps out the beat on the back of a wooden chair — the sound fades away to nothing and you think the action's over.

This'll fool a few deejays — suddenly everything starts happening again and the instrumental storm builds back to another crescendo.

"STRAWBERRY FIELDS FOREVER" was the first item The Beatles worked on when they went into the E.M.I. Recording Studios at the beginning of December. It took the best part of two weeks to complete. Two completed tapes were destroyed because the group agreed that the tempo was wrong. When they started work on the third version they took it a little faster and everything worked out right.

PAUL McCARTNEY:
'I'M NO LONGER ONE OF FOUR MOP-TOPS'

(Editor's Note: As we were going to press, The BEAT received a telegram from London announcing that the Beatles have just signed a new nine year contract with EMI and Brian Epstein. However, there was no mention of whether they signed as a group or as individuals.)

Who is getting the run-around? First come the Beatle rumors, next come the official confirmation or denial and just as soon as that's printed one of the Beatles starts talking. Result? One fat circle.

First came the rumor that the Beatles would tour no more, then at press conferences all across the U.S. last summer the Beatles professed to know nothing of any such decision. Still later came the official decree that, indeed, the Beatles would make no more personal appearances but that they would go ahead and make a third movie as well as record a new single and a new album.

The new single is, of course, now released and the album is currently being cut. And Paul McCartney has announced that the Beatles will only work together again "if we miss each other."

Paul went on to add that: "I no longer believe in the image. I'm no longer one of the four mop-tops."

The reason for the split is financial — only in reverse. Most groups break up because they haven't made it. The Beatles are breaking up because they've made it too much and any further group effort will only go into taxes.

"We've all of us grown up in a way that hasn't turned into a manly way," admitted Paul. "It's a childish way. That's why we make mistakes. We've not grown up within the machine. We've been able to live very independent lives. Now we're ready to go our own ways. We'll work together if we miss each other. Then it'll be hobby work. It's good for us to go it alone."

Since the Beatles departed the United States, they've worked together only in the recording studio. John, of course, made a movie; George went to India to learn sitar and Ringo put out the word that he's interested in doing a movie. Paul has been on safari in Africa and has put together a movie he shot in France. "It's all part of breaking up the Beatles," revealed Paul.

And all that leaves their proposed third movie where? In the hobby room?

KRLA ARCHIVES

Switching On

BEAT Art: Linda Bull

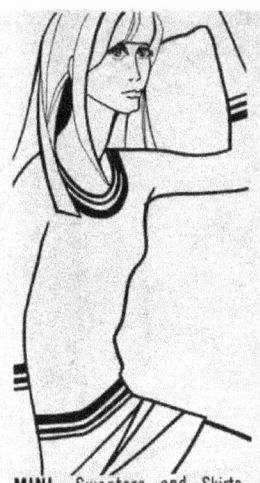

MINI — Sweaters and Skirts.

■ France, traditional land of the sweater, has come out with a new knit on the old. Mini-sweaters, or mini-Shetlands as they call them in Paris (a Shetland is a very small pony) are the rage of France. Worn barely to the waist in warmer seasons, the mini-sweater stretches below the waist (as in our drawing) during colder months. Knitted of fluffy wool, the sleeve should not quite reach the wrist. But the size is the most important — nothing larger than what might fit a 12 year old child.

■ Dress up a pants suit with a lacy, frilly blouse, letting the ruffles peek out at sleeves and neckline. Or leave the jacket unbuttoned if it isn't double-breasted. A groovy change.

■ Bangs are still big news but tend to be shorter than before — eyebrow length rather than eyelash length. Many girls are doing away with them altogether, combing the hair to the side and tucking it behind the ears.

■ Pierced earrings aren't dangling quite as large. The huge plastic type are gone but department stores are now carrying a cute set of small plastic cubes and balls — darling with op art dresses.

■ Boutique hunting is a great way to spend Saturday afternoon, and also yields fab results! We found (and snatched up) a demure military cover-up coat to go over swimsuits. Complete with rows and rows of buttons, the cover-up will be great for early spring surfing.

NEWEST LOOK for new designs.

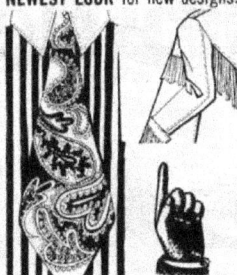

PAISLEY TO SUEDE for the aware.

■ Washed out by those harsh office or school lights? It's the pink tones in your skin which disappear so begin using a pink foundation, pink powder and keep a pink lipstick handy — preferably the glossy type. It does wonders.

■ From England comes word that the newest development in suits is a shirt to match — you buy the shirt with the suit and the suit fabric is repeated on the shirt collar.

■ Hair is getting shorter but is still longer than the "I Want To Hold Your Hand" Beatle length. Even Mick Jagger, The Seeds, Davy Jones and Sonny Bono are visiting the barbershop more often.

■ Ties are w-i-d-e and colorful. The keynote is **anything goes** — from paisley to stripes to polka dots. But make it distinctive!

■ Happening on campuses is Bear Foot gear, suede shoes styled like tennis sneakers! Worn with or without socks, they are extremely comfortable and look good with just about any type of clothes.

■ Western suede, fringed or unfringed coats are definitely on the scene. Local department stores don't have them yet but Western shops have beautiful collections — and suede coats last longer than their wool counterparts.

■ Scott Walker, American export to England, is making these double pocket pants big fashion news. Though Scott usually appears wearing his in slightly wrinkled denim, English fashion shops carry

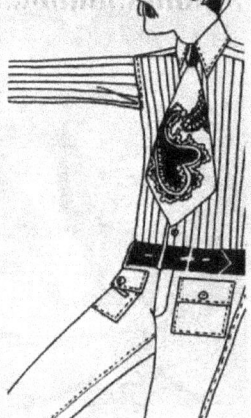

POCKETS — Two for the Tasteful.

them in all fabrics and designs. Worn with plain shirts or the striped model shown in our sketch, these trousers are suitable for casual wear and may soon be shown with suit coats for Stateside dress.

■ Mustaches, says Russ Giguere of the Association, are invariably admired by men and hated by wo-

men. Three Beatles are sporting an inverted U-type while Stateside, Russ, Sal Valentino and others are wearing them in all styles.

PAULREY VEAR AND RADISHES: PART II

(Editor's Note: This is the second and final segment of Paulrey Vear and his Radishes written exclusively for The BEAT by Mark Lindsay of the Raiders.

After a sleepless night during which the three had discussed the obvious merits of living in such a Great Society, they stiffly arose and began packing their horses for the day's journey.

"Hark!" said Paulrey, for the second time in this story. "Do you hear what I hear?" "Nope!" flatly stated Marc. "Me too!" said Black-Smith, who was busily digging white grubs from under a mossy log.

Threading their way silently through the bushes, the three musketeers came upon two disgustingly filthy hunters who, instead of discharging their bows and arrows into the herd of deer that were curiously watching, were plunking mightily upon them (the bows), producing the unmistakable strains of "I Want To Hold Your Hand."

"Ungh, Kemosavi," grunted Black-Smith, recognizing the dirty pair as none other than Philrup-the-Tooth and Harkin-the-Horn, "there is your string section, Master," and so saying, began munching on some mushrooms growing at the base of an old oak tree.

Paulrey quickly snowed the two recruits into believing he controlled the rotation of the earth, and gladly signing a lifetime contract in the blood of a turnip, the happy pair quickly picked up the horses which were fully loaded and smiling, and five-strong, the new group which Paulrey instantly christened *Paulrey Jeer and the Radishes* staggered off into the sunset.

HULLABALOO
ROCK & ROLL SHOWPLACE OF THE WORLD
presents

Friday & Saturday — Feb. 10 & 11
JOEY PAIGE
PLUS
THE WILD ONES

Friday & Saturday — Feb. 17 & 18
(The "Hello Hello" group)
SOPWITH "CAMEL"
PLUS
EAST SIDE KIDS

Friday & Saturday — Feb. 24 & 25
THE STANDELLS
PLUS
THE YELLOW PAYGES

6230 SUNSET BLVD., HOLLYWOOD — HO. 6-8281

TWICE AS MUCH (Convenience) **FOR** (Almost) **HALF THE COIN**

Limited Offer — Regular $5.00
On Newsstands — EVEN MORE!

ONE FULL YEAR — ONLY $3.00

Mail To:
The BEAT
6290 SUNSET BLVD., #504
HOLLYWOOD, CALIF. 90028

☐ New Subscription
☐ Renewal (Enclose your address label)

NAME: _____
ADDRESS: _____
CITY: _____ STATE: _____ ZIP: _____

I want BEAT for one year ☐ 3.00 or two years ☐ 5.00
Enclosed is ☐ Cash ☐ Check ☐ Money Order   Outside U.S. — 9.00

BEAT Art: Steve Mumford

KRLA ARCHIVES

Adventures of Robin Boyd...

©1965 By Shirley Poston

Never let it be said that Robin Irene Boyd is the sort who comes unhinged easily.

When no one attended the Mockingbirds' opening at the Neville Club except the Mockingbirds, did she immediately fling herself into a corner and start sniveling at the top of her lungs?

Certainly not. She remained perfectly calm for at least seven minutes, and only *then* did she fling herself into a corner and start sniveling at the top of her lungs.

Soothing Spear

The Budge rushed to comfort her, and even Ringo (as in Boydbrain) came out from behind her drooms long enough to give her distraught sister a soothing spear of the olde Loodwig. But it was no use.

"Where did we go *wrong*?" Robin blubbered, blowing her nose on a crepe paper streamer.

"You might well as in arsk," said The Budge. "Everyone *knew* about tonight. All they had to do was read the posters. And I happen to know they *can* read."

Ringo nodded. "Even some of the kids in *my* grade can read. But I'll bet they didn't show up because they couldn't!"

Robin re-blew. "Couldn't *what*?"

"Couldn't get out of the house. Some girls I know say their folks never let them go to anything but Sewing Circle. The squares," she added contemptuously.

Robin and Budgie exchanged sneaky glances, and after locking up the club, they whispered fiendishly all the way home.

The next morning, which had the good sense to be a Saturday, the three of them set out, armed with an assortment of hurriedly and clumsily drawn (surely you haven't forgotten that no one is perfect) poster which read: NIGHTLY AT THE NEVILLE CLUB! TEENAGE CHARITY QUILTING BEES!

"Why don't we add B.Y.O.B." Robin said as an after-thought. (After *what* thought I'd rather not say.) "I merely meant bring your own bee, bring your own bee," she added hastily when The Budge gave her a P.T.A. glare.

After they had skulked through the town (gnash) and plastered the posters, they stopped at the druggist's (for a coke, for a coke). At which time Robin had another after-thought.

"Budgie," she simpered. "Do me a favor?"

"No," The Budge replied pleasantly. "Next question?"

Robin paid no attention, as usual. "Go home and gather up all the ragged clothes you've been meaning to hurl out of your closet."

"I can't," The Budge replied pleasantly. "I'm wearing them."

"I'm *serious*!" Robin bellowed, lowering her voice when the behind the counter clicked his ice cream scoop in the direction of her jugular vein. "Get the stuff and come over to our house. You too, Ringo."

"I can't come-over-to-our-house," Ringo replied pleasantly. "I live there."

Hauling her sturdy 12-year-old sister off the stool (which later had to be reinforced), Robin dragged her home by the mitten string and started plowing through her own closet (using—you guessed it—the tractor she always kept handy for such purposes).

When The Budge arrived, she added her arm-load to the pile in the middle of the living room floor.

"We will now snip this crud into neat squares," Robin ordered, passing out (yay!) scissors (boo!).

"Have you dropped another one?" Budgie inquired politely. "Known as being in the Marble Bag?"

"Nope"

"Nope," said Robin. "When I say quilting bee, I *mean* quilting bee!"

Whoppers usually didn't keep Robin up nights. However, being grazed by three lightning bolts in one day, in the dead of winter, *did*.)

At seven o'clock that evening, the Neville Club was open for business. The Mockingbirds were on stage, busily praying for some of the same, when the door opened and in they crept.

They being 103 (Robin is a fast counter) (among other things) saddle-shoed Pitchforkians, who entered in single file, deposited their admission quarters in the cigar box (nothing but class) and then broke ranks and stood silently about the room (a room to stand silent *about* if there ever was one).

After Robin had picked up her teeth, she staggered to the microphone and haltingly made the speech she'd been practicing for weeks. First she told the crowd about the plans they'd made for a future Youth Center (leaving out a few minor details, such as bribes to Old Baldy, etc.). Then she got around to a more recent bribe.

"Our posters said this was going to be a quilting bee," she choked, staring nervously at the sea of expression faces. "I don't know what a quilting bee *is* exactly, but assuming it's something you do with pieces of cloth, we've provided a large box of such materials. However, if you'd rather do something else, it could—er—probably be arranged."

Robin then took a deep breath and waited for something to happen. But nothing did. No one spoke. No one moved. They just returned her stare.

Cymbal Crash

Suddenly there was a crash of cymbals and Ringo came to (it's about time) her feet. "Hey, you guys!" she yelled unceremoniously. "Do you wanna quilt bees or whatever it is you do with those thingies we spent all afternoon hacking up?"

103 heads shook a silent but fervent no.

"Well," thundered Ringo. "Do you wanna hear some music?"

103 heads nodded a silent but fervent yes.

And, giving Robin an I'm-not-as-dumb-as-I-look-look (an impossibility), Ringo banged into the opening bars of the noisiest number she could think of.

The Mockingbirds then went into action, playing everything they knew except their Beatle songs, which they'd sworn (I'll say) to save for an *ultra*-special occasion.

Finally, they stopped. Not from exhaustion; from amazement. Because, during the performance, the crowd had continued to stand motionless and stare wordlessly. And, when they did stop, the "audience," as if on cue, did an about-face, fell back into single file ranks and marched silently out the door.

Silent Sound

This was only the first of many such evenings. The same exact thing happened every night the Neville Club was open. The same 103 people showed up. In they filed, there they stood and out they went, without having said a word or moved a muscle.

After a week or so of this, the girls stopped blithering after performances and cracked funny (you bet) jokes about being appropriately dressed (in black leather of early Be-attle fame) for the occasion, and threatened to change their name to The Embalmers.

But they were still just sick about the situation. Everything was going just as planned except one. Nobody, including them, was having any am-day fun.

And they might *never* have had any (fun) if it hadn't been for the night when 103 filed in and 102 filed out.

(To Be Continued Next Issue)

GENE, DINO, FELIX AND EDDIE talk to their fans on the phone.

Rascals—Inside Looking Way Out

By Lisa Stewart

There is a crowded room filled with music, laughter and dancing ... all at once everything stops ... three hundred people become fused together as all eyes and ears focus on a small stage. There is an undercurrent of excitement, anticipation and hushed expectancy. Then suddenly the room explodes and the Rascals happen!

Hypnotic

Four perfectly combined and conditioned musicians produce a sound so overwhelmingly powerful that it is almost hypnotic in its intensity. Four heart and souls are torn apart and inside out, exposing everything that lies within them; the strength and drive, beauty and tenderness, love and hate, compassion and sensitivity, joy and sorrow. The music reaches out, surrounds, enfolds and compels you to become a part of it. Once inside there is no turning back. You cannot escape the driving, pulsating sounds, the frenetic quick-silver excitement that invades every part of you. For the moment all that exists is a frightening collage of sight, sound, light and color. There is an irreverent innocence for the conventional music forms ... a ceaseless, restless probing ... and the subtle chemistry of bashful genius and youthful awareness.

European Success

Whether it is a soft ballad or an up-tempo rocker, the same excitement prevails. They are the new spokesmen for American music. But you don't have to speak English to understand what they are saying. That became apparent on a recent trip to Europe, where the reactions of foreign-language teenagers were so enthusiastic that another trip has been set for April.

Eddie, Felix, Dino and Gene are in love with the world and they're shouting it from the rooftops in the way they know best.

It's here and now ... yesterday, today and tomorrow ... the sounds are alive and real ... the noise of the streets ... the quiet of the parks ... the eye of a hurricane ... a soft breeze on a summer's day ... the gentle brook and the onrushing tidal wave ... encompassing all before it and conquering all it touches, higher and higher until ... it's over. But the magic that occurs will take place again and again, everytime they step onto a stage and into the hearts of everyone who has had the experience of watching the Rascals happen!

EDDIE GROOVING OUT on stage.

KRLA ARCHIVES

RECORDS FREE FROM RC®
You'll Flip at the ZZZIP in RC® Cola

while you swing to your favorite stars! RC and music, perfect partners for the perfect lift

TAKE 1 ALBUM FREE

For everyone you buy... with 6 cork liners or seals from R.C. bottle caps over 100 Capitol LP's available. Order as often as you wish. Nothing to join. Look for this display at your favorite store.

Here's your best way yet to save more on the records you want. In dollars-and-cents terms you get two albums that the Capitol Record Club sells for $3.98 each time you buy one. The savings are even bigger on stereo records! And there are no shipping charges to pay, nothing else to join or buy.

What's more, you choose from top albums by today's biggest stars, including the Beatles, David McCallum, Frank Sinatra, Lou Rawls, Buck Owens, Petula Clark, the Outsiders, Nancy Wilson, Dean Martin, Sonny James, the Beach Boys and many others.

OTHER FINE BRANDS: DIET-RITE®COLA, NEHI®BEVERAGES, PART-T-PAK®BEVERAGES, UPPER 10®
"ROYAL CROWN" AND "RC" REG. U.S. PAT. OFF.; ®1966 ROYAL CROWN COLA CO.

KRLA ARCHIVES

America's Pop Music NEWSpaper

KRLA Edition
BEAT
March 11, 1967

25¢

SHEBANG IS BACK!

AND IT'S GREAT!

KRLA BEAT

Volume 2, Number 36   March 11, 1967

DAVY JONES
Met In London By A Stampeding Mob

LONDON — Beatlemania gave way to Monkeemania as Davy Jones, smallest and only British Monkee, landed at London Airport and was greeted with a mob scene! Police said that the scene, staged by about 700 teens, revived the very worst days of Beatlemania.

The crowd, consisting mainly of girls, surged through police lines, knocked down passengers (including an expectant mother) and stampeded up and down stairs in a vain search for Davy, who was hidden in a customs room.

Frantic Officials

Airport officials were frantic and angrily rerouted other passengers because "anyone walking into that mob would risk great danger of injury." The girls wept bitterly when they were blocked from Davy and the police offered their excuse by saying that they could have done much better but many of their officers had been sent to Gatwick Airport to handle the crowds and protect Soviet Premier Alexei Kosygin upon his departure from England.

For his part, Davy could not get over the enthusiastic reception his fans staged at the airport, declaring: "I'm a very happy man. I didn't expect anything like this."

Jones' fans staged a giant sit down when police attempted to move the girls along. Davy was smuggled out of the airport in a police car and then transferred into a limousine for a ride to a London hotel. However, upon reaching the hotel Davy was greeted by another 150 girls which necessitated around-the-clock police to keep the crowds moving.

The Monkees' London publicist could not even get into his office because girls were crowding every inch of the office in hopes that Davy would appear. Davy was forced to cancel his intended visit to Manchester to see his family. "There are so many girls camped outside the house," said Davy, "I had to arrange to see my family somewhere else." Davy spent a few days in London and then headed "for the hills" where he hoped to find some "peace and quiet."

Nesmith Leaves

As Davy arrived in London, fellow Monkee Mike Nesmith boarded a plane to return Stateside and Micky Dolenz, who had originally intended to leave London for the Continent, decided instead to remain in the city. He was on hand when Davy finally arrived at the hotel.

Peter Tork is the only Monkee who did not visit England. He spent his vacation in New York.

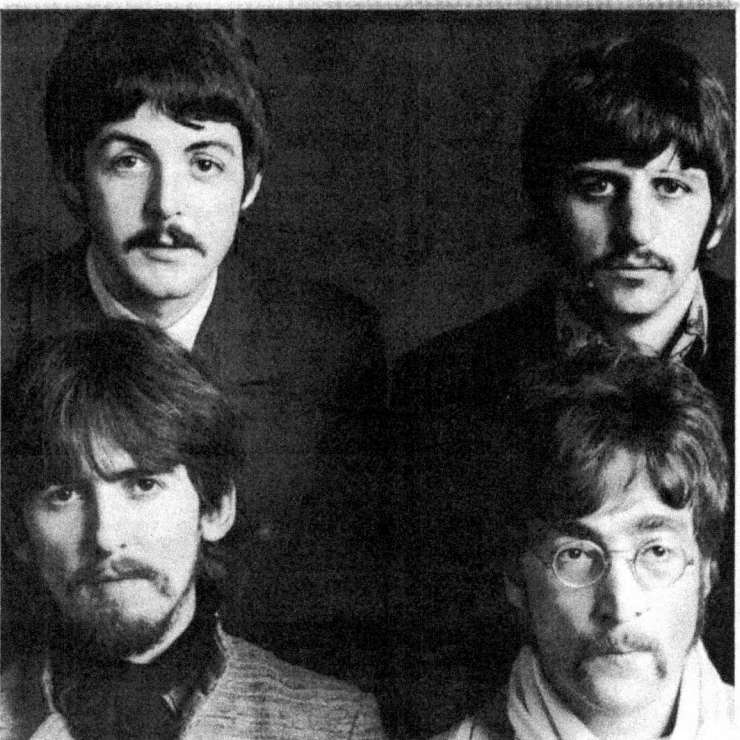

THE NEW LOOK for the Beatles — hair and more hair! Beatles, moustaches and all, will make third movie.

The Beatles Ink New Nine Year Recording Contract

The Beatles' manager, Brian Epstein, has signed a new nine year contract for the Beatles with EMI (Electric & Musical Industries, Ltd., which is the principal stockholder in Capitol Records).

In announcing the signing of the new contract, Capitol Records President, Alan Livingston, said: "We are, of course, extremely pleased to be able to continue our association with the group that has proved to be the most creative and talented foursome the recording industry has ever known.

"Since they were introduced to America, the Beatles have demonstrated that as performers and composers they have no peer. Their songs, besides earning the 'usual' Gold Records and starting industry-wide trends, have also established phenomenal sales records.

Unequalled

"For instance, 25% of all Gold Records awarded for singles by the RIAA have been earned by the Beatles. And, last year, every fourth Gold Record awarded by the RIAA for million dollar albums went to the Beatles. The overwhelming acceptance of their new single is evidence that this unmatched success will continue throughout 1967 and in years to come."

Capitol had received over one million orders for the new Beatle single, "Penny Lane/Strawberry Fields Forever," before it was ever released and, consequently, have asked the RIAA for certification of the single as a million-seller.

This will be the 22nd Gold Record earned by the Beatles. All previous Beatle million-sellers were qualified for Gold Records before being released, a sales feat no other recording group, American or foreign, has ever equalled. In fact, 22 certified Gold Records are more than any other artist has ever earned in the history of the record industry. Ten of the Beatles' Gold Records are for albums, 12 are for singles.

World's Record

The Beatles' first single, "I Want To Hold Your Hand," released in the U.S. in December, 1963 has, to date, sold over 4.5 million copies and their first album, "Meet The Beatles," is currently approaching the five million sales mark. The Beatles' total world sales figure now stands at 180 million records sold.

The Beatles' new contract came as a complete shock since Paul McCartney had recently admitted that he was "no longer one of the four mop-tops." McCartney went on to add that: "Now we're ready to go our own ways. We'll work together if we miss each other. Then it'll be hobby work. It's good for us to go it alone."

The word out of London was that the Beatles would not renew their contract with Brian Epstein when their present contract runs out. This, however, remains to be seen as there has been no official word on the subject.

PETER AND GORDON IN SEMI-SPLIT

Peter Asher and Gordon Waller announced in London last week that following their current American tour they will no longer be a full-time act.

In a joint statement to the press, Peter and Gordon said: "We shall get together once in a while when we feel like it — it's as simple as that. But basically, after our present U.S. tour, we are going our separate ways."

Peter will concentrate on becoming a record producer and will also spend part of his time managing his bookshop. Gordon will become a solo artist for Columbia and will make his first personal appearance minus Peter in British clubs this spring.

Inside the BEAT
LOVIN' SPOONFUL MEDICINE 2
MONKEES MEET BEATLES 5
SWITCHED ON FASHIONS 7

"I'M A VERY HAPPY MAN," said Davy following airport reception.

KRLA ARCHIVES

LOVIN' SPOONFUL
Washing The Bad Medicine On Down

By Louise Criscione

He stands 5'10" tall, has blue eyes, fair hair and digs Smokey Robinson, Diana Ross and Sophia Loren. His taste in clothes runs toward vests, bell bottom pants, striped shirts and suede boots. He writes the kind of songs which inevitably become hits and he despises canned orange juice. His name is John Sebastian and he's part of a Lovin' Spoonful.

He once worked as an undertaker's assistant but that lasted only a few days. He likes good microphones, fireplaces and the composing talent of Chuck Berry, Brian Wilson and Lennon/McCartney. If he had a choice he'd wear only comfortable clothes, striped shirts, flowered ties, suede jackets. His name is Joe Butler — the Spoonful beat.

For centuries, mothers everywhere have given their children a spoon full of sugar and water to help the bad-tasting medicine go down. In the southern part of the United States, this spoonful of sugar-water is known as "a lovin' spoonful" and in the 1920's Mississippi John Hurt recorded a song called "Coffee Blues" which has since become a classic in American folk music. The lyric of "Coffee Blues" is "I love my baby by the lovin' spoonful . . . by the lovin' spoonful . . . by the lovin' spoonful." The Delta Negroes borrowed the idiom of the spoonful of sugar-water to express the sweetness of their "good lovin'."

In early 1965, John Sebastian, Joe Butler, Zal Yanovsky and Steve Boone formed a group. Since every group must have a name, the four set out in search of a suitable name for their group—one which was just unique enough to be easily remembered. A friend suggested "The Lovin' Spoonful." And they've been known ever since by the phrase from Mississippi John Hurt's "Coffee Blues."

Good Time

They broke through the English-dominated pop charts with "Do You Believe In Magic?"—an entirely different sound from the hard, driving music which was everywhere. People said they sounded sort of happy-go-lucky and consequently took to calling Spoonful music "good time;" a throwback to earlier days.

With their longish hair and hip clothes, the Spoonful look like nothing but "now," belong to no other generation than today's. Their musical style has been imitated but never successfully duplicated. The Spoonful rank as one of the top American pop groups and are impossible to get to sit still together for more than two minutes.

John Sebastian, whether he admits it or not, is the head Spoonful. He was born in New York City on March 17, 1944, the son of John Sebastian, the world-famous harmonic virtuoso who is now living in Rome. John Sebastian (Spoonful) was raised in the Greenwich Village section of New York, except for two periods during his childhood when the Sebastian family resided in Italy. When he isn't on tour with the group, John lives in New York with his wife, Lorey, a New York journalist. Although all of the Spoonful are prolific writers, it is John who has composed the most Spoonful songs. He frequently handles the chore of lead-singing and also plays guitar, autoharp and harmonica.

Steve Boone is modest and definitely on the shy side – though he is quick to come forward when he's enthusiastic about something. Born in Camp Lejeune, North Carolina on September 23, 1943, Steve lived in several different parts of the U.S. during his childhood. An avid composer, Steve avoids the limelight by staying away from the microphone as much as possible while performing on stage.

Comic Approach

Zollie Yanovsky, or Zal if you prefer, is a favorite with audiences because of his comic approach to music. He was born in Toronto, Canada on December 19, 1944 where he spent his life until he turned 16. It was then that he left to travel to Israel to work on a kibbutz for a year. Returning to the States, he played with several folk groups during the time folk was beginning to pick up the influence of pop. Before joining the Spoonful, Zollie worked with Cass Elliott in a group called the Mugwumps.

Joe Butler, the beat behind the Spoonful, was born in Glen Cove, Long Island on September 16, 1943. He was the lead singer in several of the up-and-coming groups around Long Island before joining the Spoonful. Joe is particularly noted for two things: his drumming (which has acquired for him the title "Drummer of the Decade") and his personal warmth and charm. Besides playing drums, Joe also adds his talents on the autoharp and the kazoo. He sings lead on several of the Spoonful songs and now lives in an apartment in Manhattan.

These, then, are the four Lovin' Spoonful—busily making the bad-tasting pop sounds go down.

His friends call him "Stebun," he went to Suffolk College on Long Island. His favorite food is meat loaf; he's crazy about the Beatles, cars, music, blue jeans and leather jackets. He doesn't like cold weather and he digs the way Bob Dylan and Phil Spector write. He spends whatever free time he can invent (which isn't much) pursuing speed. His name is Steve Boone and he's one-fourth of the Lovin' Spoonful.

He has a name that makes people smile when they conquer it and stammer when the mispronounce it. He is a television fan but a movie addict and a student of Marvel Comic Books. He wears flowered ties and digs what he calls "Early Fop" clothes. His favorite singers are Fontella Bass, Smokey Robinson and Tim Hardin. He hates corned beef sandwiches on white bread. His name is Zalman Yanovsky — he's a Spoonful.

KRLA ARCHIVES

Their GREATEST

SONNY & CHER
International Fan Club
8560 Sunset Blvd.
Hollywood, Calif. 90028

KRLA ARCHIVES

Scene From The British Side

By Tony Barrow

MAMA CASS and P.J. PROBY—two stars who came from California to London and neither one is here to work!

Jim Proby would like to work but the authorities made him cancel an appearance in BBC Television's "Top Of The Pops." He was detained four hours at London Airport because he hadn't been granted a work permit. In the end they let him through as a vacationing tourist once he promised to refuse all offers of work during his stay. Proby still hopes to be granted a work permit so that he can pay off giant U.K. tax debts by TV and concert appearances.

Mama Cass came in much more quietly—although, by coincidence, she found herself on the same flight as Monkee MIKE NESMITH and his wife.

Cass is looking for an unfurnished house to rent in London until the end of June. Meanwhile she's been staying in a most expensive suite at Park Lane's plushy Dorchester. "BOAC are airfreighting about a ton of furniture for me," declared Cass as we lunched on *Lobster au gratin*.

Below her balcony about 100 cops held back demonstrating banner-carrying protesters—but it was nothing personal. The crowds had come to see Mr. Kosygin who was holding a Press Conference downstairs at the Dorchester as we lunched!

When I left she was trying to decide which of two luxury Mini Rolls cars to go and look at—one formerly owned by Peter Sellers (electric blue) or one which Brian Epstein had for sale (black). She's quite determined to bring home a Mini as well as a baby when she flies back to California in the summer!

★ ★ ★

30-minute TV Special filmed in London by THE FOUR TOPS previewed their new one "Bernadette"... MONKEE MICKY talking about PAUL McCARTNEY'S moustache: "One day I might grow one like it"...DUSTY SPRINGFIELD'S "I'll Try Anything" recorded in New York—but instrumental accompaniment was added in London studios!... Fastest-ever U.K. chart climber for PETULA CLARK—Chaplin's "This Is My Song"... When THE ANIMALS come to America in March ERIC BURDEN will be accompanied by 20-year-old Angie King, the girl he's known since 1965 and plans to marry later this year... Will PET CLARK star in "Finian's Rainbow" movie?... SPENCER DAVIS, MANFRED MANN, DEL SHANNON and DUANE EDDY latest Saville Theatre concert attractions lined up by Brian Epstein... MICKY on THE MONKEES' recording future: "We would like our next single to be an all-Monkee production"... PETER AND GORDON soloing after current American visit. Gordon has solo cabaret bookings and a single planned. Peter will concentrate on record production. Duo may make a limited number of records together and have said they will be willing to join up for future American tours together.

How much does a MONKEE earn each week? Would you believe 400 dollars?... BBC-TV "Top Of The Pops" show screened actual 53-year-old film sequence of fighter pilot Baron von Richtofen while ROYAL GUARDSMEN "Snoopy" single played... Herman: "I spent 400 dollars on a sporting gun but I don't like shooting things so I may trade it in for a motor bike"... MICK JAGGER taking legal action over remarks attributed to him in *News Of The World* drug-taking investigation... Album called "The Beatle Girls" by GEORGE MARTIN has nothing to do with Patti, Cyn, Mo and Jane. Title refers to George's orchestral arrangements of songs like "Anna," "Michelle" and "Eleanor Rigby"... At London's Roundhouse during pop Happening designer Mike Lesser wriggled stark naked through scarcely-set remains of a 60 gallon jelly!

BEAT Photo: Courtesy of RCA Victor

"YOU MEAN YOU were mobbed at the London Airport?" asks Micky.

Beatles Stage Happening With Monkee, Stones . . .

By Tony Barrow

41 of Britain's most accomplished classical musicians wearing formal evening dress, false noses, assorted king-size sun shades and other good-humoured embellishments.

20 or 30 lean, luverly mini-skirted and trouser-suited birds wandering at random amongst the massive orchestra.

Two dedicated young men with powerful projectors throwing onto the walls a series of curiously colored "oil slides."

DONOVAN and his mate GIPSY DAVE lighting hand-held sparklers. MONKEE MIKE NESMITH meeting recording manager GEORGE MARTIN and each exchanging words of praise about each other's diverse artistries.

MARIANNE FAITHFULL pouring a fresh cup of sparkling champagne for MICK JAGGER when the supply of regular champagne glasses ran out. MANFRED KLAUS VOORMANN and his wife Christine decorating two large balloons with Crazy Foam from a spray pack.

KEITH RICHARD taking movie-making lessons from a professional cameraman. PATTI HARRISON and CYNTHIA LENNON chatting with two (female) cousins of PAUL McCARTNEY.

These were some of the basic ingredients for a Beatles Happening which was held on a February Friday evening at the huge No. 1 studio of E.M.I. Records in St. John's Wood, London.

There were two excellent reasons for the holding of the Happening. The Beatles were using for the first time ever a 41-piece orchestra to add extra instrumental accompaniment to one of their new album tracks. At the same time they were creating the first film sequences which will be used in the 60-minute TV Special they are making to coincide with the international release of the album.

The Beatles are acting as their own TV directors for the project. In the studio were at least seven hand-held movie cameras, two used by professional cameramen while the rest were available for impromptu use by any of the forty assembled guests. Ringo, Mick, Keith and Klaus were amongst the impromptu users.

To increase the fun-atmosphere and the visual glamour of the occasion everyone had been invited to wear the brightest available gear. Indeed it bordered upon Fancy Dress.

Everything was accomplished with remarkable speed, the session lasting from eight until eleven in the evening. Paul perched himself on a tall stool in front of the orchestra and conducted. John and George hurried to and fro making last-minute suggestions. Ringo used reel after reel of 16 mm movie. Ten brilliant arc-lamps played down on everyone from high places, bathing the whole Happening in as many different colors. A balloon burst in the middle of Take 3. Paul's telephone on the conductor's rostrum rang loudly in the middle of Take 4.

At the stroke of eleven the 41 musicians, all good union guys, wrapped up their instruments, stripped off various false noses, bald-scalps and so forth.

"No, I really enjoyed it actually," said a serious-looking but convinced violinist.

"We'll get extra money for the filming, you know," declared a horn player.

"Now we'll do the choir bit," shouted John, rounding up birds and boys and gathering them round a couple of mike booms. Ten arc-lamps followed the crowd.

"I'll count you all in each time," started Paul. "Klaus will give you the notes on the piano. Klaus? You ready?"

The choir bits were put on tape. Beatles and selected guests wandered off to join George Martin in the control room. Play-back time. Each Beatle satisfied. Eleven-thirty.

"Pity you can't edit in the voices now," sighed John.

"Bag Of Nails tonight or Scotch Of St. James?" asked Paul.

"We're going home," said George and he took Patti away.

"Try the Bag first, eh?" decided Ringo.

"Goodnight, gentlemen," from George Martin.

The Bag Of Nails was too crowded and nobody had booked a table. We all finished up in a comparatively deserted Scotch Of St. James.

But everything was anti-climax after that fantastic studio Happening. There's never been a Beatles session like it. There's never been a session like it.

You'll hear the resulting track when The Beatles release their album in the Spring.

GENE PITNEY MARRIED DURING REMO FESTIVAL

SAN REMO, ITALY—Gene Pitney took time out from his fourth consecutive appearance at the annual San Remo Song Festival to marry his high school girlfriend, Lynne Gayton.

The couple was married in the picturesque church of San Giovanni Batista in Ospedaletti, near San Remo, by Father Galomo di Gwiaomo. Garry Sherman served as Gene's best man and Sherman's wife, Marie, attended Lynne as Matron of Honor. More than 70 photographers from all over the world crowded into the church to witness the ceremony and at its conclusion the newlyweds were mobbed by enthusiastic and well-wishing townspeople.

The bride, a pretty 5'4½" redhead with blue eyes was married in a street-length dress of Alencon lace on French net over a skirt of ivory re-embroidery. The A-line silhouette was finished with a bateau neckline and bishop sleeves and double peau de soie bow in the back. She wore a bouffant veil of imported silk illusion held in place by a wreath of silk peau de soie roses and carried a prayer book and a bouquet of matching, fresh-cut blossoms.

The wedding party then boarded Pitney's chartered yacht, the Odyssia, and set sail on a two-hour sea cruise prior to the final Festival performance that evening. The Pitney yacht and the dock at which it was berthed in the San Remo harbor was crowded with sightseers during the day and far into the night.

It's rather ironic that Gene Pitney is an international star—more revered abroad than Stateside. Italy has become a second home to Gene so it came as no surprise that he decided to be married there.

Immediately following the San Remo Festival and a brief personal appearance tour, Gene began work on his first motion picture which was created around a storyline based on one of the songs he performed at the Festival.

Gene's schedule also calls for a lengthy personal appearance tour in England, where his name is a household word. These activities, of course, rule out the possibility of an early honeymoon for the Pitneys but the couple have promised themselves to have one at the first opportunity.

VENTURES TO INDONESIA

While Gene Pitney takes care of American popularity in Europe, the Ventures hold down the Far Eastern front.

So popular, in fact that the Indonesian Government has asked the Ventures to perform in a series of concerts throughout Indonesia.

MQCB = 1 ON THE CHARTS. DJ's ACCLAIM QUINTETTE CLUB AS GREATEST REVELATION IN THE MUSIC WORLD!

KRLA ARCHIVES

The Minis are Here!

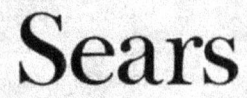

UP is where the hemlines are juniors and junior petites...
mini-dresses
FREE the Knees

14.99

Get the London Look! It's here now in the clipped hem; caper-legging it your way! Slide into a slinky shift or shirtdress ... have the knack in a knit. We've got all the Swingers! Get them in sassy stripes, impact solids, dazzle dots and high intensity prints. Junior and Junior Petite sizes 5-13. Shake a leg; Come to Sears!

CHARGE IT
on Sears Revolving Charge

FREE
Discount Coupon for
TEEN-AGE FAIR

Come in to Sears for your FREE Discount Coupon worth 50¢ on the $2 entrance fee to TEEN-AGE FAIR. See the Psychedelic Fashion Show at Sears BUG OUT.

ALL ROADS LEAD TO  SOUTHERN CALIFORNIA STORES
SEARS, ROEBUCK AND CO.

SHOP 6 NIGHTS
SHOP MONDAY THRU SATURDAY
9:30 A.M. TO 9:30 P.M.

KRLA ARCHIVES

TROUSERS — From Aztec to Paisley, they're wild!

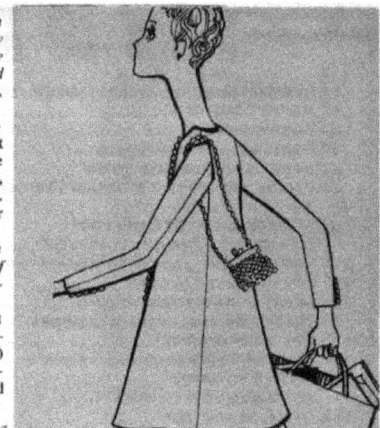

TRESSES — If they aren't long, they're short, curly!

- Sideburns or "sidies" are getting longer for everyone. Let 'em grow slightly, or exaggerate them, like the drawing at left.
- Turtleneck sweaters spell English and under a jacket are a great change from the drab shirt-coat look. Besides, gals love them.
- Slacks are louder, brighter, splashier than ever before, with Aztec prints, African prints and paisleys around the corner for Spring wear.
- Pop stars and hippies have hit on a good-looking combination: cord trousers with a velour coat the same color — blue, orange, gold, etc.
- The latest pullover shirts are showing side vents and wide spread collars.
- If you want a real change, trim your hair down to Mia Farrow length, but ultra-curl it like the drawing at right. It's the up and coming thing, the most delicate, feminine style around.
- Spectacles are in the news today — round, oval, square. Most popular utility style is tortoise shell. For groovy accessories, Monkeeshades are catching on. Next issue in BEAT, look for where to get them.
- Twiggies are the latest thing in England — named after Twiggy, of course. They are bottom eyelashes, painstakingly painted on.
- Carry the left over articles that won't fit in a tiny handbag (anything larger than six inches is out) in a straw or briefcase-type satchel. Also add books, lunches and kitchen sinks.

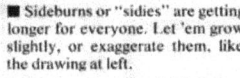

Switching On

Although they're not widespread among young adults, paper dresses *are* a happening thing. And the name most closely connected to the world of paper clothes is Judy Brewer. The young designer's shop in Beverly Hills has had such distinguished visitors as the Supremes, Carol Jones, Mrs. Steve McQueen, Phyllis Diller and Gypsy Rose Lee.

Decorated ala' hippy, Judy's shop has psychedelic mirrors, earrings made out of everything including wrapping paper, clothes hanging all over the walls and a guest book for customers or browsers to sign.

Judy came up with the idea for paper dresses while still in college. "Part of my master thesis was Fashions in the Future," says Judy, "wood, metal, foil, paper." Paper! And, thus, we have the paper dress.

"Paper is no more of a fire hazard than any kind of cloth," says Judy in answer to the accusation that paper dresses are a definite fire hazard — an accusation which made all the newspapers.

Another false theory concerning the paper clothes is that after one wear they are no longer of any value and must be discarded. Not so, says Judy. "You can wear them from five to 20 times, depending on what you're going to do. I have some that are three-years-old," she admitted.

Despite the fact that many teens feel they're trend-setters in fashion, Judy disagrees: "I think teens are reluctant to accept new styles."

Besides dresses made of every conceivable type of paper, Judy also stocks silk dresses, "invisible" raincoats, cloth dresses and hats. Her prices range from $12 on up.

Her advice to young people interested in going into fashion designing is simple: "Take any job you can get but it's always wise to go with a well-known label because you want to get experience."

One parting fact about paper clothes, says Judy, is that "if you ever tear a paper dress while you're out on a date you can always tape it back together!"

Touche to all the skeptics.

GLIMMERING SILVER — This paper dress sparkles like tin foil.

BABY DOLL LOOK — Created by rows of ruffles in light orange.

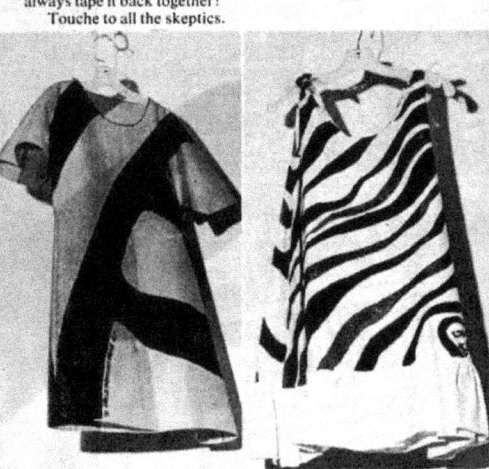

JUDY'S PAPER DRESSES are no more flammable than any other type of clothes.

MONKEE SHIRTS — Since our article about the Monkee clothiers, we've received numerous requests for "where to buy" information. Monkee shirts as shown above are available at Lenny's Boot Parlor, 1448 Gower St., Hollywood, California. Proprietor Lenny Able will send a catalog upon request. Mail orders are filled promptly. We've been seeing Monkee shirts on girls, by the way, and they're great.

TWIGGY — Though she doesn't consider herself a successor to Jean Shrimpton, England's Twiggy is the most photographed model of the day. Petite, 17 years old and 90 pounds, she has been described as the only girl who can make a man's suit look feminine. Her secret is her eyes — tiny, painted on bottom lashes, called Twiggies. It takes two hours to put them on.

KRLA ARCHIVES

Top 40 Requests

1. PENNY LANE/STRAWBERRY FIELDS FOREVER ..... Beatles
2. HAPPY TOGETHER ..... Turtles
3. RUBY TUESDAY ..... Rolling Stones
4. DARLING, BE HOME SOON ..... Lovin' Spoonful
5. 59TH STREET BRIDGE SONG ..... Harpers Bizarre
6. I HAD TOO MUCH TO DREAM LAST NIGHT ..... Electric Prunes
7. KIND OF A DRAG ..... Buckinghams
8. DEDICATED TO THE ONE I LOVE ..... Mamas and Papas
9. SIT DOWN, I THINK I LOVE YOU ..... Mojo Men
10. LOVE IS HERE AND NOW YOU'RE GONE ..... Supremes
11. FOR WHAT IT'S WORTH ..... Buffalo Springfield
12. BABY, I NEED YOUR LOVING ..... Johnny Rivers
13. THEN YOU CAN TELL ME GOODBY ..... Casinos
14. UPS AND DOWNS ..... Raiders
15. KIND OF A HUSH/NO MILK TODAY ..... Herman's Hermits
16. EPISTLE TO DIPPY ..... Donovan
17. ROCK AND ROLL GYPSIES ..... Hearts and Flowers
18. LITTLE BLACK EGG ..... Night Crawlers
19. ACAPULCO GOLD ..... Rainy Daze
20. RETURN OF THE RED BARON ..... Royal Guardsmen
21. PRETTY BALLERINA ..... Left Banke
22. LET'S FALL IN LOVE ..... Peaches and Herb
23. AIN'T GOT NOTHING YET ..... Blues Magoos
24. I'M A BELIEVER ..... Monkees
25. GIMME SOME LOVIN' ..... Spencer Davis Group
26. NO FAIR AT ALL ..... Association
27. MY CUP RUNNETH OVER ..... Ed Ames
28. MISTER FARMER ..... Seeds
29. YOU GOT TO ME ..... Neil Diamond
30. STAND BY ME ..... Spyder Turner
31. SO, YOU WANT TO BE A ROCK AND ROLL STAR ..... Byrds
32. WHAT'S THAT GOT TO DO WITH ME ..... Jim and Jean
33. 98.6 ..... Keith
34. MUSIC TO WATCH GIRLS BY ..... Bob Crewe Generation
35. MORINGTOWN RIDE ..... Seekers
36. THE LOVE I SAW IN YOU WAS JUST A MIRAGE ..... Miracles
37. THE BEAT GOES ON ..... Sonny and Cher
38. TELL IT LIKE IT IS ..... Aaron Neville
39. SHOW ME ..... Joe Tex
40. LIVE ..... Merry-Go-Round

By Pen

The following letter was written to KRLA's Program Director, Dick Moreland from a San Gabriel Valleyite:

"Dear Sir: Being born in L.A. 43 years ago I feel it is my duty to write this letter. Why do we have to listen to that noise and lamenting groans they call MUSIC? Now I know this is your living but for all of us that like real MUSIC that hog calling is on every station and it has gotten worse since they tried to mix the Beatle version in. Lately everybody is a hillbilly . . . you know if they were a little bit funny it wouldn't be so bad but even then it stinks. I love children and it hurts me to think that some day they might forget good music altogether.

Please again forgive me and let me know if you share any of my feelings. Say hello to Bob Dylan for me and tell him I just purchased a 10 ton Chevy flat bed truck to haul the wig if we do make a deal also there will be room for the DC3, if he will help me pull the wings off so we won't have to get a highway travel permit. We can take the back roads to San Gabriel. Answer this letter if you get a minute. Thanks, Bill Hebert, Rosemead Blvd., San Gabriel."

"O.K. Bill and right" says Dick Moreland. . .slowly trying to digest the clear meaning of one more listener's request.

The Spats Dig The Beat

Dear BEAT,

Here's some photos I thought you might be interested in seeing. It's the Spats taken in our backyard one Sunday afternoon when we spent two hours having a fab time interviewing them and taking photos.

As you can see, they really dig the KRLA Beat. They had all my copies from the past two years out in the yard looking through them. They're really great guys.

A loyal subscriber, Ann Irvine

Come to the Sears Psychedelic Bug Out

at the

Teen Age Fair

March 17-26 at the Hollywood Palladium

Play the Bug Out Game... win prizes! See the first Psychedelic Fashion Show. Learn a new Bug Dance. While you are there register for the free membership in the Sears Teen Record Club.

FREE Membership
Members are entitled to 10% off the regular price of any Sears Top 10 single record every week of the year.

50¢ OFF $2 Entrance Fee at The Teen Age Fair Discount coupons are available now at all Sears Jr. Bazaar and Student Shops.

ICE HOUSE GLENDALE
234 So. Brand Ave.—Reservations: 245-5043

HELD OVER THRU MARCH 13

The Nitty Gritty Dirt Band
with their new Liberty LP album "The Nitty Gritty Dirt Band" and their new hit single "Buy For Me The Dawn" b/w "Candy Man"

— Plus —

Lee Mallory
introducing his new hit single on Valiant

"Take My Hand" b/w "Love Song"

ICE HOUSE PASADENA
24 No. Mentor—Reservations: 681-9942

Feb. 28 thru March 26

Bud Dashiell
(formerly of Bud & Travis)
And Friends

KRLA ARCHIVES

Casey's 'Shebang' Returns At Night And In Color

One of the most popular teenage shows in television history, *Shebang*, has returned to the television tubes at its new, more convenient time, 7:30 P.M. in *Color*.

Although KTLA received over 2,000 cards and letters in addition to over three dozen petitions, each averaging over 1,000 names, the station manager held returning the show until the best possible time period could be had. Now that this has become reality, "Shebang" is now back with many new added and interesting features.

Each show includes an artist performing one of his top hits from the "Shebang Scrapbook of Stars." This artist library of actual performances in color is the only one in the world. Every top recording star that has visited "Shebang," has been preserved on tape and will be seen each Monday night.

Outstanding features from both the past and the present will also be featured which include the "1966 Beatle Visit To Los Angeles," a color film to be seen in four segments during the first four shows, and "The Complete Story of the Monkees," a collection of music, color pictures and film.

To continue in the same "Shebang" tradition, each week, in person, one of the nation's top recording stars will visit the show and perform at least two of their top records.

Two new innovations to the show are a "How-To-Do" portion in which viewers will be taught the latest dance steps and some refreshers on others they may have forgotten and want to brush up on as well as the biggest innovation, the introduction of the free membership cards in "The Shebang Set."

Anyone is eligible to become a charter member simply by sending a self addressed, stamped envelope to Shebang Membership Card, KTLA, Hollywood, 90028. Each card will be numbered and a record of each will be kept in the Shebang Office.

Ten times during the show, cardholders numbers will be flashed on the screen and if the cardholder is watching, and within a 24-hour period, calls in the special members number and identifies the cardholder and the number, they will win every record played on the show. There will be ten cardholder winners on each "Shebang" show.

"Shebang" has as its host, by popular demand, Casey Kasem, and is broadcast from the world's largest television soundstage where over a hundred young adults enjoy dancing to the current hits of the day. Each Monday night, "Shebang" will host in person, three times as many guests than any other current dance show.

As with the daytime "Shebang," Bob Barnett will continue to produce the show.

Tickets are available on a first-come basis and can be obtained by writing to: Shebang Tickets, KTLA, Hollywood, 90028.

Free Records From RC Cola And Capitol

Royal Crown Cola and Capitol Records have come up with a unique promotion that will prove to be of particular interest to teenagers in Los Angeles as well as the rest of the country.

RC is offering a collection of Capitol's top 'teen-oriented albums by such artists as The Beatles, Beach Boys, Lou Rawls, Peter & Gordon, Nancy Wilson, The Seekers, The Outsiders to RC buyers free with the purchase of any other 'teen or adult LP at the regular price of $3.98. In other words, you buy one at the regular price and get the other for nothing. Two albums, which normally sell for $3.98 or more *each*, will both come to you, and you've spent only $3.98, or $4.98 if you want stereo.

All you have to do is make it into the nearest supermarket or drugstore that sells RC Cola and buy a six-pack.

Check out the RC/Capitol supplement that comes with it. It lists more than 100 of the best albums around. Pick one—say "Best of The Beach Boys"—then pick another, say "Rubber Soul" by The Beatles, and you've got two LPs for the price of one!

The albums, by the way, are all best-sellers. They're not the usual albums (the ones that don't sell) you find in promotions of this type. Nearly a dozen of the albums available have already earned Gold Records for sales in excess of $1 million.

Warner Bros. unlocks all the doors of the sensation-filled best seller.

It's like you're running a big city... a unique empire... a private world with a do-not-disturb sign on every door...

HOTEL

Starring ROD TAYLOR
CATHERINE SPAAK · KARL MALDEN · MELVYN DOUGLAS · RICHARD CONTE · MICHAEL RENNIE
KEVIN McCARTHY and MERLE OBERON as "The Duchess" Original Music by Johnny Keating
Based on the novel by Arthur Hailey · Written for the Screen and Produced by WENDELL MAYES
Directed by RICHARD QUINE TECHNICOLOR® FROM WARNER BROS.

EXCLUSIVE ENGAGEMENT
NOW PLAYING! PACIFIC'S HOLLYWOOD **PANTAGES**
HOLLYWOOD BLVD. at VINE Crossroad of the Stars!
HO. 9-7161

CAN YOU DIG IT?
GLAMOUR & SOUL RETURN TO THE SUNSET STRIP

NOW APPEARING THRU MARCH 5th

THE MOTOWN SOUND OF **MARVIN GAYE** PLUS THE RAGLETS

NEXT — THE FIFTH DIMENSIONS

CIRO'S

8433 SUNSET BLVD.

DINING & DANCING TILL 2 A.M.

ALL AGES WELCOME
FOR RESERVATIONS: 654-6650

KRLA ARCHIVES

IF YOU CAN'T BELIEVE YOUR EYES .... LISTEN!

MERCURY RECORDS / MG·21111 / SR·61111

MERCURY RECORDS / MG·21112 / SR·61112

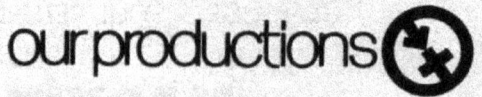

6290 SUNSET BOULEVARD, LOS ANGELES, CALIFORNIA 90028

KRLA ARCHIVES

Pop Artists Score Grammy Nominations

The finalists for the 1966 Grammy Awards have been announced and, surprisingly enough, quite a few pop artists have made it into this year's nominations.

The Mama's and Papa's, the Association, the Beatles, the New Vaudeville Band, the Beach Boys and the Sandpipers are among the pop artists nominated for Grammy Awards—the Record industry's equivalent to the motion picture Academy Awards.

Frank Sinatra and the Beatles top the nomination list with seven apiece and last year's big winner, Herb Alpert, won five nominations this time around.

Record Of Year

The Record of the Year category consists of "Almost Persuaded" by David Houston, "Monday, Monday" by the Mama's and Papa's, "Stranger In The Night" by Frank Sinatra, "What Now My Love" by Herb Alpert and the Tijuana Brass and "Winchester Cathedral" by the New Vaudeville Band.

Nominees for Album of the Year are "Color Me Barbra" by Barbra Streisand, "Dr. Zhivago (Soundtrack)" by Maruice Jarre, "Revolver" by the Beatles, "Sinatra: A Man And His Music" by Frank Sinatra and "What Now My Love" by Herb Alpert and the TJB.

In the running for Song of the Year (a composer's award) are "Born Free" by John Barry, "The Impossible Dream" by Mitch Leigh and Joe Darion, "Michelle" by John Lennon and Paul McCartney, "Somewhere My Love" by Paul Francis Webster and Maurice Jarre, "Strangers In The Night" by Bert Kaempfert, Charles Singleton and Eddie Snyder.

Sandy Posey, Barbra Streisand, Ella Fitzgerald, Eydie Gorme and Nancy Sinatra are all up for the Best Vocal Performance by a female while David Houston, Jim Reeves, Paul McCartney, Jack Jones, Andy Williams and Frank Sinatra are the nominees for Best Vocal Performance by a male.

Four of the five nominees in the Best Performance by a Vocal Group category are pop artists. The Association are in the running with "Cherish," the Beach Boys with "Good Vibrations," the Sandpipers with "Guantanamera" and the Mama's and Papa's with "Monday, Monday."

Bill Cosby and Mrs. Miller are two of the nominees for Best Comedy Performance. Bill for his "Wonderfulness" album and Mrs. Miller for "Downtown."

The Best Contemporary (R&R) Recording category lines up with "Cherish" by the Association, "Eleanor Rigby" by the Beatles, "Good Vibrations" by the Beach Boys, "Last Train To Clarksville" by the Monkees, "Monday, Monday" by the Mama's and Papa's and "Winchester Cathedral" by the New Vaudeville Band.

Nominees in the Best Contemporary (R&R) Solo Vocal Performance category are Sandy Posey for "Born A Woman," Paul McCartney for "Eleanor Rigby," Bobby Darin for "If I Were A Carpenter," Nancy Sinatra for "These Boots Are Made For Walking" and Dusty Springfield for "You Don't Have To Say You Love Me."

Pop Everywhere

The Best Contemporary (R&R) Group Performance category is made up of "Cherish" by the Association, "Good Vibrations" by the Beach Boys, "Guantanamera" by the Sandpipers, "Last Train To Clarksville" by the Monkees and "Monday, Monday" by the Mama's and Papa's.

Ray Charles, James Brown, Lou Rawls, Stevie Wonder, Percy Sledge, the Capitols, Ramsey Lewis, Sam & Dave, James and Bobby Purify and King Curtis are all nominees in the rhythm and blues categories.

In the category of Best Album Cover (Photography) some of the nominees are Bob Dylan's "Blond On Blond," the Sandpipers' "Guantanamera," the Byrds' "Turn, Turn, Turn" and Herb Alpert's "What Now My Love."

The Beatles' "Revolver" is one of the nominees for Best Album Cover (Graphic Arts) as is Barbra Streisand's "Color Me Barbra."

Ted Bluechel—The Ice Cream Suits And Licks

By Rochelle Reed

(Editor's Note: This is the fourth in a series of interviews with all members of the Association. Next week—Jim)

Fans look at him and call him "the handsome one." The Association, who supposedly know him better, have named him the "Pig."

Ted Bluechel is a little of both. With a face that is innocently handsome, he appeared for his interview wearing a white tee shirt decorated with huge chartreuse polka dots and other suitable attire. It would be fun, but not quite fair, to label him a handsome Pig.

Since the Association voted to drop their identical suits onstage, Ted assures the world that it's "getting a more honest image. But we'll keep the suits for more suitable occasions. We have a best one for really special things, though. It's an ice cream suit—a cheap one but you get your licks."

If you're the groaning type, you may not realize that to Ted "the highest form of humor is the pun. You can go up to someone you don't even know and establish a form of communication."

Launches Career

If the person thinks puns are the lowest form of humor, however, Ted says he can go the same way as people who don't like the Association: "If he refuses to see what we're laying on him, then okay, fine... man, that's his scene. There's no right or wrong."

Ted launched his musical career in high school as a classical drummer in the band. He even won first chair in the All Southern California High School Concert Band. But Ted quit classical drumming in his senior year when a minor rule infraction and petty politics stripped him of a state award. So Ted decided to make the college scene.

School books lasted until his 4th year, when a group named the Cherry Hill Singers lured him away from a degree. Then he became part of an early Association happening at a Hollywood club and voila! instant Ted, the Associate.

The Association describes Ted as a "clean, methodical drummer" and he asserts that this stems from his classical career. "Drumming has to be done rhymically," he says, "it can't be done melodically. I sort of passed a test within myself on 'Love Rushing In' which we just finished cutting. I play an old jungle beat while the song has a Mersey beat."

Never Solos

Ted never solos because "there just hasn't come an appropriate time. We do a vocal type thing. I don't do a solo just to do it—mainly because I'm to humble. To me, everything is a solo."

Everyone, according to Ted, is also a solo, an individual, to be taken alone. An articulate person, Ted remains quiet until he knows you, then pours out his thoughts in rushing streams.

If Ted is handsome, he distains it. "Male is female and female is male in the total sense," he explains. "I don't believe in the big ego-type thing—you know, the masculine, muscular he man. Where is the real he man without his muscles and good looks?"

In other words, Ted prefers to accept a person for his sum worth, and not his looks or clothes.

Wants Freedom

Ted maintains this unmaterialistic outlook towards his own life when he proclaims "freedom and happiness, that's what I'm aiming for..."

But before we relate Ted's example of true freedom and happiness, it's only fair to warn you that it's partially what earned him the nickname of Pig.

"I had five pet rats," he explains. "I bought one at a fair and it turned out to be a pregnant female, but I didn't know it at the time. So I let it run free. It ate a hole in the couch and lived there, had babies, and all of them grew up. I gave three away and kept two. I never said 'no' to them, always let them run free.

"They're groovy. I let them run anywhere they wanted to. We could communicate...if I was really uptight, they wouldn't come around, but if I was really happy, they'd come over to me and we'd freak out.

"Now I keep them in a cage (he was forced to get rid of the couch). I feel really paranoic about it. They sit up in the cage and look at me. But, you see, they proved there is a form of communication between worlds. They're really happy, warm. They just feel it in the air and freak out!"

Freak Out!

"Freak out," says Ted, is a commandment of his inner voice. "Life isn't that serious to me, yet."

Which doesn't mean that Ted couldn't care less about what goes on. He has definite ideas on everything from the Kennedy assassination ("It was a huge conspiracy") to transmigration of souls ("Christ makes references to a previous life").

Honest Image

People talk about Ted as the Associate who has changed the least since the group received their measure of success. Whether or not it's true, Ted Bluechel, from his polka dot tee shirt to his caged rats, presents "an honest image." He left our office proclaiming "Go ye therefore and multiply!"

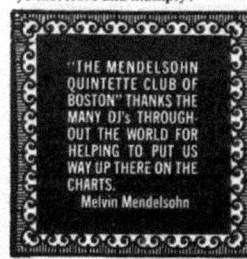

"THE MENDELSOHN QUINTETTE CLUB OF BOSTON" THANKS THE MANY DJ's THROUGHOUT THE WORLD FOR HELPING TO PUT US WAY UP THERE ON THE CHARTS.

Melvin Mendelsohn

KRLA ARCHIVES

On the BEAT
By Louise Criscione

Micky Dolenz, Davy Jones and Mike Nesmith certainly have made an impression on England during their recent vacation there. Micky was the first Monkee to land on British soil and the press lost no time in hunting him down for interviews. English or American, they're all the same and so, naturally, the first thing the British press wanted to know was whether or not the Monkees can play their own instruments. Speaking frankly, Micky said what he'd said a hundred times before — no the Monkees did not play on all their records but yes they *can* play their own instruments and yes from now on they *will* do all the instrumental tracks for their records to halt this ridiculous controversy.

As you know, Davy was mobbed at the airport and was unable to visit his family in Manchester because his fans had his house staked out. So, he arranged to meet his family elsewhere. Mike was impressed by the city of London but felt that it is too steeped in its own tradition. Peter was the only Monkee who did not go to England; he spent his time off in New York.

What a nice surprise it was to see so many pop artists in the running for Grammy Awards this year. Of course, it will be even nicer if they *win* some awards since top 40 music has been considered by many to be an illegitimate offspring of "true music."

It was Petula Clark who finally knocked the Monkees off their top spot on the British charts with her beautiful "This Is My Song." Pet, who always has something going, has now been signed for her own television series on the BBC. She's set to spend the major part of the spring and summer here in the U.S. doing personal appearances, club dates and television shows. Movie-wise, the petite international star has been offered a role in the up-coming film version of "Finian's Rainbow" but has not yet decided whether or not she will take it.

. . . MICKEY DOLENZ

QUICK ONES: Herman and the Hermits have been signed to headline a one-hour television special, "Go," to be seen over the ABC-TV network on April 23 . . . The Righteous Brothers, who attract sell-out crowds no matter where they play, are set to appear at the Cocoanut Grove . . . Everything seems to be coming up wonderfulness for the "I Spy" brothers. The show has been renewed for its third season, it picked up a Golden Globe Award for most popular television series, Cosby is set to cut his next album during his stint at Harrah's and it won't be too surprising if Bob Culp wins an Emmy for his "Warlord" script and performance . . . P. J. Proby has filed for bankruptcy . . . Don and the Goodtimes are scheduled for the Dick Clark tour beginning March 25 along with Neil Diamond, Tommy Roe and Keith . . . the Raiders are set for Minnesota and Pennsylvania in March and Michigan and Ohio and Colorado in April . . . the Turtles have changed bass players once again — this time Chip Douglas is leaving to go the producing route and is being replaced by Jim Ponce.

The Daily Flash caused quite a sensation during their stand at New York's Ondine. Lines ran all the way down the block and around the corner and members of such pop groups as the Monkees, Raiders and Animals all made it in to see the Flash.

NEWS IN THE SOUL WORLD: The Supremes are going to do college tours . . . James Brown offered to buy a Los Angeles club rather than pay $140 for three bottles of champagne.

. . . DIANA ROSS

CLASSIFIEDS

BEAT is beginning a classified column, designed to buy, sell, find, lose, trade, give, announce, notify, warn, or say whatever you wish.

Ads will be accepted for just about anything, including

for sale — wanted — pen pals
fan clubs — announcements — personals
lost guys and gals — special notices — everything else

Prices are cheap! Only 20c a word for classifieds and a mere 10c a word for personal messages (from you to someone else without an item for sale, trade, etc. involved).

Now, what's a word? Well, it's the usual thing plus two exceptions: the city and the state count as only one word (Hollywood, California) and the number and street (6290 Sunset Blvd.) are only one word.

Send all advertisements (clearly printed or typed) along with the correct amount of money to:

Classifieds
BEAT Publications
6290 Sunset Blvd.   Suite 504
Hollywood, California 90028

Paul Revere and the Raiders Strike Again!
with

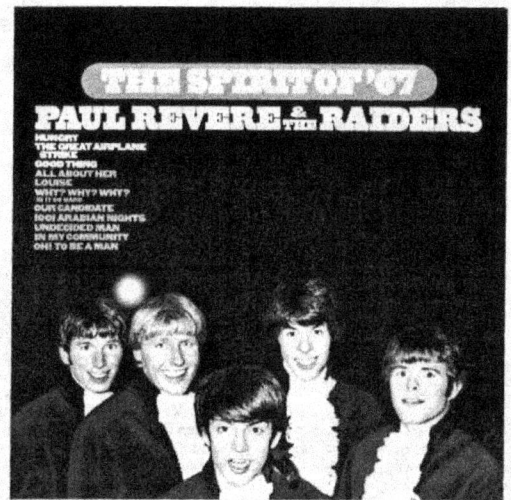

The Spirit of '67
CL 2595   CL 9395

JUST LIKE US
CL 2451   CL 9351

MIDNIGHT RIDE
CL 2508   CS 9305

HERE THEY COME
CL 2307   CS 9107

Be Sure To Get Their New Single—
"Ups and Downs" 4-44018

the NOW Sound
On COLUMBIA RECORDS

Available at your favorite record shop.

KRLA ARCHIVES

SHIRLEY
By Shirley Poston

Do you fancy yourself (I allus do iffen I think there's a man within ten miles, honey) ... well, now that I've completely blown the first paragraph, let's get to work on the second.

Do you fancy yourself a member of that collection of rare birds known as Show-Must-Go-On-People (and otherwise known as masochists)? You know the ones. Someone wrote a song about them once ... there's *no* people like show-must-go-*on* people like *no* people I know... hmmm, that isn't quite it. (Maybe it will come to me later.)

Nothing's Changed

Anyshow, I've fancied *myself* to be one of those aforementioned people since I was five years old! (Course, I couldn't spell masochist then.) (I know, I know, nothing has changed.)

Except my mind, that is. (Which leads one to believe that very *little* has changed.)

Until two weeks ago, my attitude toward my work (writing this mess *is* work, you know) (so, they tell me, is reading it) was nauseatingly saint-like.

I felt that *nothing* would keep me from writing this column except two thingies. One—Getting fired. Two—getting a net clapped over me. (Both are possible.) (Not to mention *probable*.) But nothing *else*, including snow, sleet and hail (as in the gang's all here), would ever keep Postmanly Poston from her appointed rounds. (I prefer Melba.)

In fact, I always rather hoped something would just *dare* try and make me miss a deadline. Can't you just see it all now?

Sloshing her way through Hurricane Herbert (?), dodging nuclear warheads, pursued by wolves (four-legged) (am-day), her anemic countenance covered by a sudden coat of red paint sprayed by a hovering Goodyear blimp (come to the *ween*dow,) somes good olde Shirl, with next issue's column clutched triumphantly in her remaining hand.

That's how I used to picture it. Than I got the flu.

Not the ordinary flu. The rootin'-tootin'-sonofagunfromArizona-Ragtime-Cowboy-flu!

I don't mean to bore you (not to mention *digust* you) with the gory details of my intimate biological functions, but to say I was bedfellows-with-the-bowl is putting it *mildly*.

For the first three delirious days of feeling like I'd swallowed a live goat, I didn't know a deadline from a doorknob. However, on the fourth day, I found myself still too sick to write but well enough to worry. And I had plenty to worry about, because that was the day my writty was due.

Mental Vivids

I tell you, I tried *everything*. I conjured up vivid mental pictures of the aforementioned Postmanly Postum. I crawled to the typewriter and pecked dizzily. I even made my brother play "Onward Christian Soldiers" on his harmonica. But nothing worked. And I finally reeled back to my trundle, knowing I had failed.

How, I then asked myself (and answered), would I break the news to *The BEAT*? And what would they *do* when they heard that their formerly reliable postman - er - columnist was too pooped to pop. (Gawd, how graphic can one *get*?) (Stick around and you may find out.)

Well! Whan I at last summoned up the strength and the nerve to call them, do you know what they *said*? *After* they let me go through my whole big moaning bit about how I wasn't long for this world? They said: "Oh, that's okay. We need the extra space anyway."

Actually, I was never so glad to hear anything in my life (at that moment, I couldn't have written my name) (had I been able to remember it), and they did say it very pleasnatly, but *still* ... I thought they'd at least try to kill themselves or something. (Sure, Shirl.)

Giving Thanks

Does this story remind you of the time I wrote and memorized a whole long speech when I was going to ask (as in beg openly) for George (rasp) Harrison's phone number? If it doesn't, it's because you haven't heard *that* story, and you should spend a lot of time on your knees, giving thanks for your good fortune.

Anybowl, I have now recovered. Not only from the previously stated (I get tired of saying aforementioned) (almost as tired as you get of hearing it) rootin-tootin. Also from the delusion that I can class myself amongst the martyrdom-for-lunch-bunch.

A few paragraphs back, I made mention of a net (and I don't mean Funicello). For a long time, I've been kidding around and giggling it up about how someone's going to drop same over me one of these days. I think it's about time I stopped kidding.

So help me, for the last week, there has been a huge net hovering over a certain intersection which I am forced to careen through daily. It's *tied* up there and I just *know* that very soon, someone is going to pull a little bitty string and *zap!* Away I go in a covered basket. I knew they were looking for me, but I had no *idea* they wanted me *that* bad.

To make thingies worse, when I went to lunch the other day, there was a man in the restaurant carrying a long-handled butterfly net! I am not *kidding*. Nor, I fear, was he.

I'm mainly worried about the heavy-duty jungle-weave that's hanging over the intersection though. If anyone has seen this and knows what it might be for, please explain. If it's for what I *think* it's for, please wave as they drag me away.

Oh, I almost forgot. When I was sick (and when haven't I been) a boy named Gary called and tried to cheer me up with the following conversation.

He: "Do you know what monsters eat?"
Me: "No, what?"
He: "They eat things. Do you know what monsters drink?"
Me: No, what?"
He: "They drink coke. Do you know why?"
Me: "No, why?"
He: "Because things go better with coke."

So, I have discovered (thanks to having a *lot* of friends like the aforementioned Gary), does Scotch.

THANKS TO OUR LEADER, IRVING MENDELSOHN, NO ONE CAN IMITATE "THE MENDELSOHN QUINTETTE CLUB OF BOSTON".
Sheldon Mendelsohn

STONES SET TOUR DATES

The Rolling Stones have dispelled all rumors about their alleged decision to follow the Beatles into a "no more personal appearances" decision by taking off on a tour of 12 European countries this spring.

The 21-day Stone tour will open on March 25, however, not all dates have yet been finalized. Appearances definitely set include Hamburg, Berlin, Essen, Vienna, Rome, Athens, Zurich, Paris and Bordeaux. Tentative plans call for the Stones to appear in either Norway or Holland, Belgium and Denmark.

Negotiations are currently underway for the Stones to play two or three concerts behind the Iron Curtain. The Stones' agent, Tito Burns, in announcing the forthcoming tour, said: "The demand for the group in Europe is quite unbelievable. I hate to disappoint a number of impresarios in various countries we were unable to fit into th e hectic schedule."

Immediately upon their return from the Continent, the Stones are expected to begin a major British tour. Said Mick Jagger: "We want to do something special for the British public and I can promise you that it won't be the conventional pop format."

The Rolling Stones have added another jewel to their crown by being named the best-selling British recording act for the period from July 1, 1965 to September 30, 1966 at a special Grand Gala held in Cannes, France.

The handsome trophy was given during the closing activity of the International Record and Music Publishing Market in Cannes and was attended by more than one thousand prominent executives and personalities of the world-wide record business. Over 30 countries were represented at the affair.

The Stones, who last week received their fifth consecutive Gold Record albums award for "Got Live If You Want It" are virtually assured of their sixth for "Between The Buttons", the new Stone album. Advance sales totalled very close to the necessary one million dollars required for the RIAA to certify the album for a Gold Record award.

Turning On

SONNY & CHER—IN CASE YOU'RE IN LOVE (Atco) *The Beat Goes On, Little Man, Monday, Podunk* and eight others.

Sonny's been knocking himself out composing songs for himself and Cher lately, and some of his best efforts are spotlighted on this LP. Cher's voice is the basis for most tracks, but a few are Sonny himself, singing well-written love songs and Protests. And you won't believe it if we tell you, so you've got to listen to '*Podunk!* It's hilarious, good time music!

TOMMY ROE—IT'S NOW WINTERS DAY (ABC) Produced by Steve Clark. *Leave Her, Aggravation, Have Pity On Me, It's Now Winter's Day* and eight more.

Tommy Roe has finally recorded some of the fine songs he's written over the last several years. Prettier than anything he's issued 'til now, this LP has several highlights: *Nightime, Sing Along With Me,* plus, of course, *It May Be Winters Day.*

THE SUPREMES SING HOLLAND-DOZIER-HOLLAND (Motown) Produced by Holland-Dozier. *You Keep Me Hangin' On, It's The Same Old Song, Love Is Like A Heat Wave* and nine more.

This time in tribute to their producer-writers, The Supremes continue their particular style. Though not as outstanding as other albums (like 'Supremes A Go Go), this LP is an adequate and pleasing follow-up, always maintaining the Supreme sound.

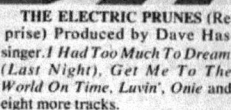

THE ELECTRIC PRUNES (Reprise) Produced by Dave Hassinger. *I Had Too Much To Dream (Last Night), Get Me To The World On Time, Luvin', Onie* and eight more tracks.

In addition to their smash disk, this LP has some truly beautiful songs among its tracks. *Onie,* especially, sings out reminiscent of 1955 music with a beautiful new treatment. From the unusual, to the new, to the pretty, this LP is a top notch venture.

THE WEST COAST POP ART EXPERIMENTAL BAND—PART ONE Produced by Bob Markley and Jimmy Bowen. *Shifting Sands, Help, I'm A Rock, Transparent Day, 'Scuse Me, Miss Rose* and seven more experiences.

Eerie wails, incredible noises of notes and soft, loving vocals make this album one of the most original man-made LP's we've heard. The great *I Won't Hurt You* is a quiet thunder of smooth singing. This group keeps their musical freak out under control at all times.

TONY RANDALL—VO, VO, DE, OH, DOE (Mercury) *Byrd, (You're The Bird Of Them All), Lucky Linda, Winchester Cathedral, You're Gonna Lose Your Gal,* and six more.

Actor-singer Tony Randall recreates the style of the thirties on this album without modernizing, twisting, or otherwise mutilating the music. Fans of old-time, good-time music will be appreciative of the respectful treatment given "Winchester Cathedral," "Doo Wacka Doo" and "Cecilia."

KRLA ARCHIVES

Adventures of Robin Boyd...

please send me
BEAT

26 issues only

$3 per year

Mail to: **BEAT Publications**
6290 Sunset Blvd. #504
Hollywood, California 90028

☐ New Subscription
☐ Renewal (please enclose mailing label from your last BEAT)
I want BEAT for ☐ 1 year at $3.00 or ☐ 2 years at $5.00
I enclose ☐ cash ☐ check ☐ money order
Outside U.S. — $9 per year

• Please print your name and address.

Name_____
Street_____
City_____
State_____Zip_____

©1965 By Shirley Poston

Everything began to change the night 103 zombies - er - customers filed silently into the Neville Club and only 102 filed silently out.

This was the first time Robin had noticed #103. The tall, sort of sandy-haired, be-spectacled young man wasn't exactly what you would call obtrusive (especially if you don't know what it means) (either).

And when she saw him standing there (repetition may rule but can plagiarism be far behind?) she didn't know quite what to think. Fortunately, she didn't have to (she should only be spared this task more often) because he spoke immediately.

Two Words

"Ummm, I notice you're having a bit of trouble with your—your audience," he said and he said it kindly because *a bit* was not the *word*. (How could it be? It's *two* words.) (Down, big fella.)

"A conservative estimate," Robin smiled ungraciously.

The stranger coughed. "Could I make a suggestion?" he asked. "Well," he continued when the three girls am-day near nodded their fool heads off, "I used to be a member of a group. One time when we were playing in Germany (Robin's ears stood straight up) ... Germany, South Dakota, that is (Robin's ears stood straight down), the owner of the club got after us for not being more lively on stage. He kept saying 'make show, make show,' and when we tried it, it worked!"

"You mean you jumped around and Stuff?" Robin demanded, becoming interested.

"A conservative estimate," the stranger smiled graciously.

Eyeing each other, Robin and her fellow Mockingbirds fell into a huddle (and very nearly hurt themselves) (keep 'em coming, kid) and agreed that it was certainly worth a try. When they looked up, the stranger was gone.

Later, having declined Budgie's and Ringo's offer of a snack (as in grind up another horse, Mable, they're here again), Robin was trudging through the deserted streets of Pitchfork, in the direction of the Boyd house (twitter) (or is it twit).

Suddenly, she heard the snow squeaking behind her.

"Good Heavens," she thought. "I'm being followed!" Changing that to *Thank* Heavens, she whirled around hopefully - er - nervously. "Nuts," she immediately added under her breath. It was only good olde #103. But, realizing that with her luck, he was probably the Masked Strangler in disguise, she snarled politely.

"Hullo again," he said, catching up with her. "Mind if I walk with you?"

"You'd have better luck walking with your legs," Robin said wittily.

The stranger larfed and when he did, Robin peered at him curiously. It wasn't that she was unaccustomed to having her clever remarks send people into stitches (at the wrist, generally). It was just that, for a second, he looked familiar. And, judging from the flash of eyes behind those round glasses, he probably *would* be if one gave him 'alf the charnce.

With this in mind, Robin was careful to keep the conversation light and impersonal. They talked mostly about the club (when he asked her how the place had been named, she merely muttered something unintelligible—there was no point in explaining the Neville Club bit to such an obviously dull thud). As usual, her ladylike tactics worked, and when they reached her darkened doorstep, he didn't start getting romantic.

Sixteen Feet High

Suddenly Robin jumped sixteen feet into the air. "How *dare* you?" she bellowed at her companion, who had fallen off the step and was rolling hysterically in a snowbank.

Then she gasped, fell off the other side of the step and rolled hysterically in a rose bush (which had frozen its bud off some months ago).

When the two of them were able to stop laughing, they struggled to their feet (each other's) and hugged each other wildly.

"I *knew* it!" Robin blithered. "I knew it the minute you pinched me!"

Robin then re-pouned on John (of Lennon frame and Genie fame) (and you can't hardly get 'em like that no more) with a series of questions. She soon learned that he was on vacation (in other words, hiding out while his hair grew back) (like Be-attle, like Genie) (and I'd like *both*) and George, who was still having transfer problems, had suggested he "coom around" to see what she was up to.

"*George!*" Robin wailed. "How is he and where is he and when will he be here and when am I getting my magic powers back and how long can you stay?"

After a brief translation of the question, John replied that George was fine, and at home visiting his folks. Also that George's arrival, the return of her powers and his departure all fell into the same category—like, *soon*.

"*How* soon?" she re-wailed. "Do you have to leave, I mean?" John thoughtfully brushed the snow off his Snow White watch. (Words fail me.) (It should only be.) "Oh, I guess I can stay another sixty seconds."

"Ratzafratz," wept Robin, but John (who, like his fellow Genie, does not mess about) re-pinched.

"Shurrup," he ordered. "Now you do what I told you about the group. You sound great, but stop acting like you have broomsticks - er - move *around*. Make show! And take off those Harley Davidson jackets! And you might sing a Beatle song once in awhile, you ingrate!"

"Anything else?" Robin inquired haughtily.

"Yes," he replied, making a grab for her.

"*John!*" she cried, outraged. (You have just visited the lie of the month.)

John shrugged. "George *said* to give you his love."

Robin gave him a suspicious glare. "He isn't going around with that genie-ess or witch-with-a-B or whatever she is, is he? That Ann Thrax individual?"

"They see each other occasionally," John said sneakily, failing to add "but not if he sees her first."

Robin's eyes narrowed. "Well, you *will* give him my love in return, won't you John?"

"Be 'appy to," John obliged, re-puckering.

Flang!!

When he vanished several hours later (it was only minutes, only minutes) Robin staggered into the house and flang herself on the couch. She felt marvelous, but also very weird. That old feeling was back. That *uh-oh* feeling she used to get in the good old daze, just before something incredible happened to her.

"Oh well," she mused to the Boyd dog, whom she was using as a pillow. "It couldn't be any more incredible than what's already happened to me."

And although she couldn't say for sure, Robin was almost *positive* that the dog laughed.

Since so many new readers will be picking up on The BEAT and on Robin Irene in the next two months, we've decided to put her on "vacation" (she needs the rest) (as in cure) during this particular portion of our expansion program. We'll then do a re-cap chapter so Robin's new victims—er—fans will at least have some idea of what the series is all about, and pick up the story where we left it in this issue.

Also, you'll be happy to hear that the previous chapters will soon be available in book form. For info on how to get a copy of Robin's past adventures, and for her further adventures, stay tuned to The BEAT!

ACCEPT NO IMITATIONS! THERE'S ONLY ONE MQCB!

CLASSIFIED

MOONRAKERS WHERE ARE YOU? Kathy—675-8831; Barbara—676-3534 (Los Angeles).

I LOVE TONY HILLARY

MOULTY MOULTON, The Barbarians' one-hand drummer and leader, is free!

Ann + Don = Tranquility

WHERE IS THE MUSIC MACHINE?

NANCY TRUBY—
Happy 18th B-Day!
Lots of Big-Sisterly Love, Linda

SONNY; CHER!

LYNNEA OR ALICE? Randy still can't make up his mind!

PIGGY—I'm the one who spilled coffee on your boots at the Freak In, remember? You've got my number so call. Red-haired Ann.

THE SECOND HELPING IS COMING!!!

HELP! I've lost a really cool hip guy. He's from England and usually wears a burgundy turtleneck and two identical rings on his left hand. I want to see him again to apologize for being rude. Call Sadala at 853-1212.

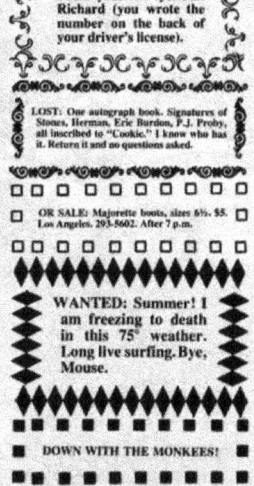

MOD GIRL, where are you? You've got a freckle under your left eye. Call Richard (you wrote the number on the back of your driver's license).

LOST: One autograph book. Signatures of Stones, Herman, Eric Burdon, P.J. Proby, all inscribed to "Cookie." I know who has it. Return it and no questions asked.

OR SALE: Majorette boots, sizes 6½. $5. Los Angeles. 295-8602. After 7 p.m.

WANTED: Summer! I am freezing to death in this 75° weather. Long live surfing. Bye, Mouse.

DOWN WITH THE MONKEES!

KRLA ARCHIVES

KRLA ARCHIVES

America's Pop Music NEWSpaper 25¢

KRLA Edition BEAT

MARCH 25, 1967

KRLA ARCHIVES

KRLA BEAT

Volume 3, Number 1 — March 25, 1967

Beach Boys Throw A Suit At Capitol

Although Capitol Records will make no statement, it is a fact that the Beach Boys have filed suit in Los Angeles Superior Court, charging that "Capitol has failed to compute royalties at the rate specified and provided for in their contract." The Beach Boys are asking for a complete audit of all books and records as well as a termination of their contract with Capitol which expires in November, 1969.

The Beach Boys claim that Capitol owes them at least $225,000 in royalties under the contract which was signed in November, 1962 allegedly giving the group a five percent royalty on records sold.

Brian Wilson's only comment on the lawsuit was: "We're (the Beach Boys) suing Capitol because we don't think they've paid us enough artists' royalties."

However, most feel that the *real* reason the Beach Boys entered the suit was to terminate their contract with Capitol so that they'll be able to record under their own company, Brother Records, which is already in existence. Brian appears quite confident that the Beach Boys will win their suit.

The Beach Boys are the hottest American group on Capitol. The Beatles are, of course, the label's hottest international group and, at least from the Beatles, Capitol is expecting no trouble. They've just signed a new nine year recording contract with the label.

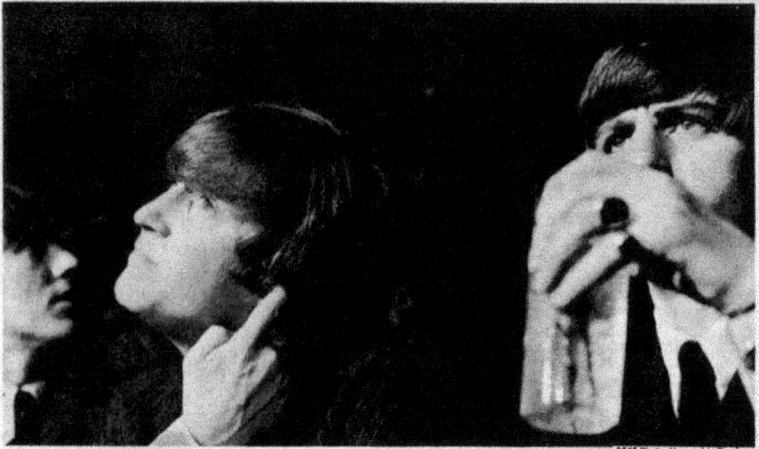
BEAT Photo: Howard L. Bingham

Boos, Jeers Greet Two Beatles At Berry Show

LONDON — John Lennon, Ringo Starr and their manager, Brian Epstein, were the object of booing and jeering from the audience at the Epstein owned Saville Theatre.

The audience, numbering over one thousand teens, booed loudly at the two Beatles and attempted to destroy the Theatre by ripping the seats, tearing down the curtains and smashing lights.

License Loss?

The rioting started when two fans jumped on stage during Chuck Berry's act. This, according to the Theatre manager, was against the Greater London Council regulations. He, therefore, ordered the safety curtain lowered. This, in turn, set off the audience who "just went wild and began tearing the place to pieces,"

according to a member of the audience.

Unfortunately, the two Beatles were seated in a box along with Epstein and the audience immediately turned on them with boos and jeers. Squads of police were called in and during the height of the rioting John and Ringo made a hasty exit but Epstein remained in the Seville pleading with the audience to restore order.

The police herded the outraged fans into the street near Piccadilly Circus where they chanted "we want our money back" while ripping life-size pictures of Berry which had been hanging out in front of the Saville.

The trouble, however, did not end there. Epstein announced that he sympathized with the audience and consequently fired his Saville manager, Michael Bullock. Epstein's dismissal of Bullock caused the National Association of Theatrical and Kine Employees to issue an ultimatum demanding an immediate withdrawal of what they termed Epstein's "irresponsible attack" on his staff. If not, they threatened to strike.

Safety Curtain

There is also the chance that Epstein will lose his Sunday license for the shows, but throughout all the hysteria and criticism Epstein is remaining calm. "If at any time my license is withdrawn," said the Beatles' manager, "I shall simply move the shows to another theatre."

JAGGER, RICHARD IN BRITISH DRUG SEARCH

LONDON — A huge drug crackdown is taking place in Britain with particular emphasis being placed upon pop entertainers. One of the first groups to gain national attention was the Rolling Stones, as it was reported in the English press that Mick Jagger and girlfriend, Marianne Faithfull, were searched at the home of fellow-Stone, Keith Richard, in West Wittering, Sussex.

Allegedly, eight people were searched at Richard's home by fifteen policemen with a search warrant issued under the Dangerous Drugs Act. Substances were taken from Keith's house but, according to the Stones' publicist, no arrests have been made and there has been no word from Scotland Yard regarding any impending arrests.

This latest "Jagger and drugs" story came on the heels of an article which was printed in "News Of The World," attributing remarks concerning drugs to Mick — remarks which Jagger claims he never made. In fact, Mick is currently in the process of suing the newspaper for libel.

"I am shocked that a responsible newspaper like the 'News Of The World' can publish such a defamatory article about me," declared Jagger. "I want to make it quite clear that this picture of me is misleading and untrue and, therefore, the only way left for me to prevent this libel being repeated is for me to ask my lawyer to take legal action in the High Court immediately."

The British police are waging an all-out war to halt, or at least curb, the flow of drugs in the country. Lord Chief Justice Parker believes that drugs are being sold on some club premises and, therefore, is introducing a bill to license "private places of entertainment." A bill which club owners feel will have "disastrous" effects on the entire pop scene.

MONKEES SET RECORD

TORONTO, CANADA — The Monkees April 2 concert here, promoted by Dick Clark Productions, Inc., sold out completely the first day tickets went on sale.

Teenagers lined up in 0-degree weather to purchase tickets at the ten box office windows of Toronto's Maple Leaf Garden. The 17,000 seat, turn-away sale resulted in gross sales of slightly more than $91,000 and constitute a new one-night record for the Monkees.

During their hiatus from "The Monkees," at least two of the members have changed their appearances slightly. Davy Jones now has a moustache growing on his upper lip and has had his hair trimmed quite a bit. It's by no means a crew cut but it is much shorter than the page-boy type style he usually wears.

Micky Dolenz has done nothing new to his hair but is in the process of acquiring a beard! However, it's safe to say that by the time "The Monkees" once again start filming all excess hair (except that on the head) will be removed!

GRAMMY AWARDS
STRIDE FORWARD OR STEP BACK?

HOLLYWOOD — Davy Jones showed up with a shorter haircut, John Phillips came dressed in tux and the Beatles scored a double victory by winning two awards. But are the Grammy Awards a fluke as far as Top 40 music is concerned? It makes one wonder.

It is certainly a surprise to no one that most over 25 consider Top 40 music to be illegitimate. No one dares knock the Establishment and, therefore, Frank Sinatra again walked off with the most awards. And "Winchester Cathedral" won the prize as Best Contemporary Rock and Roll Recording. "Winchester Cathedral" — rock 'n roll? Nostalgia is more like it. One shocked guest at the International Ballroom of the Beverly Hilton Hotel, gasped when "Cathedral" was named the winner: "It just shows who votes and what they base their opinions on. Middle-aged businessmen who think that anyone under 30 is a rock 'n roll singer!"

Still, this was the first year that so many Top 40 entertainers were even *nominated*. Surprisingly, several of them won! Paul McCartney walked off with a Grammy for "Eleanor Rigby" as the Best Contemporary Rock 'n Roll Solo Performance. The Mama's and Papa's were awarded a Grammy for Best Contemporary Rock 'n Roll Group Performance for "Monday, Monday." The biggest shock of the evening came when the announcement was made that John Lennon and Paul McCartney had won out over "Born Free," "The Impossible Dream," "Somewhere My Love" and "Strangers In The Night" for "Michelle" — the Song Of The Year.

It is interesting to note, however, that in the category of Best Performance By A Vocal Group, all but one of the nominees were from the Top 40 field. And it was that one, the Anita Kerr Singers, who copped the award — winning over the Association, the Beach Boys, the Sandpipers and the Mama's and Papa's.

HAPPENING

ROCK TREND FOR MOVIES

The Beatles started it all with their hit "Hard Day's Night" movie score acclaimed by both art critics and teenagers. Now the move is on toward using rock 'n roll soundtracks to underscore prestige movies.

The Byrds, now on European tour, will break into films when they return, singing the title song as well as the score in the Filmways-MGM production, "Don't Make Waves." Stars are Tony Curtis, Claudia Cardinale and Sharon Tate.

Kama Sutra released the John Sebastian Lovin' Spoonful score for "You're a Big Boy Now," on time for the opening of the film in New York and other cities. The Spoonful's new single, "Darling Be Home Soon," is from the Julie Harris-Geraldine Page-Elizabeth Hartman movie.

The Spoonful, of course, have already wet their feet in the film business. They appeared in Woody Allen's, "What's Up, Tiger Lily?"

The Beatles followed up their success in "Hard Day's Night" with the Capitol soundtrack for "Help!" Paul McCartney has just finished his first solo scoring job for Hayley Mills' "The Family Way," but the album has not been released yet.

The Rolling Stones are discussing a film score for "Only Lovers Left Alive" for the London label. Atco has set the Sonny & Cher "Good Times" soundtrack for March release.

BOSTON LIFTS THE BAN ON MQCB!

BEATLES IN NEW PACT

Dousing rumors of a Beatles' break-up, Alan W. Livingston, President, Capitol records, announces that a new, nine-year contract has been signed with the foursome at EMI House in London.

The Beatles are breaking records with their new record "Strawberry Fields Forever"/"Penny Lane." Three days after the group's latest single was released, Capitol had shipped one million-plus disks to dealers.

This figure chalks up a record number of any one single ever pressed and shipped in three days under the label. Guess what the previous high mark record was for a three-day period? "I Want to Hold Your Hand," the Beatles first Capitol single held the record at 750,000 and went on to sell more than 4.5 million disks.

Capitol asked the RIAA for gold record certification of the single on its release date. "Strawberry" will be the 22nd for the British quartet since their 1963 American debut. The 22 certified gold records are more than any other artist(s) have ever won in the history of the record industry.

John, Tad Seek Girl For Trio

John Stewart, one-third of the soon-to-be dissolved Kingston Trio, reports he has tapped Henry (Tad) Diltz as a second voice in a new boy-girl trio he will debut in June, as soon as the Kingstons finish their personal appearances. Stewart is still searching for the female voice to round out the trio. Tad is a former member of the Modern Folk Quartet.

Kingston member Bob Shane will continue his musical career as a single. While third member, Nick Reynolds, will become a full-time builder and driver of racing cars. He will also help his wife, Joan, operate their discotheque in North Beach, California, The Henry W. Kuh Memorial Auditorium.

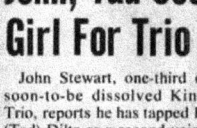

BYRDS KICK OFF ENGLISH TOUR WITH A TEA PARTY

The Byrds started their extensive, three-week European promotion tour with a London tea party for hundreds of their fans, 1700 of whom sent a petition begging them to return to England. Their current hit single, "So You Want To Be a Rock 'n Roll Star," is a musical tribute to their British fans. The screams backing up the Byrd's singing and instrumentation on the single are a recorded crowd reaction to one of their concert appearances in Bournemouth, Hampshire on their last visit to England in August, 1965.

The Byrd's latest Columbia album, "Younger Than Yesterday," has just been released.

The Byrd's London Headquarters are in an apartment near Regent's Park. Then they'll wing to the Continent to fulfill television and promotional engagements in Northern Europe.

"Purely promotional in nature," said Byrds co-manager Ed Tickner, "the trip will not include concerts." The Byrds have limited U.S. concert appearances since last summer, concentrating on developing themselves as creative musicians in their recording work.

The Byrds will break into films upon their return from Europe. MGM has asked the group to compose the title song and background score for a forthcoming feature length film.

Mel Carter To Tour London

Mel Carter kicks off an extensive European tour with a headlining appearance on "Sunday Night at the Palladium" in London on June 4. Carter will visit Copenhagen, Paris, Munich, Vienna, Milan, Madrid and Rome before he returns July 11.

"IN" PEOPLE ARE TALKING ABOUT Davy Jones flying up to Vegas . . . why Mick Jagger said no more Stones' personal appearances and then got booked into a full-scale European tour with a British tour as a follow-up . . . why Lennon and Starr really got booed in London and the question going around over all the hairy faces . . . Eddie Brigati of the Rascals buying a new home for his parents in Jersey . . . Sonny Bono winning a BMI award for "The Beat Goes On" . . . Phil Spector marrying one of the Ronnettes . . . whether or not Diana Ross and Berry Gordy will get married . . . the secret to Bill Cosby's success lying in the identifying bag—face it, everyone's heard of Noah . . . Steve McQueen wearing a paper suit . . . the Turtles switching a few more members and becoming an entirely different group . . . when the Mama's and Papa's are going to get together again and deciding that it will be quite awhile unless John, Michelle and Denny travel to England, where Cass is encamped until June

. . . how long before records go underground since movies and papers have . . . where censorship is going to end and where it's going to begin . . . whether or not there are no more teenagers past nine . . . how much the Fifth Dimension sound like the Mama's and Papa's . . . the Byrds perhaps not dropping out of the scene after all . . . how well Herman will do with "Mrs. Brown" this time around . . . Five Americans sending a telegram all over the nation . . . the Monkees making believers out of the British . . . the Righteous Brothers going into movies and probably doing very well for themselves—thereby making them a success in all three entertainment medias . . . the fact that Aaron Neville really does exist . . . why the entire world thinks we can locate the Association any hour of the day . . . how much it's all really worth

. . . Mitch Ryder doing a whole lot better than most people expect-

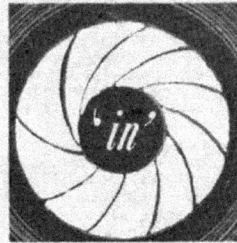

ed . . . the Who and the Hollies coming Stateside . . . new groups generally being a large pain in the neck but a necessary evil if we are to have the Beatles, Stones, ad infinitum . . . whether or not Neil Diamond will actually get his show

to Russia and deciding that he probably won't, unfortunately . . . why Herman is bringing no milk today . . . what happens when you raise your hand?

. . . whether or not "Ruby Tuesday" made it to the top spot on the nation's charts because the other side was unofficially banned . . . Tom Jones being one of the sexiest men alive . . . how many promoters making their mint off teens really despise them . . . Penny Lane being the most well-known street in Liverpool—thanks to the Beatles . . . Herbie Alpert and his TJB exceeding the 18 million sales mark for their albums . . . with "Mairzy Doats" back on the charts, the cycle is complete . . . how high is up and how deep is down? About an inch

. . . the theory that all rock 'n' roll singers with long hair smell, being basically untrue — with several notable exceptions, of course . . . what happens when the hunter gets captured . . . "Action" and "American Bandstand" both going off the air—thus making the defeat of the national teen shows complete . . . how unbelievable it is that hundreds of people would turn out to welcome Elvis' guitar into Canada . . . the Grateful Dead having one of the most original names in the business . . . why the Fascinations think "Girls Are Out To Get You" and deciding that it's probably because they are . . . how many versions of "Everybody Needs Somebody To Love" we're going to get within the next month.

Beat Publications, Inc.
Executive Editor . . . . Cecil L. Tuck
Publisher . . . . Gayle Tuck
Editor . . . . Louise Criscione
Staff Writers
Carol Deck   Bobby Farrow
Ron Koslow   Shirley Poston
Rochelle Reed
Contributing Writers
Tony Barrow   Sue Barry
Lawrence Charles   Eden
Tammy Hitchcock   Rochelle Sach
Jamie McCluskey, III
Photographers
Chuck Boyd   Dwight Carter
Advertising
Dick Jacobson   Jerry Lass
Winona Price   Dick Stricklin
Ron Woodlin
Business Manager . . . . Judy Felice
Subscriptions . . . . Nancy Arena
Distribution
Miller Freeway Publications
500 Howard Street, San Francisco, Calif.

The BEAT is published bi-weekly by BEAT Publications, Inc., editorial and advertising offices at 6290 Sunset Blvd., Suite 504, Hollywood, California 90028. U. S. bureaus in Hollywood, San Francisco, New York, Chicago and Nashville, overseas correspondents in London, Liverpool and Manchester, England. Sale price 25 cents. Subscription price, U.S. and possessions, $5 per year; Canada and foreign rates, $9 per year. Second class postage prepaid at Los Angeles, California.

KRLA ARCHIVES

PET CLARK SIGNED FOR 'FINIAN' FILM

Petula Clark has definitely signed to play the part of the daughter in the movie version of "Finian's Rainbow" which will be shot in Hollywood during the summer. Fred Astaire is set to play the title role in the film.

There had been a delay in casting Petula in the role because of a disagreement over which record company would release the soundtrack album. The problem still hasn't been settled but it now looks as if either Warner Brothers or Pet's international label, Vogue, will issue the soundtrack.

Tommy Steele is being sought to co-star in the film but he has not yet been signed. He, of course, is the young British actor who starred in "Half A Sixpence." Tommy is already being considered for two other movies which means that he may not be able to fit "Finian's Rainbow" into his schedule.

ON THE BEAT
BY LOUISE CRISCIONE

What a week for pop news this was. Fifteen British police officers allegedly searched Keith Richard's house for drugs, Petula Clark announced that she thinks "This Is My Song" is "awful in some ways," Davy Jones' fans did a fine job of damaging his dad's house in Manchester, Diana Ross visited Doris Day on the set of "Josie," Bill Cosby signed a new four million dollar recording contract, the Byrds were signed to compose and record the title tune for "Don't Make Waves," and Sammy Davis Jr. presented the Righteous Brothers with a Gold Record for "Soul And Inspiration."

Beatle Impression

The Beatles made quite an impression with their Liverpool-shot appearance on "Hollywood Palace." As always with the Beatles, there were pro and con opinions on the new Beatle look—hair and more hair. The funniest comment heard was "it looked like all the cameramen were high!" But with movies and records taking the psychedelic route, why not television?

Tom Jones is up for a role in a dramatic movie. "It's a marvelous role," says Tom, "and I can't afford to miss it. It's a drama and that's about the only thing I'd want to do in films. I need something aggressive, moody-like." Tom refused to offer any more information but as soon as contracts are all signed, Tom will let the whole world know.

P.J. Proby arrived back in London and immediately sought to get the Jones vs. Proby fire roaring again. "I've never been able to understand this P.J. Proby thing," admitted Tom. "People say I'm like P.J. Proby, I look like him, I copy his actions. I sing like him. I honestly just don't see it and I've never been able to."

...JIM McGUINN

Tom's not alone. I don't see any resemblance either. As a matter of fact, I'm inclined to toss the whole thing off as a "press agent's dream."

Neil Diamond

With my inimitably beautiful luck, I missed Neil Diamond when he stopped by the office the other day. So, I'm still not sure if Neil got the movie role he was up for. He did, however, write another one for the Monkees, "A Little Bit Me, A Little Bit You." As you know, it was Neil who penned their fantastically successful "I'm A Believer."

Going for himself, Neil has a sizeable hit with "You Got To Me" and should by now have his second album cut. To show you what kind of a man Neil is; he flew all the way into Hollywood (at his own expense) just to accept an award from a magazine. And, it's not the first time Neil's done something like that. He's flown into cities for the sole purpose of doing a charity show. Tell you the truth, it's hard to believe someone like Neil actually exists in this business.

Herman and his Hermits are set to begin filming on their second movie for MGM, "Mrs. Brown You've Got A Lovely Daughter," on April 3 in London. The movie, based roughly on the group's hit single by the same name is expected to take about ten weeks to complete.

Besides filming in London, the company is scheduled to go on location in Herman's hometown of Manchester. Rehearsals and recording for the soundtrack began in March under the watchful eye of Mickie Most.

...TOM JONES

QUICK ONES: The Lovin' Spoonful are currently "out" with the hippies. In fact, one psychedelic shop is using a Spoonful poster as a doormat . . . Mick Jagger supposedly arrived in Los Angeles but up until press time no one's been able to find him . . . the Buckinghams have signed with Columbia Records and are set to visit 30 cities within the next two months . . . Paul McCartney likes "the end bit" of the Spoonful's "Darling Be Home Soon" . . . the Spencer Davis Group will tour the U.S. and Canada from July 17 to August 20 and will go the college circuit from October 13 to November 19 . . . Herbie Alpert and his TJB received "the Beatle treatment" when they filmed part of their April 24 television special in the Tijuana bullring. "It was one of the wildest experiences we ever had," said Herbie. "We had to leave from the stage directly into getaway cars."

SPRINGFIELD SETS MAJOR CLUB DATES

Dusty Springfield is set to spend two months of her summer vacation here in the United States, playing three of the top night clubs in the country.

She opens for three weeks at New York's Copacabana on July 7 and then immediately moves on to Mr. Kelly's in Chicago and the Fairmont Hotel in San Francisco.

Dusty was the only British female nominated for a Grammy Award. The other British nominations went to the Beatles and to the New Vaudeville Band.

Hollies Cancel Part Of Tour: Drummer In Hamburg Hospital

The Hollies' drummer, Bobby Elliott, was taken seriously ill to a hospital in Hamburg during the group's German tour. The hospital announced that Bobby was "very ill with an inflamed appendix, but responding to treatment." Bobby is under constant sedation and is being cared for by five specialists.

Bobby's parents flew into Hamburg when they received news of their son's condition and are expected to remain with him until he is able to leave the hospital.

Meanwhile, the Hollies hired another drummer to substitute for Bobby and will go ahead with their recording plans. They're due to open a British tour with Spencer Davis but they're holding up hiring a drummer until they're sure that Bobby will not be able to perform.

The Hollies did, however, cancel their scheduled tour of Yugoslavia which was to have started last week.

THE WHO VISIT US

LONDON ENGLAND—The Who, whose biggest hit was "My Generation," make their first American visit starting March 22. After preliminary interviews and promotion, they appear at a special Murray the K Easter show in New York. Splitting the bill are Wilson Pickett, Smokey Robinson and the Miracles and Mitch Ryder.

The Who will guest star on DJ Murray the K's TV show, Colliseum, on April 2. Then the group will jet immediately to Germany to start a two-week tour.

WE ARE GRATEFUL THAT THE PEOPLE OF BOSTON NOW HAVE THE OPPORTUNITY TO OPENLY ENJOY THE GREATNESS OF "THE MENDELSOHN QUINTETTE CLUB".
Sam Mendelsohn

Nancy Sinatra Sues, Angry About Album

Nancy Sinatra is suing Capitol and Tower Records for $100,000 in damages to stop her picture and name from being used on the soundtrack album cover of the movie, "The Wild Angels." She has also named American International Pictures in the suit.

Nancy claims the album was made without her consent and although she starred in the film, she never gave her permission to use her name and picture on the record jacket.

Gary Lewis Wed In LA

Gary Lewis married Jinky Suzara March 11 in Los Angeles. They were engaged after an eight week courtship during which they could only visit each other from opposite sides of the fence at Fort Ord Army Base where Gary is stationed.

Jinky's sister, Gemma, who was maid of honor, flew in from Manila, Philippines for the wedding.

Write to:
THE SANDPIPERS FAN CLUB
247 So. Beverly Drive,
Beverly Hills, California

KRLA ARCHIVES

The Generation G-a-p

By Lawrence Charles

Young people have inherited a world that is very different from the one their parents knew in their teens.

Computers can do calculations a man could not complete in a lifetime.

Since the first atomic bomb exploded over 20 years ago, Dick Clark points out, "Someone other than God can blow up the whole scene."

This generation is challenging not only their parents' authority, but their very way of looking at the world. Widely different views of life create communication problems and have given rise to a growing "Generation Gap."

"The real gap is in the rules, regulations, morals and codes," says Lou Adler who produces records by the Mama's and Papa's and Johnny Rivers.

"The kids aren't sitting back and taking it anymore; they're questioning the old codes. This is a brighter more intelligent generation. A 16-year-old talking to a policeman usually knows more than he does."

During the 50's parents were urging their children to break out of their silence and apathy. In the last six years young people have become concerned and outspoken about their world. At civil rights demonstrations, war protests and campus rallies, they have become the most visible generation.

Adults often act as if they expected young people to be radical and non-conformist in tidy rows. They are often startled and dismayed by the force and spontaneity of the youth movement.

Members of this generation resist attempts to standardize them. Their long hair and mod clothes express their taste and establish them as individuals.

"I think the grown-ups have to open their minds to the fact that kids with long hair are not just idiots carrying signs," says Tommy Roe, "they have opinions—some good, some bad. I think both sides, the kids and the grown-ups, have to open their minds."

Grownups who impatiently order teenagers to cut their hair or change their habits can learn from the experience of one woman at a Sunset Strip demonstration who asked Bobby Jameson, "How much does that hair really mean to you?"

"Exactly as much as it means to you to have me take it off," he answered.

"Grownups don't like our hair long because it shows disrespect to them," said Doug, a Los Angeles teenager, "but long hair shows masculinity. Look at Sampson. Caesar wore his hair short in Christ's time."

Young people are subjecting the adult world to a harsh, critical examination and often finding it undesirable. They question the fierce competition, the brutalizing rat race for money and power.

Tense, defensive adults in a bitter contest for goals with no humane basis can't appreciate each other as people. Is it worth sacrificing human kindness, spontaneity and the joy of living to compete for anything?

Many young people say no.

"The older generation's darkest fears may be justified," warned Robert A. Gross, 21, general secretary of the U.S. Student Press Association.

"While a majority of students passively accept the values of their parents, a significant minority is turning off and opting out of the system," he told an audience of 300 college newspaper editors, Washington officials, professors and journalists gathered in the nation's capital to discuss "The Generation Gap-Translators Wanted" a month ago.

Today's youth values decency, tolerance and honesty. Grownups pre-occupation with expensive homes, lavish cars and material status symbols tarnish them in the eyes of many young people. In a 1966 Look Magazine survey 550 teenagers were asked if they had any heroes. Most of them weren't sure they had any or even knew what a hero was.

They struggled to list JFK, Mickey Mantle and Elvis Presley—but not one of them mentioned the current President of the United States.

As historian Arthur Schlesinger Jr. points out, "Our statesmen become bores, while our folksingers are the rage ... The Multi-Lateral Force is out. The Beach Boys are in.

The message the young are digging and supporting (over $100 million worth of 45's were sold in 1966) comes from their heroes—singers like Bob Dylan, the Beatles and the Monkees. What speaks more directly and honestly to the concerns of young people than these lyrics by Bobby Jameson from his forthcoming album, "Jameson, Color Him In."

"*My friends there's no one who can tell you more than you know within yourself
And all the thoughts that are inside you
They don't belong to no one else ...
For all those thoughts that are inside you are not controlled by someone else.*"

Young people in this country take the current level of unprecedented prosperity for granted. They have never known a depression. They see no reason to delay spending their money.

Last year they swelled the economy by purchasing over $18 billion in goods and services. Since luxuries have always been plentiful for them, teenagers don't regard their attainments as the major achievement their parents do. Young people are turning inward, searching their souls and trying to develop their minds. (See Next Page).

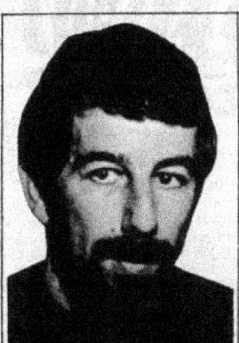

LOU ADLER: "*The real gap is in the rules, regulations, morals and codes.*"

DICK CLARK: "*Someone other than God can blow up the whole scene.*"

DAVY: *I think most of the generations have the same problems. The difference between teenagers today and their parents is not any different than that between teenagers 50 years ago and their parents.*

MICKY: *No matter how you look at it, this generation is kind of a good generation.*

TOMMY ROE: "*I think both sides, the kids and the grownups, have to open their minds.*"

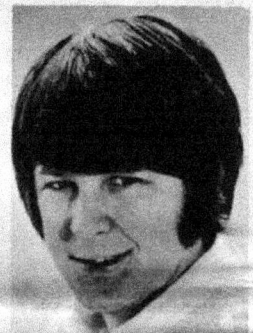

BRIAN WILSON: "*The gap has resulted in an extreme polarity which makes life very interesting and spicy.*"

PETER: *Parents never understand their children. I do not expect to understand mine.*

MIKE: *I don't know—I think it is overrated. Everybody does what they have to do when they have to do it.*

And so have I heard it said that the young will always disagree with the elder until the young learn the way of the elder. Or could it possibly be said that the time it takes to hypnotize the young into standardization is called growing up.
There is now a double standard of regard toward everything. A difference in expectations of situations, a gathering of the seekers of the unseekable. There are two sides and both see themselves as right and duly licensed to express their natures. Communication between the two entities becomes less and less. Reaction toward one another becomes totally abrupt, and lacks control. Thus a war of standards!

Bobby Jameson
21-year-old singer-poet

KRLA ARCHIVES

They're Hardly-Worthit

By Marsha Provost

■ "This is insane. Can you believe the three of us are here, talking to you people at The *BEAT*? And we're going over to film 'Hollywood Palace' tomorrow. Us!

"Look at us. Can you imagine us doing record hops? We did one yesterday at a shoe store and sold 18 pairs of shoes."

That was our introduction to the Hardly-Worthit Players, who have blown as few cools with their rendition of "Wild Thing" by Senator Bobby.

Taken together they really don't make it as a pop group. They've got far too much education and far too little hair. But taken individually they really become the least likely candidates for pop stardom.

Take Bill Minkin, who thought up the original concept for the entire Hardly-Worthit Report. This guy has a masters degree in communication from New York University and is a teacher at Brooklyn College.

Super Cool

He likes to tell about his students and how they all try to be so super cool about their teacher having a record on the national charts.

And there's Dennis Wholey, who is well known to New York Television stars and radio listeners for his works as host and interviewer. He worked for a while in the theater as director, stage manager and a little bit of everything else before going into television and radio. His major complaint against the world right now seems to be "they don't even sell Chinese food at Grauman's Chinese." (Grauman's Chinese is a movie theater).

Then there's Steve Baron. Of all three of the guys, Steve is the only one who might conceivably have been on the pop charts at any given time.

Steven's a folk singer and composer and has appeared often in various coffee houses in New York. He has a degree from the University of Wyoming.

Mirrors

Describing the Hardly-Worthit Players, he says "The world's flipped out and we're just mirroring it."

The three met in the summer of 1964 when they were, honest, all pages at NBC. When they outgrew their paper collars (that all pages are required to wear) they became the Hardly-Worthit Players.

... THE HARDLY-WORTHIT PLAYERS (l. to r.) Steve, Bill and Dennis — Senator Bobby's "Wild Things."

They got together with a few dozen friends and recorded the "Hardly-Worthit Report" album. According to the liner notes, "Some came over directly from their offices; some came from their almost-paid-for houses in the suburbs; some came from the Village; some came from the East Side; some came from the West Side. Others, as usual, came late."

After weeks of writing and re-writing and arguing and trying everything out on each other, they put in a grand total of one and one half hours of recording time and came up with an album.

It sold twelve copies. According to Dennis, Bill's mother bought five. Steve was going to give one to his mother, but a friend told him not to, so he didn't.

A few disappointed days later, they heard the album put out by Senator Everett Dirksen. Now, if Dirksen could put out a successful album, surely they could too, they figured.

They came up with this idea to cut "Wild Thing" sounding like Dirksen on a Sunday. They rehearsed it on Monday, recorded it on Tuesday, sold it to a record company on Wednesday and Thursday it was on the air. The album, with "Wild Thing" added, then began to sell.

However it was the other side of the single that got the air play. At the end of the session they had a little time left over and decided to try the same thing with one of the Kennedy voices that Bill is so good at. Thus came about "Wild Thing" by Senator Bobby.

That seems to be the way their whole careers came about. Even the name was an accident.

"We originally called ourselves the Hardly-Worthly Players," recalls Bill, "but everyone kept mispronouncing it."

There are two other vital people to this whole insanity.

One is Chip Taylor, who produced the record along with Dennis. Chip wrote "Wild Thing" which was originally done by The Troggs.

Girl Involved

And there's a girl involved too. All of the female voices on the album are done by Carol Morley, currently appearing with The Mad Show in New York.

Carol didn't come out to Carol didn't come out to film 'Palace' with the three guys because of her engagement with the Mad Show.

"Lets talk about Carol," they said during their visit to The *BEAT*, and then didn't.

Asked what they were going to do when they returned to New York, they replied:

"I've got a class to teach Monday morning," — Bill.

"I open at the Gaslight Club Monday night." — Steve.

"I think I'll go look for a new job." — Dennis.

With that they shook hands with us, each other and some stranger they picked up in the elevator and left us with the world's only copy of a picture of the Troggs personally autographed by the Hardly-Worthit Players, including Chip, who wasn't even there.

TRINI LOPEZ
Best Export Since Coke

... TRINI AND FRANK Sinatra smiling it up at a party

TRINI PUTS ON a big smile as he steps aboard Paris-bound plane

The miracle of Trinidad Lopez III is this: Over half the man's young life was spent in the jungle atmosphere of Dallas' "Little Mexico" where his playground was rooted in the narrow dirty streets and his family slept and lived eight in a room and fought a daily war to keep a sense of dignity alive. Today, not yet 30, Trini lives in a magnificent apartment in one of Hollywood's most elegant buildings where the monthly rent would pay for at least a square mile of those Dallas slums.

Forget It

So if you expect the talent of Trini Lopez to resemble that of a proper Anglo-Saxon hatched out of a protected childhood and a comfortable, full-filled adolescence — forget it. The gifts which constitute the natural property of this handsome, bullfighter-lean young Latin were forged out of a deep passion for music, a burning hatred of poverty, a profound pride nursed by parents determined that their children would escape from poverty row, and a resulting sensitive and driving ambition to make it big and be recognized purely on the strength of talent.

He was only eleven when he had already decided what he wanted to do; having watched his father play the guitar and sing since he was a tot, he decided that music would be his life. His father bought him a $12.00 instrument. "It was like an ordinary family spending $500 for a kid's gift," says Trini. He worked every day and began to develop a singing style. By the time he was 15 he had formed his own combo and was playing at a Dallas restaurant.

Enter Sinatra

In 1960 Trini arrived on the West Coast and was playing PJ's, a popular night club. He played several other clubs in the Los Angeles area, during which time he was discovered by a variety of people, including Don Costa, well-known conductor, who called Frank Sinatra and arranged for the singer to hear Trini. Sinatra did and it was the beginning of a fast friendship and a meteoric career.

Trini was signed to an exclusive contract with Sinatra's Reprise Records in April, 1963. His first album released in June of 1963 titled "Trini Lopez at PJ's" was in No. 2 position in the nation's record charts only six weeks after it was released. One of the cuts from that album, "If I Had A Hammer," was released by Reprise as a single record and was an instant success, not only in this country but introduced Trini to audiences in 20 foreign countries and sold over 4,500,000 records.

Mexico's newspaper NOVEDADES proudly hailed the success of the young Spanish-American Lopez with "That Trini Lopez is the greatest United States export since Coca-Cola."

Now, a little more than three years after his initial album was released, Trini is one of the outstanding and best-selling recording artists on the North American continent. He has produced 13 albums which have sold well over two million copies. Now he looks to new horizons for his talents and only recently co-starred with Lee Marvin, Robert Ryan, Telly Savalas and Ernest Borgnine in the MGM film "The Dirty Dozen," scheduled to be released in the summer of 1967. While he states positively that he will never abandon the music field, he admits that he has a very strong interest in acting.

Trini's younger brother Jesse, now a student at North Texas State College, is giving strong evidence that he wants to follow in the singer's footsteps. Trini is giving him every encouragement, while insisting that he finish his college career.

His four sisters are married now, and his parents live comfortably in Dallas, enormously proud of their son's success. Trini is devoted to his family and has no hesitation in stating that it was the principles and outlook that his parents instilled in him, and particularly their insistance that he look beyond the borders of the slums in which he was born and find his way to a better life, that contributed in great measure to the success he enjoys today.

KRLA ARCHIVES

Mobs, Chaos, Knockers — For Monkees What Price Fame?

By Louise Criscione

Davy Jones is not physically big anyway — not that it matters much how huge you are when you find yourself the object of so powerful a fan force that they'd tear you apart like a piece of paper if given half a chance.

"I don't mind admitting I'm frightened by this whole thing," said Davy. "Frightened" has to be the understatement of the century. "Terrified" would be much more appropriate.

When "The Monkees" recently took a three week break from filming, Davy, Micky and Mike headed for England. Mike didn't stay long, Micky extended his visit several days but it was Davy who caused an uproar England won't soon forget — and all because he wanted to visit his family.

Mob Scene

Met at the London Airport by a mob 700 strong, Davy was hidden in a customs room while police attempted (unsuccessfully) to move the crowd along. Driven out in a police car and then transferred into a limousine, Davy arrived at the hotel only to find over a hundred fans encircling the entire premises.

But the worst was yet to come. Davy's father lives in Manchester and his fans know it. Consequently, when Davy arrived at his family's home looking for a little peace after the chaos in London he found anything but. "We found that there were hundreds of them (fans) outside the house," said Davy. "We made several attempts to stop so that I could go in the house but it was too dangerous. The girls had already smashed the front gate."

Impersonation

In desperation, Davy dressed up as a woman, got some neighborhood kids to walk along with him as if he were their mother and succeeded in getting around to the back of the house, climbing a fence and making it inside. Davy didn't think the fans knew he was there but it made little difference as they merrily went about their business of smashing all the windows and breaking down a door. A phone call brought every available police car to the Jones' residence and the risky job of getting the girls out of the area and Davy safely out of the house got underway.

Davy left uninjured but disgustedly reported: "In a whole week, I've been able to see my father for just two hours." Lovely price for fame. "If they can cause so much damage to the car, what would they do to me?" asked Davy. Not much. Break an arm, a leg, smash a head. Not much at all.

Those of you who think the Monkees are already rich are wrong. They reportedly make a flat $400 a week on the show and another 30 per cent of the gross from their personal appearances — after all expenses are taken out. Of course, they make record royalties — but, generally, royalties are notoriously late in arriving.

The future for the Monkees is assured for at least another year. Their television show has been picked up for another season, they're set to make a movie, they've been booked to play the World's Fair in April and, of course, they will continue recording and making personal appearances.

In the far away future, Davy thinks he'll stick with acting, Mike and Peter will go solo and Micky will become a comedian. As for the knockers who have been constantly chipping away at the Monkees, Micky, Peter, Mike and Davy sort of shrug their shoulders at the inevitability of success bringing jealousy and whistle on their way to the bank.

Ad Lib

The scripts for their show are more of a guide line than a Bible. Roughly 85 per cent of the series is strictly ad lib. Whole scenes are discarded if the Monkees don't feel they're right and each Monkee changes his lines if they don't suit his personality.

The Monkees each have their own dressing room which assures them of at least a small domain of privacy, though the set itself is always overrun with visitors who pay no heed to the "closed set" sign which is obviously more of an ornament than a law.

Home-based in Hollywood, the Monkees have little or no trouble with wild mob scenes, although their fans stage all-out searches to find their homes and phone numbers. The grapevine system is amazing and fans knock on Davy's door at all hours of the day and night. But compared to the mess in England, Davy's apartment is a real bed of tranquility.

Safe At Home

The Monkees are rarely bothered in clubs and are relatively free to come and go as they please. In fact, Davy and Micky once visited a Sunset Strip club and were not even asked for so much as an autograph the entire evening! Another time, Micky went to an after-hours club and no one seemed the slightest bit ruffled because a Monkee was in their midst.

Once out of Hollywood or once on a stage, however, everything changes. Mob scenes break out with regularity, extra squadrons of police are needed, objects hurled through the air manage to hit at least one Monkee (not to mention unfortunate fans seated in the line of fire) and pandemonium reigns supreme. "When something like that happens," says Davy, "you feel you want to walk off."

But you can't. You're a star and it's all part of the game.

MICKY THE TOUGH GUY? Not on your life — he's a comedian.

DAVY AND HIS dad — long ago when there was privacy.

PETER TORK AND LEAH (Cass Elliott's sister) on the Monkee set.

MIKE NESMITH PUTS on a serious face for some guitar playing.

Lenny's Salutes The No. 1 Group In The United States

LENNY'S BOOT PARLOR

1448 GOWER STREET

HOLLYWOOD, CALIFORNIA 90028

WRITE FOR FREE CATALOG

KRLA ARCHIVES

Image Of Tommy Roe: 'What Difference Does It Make?'

By Carol Deck

BEAT Art: Jan Walker

In the process of being a pop reporter, we usually see an artist on stage or television and hear him on record before we ever get to meet him. We know his stage personality, which sometimes, but not always, is the same thing.

But with Tommy Roe, we played the game in reverse. We got to know Tommy off stage before any of us ever got to see his stage act. And did he ever blow our minds!

The first time we met Tommy, he came out our way on a promotional tour when "Sweet Pea" was jumping up the charts. He came by the office, had a cup of coffee and chatted for a while and we discovered one very friendly, polite Southerner who talked freely and frankly.

A few weeks later he moved to our city, for many reasons, mainly because he wanted to be nearer the movie industry which he would very much like to get into, and because he had been signed to be a regular on Dick Clark's "Where The Action Is" series.

More & More

We began to see more and more of Tommy Roe—in the elevator of our building, and every now and then on "Action" whenever one of us would get off early.

We saw him when he was happy, when he was tired and when he was sick, but we still hadn't seen him on stage.

We ran into him at one of his sessions, when he was on the verge of collapsing from exhaustion. It seemed strange then, because most people when they are ill tend to seek sympahty, but Tommy seemed genuinely embarrassed that we should see him ill.

Later that same night, he actually collapsed and was taken to the hospital. He's done this before and will probably do it again. He gets wrapped up in his career and forgets to watch his health.

And so we came to know Tommy Roe—Tommy who tells you he hates parties, then somehow finds himself hosting one in his new Hollywood hills home: the Tommy who paints a picture over five one-dollar bills so no one will ever be able to tell him it's worthless; the Tommy who calls his friends "Pinhead" or "Birdwell"; the Tommy who is one of the gentlest people in the world, yet collects firearms.

Then one day we got to see another side of Tommy that we never dreamed existed. He invted us to come see his show at the world famous Disneyland, and of course we went.

We saw him standing back stage before the show, calm and confident, nothing different.

But then he slid onto the stage, took mike in hand and started into a pretty darn sexy version of the Stones' old smash and the audience full of young teenagers went wild. In the middle of one number, Tommy leaned down and kissed one young girl, who almost fainted.

And there we sat with our mouths open. It's hard to accept girls getting hysterical over a guy you run into in the elevator who calls you "Birdwell."

He did four shows that night, once more driving himself, and allowing others to drive him, to the verge of exhaustion. And the girls come back, set after set, and so do we, amazed.

New Side

It's a whole new side of Tommy, but not a side that he's been hiding, for, unlike some pop singers, Tommy doesn't attempt to build an image or only let people see one part of him.

He realizes that all most people know of him is what they see on stage or television and hear on record, but, he says "What can I do? They don't really know me, true, but, in a way, what difference does it make? Whatever they know of me, it's selling, and I don't know how I can show them any more of me."

So now, with this new slice of Tommy firmly implanted in our minds, we sit back to watch the progress of his new single.

"I don't think I'll write anymore sad songs, 'cause I'm pretty happy now. Besides, anything that brings people up has got to be better than something that brings them down."

Beat Bows To Ballad—Where From Here?

By Tony Barrow

According to SONNY AND CHER "The Beat Goes On." Indeed they took their song of that title way up high into your Top Ten. But not in Britain. It's not beaten its way into the U.K. Top Thirty—despite the duo's carefully promoted, expertly exploited visit to London.

OF THE CURRENT BRITISH TOP THIRTY RECORDS NO LESS THAN EIGHTEEN ARE BY SOLO SINGERS. THIRTEEN RECORDINGS ARE OUT-AND-OUT BALLADS INCLUDING THE SENSATIONAL "THIS IS MY SONG" BY PET CLARK, NANCY SINATRA'S SUPERBLY LAZY "SUGAR TOWN," DONOVAN'S "MELLOW YELLOW," SANDY POSEY'S "SINGLE GIRL" AND DUSTY SPRINGFIELD'S NEWIE "I'LL TRY ANYTHING."

AT LEAST ANOTHER SIX OF THE BIG-SELLING THIRTY SINGLES ARE FRINGE-AREA BALLADS LIKE HERMAN'S "THERE'S A KIND OF HUSH," CAT STEVENS' "MATTHEW AND SON" AND GENO WASHINGTON'S "MICHAEL."

Of course The Beat does go on—via hard-hitting things such as "I'M A MAN" by SPENCER DAVIS, the second-time-around success of "LAST TRAIN TO CLARKSVILLE" by the monstrously popular MONKEES and "ON A CAROUSEL" by THE HOLLIES.

By and large beat has backed down to make way for ballads. Even the big boys like The Stones, The Beatles and The Troggs are balladeering via "Ruby Tuesday," "Penny Lane" and "Give It To Me."

Where we would have had hefty barrages of percussion and avalanches of guitar all through our charts a year ago, we find sugar-soaked slabs of romantic sentimentality selling the love-along singers into the Top Ten.

The division between Beat and Ballad is greater than ever before. On the one hand we've got all those string-draped orchestras and sympathetic choirs. On the other we have an entirely new wave of beat groups determined to reach an ultimate target of musical eccentricity by the use of electronics and an assortment of tricks tied together with an unsatisfactory label which reads "Psychedelia." On the one hand a return to total convention, on the other much freaking from a frugal minority.

In Britain—and in America too, I suspect—the fans are still waiting to hear something spectacular for '67. The whole pop scene is diversified. Ask six different people the way and they'll give you six different directions. Beat, ballad, Motown, Thirties, Monkees and Country & Western.

Who will win? Who will draw everyone else onto some kind of pop Main Street for the rest of the year? Will it be The Seekers and Tom Jones or The Sopwith Camel and The New Vaudeville Band? Will it be The Tops and Mitch Ryder or Keith and Cat Stevens? Is it all down to the pseudo-Thirties or the psyche-Sixties?

You tell me. I haven't got it together yet.

Sonny & Cher Win Award

Sonny & Cher are the winners of their 12th BMI Award for the duo's top ten recording of "The Beat Goes On" on the ATCO label.

Billboard and Cashbox music trade publications have placed the disc in the top ten of their best selling lists.

THE HOTTEST QUINTETTE CLUB GOING, IS COMING!

...DOES THE BEAT really go on?

...IF THE MONKEES are a measuring stick, it certainly does!

KRLA ARCHIVES

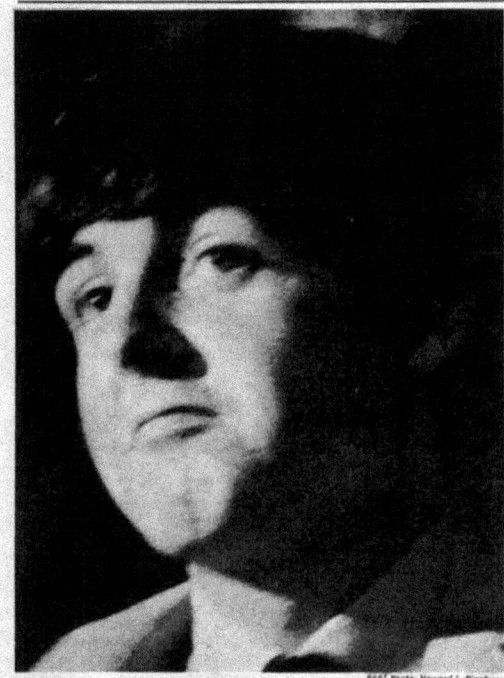

...MARTHA McCARTNEY dislikes Paul's trumpet playing.

JANE ASHER DENIES SPLIT WITH BEATLE

Whether she meant it to happen or not, Jane Asher is a well-known name today because of Paul McCartney. Perhaps she would have made it on her own talent—perhaps not. Jane is currently in the United States touring with the Bristol Old Vic Repertory Company.

Reporters don't care about that. They want to know what gives between Jane and Paul. "I'm in this country as a Shakespearean actress," said Jane, "not just a friend of a Beatle."

Word out of England is that the Asher/McCartney romance is now in the past tense. Jane obviously doesn't think so. "I love Paul very deeply and he feels the same," she declared. "I certainly should be very surprised indeed if I married anyone but Paul."

Paul did not see her off at the airport but reportedly the couple shared a candlelight dinner the night before her plane departed for the United States.

American reporters met Jane at the airport and demanded to know about McCartney, because "the public wants to know." "I don't *care* what the public wants to know," sniffed Jane. "If I even said I'd had a letter from him, everybody would pounce on me and say, 'what was in it?'"

Jane, who is now 20, began her acting career when she was five playing the part of a deaf mute in the movie, "Mandy." Her father is a doctor but Jane says that both sides of her family have always been involved in the theater, if only on an amateur level.

"I think mother took her children to auditions because a neighbor said, 'with that hair, they're naturals.'" Jane, her brother Peter (one-half of the Peter & Gordon duo) and her 18 year old sister, Claire, all have an unusual shade of hair which has been described as everything from Marmalade to "just plain red." "I think 'orange' best describes the shade," said Jane. "I grew up with the nicknames 'carrots' and 'copper knob'."

Jane has done several dramatic roles in British films but is best known to U.S. moviegoers as one of the girls opposite Michael Caine in "Alfie." She has never formally studied acting, although she says "you learn new methods from each director."

With the Old Vic, Jane is playing Juliet in "Romeo and Juliet" as well as Julietta in "Measure For Measure." This is the company's first American tour and by May they will have played in Boston, Philadelphia, Washington D.C., New York, Los Angeles, San Francisco, San Diego, Denver, Dallas, Chicago, Champaign, Lafayette, Indianapolis, Bloomington, Detroit and Cleveland. They will then head to Canada to appear at the Expo 67.

"American audiences so far have been wonderfully receptive to Shakespear," Jane said. "They're so quiet. I think the English have become a bit blase."

There was quite a bit of speculation to the effect that Paul would accompany Jane on her tour. Up until press time, however, he has remained in England.

U.K. POP NEWS ROUND-UP

Beatle 'Babies' Identified

FOR ALL BEATLE PEOPLE WHO ARE STILL TRYING TO GUESS THE CORRECT IDENTITIES OF THE FOUR BABIES PICTURED ON THE CAPITOL SLEEVE WHICH CAME WITH "PENNY LANE" AND "STRAWBERRY FIELDS FOREVER" HERE'S THE RUN-DOWN THAT WINS OR LOSES SO MANY BETS! THE BABY SITTING BESIDE A TOY DOG IS JOHN LENNON. THE BABY IN THE PRAM IS PAUL McCARTNEY. THE CLOSE-UP PICTURE OF A LITTLE BOY WEARING A KNITTED JERSEY IS GEORGE HARRISON. AND THAT LEAVES RINGO STARR—HE'S THE TINY 6-MONTHS-OLD TOT SITTING ON A BIG CUSHION.

Recordings made in their pre-Monkee days by MICKY DOLENZ and DAVY JONES are being released or re-issued this month in Britain.

Davy-Solo

The Davy Jones material is in the hands of Pye Records; I understand they have enough tracks to make up an album and at least one single. The recordings, made for the Colipix label, consist of solo vocals which Davy describes as "garbage."

"Don't Do It," written and recorded by Micky Dolenz, has already hit the U.K. market on the top deck of a London single.

THE ROLLING STONES are to spend three weeks touring Europe at the end of this month and the first half of April. Included are concert dates in Norway, Denmark, Holland, Germany, Belgium and France. They'll play five nights in Athens and visit Vienna and Zurich. Other dates in Eastern Europe are to be added.

A few weeks after their return to Britain the Stones will set off on a short U.K. concert tour playing key cities in England, Scotland and Wales late April and early May.

P.J. PROBY, presumably back home in the U.S. with you by now, was given a last-minute reprieve by London's work-permit authorities so that he could plug "Niki Hoeky" on BBC Television's "Tops Of The Pops."

Before flying out of London Jim starred in a week-long cabaret presentation at Newcastle in North East England. Agent Tito Burns is hopeful that a further work permit will allow Proby to undertake a full-length cabaret and/or concert tour of Britain early this summer.

Mini-Marriage

Talking in London of his recent mini-marriage (which lasted only one week, he claimed!) Proby said: "I had known Judith Howard for 8 months before we married on my birthday last November. She didn't like my long hair and had me cut off my pony-tail. Then she didn't like my new haircut."

BARRY BENSON, once Jim Proby's hairdresser, chart-climbing here with "Cousin Jane," an off-beat ballad borrowed from The Troggs' album... PAUL'S fast-growing dog Martha McCartney dislikes her master's trumpet playing!... My formal congratulations to NANCY and RON on their formal announcement!... JEFF BECK solo debut disc is "Hi Ho Silver Lining."

London journalists found SANDY POSEY a difficult interview subject... Elektra label released self-penned DOORS single "Break On Through" in U.K.... Have the MOTHERS OF INVENTION stopped inventing?... STEVIE WINWOOD finally quit The Spencer Davis Group to concentrate on songwriting... Birthday telegram to GEORGE was signed "Magnetes, Moscou"... Secret Wedding Congratulations to TURTLE Mark Volman... Ravi Shankar's brother a guest of GEORGE HARRISON at recording sessions... BEATLES hope to acquire their own private recording studios in London's West End.

Byrd News

On their first night in town BYRDS down at London's most "in" discotheque, The Bag O' Nails, after visiting BEATLES recording session... According to P.J. PROBY: "The Monkees will last as long as the public remains ignorant."

MONKEE MICKY's most constant London companion was "Top Of The Pops" TV deejay SAMANTHA JUSTE. Said Sammy: "He's very thoughtful, kind and generous."

From Basil Foster, boss of the Yorkshire stables where he once worked for 12 dollars a week.

DAVY JONES: album of "garbage"

BEATLES TO buy recording studio

MONKEE DAVY is buying his own race horse. Hopes to fly to Britain to see his purchase a couple of months from now.

On current ROY ORBISON/SMALL FACES U.K. concert tour, JEFF BECK'S group makes stage debut... Will SONNY AND CHER use Trogg Reg Presley's "Our Love Will Still Be There" on next single?

B-Flat Solo

Pleased to hear PETULA CLARK confirmed for starring role (as veteran FRED ASTAIRE'S daughter) in Warner Bros. screen version of "Finian's Rainbow"... Top Australian singer NORMIE ROWE appearing without fee throughout current GENE PITNEY/TROGGS package tour... Top Australian group THE BEE GEES (average age of the foursome is just 17 years!) signed to management/agency contract by Brian Epstein's NEMS Enterprises... Spring seasons at the London Palladium for FRANK IFIELD, THE SEEKERS and TOM JONES... To be very precise that's a B Flat Piccolo Trumpet on "Penny Lane"... Will P.J. PROBY star in Western movie "Johnny Vengenace" scheduled for summer production in Spain?... Two weeks stint at London Palladium will delay appearance of FRANK IFIELD on "The Ed Sullivan Show" until the end of April... KEITH in London now to promote his new Hollies-penned single "Tell Me To My Face."

Because iron curtain was lowered at Saville Theatre before CHUCK BERRY had finished his Sunday concert, 1200 fans rioted doing damage estimated at a thousand dollars. As a result of the incident Saville boss BRIAN EPSTEIN fired theatre manager Michael Bullock... BRIAN EPSTEIN now in New York prior to Mexico visit.

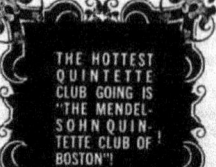

THE HOTTEST QUINTETTE CLUB GOING IS "THE MENDELSOHN QUINTETTE CLUB OF BOSTON"!
Irving Mendelsohn

KRLA ARCHIVES

TURTLES
From Machine to Group

By Carol Deck

Some old friends of *The BEAT's* have come up with another huge hit — their fourth, fifth, sixth or seventh, depending on what part of the country you live in.

Despite some inconsistency in their careers, the Turtles are rapidly climbing charts again with "Happy Together." It all began a few years ago with "It Ain't Me Babe," which was followed by a couple more hits, and then things began to get a little messy and the Turtles found they had less and less control over their own careers.

"We found ourselves becoming more and more the product of all the people who said the Turtles must be this and this and this. They said we had a hit with 'It Ain't Me Babe' and so everything we do must sound like 'It Ain't Me Babe'," explained Howard in the midst of a group rehearsal. "We became a Turtle machine."

Confusion

There was some confusion in releasing singles and the group seemed to have several out at the same time in different parts of the country. In one performance, they would announce as many as three different tunes as "our latest single."

But things have changed now and the Turtles are truly "Happy Together." They've gotten rid of a lot of the hangers on who were trying to tie them down, cut an unbelievably great commercial, changed bass players, filmed a movie, set a number of tours including a European one, and one of them has gotten married.

"We've changed from a Turtle machine to a Turtle group," noted Al.

"Hey, be sure and tell them we did the Camaro mod commercials," reminded Howard. "Everyone thinks it's the Cyrkle," he added and then proceeded to sing the entire 60 second spot.

Two Jims

"And have you met Jim, our new bassplayer? We have two Jims now but it doesn't bother us because we don't call either Jim. Tucker is Tuco and Pons is JP," explained Howard.

The new member, Jim Pons, formerly of the Leaves, replaces Chip Douglas, formerly of the MFQ and the Gene Clark Group, who has decided he's more of a producer than a bass player and is going into production, full time.

"I've been friends with the guys for quite a while," said Jim, explaining how he joined the group. "I've always admired the Turtles, second almost to the Beatles. I wouldn't have quit the Leaves for any other group."

The night Jim joined the group Johnny and Al were out walking the streets looking for a new bass player and someone mentioned Jim's name to them. They knew he was recording at the moment, so they went into the session and Jim became a Turtle.

Ask what they've been doing between hits and you get 47 different answers from these characters. "Oh, we've been working at Hughes Aircraft." "Yeah, and getting a lot of sleep."

"Hey, I got married," shouts Mark from across the room, "to a girl named Patricia Hicky."

But sudden seriousness sets in as Al pulls everything together and says, "A lot of groovy things happen between records. We're not as concerned about so many things and we have time to put our heads together and work on new material and arrangements. Yeah, a lot of groovy things happen between records."

Groovy Things

A couple of those groovy things are an appearance on the Smothers Brother's Show and being signed for two more, cutting a new album, definitely not titled "Turtle Soup" ("We ate that," said Tuco), being signed for the Ed Sullivan Show, Hollywood Palace and the Dating Game, filming a movie titled "The Russians Are Swinging" with Paul Revere and the Raiders and making plans for a European tour.

The group would publicly like to thank "all the people who helped make the new record a hit. It's like we've come back and we're better than before. We're glad they remembered us."

CAREER TIPS
Want to be a writer?

By Shirley Poston

For the next few issues of *The BEAT*, I'll be doing a series that will give you lots of information about all kinds of groovy careers.

I'm going to start with the grooviest career I can think of. The one I've been thinking of all my life . . . writing.

Writing isn't like any of the other careers we'll be discussing in this series. Going to college doesn't automatically make you a writer, which is really very unfortunate because so many people don't take this into consideration when they decide to pursue a writing career.

Old Adage

An old adage claims that writers are born and not taught. From what I've heard and learned, this is part wrong and part right. Writers are born and *then* taught. So, if you don't have a natural flair for putting words together, do yourself a favor and set your sights on some other goal.

A great many have this gift, and if you're one of them, now is the time to start developing it, no matter what your age might be.

Writing, like charity, begins at home. If you want to write, don't just talk about it. *Do* it. Writing just for your own enjoyment is the best possible way of developing a style, learning how to say what, and learning what to say when.

Reading is just as important. Read everything you can find, including advertisements on bus benches. (?) Reading helps you learn new words, gives you ideas, familiarizes you with different types of writing and gives you a daily lesson in grammar and sentence structure without boring you senseless.

A good command of the English language is a must. So is a knowledge of punctuation. But don't get too carried away with details or technicalities. If you try to follow every rule to the last letter, your natural creativity suffers and your writing may end up sounding stilted and un-natural.

School is another place where you can learn writing by doing. Involve yourself in every possible activity which has anything to do with writing. Take journalism, literature, drama, work on the school paper, the annual, and the literary magazine if there is one. Then follow the same course throughout college.

Don't wait for a degree to start peddling your wares. Don't wait, *period*. There are many publications where your writing can be sold or at least printed, right *now*.

Teen-slanted

Teen-slanted publications are an excellent market. Don't make the mistake of contacting them and asking if you can interview the Beatles (yay!) or write a column. Most of the star interviews are either staff written or purchased from regular contributors. But most of these publications are always looking for material such as fiction stories, poetry, impressions of favorite stars, discussions of teen problems, beauty and fashion hints, etc.

It's best to make your contact by mail. Don't write a letter first and ask if they'd be interested in such and such. Send the article without any prior correspondence. Make sure it's typed, and double-spacing is another must. Enclose a stamped, self-addressed envelope and, if you like, a *brief* letter. If you don't hear from the publication within the next two months, write and ask them if they intend to use your story.

Although your material is welcome, it still falls into the "Unsolicited Manuscript" category and most teen publications aren't equipped to handle an overload of outside contributions. Instead of making a fuss, re-type the article from your carbon copy (still another must) and either send it to them again or send it to another publication.

Every successful writer can look back and remember the good old days of waiting hysterically by the mail box and having manuscripts lost forever.

There are hundreds and hundreds of available markets, besides the teen publications, where young writers have a chance. The best way to find them is through a monthly magazine called the Writer's Digest. Each issue contains a list of publications, where young list of publications, complete with addresses and information about what type of stories they prefer. Also, this same magazine publishes a book each year titled The Writer's Market, where practically every publication on earth is listed.

The publications you see on the newstands are only a few of the thousands printed each month. Among those you rarely see on sale are technical trade journals, and highly-specialized magazines which deal with one subject only.

The Writer's Market (which costs about $5 but is the world's best investment for a writer) lists most if not all of these smaller publications. And even if it seems silly to you, if your cat did something funny or brilliant, write about it and mail it off. Perhaps this wasn't quite the way you'd intended to begin your writing career, but if you find a check in the aforementioned mail box, the whole thing will stop seeming the least *bit* silly.

I'm so sold on starting with smaller publications for two reasons. One — you can start *now* because you don't have to be another Agatha Christie to have your work accepted. Two — that's how I got started, so I *know* it works.

First Story

My first story appeared in a 12-page magazine that is distributed free to members of a youth organization. I found the address in the Writer's Digest, sent them the story and soon received a small but beautiful check. And don't think this was my first attempt.

Just to show you how things can and do work out, that first story was written when I was in a particularly morbid mood and was about a girl named Robin who was dying of some ghastly disease.

After I sold the story, my writing started to change (probably because I finally had at least a fly-spec of confidence in myself) and got off onto lighter subjects.

Every time I become embarrassed about the way I got started in writing, I begin to wonder what might have happened if I *hadn't* kept sending out story after story.

KRLA ARCHIVES

YESTER EXPLAINS
Association Is Subtle Insanity

By Rochelle Reed

"Subtle insanity," explains Jim Yester, is when the Association sings "Ba-nan-a Won-der-ful" in place of "bop-do-waah" at one point on their album track, "Another Time, Another Place."

Jim, prominent singer-guitarist of the Association, can get away with this casual explanation. He passes it off like a scientific fact because while the Association is noted for their comic view of the world, Jim also has a reputation for keeping both feet on the ground.

If Jim is firmly planted on Mother Earth intellectually, his eyes are in the air following some of the vultures he has trained for 10 years. A member of that often-joked about group, bird lovers, Jim no longer keeps vultures in his backyard but feeds pigeons on his front lawn. It's his temporary sacrifice to success.

One of the nicknames tagged on Jim is "Owl," which he earned for his interest in birds of all sorts. "Actually, it was a toss up between Owl and Troupe," he explains. "The group always called me Yester until one day when I said, 'Hey, I've got a first name, troupe!'." From that day on, Jim has been occasionally known as Troupe.

Still Grows

The 24-year-old Associate who would be a game warden if he weren't a singer was born in Birmingham, Ala., but grew up in Burbank, Calif., adding "the process still goes on, hopefully."

He began singing in the folk music bag of 1960 with his younger brother Jerry (producer of the Association) as an act called, originally enough, the Yester Brothers, and sometimes known as Jim and Jerry.

They sang around the Southland in local coffee houses before Jim took the big step and joined the Army. He attended radar school and wound up in Germany where the Bavarian atmosphere got to him and he performed in service shows as Jim Yester Alone.

"When I came back to the U.S., my brother was in the MFQ so I sang in the restaurant (owned by his parents) to replace my father behind the piano bar," he relates.

"Then I came to the big city and stopped by the Ice House where the Association was auditioning, looking for a tenor. To complete the circle of insanity, they had me committed."

Solo Recut

Institutionalization of the Association-type has done wonders for Jim, and he returned the favor by writing and soloing (on the album version) of "No Fair At All." (The song was recut for the single release without a solo.)

"I was just sitting at the piano going through cord changes when I wrote 'No Fair At All'," Jim explains. But when the Association finally recorded the disc, Jim's part was done in a rather unusual manner — in total darkness.

"Cutting in the dark got to be a habit at the studio," Jim explains. "Solo work is easier when you know everyone in the studio isn't looking at you. You can laugh or cry if you want. It's fun to get involved in singing, though singing in the dark is really no fair at all...

"Actually, it all started after seeing Brian Wilson, who is one of our favorite singers by the way, cut in the dark. All the guys said, 'Hey, look at that, that's sharp, we'll have to try it.'"

Jim jokingly says he's torn between being "skinny and careful" as his major emphasis in life, but seriously he advocates enjoying life without asking too many questions. "Become very analytical without being critical," he says.

Great Watcher

"I guess I'm The Great Watcher. I analyze a situation to find out what groovy things there are in it."

In life, Jim finds many groovy things. He is fond of quoting Einstein: "The center of the universe is where you see it from." Jim's point of view is also the message for the year that he left with BEAT.

"Love is the only way," he said as he left the office. "If you can relate to that, a whole lot of other problems drop away!"

JIM YESTER: "The process still goes on, hopefully."

GUITARISTS!
- Improve your ability • Increase your income
with "The Guitar" by Barney Kessel

Now you can profit by Barney Kessel's 30 years of experience as a guitar-pro in Rock, R & B, Folk Jazz and the "Nashville" sound. This book shows you how to select the proper guitar and equipment, accompany singers, read music and improvise. Learn the commercial recording techniques and how to "BREAK" INTO THE BUSINESS. Easy-to-read book has 211 pages of text and music examples.

-- -- -- -- -- -- -- -- -- MAIL COUPON TODAY -- -- -- -- -- -- -- --

WINDSOR MUSIC COMPANY, DEPT. KB
P. O. Box 2629
Hollywood, Calif. 90028

Enclosed is $_____ Please send me _____ copies of "The Guitar" by Barney Kessel, at $15 each.
(California residents add 4% Sales Tax).
___ Check ___ Money Order ___ Send free brochure

(Please Print)

NAME_____

ADDRESS_____

CITY_____ STATE_____ ZIP_____

(Tax deductible for professional musicians)

MUSIC MAKERS PT. 1
Power Behind The Lovin' Spoonful

(Editor's note: Responding to a growing interest in record producers and recording companies, The BEAT begins a new series about the music makers — the men behind the sounds. Here we take an inside look at Kama Sutra. Look for behind-the-scene profiles of the recording industry in upcoming issues).

By Ron Kostow

Bob Krasnow, West Coast Vice-President of Kama Sutra Records Inc., was deep in thought. As he sat concentrating to the sounds throbbing from the two large speakers at the other end of the long, red-carpeted conference room, he seemed oblivious to all else around him. An aspiring young songwriter sat opposite him waiting from some sign of reaction from behind Krasnow's steel-rimmed sunglasses. A secretary, blonde and mini-skirted, scurried in and out, bringing coffee, telegrams and assorted memos to the large oak conference table.

Kind Of Hush

As the song ended, an extended hush fell over the room. Now, Bob Krasnow knows music; most of his formative years have been spent in the recording business with people like James Brown, The Olympics and Ike and Tina Turner. Thus, when he is confronted with any new piece of material it is automatically filtered through the store-house of musical knowledge and taste in his mind, weighed and judged according to what he knows of past trends and what he foresees for the future.

Bob began to shake his head, "No, I'm sorry man, we just can't take it."

The young songwriter looked crushed, "But why, what's wrong with it?"

Krasnow looked up at him, "It's about drugs man; it lacks taste."

The songwriter was indignant, "But that's where it's at, that's what's happening in music now."

"Look," Krasnow spoke firmly, "there's a difference between psychedelic music, sounds that stimulate the mind, and music that tells kids to go out and take things. The song has possibilities, why don't you clean it up and bring it back."

The songwriter picked up the demo disc he had brought and started to leave.

"Any Time"

"If you've got anything else you'd like me to hear, come in any time," Krasnow reassured him.

The young writer smiled and walked out, calling back behind him, "I'll be back."

In just four short years Kama Sutra has risen to a position of respect and influence in the recording industry, for the reason that they are receptive to all new material and strive for perfection and good taste. At this writing, there are five Kama Sutra records on the national charts; they have to date, sold over 25 million records, and this year promises to be their best ever.

Founded in 1963 by Phil Steinberg, Artie Ripp and Hi Mizraki, with $400 and an unknown group called the Shangrilas, their first release was "Remember Walking in the Sand." Then came "Leader of the Pack" and their first good record.

Next they signed Jay and the Americans and immediately clicked with "Come A Little Bit Closer."

As always in the entertainment business, when things start to happen, they happen fast; when Artie Ripp stumbled into the Cafe Wah, a little club in New York's Greenwich Village, a new era in sound was born. He was so turned on by the group playing there, he signed them on the spot. That group was the Lovin' Spoonful.

Kama Sutra provided the "Spoonful" with an atmosphere which allowed them to truly, "bloom." And as the "Spoonful" emerged as one of the most admired groups on today's scene, so Kama Sutra grew, acquiring Tommy James and the Shondells, The Tradewinds, The Sopwith Camel, and the great Gene Pitney.

...SPOONFUL allowed to bloom.

KRLA ARCHIVES

REBEL FOSTER, newest addition to the KRLA DJ's, backstage at Gazarri's, where he dropped in to see the Teddy Neely Five. From left, Billy Patton, Teddy Neely, Lynn Ready, Reb, Paul Tabet, Jerry LeMire.

KRLA's Electric Circus Set For Teen Age Fair

It's Teen Age Fair time again and a big part of the Fair this year is KRLA.

The Fair will be held from March 17 to 26 at the Hollywood Palladium on Sunset and KRLA will be taking over a large part of the outdoor area for an exciting Electric Circus.

Gold Diggin'

Stop by the Electric Circus and you can go hunting for Acapulco gold in a psychedelic sand box. The box will be 10 feet by 20 feet, filled with sand, and you'll climb into it with a sift and search for the gold while listening to ear drum to ear drum psychedelic sounds.

And there are many other goodies in store at KRLA's Electric Circus. You can turn on a KRLA dancer, win funny money, and take part in turtle and rabbit races.

Dancing, Too

And of course no Fair's complete without dancing so KRLA will set up a dance area and bring in many top name and local groups to play for your dancing enjoyment.

All of the KRLA DJ's as well as many well known singers and entertainers will also drop by the Electric Circus at various times during the fabulous annual Teen Age Fair.

Also at the Fair will be the usual highlights featured every year—the crowning of Miss Teen Age Fair plus exhibits and demonstrations by scores of manufacturers who produce things for the teen market.

And watch for hotrodding, surfing, hairstyling and makeup displays as well as performances by many top name performers and food, food and food.

KRLA TOP 40

1. PENNY LANE/STRAWBERRY FIELDS FOREVER ... Beatles
2. NO MILK TODAY/KIND OF A HUSH ... Herman's Hermits
3. HAPPY TOGETHER ... Turtles
4. CONNECTIONS ... Rolling Stones
5. LIVE ... Merry Go-Round
6. SHE ... Monkees
7. DEDICATED TO THE ONE I LOVE ... Mamas and Papas
8. 59th STREET BRIDGE SONG ... Harpers Bizarre
9. RETURN OF THE RED BARON ... Royal Guardsmen
10. RUBY TUESDAY ... Rolling Stones
11. SOCK IT TO ME ... Mitch Ryder
12. UPS AND DOWNS ... Paul Revere & Raiders
13. LITTLE BLACK EGG ... Night Crawlers
14. KIND OF A DRAG ... Buckinghams
15. SIT DOWN I THINK I LOVE YOU ... Mojo Men
16. WESTERN UNION ... Five Americans
17. EVERYBODY NEEDS SOMEBODY ... Three Midnighters
18. DARLING, BE HOME SOON ... Lovin' Spoonful
19. I HAD TOO MUCH TO DREAM LAST NIGHT ... Electric Prunes
20. THEN YOU CAN TELL ME GOODBY ... Casinos
21. BABY, I NEED YOUR LOVING ... Johnny Rivers
22. ACAPULCO GOLD ... Rainy Daze
23. EPISTLE TO DIPPY ... Donovan
24. LOVE IS HERE AND NOW YOU'RE GONE ... Supremes
25. FOR WHAT IT'S WORTH ... Buffalo Springfield
26. ROCK AND ROLL GYPSIES ... Hearts and Flowers
27. LET'S FALL IN LOVE ... Peaches and Herb
28. WE AIN'T GOT NOTHING YET ... Blues Magoos
29. IT TAKES TWO ... Marvin Gaye & Kim Weston
30. I'M A BELIEVER/STEPPING STONE ... Monkees
31. YOU GOT TO ME ... Neil Diamond
32. GIMME SOME LOVING ... Spencer Davis Group
33. NO FAIR AT ALL ... Association
34. PRETTY BALLERINA ... Left Banke
35. MY CUP RUNNETH OVER WITH LOVE ... Ed Ames
36. GO WHERE YOU WANNA GO ... 5th Dimension
37. THE LOVE I SAW IN YOU WAS JUST A MIRAGE ... Miracles
38. STAND BY ME ... Spyder Turner
39. SO YOU WANT TO BE A ROCK AND ROLL STAR ... Byrds
40. 98.6 ... Keith

Inside KRLA
By Eden

If you're looking for a new car this week, the All-American Boy—Jack Armstrong—is the man to see. Just head out on the nearest freeway to nearby pleasant Palmdale and when you spot those road-hungry Packards ... you know you're there. Jack Armstrong can take care of *you*, too!

Visiting the KRLA studios recently was Mitch Ryder, now singing solo minus the talents of the Detroit Wheels who have been with him on all of his hit records.

At present, Mitch is on the KRLA Most Requested list with "Sock It To Me," recorded with the Detroit Wheels; in the future, however, Mitch will be recording alone. He also hopes to put together a real "soul show"—an entertainment package, much like that of James Brown, in which he will be featured with a large back-up band.

Mitch has often been praised as one of the top white R&B artists in the country, and certainly if there is such a thing as "blue-eyed soul," this brown-eyed young man from the Motor City has it in abundance.

March is Monkee Month on KRLA—so if you want to be a part of the many exciting daily prizes to be given away throughout the month, be sure and listen to KRLA for details. You can also join KRLA's exclusive Monkee fan club and receive pictures and exclusive information on the boys

By Pen

March is Monkee Month at KRLA. And now you're able to pick up your Monkee fan club kit (complete with Monkee photos, news of the Monkee's activities and Monkee fan club cards) at your nearest Thom McAn Shoe Store. But that's not all.

Each of the fan club cards is numbered. Beginning March 1st, KRLA started reading card numbers selected at random on the air. When you hear your number, you will be allowed five minutes to call KRLA and claim your prize.

You could win Monkee sun glasses, Monkee stocking caps, Monkee records and albums, Monkee money (approximately $111.00 per week) and a grand prize which allows you to view the filming of a Monkee TV show.

Remember to keep listening for more details of when you can pick up your kit and how those prizes can be yours. You'll hear it only on KRLA.

Warner Bros. unlocks all the doors of the sensation-filled best seller.

It's like you're running a big city... a unique empire... a private world with a do-not-disturb sign on every door...

HOTEL

Starring ROD TAYLOR
CATHERINE SPAAK · KARL MALDEN · MELVYN DOUGLAS · RICHARD CONTE · MICHAEL RENNIE
KEVIN McCARTHY and MERLE OBERON as "The Duchess" Original Music by Johnny Keating
Based on the novel by Arthur Hailey · Written for the Screen and Produced by WENDELL MAYES
Directed by RICHARD QUINE TECHNICOLOR® FROM WARNER BROS.

NOW PLAYING AT A THEATER OR DRIVE-IN NEAR YOU

KRLA ARCHIVES

This Casey Doesn't Strike Out Often

Casey Kasem was in high school when he decided that he wanted to be a Major League baseball player *and* an actor.

Not one or the other but both.

His ambition was to find a way to combine sports and acting. In those days, he managed to do so by participating in high school plays, portraying straight dramatic roles as well as doing comedy. He even appeared in musical productions. ("Although I can't even hum on key.")

He was a letterman in baseball and became a sports announcer. He was president of the Letterman's Club, and vice-president of his graduating class.

It was at Wayne State University that he realized he wasn't quite Major League material. (He got the name "Casey" from striking out too often in baseball, in spite of his exuberance for the game.) So he decided to devote most of his time to acting. He also became a disc jockey and hosted several television shows.

Casey served in the Army in Korea where he was Radio Program and Production Coordinator for the American Armed Forces Korean Network.

Casey was born April 17, 1932, in Detroit, Michigan where his parents were in the grocery business. His family background, rich in the Lebanese tradition of family pride and devotion, was filled with happiness.

One learned gentleman, who not only understands teenagers, but stoutly defends them and actually "digs" them is Casey Kasem.

He not only loves the rock-and-roll music but thinks the stars are great, and he loves the teenagers. He appreciates their thinking, their alertness and awareness of things and even admires the clothes they wear. He feels their styles are way ahead of everything.

He looks forward each week to his television show because of their vital participation and especially to see their clothes. The Mod style is very original and exciting to Casey, and he maintains that manufacturers watch the "Shebang" show to "get new ideas from the teenagers; they are so inventive and imaginative in the combinations they create. They set the styles and the trends."

Casey feels that "Shebang" is much more than a teenage entertainment show, he believes it is a public service show in many aspects. It is not only a place for them to let off steam, it is a place for them to grow, to learn and to be accepted for what they are.

"Teenagers are very critical... you can't fool them, though. They are a little fickle, but that is because they like to identify with a winner," he says.

The beat used to be the most important thing. The beat was the thing that was emphasized, but today it's the lyrics as well as the beat — they are equally important now.

"Each person hears something different... the words and the music have a different meaning for each individual. Word pictures and colors are evoked that stimulate an emotion within. I believe that some of the most beautiful and meaningful poetry of our time will certainly come from the rock-and-roll period," Casey says proudly.

Recently something new and exciting happened to Casey — READ the next issue of the *KRLA BEAT*.

Troubadour CR. 6-6168 9081 SANTA MONICA BLVD.
NOW **GLENN YARBROUGH** THROUGH MARCH 19 **ODETTA**
OPEN EVERY NIGHT — NO AGE LIMIT

ENJOY YOUR TEENAGE FAIR,
AND THEN VISIT
THE "IN" STORE OF HOLLYWOOD
LOU LEWIN'S RECORD PARADISE
Featuring all British Imports. STONES, BEATLES, WHO, YARDBIRDS, SPENCER DAVIS, PRETTY THINGS, ETC., ETC. L.P.'s, E.P.'s, singles.
Also all the latest "POPS" at lowest prices anywhere.
And, Exclusive POSTERS, PHOTOGRAPHS — GALORE.
"WE DIG THE MOST"
6507 Hollywood Blvd., L.A. 28 — HO 4-8055

ICE HOUSE GLENDALE
234 So. Brand Ave. Reservations: 245-5043

NOW THRU MARCH 12

The Nitty Gritty Dirt Band
with their new hit
"Buy For Me The Rain"
— and —
Lee Mallory
introducing his hit
"Take My Hand"

MARCH 14-26

Travelers 3
— and —
Hypnotist
George Sharp

ICE HOUSE PASADENA
24 No. Mentor — Reservations: 681-9942

Ends March 26
Bud Dashiell
Bill Morrison
Rusty Stegall

=== DOUG WESTON PROUDLY PRESENTS ===

ONE NITE ONLY
SUN. MARCH 19
8:30 P.M.

IAN & SYLVIA
EXCITING CANADIAN FOLK ARTISTS

BUFFY SAINTE-MARIE
WORLD FAMOUS AMERICAN INDIAN FOLK SINGER

TWO NITES ONLY
FRI.-SAT.
MAR. 24, 25
8:30 P.M.

LINDY OPERA HOUSE
5212 WILSHIRE AT LA BREA
TICKETS: 4.00, 3.50, 3.00. AVAILABLE AT TROUBADOUR BOX OFFICE, FREE PRESS BOOKSTORE, ALL MUTUAL AGENCIES, WALLICHS MUSIC CITY
=== INFORMATION WE. 7-3500 ===

CAN YOU DIG IT?
GLAMOUR & SOUL RETURN TO THE SUNSET STRIP

NOW APPEARING THRU MARCH 18th

THE EXCITING SOUND OF **BROOK BENTON** with THE 5th DIMENSION

CIRO'S
8433 SUNSET BLVD.

DINING & DANCING TILL 2 A.M.

ALL AGES WELCOME
FOR RESERVATIONS: 654-6650

KRLA ARCHIVES

IF YOU CAN'T BELIEVE YOUR EYES ....LISTEN!

MERCURY RECORDS / MG•21111 / SR•61111

MERCURY RECORDS / MG•21112 / SR•61112

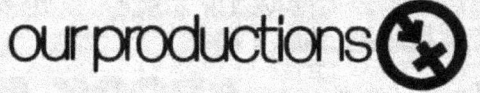

our productions

6290 SUNSET BOULEVARD, LOS ANGELES, CALIFORNIA 90028

KRLA ARCHIVES

TEEN PANEL

Time to Cool Easter Week?

It's that time of year again. All over the country, teenagers and college students are getting ready for the annual (and annually controversial) celebration of Easter Vacation.

In this issue, The BEAT's teen panel discusses this same subject. Participating are Judy (18), Gordon (17), Sharrie (17) and Bob (20).

If you would like to suggest a topic for a future teen panel discussion, please drop a postcard to The BEAT.

* * *

Judy – "I'd like to start things off by saying I think the newspapers are mostly at fault for making Easter Week sound like something it really isn't. When you get that many kids together in one place at the same time, there's bound to be a lot of uproar, but these 'celebrations' certainly aren't the orgies they're written up to be."

Bob – "Have you ever spent Easter Week in one of the big resorts, like Fort Lauderdale?"

Judy – "No, but kids get together in other parts of the country too, you know, and they have just as much fun as they do in the 'famous' places. And they have as much trouble with the papers and the police. I still think this is because of the publicity. Nothing goes on that week that doesn't go on the rest of the year. It's just that everyone's attention is drawn to the kids during this week."

Gordon – "What I can't figure out is why there's so much objection by adults, even when there isn't anything going on that could be considered out-of-line. It's just a holiday, and just a celebration. *Some* adults sure don't object! Not the ones who rent their houses to students for something like five hundred dollars for a weekend. They don't mind a bit."

Sharrie – "Don't you think it could be the *nature* of the holiday that causes a lot of the objection? When you really think about it, Easter Week isn't really a very appropriate time for living it up and letting off steam. It *is* a religious holiday; still, it's about the only time we have during school to really let go."

Bob – "You could be right about some people objecting for religious reasons, but I don't see these people objecting about the thousands and thousands of drunk drivers who are picked up during the Christmas holidays. I'm not saying they *don't* object, but you don't hear about it because it's adults who are involved, not young people."

Sharrie – "It might help if things didn't get quite so wild that week. Help the image of the whole thing, I mean."

Bob – "Why do you think things *do* get wild in some places?"

Sharrie – "Because you're either away from home or away from the pressure of school for awhile. The atmosphere doesn't help either. It's like everyone is expecting you to do something horrible. Not horrible just *wild*."

Judy – "I'm not sure I know what you mean by wild. If you're talking about crowds of people getting together on a beach and drinking beer and whooping around, that happens all the time in smaller numbers. I have a fight every year with my folks about this subject. They start right after Christmas telling me I'm going to stay home during Easter Week, and I know it's not because they think I'm going to drink beer or act like a nut. They think I'm going to do a lot worse than that."

Gordon – "I take it that you usually end up getting to go anyway."

Judy – "Yes, but it's always a battle."

Gordon – "It probably wouldn't be if you were a boy. The newspapers *have* made Easter Week sound like a national orgy. I don't honestly know if I'd want my daughter going to something that even *sounds* like that. I guess you really have to trust a girl before you'd let her go."

Bob – "It isn't a matter of trust; it's fear. Your folks trust you the rest of the year don't they? I doubt if your folks or any girl's folks *think* you're going to do, as you put it, a lot worse than drink beer. They're *afraid* you *might*, and afraid of what might happen if you did. That's only natural."

Sharrie – "I don't think there's anything very natural about *any* of this, with the exception of everyone wanting to get together and have fun. The rest of it is all distorted. That's why it does get too wild in some places. Everyone's watching you like hawks; you're in a side-show. A lot of the action is just an act on the part of the kids. They want to give the audience their money's worth. By the way, I have the same trouble with my folks. They like the boy I go steady with until Easter Week. Then, when we want to get together with our friends and go somewhere my boyfriend is suddenly a sex-fiend or something in their eyes. I wish I knew what would help stop this image or attitude or whatever it is. By the time I get through fighting to get to go, I don't have any fun."

Bob – "The only thing that would help would be if we'd all cool it and keep it down to a dull roar, when the 'audience' is looking, I mean. There isn't any way we can *explain* that Easter Week isn't what it seems to be. We'd have to show them it's not as wild as they think. Sharrie made a great point about a lot of it being an act just to put people on and shake them up a little. If we'd stop that, they'd let us alone and then we could have some fun. Maybe."

Gordon – "I agree there's no point in trying to explain because the image is already created and it'll stay until people actually see it changing. We don't have to be as obvious as we are, and if we *weren't* being so obvious, there wouldn't be houses wrecked and that crap. That's usually nice kids getting too carried away with the idea that the world is watching them on a cinemascope screen, so they really sock it to 'em, baby. Cooling it is almost a necessity at this point – a lot of places won't let us in *now*. Like the Springfield song says, nobody's right if everybody's wrong."

Minister Becomes California Hippie

(Continued from page 5)

but no more dangerous nor harmful than that accepted by adults – is not the significant characterization which they should be judged. It is a symptom of impatience and curiosity common to most generations. It is also an expression of contempt for the hypocritical standards of their elders.

The group populating the Haight-Ashbury district and their fellow hippies on the Sunset Strip are extreme examples. But their beliefs and behavior are being followed to a growing extent by young people in other major cities throughout America.

The adult generation sees their wild, uninhibited appearance and behavior and is turned off by it – convinced that these young people are going lickety-split to hell.

Look magazine recently stated that most students on U.S. college campuses – and even some high school campuses – have either tried marijuana or know someone who has.

Many of them regard it as a non-addictive, apparently harmless way to groove – its principal dangers being legal. A few years ago students obtained the same vicarious thrill by breaking similar taboos regarding alcohol.

Grownups, who sometimes drink to the point of ruining their health and disrupting their families – and pay no attention to the warning labels on their own cigaret packages – react with outrage and alarm at the increasing experimentation with marijuana among young people.

Timothy Leary and other leaders of the so-called psychedelic revolution, speak of revelation, spiritual illumination, sensual contact with nature and love when describing the effects of psychedelic drugs such as LSD.

The majority of young people who don't smoke marijuana respond strongly to such talk, for they are searching for the same emotional values in their lives.

Many adults feel that the simple way to deal with the rapidly spreading interest in drugs among the under-25 generation is to outlaw it. The same solution was once offered for alcohol.

I fear the results will be equally disappointing. No laws can stop the writing and even singing about the possibilities of Utopia spawned by psychedelic contact. Using the nightstick approach will only drive the forbidden fruit farther underground and make it more tantalizing.

I am hopeful these symptoms of impatience and curiosity will moderate with time and maturity. But even as they exist now, I am convinced this generation is far more moral than the preceeding generation.

The truly important characteristic of today's generation is its sense of awareness, its sense of justice and its sense of values as to what life is really all about.

They are painfully honest with themselves, overly idealistic and will often get their ears slapped down in a cruel world which masks its selfish motives with pious pronouncements – a world which punishes a single, direct act of murder but often acclaims mass murder.

But this generation will not be put off.

After seeing the best and the worst that it has to offer I am more encouraged than ever before. This generation will make the most important contribution to mankind in recent history.

Naively, its aim is to save the world. And I think it will succeed.

MONO-TEM 3004 STEREO-TES 4004

Lets Fall In Love

PEACHES AND HERB'S NEW SINGLE
'CLOSE YOUR EYES'
2-1549

Available At Your Favorite Record Store

KRLA ARCHIVES

Vox is the sound—the sound at the top. Like Paul Revere and the Raiders, the Beatles, the Rolling Stones. If you want to sound like the sound at the top, buy Vox. That's what's happening. Write: 8345 Hayvenhurst Ave., Dept. BP325, Sepulveda, Calif. We'll tell you where to get **Vox guitars, amplifiers and Continental organ.**

KRLA ARCHIVES

ROD McKUEN
'THERE'S NO SUCH THING AS TEENAGERS OVER NINE'

You might not think you know him. But you do. He was born in Oakland, raised in California, Nevada, Washington and Oregon. He had a wild love affair going with San Francisco, worked as a laborer, stunt man, disc jockey and newspaper columnist before serving with the army in Japan and Korea. He has performed in major clubs all over the world, appeared in practically every large concert hall and written more than 700 songs.

He's Rod McKuen and he believes that "there is no such thing as teenagers anymore unless they're about nine. I think after that they become pretty intelligent."

Rod is proclaimed by many to be the most sensitive and certainly one of the most recorded composers in the fast-paced, hyper-unsensitive world of the 60's. If all goes as scheduled, close to 80 McKuen compositions will hit the market this month alone. His songs have been performed by everyone from Andy Williams to the Kingston Trio and from the Righteous Brothers to Danny Kaye.

The sensitivity of McKuen seeps out of his songs like tea out of the bag. Perhaps it is because Rod is something of "an outdoor man." "I like living close to the ground," says Rod. "The sea has always had a strange fascination for me and I've attempted over the last several years to write about the sea but I never got to it 'til this time." *This time* is a hauntingly beautiful album simply entitled "The Sea." It is entirely spoken word with the tremendously exciting background music supplied by Anita Kerr.

Unlike the majority of composers, Rod does not aim his material at any one particular market. "I never try to think of whom I appeal to. I think if something is good it should have a wide appeal to everybody."

Rod spreads his literary talent over the entire spectrum. Besides his songs, McKuen is quite a poet. One of his collected works, "Stanyan Street & Other Sorrows," has sold more than 30,000 copies, making it the biggest selling book of poetry in 20 years. His next work, "Listen To The Warm," has already been grabbed by Random House and will be published in September.

Also in the works for Rod are a recording session with Al Hirt in South America and in September an appearance at the famed Carnegie Hall. Rod runs a growing publishing and recording firm, and is currently working on a novel and finishing up a musical play, "Lonesome Cities."

The following is an excerpt from "The Sea." We chose it because, we feel, in "The Days Of The Dancing" McKuen has a valid and valuable comment on what is happening today, right now, to everyone in the world over nine.

THE DAYS OF THE DANCING

Words by Rod McKuen   Music by Anita Kerr
From the Anro Production for Warner Brothers Records "The Sea"

These are the days of dancing . . . six feet apart
You see people
in bars or places
and they look at each other
just look
and they don't do anything about it.

Suddenly it's two o'clock
and they don't do anything about it.

Let's be different.
Let's not wear mustaches and funny clothes.
Let's not let our hair grow so long
it covers up our eyes and makes us unable to see the world

Never mind the world.
Let's not miss each other.

They can keep their wedgie shoes
butterfly collections
and their nineteen thirties songs
I'm tired of dancing anyway.

I feel like going somewhere somewhere I've never been.
They can have their one room trips.

If these are the days of dancing
let's keep the nights for love.
And what was your first name anyway?

Copyright 1967 by Rod McKuen and Anita Kerr
Assigned to Warm Music, Box 2783, Hollywood, California
Published in book form in "Listen To The Warm" by Random House, New York
All rights reserved
Used by permission

Switching On

FURRY FANTASY — Cher models luxurious three-quarter length coat of red fox on white suede with large zipper opening. Underneath the coat, Cher wears a white turtleneck short sleeve sweater and white suede pants.

Cher Designs

The exclusive *BEAT* pictures on this page feature Sonny and Cher styles designed by Cher for their movie, "Good Times." The styles are striking, practical, and best of all, can be worn by the average "Switched On" person. Cher, recently featured in a number of magazine layouts (Vogue, Ebony), is becoming a strong name in the fashion world for her outstanding designs.

ORIGINALS BY CHER — She wears an outfit in large mother-of-pearl sequins on silk. Note especially the black and white boots. Sonny wears a suede suit with leather pocket flaps and cuffs.

CASUAL PANTS AND TOP — This outfit is sewn in a cotton stripe fabric with the flower print area in velveteen. The high bodice belt creates an empire style.

DOUBLE BUTTONS — Sonny's shirt features small double buttons closer set than Monkee style, on a cotton flannel. Cher owns an identical belt.

KRLA ARCHIVES

BEAT EXCLUSIVE
Inside Cosby's Mind

By Eden

Laughter should be an easy thing—it isn't very difficult to smile. We all enjoy a happy moment or two of humor, some funny thing which we can all share and enjoy. But the difficult part is making someone *else* laugh—and that can be a very serious business.

It isn't very often that we get an opportunity to go *inside* the mind of a comedian—to see just how he goes about the business of making people laugh. So, we are indeed fortunate to be able to spend at least a short time with Bill Cosby —probably one of the funniest comedians of all time—learning about his humor, from the inside looking out.

"Usually I do what I call 'Bobbing and Weaving.' The *attitude* is paramount. I let the attitude kind of shove the mind around and we Bob and Weave to see if we can get a smile or a laugh or if something can register itself.

"Now, if the people laugh—then, I think about it and I *study* to see what they're laughing at. Sometimes I get a laugh and I don't know what really caused them to laugh that hard, and I study it. This is all within a split second, because I'm still talking while this is going on.

Why?

"They laughed... *why* did they laugh?... so forth and so on... okay, let's try to stay within the same framework of what they're laughing at. Can we follow this line with another? Yes, we can; we have a beautiful picture to paint here. Right!... I have a picture to paint after I throw in *this* punchline... the punchline goes *boom*, the people laugh... ah hah... all right, let's take it up carefully and build a little tension here and relax the tension with the line here, *wack!*... now, did you hit it right?... yes... got a good laugh; did you hit it right?... no... I think it was off a little... what was the response?... well, it was mild, but not as good as it could have been... all right—remember that the next time, not to put the line before the picture, and so forth and so on... and that's how something funny develops."

If the preceding seems a bit miraculous to you, you're not alone; it does seem astounding that anyone could be so involved in so much at one time and still entertain a huge crowd of people as well as Bill does.

However, Bill denies any possibility of miracles in his comedy.

"It's like a man that runs a lathe. You look at the guy who has three, four things to do and you say, 'Gee whiz—if I had all those things to do I'd cut my hand off!' Well, he practices, and of course he hits his thumb, or he bangs up his finger and he may have a few scars, but nevertheless, he knows how to run it.

"Now, comedians, of course, have had to run the same kind of a machine — *mentally* — and they have scars and they've made plenty of mistakes, and they're *still* making them! So, it's nothing *that* great. I, for one, think that my talent is a *natural* thing. I like to think of it as a natural thing because I've been trying to do it *unprofessionally* for 23 years."

With any kind of humor, it is usually a two-way affair. Someone, or something, is making someone else laugh. In the case of a professional laugh-maker, the other person is of the utmost importance, for without them—there would be just empty jokes with no one around to laugh at them.

Attitudes

"That's what comedians are concerned with: the attitude that the people have, the attitude of the audience. You cannot perform without an audience; *I* cannot perform without an audience. I can go on and say some stories, but I wouldn't know where, exactly, to go without an audience — that's how heavily I lean on them.

"Woody Allen can *write* without an audience, knowing that something is funny—he will take it, and know that at least 70 per cent of it

SAYS COSBY of his co-star: "Bob Culp could make mincemeat out of me in front of the cameras if he felt like it." Culp disagrees.

is good, go up and try it... and in that way he can tell what is really funny, and how he can place another line. We *all* depend upon this. All comedians work the same way—they have *to*.

"Now, in the *response* to the attitude, we all differ, I think. Some comedians get hostile, others fold under it and get worse. I, for one, when I find that an audience is unresponsive, take my act and chop it down. Where I would go maybe an hour and a half, I may just go 35 minutes; I cut it down from maybe one-half to one-fourth, depending upon how hostile I am. I never make any mention to the audience that *they're dead* or that

there's something wrong with me. I just go faster.

"I make attempts, trying to work harder. But when you're pressed—at times an individual does not work as hard as he can, or he's not working as *well* as he can. This is only in a night club; if I have a bad evening at a concert, I try different things—I may stay in there a little longer, but I usually come off much quicker than I expected."

Humor is a wonderful thing—one of the most precious gifts we can share with one another. And when it is coming from the mind of a man like Bill Cosby—it *has* to be a very funny business!

Righteous Two: 'Our Next Move Is Movies'

By Bob Levinson

Bobby Hatfield wanted a map to the movie stars' homes, the kind sold on street corners by kids and crones, and he would ask for one every time the family devoted Sunday afternoon to a motor tour of Beverly Hills.

He never got one, so he could only guess what celebrities might live in the lavish homes on elegant streets.

Today, Bobby lives in Beverly Hills in a hilltop home in one of the city's most exclusive sections. Were those gawkers' guides ever updated, his name and address would be included.

He's one half of the Righteous Brothers, the blond one with the outgoing demeanor, who hits the high notes with unerring accuracy. He's 50 per cent of a singing duo that gives all indication of staying part of the entertainment scene regardless of musical trends or teenage tastes.

The other half is Bill Medley, the taller, dark-haired, more introspective one, whose echo of a voice hits fathoms otherwise reached only with diving gear.

Together they have a sound that puts a modern interpretation on soul music, distinctive combinations of rhythm and rock that sell records and sell out night clubs and concert halls.

It's been that way virtually since the two disbanded competing musical groups in the Santa Ana, California area and merged their voices four years ago.

Their Verve recording of "Soul And Inspiration" was the nation's number one song and million seller within five weeks of its release. Their new album, "Sayin' Something," is enroute to Gold Record status as well.

If the young men, both 26, have any career objective, it's further to solidify their standing as an act with appeal to all age groups. They still suffer the stigma adults arbitrarily attach to all talents discovered by teens.

"We like to work the teenagers, but we also like to work our own age and up to 30-35," Bill explained.

Said Bobby: "We just want to progress and, like any act, do concerts and TV work. When we started night clubs, we didn't plan so many right in a row."

We Didn't Think

Bill: "When we drove into the night clubs, we didn't think, 'Let's capture an older audience,' although we did want to ensure our careers. When we played the Sands in Las Vegas, for example, they came in thinking of us as a rock and roll show, and the adults were pleasantly surprised."

Bobby: "Although we still do a lot of up-tempo stuff, we're doing more ballads. If we were still doing only the hard, hard screamers, we wouldn't be singing at all."

Bill: "We do a medley of our well-known hits in three minutes. Then we get on with the show."

"The more people who see you, the more people you get on your side, and the more bread you make," Bobby observed. Bill adding: "Our next move is definitely movies. We've had offers, but we're waiting for the right one."

Separate Ways

The Brothers, when not working, go their separate ways—Bobby in Beverly Hills and Bill in a Spanish-style casa grande in the Hollywood Hills.

"Before either of us was married, we thought about moving in together in Hollywood and, man, all that action," Bill recalled. "But it's too easy to kill a good thing."

Added Bobby: "Willie doesn't wake up too good. You just don't talk to Willie in the morning.

"In the old days, I used to stay over at his house some nights. I've seen him wake up with the phone next to his ear from the night before."

(Editor's note: Bob Levinson covers the teen scene regularly for the Sunday "Around LA" entertainment section of the Los Angeles Herald-Examiner. This feature is reprinted through the courtesy of the Herald-Examiner.)

BEAT Photo: Robert Young
FOLLOWING HIT medley "We get on with the show."

KRLA ARCHIVES

'Hey, Paul, Heavy On The Relish!'

By Ron Koslow

See, there was a guy named Paul, who owned a drive-in restaurant in Napa, Idaho. And every day, Mark, the delivery boy from neighborhood bakery would deliver buns for Paul's burgers. One day, as a promotional scheme, Paul hired a rock and roll band to play at the restaurant; now Paul had always kept his secret ambition under cover, until the band's piano player didn't show.

Now was his chance to bring out in the open what he had kept behind locked doors all his life—Paul took over that piano and began to play in a way that would have done Jerry Lee Lewis proud. While Paul was grooving on the keyboard, Mark drove his bakery truck into the parking lot. Like a man in a trance, Mark moved toward the band platform. He stood beside Paul, who was oblivious to everything but his hands flying across the keyboard of the piano. When the number was over Mark tapped Paul on the shoulder. Paul looked up and saw it was the boy from the bakery. "Just leave them around the back by the kitchen door," the restaurant owner told the delivery boy.

Mark stammered, "Do you... Do you think I could sing?"

Lindsay Shy

Paul seemed surprised and then he nodded. Mark moved to the microphone and stood waiting. Always shy and introverted, Mark was now so nervous his knees were literally knocking together, but when the band broke into "Crazy Arms," all the musical hopes and ambitions that had only come forth while on deliveries, and in the shower, now exploded. He could hardly believe the rich, powerful voice that filled the drive-in parking lot was his own, and neither could Paul. And at that moment both Paul Revere and Mark Lindsay realized the burgers and buns just weren't their bag.

Paul decided to move to Portland, Oregon and took Mark with him. Once there they began to piece together the group that is today known as Paul Revere and the Raiders. They enlisted Mike Smith, a hot little drummer who owned a thriving teenage night club in Portland and with the help of disc jockey, Robert Hart, they began promoting dances featuring the Raiders.

Setback

In January, 1963 they signed with Columbia Records and recorded the original version of "Louie, Louie." The single released that June, was unfortunately beaten to the national charts by a cover version recorded by the Kingsmen.

This minor setback only increased their determination and by 1964 they were the top rated group in the Northwest and Hawaii, making continual appearances and setting attendance records wherever they played.

In January, 1965 Phil Volk joined the group as their bass guitarist and all signs pointed toward the big move—the move into national popularity. Their timing was right and Dick Clark, who knows just a little bit about Pop music, decided that this was the group he wanted to feature on his forthcoming "Where the Action Is" series.

In April, 1965, Paul Revere and the Raiders were introduced to the nation and within a matter of months became nationally acclaimed as one of the hottest groups ever. Columbia Records backed them with the full force of their production and promotional facilities and soon an unbroken chain of hit records was established.

The most important asset the group possesses, however, is their incredible stage presence. They are more than just a group, they're an act—tightly structured and ex-

...THE RAIDERS (l. to r.) Harpo, Fang, Smitty, Mark and Paul waiting to go on a local TV show

tremely well rehearsed, yet still open to the spontaneous humor and excitement that makes their act unique.

Their dynamic and sometimes zany act tends to obscure Paul Revere and the Raiders as individuals. It is an easy mistake for one to attribute their on-stage personalities to the off-stage individuals, and this writer was no exception. I was fully prepared for an interview with five raving maniacs, but I was pleasantly surprised and impressed. Off stage, the Raiders (all of them) are intelligent, serious minded, warm and really beautiful people.

Uncle Paul

Paul is the leader of the group and their great success attests to his keen business mind and skillful direction. Nicknamed by the others, "Uncle Paul," he maintains a complete equilibrium within the group making sure that everyone is happy and satisfied.

He is a man of great honesty and admits quite openly that what he would most like to do in the future is devote more time to his wife and two children. He is managing his money wisely, in stocks and municipal bonds plus ownership of several apartment buildings, an oil well, a chain of drive-ins and a real estate company.

Hopes to Return

He some day hopes to return to the Northwest where he loves the clearn, cold winters and change of seasons. At the moment though, he is busy pounding out the rhythmic background for the Raiders, and devising much of their comedy on the spot.

Mike Smith is the "gutsy" little drummer who provides the foundation for the dynamic Raider sound. Anyone who has watched him work out, knows that Smitty is an accomplished musician and moreover a brilliant clown. His facial expressions are priceless, in the tradition of Jonathan Winters and his talent for the subtle "shtick" is fantastic.

Youth Insight

Having been the owner of a teenage night club in Portland, Smitty has a keen insight on youth and what's happening today and is able to articulate his views with sincerity.

An entirely self-taught musician, he is most inspired by the music of the "Spoonful," the Beatles and the Byrds, and hopes that the present musical trend of "down home blues-rock" as exemplified by their latest hit, "Ups and Downs" continues.

Phil Volk (affectionately known as Fang) is a bright and interested 21-year-old. He feels that today's music has transcended the label of rock and roll, and should now be considered "contemporary music." He is anxious to develop himself in other phases of the business and eventually would like to write (music, novels, films) and possibly try his hand at acting. As far as immediate plans go, Phil would like to travel to Europe (if and when the Raiders busy schedule allows). Meanwhile he never ceases to be stimulated by the new places he visits and people he meets while touring the U.S.

Sensitivity

Jim Valley, "the new Raider," replaced Drake Levin who is now serving in the National Guard, and Raider fans wasted no time in taking Harpo to their hearts. His smile could charm just about anyone, and his sensitivity is something beautiful.

Jim was playing with Don and the Goodtimes when Paul asked him to join the group. At first Harpo was reluctant, but he then realized that this was "a once in a lifetime opportunity."

His sense of humor and warmth made him a natural for the Raiders and he is now "one of the family."

Jim is especially fond of children and ever amazed at their vitality and honesty. He is now in the process of writing a book of fairy tales, fables, and songs for children.

A Loner

Mark Lindsay is considered, today, one of the finest lead singers in the business. He is a deep and serious person who spends much of his off-stage time alone and in thought. He admits to the existence of two Mark Lindsays—one who loves performing and really digs the incredible audience response he invariable evokes; the other, still basically the shy, somewhat introverted boy from Napa, Idaho. Coming from a relatively poor family (Mark's father is a school teacher) he still can't believe his phenomenal success and feels a great responsibility to those who put him where he is today.

Film Plans

Mark, also, would like to try acting and no doubt he will be cast in a key role in the Raiders' upcoming film. His songwriting has produced several of their big hits and he plans to continue in that field in conjunction with an attempt at fiction (see Mark's fairy tale in BEAT, Feb. 11.)

Last year the Raiders grossed over 1.5 million dollars; this year they expect to double that mark, but no matter how great their success, they will continue their backbreaking schedule of nation-wide performances as a sign of appreciation to their fans. With this kind of approach, Paul Revere and the Raiders will be around for quite a while.

RON KOSLOW takes notes while Smitty gets his shoes shined

...HEAD MAN—Paul Revere

KRLA ARCHIVES

...THE MOTHERS OF INVENTION, one of the leading groups in the generation gap, are pictured here with dancer, Karl, and three girls from the Mother's stage show.

... It's Widening

Lashing out at the values of the adult world, Bobby Jameson said, "It's a competitive economic state of being, it's not living." Young people who turn away from the world their parents expect them to inherit, he continued, "Would be dropouts from society, but not dropouts from life."

The young often accuse the adult world of hypocracy, materialism and act as if the grownups had the power to set right all the evils of war and poverty. They sometimes widen the generation gap by underrating the adults.

They forget that the older generation eliminated polio, struggled to erradicate tuberculosis and fought World War II to defeat the racial terror preached by Nazi Germany.

But the young remain suspicious of the leaders of the adult world. Upset by "apparent contradictions" between what we say about Vietnam and what we are doing there, 100 student body presidents and campus editors wrote to President Johnson:

"Unless this conflict can be eased, the United States will find some of her most loyal and courageous young people choosing to go to jail rather than bear their country's arms."

The letter was signed by leaders popularly elected at Duke, Indiana, North Carolina, Columbia, UCLA, Berkeley, Stanford and 93 other capuses all over the nation. The signers are intelligent, well bred, close-cropped, concerned young people, not easily dismissed as hippies or pot smokers.

By 1970 half the population of the U.S. will be under 25. What are they after and what are they protesting?

It is hard for even this articulate generation to say what they want. Young people are more vocal about what they don't want.

Addressing a teenage audience recently, 22-year-old broadcaster Elliott Mintz said:

"A lot of you probably, in the privacy of your own heads, entertain ideas of where it's at and where it's going. We are going to turn this world into an incredibly beautiful place for all of us to live and groove and do our thing."

The world has changed more in the last 20 years than in any other 20-year period in history. Today's teenagers will face a world even more radically different in their adult years.

Experts feel that technology is advanced enough to eliminate many tedious industrial jobs in the next generation. If many of us are only putting in two or three days on the job by the year 2,000, we will have to know how *not* to work.

A society like ours which preaches that "hard work is the road to happiness" might find itself in trouble. With more leisure time than work hours on our hands, song, dance and the exchance of ideas could become the most important activities.

Today's societal dropouts, the hippies whose weird dress and habits make them easy to dismiss, might be in the vanguard of society.

Many speak of this generation of teenagers as swinging, open, free and honest. Will this help them make a world less uptight than their parents? One observer of the teen scene, Dick Clark, doesn't think so:

"The kids are going to get just as uptight as their parents. Life is hard. They may not see their way clear now but they'll have to change."

More optimistic viewers feel the country will benefit from today's youth explosion.

"I think its very healthy that the (youth) movement is growing," said Andy Wickham. "In America the movement is all toward personal emancipation and the kids are more aware of the human element."

Andy feels the generation gap is "more painful and obvious now." Young people are more concerned about individualism and human rights and "have reached a tremendous enlightenment and it is expressed now in music and the arts."

Brian Wilson thinks the generation gap has resulted in "An extreme polarity" which makes life very "interesting and spicy."

If so, then it's apt to become even spicier. The generation gap appears to be widening.

MORAL OR IMMORAL?
Minister Beomes California Hippie

(Almost 18 months ago the author, in his second year as assistant pastor of a large church in the Midwest, exchanged his black clerical suit for corduroy pants and a paisley shirt. Aware of the growing gulf between today's generation and established society, he set out to observe and grasp the new morality represented by today's rapidly-shifting values. On leave from the church, he traveled to Chicago, New York, San Francisco and Los Angeles, becoming a member of the new society known as the Underground. — The Editor)

By Rev. Ansel Stubbs

An odd thought struck me as we sat around cross-legged on the floor of a bare apartment in San Francisco's Haight-Ashbury district — a rag-tag collection of misfits, dropouts and rebels vigorously arguing a mixture of philosophy and theology.

Looking at their scraggly beards and long hair, most of them wrapped in blankets or panchos in the unheated room, I was struck by the resemblance to paintings of a familiar Biblical scene.

"This looks like a scene from the Last Supper," I thought. And in many ways the comparison was not as ridiculous as it sounds.

The smoke curling around the small room was not incense and the bottle of wine they passed around was hardly a sacrament. And yet I have never heard more fervent sincerity nor total dedication to the true spirit of religion — brotherly love — at any Wednesday night prayer meeting.

The experience was typical of several I have encountered since becoming a member of this young, adventurous, impatient, rebellious and idealistic society which sprang up only yesterday and is determined to find all the answers and to correct all the wrongs today.

I am still appalled by some of their personal behavior, their deliberate violation of so many of society's and Christianity's moral taboos. Some of their practices appear degrading and depressing at best, dangerous and self-injurious at worst.

And yet I am now convinced such behavior — more spectacular

(Turn to page 15)

KRLA ARCHIVES

Supremes – Capricious But Cautious

By Bob Levinson

They're called the Supremes, but people would understand were the president of Motown Records to change it to The Dollar Signs.

The company's success in the six years since Berry Gordy Jr. began carving out a recording empire in an area of Detroit — where most of the carving is done by wrecking crews — is substantially due to these young ladies.

Diana Ross, Mary Wilson and Florence Ballard became the country's foremost female singing trio virtually the moment Gordy gave them a Motown contract as a high school graduation present.

No one will say just how rich the girls became, but it's evident Diana, Mary and Florence recognize poverty only because they lived with it so long.

"We lived in the Brewster Douglas housing project, where you *have* to be poor," Diana related. "The first thing we did when we were able was to buy our parents homes."

Berry, on hand to mother-hen his mint, remembered: "They bought fantastic homes. But by the time the deals went through, they had outgrown them financially. So, they spent twice the cost furnishing the homes."

Each of the girls has become a fashion plate, the area in which they can complete as individuals, rather than one-third of an impression.

The company protects the purse strings.

"We invest in stocks," said Gordy. "The company has top auditors and accountants who look for tax shelters and teach the girls how to pay taxes."

The young women appear to take their success and solvency capriciously, but cautiously. It's almost as if each morning a pinch is necessary to verify reality. Then, having done so, whoopee!

There is every likelihood the Supremes' popularity will be maintained and move onto more adult plateaus, because Gordy is keeping them keyed to current market tastes at all times.

He explained: "Their records are essentially the same, and they're commercial, but they're doing more now, all types of music — ballads, show tunes, folk. They're increasing their repertoire but the original feeling has not changed.

"Their voices have mellowed to a great extent. Their sound is much more refined and it's much more dynamic because of their confidence."

Diana, Mary and Florence hadn't done much talking.

It's their singing that sells.

(Editor's note: Bob Levinson covers the teen scene regularly for the "Around LA" entertainment section of the Los Angeles Herald-Examiner. This feature is reprinted through the courtesy of the Herald-Examiner.)

THE SUPREMES — "Their voices have mellowed to a great extent." *BEAT Photo: Chuck Boyd*

SPECIAL OFFER TO BEAT READERS!!

TEEN INTERNATIONAL APPROVED

AUTHENTIC MONKEESHADES by DEBS®

ONLY $1.98 PLUS .02 HANDLING CHARGE

★ Created & Designed by Davy Jones in London

★ 5 Groovy Colors...rose...yellow...blue...grey...green

★ Heavy Mod Golden Chain

★ Just Like the MONKEES Wear On Their Swingin' TV Show

★ MONKEESHADES are the Wildest!

Send to: **MONKEESHADES, 81 W. State St., Pasadena, California 91105**
PLEASE SEND ME THE MONKEESHADES AS INDICATED. I ENCLOSE $2.00 FOR EACH PAIR

COLOR_____ NO. PAIRS_____ TOTAL AMOUNT ENCLOSED_____
Name_____
Address_____
City_____ State_____ Zip Code_____

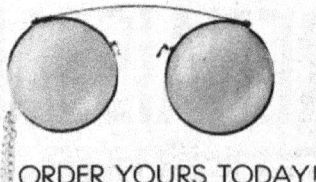

ORDER YOURS TODAY!!

KRLA ARCHIVES

SHIRLEY
By Shirley Poston

I'm about to say something that's going to sound exactly like something you'd expect me to say (as in ridioulous). In fact, I think I just *did*.

Anygoat (just kidding) (Gawd), here it is. I *hope* I met someone very gloovy (that's Chinese for groovy) the other night. It isn't that I don't remember. It's just that gloovy is the only word I know in Chinese.

I'd ask you if you've ever spent quite a bit of time listening to someone without ever having the froggiest (*hah?*) notion what the someone was talking about, but I'm afraid some of my (ir)regular victims - er - readers would be only too happy to answer than question. (I have found that the word *answer* is much more interesting when you pronounce the w.) (I have also lost my mind.)

Now don't get the idea that the possibly gloovy person was actually speaking Chinese. Get the idea that he might as *well* have been.

Two Languages

I speak two languages in addition to English. (or would if I *could* speak English.) They are called "Blither" and "Pop Star." But the someone in question was neither nut nor musician; he was something else. (I'll say.) Which rather leads me (by the collar) to believe that every crowd-bunch-gang-or-whatever thingy has it's very own tongue. (Which is always nice if you have a lot of stamps to lick.)

I was able to glean one comment from the un-translated version of our meeting. When something is really rare and choice, it is referred to as "antique."

Well, I must say that this someone is certainly antique enough for me to make every effort to collect him. And even if I never do figure out what he's babbling about, I feel I could learn to overlook our differences. (From a hilltop sanitarium, no doubt.)

Course, there's always the possibility that I just wasn't listening closely enough. You see, all this took place just after a certain date, and I don't mean Dromedary — I mean February 25th! (Bow, bow toward the East, all believers!) (East as in Surrey.)

I was so exhausted from the annual hysteria of celebrating George L. M. Harrison's birthday (the L.M. stands for Low Moan), I really wasn't at me best. No, no, I'm not going to start *that* again and go through the whole Beatle Birthday bit and tell you about the cake and the pageant and the 24 people we had to find named George.

Leap Year

Speaking of George (I've been known to) (I've also been known to speak of George), another of my favorite Georges was born in February. Only he was born on February 29th, so he didn't get to have a birthday this year. When Leap Year comes around, I'll be sure to leap on him (with expensive gifts and good wishes, that is.)

I don't know why that reminds me of what I'm about to blither about, but then I don't know much of anything.

It seems that every time I wear my hair in braids, I get into trouble. If you're a new reader - er - victim, you are fortunate enough to have missed the story about the time I had "words" (and never mind *what* words) with the checker at a supermarket because he insisted that I had to buy a whole box of orange popsicles (if you love them too, keep reading this insanity and you'll soon learn to hate them) (not to mention me) instead of *one* orange popsicle.

Let it suffice to say that when I politely refused (in the key of High C) to do any such am-day thing, he looked me right square in the braids and said "Sorry about that, Becky-poo."

I didn't give him time to add "of Sunnybrook Funny-Farm."

This is *mild* compared to what happened recently. I was walking down the street, minding my own business (for a change.) When I stopped for a traffic light, I noticed that a man standing beside me was giving me the eye. Although I'm not the type to go around encouraging D.O.M., the way he was looking at my hair (which was in braids tied with rawhide) kindof tickled me. So, thinking *he* was probably thinking I closely resembled a somewhat sappy Seminole, I laughed.

He drew himself (just 'appened to have pen and paper there wif him, he did) up haughtily. "It's not funny," he said.

I immediately gave *him* the eye and stalked off, wondering *what* wasn't funny. Well, I soon found out because he bounded after me and added the following comment in all seriousness: "You're anti-American! I can tell by the way you wear your hair!"

With that, he re-bounded in another direction. And before I could recover, another man said: "Hey kid, you've got the hair and I've got a protest. Let's go picket!"

I thought the whole thingy was pretty funny at first. Now it makes me about half mad (my usual condition.) The last commentator was just being smart, but the first one was dead serious, and in essence they both said the same thing — like, burned any good draft cards lately?

Good grief. Do grown-up supposedly rational people actually think they can judge someone's political feelings by a *hairstyle?* I shudder to think what might have taken place on that street corner if my hair had been *red*.

Me Pocohontas

Next time I venture out of the house in braids, I'm going to wear a large sign that says "Me Pocohontas." And I'll take John Lennon along just for further proof. (I know, I know, it was John *Alden*, but you take who *you* want and I'll take who *I* want.)

Before I close (my gabbling trap), I'd like to comment on a certain rumor which several of you have written and asked my opinion of (?). I'd rather not say what the rumor is because the only thing I believe in spreading is peanut butter. Let's just say that although it doesn't concern *me*, it *concerns* me. (Keep it up, girl. That kind of writing is bound to catapault you to fame.)

The happiness of the someone the rumor's about is very important to me, and to answer your questions. No, I don't believe it, and re-no. I'm not happy to hear it. And I never will be. Not ever.

Well, would you believe *hardly* ever?

LEWIS TAKES CONCERT HONORS

PHOENIX, Arizona—A big line-up of stars and Jerry Lee Lewis will perform at a concert on June 2 at the Memorial Coliseum here to honor Jerry's 10th anniversary as a recording artist. A 90-minute film will be shot during the show produced by Bobby Boyd in connection with the Glenn Development Corp. of Phoenix.

Turning On

THE MAMA'S AND PAPA'S DELIVER (Dunhill) *Dedicated To The One I Love, Creeque Alley, John's Music Box* and nine more tracks.

The third LP by the big four features less original material than other albums and consequently lacks the exclusively original sound of the group. However, it is still an excellent LP. *Creeque Alley*, musical history of the four, and *Dedicated* are great, as well as Cass' *Sing For Your Supper*.

ERIC IS HERE—ERIC BURDON AND THE ANIMALS (MGM) *Help Me Girl, It's Been A Long Time Comin', That Ain't Where It's At*, and nine others.

Eric, as a solo artist, has arrived just as the album title states. The Animals stay in the background behind Eric's soulful and powerful voice—used to it's fullest advantage on *Help Me Girl, Wait Til Next Year, Losin' Control* and *It's Not Easy* are some of the better tracks.

SAYIN' SOMETHING—THE RIGHTEOUS BROTHERS (Verve) *Along Comes Jones, I Who Have Nothing, Yes Indeed* and nine more tracks.

Once again the Righteous Brothers have issued a top notch album. *I Who Have Nothing* is probably the most outstanding track, and incidentally, the twosome's new single release. It's backed with *Along Comes Jones*, also on the LP.

DISCussion

One of the best of the new releases this week comes to us from the talented Mama's and Papa's with their latest, "Dedicated To The One I Love." More than just a new rendition of an old Shirelles' hit, the disk is a beautiful combination of production which borders on the brilliant, outstanding vocal harmonies, and an ingenious arrangement to support the entire record. This has to be one of the biggest for the talented M's and P's.

* * *

First spin around the turn table for the Merry Go Round with "Live" and they may come up with a fair-sized hit on this first time out. You may be reminded of early Beatles or even middle-Lovin' Spoonful with this one, but that's primarily due to the vocal sounds of lead-singer Emmitt Rhodes and arrangements of producer Larry Marks. Good instrumentally and vocally this might be the beginning of a winning streak for the new, young quartet.

* * *

Motown has sent us a big, shiny new package of goodies from their New Releases Dept., and as usual — they're all outstanding. Heading up the list is a beautiful record from Smokey and the Miracles—"The Love I Saw In You Was Just A Mirage." If you ever finish saying the title, listen for some unusual and beautiful instrumental work here, including the unusual combination of 12-string guitars and bells. A great record.

The Tops are spinning back to the chart-tops with their latest — another Holland-Dozier-Holland composition — "Bernadette." Although there are many immediately familiar elements taken from their recent releases on this record, it is still very new and unique. The talented Holland-Dozier producing team seems to be getting more and more involved with the use of a musical pause and sustained note. Listen for this in the new Tops single.

Stevie Wonder joins the list of Motown Movers this week with a beautiful new uptempo ballad, "Traveling Man." Very poignant lyrics and an excellent vocal performance, coupled with the usual high standard of production at Motown should send this one to the top for this phenomenal lad.

Martha and the Vandellas have also returned to the chart race — *at last!* — with a Holland-Dozier-Holland effort entitled "Jimmy Mack." The use of the Vandellas' harmony as background for Martha on this disk is slightly reminiscent of the Supremes' earlier work, but Martha's distinctive lead-vocalizing gives this disc the personal signature of Martha and the Vandellas ... which should have them signing into the Top 20 again very soon.

THE ASSOCIATION
new hit single
NO FAIR AT ALL
V 758
from their latest hit album
RENAISSANCE
Valiant RECORDS

KRLA ARCHIVES

please send me
BEAT

26 issues only
$3 per year

Mail to: **BEAT Publications**
6290 Sunset Blvd. #504
Hollywood, California 90028

☐ **New Subscription**
☐ **Renewal** (please enclose mailing label from your last BEAT)
I want BEAT for ☐ 1 year at $3.00 or ☐ 2 years at $5.00
I enclose ☐ cash ☐ check ☐ money order
Outside U.S. — $9 per year

* Please print your name and address.

Name_____

Street_____

City_____

State_____ Zip_____

FOUND: The Knack

The search is on. At least once every working day someone dashes into *The BEAT* offices and declares, "I've found a new group that's the greatest thing since the Beatles."

But when Capitol Records tells us they've found a group that they think just might be that, we listen, for, after all, who brought the Beatles to us?

And Capitol thinks they have, in a group called the Knack. They have been appearing in and around their home town and Capitol's home office, Los Angeles, for some time and they've just released their first single, an original composition titled "I'm Aware."

The Knack is Mike Chain, Larry Gould, Dink Kaplan and Pug Baker. As to how they came about the name, their official biography states, "Mike, Larry, Pug and Dink, once having found it, defined it and created it, realized that having the knack was not enough ... and so, they became it."

18 year old Mike is leader and most outspoken member of the group. "I think we have something unusual to offer," he says. "For instance, we're one of the few groups around who can write, arrange, produce, play and sing. If necessary, we could produce and record a disc by ourselves. We're not just three rock guitarists and a drummer. Each person has something unique to contribute."

Mike, along with Dink, writes most of the group's material, and his imitations of other singers has become the highlight of the act.

Tall, easy going, bass playing Larry comes nearest to actually having the knack when it comes to girls. Although he hasn't "zeroed in yet on any particular dolly," he explains that he's looking for "someone who's easy going and extra understanding. She's got to be extra understanding because an entertainer is always going to be around other girls. She's got to understand that because I'm around them doesn't mean I'm after them."

Dink is the group's prize musician, an excellent guitarist who also tends to be the funnyman. His guitar playing, which he's been doing for almost six years, is entirely self taught. "I took four lessons when I first started, but then I quit. I got tired of playing 'Jingle Bells.'"

London born Pug is the silent member of the group, and their drummer. He doesn't sing, and often doesn't talk either. "I got the habit of just sitting quietly in one place a long time ago because I didn't want to seem out of place. I guess I'm still used to sitting in one place whenever we go somewhere because I still don't want to seem out of place."

CLASSIFIED

FOR SALE

'66 HONDA 90 cc. low mileage, excellent condition. Best offer, call Francine (Hollywood, Calif.) 659-3641, eves. 466-5730. (F)

WANTED

WANTED: BEATLE PHOTOGRAPHS. Will pay good prices for quality photos. J. Cook, 395 31st Ave., San Francisco, Calif.

TWO GIRLS need other hippie girls to share house in Laurel Canyon. Bonnee 645-0274 or Cheree 645-8279 (Hollywood, Calif.).

WANTED: ROCK BAND to record. Must have excellent harmony and lead guitar. Orange County area, Calif. 524-0753.

WANTS DATE with John Senne.

WANTED: PEN PAL, 16 or over, with Mad Interest in Absolutely Everything! (Especially Baron Manfred von Richthofen!) Loretta Kelley, 24727 Bombay Ave., Wilmington, Calif. 90745.

CLEFER WILL FINANCE Cykle-type group to cut 3 or 4 prof. studio demos. DU 2-4707 after 9 p.m.

THE MAGICAL MYTHICAL RYTHMICALS will play at your party or dance with ease. 289-9836.

LOST GUYS & GALS

MARS — Can't find you skiing. Write: 636 Toper Drive, Seal Beach, Calif. Blonde-haired Linda.

WHO LIVES AT 721 N. Alfred Street? Please write: Janet Burchett, 5567 Hamill Ave., San Diego, Calif.

LOST — on Jersey Turnpike. Two neat guys in a red Corvet. We were in the blue Corvair. Meet us same place, March 20. Doris and Karen.

PERSONALS

PETER TORK — I won the date two months ago. I'm still waiting!! Janet Gellman.

KEITH RICHARD belongs to me! ... Joni

SALLEY LOVES JOE.

BAKERSFIELD! FREAK OUT with the **THIRD STORY**. Coalinga, Calif. Coming Soon!

I LOVE YOU and someday I'll meet you PAUL! Linda.

HELLO JULIE OF CAGE 57. LOVE JFB.

THE MARK DAVIDSON TRIO GROOVES!!

BOSCO RABBIT WALKS AMONG US! ... beware the unbeliever!

MR. HARRISON: Does it tickle? Sue

I LOVE LARRY MON

ALBUM CUT of "No Fair At All" — better than single!

JOYCE IS GROOVY!

MIKE CHAPMAN is a cool guy!

THE MONKEES ARE THE GROOVIEST!

THE ASSOCIATION IS UNNECESSARY — just like food, sleep, happiness and love.

LYNNEA, ALICE, RANDY: you'll NEVER find out who I am, but I KNOW ALL! signed: SECRET PAL.

CANOGA PARK HIGH RULES.

CLASSIFIEDS ... 10¢ a word for personal messages from you to someone else without an object for sale or trade, etc. Everything else (for sale, wanted, etc.) ¼ 20¢ a word. When counting words, the street and number (6290 Sunset Blvd.) count as one word. Telephone numbers are one word. City and state (Hollywood, Calif.) count as one word. Classifieds must be mailed with the correct amount of money to BEAT CLASSIFIEDS, 6290 Sunset Blvd., Hollywood, Calif. 90028.

... **DAVID McCALLUM** and **BEAT** reporters, Rochelle and Louise at a party for the Knack

KRLA ARCHIVES

America's Pop Music NEWSpaper

KRLA Edition BEAT

APRIL 8, 1967

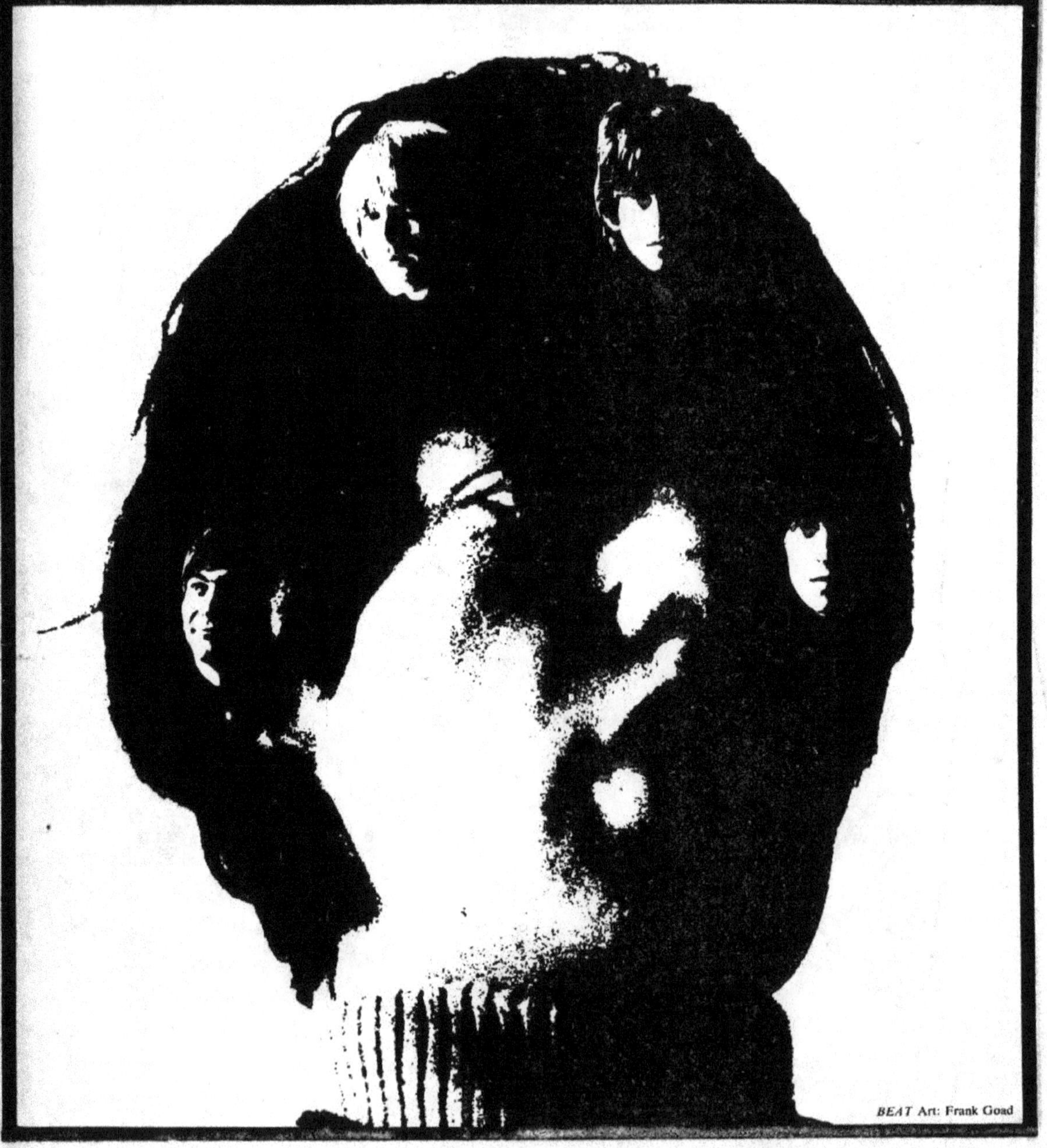

25¢

BEAT Art: Frank Goad

KRLA BEAT

Volume 3, Number 2 April 8, 1967

BEACH BOYS SET THEIR EUROPEAN TOUR MINUS CHIEF BRIAN WILSON

The Beach Boys, minus Brian Wilson, will revisit Europe. In May they start a six-nation tour in Dublin, Ireland. Then they'll play Belfast in British Northern Ireland and hop over the Irish Sea on May 4 for their first London Concert. Following their British tour, the group will visit Norway, Holland, Germany and Sweden.

The group's latest single, "Heroes and Villains" is the first collaboration between Brian Wilson and Van Dyke Parks, who are also writing the new album, "Smile" to debut this spring. The album has a 12-page insert book of color photos of the group.

Brother Records, Inc., The Beach Boys' own recording company, has opened offices in Los Angeles. The group is currently developing a TV and films production operation at the same office.

Draft Looms In Monkee Future

HOLLYWOOD — If anything splits the phenominally popular Monkees, it will be the United States Army! And the Monkee closest to being called up is Britain's Davy Jones.

Davy, although still a British citizen, is eligible for the U.S. draft because he lives and works in this country. He's due to take his Army physical shortly but everyone connected with the Monkees is confident that Davy will not be called up.

"Eligible"

The Monkees' American publicist refused to comment on the subject, except to say that Davy is "registered and eligible." However, the group's English publicity office was a bit more talkative. "Obviously Davy doesn't want to go," said publicist David Cardwell, "but he certainly won't kick if he is called up. He has no plans to appeal against it, as far as we know."

Another spokesman for the Monkees said: "It is true that Davy is eligible for service, but the fact that he has dependent relatives and is not of the required height will almost certainly exclude him."

Needless to say, the millions of Monkee fans all over the world are keeping their fingers crossed but in the end it will be entirely up to Davy's draft board whether or not he is called up.

On the record front, the Monkees' fantastic sales pace has not lessened at all. As usual they were awarded a Gold Record simultaneously with the release of their latest single, "A Little Bit Me, A Little Bit You" b/w "A Girl I Knew Somewhere." The single had orders in excess of 1.5 million copies at the time of its release and was immediately audited and certified by the RIAA.

Since August 16, 1966 the Monkees have sold over six million albums and nearly six million singles in the United States alone.

Meanwhile, the Monkees have landed right in the middle. of a $35,000,000 lawsuit filed by Don Kirshner. The Monkees themselves were not named in the suit filed by the former executive of Screen Gems/Columbia music. However, the suit revolves directly around them as Kirshner charges that he was "fired without cause" from a five year contract signed last August and that Columbia Pictures and Bert Schneider, Monkees' manager, were involved in a "conspiracy" against him.

Allegedly, the story is that Schneider asked Kirshner to leave "The Monkees" television show because of a disagreement over how the group's music was being handled on the show and also over who was getting the credit for the music.

A further allegation is that the Monkees would like to write more of their own material instead of using the compositions of other writers. Of course, no one is kicking (indeed, can kick) about the Monkees' sales figures.

Denials

For their part, both Columbia and Schneider emphatically deny that there is any foundation to Kirshner's allegations. A statement issued by Columbia said, in part: "in the opinion of our counsel the suit is totally without merit and the personal charges which Mr. Kirshner has made against the individuals are wholly groundless. We are confident that the court will agree that the actions were well justified and that the corporations acted within their legal rights and in the best interests of their stockholders."

Schneider said only that "there is no basis whatsoever for the accusations."

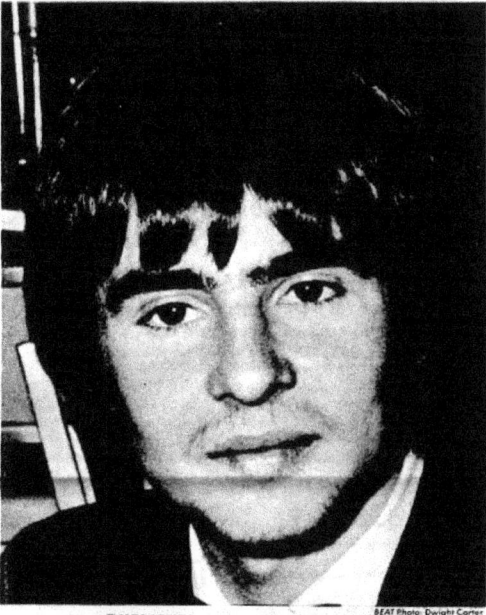

...DAVY JONES will go without a fight if drafted

Gary Lewis and "Jinky" Suzara were married at St. Paul the Apostle Church in Westwood, California. In the next issue of The BEAT we'll have exclusive pictures of the bridal couple taken at the church and at the reception which was held in the home of Gary's parents, Mr. and Mrs. Jerry Lewis.

We'll also have an exclusive story on how Gary and Jinky met, the problems they encountered when they went to obtain their licence, etc. So, don't forget to see the next issue of BEAT.

BRIAN JONES COMPOSES FILM SCORE: STONES' 'RUBY' IS CERTIFIED A GOLDIE

Brian Jones of the Rolling Stones has opened up a whole new facet in his career by composing and producing the background score for the forthcoming motion picture, "A Degree Of Murder."

The movie is a full-length film which was filmed in Munich, Germany and will be exhibited at the Cannes Film Festival from April 27 through May 12. The film was chosen for the Festival because of its camera effects, its meter and Brian's musical score.

After completing the score, Brian and fellow Stone, Keith Richard, left for North Africa for a vacation. Mick Jagger is also on a vacation but is attemping to keep the location a top secret.

The Stones' last single, "Ruby Tuesday" b/w "Let's Spend The Night Together," has been certified by the RIAA for a Gold Record. Both sides were penned by the Jagger/Richard team who, as you know, are currently working under a million dollar writing deal signed through Gideon Music in the United States.

Both "Ruby Tuesday" and the highly controversial "Let's Spend The Night Together" were taken off the Stones' latest album, "Between The Buttons." The album became the sixth consecutive Stones' album to qualify for a Gold Record with sales numbering over the million mark. With the success of "Between The Buttons," the Stones now number four albums in the nation's charts—the other albums being "Big Hits—High Tide and Green Grass," "Aftermath" and "Got Live If You Want It."

THE ROLLING STONES are set to tour Europe and England.

KRLA ARCHIVES

HUNDREDS TURN OUT TO GREET PRESLEY'S GUITAR

It is a well-known fact that Elvis Presley makes no personal appearances. However, he did relent slightly by allowing his guitar to be exhibited at Expo 67, Montreal's Universal Exhibition.

Hundreds of Montreal teenagers staged a huge welcoming party for the Presley guitar when it arrived at the Montreal airport! The guitar will be placed in the Popular Music exhibit at the U.S. Pavilion. The guitar (which has been termed priceless) is the one with which Elvis recorded some of his biggest hits, including "Heartbreak Hotel." This is also the guitar he played at the time of his television debut.

It's only fitting that the Presley guitar be placed in a special section of the U.S. Pavilion, the one devoted to "The American Spirit." And what spirit the Presley fans still have—turning out in the hundreds to welcome his guitar into their country!

DEAFENING APPLAUSE GREETS MQCB IN ALL CIVILIZED AND BARBARIC COUNTRIES OF THE WORLD!

U.S. Rallies On UK Charts

LONDON — American music is finally staging a comback on the British scene. A detailed analysis of record store sales in Britain during the last three months of 1966, shows that U.S. artists, labels, and producers are cutting into British dominance of the charts here for the last three years.

Record Retailer, a British weekly, checked its top 50 charts and found that the Beach Boys took the top album position and the Four Tops the top singles place. The Beatles and the Kinks claimed the next two album slots. America's English residents, the Walker Brothers, were fourth, followed by the Rolling Stones.

Dave Clark Makes Film

Dave Clark has formed his own movie production company, Big 5 Films. He has just finished a 15-minute short, "The Dave Clark Five Hits in Action," which features all of the boys with their million-plus hits as a background score.

The film which shows the group water skiing, horseback riding, racing and clowning around, was directed by Dick Clark and has no dialogue. It has been sold for American distribution.

We're Sorry About That!

Dear Reader,
Here is a little map to reading the March 25 BEAT. Page 20 and 5 were mistakenly switched by our printer, thereby breaking up "The Generation Gap...It's Widening." Sorry if we confused you. Hope you enjoyed it anyway.
— The Editor

TURTLES HIT SOUTH; EUROPE THIS SUMMER

The Turtles, enjoying their recent hit success, "Happy Together," have lined up their schedule of personal appearances. The group has just completed arrangements for their first European tour, starting in London on June 1, with dates booked for Paris and Copenhagen.

The group is currently on a tour of the Southern U.S. appearing at: Lake Worth, Florida, April 1; Jacksonville, April 7; and Montgomery, Alabama, April 8. The Turtles will then fly to California to appear at: San Francisco University, April 14; University of Redlands, April 15; and San Bernardino Auditorium, April 15.

Then the group will fly to Des Moines, Minneapolis and wind up in Chicago.

Kink Hurt By Surging Paris Fans

Over 2,500 Paris fans became so frenzied during a performance by the Kinks that they broke through guard lines and poured onto the stage. Bass guitarist Pete Quaife suffered a broken leg in the melee but the rest of the group escaped unhurt.

Quaife was knocked down by about 150 girls who tore at his clothes and hair before guards could hustle the injured Kink offstage.

He completed the remainder of the group's Continental tour with his leg in a cast.

PEOPLE ARE TALKING ABOUT when the **Beatles** are going to finish up their album . . . whether or not the **Rolling Stones** will ever get good publicity from an adult-oriented magazine . . . the rumor that one of the **Raiders** may soon make his exit from the group . . . the soothsayer predicting the end of the **Monkees** within a year—very reminiscent of the predictions that the **Beatles** were just a passing fad

. . . the decision not to release "Epistle To Dippy" in England . . . the Boston soul of the **Hardly-Worthit Players** . . . the hilarity of Kenny Solms and Gail Parent and their "1 Were A High School Graduate" carrying a "not recommended for adults" tag with it . . . the disappointment of **Jeff Beck's** debut . . . "American Bandstand" not going off the air after all; it was Clark's "Swingin' Country" and "Action" which got the axe

. . . the Boston Airport phoning *The BEAT* office to ask where they might locate **Russ Giguere** of the **Association** . . . whether or not the **Beach Boys** will succeed in breaking their contract with Capitol Records and what **Brian Wilson** will do if they don't . . . how many groups are now imitating the **Monkees**, sound-wise—which is only to be expected since success always breeds imitation . . . whether or not the **Walker Brothers** will accept that offer to appear in Las Vegas . . . how embarrassing it must be for Davy and Micky to have their old records re-released for sale. Davy's old album features pictures of him with his short, combed-back hair

. . . what a good laugh it is on those people who are trying desperately to start a controversy going between the **Beatles** and **Monkees** that neither group will bite . . . **Grace** of the **Jefferson Airplane** being in the hospital recovering from exhaustion . . . *BEAT* being in the *Saturday Evening Post* thanks to the **Mamas** and **Papas** . . . those horrible photographs that the Stones are letting slip into the

British papers . . . **Hayley Mills** trying to be the Mia Farrow of England by marrying a much older man . . . **Diana Ross** flying all the way from Detroit to Los Angeles just to keep a dentist's appointment . . . the **Knack** and their manager splitting and leaving some very hard feelings all the way around. As a matter of fact, people are wondering what the group will do when they have a hit.

. . . how wide the generation gap really is . . . whether or not that mini-castle will be purchased by Mick Jagger . . . Sonny and Cher being surprisingly good on their "Man From U.N.C.L.E." stint . . . how everyone wishes they really knew what gives between Paul McCartney and Jane Asher . . . "Crank Your Spreaders" finally hitting the newsstands and what a gas it really is . . . what will happen to the **Raiders** if one member is drafted and another leaves to go his own way

. . . the return of the English rockers . . . British teens complaining that the **Beatles** are trying to sound like the **Beach Boys**

. . . the return of greasy hair becoming something of a fact in Britain . . . **Dave Clark** arriving late for his own party and finding dirty breakfast dishes still piled in his room . . . the **Happenings'** "I've Got Rhythm" sounding more like the Four Seasons than the Four Seasons . . . **Lawrence Welk** covering "The Beat Goes On" and **Enoch Light** covering "Sunshine Superman" . . . **Lamont** of the 5th Dimension and his "soap and

water" . . . **Herb Alpert** going mod with checked pants and turtleneck sweater . . . the trouble **Frank Zappa** got into because of the music coming from his all-night party—now he just plays his record player.

Beat Publications, Inc.

Executive Editor . . . . Cecil I. Tuck
Publisher . . . . Gayle Tuck
Editor . . . . Louise Criscione

Staff Writers
Carol Deck   Bobby Farrow
Ron Koslow   Shirley Poston
Rochelle Reed

Contributing Writers
Tony Barrow   Sue Barry
Lawrence Charles   Eden
Tommy Hitchcock   Rochelle Sech
Bob Levinson   Jamie McCluskey, III

Photographers
Chuck Boyd   Dwight Carter

Advertising
Dick Jacobson   Jerry Loss
Winona Price   Dick Stricklin
Ron Woodlin

Business Manager . . . . Judy Felice
Subscriptions . . . . Nancy Arena

Distribution
Miller Freeway Publications
500 Howard Street, San Francisco, Calif.

The BEAT is published bi-weekly by BEAT Publications, Inc., editorial and advertising offices at 6290 Sunset Blvd., Suite 504, Hollywood, California 90028. U.S. bureaus in Hollywood, San Francisco, New York, Chicago and Nashville; overseas correspondents in London, Liverpool and Manchester, England. Sale price 25 cents. Subscription price: U.S. and possessions, $5 per year, Canada and foreign rates, $9 per year. Second class postage prepaid at Los Angeles, California.

KRLA ARCHIVES

GOODTIMES' TOUR DATES AND CITIES

Don and the Goodtimes announced their signing with Epic Records. The quintet's first single on the label, "I Could Be So Good to You," has been rushed out.

The Goodtimes, the group Dick Clark calls, "a hit in the making," finished their first album before leaving on a three-week U.S. tour. Still untitled, the album includes a number of original compositions by Buz Overman. It was produced by Jack Nitzche and Stu Phillips.

The group is featured on Dick Clark's, "Where The Action Is," and are on an extensive April tour with the Dick Clark Caravan.

Following is Don and the Goodtimes April tour schedule:

1, Paducah, Kentucky; 2, Cincinnati, Ohio and Muncy, Ind.; 3, Murray, Kentucky; 4, Jackson, Tenn.; 5, Martin, Tenn.; 6, Birmingham, Ala.; 7, Augusta, Ga.; 8, Winston-Salem, N.C.; 10, Cookville, Tenn.; 11, Ashville, N.C.; 13, Melbourne, Fla.; 14, Orlando, Fla.; 15, Columbus, Ga.; 16, Chattanoga, Tenn.; 17, Lafayette, La.; 18, Jackson, Miss.; 19, Little Rock, Ark.; 20, Nashville, Tenn.; 21, Florence, Ala.; 22, Huntsville, Ala.; 23, Owensboro, Kentucky and Evensville, Indiana.

Hollies And Herman on TV

Herman and the Hollies are both featured in a CBS documentary on youth to be screened in April. The show devotes a large segment to the recent outbursts on the Sunset Strip.

Hollies' drummer, Bobby Elliott, who has been in a German hospital with appendicitis, is making a rapid recovery and hopes to return to England soon.

'BANDSTAND' TO CONTINUE

Dick Clark's "American Bandstand" has survived network scrutiny and will continue to broadcast Saturday afternoons. "Where The Action Is" and "Swingin' Country," however, were not so lucky. Both shows have been terminated.

"American Bandstand," now in its 12th year, has become a teenage institution. It began airing in 1956 from Philadelphia. Shortly afterwards, Dick Clark took over hosting duties and the popularity of the show zoomed. It has been carried over national television since then.

"OUR SINCERE THANKS FOR THE DEAFENING APPLAUSE AFFORDED "THE MENDELSOHN QUINTETTE CLUB OF BOSTON"
Hymie Mendelsohn

The Spencer Davis Group Loses Stevie Winwood

England's pop scene is in widespread shock at the news that Stevie Winwood, member of the Spencer Davis Group, has completely quit the performance end of the music business.

Stevie, one of the country's top musicians, walked away from the Davis Group, last year voted #1 R & B singers over the Rolling Stones, saying that he hopes to experience some of the teenage years he has missed.

Relax And Think

Eighteen year old Stevie has been performing since he joined a skiffle group at the age of 11. Now, he plans to relax and "think out my music" for at least six months.

First, however, he must finish composing music for two feature films. After his half year hiatus, he plans to devote all his talents to songwriting and producing.

Another chapter of the story indicates that something besides just the desire to quit performing was responsible for his decision. Stevie is reportedly upset that during his three years with the group, he has received fame but no money for his efforts.

One British paper even quoted him as saying "I want lots of money!"

Ever since Winwood joined the Spencer Davis Group, rumors have followed him reporting that he would leave the group shortly. But until now, he had never said he was definitely exiting the act. So it is accepted that Winwood's action is completed, final and permanent.

While Davis fans are unhappy with the news, Stevie is reportedly relieved and satisfied with his action. He adds that he is indeed serious about becoming a writer and producer. He penned the Davis Group's latest hit, "I'm A Man."

Spencer Davis is currently looking for a replacement for Stevie and will tour the U.S. as scheduled.

Inevitable

According to informed British sources, the Davis-Winwood split was inevitable because of the necessity for both singers to go their own way. In addition, Stevie had been getting progressively more restless with the pop performer's life.

Rumors are rampant, but unconfirmed, that lead guitar player Muff Winwood, Stevie's brother, is also departing the group to return to his former occupation, accounting. If he does, only Spencer Davis and Peter York will remain of the original foursome.

D. Payton of DC5 Weds

Denis Payton, 23 year old tenor sax and guitar player with the Dave Clark Five, married blonde Lyn Griffiths in Epping, England, early this month.

Lyn, 21, is a secretary. She wore a traditional white bridal gown at the mid-day wedding. Dave Clark was best man.

Denis is the third member of the DC5 to marry. Only Dave Clark and Michael Smith are bachelors. Dave has been rumored to be engaged to Cathy McGowan, hostess of the BBC's now-defunct "Ready, Steady, Go" television program, both Dave and Cathy deny that they are betrothed.

ON THE BEAT BY LOUISE CRISCIONE

Despite the fact that the Beatles won't be coming and the Stones are doubtful, you can expect a full-scale tour from Herman and the Hermits during the summer. Their Stateside tour is scheduled to follow upon the heels of the completion of their movie, "Mrs. Brown You've Got A Lovely Daughter." Which means that if all goes with realtively few hitches the group will spend four to five weeks in the U.S. during July and August. However, none of the dates and cities have yet been set.

Jeff Beck, former lead guitar man for the Yardbirds, seems to find trouble no matter where he goes or what he does. He left the Yardbirds to form his own group, which he did one week before they made their debut in England. Unfortunately, their opening night turned into a disaster instead of a triumph.

Beck Leaves

Our reporters in London revealed that because the group had only formed days before the show they had not had time to sufficiently rehearse their act. During the first house, the power failed and Jeff walked off the stage. Following the poor reception accorded the group during the second house, Jeff announced that they were leaving the tour.

All I could get out of Davy Jones about his fantastic return to England was that it was "wild." He certainly looked none the worse for wear – though our British spies reported that he had some very narrow escapes from his English fans. He's looking perfectly fit with his new shorter haircut and his pencil-thin moustache and newly-acquired beard.

BEAT Photo: Chuck Boyd
...HERMAN

"Wild" Says Davy

In contrast to Davy's shorter hair, I spotted Micky Dolenz the other day and he has let his hair grow out a bit. Micky was also engulfed by fans during his stay in London, but he too escaped uninjured. The Monkees' visit was supposed to be a vacation, though it didn't quite turn out that way. They certainly accomplished something with the press over there. Ever since their visit, the British papers have been filled with Monkee stories and pictures – very reminiscent of what went on over here with the advent of the Beatles.

Speaking of the Beatles and Monkees – the Beatles have just been awarded their 13th Norwegian silver record (signifying 250,000 sales) for "Yellow Submarine." Their "Penny Lane" should be number one there by now and will in all probability be their 14th silver record. Meanwhile, the Norwegian television network has purchased six episodes of "The Monkees" for airing during the next couple of months. The Monks' "I'm A Believer" has already topped the Norwegian charts.

A Canadian group, the Mandela, caused quite a stir when they played the Scene in New York. Among those who dropped by to see them were Herman, the Young Rascals, Brian Epstein, the Casinos, Andrew Oldham and Andy Warhol.

Soul Revival

The Mandela have come up with something which has to be seen to be believed. They've started a nationwide *tent* tour. I swear! It's derived from the religious revival meetings which are held in tents – only the Mandela's is a soul *music* revival.

...SKY SAXON

Another group causing a sensation across the nation, but especially around the Los Angeles area is the Seeds. Led by Sky Saxon, the Seeds recently played a gig at the celebrity infested Daisy Club where they drew people like Jane Asher (touring Stateside with the Old Vic Company), Tommy Smothers and Mickey Callan in to see them. The group is currently on a cross-country tour plugging their latest hit, "I Can't Seem To Make You Mine."

KRLA ARCHIVES

Letters TO THE EDITOR

ADDITION TO MONKEE SIDE

Dear *BEAT*:

Thanks for the swell article defending the Monkees. It was really fantabulous!

I'd like to add something, though. It's said that they owe their popularity to mass TV exposure. True, they were first seen on TV, but stop and think. Where were the Righteous Brothers before "Shindig?" Where were Paul Revere and the Raiders before "Action?" Even the Robbs and Hard Times on "Action." From the space they take up in fan mags, they must be terrif, but we don't get "Action" in Decatur, Indiana and I've never heard them sing — or Keith Allison either for that matter. They must have gotten their popularity from TV!

Long live the Monkees — and all other pop groups, for that matter.
Pat Miller

Davy Jones On Casey?

Dear *BEAT*:

I enjoy your paper very much. All of my friends read it too. I think the Monkees are the greatest! When I first saw a picture of them in The *BEAT* I was sure I had seen David Jones on one of the Ben Casey shows. It seems to me Davy played a glue-sniffing addict. My friends say I must be wrong. Am I?

I would appreciate it very much if you could clear this matter up for us. If you can't, could you please let me know how to get this straight?

Thank you very much for any help you can give. In the meantime, please do more on the Monkees.   *Buttons*

You're right, Buttons, Davy did portray a glue-sniffing teen on a Ben Casey segment.
The Editor

BEATLES AND CHANGES

Dear *BEAT*:

I didn't write to you to compete with any letters, or to even agree with them. I just wrote to you about the Beatles. No words can describe how I feel about them. Well, maybe there's one, SHAGGY, which I think is very cute.

When the Beatles first came to the U.S., to me they were four mop tops with big eyes who made a lot of noise. But after awhile, they made great movies, they appeared in the newspapers and then I heard "Yesterday," "Michelle," "Girl" and "And I Love Her" and I also noticed Paul. I feel silly saying this but in the beginning I thought that John was Paul and Paul was John. So, everyone said they liked Paul because he was so pretty. But not me. I just loved John because I didn't know who was who — except for Ringo.

Later I got things cleared up. Paul was the hazel-eyed, left-handed, adorable one. John was the slanty-eyed, fresh-looking, sexy one. The first time my father saw them in the newspaper, he said: "Look what England's sending us now."

Yet, I wouldn't want to see them as a fan and start to chase them up the street. If I saw Paul walking up the street, I wouldn't run out and ask for his autograph. I'd invite him in for tea and English muffins and then ask him for his autograph.

Do you get my point? I think so.
Jeannine Raber

A Request For Dylan

Dear *BEAT*:

May I first say that I enjoy The *BEAT* very much and I hope you continue to write up the kind of paper you do now.

I have a request to make. I feel that Bob Dylan is the most influential writer-composer of our time and I feel that what he has to say should be heard. Do you think that maybe in one of your up-coming issues of The *BEAT*, you could print a large article or maybe an interview with Bob Dylan?

Also, the Young Rascals have a semi-hit. I think that if there had been more promotion behind this record they could have had a smash hit. I feel that the Young Rascals are the greatest group. Felix Cavaliere is one of the greatest soul singers of our time, next to Eric Burdon and Mitch Ryder. I do hope you answer my requests.
Dave Bloom

MONKEES FAN CLUB

Dear *BEAT*:

I first got an edition of The *BEAT* yesterday. I was very pleased and here is my money for a year's subscription!

Please give some information on the Monkees Fan Club. I don't know where to send for it.
Barb Ward

For information on the Monkees Fan Club write to 1334 North Beachwood Drive, Hollywood, California 90028. The Editor

THE SOUL OF MITCH RYDER

Dear *BEAT*:

I doubt that anyone in their right minds ever termed Mitch Ryder as a "white Negro." He doesn't possess that much soul — would you believe an American Eric Burdon, a bit closer I might say.

As for giving James Brown a run for his money — that's like saying the Seeds are giving the Beatles a run for the money (not even to talk about talent.) Might I add that as far as Mitch Ryder traveling without his Detroit Wheels, well, they really made the group. Guess this is the end anyway for groups and another fad will try to replace this one.

Thank you for taking the time to read my thoughts.
John D. Vland Jr.

MAY YOU OPEN YOUR MIND TO THE TALENTS OF NEIL

Dear *BEAT*:

My reason for writing is that I feel that the only way I can express myself to people is by doing it through The *BEAT*. I feel the need that people should start opening up their eyes and ears to a great guy, a guy who has been noticed but in so many ways unnoticed; of course, I'm speaking of Neil Diamond. To me, Neil Diamond is one of the most fantastic performers in the music world today. He not only sings his songs, but writes them with a great style of his own.

When Neil Diamond came out with his first hit called "Solitary Man," I thought, "so what . . . just another singer" and thought no more of him or his song. Finally, when he released "Cherry, Cherry" my eyes began awaking to him and I'm glad they did.

Like most songwriters when they have a hit record, their follow-up record sounds just like the first one. Of course, there have been others, but have you ever really noticed how different Neil Diamond is? His first hit was a beautiful slow ballad with great lyrics. His second hit seemed to be just the opposite — a fast moving song with a lot of rhythm and beat. One thing that you can be assured of when Neil Diamond sings is that he leaves that feeling with you. He can set you in the mood and makes you often feel as though the song he is singing is about you. Not too many singers can do that.

I, myself, had the chance of being able to see Neil Diamond and if I could have the chance to turn the clock back, I think I'd like to turn it back to that one night. You see, I'll always regret that night because then I really wasn't aware of how talented he was. I didn't take the time to really sit down and watch and listen to him, but now I hope that in the near future I will have this chance.

You can tell just by looking at Neil that he isn't the type of guy who is in the music world just for the money, but because he feels it's a part of him and that this is what he should be doing.

He also seems to be doing it for the pleasure of entertaining and expressing himself through his songs. Some people believe that Neil is an angry-looking young man, but what they really don't know is that beneath that hidden smile is a very serious man with a friendly attitude about him. He seems to take his music very seriously and at times too seriously, but look how it's turned out so far . . . fantastic!

Of course, this is only one fan's point of view, but at least I've noticed the talents of Neil Diamond. Maybe he hasn't gotten to you but, believe me, he's sure "Got To Me." I hope you can find room to print this letter because maybe it'll bring some people into noticing Neil Diamond. I hope so!
Cherry Cherry

Married Raiders?

Dear *BEAT*:

For my sake and for that of every Raider-Rooter, answer me this one question: is Paul Revere really the only married Raider, or do Smitty and Harpo both have secret wives?

I hope that this rumor is not true, not because I don't want Harpo and Smitty to get married, but because I can't believe that any of the Raiders would think it necessary to hide the fact that they are married.

Thank you very much.
Karen Moss

According to the Raiders' publicity office, Paul is the only married Raider. The Editor

BIG ENOUGH FOR TWO

Dear *BEAT*:

I am a Beatle fan. I always have been. I have all of their records and I have been to two of their three shows in San Francisco. Now people are saying that the Beatle fans don't care about them any more and instead have turned to the Monkees. People are putting down the Beatles by saying that they've changed and they're old men.

They *have* changed. You have to change. Everything changes. They aren't exactly what I would call old men. I think that they are wise not to stay in the whole business and to just do records. John's right. Who would want to see a Beatle at 80 up on the stage? I don't think I would. Of course, I'll miss them a lot.

But now there's the Monkees taking over. I'm not ashamed to admit that I also have all of their records. I can't understand why people put them down because they don't play all of their own music. Lots of groups use other musicians. As long as they make people happy, so what? I say thanks to the Beatles for making so many people happy and may the Monkees make just as many people happy.
Vicki Braun

KRLA ARCHIVES

The 'Trouble' With Stones

By Louise Criscione

Their middle name has always been "trouble." Some of it real, most of it imagined. The Rolling Stones were the first of the pop group anti-heroes. Right from the very beginning only their fans accepted them—the rest of the world merely dismissed them as some sort of a group disease which would die by the sterilized point of the good-taste needle.

From The Top

From the smallness of the Crawdaddy to the emensity of the top U.S. variety shows, the Rolling Stones were heralded by most critics with something far less than respect. Emerging from their debut at the Crawdaddy, the Stones were met with cries of "would you want your daughter to marry a Rolling Stone?" No mother did.

Eventually finding themselves with a hit record, the Stones overheard the plaintive cry of anguished parents: "They don't even wash, you know!" Worried about the sanity of their daughters, mothers pointed up the fact that "surely they smell." Stone fans didn't buy it.

Stateside with a fairly large name already made for themselves, the Stones appeared on "Hollywood Palace." It was pure fiasco. Sandwiched between animal acts and introduced with highly uncomplimentary remarks, Mick admitsing." Seething anger churned inside the Stones but they went on with their performance as if nothing had happened. It was, after all, only another in a long line of insults. Months later, Mick termed their appearance on the show "our biggest mistake"—but other than that, he said nothing.

The "Facts"

By this time, reporters had wind of the "fact" that the Stones were smart-aleck, smelly kids. They interviewed them as such. They wised-off before the Stones could open their mouths. Others who approached the Stones with intelligent, thought-out questions received intelligent, thought-out answers. But they were by far in the minority.

The Stones, for their part, shot-off when provoked and acted like polite human beings when treated as such. In fact, many times Mick and Keith wore themselves out attempting to make a good impression on a reporter. After the reporter had left, they congratulated themselves "on getting on well" with him only to open the next morning's paper to find themselves kicked from A to Z and all the way back again. It left a bad taste no matter how many times it happened.

I especially remember one time when I was speaking to Mick in a crowded dressing room. People were pushing and shoving like there was no tomorrow. Elbows were painfully stuck into sides and feet were stepped on with a particular vengence. Yet, through it all Mick took his time answering each and every question I asked him.

Another reporter stalked up to us, planted his ample body between us and began firing ridiculous questions at Mick. The chief Stone gently but firmly moved the man aside explaining that he was busy and as soon as he finished he would answer his questions. The reporter didn't wait. He shuffled off with a disgusted look on his face and unprintable words tumbling from his mouth. No doubt he returned to his typewriter to tell his readers what a rude and insulting person Mick Jagger was.

Obscene?

Still later, the anti-hero Stones had the distinction of having their records termed "obscene." And the cry changed to: "You know why they sing so you can't understand them? It's because everything they sing is dirty!" Dirt, reminded the Stone fans, is in the mind of the listener.

And now the headlines in England scream out the alleged raid by police officers on Keith Richards' house. A tasty morsel of flesh for those who had started out knocking the Stones only because they "smelled."

Trouble

It made little difference that the police evidently did not find any traces of drugs because no arrests were made. It was enough that they had apparently searched the house. "It must be true," say the righteous people. "Those Stones are nothing but trouble."

But are they really? Or are they merely victims of the giant publicity machine?

...**STONES** (left to right) Bill, Brian, Mick, Charlie and Keith rehearsing for "Sullivan Show."

KRLA ARCHIVES

'More Popular Than Jesus?'

KRLA ARCHIVES

KRLA ARCHIVES

U.K. POP NEWS ROUND-UP
British Drug Crackdown

By Tony Barrow

The British national press has carried headline stories about widespread drug-taking investigations over the past few weeks. The homes, the parties and the persons of various pop stars have been subjected to raid and search.

"Several pretty big names are really going to get crucified when the police start making their charges" commented one wise pop colleague of mine in the pub.

First step...crucification. Second step...martyrdom? It doesn't sould like a clever way to solve a problem.

No Epistle

But more immediately the current controversy has led to a decision NOT to release in Britain DONOVAN'S "Epistle to Dippy" single. Don't manager Ashley Kozak admits that the reason is "to avoid letting the press look for any controversial implications in the lyrics."

So Donovan's next single—likely to be released simultaneously on both sides of the Atlantic—will be "Tinker And The Crab." Meanwhile Don is set to put on his own one-man show for a week at Brian Epstein's Saville Theatre week of April 24.

Screen time allocated to pop programmes on our various TV channels in Britain has shrunk to an all-time low. Partly because of last year's effective union ban on lip-sync shows. Suddenly the springtime prospect brightens with the BBC ready to start a new twice-weekly series called "Dee Time" early in April. Host will be DJ SIMON DEE, one of the very few "new wave" jocks to graduate all the way from pirate radio to establishment-type television. Dee just spent a week in New York studying American pop TV techniques. Another show—using dedications from troops stationed overseas and called "As You Like It"—is getting a try-out run in local ITV(commercial television) areas and could build to network proportions if the ratings look good.

Many tears flowed from many teeny-boppers' eyes when London was hit by rumours that DAVY JONES might be drafted this summer and all prospect of a U.K. visit by the Monkees would be ruled out. By now everyone is convinced that Jones will not be called upon to serve the cause of battle. Apart from stage-door battles that is.

RCA Victor will bring out The Monkees' "A Little Bit Me, A Little Bit You" in Britain on March 31. Other side of the single will feature Mike Nesmith's "A Girl I Knew Somewhere." The group's second LP album will reach British record stores on the same day as the new single.

Jagger & Faithfull

MICK JAGGER AND MARI-ANNE FAITHFULL took time out to look over a country mansion close to the tiny village of Little Chalfont in Buckinghamshire...situated no more than a mile or two from Burnham, the home of CHRISSIE SHRIMPTON! The property, belonging to movie tycoon Basil Dearden, is for sale at something over 200,000 dollars and is described as a "mini-mansion!"

Vocalist/composer/guitarist STEVIE WINWOOD and his bass-guitarist brother MUFF WINWOOD quit THE SPENCER DAVIS GROUP after a final appearance with the Hollies/Paul Jones package tour at Liverpool Empire April 2. Stevie plans to concentrate on composing and is interested in working on movie soundtrack scores. Muff is leaving the pop world to go into business.

Dave's Thriller

DAVE CLARK FIVE, using Dave's own production company, to make non-musical thriller movie later this year...ROY ORBISON talent-hunting in U.K. for his new Nashville record production company...BRIAN JONES is the composer of soundtrack music featured in short movie starring the Stone's steady date Anita Pallenburg...ROY ORBISON filmed his own 60-minute TV Special in London. Made in color the show is to be screened on both sides of the Atlantic.

Good chance of FRANK SINATRA flying 6,000 miles to attend the June premiere of his "Naked Runner" movie in London. Around the same time TOMMY STEELE may fly in the opposite direction to be at the Hollywood Pantages Theatre when Disney's "Happiest Millionaire" is unveiled...Seems like bells stopped ringing for STEVIE (Faces, Small) and CHRISSIE (Shrimp, Jr.)...MICKY DOLENZ a big Spencer Davis fan.

School drawing by JOHN JULIAN LENNON provides inspiration for one of dad's new album compositions...MARI-ANNE FAITHFULL makes her legit theatre acting debut in Russian play "Three Sisters" April 14 at London't Royal Court...Midsummer Vegas cabaret offer for THE WALKER BROTHERS under consideration...MANFRED MANN guitarist KLAUS VOORMANN very proud of his "Grammy" album cover award for "Revolver" design...Dave Harman (the first part of DAVE DEE, DOZY, BEAKY, MICK AND TICH) "kept the kids in order" outside his local ballroom at Swindon, Wiltshire, four years ago when he was a police constable!

Britain's first beat group, THE SHADOWS, split from CLIFF RICHARD for all future work apart from possible joint recording sessions...New SMALL FACES album a year in the making...Six 30-minute BBC TV shows this summer for DUSTY SPRING-

BEAT Photo: Chuck Boyd
DONOVAN'S "Epistle To Dippy" not released in England in order to avoid "controversial complications."

FIELD..."Something Stupid" from NANCY and FRANK is something superb...DAVY JONES, who once appeared with HARRY SECOMBE in the stage production of "Pickwick," makes guest appearance in hour-long "Secombe and Friends" TV Spec due for U.K. screening April 16...NEW VAUDEVILLE BAND paid 300 dollars in excess baggage charges when they flew to America...Medical check-up for BRIAN JONES following respiratory trouble...American concert dated between May 6 and 29 for THE HOLLIES following their down-under tour of Australia and New Zealand.

Pye Records in London rushed out with DAVY JONES album which includes his vintage versions of "Any Old Iron," "Maybe It's Because I'm A Londoner," "It Ain't Me Babe" and "Dream Girl."

BEATLE FIRM'S PROFITS SOAR

LONDON—Northern Songs, the firm owning copyright to 99 of the tunes composed by John Lennon and Paul McCartney and seven others by George Harrison, doubled profits for the last half year. Pre-tax earnings went soaring up to 422,000 pounds against 204,000 pounds.

Share holders prospering include John and Paul whose stake in the company runs about one million pounds. George and Ringo Starr own 40,000 shares each which would fetch up 56,000 pounds on the stock market. Is there anywhere to go but up?

BEAT Photo: Howard L. Bingham
...PAUL McCARTNEY

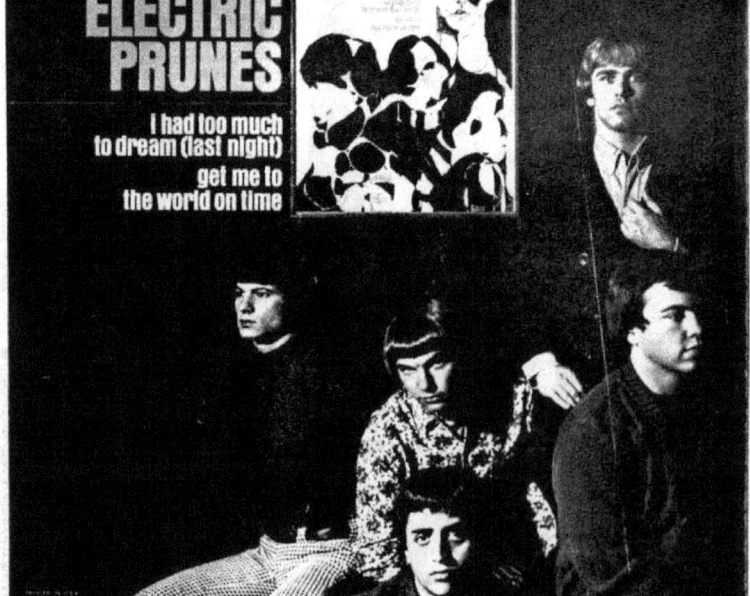

KRLA ARCHIVES

Monkee Session Revisited

Because people are more apt to believe what they *see* than what they hear, we've decided to disprove the "story" that the Monkees do not sing on their own records by printing these pictures of the Monkees taken at the RCA Victor recording studios in Hollywood.

As you can see, Monkees will be Monkees no matter where they are! So, sandwiched in between all the hard work which goes into recording, Davy, Mike, Peter and Micky manage to get a bit of Monkeeshines going. Helps relieve the pressure, you know!

These pictures were taken during the session which created "A Little Bit Me, A Little Bit You." The song was penned by Neil Diamond who also wrote "I'm A Believer" for the Monkees. Jeff Berry, who incidentally happens to be Neil's producer, again took on the producing chores for the Monkees.

BEAT Photos Courtesy of RCA Victor

MIKE, PETER, MICKY AND DAVY wait to hear playback on a take of "A Little Bit You, A Little Bit Me."

...DAVY AND MICKY indulge in a little game of "catch the imaginary ball."

"I ONLY THOUGHT if we changed it here..." Producer Jeff Berry doesn't seem to see the light, but Davy's making sure Jeff sees him!

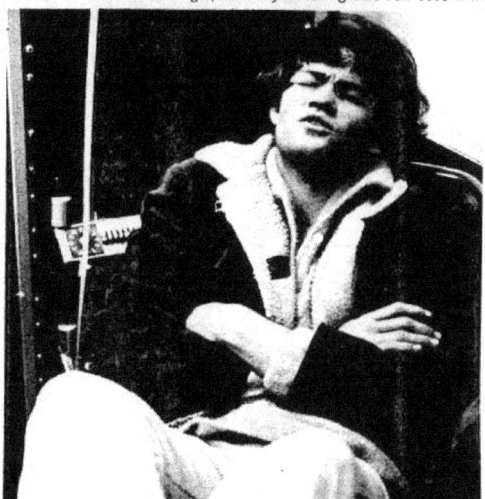

DAVY AND PETER rehearse their background music.   **INTENT LOOK** crosses Mike's face during playback.   **...THAT'S IT,** guys, I'm through for this session."

KRLA ARCHIVES

Harpers Bizarre—From A Nut House To A Studio

By Bobby Farrow

Back in the days when Scap and Dick were just a couple of teenagers in Santa Cruz, Calif. their big dream was to become a famous folk song duo and sing to standing room-only audiences in huge concerts all over the country. As a modest beginning they sang in pizza joints, high schools and clubs around Santa Cruz for about a year. They even cut a record— over a drugstore in Santa Cruz — at their own expense. The record was an immediate failure. But our heroes thought it was so groovy just being in front of tape recorder.

"Wow, look at those little wheels going around," Scap said in amazement at the time. So even though the record was a dud, they really dug making it.

Scap and Dick were getting nowhere as folksingers when suddenly the Beatles exploded on the scene and changed everything. Now even top folksingers were edged off the charts. Everything was rock 'n roll. So after a very significant 5 minutes of thinking, Scap and Dick decided they were rock 'n roll singers.

So they called up Ed and Ted, old friends from around Santa Cruz. Ted was playing trumpet with a jazz group, Ed was a classical guitarist and had never played a rock 'n roll song in his life. But he grew a mustache and locked himself up in a closet and listened to rock 'n roll records. When he got out of the closet, totally recast as a lead rock guitarist, the group chose a name, the Tikis (since changed to their present name, Harpers Bizarre) and began to play.

Today the Harpers Bizarre has hit the charts with their first success "Feelin Groovy, The 59th St. Bridge Song," a Simon and Garfunkel tune.

Dick Young, 22, the group's bass player is a clown with curly yellow hair. What did you do to make ends meet before the group's success, the BEAT staff asked Dick.

"I worked in a walnut shelling place, you know a nut house. I must have shelled millions, it had to be millions of walnuts. Can't look at them now. Loved them before I took the job."

A serious look comes over Dick's face and he says, "But I picked up a lot of good things in the nut factory."

So the BEAT staff falls for it and we say, "Really, what good things?"

Nut Shells

"Mostly nut shells," he said and we all cracked up.

John Peterson, 22, is on drums. He's the one who switched from classical. He's very shy and blushes a lot behind his new blonde mustache.

We asked Ted Templeman, 22-year-old guitarist the meaning of the title "59th Street Bridge Song." He explained: "It's just a very groovy bridge in New York, old and cobble-stoned. None of the group has ever visited New York, but that bridge is number one for our first sightseeing tour there."

Scap, Dick Scoppettone, 22, plays guitar in the group. He says the group is still "unbelieving" about their success. "We want to see if we can sustain it. We know that we can do it now, so we have much more confidence."

Sweet Success

Says Ted, "A lot of people back home talk to us in the street. They say things like, 'We always knew you could do it.'"

"But what was the line two years ago?" interrupts Scap. "They told us, 'Look kid we don't want to hurt your feelings but why don't you forget this singing business and study to be something else?'"

"Now when we go to Warner Brothers to record, they find us chairs to sit in," says John.

"We've really been busy," says Scap. "Up to two months ago, we rehearsed all the time, because we never had anything to do."

The Harpers Bizarre intends to maintain their "easy listening, fun sound" introduced with their first single throughout their upcoming album, "Harpers Bizarre Feelin' Groovy."

Happy Titles

Some of the titles off the album even suggest the light, happy sound: "Happy Land," "Simon Smith and The Dancing Bear," and "Debutantes Ball."

Suddenly Ted just can't resist giving us a sample and he breaks into a few bars of "Debutante."

The group will be touring the Midwest with the Beach Boys and then have a 20-day tour scheduled with the Turtles.

"We don't have top billing on these tours," says Scap, "but someday we'll headline."

BEAT Photos: Jim Marshall
HARPERS BIZARRE — Still unbelieving about success.

JOHN PETERSON — From classical to groovy music.

59TH ST. BRIDGE — First on their sightseeing list.

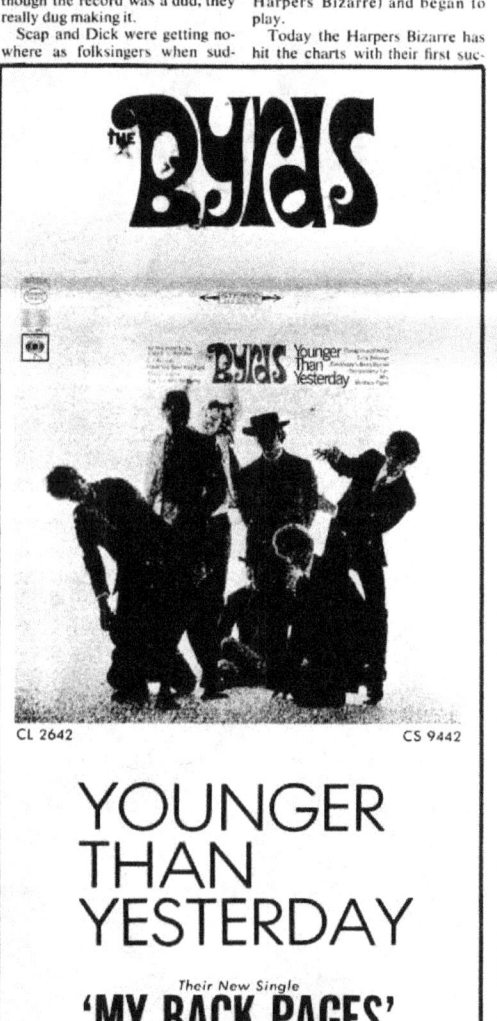
The Byrds
CL 2642 CS 9442
YOUNGER THAN YESTERDAY
Their New Single
'MY BACK PAGES'
4-44054
On COLUMBIA RECORDS
Available At Your Favorite Record Shop

KRLA ARCHIVES

BEAT EXCLUSIVE
Reader Spends A Day With Beatle Family In England

(Editor's note: If you're lucky enough, it can be done. Beatle fan, Patty Juliono, spent a fantastic day at the home of Mr. & Mrs. Harrison. A surprise twosome greeted Patty inside the house and the following is Patty's story of the day she'll never forget. We hope you'll enjoy it as much as we did.)

By Patty Juliono

I've been writing to Mrs. Harrison ever since I got her address a few years ago and I have always gotten an answer from her. Last February I went to Paris with my father. Before I left I wrote Mrs. Harrison a letter telling her I was coming to Europe and if I ever came to England, I would love to see her. When I got to Paris I was surprised to find a letter from her. She said she would love to see me and gave me directions on how to get to her house.

Phone Call

I called her the day we were going to Germany. She sounded so nice. I told her about coming to see her. I asked what would be the best day, Saturday or Sunday. She said either so I picked Sunday. I had to hang up then because we had to hurry to the airport.

My dad asked me to call Mrs. Harrison and ask if we could come on Saturday instead of Sunday because we had to leave Sunday so we could go to Switzerland on Monday because I had to start school.

When I called, she wasn't home, so my father called later and asked her. She said it was just fine and that she was looking forward to meeting me. So on Friday, March 4, we landed in London, England. I was so excited I couldn't believe I was in England! All Friday we went sightseeing. I even had lunch in an English pub!

The next morning we got up at eight, had breakfast and then took a bus to the London airport. We had to fly from London to Manchester and then take a train from Manchester to Warrington. When we got to Manchester, my dad decided to take a taxi to Warrington. When we got to Warrington, we had to stop at the train station so we could call Mrs. Harrison and ask how to get to her house from the station.

George Answers

My dad called and when he got off the phone he had a smile on his face. I asked him why he was smiling – he didn't say anything. What he was smiling about was that George had answered the phone and he was just thinking of what would happen if I had called and George answered the phone. All the way to her house I kept saying wouldn't that be neat if George was there.

Finally we turned down the road to Mrs. Harrison's house. Mrs. Harrison was out in the front waiting. I got out of the taxi and gave Mrs. Harrison a box of candy I had bought her. We walked into the house. The door leading to the living room is made of glass. I looked through and saw someone sitting in there. Then Mrs. Harrison opened the door and who should be sitting there but Patti – she is so pretty in person.

Mrs. Harrison introduced us and we sat and talked. Then my dad came in and I introduced them. Then Mr. Harrison came in and we all started talking. I asked Patti if she got a lot of mean letters from girls after she married George. She said she got a few saying "I hate you so much." After awhile, my dad looked up and smiled and then said: "Well, here's our boy." I turned around and there stood George with a big smile on his face!

He came over and shook my hand and sat in the chair next to me. He offered everyone a cigarette – even me! I joked and started to take one. He laughed and said: "Aren't you too young?" I never did get one.

My dad and George started to talk about Vietnam. Patti and I just sat and listened and threw in our two-cents once in awhile. Then George started talking about the police protection they get when they're in America. He said the English police were better. He told me how he's seen policemen take kids and hit them with their clubs. He said English policemen don't do that.

Then Mrs. Harrison called us in for a small lunch. We had tea sausages, cheese and bread. I sat between Mrs. Harrison and Patti and George sat across from me. Mrs. Harrison showed me a scrapbook of fans from all over the world. I found a lot of pictures of kids from the United States. I even found a picture of me!

After we ate, I cleared off the table and helped Mrs. Harrison with the dishes. Then my dad suggested we take pictures before the sun went down. We took six pictures outside. After we took the pictures, George's two brothers, Peter and Henry, came with their wives and George's little niece and nephew, Janet and Paul. We got one picture of Janet. She was very shy. We started talking about cars because George just got a new car which was out in front. I think it was a GTO. George started talking about the Munsters' car.

Good-Byes

Around five o'clock, my dad said it was time to go. I didn't want to but we had to catch a train at 5:30. Mr. Harrison drove us to the train station. I really hated to say good-bye. George and Patti stood in the doorway holding hands. George's brothers all shook my hand and said they enjoyed meeting me. I told Mrs. Harrison I really had a wonderful time. She was glad.

I got in the car and as we drove out the driveway, I turned around and saw Mrs. Harrison standing there waving good-bye. I'll never forget that day. I really couldn't believe I had met one of the Beatles!

I did learn one thing about George – he is supposed to be a real good cook, his father told me. Well, I still write to Mrs. Harrison and she writes to me. Maybe someday I'll meet her again.

PATTY POSES with George and Patti and Mr. & Mrs. Harrison.

KRLA ARCHIVES

KRLA ARCHIVES

PART II
Casey Kasem — A Man Of Radio, TV And Movies

...CASEY KASEM

Casey Kasem, who first won big time disc jockey fame in Detroit, is now a top television host of his own television series, "Shebang," as well as a popular KRLA disc jockey. He also can be called a recording artist, although he doesn't sing a note. He has a hit record, "A Letter From Elaina," on the Warner Bros. label, to his credit.

Film Debut

An exciting new career has just opened up for Casey. He has extended his many activities to include acting in motion pictures. His first film portrayla, appropriately, was that of a KRLA disc jockey named Casey Kasem for Allied Artists, in a comedy science-fiction production, "2000 Years Later," starring the talented British actor, Terry-Thomas.

It wasn't type casting, however, for only the name and the station are the same. The disc jockey Casey played was the director's interpretation of what a disc jockey should be: fast-talking, wild, hippy, swinging and verbose. In fact a little obnoxious. This role was a test of real acting. In his second Allied Artists Production, a serious science-fiction picture, "Doom's Day 1975," starring Ruta Lee, Casey was Major Peters, a dignified, conservative ground central operations officer who directs sending a space ship to Venus.

Reaction to Casey's motion picture debut was immediate and enthusiastic, and observers are already predicting his motion picture career as a solid hit.

Both productions are slated for release within the next few months. Casey thrives on the challenges and the variety that the movie industry offers. He loves all three mediums — radio, television and motion pictures — and he excels equally in all three.

These days, however, Casey needs roller skates or a bicycle to keep up with all his activities. His motion picture duties, his disc jockey chores, his television show, his Friday and Saturday night dances, plus his active participation in the KRLA baseball and basketball games . . . He still finds time, nonetheless, to answer the many requests for guest appearances from charitable organizations, to speak before various groups, and to take part in community events which he considers "part of my civic duty."

Dedication

Let no one think that Casey's assent to the heights of his profession was casual or due to accident. It was the result of dedication, talent and plain hard work and knowing what direction he wanted his life to take at a very early age.

THE GOLDEN BEAR
306 OCEAN AVENUE (HWY 101) HUNTINGTON BEACH

IAN & SYLVIA   MAR. 20 — APR. 2

PHONE 536-9600

PLUS Steve GILLETE

William Jarvis Presents
His Rock & Roll CoMODy
"VILLAINS V's HEROINES A LA MOD"

THE D. J. CLUB
5955 VAN NUYS BOULEVARD AT OXNARD, VAN NUYS, CALIF.

with
A TOP ROCK AND ROLL BAND and AN ALL TEENAGE CAST
DUNCAN BEGG Presents THE LATEST MOD FASHIONS FROM LONDON

* Disc Jockettes
* Pizza
* Soft Drinks
* Hamburgers
* Hot Dogs
* Steak Dinners
* Steak Sandwiches

★ **SPECIAL** ★
PARTY PACKAGE
Including:
Admission
Steak Dinner and
2 Drinks

ALL AGES WELCOME
Admission — Teenagers $1   Adults $2

2 SHOWS NITELY—FRIDAYS & SATURDAYS 8:30 P.M. & 10:30 P.M.

* **ATTENTION** TO ASSURE **YOUR** ROCK & ROLL TABLE
Phone 785-3303

KRLA TOP 40

1. PENNY LANE/STRAWBERRY FIELDS FOREVER .... Beatles
2. NO MILK TODAY/KIND OF A HUSH .... Herman
3. YELLOW BALLOON .... Yellow Balloons
4. BUY FOR ME THE RAIN .... Nitty Gritty Dirt Band
5. GIRL I KNEW SOMEWHERE/LITTLE BIT ME, LITTLE BIT YOU .... Monkees
6. LIVE .... Merry Go Round
7. HAPPY TOGETHER .... Turtles
8. WESTERN UNION .... Five Americans
9. CONNECTIONS .... Rolling Stones
10. CAN'T SEEM TO MAKE YOU MINE .... Seeds
11. BLUES THEME .... Davy Allen and The Arrows
12. YOU'VE GOT WHAT IT TAKES .... Dave Clark 5
13. MY BACK PAGES .... The Byrds
14. THIS IS MY SONG .... Petula Clark
15. SHE .... Monkees
16. UPS AND DOWNS .... Paul Revere & Raiders
17. 59TH STREET BRIDGE SONG .... Harpers Bizarre
18. DEDICATED TO THE ONE I LOVE .... Mamas & Papas
19. BABY I NEED YOUR LOVIN' .... Johnny Rivers
20. RUBY TUESDAY .... Rolling Stones
21. SHE'S LOOKIN' GOOD .... Roger Collins
22. THEN YOU CAN TELL ME GOODBYE .... The Casinos
23. LITTLE BLACK EGG .... Night Crawlers
24. AT THE ZOO .... Simon & Garfunkel
25. SOCK IT TO ME .... Mitch Ryder
26. GO WHERE YOU WANNA GO .... 5th Dimension
27. SUMMER WINE .... Nancy Sinatra
28. BERNADETTE .... Four Tops
29. SOMETHING STUPID .... Nancy & Frank Sinatra
30. BREAK ON THROUGH .... Doors
31. GET ME TO THE WORLD ON TIME .... Electric Prunes
32. I GOT RHYTHM .... Happenings
33. SHE HANGS OUT .... Monkees
34. I NEVER LOVED A MAN .... Aretha Franklin
35. LET'S FALL IN LOVE .... Peaches & Herb
36. IT TAKES TWO .... Marvin Gaye & Kim Weston
37. MY CUP RUNNETH OVER .... Ed Ames
38. ACAPULCO GOLD .... Rainy Daze
39. THE LOVE I SAW IN YOU WAS JUST A MIRAGE .... Miracles
40. I HAD TOO MUCH TO DREAM LAST NIGHT .... Electric Prunes

KRLA ARCHIVES

...MINI-SURFER WINNER PAM METHVIN

Winners Announced

Debi Blasingame is the proud possessor of a "Oh Dad, Poor Dad..." closet after she submitted the winning entry in KRLA's "Oh Dad, Poor Dad..." contest.

Debi's entry read: "I'd like to have Dick Biondi hanging in my closet because my room needs laughter and I want a souvenir from my favorite station—KRLA. He will also scare away the moths."

Pamela Methvin, winner of the Beach Boys' Mini-Surfer, received her prize last month. KRLA held the car for Pamela until she moved from Oklahoma to San Bernardino.

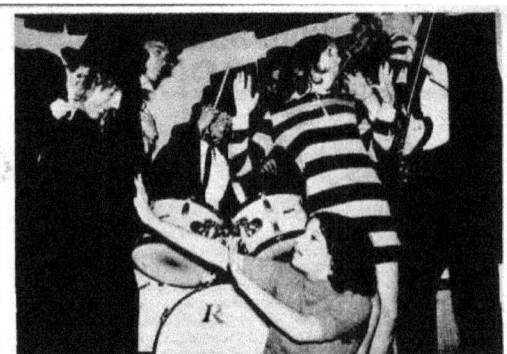

THE NU-TREND VILLAINS menace the Heroines at the D.J. Club in Van Nuys, a newly opened teen and young adult night club.

RC Offers Capitol LP's 2 For 1

Capitol Records and RC Cola have come up with a unique promotion that will prove to be of particular interest to teenagers in Los Angeles as well as the rest of the country.

RC is offering a collection of Capitol's top teen-oriented albums by such artists as The Beatles, Beach Boys, Lou Rawls, Peter & Gordon, Nancy Wilson, The Seekers, and The Outsiders to RC buyers free with the purchase of any other offered teen or adult LP at the regular price of $3.98.

In other words, you buy one at the regular price and get the other for six RC branded cork liners. Two albums, which normally sell for $4.98 or more each, will both come to you and you've spent only $3.98 or $4.98 if you want stereo.

It's the same deal as the regular record club except you don't have to agree to buy "X" number of records over a year. Two for the price of one!

All you have to do is make it into your nearest RC dealer. Look for the special display card that holds the 100 Top Hit Records selector folders.

If there *is* no display, ask the dealer about them. He will have a supply on hand... if he's not already out! Then take home a 6-Pak or ask your mom to bring some home the next time she goes shopping.

The albums, by the way, are all best sellers. They're not the usual albums (the ones that don't sell) you find in other promotions of this type. Nearly a dozen of the albums available have already earned Gold Records for sales of $1 million.

FROM **RC.**

RICHARDS SHOES
HOUSE OF IMPORTS

LARGEST SELECTION OF MEN'S BOOTS & SHOES IN THE CITY!

"OUR BIZ IS SHOE BIZ"

8106 Santa Monica Blvd.
Los Angeles 46, Calif.
656-2153

COME IN 'N BROWSE

WE HONOR DINER'S CLUB & BANKAMERICARD

ROBERT STACK
ELKE SOMMER
And **NANCY KWAN** as TINA
CHRISTIAN MARQUAND

The deadly search for the Peking Medallion that turned them all into...

THE CORRUPT ONES

WITH MAURIZIO ARENA · WERNER PETERS · SCREENPLAY BY BRIAN CLEMENS · STORY BY LADISLAS FODOR
MUSIC BY GEORGES GARVARENTZ · EXECUTIVE PRODUCER NAT WACHSBERGER · DIRECTED BY JAMES HILL
WORLD SALES OMNIA FILM · TECHNICOLOR® and TECHNISCOPE® · Distributed by WARNER BROS.

STARTS MAR. 29th AT A THEATER OR DRIVE-IN NEAR YOU

ICE HOUSE GLENDALE
234 So. Brand Ave. Reservations: 245-5043

March 28th to April 2nd

The Yellow Balloon
with their hit
"The Yellow Balloon"

— ALSO —

Comedian Pat Paulsen
As seen on the Smothers Bros. Show

OPENING THE SAME NIGHT
Bob Lind
with his hit
"Elusive Butterfly Of Love"
AT THE

ICE HOUSE PASADENA
24 No. Mentor — Reservations: 681-9942

CAN YOU DIG IT?
GLAMOUR & SOUL RETURN TO THE SUNSET STRIP

NOW APPEARING THRU APRIL 2nd

Comedian **RICHARD PRYOR** with **THE CHECKMATES LTD.**

CIRO'S
8433 SUNSET BLVD.

DINING & DANCING
TILL 2 A.M.

ALL AGES WELCOME
FOR RESERVATIONS: 654-6650

KRLA ARCHIVES

Eric Burdon: 'I Am Just Responsible For Myself'

...ERIC'S NEW ANIMALS — talent and versatility.

Once upon the Tyne, there were five young men from Newcastle, England, and the smallest of these was Eric Burdon. They became the Animals, a force-field of pop music, and the voice of these was Eric Burdon. Now they are no more and the New Animals have arisen and the most of these is Eric Burdon.

It was in 1962 that Eric Burdon joined the Newcastle quartet, the Alan Price Combo. He'd studied art and was a designer, but blues music was his love. So, Eric put his blues instrumental sound of the other four and the sound they made, the feeling they put across drove their audiences to nickname them the Animals. In tribute to the fans and with regard for the aptness of the name, the Animals they became and as the Animals they rose.

Eric's "Sun"

"House Of The Rising Sun" shone upon them and Eric's wailing, crying, aching voice pouring out the story of a youth's ruin in New Orleans was heard throughout the world. Eric became the image of the Animals—face contorted in song, compact body tense with effort, oblivious to the world outside the music. And the boy with the sleep-lidded eyes with the glint of mischief in their depths became every girl's idea of sexiness and every boy's idea of a real blues singer.

In the years of their reign, the Animals saw many of their dreams come true. They toured with Chuck Berry, saw the world from behind massive security protection and gained respect as one of the world's foremost rhythm 'n' blues groups. They had nine hit singles and four hit albums.

A Shock

So, it was that it came as a shock when in the summer of 1966 Eric Burdon announced that the Animals were disbanding. Amid the moans and weeping of his fans and followers, Eric held to his intention to take over the Animals and started along his new road.

"I'm happier now than I have been in a long time," says Eric, "and things are getting better. I can progress now. I enjoyed my life with the Animals, but there comes a time when you have to think of the future. In a co-operative group, you are responsible for the well-being of four other people besides yourself and this makes you reluctant to take chances and try new things. Now, I'm just responsible for myself."

What Eric wanted was a group with talent and versatility. First to join his New Animals was an old Animal, drummer Barry Jenkins. Then came Johnny Weider, a tall, skinny towhead who doubles on lead guitar and electric violin, and Danny McCulloch, a big, broad, bass guitarist. Finally completing the line-up was blond, sometimes bearded Vic Briggs. Eric took them into weeks of intensive rehearsal and emerged with a "Bring Back The Rock" flavor and one of the most varied repertoires in pop. Eric's belting blues voice is still in the fore, his "leaping, over-fed gnome" figure still uses mike stands as pogo sticks and jerks spasmodically as the music comes tearing from him.

With Eric, appearances definitely are deceiving. Despite his tough-guy looks and earthy manner, he is in truth very shy. Even when being interviewed it takes time for him to relax with a stranger. Privately, though his friends are numberless, he sticks to a small circle of very close friends. So, his outspokenness and willingness to express frank opinions could mislead you into thinking him aggressive, which he is not.

SPECIAL OFFER TO BEAT READERS!!

AUTHENTIC MONKEESHADES by DEBS®

* Created & Designed by Davy Jones in London
* 5 Groovy Colors...rose...yellow... blue...grey...green
* Heavy Mod Golden Chain
* Just Like the MONKEES Wear On Their Swingin' TV Show
* MONKEESHADES are the Wildest!

ONLY $1.98 PLUS .02 HANDLING CHARGE

Send to: MONKEESHADES, 81 W. State St., Pasadena, California 91105
PLEASE SEND ME THE MONKEESHADES AS INDICATED. I ENCLOSE $2.00 FOR EACH PAIR
COLOR_____ NO. PAIRS_____ TOTAL AMOUNT ENCLOSED_____
Name_____
Address_____
City_____ State_____ Zip Code_____

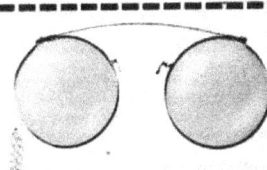

ORDER YOURS TODAY!!

KRLA ARCHIVES

Switching On WITH TENT DRESSES, BOOTS

Bermuda Pants Suits, Safari Jackets Adorn London, U.S., For Springtime

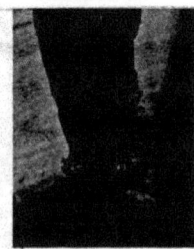

...MONKEE MIKE'S BOOTS

London fashion sprouted forth recently with African prints, safari clothes, gay tent dresses and sailcloth outfits parading on a stage covered by giant sunflowers and under a sky filled with rain. One fashion house, Marlborough, even water-proofed its entire line in case the weather got too damp.

To the lament of high school principals, hemlines in the show remained nearly a foot above the knee. Bloomers, the Paris-inspired creation which made mini-skirts modest, were completely absent from the showing, sponsored by the Associated Fashion Designers of London.

Cone-shaped tent dresses and coats, launched originally in Paris, were everywhere. Colors were frosty yellows, oranges and lime greens, and stand-up collars (usually white) decorated the majority of styles. Cuts were either the conventional straight line or unusual diagonal styles.

Safari suit jackets brought the jungle to the city. Belted and multi-buttoned, the suits resembled the bush jackets men wear hunting on the veldt. Another masculine influence was the trouser suit complete with vest and tie.

Trouser suits also went springtime with bermuda shorts taking the place of full-length pants. Knee-socks, or simply bare legs, completed the outfit.

On the London make-up scene, Mary Quant quit complaining about the widespread standardization of eye shadow at brown or black. She designed a pure silver liquid shadow, applied with a sable brush and outlined in blue. She also advocated either covering or creating freckles with the silver liquid. It's a neat look for party time.

Bikinis, some say, can't get any briefer. But leave it to Paris! However, the French also did the unusual and made bikinis modest by attaching cotton legs (much like capris) to the bikini bottom. Sleeves and blouse yoke were added to the bikini top for a covered-up look. All together, this modest bikini is an unusual but ultra-attractive outfit, certain to catch on when it is time for summer evenings.

Hairstyles in both Paris and Britain, as well as the U.S., are curly. The long, straight look is lingering on in some parts of the States but only with the Unswitched On. The stylish haven't necessarily trimmed their locks but wear them with body, style, curl, bounce and more curl. Curled tresses, in case you've forgotten, are created with a permanent wave or sets as needed.

BEAT Photo: Chuck Boyd

TENT DRESSES, colorful and airy, are sweeping both continents! Mama Cass, noted for her huge bulkage as well as her powerful voice, helped inspire this current rage when she began disguising her immense proportions by wearing Parisian tents. Cass' dresses are usually in bright, startling prints or pink and orange chiffon, but girls from Sunset Strip to Liverpool are switching on with cotton fabrics of all types. The secret is to wear them short!

Guys

■ **Mike Nesmith,** the Monkees' representative from the wild world of Western, favors leather knee-high moccasins complete with rawhide strings and fringed edges (shown above.) Department stores and larger shoe shops are beginning to stock them but the best moccasins are still obtained at smaller Western shops.

■ **Speaking of Western,** we've been preaching the glories of suede and leather jackets and apparently someone has been listening. Pop stars caught in them lately include Donovan, Neil Diamond and Mick Jagger (his is black).

■ **Mustaches,** still a thorn in the side of school authorities, have further premeated the entertainment scene. With hair: Sean Connery (Bond, he says, would never wear a mustache), Michael Caine and Hollie Graham Nash.

■ *England is featuring the trench coat look once more, combined with trim trousers in charcoal, satin shirts with puffed sleeves. Harrison, formerly a mop top, now favors Indian garb with a special attachment to the Indian coat and high collar.*

■ **White linen** summer suits and two-tone shoes will be the word for the office crowd come spring. Also, they'll wear Mod shirts and wide, colorful ties.

■ *Monkeeshades,* or op art glasses, are gaining on conventional frames, both sunglass and optical types.

Gals
In The Office

We've received letters pleading with us to try out our reporting on styles for gals who prefer the typewriter to school books. "We're tired of being a dowdy bunch," said one reader, "but our bosses are such old fogies they'd have a heart-attack if a mini-skirt got within two blocks!"

Surveying the office scene, we definitely decided "dowdy" was the right word, unfortunately, for most gals. So the following are hints for the working lass who wishes to boost both her looks and her morale.

■ **Fishnet stockings** are appropirate for working wear. Don't wear them in black, however, for fear that Mr. Boss will send you away to the nearest chorus line. Instead, do try them in white or pastel colors. They can be purchased for under $2 at most stores (and they don't run).

■ **Keep those typewriter-length** fingernails immaculate and looking longer than they actually are by covering them with white pearlized nail polish.

■ **Unless your boss is a beat-type,** do not wear long dangling earrings, either pierced or unpierced. Stick with the button-size. Buy them cheaply in all colors of the rainbow to match your various outfits.

■ **Don't wear spike heels** even if you are under three feet tall. Heels today are stacked, low and comfortable.

■ **Likewise,** ratted hair went out with bucket purses, and you know how long ago that was!

■ **Hemlines are a problem.** Wear them a fraction shorter each day til you reach the supervisor frown stage (if you are the daring type). Or discuss the issue with the boss if you are on friendly terms. Mid-knee lengths, however, shouldn't be objectionable to anyone.

■ **Stay away** from skirts and blouses. They mark you as just-out-of-school. Invest in dresses which give a more sophisticated look.

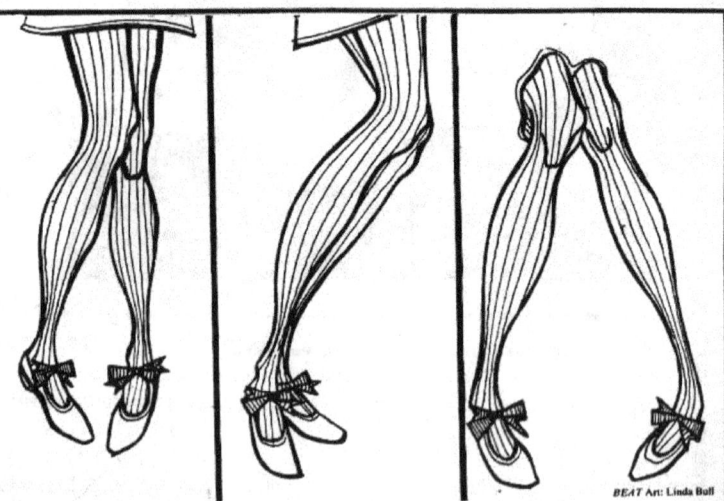

BEAT Art: Linda Bull

MINI-SKIRT MANEUVERS — Designed to prevent your mini-skirt from losing its glamour. Instead of a twist and tug battle with your hemline, our **BEAT** artist gives us her version of three baby doll ways to sit in your little girl skirt.

KRLA ARCHIVES

Dear Anne,
At a slumber party last weekend one of the girls brought a bottle of peroxide and bleached a streak in her hair. Well, it seemed like a good idea at the time and so the rest of us did too, just a little streak in the front. The problem is when my father saw it he hit the roof and says I can't go out until the streak is grown out. It will probably take months to grow out and I don't think it's fair of my father to make me stay in all the time because it's just a small streak and not real blonde, just lighter than the rest of my hair. None of the other girls were punished – please say whether or not that's fair.

Bottled Up

Dear Bottled,
The point your father is probably trying to make is that there is great danger of your injuring yourself with hair coloring solutions if you don't know exactly what you are doing. When my best friend in High School bleached her hair, it all fell out – she had horrible scars all over her head as a result of her allergy to the ingredients of the product she had used, and the equivalent of a crew cut for many months afterwards. Tell your father that you understand his point of view, and offer to pay for a trip to the beauty parlor to have the streak dyed back to match the rest of your hair. Once he gets over his initial upset, he should relent, if you tell him straight out that you will defer his wishes by not tampering with your hair color again. All Dads should realize that sooner or later every girl gets the urge to play around with the color of her hair – and that the best way to react is not to fly off the handle but to explain the risk involved when inexperienced hands mix and apply the potent chemicals contained in hair coloring mixes.

Anne

Dear Miss Anderson,
I have a very bad case of teenage skin. I've tried every cream and lotion in the store and nothing seems to work. It just gets worse. I asked my mother to let me go to a dermatologist, but she says it is a waste of money and I will grow out of it. I may grow out of it but right now I need help badly. Please tell me the right thing to do for my skin.

Zit City

Dear Zit,
The first thing to do is to ask your school nurse to write your mother a letter requesting permission for you to see a doctor. Your mother doesn't seem to realize that your skin problem if it is as bad and consistent as you say, may not be just "teenage skin" but the physical evidence of a lack in your system – a vitamin or thyroid deficiency – which affects the whole state of your health, not just your face. Exactly what causes your skin problem and what to do about it should be decided by a doctor, and no one else. If cost is a factor, offer to pay the bills for the visit and any medication prescribed, either out of your allowance or by taking on extra chores around the house. You probably will "grow out of it," but that's no help now, and it is unfair of your mother to prevent you from seeking help for an ugly and embarrassing problem.

Anne

Dear Miss Anderson,
I have the world's ugliest nose. It is very large and it ruins my face. I would like to have plastic surgery but my parents say I am too young. (I am 15.) I am so ugly with my nose the way it is – please tell me how much does plastic surgery cost and will you please recommend someone I could go to for this?

Judy
P.S. – My friend just had her nose done and it looks just great. We are the same age.

Dear Judy,
Is your nose really all that big – or do you want a nose job because your friend has had one? Playing around with the basic structure of your face is not a thing to be undertaken lightly – a nose that seems monstrous now may be your best feature in three or four years. Look at Barbra Streisand for example, whose profile has been likened to that of Nefertiti, beautiful queen of ancient Egypt – and the main similarity is that of the noses. Abide by your parents' decision to wait a few years. If your nose still seems terribly out of proportion when you are 18, that will be the time to discuss plastic surgery.

Anne

P.S. – I couldn't possibly recommend a surgeon or give advice as to cost – in the first place it isn't ethical and in the second place I know absolutely nothing about it.

GUITARISTS!

- Improve your ability • Increase your income

with

"The Guitar" by Barney Kessel

$15

Now you can profit by Barney Kessel's 30 years of experience as a guitar-pro in Rock, R & B, Folk, Jazz and the "Nashville" sound. This book shows you how to select the proper guitar and equipment, accompany singers, read music and improvise. Learn the commercial recording techniques and how to "BREAK" INTO THE BUSINESS. Easy-to-read book has 211 pages of text and music examples.

— — — MAIL COUPON TODAY — — —

WINDSOR MUSIC COMPANY, DEPT. KB
P. O. Box 2629
Hollywood, Calif. 90028

Enclosed is $_____ Please send me _____ copies of "The Guitar" by Barney Kessel, at $15 each.
(California residents add 4% Sales Tax).

____ Check   ____ Money Order   ____ Send free brochure

(Please Print)

NAME_____

ADDRESS_____

CITY_____ STATE_____ ZIP_____

(Tax deductible for professional musicians)

The Man Of My Dreams...

Dear BEAT:
I thought you might be interested in meeting my ideal rock 'n' roll star. He has the intelligence and sense of humor of John Lennon. He can sing softly, like a poet, with the sweet voice of Garfunkel. But when he wants he can have the fabulous, strong beat of the Turtles' groovy drummer, John Barbata. And best of all – he has the cutest dimples like Peter Tork.

Barbara Fox

We found Barbara's letter in the BEAT mailbag and liked it so much, we decided to share it with our readers. The BEAT artist had some fun and came up with a composite of Barbara's idol. Send us a description of the rock 'n' roll singer you dream about. We'll print the best one received in the next issue. No pictures please! We have a photographic specialist standing by to create your ideal's face.
– The Editor

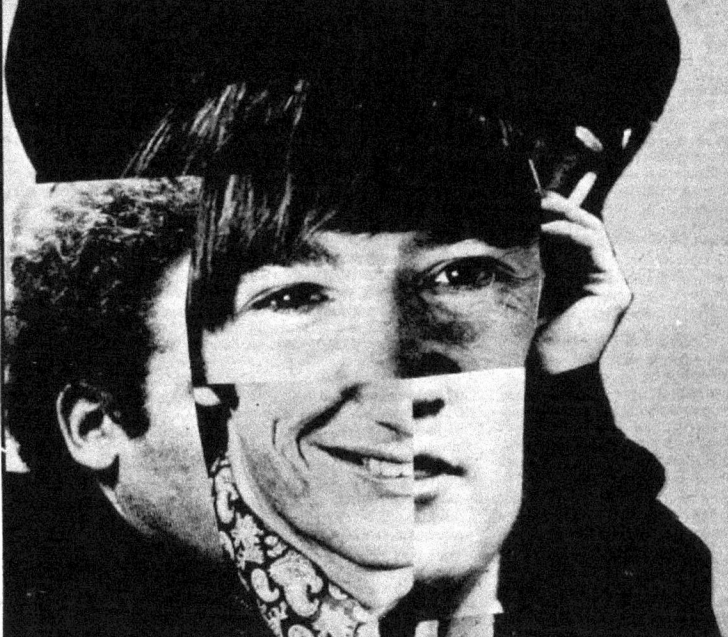

KRLA ARCHIVES

Get Set To GO

Here are some coming attractions from *Go*, a one-hour special featuring a line-up of top stars to be aired on April 23 on ABC-TV in the time slot normally filled by *Voyage to the Bottom of the Sea*.

Below are (l. to r.): Rudy Valley with a megaphone; A group shot of Noel Harrison, Ryan O'Neil and Peter Noone; and the Buffalo Springfield. Herman's Hermits (upper right) sing to a group of *Go*-girls.

Brian Hyland and the Jokers will join in the fun and the Swingin' Six will sing. Abigail Van Buren, "Dear Abby," will be on hand with tremendously funny comment. Noel and Ryan will blend their talents in a specially arranged duet. Then Peter and Noel have a riotous spoof of the way-out mod mod mod world of fashions. There will be a look at the fashions and fancies of tomorrow.

Buffalo Springfield Unwind

By Jamie McCluskey III

Now, you've got to admit: there aren't *many* people who come to Los Angeles from Canada ... by way of *hearse*! However, Neil Young of the Buffalo Springfield did. Sometime after his arrival in L.A., Neil happened to be stopped at a very important stoplight on Sunset Blvd. (a very important street) when he spotted Steve Stills, also at the stoplight. Needless to say, it was one of those happy reunion scenes, marred only by the 500,000 cars passing by that could have *cared less* that Neil and Steve were old friends.

Meanwhile, back in New York, another old friend – Richie Furay – received a get-out-here-fast notification from Neil and Steve (who are old friends), and after pawning everything in sight, he did so – post haste.

A Threesome

Shortly thereafter, the growing group, now a threesome, "acquired" – und *no one* is willing to say *how*! – an articulate and talented drummer by the name of Dewey Martin – who at various times in his career has played with the MFQ, the Grand Ole Opry, Roy Orbison, and Sir Walter Raleigh and the Coupons (*He* was Sir Walter!).

In quick acquisition Jim Fielder, formerly a Mother of Invention, cut his hair and became both *human* and a member of the Buffalo Springfield – quite a feat for any one!

Now that we have all five of them together, the question which must inevitably arise is, What does one *do* with five Buffalo Springfield – for whatever they're worth?

Obviously – one *attempts* to conduct an interview. Now, depending on the day of the week, the moods of the group, the events of the preceding week, and the rain fall in Argentina at that precise moment – you may or may not succeed. However, it would be well for you to keep in mind that we are all only human – even the Buffalo Springfield – and of course, every Buffalo has his day. (?)

Inner Insanity

Our interview took place in a suite of offices generally referred to (affectionately, of course!) as Inner Insanity. Other people (the "straight guys") would probably tell you that they are the offices of Charlie Greene and Brian Stone, which they are.

When they are in the proper frame of mind, all five of the Springfield can be articulate, glib, intelligent, humorous individuals. This particular day, however, they were merely exhausted and subdued. (That may have had something or another to do with the Argentinian rainfall – but more likely it involved the heavy work and recording schedule of the group).

At one point, Steve – be-spectacled and be-Cowboy hatted, explained to us the way in which "For What It's Worth" was written. "It was written on Saturday .. recorded .. on Monday ... and on the radio on Tuesday." The song was written in about 15 minutes during a week when the group was playing an engagement at the Whisky A Go Go in Hollywood.

Big Trouble

"That was the week when we came back from San Francisco and we'd been hearing about 'Big Trouble on the Strip!' We went to work at the Whisky, but it was pretty dull all week 'cause everybody was having a much better time down the street at the *riot*!

"So, I went down to see what it was about – or, *drove past it*, actually – and later on that night I went to Terry's (a friend's home at which the song was written) and it just sort of fell out."

Later on, Steve defined a "generation gap" for me as being 'two generations, separated by time, who are unable to communicate.' We all discussed the recent activities on the Strip and in other places all over the country and the group seemed pretty well agreed that the only possible solution is to *find* a means of communication between the generations. Dewey commented that there always has been and always will be a gap between the two, but the group as a whole seems hopeful of some eventual peaceful resolution of the tensions currently surrounding the relationships between the two generations.

Neil fell asleep under his huge black cowboy hat a lot – but he explained that it's hard work being and Indian, so of course we all forgave him. Besides, he woke up later – just before we left – and was very funny and very polite, several times offering to "pay your carfare if you'd like to come back and do this interview all over again!"

Dewey was effervescent and dynamic, as usual – he'll probably never be able to be contained by *anything*! Richie was quiet and polite, and Jim smiled quietly beneath his light brown fringe of hair.

Later on, Steve – a very gentle and sincere young man – sang "For What It's Worth" – one of the most phenomenally successful, and long-lasting hit records to come along – for me with just one guitar which he strummed softly.

What's it all worth? Well, the Buffalo Springfield are a *good* group of *talented* musicians who work hard and believe in their music. They put a lot of time and effort into their music, and when their supply of inexhaustable energy temporarily runs low – they are honest enough to politely tell you so, and apologize for not being their usual, zany selves.

But, that's cool – after all, even the Buffalo Springfield are *human* . . . and that's worth *a lot* in this funny world of pop!

KRLA ARCHIVES

Their New Single
'DARK ON YOU'
4-44063

On COLUMBIA RECORDS

Available at your favorite record shop.

KRLA ARCHIVES

HERB ALPERT clutches Grammy
BEAT Photos: Dwight Carter

MICHELLE AND JOHN toast the occasion

BEHIND THE
GRAMMY AWARDS

DAVY JONES sits alone at his table but not for long!

NOMINEE LOU RAWLS

TWO PAPAS, ONE MAMA happy over their Grammy.

HOLLYWOOD – The 1966 Grammy Awards went off in the International Ballroom of the Beverly Hilton Hotel with very few surprises, a bit of glamor and a lot of talk.

The big winner was, of course, Frank Sinatra who managed to cop awards for the Album of the Year, the Record of the Year and the Best Vocal Performance – Male.

The Beatles, Mamas and Papas and the New Vaudeville Band represented the pop field in the list of Grammy winners and, in fact, John and Michelle Phillips and Davy Jones presented awards this time around.

Davy Jones showed up with the beginnings of a beard and mustache and Michelle appeared in a floor-length gown accompanied by her husband, John neatly attired in a tux. Quite a change from the usual Mamas and Papas outfits.

Ray Charles received the biggest ovation from the crowd when he was named winner of the Best Rhythm & Blues Solo Vocal Performance and the Best Rhythm & Blues Recording.

Bill Dana took off his Jose Jiminez voice for part of the night and took on the master of ceremonies chores for this year's awards.

Performing the nominated songs were Jack Jones ("The Impossible Dream"), Roger Williams ("Born Free"), the Anita Kerr Singers ("Michelle"), Julius La Rosa ("Somewhere My Love") and Keely Smith ("Strangers In The Night"). As you know, Paul McCartney and John Lennon won the Song of the Year award for their "Michelle."

Herb Alpert, last year's big winner, walked away with two awards and when Bob Newhart failed to show, Davy Jones took over his spot to present the two biggest awards (Song of the Year and Record of the Year) with June Hutton.

LOUISE, DAVY, CAROL

JACK JONES awaits dinner

...AWARD WINNERS POSE WITH HERB ALPERT.

DAVY JONES SMILES with Keely Smith

JACKIE DESHANNON

A VERY HAPPY PAPA JOHN

...JODY MILLER AND SHEB WOOLEY.

RAY CHARLES

KRLA ARCHIVES

Shirley You Jest

Would you believe I dreamed I was a Beatle in my maidenform bra?

I didn't think you would. Well, would you believe I did dream something almost as weird?

I've told you how I lie awake nights making up wild whoppers (as in Wishful-Thinkies) about George N. Harrison (N as in Nibble). I've also told you I seldom ever manage to *really* dream about the Beatles (asleep-style), and that when I do, my poor brain gets confused (make that *got*) (then add *years ago*) and I end up dreaming about John instead of George. (Worse things could come to pass, I tell you.) (And have.)

In my dream I had somehow finagled John Lennon's telephone number. Clutching my throat with one hand, I dialed same (the phone, not my throat) with the other. (Yes, yes, I realize it's impossible to direct-dial from America to England, but when I dream, kiddo, I DREAM!)

John answered immediately, but instead of saying hello, he said: "Are you on the Mudvale Road?"

I looked around me. (One never knows.) (Especially *this* one.) "Why do you ask?" I answered. (Yes, yes, I realize it would have been cooler to have said *arsk*, but no one is perfect.)

"Because," he explained fully. "Will you stop at the store and bring me something?"

"Certainly," I replied. "If you're not in too big a hurry, that is. I'm calling from California."

"You Americans," snorted John. "Always worrying about details."

Would you believe (not to mention *hope*) that was the end of the dream. Naturally, I woke up in a cold sweat (also in a bed) (a pleasant change) and raced to my life-sized map of England (a slight exaggeration) only to find no Mudvale Road. I did, however, find several more marbles.

Socially Retarded

Speaking of calling people, my socially retarded brother gets this enormous charge out of calling people and asking for himself. He always picks someone who knows his voice but doesn't know him well enough to say "look, you boob, go play under the overpass."

What they usually do say (after a series of noisy gulps and frantic glances) is: "No, you aren't here—I mean no, *he* isn't here." Then Stupid - sorry - my brother leaves a message for himself, hangs up, and chortles gleefully for hours, knowing that still *another* person is fearing for his sanity.

Speaking of George (yep, I'm gonna start *that* again), my favorite Beatle spy tells me he's re-shaved off his mustache again. I'm kindof glad to hear it on account of because I prefer the way he looked before he went to India. (Sari about that.) (Gawd and re-Gawd.)

Dunno why, but what I just wrote (and I use the term with reservations) (Sioux, preferably) reminded me of the way some adults used to call George homely when the Beatles were just starting to become a big thingy. That really used to cut me to the quick (a painful experience despite the fact that I have an unusually slow quick) (among other things.)

Oh well, like they always say (giving me further cause to wonder about them), beauty is only derma-deep. (*Whew*.)

New Look

It's been awhile since I've heard this sort of comment, though. Not just about M. George (M. as in MY) — about pop stars in general. I guess older people (fifteen minutes older than the Roman Empire, that is) are finally adjusting to the new look. Either that or they've given up on trying to put it down.

As long as I'm in such a Be-attly mood today, I might as well throw this in (the fire would be nice). When Jane Asher came to America a few weeks ago, a reporter asked her why she didn't clear up the Paul-Romance issue once and for all because the public wants to know.

Jane replied: "I don't care what the public wants to know. If I even said I'd had a letter from him, everybody would pounce on me and say 'what was in it?'"

When I first read this, I thought it sounded pretty snippy. In a way, I still think so, but I do admire her for being honest. If she doesn't care who wants to know what, at least she admits it. And, I suppose it does get a bit tiresome being asked the same question nine million times.

There's another factor I didn't even think of until just now. When you're engaged-to-be-engaged-or-married-or-whatever, I suppose you have enough on your mind without having to worry about the public, too. Especially if everything isn't going too smoothly.

Most of us are lucky enough (or unlucky, as the case may be) (and in this case, *is*) to only have a few people to answer to. I don't think I'd want to tell the whole world about *my* personal life.

However, I do hesitantly and blushingly admit that I'm going to miss a certain boy named Larry Pierce. He just left for the Marine Crops (sorry – Corps), which leaves me without a Geography partner.

If you don't know what Geography is, it's a very *fascinating*, very *daring* game where he, for instance, would name a place that ends in the letter A. Then *I'd* have to name a place that starts with the letter A. (Oh, the *shame* of it!)

And now you know *why* I don't think I'd want to tell the world about my personal life. I just *hate* the sound of uncontrollable snoring.

BOOK REVIEW

'NEW SOUND'—A SOCIAL REGISTER OF POP MUSIC

The New Sound/Yes!, edited by Ira Peck, The Four Winds Press, New York.

Here it is, fans. A short, quick book that tells you all about the "What, Who and Why" of the rock 'n' roll business. DJ Murray the K leads off with a bit of explosion for an introduction. "Today's songs," says the K, "reflect attitudes of children born after the close of World War II, whose psyche was fathered by the atom bomb!"

The book is full of fascinating tidbits from rock 'n' roll history. Remember when it all began? Bill Haley and his Comets unleashed tremors with *Rock Around the Clock* that are still rocking the music business. Did you know who coined the term rock 'n' roll? The credit goes to Cleveland DJ Alan Freed, a rapid-fire pitchman who sang with the records, slamming his hand down on a telephone book to accentuate each beat.

They all said the big beat was a fad but then in the fall of 1956, Elvis came along with his three-inch sideburns and gyrating hips. Parents objected but their teenagers kept giving Elvis gold records. Now that everyone is twisting, Elvis' wiggling act seems tame. Did you know this interesting sidelight? The book's penetrating profile of Elvis says he lives in a sprawling Tennessee mansion with some hometown friends. He rarely mixes with the Hollywood set or rock 'n' roll personalities. He is kind of a mystery.

"C'mon, baby, let's do the Twist!" was the invitation of a onetime Philadelphia chicken plucker, Chubby Checker. And the big beat went into high gear for the sound of the 60's.

Step behind the scenes, into the sound studios with revealing studies of the singers and the song makers. Meet "The First Tycoon of Teen," Phil Spector who made his first million by age 21 producing rock sounds. Follow the antics of "Music's Gold Bugs: The Beatles." If you're a folk purist forever down on Dylan for joining the big beat, then you'll have to read, "In Defense of Dylan."

It's a funny, easy-reading book.

Turning On

THE LOVIN' SPOONFUL (Kama Sutra) The original film sound track from *You're a Big Boy Now* with the title song *Darling Be Home Soon*, and 12 other tracks (8 are instrumentals).

Save your money for the movie. We hope that's better than the track otherwise the Lovin' Spoonful might have a double financial disaster on their hands. John Sebastian, 22, composed all the songs, best of which is *Darling, Be Home Soon*.

DISCussion

BETWEEN THE BUTTONS (London) by The Rolling Stones with *Let's Spend the Night Together, Yesterdays Papers, Ruby Tuesday* and nine other tracks. Mick Jagger and Keith Richards wrote all the songs. The group has fun switching between a honky tonk piano sound and Indian-oriental strains. It's great listening.

THE NITTY GRITTY DIRT BAND (liberty) with *Buy For Me The Rain, Euphoria, Melissa* and nine other tracks. The Dirty six create a very happy-go-lucky sound of the Roaring 20's. They hum, strum, cavort with a number of primitive instruments like a washboard, megaphone, wash basin bass, harmonicas and banjos.

JANIS IAN (Verve Folkways) *Society's Child, Go 'Way Little Girl, Hair of Spun Gold, Younger Generation Blues* and seven more tracks.

15-year-old Janis Ian emerges on her first LP as an exciting new voice and song writer in the folk-rock vein. Already tagged "a female Bob Dylan," she needles uptight parents and sings with a biting wit about the problems teenagers are hung up on.

LET'S FALL IN LOVE, THE SWEETHEARTS OF SOUL, PEACHES & HERB (Date) *Close Your Eyes, I Will Watch Over You, Let's Fall in Love* and eight other tracks.

Peaches & Herb have a very pleasant R&B sound, though it's not outstanding. Their voices come through strong without electronic gimmickry. They are unfortunately short on original songs. Their repertoire is crowded with top 40 hits and old standards.

MONKEES, "A Little Bit Me, A Little Bit You"/ The Girl I Knew Somewhere." (Colgems) The Monkees' latest smash hit single is destined to rocket this great group into their fourth million-selling cut in a row. Neil Diamond who wrote the lyrics of "I'm A Believer" composed the words to "A Little Bit." Mike Nesmith did the lyrics on "The Girl."...SIMON & GARFUNKEL "At The Zoo," (Columbia) What's happening at the zoo is plenty of beautiful S&G harmonizing in a fun mood song about the funny-looking animals.... JEFFERSON AIRPLANE, "She Has Funny Cars," (RCA Victor) The single off the Airplane album "Surrealistic Pillow" uses conga-drum-type beat to set off a strong vocal arrangement with a wild wailing sound... THE SYNDICATE OF SOUND, "Mary," (Bell) This single leans too far on the repetitious side. Not very inspired but has a good, hard driving rock beat and you can sing along with it... TERRY KNIGHT AND THE PACK, "The Train," (Lucky Eleven) This group, big in the Mid-West, is looking for a national breakthrough but they won't have it with this single. Sounds like tunes 6 months back... THE BUCKINGHAMS, "Don't You Care," (Columbia) The B's new single is a very pretty follow-up to "Kind of a Drag" and it's anything but a drag

KRLA ARCHIVES

please send me
BEAT

26 issues only

$3 per year

Mail to: **BEAT Publications**
6290 Sunset Blvd. #504
Hollywood, California 90028

☐ New Subscription
☐ Renewal (please enclose mailing label from your last BEAT)
I want BEAT for ☐ 1 year at $3.00 or ☐ 2 years at $5.00
I enclose ☐ cash ☐ check ☐ money order
Outside U.S. − $9 per year

* Please print your name and address.

Name_____

Street_____

City_____

State_____ Zip_____

MERRY-GO-ROUND (left to right) Bill Rinehart, Emmitt Rhodes, Gary Kato and Joe Larsen

Merry-Go-Round of Emotions

By Lawrence Charles

A merry-go-round is colorful, wooden horses prancing to bubbly music and lots of laughing children. But The Merry-Go-Round is also the newest and youngest group of recording artists to add their names to the A&M Records' roster.

As is the case with their A&M teammates, Herb Alpert and the Tijuana Brass, the Baja Marimba Band, Sergio Mendes and Brasil '66, the Sandpipers and Chris Montez, the Merry-Go-Round hopes to make a fresh, individual contribution to the popular music scene. The group have already released their first single on the label, "Live"/"Time Will Show The Wiser."

Own Combo

The Merry-Go-Round members each headed his own combo while in high school. They began separate careers playing weekend dances to earn pocket money.

In July of 1966, the four members of the group decided to go professional. The boys worked hard in long months of rehearsal before A&M executive, Larry Marks discovered them. He also helped the group gather material for their first recording session.

Explaining how they chose the name Merry-Go-Round, 18-year-old rhythm guitarist, Emmett Rhodes, says, "We all felt that life is sort of a merry-go-round of emotions and we planned to sing songs about how we live, so Merry-Go-Round seemed appropriate."

The Merry-Go-Round are four very likeable young men between 18 and 20 years old. They compose and write the lyrics for their own songs. They sing of a subject they live with constantly and understand well — the current generation of young people.

Joe Larson, the drummer, Bill Rinehart, the bass player; Emmett Rhodes, the rhythm guitarist and Gary Kato, lead guitarist, feel their music is truthfully exciting because it is the joys and sorrows of their generation.

Twenty-year-old Bill Rinehart says, "We are not producing songs of protest or message music. We are singing about the things that happen to young people. We sing about things that have happened to us personally. Some of our songs are very happy and some not so happy. We are just singing about life as we have experienced it."

Sing For Selves

The Merry-Go-Round sing for themselves as much as for their audience.

Says Emmett Rhodes, "The most important thing we hope to achieve through our music is personal satisfaction."

Emmett writes most of the lyrics but says, "We really write as a group. One of us will get an idea for a tune. Then the four of us work on it together until we are all satisfied."

CLASSIFIED

FOR SALE

RECORD SPECIAL! 40 different (45 rpm) records only $3.95. 100−$8.95. Many recent hits by top artists. Don Stevens, 318 Lakeview Street, (TB) Bristol, Tenn. 37620

FENDER BANDMASTER, near new − covers, $275. 447-5256 (Arcadia, Calif.).

FOR SALE: Suede boot. Belonged to Rolling Stone. Autographed: Mick, Charlie, Brian. Call Karen: 987-2673 (Calif.).

MAMA'S & PAPA'S POSTERS 22"x28" $1.00 each postpaid. The Seper Co., 5273 Tendilla, Woodland Hills, California.

BEAUTIFUL RICKENBACKER − 12 string − OR 1-8662 (Inglewood, Calif.).

PERSONALS

I LOVE DIANNE

I LOVE BARRY PETERS and my girlfriend loves Scott Peters

"JOAN"

I Love SHERRY MILLER

MOD GIRL − Would like to hear from any band member. Write to Mandi, 400 N. E. 90th, Portland, Oregon, Box 15. College Co-ed. Age 18.

am serious dylan, simon & garfunkle disciple. you too? lets discuss, analyze their songs-poetry. write ed janci, 426 e. 12th st., northampton, pa.

Welcome Back **LIVERPOOL FIVE**

HAPPY (late) BIRTHDAY, George. Your sister-in-law.

BON VOYAGE Rita and Lee. Big Mar.

BUTTON WILLOW is coming soon.

JEFFERSON AIRPLANE BUFFALO SPRINGFIELD

JULIE PETRIE − Happy 14th Birthday! Karen.

HAPPY 2nd Birthday, Melissa. Aunt Mousie.

Reflect on The Mirro's Impression Coming Soon, the new sound from the South.

UP WITH THE MONKEES!

RANDY SCHOFIELD CLARK I love you. Mike's Shelley, Summer 1966.

KINGSTON TRIO PLUS GEORGE and "Mad-Dog" − tell us you're coming next time! We still love you! Linda and Beth (714) 962-9816.

CHARLOTTE=Monkee Lover.

Tonni, Tinga, BN, Inez & Les: JAXO ON WARPATH!

Davy − 69'er

"Micky, we'll get you. M.O.D."

"Strawberry Phil Forever"

TO DON & GOODTIMES, Robbs, Leaves, Lost, Barbarians, Hard Times: Sketches took long TIME . . . Write back, Luvs! Lynn Pope, 28 Topeka Ave., San Jose, Calif. 95128, Phone (408) 295-0202.

LARRY HORNE OF LYNWOOD HIGH − you're OUT-ASITE!!! Susan.

"THE BUSH are greatly growing."

Hi P.F.C. John! From Terry.

QUICKSILVER MESSENGER SERVICE FOREVER!

Dan & Sharon, Julie, Jordan, Tony, Robin.

HAPPY (late) Birthday, Harpo! Love, Sally.

Cindy − Ditch Riverside, join me on The Strip, we'll freak off. Randy.

MONKEES − PLEASE come to New Haven, Connecticut.

"CRANK YOUR SPREADERS" L.W.

YEAH MONKEES!

THE BEST OF FRIENDS

RANDY & ROBIN, VERY TRUE!

KNIGHTS OF DAY

JUDY LOVES BILL

"ZEMEL PLUS JULIE"

I LOVE YOU CHARLIE PRICE!

THE CHAIN REACTION continues . . .

FAN CLUBS

DAVE CLARK FIVE FAN CLUB, 9416 Cedar Avenue, Bloomington, Calif. 92316

HERMAN'S HERMITS OFFICIAL CHAPTER FAN CLUB. Send $1.25, name, address to: Edith Eskridge, 1900 Cabrillo St., San Francisco, Calif.

CLASSIFIEDS . . . 10¢ a word for personal messages from you to someone else without an object for sale or trade, etc. Everything else (for sale, wanted, etc.) is 20¢ a word.

When counting words, the street and number (6290 Sunset Blvd.) count as one word. City and state count as one word (Hollywood, Calif.). Telephone numbers are one word (please include area code or city).

Classifieds must be mailed with the correct amount of money to BEAT CLASSIFIED, 6290 Sunset Blvd., Suite 504, Hollywood, Calif. 90028

KRLA ARCHIVES

RECORDS FREE FROM RC®
You'll Flip at the ZZZIP in RC® Cola

while you swing to your favorite stars!
RC and music, perfect partners for the perfect lift

TAKE 1 ALBUM FREE

For everyone you buy... with 6 cork liners or seals from R.C. bottle caps over 100 Capitol LP's available. Order as often as you wish. Nothing to join. Look for this display at your favorite store.

Here's your best way yet to save more on the records you want. In dollars-and-cents terms you get two albums that the Capitol Record Club sells for $3.98 each time you buy one. The savings are even bigger on stereo records! And there are no shipping charges to pay, nothing else to join or buy.

What's more, you choose from top albums by today's biggest stars, including the Beatles, David McCallum, Frank Sinatra, Lou Rawls, Buck Owens, Petula Clark, the Outsiders, Nancy Wilson, Dean Martin, Sonny James, the Beach Boys and many others.

OTHER FINE BRANDS: DIET-RITE®COLA, NEHI®BEVERAGES, PART-T-PAK®BEVERAGES, UPPER 10®
"ROYAL CROWN" AND "RC" REG. U.S. PAT. OFF.; ®1966 ROYAL CROWN COLA CO.

www.ingramcontent.com/pod-product-compliance
Lightning Source LLC
Chambersburg PA
CBHW080450170426
43196CB00016B/2744